Sexual Violence and Abuse

Sexual Violence and Abuse

AN ENCYCLOPEDIA OF PREVENTION, IMPACTS, AND RECOVERY

Volume 2: O–Y

Judy L. Postmus, Editor

ABC-CLIO

Santa Barbara, California • Denver, Colorado • Oxford, England

Library of Congress Cataloging-in-Publication Data

   Sexual violence and abuse : an encyclopedia of prevention, impacts, and recovery / Judy L. Postmus, editor.

     v. ; cm.

  Includes bibliographical references and index.

   ISBN 978–1–59884–755–0 (hard copy : alk. paper) — ISBN 978–1–59884–756–7 (ebook)

1. Sex crimes. 2. Sex crimes—Prevention. I. Postmus, Judy L.

HV6556.S458   2013

364.15′3—dc23   2012018355

ISBN: 978–1–59884–755–0
EISBN: 978–1–59884–756–7

17 16 15 14 13   1 2 3 4 5

This book is also available on the World Wide Web as an eBook.
Visit www.abc-clio.com for details.

ABC-CLIO, LLC
130 Cremona Drive, P.O. Box 1911
Santa Barbara, California 93116-1911

This book is printed on acid-free paper ∞

Manufactured in the United States of America

Contents

Alphabetical List of Entries

SARTs (Sexual Assault Response Teams)

SCREAM Theater (Program)

Sex Industry (Overview)

Sex Offender Registries

Sex Workers

Sexting

Sexual Assault

Sexual Coercion

Sexual Freedom

Sexual Harassment

Sexual Harassment at Work

Sexually Acting Out

Sibling Abuse, Defining

Sibling Abuse, Identifying and Impact of

Simple Rape

Social Norms Approach

Solution-Focused Brief Therapy

South Asians in the United States

Specialized Victims Units (Police)

Spirituality

Sports Teams

Stalking

Statistics

Statutory Rape

STDS and HIV/AIDS

Stranger Rape

Strengths Perspective

Stress Inoculation Training

Strip Clubs

Substance Abuse as a Consequence

Substantiation (of Legal Charges)

Suicidality

Support Groups

T

Technology, Use of (Overview)

Teen Dating Abuse

Theories (Overview)

Theories, Psychological

Theories, Sociobiological

Theories, Sociocultural

Theory, Coercive Control

Theory, Continuum of Violence

Theory, Diffusion of Innovations

Theory, Ecological Approach

Theory, Feminist

Theory, General Theory of Crime

Theory, Hegemonic Masculinity

Theory, Male Peer Support

Therapeutic Interviewing Strategies

Trafficking in Persons

Trauma, Secondary

Trauma Therapy

Traumatic Bonding

Treatment Programs for Sexual Offenders

U

Underreporting

Undetected Rapists

Unintended Rape

Topical List of Entries

O

Organizational Response (Overview)

Following a sexual victimization, victims may have multiple needs including rees-tablishing a sense of safety, seeking justice, addressing immediate medical concerns, and processing emotional reactions. Victims may worry that their perpetrator will harm them or their family after the victimization and may seek assistance from the criminal justice system by reporting the assault to law enforcement. In addition, victims may report the assault if they believe it will prevent the offender from sexually assaulting additional victims.

After a sexual victimization, victims have multiple acute medical needs including screening and treatment for sexually transmitted infections, information about pregnancy risk and sexually transmitted infections, and pregnancy testing and emergency contraception. Victims might also have a medical forensic examination, which involves documenting injuries; collecting loose hairs by combing the head and pubis; swabbing the vagina, rectum, and/or mouth to collect semen, blood, or saliva; and obtaining fingernail scrapings in the event the victim scratched the assailant. Blood samples could be collected for DNA, toxicology, and ethanol testing. The findings of this examination can link the suspect to the crime if the suspect's DNA is found on the victim's body or clothing, or at the crime scene.

A lost sense of safety, a loss of control over their lives, distrust of others, and shame are common feelings that victims experience following a sexual assault. Some victims demonstrate long-term psychological reactions following a sex crime. Approximately 38 to 43 percent of victims meet the diagnostic criteria for major depression (Rothbaum, Foa, Riggs, Murdock, & Walsh, 1992), and 31 to 65 percent develop post-traumatic stress disorder (Foa & Rothbaum, 1998). Because most sex crimes are committed by someone the victim knows, there may be conflicts with friends or family. For example, friends or family may be misinformed about sexual violence and respond to the victim in a hurtful manner. These supports may try to make decisions for the victim, such as reporting to the police without the victim's consent. While this action is often well intentioned, it may intensify the victims' feelings of loss of control over their lives. In some cases, friends and family may believe and support the offender instead of the victim. All of these reactions may serve to socially isolate the victim and lead to further feelings of stigma and shame. Depending on the level of psychological distress or reactions from their support systems, victims may need to seek emotional support from a support group or a mental health professional.

There are multiple types of organizations that can address these complex needs. For safety concerns, victims may report their victimization to law enforcement to prevent their perpetrator from assaulting them again. Concerned individuals may also contact authorities to report a sexual victimization, particularly for child victims. For example, a teacher may report suspected abuse of a student to Child Protective Services. Victims who need medical care may seek help from a hospital emergency department or a sexual assault nurse examiner program. Victims who seek help to cope with the emotional reactions of the victimization may look to a rape crisis center or their clergy.

Several entries in the encyclopedia examine how different organizations respond to victims of sexual violence. This entry begins with a description of how organizational response can hurt victims (known as revictimization), and the advocacy efforts that aim to reduce those hurtful interactions. Next, this entry will explore organizations that address victims' safety concerns including Child Protective Services, Child Advocacy Centers, and specialized sex crime units within police departments. In addition, this area focuses on the prosecution rates of sex crimes and what makes prosecution likely in these cases. Further, this entry will discuss the role of secondary schools and colleges in creating safe environments for their students by implementing both protocols to respond to sexual and prevention programming. Then, in order to understand the organizations and professionals that address victims' medical needs, this entry examines the traditional approach to medical care in hospital emergency departments. This entry will also include a discussion of innovative patient-centered approaches to medical care, including forensic nursing, sexual assault nurse examiner programs, and sexual assault response teams. This entry concludes with an examination of organizations and professionals that address victims' emotional needs, including rape crisis centers, clergy, and services to victims in prison settings.

Revictimization by Professionals

When victims seek help from organizations, they need professionals working in those organizations to provide services in an empathic, supportive manner to aid their recovery. However, if professionals treat victims in an insensitive or hurtful manner, it can worsen victims' feelings of powerlessness, shame, and guilt. Unfortunately, many victims have negative experiences when they seek help from professionals within organizations. These negative interactions have been called "revictimization" or "secondary victimization" because victims often report that they feel like a "second rape" has occurred. In the entry, **Revictimization, Organizations**, Patterson highlights research about the occurrence of revictimization in the criminal justice, medical, and mental health settings. These studies report revictimization experiences that ranged from professionals being inattentive to victims' emotional needs to blaming victims for their assaults (Campbell & Raja, 2005). The research also suggests that criminal justice and medical professionals are more likely to revictimize than mental health professionals. These hurtful interactions can have a profoundly negative impact on victims' emotional well-being, increasing the risk of psychological and physical health distress (Campbell, Wasco, Ahrens, Sefl, & Barnes, 2001). Victims report that as a result, they feel distrustful of others, feel depressed, and blame themselves for the victimization. Fortunately, mental health services such as counseling have been found to be helpful in reducing post-traumatic stress symptoms for victims who have had revictimizing experiences with legal and/or medical professionals (Campbell et al., 1999).

Criminal Justice Interventions

Victim advocacy services were created to reduce victims' experiences of revictimization, particularly by criminal justice staff. Victim advocates may be housed in rape crisis centers, police departments, or prosecutors' offices. In the entry **Criminal Justice and Victims**, Kelly explains that victim advocates can be a source of support for victims by guiding them through the reporting and prosecuting process, while attending to their emotional needs. Research has suggested that victims find this source of support helpful (Wasco et al., 2004). In addition, preliminary research has found that victims who had advocates were less likely to experience revictimization by criminal justice personnel compared to victims without advocates (Campbell, 2006). When victims do experience revictimization, victim advocates may be able to alleviate the emotional distress caused by the hurtful interactions.

Organizations That Address Safety and Justice

Child Protective Services

Victims may seek help from organizations to address safety concerns resulting from a single or ongoing experience of sexual violence. In the case of child victims of sexual abuse, concerned individuals may contact authorities to seek help on behalf of the child. For example, adults who have witnessed or suspect child sexual abuse may report their concerns to Child Protective Services. Professionals such as social workers and counselors, medical professionals, day care providers, and teachers are "mandated reporters," meaning they are required by law to report suspected cases of child maltreatment, including sexual abuse, to Child Protective Services. Concerned family members or other citizens such as neighbors may also make a report to Child Protective Services, but are not legally required to do so. Thus most reports of child maltreatment to Child Protective Services come from mandated reporters.

In the entry **Child Protective Services**, Lee describes how Child Protective Services handles allegations of child maltreatment in two stages. In the first stage, a local Child Protective Services hotline or intake unit worker screens incoming reports of allegation to determine whether the referral is appropriate for further action. Referrals may be screened out if they do not meet the state's standard for investigation or if there is insufficient information to allow for an investigation. For example, it would be difficult for Child Protective Services to investigate a report that did not include enough information to identify the child or his or her whereabouts. The second stage involves further investigating of those cases that were not screened out. Child Protective Services places higher priority on cases where there is an immediate threat to the child and thus requires an immediate response. For sexual abuse, immediate threats may include allegations of oral sex, anal sex, or vaginal intercourse with a minor, as well as sexual abuse accompanied by physical abuse, sexual abuse consisting of bizarre sexual practices, and pornographic/sexual exploitation. After an investigation, Child Protective Services may take actions that include removing the accused party from the home, taking legal action against them, and in extreme cases, removing the child from the home if the parent or guardian is unable to protect the child from the abuse.

Child Advocacy Centers

The investigation process for child victims of sexual abuse can be overwhelming, intimidating, and potentially traumatizing. The child may have to disclose the abuse to multiple professionals including Child Protective Services, law enforcement, and medical professionals. Child victims of sexual abuse may also need to be examined by a medical professional to assess for, and document, injuries. Children may be easily frightened by interviews in a police station or an intrusive medical exam. As such, Child Advocacy Centers were developed to improve the response to child victims, as well as to improve the coordination between Child Protective Services and the criminal justice system. In addition to Child Protective Services, the interdisciplinary teams may include representatives from law enforcement, prosecution, mental health providers, medical providers, and victim advocates.

In the entry, **Child Advocacy Centers**, Lee describes a Child Advocacy Center as a multiservice model with four key components. First, there is a child interview that may include multiple team members conducting or observing the interview on a monitor in a different room. This process aims to reduce the number of times the child needs to be interviewed about the allegations. Second, the Child Advocacy Center may provide a medical examination in a child-friendly setting to collect medical forensic evidence (e.g., DNA) or document injuries related to the sexual abuse allegations, as well as treat any health issues (Jackson, 2004). This medical forensic evidence may be used in the prosecution of the offender. Third, some Child Advocacy Centers provide victim advocacy and legal information to help the child and nonoffending caregivers through the investigation process. Finally, Child Advocacy Centers may help the child victim and family members in accessing mental health services to help them cope and recover from the abuse.

Criminal Justice Organizations (Police and Prosecutors)

Prosecution rates for child sexual abuse vary greatly. Research has found that between 28 and 94 percent of cases are prosecuted (Cross, Walsh, Simone, & Jones, 2003). Substantiation of child sexual abuse may be difficult because most cases lack physical evidence to support the allegations (Faller & Henry, 2000). In addition, child victims may be unable, or too afraid, to describe the abuse because of their age and development stage. Adult sex crime cases also have unique challenges, with prosecution rates being substantially lower than child cases. In fact, only 14 to 18 percent of reported adult sexual assault cases are ever prosecuted. In the entry, **Substantiation (of Legal Charges)**, Patterson explains that adult cases are more likely to be prosecuted if law enforcement and prosecutors view the victim as credible (i.e., believable) or the case as "winnable." Victims are more likely to be perceived as credible if they have injuries from the victimization, did not consume alcohol or drugs prior to the assault, and reported the assault to the police immediately. In addition, the criminal justice system tends to view victims as credible if the offenders used weapons or force in order to carry out the assault. While state laws do not require these factors (e.g., force, injury, or weapon) for a case to be prosecuted, most criminal justice personnel do not believe a perpetrator can be convicted without them.

Specialized Sex Crimes Units (Police)

While criminal justice personnel tend to prosecute cases viewed as winnable or credible, the quality of the investigation itself is critical to the prosecution. Law enforcement detectives are responsible for collecting evidence from sex crime scenes and interviewing the victim and the suspect (if identified). The detective's role requires a high level of knowledge and skills in investigating sex crimes. Thus detectives must have expertise in forensic evidence, collecting evidence from crime scenes, interviewing victims in a sensitive manner, and getting confessions from offenders.

In the entry **Specialized Victims Units (Police)**, Patterson describes specialized units within police departments whose primary responsibility is handling all sex crimes reported to their jurisdiction. These units have become more known to the general public through television programs such as *Law & Order SVU* (Special Victims Unit). While it is unknown how many police departments in the United

States have specialized sex crime units, it is believed that departments with these units have some advantages over those that do not. For example, detectives may be able to sharpen their investigation skills quicker when their primary role focuses on sex crime investigation. In addition, these units may be more likely to have written procedures to guide their detectives' investigations, which provide consistency in how sex crimes are handled. These specialized sex crime units may be more likely to develop collaborative relationships with other organizations that work with victims, which would improve coordination of services for victims. For example, a collaborative relationship with rape crisis centers could increase detective referrals to these organizations for victims to receive emotional support. The hope is that this may help increase sex crime arrest and prosecution rates.

Secondary Schools and Colleges

Research has shown that sexual violence is a pervasive problem for high school and college student populations. The awareness of this problem has resulted in legislation that requires these academic institutions to respond to sexual violence on campus. In the entry **Response, Schools and Colleges**, Schwartz describes legislation such as Title IX, which requires schools to respond to sexual violence, including any acts of sexual harassment that contribute to a hostile environment. The Clery Act requires universities and colleges to publish annual reports of crime statistics and security policies, as well as provide timely notifications to the campus community (e.g., students, employees) of crimes that may pose a threat to their safety. The Clery Act also includes the "Campus Sexual Assault Victims' Bill of Rights," which requires that all colleges and universities provide victims of sexual assault with certain rights, such as being informed of options for counseling and for changing academic schedules and residency.

While these legislative initiatives aim to improve the response to sexual violence, barriers to reporting such incidents to academic institutions still exist. For example, students may be less likely to report if their colleges have vague definitions of sexual violence or when the institutions' policies do not specify the victims' options for seeking help or reporting after an incident. Although academic institutions are obligated to respond to sexual violence, variation exists in their policies, including reporting procedures, and the types of responses victims receive from formal sources of support on campus.

Organizations That Address Medical Needs

Emergency Departments

Traditionally, victims have been sent to hospital emergency departments because of their 24/7 accessibility. In the entry **Emergency Rooms and Other Medical Settings**, Diegel and Wyatt describe the role of emergency department personnel in treating patients who experience interpersonal victimizations. The role of emergency department staff (e.g., doctors, nurses) includes treating physical injuries, providing information about pregnancy risks and sexually transmitted infections, providing emergency contraception and prophylaxis (e.g., medication to treat sexually transmitted infections) and conducting medical forensic evidence examinations.

While sexual assault survivors may go to emergency departments as an easily accessible and opportune location, they often experience long waiting times because sexual violence is rarely an emergent health threat. This long wait can be uncomfortable for victims because they are not allowed to eat, drink, shower, or urinate as this would destroy physical evidence of the assault. In addition, medical professionals often lack specialized training on responding to victims in a sensitive manner. Thus many victims describe medical personnel as cold or impersonal (Campbell, 2006). Furthermore, emergency department clinicians may lack training to conduct medical forensic evidence examinations, so important evidence collection procedures are often performed incorrectly. Research also suggests that many victims of sexual violence do not receive complete care in emergency departments. For example, patients are infrequently advised about risks of pregnancy and sexually transmitted infections. Approximately half of sexual assault patients do not receive emergency contraception (e.g., Plan B contraceptive medication); however, most patients receive preventative antibiotics to treat curable sexually transmitted infections (Campbell, Wasco, Ahrens, Sefl, & Barnes, 2001).

Forensic Nursing

Some medical professionals, particularly nurses, have sought specialized training to provide quality comprehensive care to victims of crime. In the entry **Forensic Nursing**, Diegel and Wyatt describe the role of forensic nurses as providing specialized care to patients who experienced sexual violence or other crimes. These nurses may provide diagnosis and treatment for injuries, collection of medical forensic evidence from the victim's body, proper storage of evidence, referring patients for follow-up treatment for medical and emotional needs, testifying in court if the case is prosecuted, and engaging in collaborative relationships with other professionals who work with victims.

Forensic nurses practice in a variety of settings, including hospitals, doctor's offices, jails or prisons, or medical examiner/coroner offices. In addition to victims, forensic nurses might care for and collect medical forensic evidence from suspects/offenders. This evidence can help in the investigation and prosecution of the case. Forensic nurses receive specialized classroom and clinical training on medical forensic evidence collection techniques, injury detection, chain-of-evidence requirements, and expert witness testimony. Forensic nurses who work with sexual assault patients also receive training on sexually transmitted infections screening and treatment, and sexual assault trauma response.

Sexual Assault Nurse Examiner Programs

Many forensic nurses provide care to victims in sexual assault nurse examiner (SANE) programs. In the entry **SANE (Sexual Assault Nurse Examiner)**, Campbell explains that these programs were created to address problems with traditional hospital emergency department care (e.g., impersonal care, inaccurate forensic evidence collection). There are over 700 SANE programs in the United States, Canada, and other countries. Sexual assault nurse examiner programs are typically staffed by forensic nurses or other specially trained health care clinicians. Most SANE programs are located in hospitals, particularly emergency departments, but some are located in clinics or other community settings such as rape crisis centers. SANE programs serve adolescents and adults, and some programs provide services to child victims of sexual abuse.

SANE programs aim to improve key aspects of the medical response to victims of sexual violence by: (1) providing complete medical care, including information and treatment of sexually transmitted infections, and emergency contraception; (2) treating victims with dignity and respect to prevent them from being retraumatized or experiencing revictimization; (3) providing a thorough and accurate medical forensic exam and detailed documentation of the exam findings; and (4) improving prosecution rates through accurate medical forensic evidence collection and expert witness testimony.

There has been limited research to examine if SANE programs have been effective in meeting these aims, but preliminary studies have found promising results. For example, two studies have examined whether SANE programs contribute to increased prosecution rates. Both studies found that prosecution rates significantly increased after the development of SANE programs. This may be due to the SANE services provided to both victims and members of the legal community, such as consulting with law enforcement (Campbell, Patterson, Bybee, & Dworkin, 2009; Crandall & Helitzer, 2003). Overall, the research has suggested that SANE programs hold promise in improving the response to victims, but additional research is needed to replicate these findings.

Sexual Assault Response Teams

There are many types of organizations and professionals who work with victims of sexual violence. In order to improve coordination of services among professionals, some communities have developed a sexual assault response team (SART). In the entry **SARTs (Sexual Assault Response Teams)**, Campbell describes these teams as coordinated, multidisciplinary community efforts to address victim needs following the assault, such as injury treatment, forensic medical exams, pregnancy evaluation, sexually transmitted infection screening, police reporting, and psychological crisis intervention. The primary goal is to bring professionals together to promote victims' well-being and create community change. SART membership can vary by community, but most SARTs include victim advocates, medical personnel, police, and prosecutors. Sometimes SART members include members of the faith community, agencies serving marginalized populations (e.g., people with disabilities), and other social service agencies (such as drug treatment programs).

While specific goals can vary depending on the SART, most teams aim to: (1) promote offender accountability through increasing reporting and prosecution rates; (2) enhance victim recovery by addressing barriers to help seeking and gaps in services delivery, as well as improving how system personnel treat victims; and (3) increase community-wide education to prevent and increase awareness about sexual assault. SARTs can also vary in how they are structured, with some teams having formal roles (e.g., a designated leader), a defined mission statement, and written policies and procedures of operation. However, some SARTs have less structure and may have informal collaboration and communication among members. To meet their goals, SARTs may carry out activities including: (1) regular review of cases to assess their progress through the legal system; (2) cross-training among SART members to provide information about issues related to roles and areas of expertise; (3) developing and monitoring policies and protocols to guide each system's response to victims and sex crime cases; and (4) development of resources for professionals who work with victims directly (e.g., checklists) and victims (e.g., pamphlets on community resources). While there may be at least 500 SARTs throughout the United States and Canada, there has been very limited research to examine their effectiveness and the findings have been mixed. Further research is needed on SARTs' structure and function and how different practices may affect victims' services and criminal justice outcomes.

Organizations That Address Emotional and Spiritual Needs

Rape Crisis Centers

In the early 1970s, rape crisis centers (also known as sexual assault programs) were developed in many communities to meet the multiple needs of sexual assault victims and their significant others. In the entry **Rape Crisis Centers**, Patterson describes the services provided by rape crisis centers to meet victims' needs. To meet victims' emotional needs, many rape crisis centers provide hotlines, crisis intervention, and individualized counseling. In addition, rape crisis centers may offer support groups to decrease victims' feelings of social isolation, stigma, or shame. Because victims often experience hurtful interactions with those in the medical and legal systems, rape crisis centers often accompany victims to the hospital, police station, or court. Emerging research suggests that advocacy from rape crisis centers may help prevent survivors from being treated poorly by medical and law enforcement personnel (Campbell, 2006). Finally, many rape crisis centers focus on social change with the aim of eliminating society's tolerance of sexual violence. These activities may include community education, protests, survivor speak-outs, lobbying, and training other professional agencies on how to improve responsiveness to survivors. Many rape crisis centers have engaged in social change activities since their inception.

Rape crisis centers can be freestanding and without connection to other organizations, or they may work with domestic violence agencies or other organizations focused on social or health issues (e.g., hospitals, universities, county services, criminal justice organizations, and community mental health organizations). Rape crisis centers may be housed as separate programs with their own staff and budgets, or they may be housed within larger organizations—whereby funding and decision making are not separated from the overall operations of the agency. There have been few studies examining the effectiveness of rape crisis centers, but the preliminary findings suggest they are responsive to the needs of survivors and engage in social change efforts when they are compared to typical social service organizations. However, recent research suggests that freestanding centers provide more complete services than rape crisis centers affiliated with other organizations (Martin, 2005).

Prison Interventions

The needs of victims who are prisoners within correctional facilities are often overlooked. In the entry, **Criminal Justice and Victims**, Kelly describes recent programs to address inmates' past experiences of sexual violence, as well as victimizations that occur within prisons. Prisoners are more likely to have experienced past sexual violence than the general public, and they may experience sexual victimization during their time in the correctional facility from other prisoners or guards. To address in-prison sexual violence, some prisons and correctional systems have implemented policies to discourage prison rape, including a zero-tolerance policy and training for officers to identify sexual misconduct. In addition, some prisons have developed procedures to respond to in-prison sexual violence, including addressing victims' immediate medical needs and short- and long-term psychological and emotional distress.

This entry also describes a model program in Delaware (Survivors of Abuse in Recovery [SOAR]) to address prison inmates' past experiences with sexual violence. In the Delaware prison, female inmates are offered the option to receive group counseling following by individual therapy. Evaluation of the program suggests that SOAR has been effective in increasing the inmates' coping skills and reducing the anxiety related to their past victimizations.

Faith-Based Organizations

Victims may be hesitant to seek help from formal professionals such as therapists or law enforcement for multiple reasons. One reason is that victims are afraid that these professionals may respond with hurtful comments or blame them for the victimization. As such, some victims may view their faith-based communities as sources of support and healing, and prefer to seek help from the leaders of their faith-based communities. In the entry, **Clergy Response** to sexual assault victims, Bent-Goodley describes the important role that faith-based communities (i.e., churches, synagogues) can play in the prevention and response to sexual violence. For prevention efforts, the clergy can work with youth and adult ministries to implement programs that promote messages against sexual violence, and encourage discussion of how faith-based communities can address the needs of those impacted by sexual assault. Clergy also can send the message that sexual violence is wrong, requires treatment, and will not be tolerated. Furthermore, faith-based communities can increase awareness of local resources (e.g., rape crisis center, child advocacy center) in their church bulletins, pews, and bathroom stalls. These activities can diminish the silence that surrounds sexual violence, which may encourage victims who may be members of the congregation to seek help from the clergy or local services.

Similar to other professionals, it is important that clergy receive training on the appropriate response to sexual violence to ensure that their messages are healing and supportive. Collaborations with local providers (e.g., rape crisis centers) can provide opportunity for cross-training and increase victims' access to services. For example, cross-training can provide clergy members with information on sexual violence, while local providers can receive information on the cultural and social needs of the population to advance the cultural competence of local services. To increase access to local services, faith-based leaders can offer legitimacy to local providers by encouraging the congregation to extend trust to these providers to respond to their needs. In addition, faith-based communities can offer space for jointly sponsored events that aim to reduce sexual violence in the community. Holding events or services in churches decreases access problems such as lack of transportation. Together, faith-based communities and local service providers may be able to promote holistic healing for victims.

In conclusion, many organizations exist to meet the short- and long-term needs of survivors. Overall, research has found some organizations to be less responsive to survivors than others. In particular, survivors report being treated in a hurtful manner more often by personnel from criminal justice organizations and hospital emergency departments than rape crisis centers and faith-based organizations. Fortunately, new organizations and services have been developed in recent years to improve the response to survivors such as sexual assault nurse examiner programs, sexual assault response teams, and child advocacy centers.

Debra Patterson

Further Reading

Campbell, R. (2006). Rape survivors' experiences with the legal and medical systems: Do rape victim advocates make a difference? *Violence Against Women, 12*(1), 30–45.

Campbell, R., Patterson, D., Bybee, D. & Dworkin, E. R. (2009). Predicting sexual assault prosecution outcomes: The role of medical forensic evidence collected by sexual assault nurse examiners (SANEs). *Criminal Justice and Behavior, 36*(7), 712–727.

Campbell, R., & Raja, S. (2005). The sexual assault and secondary victimization of female veterans: Help-seeking experiences with military and civilian social systems. *Psychology of Women Quarterly, 29*, 97–106.

Campbell, R., Sefl, T., Barnes, H. E., Ahrens, C. E., Wasco, S. M., & Zaragoza-Diesfeld, Y. (1999). Community services for rape survivors: Enhancing psychological well-being or increasing trauma? *Journal of Consulting and Clinical Psychology, 67*, 847–858.

Campbell, R., Wasco, S., Ahrens, C., Sefl, T., & Barnes, H. (2001). Preventing the "second rape": Rape survivors' experiences with community service providers. *Journal of Interpersonal Violence, 16*(12), 1239–1259.

Crandall, C., & Helitzer, D. (2003). *Impact evaluation of a Sexual Assault Nurse Examiner (SANE) program.* NIJ Document No. 203276. Award No. 98-WT-VX-0027.

Cross, T., Walsh, W., Simone, M., & Jones, L. (2003). Prosecution of child abuse: A meta-analysis of rates of criminal justice decisions. *Trauma, Violence & Abuse, 4*, 323–340.

Faller, K. C., & Henry, J. (2000). Child sexual abuse: A case study in community collaboration. *Child Abuse & Neglect, 24*, 1215–1224.

Foa, E. B., & Rothbaum, B. O. (1998). *Treating the trauma of rape: Cognitive-behavioral therapy for PTSD.* New York, NY: Guilford Press.

Jackson, S. L. (2004). A USA national survey of program services provided by child advocacy centers. *Child Abuse & Neglect, 28*, 411–421.

Martin, P. Y. (2005). *Rape work: Victims, gender, and emotions in organization and community context.* New York, NY: Routledge.

Rothbaum, B. O., Foa, E. B., Riggs, D. S., Murdock, T., & Walsh, W. (1992). A prospective examination of posttraumatic stress disorder in rape victims. *Journal of Traumatic Stress, 5*, 455–475.

Wasco, S. M., Campbell, R., Howard, A., Mason, G. E., Staggs, S. L., Schewe, P. A., & Riger, S. (2004). A statewide evaluation of services provided to rape survivors. *Journal of Interpersonal Violence, 19*(2), 252–263.

P

Perpetrators (Overview)

In examining the research on sex offenders, there are several ways in which offenders and their offenses can be categorized. In legal definitions, offenses can be categorized as contact and noncontact offenses. Contact offenses include those that require actually physical contact between the perpetrator and the victim, such as penetration or touching. Noncontact offenses include those in which there is no physical contact, such as exhibitionism, voyeurism, and child pornography. In classifying the cases, it is also common to differentiate the type of crime based on the age of victim. Those individuals who have committed a crime against a minor are commonly referred to as child molesters, whereas those who have offended against someone over the age of consent are referred to as rapists. The relationship of the victim to the offender is also used in differentiating cases, with sexual crimes committed against children in the family referred to as incest, and assault against a spouse referred to as spousal rape or marital rape.

There are important differences between each of these types of offenses and the individuals who commit them. However, many similarities exist in the process of the offense and cognitions related to offending across types of perpetrators. Understanding these processes is important as it informs the policy and practice associated with preventing sexual violence and intervening with the offenders to prevent further victimization.

Who Are Sexual Offenders?

Available data on sexual offenders are based on the national crime victimization surveys and police data. Although these provide some insight into the patterns of perpetration in the United States, they miss the majority of cases in which the assault is never reported to police or, in many cases, the victim never tells anyone. However, these data provide us the best estimates of the characteristics of offenders.

It is known that the majority of offenders are someone who is known to and trusted by the victims. This is particularly true among child victims, about which it is believed that up to 90 percent are abused by someone they know. Of these, nearly half were a family member. Approximately 60 percent of sexual crimes are committed in the victim's home or the home of someone she or he knows. Among those who have been arrested or adjudicated for a sexual offense, 99 percent of those arrested forcible rape and 92 percent of those for other sex crimes are males. The majority of those arrested for forcible rape (56%) are Caucasian, with 42 percent black and 2 percent of other races. When including all sexual crimes, Caucasians represent a large proportion of all arrests (75%). Approximately one-third of those arrested for rape and a quarter of those arrested for other sex offenses were between 20 and 30 years old, representing the largest proportion of offenders. Juveniles account for 16 percent of all sexual offenses (Greenfeld, 1997).

Although females represent only a small proportion of those convicted or adjudicated for a sexual offense, some research indicates they go undetected in official rates of sexual violence due to lower reporting rates. As Kernsmith describes in her entry on **Female Sex Offenders**, these rates may be lower due to increased shame or guilt felt by victims or perceptions of less culpability of female offenders.

Research also indicates that sexual offenders have disproportionately high exposure to abuse and trauma in childhood. It is estimated that between 20 and 50 percent of juvenile sex offenders have been physically abused and 40 to 80 percent have been sexually abused (Hunter & Becker, 1998). These individuals are also more likely to have experienced other forms of trauma such as neglect or abandonment by a parent, exposure to violence in the home or community, or traumatic loss. Among female offenders, rates of trauma are higher, with women identifying more severe, frequent, and ongoing traumatic experiences. However, this is not to say that these traumatic experiences, or even the lack of effective intervention with these traumatic events, cause someone to offend. Most individuals who experience childhood trauma do not perpetrate against others. However, the cumulative impact of trauma, family response to disclosure of the incident, social supports, mental health, and coping strategies can be risk or protective factors that are associated with sexual offending.

However, because the majority of sexual crimes are never reported to law enforcement or other formal supports, and many victims may never even seek help from informal supports, many sexual assaults go undetected. As Craun describes in her entry on **Undetected Rapists**, research generally indicates that less than half, or as little as 10 percent of sexual assaults are ever reported. This number is even smaller among child victims, particularly when the perpetrator is a family member. Assaults may not be reported because the victim feels afraid or ashamed by what has happened. Among children, they may not have the language to discuss what has happened. Fear of the response of others may also discourage reporting. A victim may be afraid that he or she will not be believed. When the perpetrator is known, particularly when it is a family member, the victim may not want the perpetrator to be arrested or go to jail. Fear of the perpetrator may also inhibit reporting, particularly among children, vulnerable adults, and assaults that co-occur in relationships where other forms of domestic violence are present.

The victim may fear further harm or repercussions from the perpetrator if he or she tells anyone about the assault.

A victim may also want to minimize the assault or try to just get over it, not wanting to participate in a lengthy trial that requires the victim and family to be exposed to the details and memories of the assault for a prolonged time. The victim may also feel confused and not define it as sexual assault. When the victim is a child, he or she may not have a context for understanding the experience. When the assault is more coercive and less physically violent, a victim might not believe it is really rape. This may be particularly true if the perpetrator is known and trusted. The presence of drugs and alcohol can create further confusion, as the victim may not have clear memories of what has happened.

Awareness that sexual assault often goes unreported has important implications for prevention and intervention. Some critics of the sex offender registry assert that registration gives the public a false sense of security as individuals may believe they can avoid dangerous individuals by knowing who in their neighborhood has been convicted of a sexual crime. Low reporting rates also prevent legal and therapeutic intervention with offenders to help deter future offending. Victims who do not seek help may continue to experience the long-term impacts of the trauma. Unresolved trauma is identified as a risk factor for such things as drug and alcohol abuse, self-injurious behavior, eating disorders, mental health conditions such as PTSD, anxiety, and depression, and perpetration of violence against others.

Behavioral Thought Processes in Offending

The vast majority of people, even habitual sexual offenders, have internal inhibitors that dissuade an individual from abusing or assaulting another. Even a person with fixated deviant fantasies that primarily involve violence or abuse of children knows that this behavior is wrong and dangerous. Alternatively, many people who will never offend against another person may have fantasies that involve behavior that is illegal or abusive. It is thought that the difference in whether or not to act on the behavior is based in large part on cognitive processes and access to a victim.

Cognitive distortions are those thoughts and beliefs that allow perpetrators to deny their own culpability or the harm caused by the sexually abusive behavior. This denial is a coping mechanism that allows the perpetrator to give him or herself permission to commit the act or to relieve the guilt and shame of the behavior following the incident. External denial refers to the outward statements to others that he or she did not, in fact, commit the abusive act. Alternatively, the offender may minimize the frequency or duration of the abuse, deny specific acts, or attempt to shift blame to the victim. Commonly, blaming the victim would include statements that he or she was a willing participant, initiated the sexual relationship, or was not harmed significantly. Offenders of all types of crimes will

commonly engage in this external denial to avoid legal, social, or personal consequences. This form of denial may not actually be a cognitive distortion, unless the
perpetrator actually believes it to be true. In **Rape, Denial**, Boianelli further
describes these issues.

Other cognitive distortions may play a role in internally denying or minimizing
the offense. Minimizations of the nature of harm are other forms of cognitive distortion that help to ease culpability. These minimizations allow the perpetrator to
believe either that no harm was done or that the victim will be able to emotionally
recover without difficulty. One means of adapting this cognitive distortion is the
reinterpretation of his or her own victimization as loving or caring. A cognitive
distortion specific for those who offend against children is the belief that children
are sexual beings. This distortion includes the beliefs that children not only are
interested in having sex with adults, but are developmentally capable of freely
consenting to sexual behavior. Two additional distortions that allow offenders to
forgive the behavior despite knowledge of harm are the belief that they cannot
control their sexuality and that they are entitled to have the sexual relationships
they desire.

In some cases, the line between cognitive distortion and reality may be complex. Among female offenders, it is believed that approximately two-thirds of
cases involve a co-offender. In some of these cases, it is thought that the female
may be coerced or forced into the sexually abusive behavior through coercion,
intimidation, and threat of violence. It may be difficult, if not impossible, to identify to what degree the behavior was done only out of self-protection. In either
case, the perpetrator must be accountable for her actions while attending to the
experience of victimization. Similarities and differences in the histories and
offense characteristics of female sexual offenders are further discussed in the entry
by Kernsmith.

The process of moving toward a sexual offense begins with accepting cognitive
distortions that justify the behavior and minimize the perceived harm to the victim
(Mihailides, Devilly, & Ward, 2004). These thoughts begin to minimize the inhibitions to abusive behavior. These techniques of neutralization allow the individual
to ignore morals or values that would normally inhibit the behavior. They relieve
the cognitive dissonance cases by the conflict between these desires or behaviors
with morals and values, and form the foundation for sexual offending. This process may begin years before the first sexual offense or may arise more quickly
when the individual experiences a trigger.

A trigger is a situational or emotional event that challenges the inhibitions
through strong, usually negative emotions. This could include an incident that
reminds the individual of his or her own abuse, causing feelings that may either
be shame-filled or involve feelings of being loved or cared for. Triggers may also
be brought on by feelings of inadequacy or powerlessness unrelated to a previous

trauma. At this point, a potential offender may begin to plan or rehearse the crime, further overcoming the inhibitions with the positive feelings that may arise from these thoughts and fantasies. From here, the offender may begin the process of grooming a potential victim.

Grooming refers to the process through which an offender gains access to his or her intended victim, either an adult or a child, and is described more fully in the entry by Boianelli (**Grooming the Victim**). The process begins subtly, in order to avoid alarming the potential victim by building trust and a pseudo- or real relationship with the victim. Others, such as parents in the case of a minor or friends of an adult victim, may also be included in the grooming process to facilitate isolated access to the victim. This intentional process systematically works to decrease boundaries and increase access to the victim. These boundaries may include sharing intimate secrets, nonsexual touching, and eventually other sexualized behavior. By gaining trust and then engaging in a process of systematically violating personal and emotional boundaries, the offender desensitizes the victim to the behaviors that he or she initially resists. The illusion of a caring relationship encourages the victim to forgive and accept these violations. The strengthened relationship and trust built through this process may also decrease the likelihood of resisting or reporting the assault. The confusion and guilt for the victim that is brought about through the grooming process may also cause the victim to feel ashamed that he or she caused or allowed the abuse to happen.

Following the assault, if the offense is not reported, the offender may feel either remorse or relief from the event. If the offender feels relief, the behavior and cognitive patterns are reinforced, increasing the chance it will occur again with the same or a new victim. If the offender feels remorse, this emotional experience may further fuel the self-loathing or guilt that initially triggered the process. Alternatively, this may reinforce the inhibitions against the behavior, requiring the offender to begin developing the cognitive distortions again or choose to avoid the behavior in the future.

Social Justifications

In addition to the cognitive distortions of an offender, many social messages exist that shift the blame of sexual abuse or assault from the perpetrator to the victim. Many of these are widely socially acceptable norms, commonly referred to as rape myths, that run parallel to the cognitive distortions of the offender. These justifications help to support the cognitive distortions of the perpetrator, increase feelings of guilt and shame among victims, decrease emotional support for victims, and create barriers to legal intervention with perpetrators.

As Comartin describes in her entry, "**Rape Justification**" is rooted in patriarchal beliefs and gender stereotypes. Some rape myths include the belief that individuals might be obligated to engage in sexual behavior because they are acting or dressing provocatively, are on a date, or are married. Those who believe that women are manipulative or dishonest may also be more likely to engage in sexual violence. If an offender believes the victim is being a "tease" or "playing games" in order to make the male work through the initial resistance to sex, the perpetrator may choose to ignore real statements that she does not want to have sex. Paired with beliefs about sexual entitlement and uncontrollability of his sexuality, this may support sexual abuse. A belief about men that supports sexual assault is that men have an insatiable sexual appetite and should always want to have sex. This may lead to the belief that he is entitled to sex or cannot control his behavior when aroused. Alternatively, this supports the belief that males cannot be sexually coerced or assaulted because they should always be willing to have sex. This belief is particularly strong as a justification of female assaults of males, even when the male victim is below the legal age of consent.

The linking of sex with violence may be another social support for sexual assault and rape. Although research is mixed on the role of media and pornography in the acceptance of rape myths and actual sexually violent behavior, there is some indication that media representations of violence and sex may desensitize both women and men to the actual harm caused by rape. When rape can be seen as "just sex" or coercion is viewed as foreplay, it may be easier to overcome the internal morals that would normally inhibit sexual assault.

Motivations for Sexual Violence

Although the motivation for sexual assault may seem to be sexual gratification, this is typically only a minor component, if at all. Although some pedophiles will identify a primary sexual attraction to children, some research indicates that this attraction may actually be based in a fixation at an age when the perpetrator was sexually abused. This attraction may also be masking a fear of intimacy with adults. Children are viewed as less intimidating, due to their naiveté and innocence. Few individuals who have molested children are diagnosable with pedophilia, a metal health condition characterized by primary or exclusive sexual attraction to children.

Most research indicates that sexual violence and abuse is more often motivated by feelings of powerlessness or anger. Power rape is characterized by the motivation to overcome feelings of inadequacy or powerlessness through the sexually abusive behavior. By overpowering another individual, the perpetrator regains a sense that they are worthwhile, valuable and in control. This is believed to be the most common motivation for offenses against both adults and children. An anger rapist uses the acts of sexual violence as revenge or retaliation against a real or imagined offense against themselves. The assault may be a way of retaliating against the victim or of expressing rage and anger that is not related to the victim. These assaults are often characterized by higher levels of violence. A small proportion of sexual assaults and abuse are believed to be characterized by sadism. This is characterized by gaining sexual gratification from violence.

Conclusion

Prevention of sexual violence is reliant on intervention with perpetrators and prevention efforts with potential offenders. Risk reduction strategies with potential victims will never be sufficient to eliminate sexual violence. Greater understanding of the social and psychological factors that contribute to these types of crimes is needed to more effectively address violence and abuse.

Poco Donna Kernsmith

Further Reading

Eldridge, H. (1998). *Therapist guide for maintaining change: Relapse prevention for adult perpetrators of child sexual abuse*. Thousand Oaks, CA: Sage.

Greenfeld, L. A. (1997). *Sex offenses and offenders: An analysis of data on rape and sexual assault* (Vol. NCJ #163392). Washington, DC: U.S. Department of Justice.

Hunter, J., & Becker, J. (1998). Motivators of adolescent sex offenders and treatment perspectives. In J. Shaw (Ed.), *Sexual aggression* (pp. 211–234). Washington, DC: American Psychiatric Press.

Mihailides, S., Devilly, G. J., & Ward, T. (2004). Implicit cognitive distortions and sexual offending. *Sexual Abuse: A Journal of Research and Treatment, 16*(4), 333–350.

Perpetrators, Interventions with (Overview)

Intervention with perpetrators of sexual violence can take several forms, including therapeutic intervention, incarceration, and community management. These interventions are highly interrelated as they may occur simultaneously as directed by the court system. Only rarely will an offender enter treatment voluntarily.

Although there are commonalities between different forms of interventions with perpetrators of sexual violence, variations do exist based on the population served. Interventions with juveniles and female offenders are found to address issues of trauma or focus on more process-oriented approaches. Interventions with males and adult offenders are more often rooted in cognitive behavioral or educational models. More recently, interventions have begun to emerge that are culturally specific or attend to coexisting issues such as mental health or substance abuse. Consistent across all forms of intervention is the goal of increasing accountability for abusive behavior and decreasing risk of future offenses.

Treatment Programs

Perpetrators of sexual violence may enter treatment programs either as part of a prison or civil commitment sentence, at the time of release as part of a probation requirement, or voluntarily. It is believed that the vast majority of those participating in treatment are ordered through Child Protective Services or criminal court. However, treatment is available through individual counseling, online discussion groups, or support groups such as Sex Addicts Anonymous and Sex and Love Addicts Anonymous. As Kernsmith discusses in her entry on **Treatment Programs for Sexual Offenders**, little is known about the frequency of use or the impact of these interventions.

More commonly, court-ordered group counseling is provided using a variety of therapeutic approaches. The goal of these interventions is to eliminate the sexually abusive behaviors, although the means of achieving these goals is varied. Some interventions may attempt to increase empathy for the victim and decrease cognitive distortions related to offending (see the entries on **Rape, Denial** by Boianelli and **Perpetrators [Overview]** by Kernsmith for more information). Other approaches focus on the development of prosocial behavior and positive self-concept. Still others seek to eliminate sexual violence by addressing underlying issues such as trauma, mental health, and disabilities. Each of these approaches also strives to increase coping mechanisms and develop strategies to minimize urges to offend. The entry on **Treatment Programs for Sexual Offenders** provides greater detail on these intervention approaches.

Incarceration

Although incarceration has commonly been an aspect of the criminal justice response to sexual violence, recent policy changes have resulted in increasingly lengthy sentences for offenders. These sentences vary between states as they are based in the sentencing guidelines stated in the policies. For misdemeanor charges considered to be less severe, sentences can be as brief as 90 days. More severe, repeated, or violent offenses may involve lifetime imprisonment. Although youth are less likely to be incarcerated, they may be treated in residential facilities or juvenile detention facilities. In some cases, a youth may be tried as an adult and sentenced to serve time in an adult prison or jail facility. Therapeutic treatment is commonly available for both juveniles and adults for some length of time prior to release. Among juveniles, this intervention may span the duration of the incarceration. For adult offenders, treatment may be required for many years or only a few weeks.

In contrast to criminal incarceration is civil confinement. These sentences differ from incarceration as the length is determined by rehabilitation, not a predetermined sentence. Commonly, civil confinement is used in cases where the offender is believed to be a habitual offender, referred to as a sexually violent predator, with severe mental health issues that make typical intervention approaches ineffective or inappropriate. These offenders are deemed to be at the highest risk for reoffending. Civil commitment may be required following incarceration or in lieu of prison time. A discussion of the advantages and disadvantages of this approach is included in the entry on **Civil Commitment of Sex Offenders** by Wood.

Community Management

Upon reentry to the community from jail or prison, an offender will commonly be required to participate in a community management program through probation or parole. D'Orio describes the containment and comprehensive approaches to providing these services in her entry on **Criminal Justice and Perpetrators**. In the containment approach, the treatment provider and probation or parole offices maintain frequent contact to decrease the risk of offending through therapeutic intervention and monitoring. A forensic polygraph examiner is involved to ensure the truthfulness of communications. This process begins at the time of release from incarceration, or sentencing if incarceration is not required, and continues for a duration determined by the judge.

A comprehensive approach, sometimes referred to as a coordinated community response, begins at the time of the initial report of the sexual crime and continues throughout the investigation, court process, incarceration, and community reentry. This process involves a wide range of community entities including victim's services, medical, criminal justice, and education. The approach is focused more broadly than the individual offender and victim, with the goal of preventing sexual violence, improving institutional responses to victims of violence, and increasing accountability of offenders. The techniques of community management, such as registration and monitoring, may be similar in each of these approaches.

Sex offender registries are databases that contain personal information, location of residence, workplaces and school affiliation, and information on the crime for which he or she was convicted. Originally, these databases were maintained only for law enforcement and probation officers. In the 1990s, legislation was enacted that required states to make this information available to the public. In most cases, this is a passive approach in which offender information is made available through a website and at the police department. In some jurisdictions, active community notification is used, in which residents of a neighborhood will be alerted every time a registered offender moves into the neighborhood. States have the ability to determine which crimes may be included within the registry, including those that are sexually based, such as indecent exposure, lewd behavior, and sexual assault, and nonsexual crimes against children, such as kidnapping.

In addition to assisting law enforcement in monitoring the location of convicted offenders, the stated goal of public registration is to deter future criminal behavior and to allow the public the means to avoid potentially dangerous individuals. Evaluation research has found that registration information that is available to law enforcement is effective in reducing recidivism. However, public registries have not been found to decrease rates of recidivism, and may actually increase offense rates, particularly in states that have large, overly inclusive registries.

Critics argue that the registry focuses the attention of the public on the fear of the assault by a stranger, when in fact, the assailant is most often someone known to and trusted by the victim. The false sense of security may decrease other prevention efforts such as talking to children about boundaries and risk reduction. In a time when funding for sexual assault prevention is being cut in schools and universities, the role of parents in talking about sexual abuse and assault is even more crucial.

Additionally, critics argue that registration poses undue barrier to reintegration for offenders. The stigma associated with being labeled as a sex offender results in stigmatization, alienation, housing instability, difficulty maintaining employment, and harassment. These may increase the likelihood of recidivism. Additionally, as the repercussions of registration also impact the families of registered offenders, victims of sexual violence who are known to or related to the offender may be more hesitant to report due to fear of the public implications of registration for the whole family. Kernsmith provides further discussion of the legislative issues and impacts in his entry on **Sex Offender Registries**.

In addition to registration, statutes may restrict the areas in which a convicted offender may reside, work, or spend time. Residency restrictions require that a convicted offender cannot live near schools, day care centers, or other areas where children congregate, such as parks. Some jurisdictions have also included school bus stops. In some communities this results in difficulty locating allowable housing and commonly results in clustering of offenders in certain neighborhoods that are not within these boundaries. The most public example of these was a community in Florida where large numbers of registered offenders were living under a highway overpass as it was one of the few available locations to reside in. The community later removed the offenders by declaring a small area nearby to be a park. Supporters of the policies believe that these policies keep predators away from children. Critics of these policies assert that research indicates that most sexual crimes are committed in the home of the victim or more than one mile from the home of the perpetrator, indicating that residency restrictions are irrelevant.

These policies can also limit the employment of a registered sex offender in schools, day care centers, and other companies that primarily serve children as well as limit loitering in these areas. On the surface, it seems a logical strategy to keep child molesters away from places where they could foster relationships with and groom potential victims. However, like registration requirements, they may create a false sense of security and decrease the likelihood that parents will employ prevention strategies and talk to their children about potential abuse. In addition, although it is a common assumption among the public that registered sex offender is synonymous with child molester, many registered sex offenders are not a danger to a child as they have only adult victims or noncontact offenses such as public urination. Policies on loitering are an additional challenge for registered offenders who are parents and may not be able to pick up their children, attend school events, or participate in teacher conferences.

Additional means of supervision may include electronic monitoring through tethering and GPS monitoring. Tethering involves requiring an offender to wear a device that alerts law enforcement if he or she leaves a designated area. Most commonly, this is used for what is sometimes called "house arrest" in which the individual must stay in his or her home or within the boundaries of the property. GPS monitoring involves the requirement that an offender where a monitoring device that records the location of the individual at all times. These may be used in conjunction with other strategies, such as curfews, that restrict where an individual can go at night, on holidays such as Halloween, or during school hours. D'Orio provides further discussion of the ethical considerations of each of the monitoring approaches as well as other criminal justice interventions in her entry.

Another approach to managing sexual offenders is the use of physical or chemical castration, used almost exclusively with male offenders. Physical castration is the removal of sex organs associate with the production of hormones controlling sexual desire and functioning, the testicles for males and ovaries for females. Only two states allow physical castration and they are rarely used in either state. Most criticism of physical castration relates to the permanency of the procedure. Chemical castration is a process in which drugs are administered to reduce the capacity for sexual arousal and physical sexual response. The procedure is believed to be almost completely reversible once the treatment. In addition to the invasive nature of castration, criticisms of the procedure commonly relate to physical side effects.

Another critique is that the approach is based in the myth that sexual violence is primarily derived by sexual arousal, when it is more commonly a result of a myriad of emotional and cognitive distortions, including anger, shame, and desire for power. Chemical castration has been found to be effective in reducing recidivism among only those offenders driven by paraphilic sexual desires for children and/or violence. See the entry on **Castration, Chemical** by Kernsmith for his discussion of the procedures, and legal and ethical considerations.

Effectiveness of Treatment and Intervention

For sex offender treatment, effectiveness is typically defined as a decrease in recidivism rates among sexual offenders. A more complete discussion of the implications of research design and measurement choices is included in the entry on **Treatment Programs for Sexual Offenders**. Essentially, research explores the degree to which dangerous or abusive behaviors are exhibited. Less commonly, increases in prosocial behaviors, such as peer relationships, employment, and housing stability, may also be considered. Recidivism patterns vary considerably based on the age and gender of the offender and the type of offense, such as child molestation, rape, and noncontact offenses including exhibitionism or child pornography. In general, it is found that recidivism rates for juveniles and female offenders are significantly lower than adults and male offenders, particularly following participation in treatment programs.

Although research indicates a wide variation in the success rates of treatment programs, it is generally believed that those offenders who participate in treatment will have lower rates of recidivism than those who do not, particularly for sexual crimes. Nonsexual recidivism is also reduced when programs attend to challenges of reentry and reintegration into society. See the entry on **Treatment Programs for Sexual Offenders** for more information on treatment approaches.

Conclusion

There are many challenges in considering the most appropriate and effective means of intervening with sexual offenders. In all of these considerations, the safety of victims and potential victims must be the primary concern. Research indicates that treatment may be the most effective. However, it is also the most costly. Other community management approaches may have unintended consequences that may provide barriers to reintegration and increase recidivism. Further research is needed to provide a more holistic understanding of the impacts of each form of intervention on the offender, the victim, their families, and the community to inform the thoughtful development of policy approaches to increase public safety.

Poco Donna Kernsmith

Play Therapy

Child sexual abuse and other forms of child maltreatment that have the potential to be traumatic compromise children's normative development and can result in brief to long-standing or mild to severe emotional consequences. Immediate therapeutic intervention provided by adequately trained clinicians and support of nonoffending caretakers after the incidence of sexual abuse contribute to, and often predict, successful outcomes.

Providing therapy to children who have experienced sexual abuse requires clinicians to engage with them at their individual developmental levels and to invite their participation in creative and compelling ways. Play therapy is one of a number of "expressive therapies," a term used to define the therapeutic use of the arts and play, including music, dance, drama, writing, play, art, and sand play.

Although people of all ages may benefit from the use of play in treatment, play therapy is especially appropriate for children ages 3–12 years old and is particularly effective in engaging nonverbal and acutely resistant children. Therapists use play therapy to help children express what is troubling them when they do not yet have the verbal language or the emotional strength or motivation to express their thoughts and feelings. Play therapists believe that whatever is distressing to the child will eventually be "acted out" or brought to the surface through the use of toys and play. Qualified play therapists will manage the child's play and create a "safe enough distance" in which the child may gradually expose him or herself to intolerable memories and begin to tolerate the painful emotions associated with a traumatic event.

When initiating play therapy with children who have experienced sexual abuse, establishing safety in the relationship is a necessary first step. In addition, reviewing limits to confidentiality, conducting a comprehensive assessment, creating a treatment plan, and including supportive nonoffending family members are initial steps in treatment. Each play therapy session varies in length but usually lasts about 30–50 minutes, once weekly. The length of treatment varies from child to child depending on severity of symptoms, yet some research indicates that it takes an average of 20 play therapy sessions to resolve the problems of a typical child referred for treatment (Landreth, 2002). Treating victims of complex trauma may require longer time frames in order to establish necessary relational trust and address complex symptoms.

There are several known and valued theories of play therapy (e.g., psychoanalytic, Gestalt, behavioral, Jungian, Adlerian, ecosystemic, child centered, filial) that serve as an anchor for the toys, approaches, and therapist posture that are selected. Depending on the theoretical orientation of the therapist and the treatment goals, a therapist may be directive, which involves the therapist guiding the play (e.g., the clinician initiates playing a board game that generates specific dialogue about children's thoughts and feelings about traumatic events). The therapist may also take a nondirective posture, allowing and encouraging the child to guide the play. Utilizing either approach, the therapist may ask open-ended questions regarding the play, reflect on what she or he observes in the child's play, while accepting the child's metaphorical or literal responses and perspectives.

Clinicians who specialize in play therapy typically stock their offices with a standard list of toys selected purposely for symbolic possibilities. Those toys can include dollhouses, medical kits, puppets, dress-up materials, kitchen utensils and food, baby dolls, trucks, cars, therapeutic board games, and miniatures. Toys are selected to have a broad developmental range, and to be gender- and culture-appropriate. Children who interact with play therapy possess the ability to use creative imagination, pretend, and role-play to assign various meanings to the objects in their play. Children respond differently to play therapy. Some may engage in an absorbed, focused, and solitary way while others crave and request interactions with the therapist. Some children appear to need a great deal of approval, attention, or direction and may insist that the therapist become an active participant in the play. At the clinician's discretion, based on his or her theoretical model, training, and expertise, as well as his or her assessment of the child's readiness and developmental level, direct questions may be asked and interpretations of the child's play can be carefully offered.

The Association for Play Therapy (APT) was founded in 1982 and has established guidelines for the educational requirements to become a registered play therapist (RPT) and registered play therapy supervisor (RPT-S). Registered play therapists are licensed (or certified) mental health professionals who have earned a master's or doctorate degree in a mental health field and have provided the APT with documentation that verifies their graduate degrees, their completion of a minimum number of play therapy training and supervision hours, and their completion of required continuing education hours.

Kristin Briggs and Eliana Gil

See also Child Maltreatment (Neglect and Physical); Child Sexual Abuse

Further Reading

Carmichael, K. D. (2006). *Play therapy: An introduction.* Glenview, IL: Prentice Hall.

Gil, E. (1991). *Healing power of play: Working with abused children.* New York, NY: Guilford Press.

Gil, E. (2006). *Helping abused and traumatized children: Integrating directive and nondirective approaches.* New York, NY: Guilford Press.

Landreth, G. L. (2002). *Play therapy: The art of the relationship.* New York, NY: Brunner-Routledge.

O'Connor, K. J., & Braverman, L. D. (2009). *Play therapy theory and practice: Comparing theories and techniques* (2nd ed.). Hoboken, NJ: Wiley.

Schaefer, C. E. (1993). *The therapeutic power of play.* Northvale, NJ: Jason Aronson.

Selected Website

The Association for Play Therapy. Retrieved from http://www.a4pt.org/

Pornography

Throughout history people have represented sexuality in literature and art, but pornography did not emerge as a mass industry until the late 1950s, eventually breaking into mainstream distribution outlets and growing to an estimated $12 billion-a-year business in the United States by the end of the twentieth century. Although still proscribed by law in a variety of ways, pornography is increasingly accepted in contemporary culture, and contemporary pop culture has become increasingly pornographic.

"Pornography" is sometimes used to describe all sexually explicit books, magazines, movies, and websites, with a distinction made between soft core (nudity with limited sexual activity not including penetration) and hard core (graphic images of actual, not simulated, sexual activity including penetration). Pornography also is often distinguished from erotica (material that depicts sexual behavior with mutuality and respect), leaving pornography as the term for material depicting sex with domination or degradation. Laboratory studies of pornography's effects commonly use three categories: overtly violent; nonviolent but degrading; and sexually explicit but neither violent nor degrading.

The terms "obscenity" and "indecency" have specific legal meanings. Indecency defines a category of words and images that can be regulated in broadcasting (over-the-air radio and television)—language or material that, in context, depicts or describes sexual or excretory organs or activities, in terms patently offensive as measured by contemporary community standards for the broadcast medium. The Federal Communications Commission administers indecency regulations.

In the 1973 *Miller v. California* decision, the Supreme Court established a three-part test for defining obscenity (material that appeals to the prurient interest; portrays sexual conduct in a patently offensive way; and does not have serious literary, artistic, political, or scientific value) and set contemporary community standards as the measure of evaluation. Although a strict application of state and federal obscenity laws could lead to prosecution of much contemporary pornography, enforcement usually occurs only where there is political support. This prosecutorial discretion means material for sale openly in one jurisdiction may not be available in another. However, the availability of computer-based pornography ensures that graphic, sexually explicit material can be obtained easily anywhere. The only exception is child pornography—material that is either made using children or, in the digital age, made through the use of technology that makes it appear the sexual activity uses children. The former is illegal without question (*New York v. Ferber*, 1982) and available only underground; the legal status of the latter remains uncertain (*Ashcroft v. Free Speech Coalition*, 2002).

As legal prohibitions have lessened, a once-underground pornography industry with ties to organized crime has become a routine business with its own trade magazines, *Adult Video News* and *XBIZ*. Heterosexual pornography makes up the bulk of the commercial market, with a significant amount of gay male pornography available and a smaller amount of commercial material produced for lesbians. Pornography is distributed using all communication technologies: printing, photographs, film, telephones, video, DVD, and digital technology.

Playboy Magazine, which debuted in December 1953, was the first sex magazine to break into mainstream distribution channels. In the 1960s and 1970s, pornographic films moved into public theaters. In the 1980s, video swamped other forms, with the number of new pornographic video/DVD titles released each year increasing from 1,500 in 1986 to about 13,000 in the mid-2000s. Computers emerged as a major vehicle for pornography in the 1990s, moving into the Internet and mobile devices in the 2000s. In the 2000s, ease of unauthorized digital copying by consumers and the increase in amateur pornography have posed threats to the profitability of the pornography industry.

The main categories in today's pornographic movie industry are "features" and "wall-to-wall/gonzo." Features have a traditional three-act narrative with some plot and characters. The industry markets these as "couples movies" that hope to appeal to women as well as the traditional male audience, although the vast majority of pornography consumers are men. Wall-to-wall movies are all-sex productions with no pretense of plot or dialogue. Many of these movies are shot gonzo style, in which performers acknowledge the camera and often speak directly to the audience. In addition, there are specialty titles—movies that feature sadomasochism and bondage, fetish material, transsexuals—that fill niche markets.

The majority of hard-core movies include oral, vaginal, and anal sex, almost always ending with ejaculation on the woman. In the wall-to-wall/gonzo movies, double penetration (anal and vaginal penetration by two men at the same time) and aggressive oral penetration of women are increasingly common, as are hair pulling, slapping, and rough treatment. As these movies push the limits of overt violence and brutality, pornography producers search for new ways to attract male viewers looking for increased stimulation, leading to practices such as "ass-to-mouth," in which a man removes his penis from a woman's anus and places it directly into her mouth.

Debates over pornography traditionally pitted liberal advocates of sexual freedom against conservative proponents of traditional sexual morality. That changed in the 1970s with the feminist critique of pornography, which emerged out of the struggle against sexual violence during the women's movement in the 1960s and focused on the way in which pornography eroticizes domination and subordination. Feminist critics argued for a focus not on subjective sexual mores but on the harm to women used in pornography and against whom pornography is used.

Much of the debate about pornography concerns the question of effects. Does pornography, particularly material that explicitly eroticizes violence and/or domination, result in sexual violence against women, children, and other vulnerable people? Pornography's supporters and some researchers argue there is no conclusive evidence. Other researchers contend the evidence points to some kind of effects with some groups of men. No one argues that pornography is the sole causal factor in rape; the question is whether the use of pornography can be considered a sufficient condition for triggering a sexual assault.

Research also investigates the effects of heterosexual men's habitual use of pornography on consensual relationships. Evidence suggests some men withdraw from sex and intimacy with female partners when pornography use begins to dominate their lives. Other men's sexual desires begin to mimic pornographic practices, leading to requests or demands for sexual activity that female partners find uncomfortable, painful, or degrading.

Many feminists have argued that attention to the experiences of men and women—both those who use pornography and those against whom pornography is used—makes the connection clear. Such accounts provide specific examples of how pornography can (1) be an important factor in shaping a male-dominant view of sexuality, (2) contribute to a user's difficulty in separating sexual fantasy and reality, (3) be used to initiate victims and break down resistance to sexual activity, and (4) provide a training manual for abuse.

Robert Jensen

See also Child Pornography; Pornography, Internet

Further Reading

Dines, Gail. (2010). *Pornland: How porn hijacked our sexuality.* Boston, MA: Beacon.

Dworkin, A. (1981). *Pornography: Men possessing women.* New York, NY: Perigee. (Reprint edition, 1989, Plume)

Jensen, R. (2007). *Getting off: Pornography and the end of masculinity.* Cambridge, MA: South End Press.

MacKinnon, C. A., & Dworkin, A. (1997). *In harm's way: The pornography civil rights hearings.* Cambridge, MA: Harvard University Press.

Paul, P. (2005). *Pornified: How pornography is transforming our lives, our relationships, and our families.* New York, NY: Times Books.

Strossen, N. (1995). *Defending pornography: Free speech, sex, and the fight for women's rights.* New York, NY: Scribner.

Williams, L. (1989). *Hard core: Power, pleasure and the "frenzy of the visible."* Berkeley, CA: University of California Press.

Pornography, Internet

Cyber pornography is sexually explicit imagery that is transmitted via the Internet. Pornographic content can be found in the form of still images, videos, and live web shows in which viewers can direct the models' actions. Such imagery is available via a number of avenues, most commonly websites. Contents are available to suit a wide range of potential interests, ranging from "soft-core" imagery such as photos of naked models and adults engaging in conventional sex acts to deviant imagery, such as sadism, animal sex, or child pornography. The advent of the Internet has promoted the availability and easy accessibility of such imagery. Hundreds of thousands of websites exist that feature sexual content, and some pornographic websites have reported as many as 50 million or more hits annually (Worden, 2001). These websites are easily accessed, requiring users only to point and click, often free of charge. The Internet offers the additional perceived benefit of anonymity, allowing users to indulge their interests within the privacy of their homes.

Cyber pornography was not always so accessible as it is today. Although the first IBM PC appeared in 1981, public Internet access did not become available until the early 1990s. The first Web browser was developed by Sir Berners-Lee in 1990, and the first browser software was developed in 1993. The version of HTTP (hypertext transfer protocol), the standardized communication mode for computer networks and the dominant means of information transfer over the Internet, that is used today did not appear until 1999. Early Internet usage was mainly by individuals in the military and academic sectors. Content was limited, and access was not readily available to the general public. Pornographic imagery was initially introduced onto the Internet using a text-based imagery format called ASCII art, in which pictures are pieced together from strategic arrangements of letters, numbers, and other characters available on a standard keyboard. These files were small and could be easily and quickly transmitted from user to user; this format was preferable to image files, which were larger and required computers with more advanced graphics technology and a network with greater processing speed.

As noted above, the first point-and-click software, which is now second nature for users of the Internet, was first introduced in 1993. During the same time period, ASCII images were shared among users via Usenet groups, a form of online message board. This method developed as a way to share images in spite of slow network speeds. Users could scan images from adult magazines, encode them as ASCII art, and break those files into smaller files that could be transferred more quickly. Viewers could then reassemble the smaller files to re-create a whole image. Although initially free, entrepreneurs began to charge for access, laying the groundwork for a booming business. The advent of the World Wide Web widely expanded the market due to increases in accessibility and speed. As technology has continued to grow, so too have the available offerings, which now include high-definition imagery, streaming videos, and live web shows.

Despite the prevalence of commercial pornography websites, free sites remain. Some free websites offer only a sampling of images or only thumbnail images that cannot be enlarged; such websites direct users to commercial sites to access a more extensive catalog of full-size images. Peer-to-peer (P2P) file-sharing networks present an additional cost-free option. Using a format similar to that of illegal music and movie-sharing websites, such as Napster or ThePirateBay, users can upload their images and download the images of other users. The availability of free content is now so prevalent that it has begun to undercut the commercial cyber pornography market. A shift toward free material is clearly demonstrated in a decline in online sales beginning in 2005: between 2005 and 2006, sales of pornographic materials dropped from $4.28 billion to $3.62 billion (Richtel, 2007).

Cyber pornography is available in multiple formats, the most common being still images, videos, and webcams. Still images remain popular and include images scanned from print material and uploaded from digital cameras, as well as stills taken from videos. Videos and streaming videos are widely available in a variety of formats, including MPEG, WMV, and QuickTime. Although commercial video sites are available, free sites have gained a great deal of popularity, particularly those that allow users to upload their own content in a format similar to that of YouTube. Live acts are also available via webcam and may be either free or paid. Such formats often include a chat component in which viewers may request that the actors engage in particular erotic acts.

There are currently no international laws regulating cyber pornography. Each country has its own laws regarding what is protected and what is illegal. The first law in the United States aimed at regulating Internet pornography was the Communications Decency Act of 1996, which criminalized the distribution of sexual materials to children. This law was immediately blocked by the courts and in 1997 was declared to be unconstitutional as a violation of First Amendment right to free speech. Currently, laws regulating the legality of various types of pornography vary by state. If an act depicted is legal in the jurisdiction in which it is produced, it can be distributed, regardless of the jurisdiction in which it might be accessed and viewed. This standard does not apply, however, to viewers: regardless of where the imagery is produced, users can be prosecuted for being in possession of content considered illegal in the jurisdiction in which they live.

Legislation has targeted the creation and distribution of child pornography. The Child Pornography Prevention Act (CPPA) was introduced in 1996, but was struck down in 2002 by the U.S. Supreme Court. CPPA criminalized material that "appears to be" or "conveys the impression" of children engaged in sexual acts, which opponents argued would unfairly prohibit distribution of material that was neither overtly pornographic in nature nor produced by exploiting real children. Congress passed the Child Online Protection Act of 1998, which prohibits commercial websites from publishing materials that may be harmful to minors unless those sites can prove that some effort has been made to block their access (e.g., requiring a credit card for access). This legislation remains in effect.

Adeena M. Gabriel and Raina V. Lamade

See also Pornography; Rape, Cyber; Sex Workers

Further Reading

Richtel, M. (2007, June 2). For pornographers, Internet's virtues turn to vices. *New York Times*. Retrieved from http://www.nytimes.com/2007/06/02/technology/02porn.html

Worden, S. (2001, March 1). E-trafficking. *Foreign Policy*, 92–97.

Pregnancy

The physical and psychological trauma of sexual assault is considerable. To learn that one is pregnant as a result of the violence adds another layer of fear, stress, and confusion for the woman. It is a time when a woman needs information, support, and comfort.

Physical violence is frequently accompanied by sexual violence. In North America, it is estimated that 40 to 60 percent of women who are physically abused are also sexually abused (Humphreys, 2011). Research on the relationship between abuse and pregnancy often does not distinguish between the physical and sexual aspects of assaults. Whether the violence is of a physical nature, sexual nature, or both, male dominance and power is often the underlying basis of the assault.

Sexual violence includes rape and other efforts to control women's reproductive decision making, such as pregnancy coercion (e.g., pressuring women to get pregnant through physical violence and/or psychological threat; economic abuse by not giving a woman money to get birth control) and birth control sabotage (e.g., putting holes in condoms, hiding birth control pills). According to recent data, in the United States about 25 percent of women between 18 and 44 who have had at least one birth have experienced some coercion the first time they had intercourse (Williams, Brett, & Abma, 2009). This statistic does not include women who aborted or miscarried, so the number of women who have been coerced and became pregnant is likely to be much higher. It is estimated that there are 32,000 pregnancies in the United States each year as a result of rape (Holmes, Resnick, Kilpatrick, & Best, 1996).

Women who have been sexually abused as teens are more likely to undertake risky sexual practices such as trading sex for money and not using birth control (possibly resulting in unintended pregnancy). As well, women who are pregnant as a result of rape (compared to women who are not raped and become pregnant) are more likely to have sexually transmitted infections (McFarlene, 2007), which can interfere with childbearing at a later time when it may be desired.

In developing countries where the frequency of sexual violence is much higher than in the United States, women are at increased risk of illness and death when they become pregnant because of poverty, inadequate medical care, lack of access to safe (and legal) abortion services, misogynistic cultural norms that severely punish women who have been raped, and continued abuse.

Moore, Frohwirth, and Miller (2010) report that women who became pregnant as a result of a rape are often pressured into resolving the pregnancy in the way that the partner desires, through his insistence either that she maintain the pregnancy or that she get an abortion. This form of abuse further limits women's reproductive freedom.

Sexual violence and physical and psychological abuse often continue during pregnancy and can result in serious problems to both the mother and the developing child. The woman can be badly injured during assaults with resultant trauma to the fetus. Knowing that she is carrying an unwanted pregnancy, the woman may be depressed and anxious and thus may resort to smoking or drinking, which can affect the fetus. Post-traumatic stress disorder may also result. Additionally, when there is abuse, early labor or miscarriage are more likely to occur. A recent study found that women who have been raped are more likely to have a longer second stage of labor and a cesarean section (Nerum et al., 2010). Unintended pregnancies are also associated with a lower likelihood that women will breastfeed. Although once not considered a crime in the United States, spousal rape is now illegal in all 50 states and the District of Columbia; however, the likelihood that a woman will report it to the authorities is small.

If a woman has been raped and thinks it is possible she is pregnant and does not wish to maintain the pregnancy, she may want to consider using emergency contraception, that is, either the morning-after pill or the insertion of an intrauterine device (IUD). The morning-after pill (also called "Plan B") may be purchased at a pharmacy by anyone 17 and over without a prescription. The IUD must be inserted by a health care professional. Either method must be used within five days of unprotected intercourse and preferably as soon as possible. Although emergency contraception is not 100 percent effective, it is a safe means of pregnancy prevention.

When using the Internet to learn about rape and pregnancy, women should be cautious because many of the first websites that appear on search engines are supported by antichoice organizations and/or religious groups that are antiabortion. The websites selected below will provide more reliable information.

Michele G. Greene

See also Abortion; Depression and Anxiety; Prostitution; PTSD and Stress; STDs and HIV/AIDS

Further Reading

Holmes, M., Resnick, S. H., Kilpatrick, D. G., & Best, C. L. (1996). Rape-related pregnancy: Estimates and descriptive characteristics from a national sample of women. *American Journal of Obstetrics and Gynecology, 175,* 320–324.

Humphreys, J. (2011). Sexually transmitted infections, pregnancy, and intimate partner violence. *Health Care for Women International, 32*, 23–38.

McFarlene, J. (2007). Pregnancy following partner rape: What we know and what we need to know. *Trauma, Violence, & Abuse, 8*, 127–134.

Moore, A. M., Frohwirth, L., & Miller, E. (2010). Male reproductive control of women who have experienced intimate partner violence in the United States. *Social Science & Medicine, 70*, 1737–1744.

Nerum, H., Halvorsen, L., Oian, P., Sorlie, T., Straume, B., & Blix, E. (2010). Birth outcomes in primiparous women who were raped as adults: A matched controlled study. *BJOG: An International Journal of Obstetrics and Gynaecology, 117*, 288–294.

Williams, C. M., Brett, K. M., & Abma, J. C. (2009). Coercive first intercourse and unintended first births. *Violence and Victims, 24*, 351–363.

Selected Websites

The Facts on Reproductive Health and Partner Abuse. Futures without Violence. Retrieved from http://www.futureswithoutviolence.org/userfiles/file/Children_and _Families/Reproductive.pdf

The Morning-After Pill. Emergency Contraception. Planned Parenthood. Retrieved from http://www.plannedparenthood.org/health-topics/emergency-contraception -morning-after-pill-4363.asp

Rape and pregnancy. Pandora's Project: Support and Resources for Survivors of Rape and Sexual Abuse. Retrieved from http://www.pandys.org/articles/rapeandpregnancy .html

Sexual assault fact sheet. Womenshealth.gov. Retrieved from http://womenshealth.gov/ publications/our-publications/fact-sheet/sexual-assault.cfm

Prevention (Overview)

Sexual violence (SV) against women and children has been identified as a major social problem in the United States over the past few decades, largely due to the efforts of the civil rights and feminist movements in the 1960s and 1970s. As awareness of the problem increased, services for victims proliferated, providing assistance to survivors coping with the aftermath of sexual abuse. In addition to the provision of these services after SV occurs, efforts to address the prevention of sexual violence have expanded over the years. The *prevention* of sexual violence means addressing the problem before it occurs.

Understanding the prevention of sexual violence is complex, has evolved over time, and continues to be debated. What prevention looks like is often shaped by views of the causes of sexual violence. For example, a feminist perspective contends that we are living in a "rape-supportive culture" that sustains gender stereotypes and sexism, and thus normalizes certain behaviors acts of violence against women. Based on this view, rape prevention efforts must then address the underlying assumptions about gender and sexual violence. Changing rape-supportive ideologies and social norms will ultimately decrease sexual violence perpetration. Those who view sexual violence as more of a criminal issue might argue that prevention efforts should be heavily focused on defining SV as a crime, thereby seeking effective deterrents, and punishing perpetrators. Yet those subscribing to other theories to explain the cause of SV would likely suggest a different purpose of prevention efforts (see entry on **Theories [Overview]** for a complete review of viewpoints for the cause of SV).

In this entry, we begin by providing a general definition of SV prevention and the various types of prevention. Next, the various theoretical frameworks used to support SV prevention are reviewed. Efforts to involve the community and men in SV prevention are then presented, and followed by a discussion of how SV prevention efforts are directed at different age groups.

What Is Sexual Violence Prevention?

Prevention can most generally be regarded as a thoughtful way to reduce the potential of something negative happening while promoting positive behaviors and contexts. Translated to the field of SV, prevention means creating healthy, safe environments and behaviors that will hinder the perpetration of sexually violent acts before they happen. To further understand the definition of SV prevention, the field of public health is instrumental, as it has long engaged in developing our understanding of the prevention of a number of issues such as smoking, and began to recognize violence as a public health issue in the mid-1980s. The public health model is focused on addressing actions that prevent SV from initially occurring. In particular, the public health model defines prevention as both decreasing risk factors and increasing protective factors for SV. Research has identified some risk factors for SV, such as individuals holding negative attitudes and beliefs toward sexual violence, the absence of community standards and laws to sanction perpetrators of SV, and societal norms that support SV. *Protective factors* are attributes that increase the health and well-being of individuals and communities, thereby protecting them from SV. Less research has been conducted on protective factors but suggests that egalitarian gender roles, and social norms that disapprove of SV are related to less SV perpetration.

There are multiple ways in which SV can be prevented. Within our understanding of prevention, there are distinctions that help to describe the various types of prevention. In her entry on **Prevention, Levels**, Victoria L. Banyard explains the different ways in which SV prevention can be categorized. One distinction is based on who is the target of the prevention efforts, including universal (whole population), selective (considered high risk), or indicated (where problem may have already started). Additionally, Banyard explains the commonly utilized distinction of primary prevention (occurring before the problem's onset), secondary (high-risk situations), or tertiary (after an assault occurs, to increase the health of survivors and prevent perpetrators from reoffending). She also presents expanded models of prevention that address multiple locations for prevention such as Cohen and Swift's (1999) Spectrum of Prevention, which defines prevention as needing to occur from the individual level up through the organizational level to legislative levels.

In defining prevention, it is important to distinguish these types of prevention from risk reduction. Efforts to reduce the risk of potential victims have historically and erroneously been labeled as prevention efforts, when the two ideas have important differences. As explained in the entry by Grove and Zadnik, **Prevention versus Risk Reduction**, prevention focuses on stopping the action of SV from occurring, which therefore must be focused on the actions of the potential perpetrators. Risk reduction, on the other hand, serves as a safety measure to help reduce the risk of victimization, but places the responsibility on potential victims. As Grove and Zadnik explain, there is room for both strategies but true prevention must focus on addressing the root causes of SV.

Theoretical Frameworks for SV Prevention

Prevention is argued to be essential because it works to decrease or eliminate SV before it even occurs. Understanding how prevention works can be explained in part by a number of theoretical frameworks. These frameworks provide a foundation for developing effective SV strategies.

A prominent framework used for understanding SV prevention is the ecological model. As explained by Erin A. Casey in **Prevention, Ecological Model of**, the ecological framework is based on the understanding that human behavior is shaped by multiple levels of interaction, including individuals, relationships, community, and society (see the **Theory, Ecological Approach** entry for an expanded discussion). These various levels are used to explain both the causes of SV as well as points for potential intervention and prevention. As Casey discusses, ecological approaches maintain that SV prevention efforts must target risk factors for SV perpetration simultaneously at these various levels. As a result, factors that contribute to SV will be reduced within individuals, families, peer groups, communities, and society at large. Examples of SV prevention at the individual level include educational programs to change individuals' attitudes, beliefs, knowledge, and behaviors about SV. At the relationship level, SV prevention efforts work to build family and peer group norms that are rooted in respect and disapprove of coercion and violence. At the community level, SV prevention involves strategies to create climates of safety and respect, and at the societal level, prevention addresses policy and legislative change at the local, state, and federal levels. As Casey notes, there are many strengths to the ecological framework because of its comprehensive approach to addressing SV prevention. However, further research is needed to understand how change at these multiple levels can most effectively be produced.

A related theory that is significant to understanding SV prevention is social norms theory, discussed in the entry by Alan D. Berkowitz (**Theory, Social Norms**). Social norms theory holds the premise that behavior is often based on individuals' misperceptions of others' attitudes or behavior as well as perceptions of their approval or disapproval of behavior. Oftentimes, perceptions of risk behaviors (such as engaging in behaviors supportive of SV) are overestimated, and perceptions of protective or healthy behaviors (such as engaging in healthy relationships or intervening with SV situations) are underestimated. As a result, individuals may become passive bystanders to others' problem behaviors, or, in the worst-case situation, may use their misperceptions to justify their own abusive behavior. Berkowitz explains that correcting these misperceptions is key to SV prevention, and emerging research supports the positive impact of social norms prevention efforts. Further research is needed to confirm the effectiveness of addressing social norms.

Another set of theories have been put forth by the public health field to provide a foundation for SV prevention, including **Theory, Diffusion of Innovations**, **Reasoned Action Approach**, and **Health Belief Model**. The Centers for Disease Control and Prevention (CDC) highlight these theories as important for developing SV prevention efforts. In her entries, Sheila McMahon discusses each of these. She explains that Diffusion of Innovations (DOI) is used to understand community-level social change, based largely on the work of Rogers (1983). DOI explains how innovations—or new ideas or behaviors—are introduced and adopted throughout communities. The adoption of the new behavior by leaders is a key element of DOI and the success of widespread acceptance in the community. In the case of SV prevention, DOI would function by having communities adopt new ideas and behaviors that do not support SV, and are based on respect. Although DOI has not yet been empirically tested with SV prevention, it has been utilized as a foundation for work in the field of HIV prevention.

While DOI represents a community-level theory of behavior change, the Reasoned Action Approach (RAA) is a model for predicting individual behavior. McMahon explains that RAA is a culmination of theoretical development work by Martin Fishbein and Icek Ajzen, and posits that an individual's behavior is influenced by a number of key factors, including attitudes and beliefs about the behavior, perceived norms (perceived social pressure to perform or not perform the behavior), and actual control to perform the behavior (based on a person's skills and environmental factors). Applied to SV, RAA suggests that prevention efforts need to address each of these key constructs (beliefs, attitudes, perceived norms, and control).

Lastly, the Health Belief Model provides another model of individual-level behavior change. McMahon explains that the model, based on the work of Rosenstock and Becker, states that an individual's health behavior can be predicted by a number of perceptions about the impact of the behavior on the person's own health. These include: (1) a person's perception of a threat to her or his health, (2) the person's perception of the consequences of this health threat, (3) the person's evaluation of the benefits of self-protective behavior, (4) perceived barriers or costs to acting in a protective way, (5) action cues such as mass media or symptoms, and (6) enabling factors such as demographics, structural, or social psychological factors.

Current Trends in SV Prevention

Currently, there is a trend in SV prevention to emphasize the need to move beyond an exclusive focus on individuals and include the community in efforts to address SV. In particular, bystander intervention is an approach to SV prevention that frames SV as a community level issue that involves everyone, not just potential perpetrators or victims. In her entry on **Bystander Intervention**, Victoria L. Banyard explains that due to their proximity to contexts involving sexual violence, bystanders have a potentially important role to play in how the situation unfolds. She discusses the process an individual must go through to become an active bystander, including recognition of the situation as a problem and making decisions about what to do. Research has provided us with insight as to factors that influence a person's decision to help including personal factors (personality, mood, gender, personal experiences) and situational factors (relationship to victim and/or perpetrator, presence of other people). Banyard explains that a number of sexual violence prevention programs focus on the role of bystanders. Thus far, evaluation efforts are in their early stages but offer promising results.

Examples of bystander intervention programs include the **Mentors in Violence Prevention** program, developed almost two decades ago at Northeastern University's Center for the Study of Sport in Society. As explained by Jackson Katz, the MVP model addresses gender violence and bullying prevention utilizing a bystander approach that encourages individuals to speak out against abusive behavior. Originally, the MVP program was utilized for sports organizations but has expanded as a tool for diverse groups including high school and college students and the military. Victoria L. Banyard describes another prevention program, **Bringing in the Bystander**, developed at the University of New Hampshire and built upon the work of Jackson Katz and Alan Berkowitz, addressing a range of issues including sexual violence, relationship abuse, and stalking. Banyard describes the program as inclusive of a number of prevention tools including curricula for educational workshops and a bystander social marketing campaign. The program is based on the notion that all individuals have a role to play in ending violence against women. **SCREAM Theater** is another model of a bystander intervention program, developed at Rutgers University nearly two decades ago. As described by Sharon Zucker, this program utilizes peer education and theater as its foundation for delivering awareness about issues including sexual assault, dating violence, stalking, and bullying. The program was created by and for college students, but has expanded over the years to provide presentations for a range of audiences including high schools, middle schools, community groups, and professional organizations. In his entry, John D. Foubert outlines **The Men's Program**, another well-established bystander program, also in existence for almost 20 years. The program is an all-male, peer education workshop that focuses on increasing bystander intervention and victim empathy. Finally, a newer yet popular bystander intervention program is **The Green Dot**, originated by Dr. Dorothy Edwards at the University of Kentucky in 2003. As explained by Jackie Dietch Stackhouse, The Green Dot is a primary prevention strategy aimed at increasing positive bystander intervention to end a range of violent and abusive behaviors, including sexual violence, domestic violence, and stalking. The program is based on the notion that sexual violence and other forms of abuse occur because of negative individual actions (red dots), which can be replaced by positive attitudes, choices, and behaviors that do not support violence (green dots). The Green Dot is based on social diffusion theories, meaning that once leaders in a community start adopting positive actions to end violence, their influence will transmit to other individuals in their community, thereby creating a "viral" effect and promoting cultural shifts.

A common thread among these various bystander programs is their community-inclusive framework, which expands previous approaches to sexual violence prevention by maintaining that all community members have a role to play. One of the results of this perspective is an increased role for men to play in SV prevention. Traditionally, SV was regarded as a "women's issue" and one that men did not necessarily regard as relevant. However, as explained by John Horowitz in his entry on the **Prevention, Involving Men**, men have become increasingly visible in the antirape movement over recent decades. Their involvement in SV prevention is especially important because of their ability to challenge their male peers to consider how their actions may contribute to sexism and SV. Horowitz outlines a number of ways men have become involved in SV prevention, including participating in activism to end SV such as Take Back the Night, engaging in educational efforts to prevent SV, boycotting sexist media, and forming national organizations against SV.

An example of ways that men are becoming more actively engaged in SV prevention is provided by Brian O'Connor in his description of the **Coaching Boys into Men** program, sponsored by Futures without Violence (formerly the Family Violence Prevention Fund). This program delivers media messages about the importance for men to teach boys about treating girls and women with respect, having healthy relationships, and preventing SV and other forms of violence against women. A number of other organizations address the importance of SV prevention. In her entry, Melanie Hoffman reviews the proliferation of **Prevention, Organizations for** and their role in assisting communities. There are a number of diverse organizations worldwide that have been created to address SV, with some focusing on victims and survivors, and others providing education to the larger community.

SV Prevention and Young Women

Research consistently demonstrates that SV disproportionately impacts young women, with national studies indicating that over half of all rapes occur before age 18 (Tjaden & Thoennes, 2000). Additionally, females ages 16–19 have been identified as particularly at risk for experiencing completed or attempted sexual assault as compared to the general population (Bureau of Justice Statistics, 2000). Therefore addressing prevention with young people is of particular concern.

In her entry on **Prevention, Dating Violence**, Weisz explains that sexual assault may occur as one of many forms of violence, along with physical and psychological abuse. Increasingly, there is evidence that teens use technology when engaging in abusive actions. Weisz emphasizes the need for prevention programs on teen dating violence to address the issue of technology, as well as addressing multiple levels including the media, community, family, peer groups, and individuals. Currently, many teen dating violence prevention programs are based in schools, and range in their length, content, and focus. Other key issues when addressing teens and sexual assault are alcohol and consent (see entries on **Alcohol and Drug Abuse [Overview]**).

On college campuses, awareness of the widespread problem of sexual assault has increased over recent years, with statistics indicating that one-fifth to one-fourth of all women experience a completed or attempted rape during their college career (Fisher, Cullen, & Turner, 2000). As such, many universities and colleges have developed SV prevention programs. Venezia and Fisher review the different types of SV prevention programs that occur on college campuses, including those that address primary, secondary, and tertiary prevention (see **Prevention, Colleges and Universities**). While research is mixed on the effectiveness of these various programs, there are a number that show promise such as bystander education.

Childhood SV Prevention

In addition to the disproportionate impact of SV on young women, we know that childhood sexual abuse is a major social problem affecting millions of children worldwide each year. In their entry on **Prevention, Child Sexual Abuse**, Fuentes and Truffin explain the complexity of the problem and some of the unique aspects of child sexual abuse (CSA) prevention efforts. The authors present a review of CSA prevention efforts, stating that effective programs are supported by research, developmentally appropriate for children, and address a broad audience including special-needs children. Fuentes and Truffin outline the various types of CSA prevention efforts, including those directed at parents, those occurring within schools, and those taking place in the community to address broader, societal-level messages that may contribute to CSA.

In conclusion, the prevention of SV is a complex and emerging field. Researchers and practitioners continue to develop an understanding of how to best define and theoretically support SV prevention. Current trends suggest that SV prevention needs to be broad and inclusive of multiple levels, including efforts to address individuals, groups, families, communities, and society as a whole. A number of promising SV prevention efforts are under way, but further work is needed to determine if these approaches are successful in creating social change and communities that do not tolerate SV.

Sarah McMahon

Further Reading

Bureau of Justice Statistics (2000). *National Crime Victimization Survey.* Washington, DC: U.S. Department of Justice.

Centers for Disease Control and Prevention (2004). *Sexual violence prevention: Beginning the dialogue.* Atlanta, GA: Author. Retrieved from: http://www.cdc.gov/violenceprevention/pdf/SVPrevention-a.pdf

Cohen, L., Davis, R., & Mikkelsen, L. (2000). Comprehensive prevention: Improving health outcomes through practice. *Minority Health Today, 1*, 38–41.

Cohen, L., & Swift, S. (1999). The Spectrum of Prevention: Developing a comprehensive approach to injury prevention. *Injury Prevention, 5*, 203–207.

Fisher, B. S., Cullen, F. T., & Turner, M. G. (2000). *The sexual victimization of college women* (Publication No. NCJ 182369). Washington, DC: U.S. Department of Justice, National Institute of Justice.

Tjaden, P., & Thoennes, N. (2000). *Full report of prevalence, incidence, and consequences of violence against women* (Publication No. NCJ 181867). Retrieved from http://www.ojp.usdoj.gov/nij/pubs-sum/181867.htm

Selected Websites

Futures without Violence. Retrieved from http://www.endabuse.org/

National Sexual Violence Resource Center. Retrieved from http://www.nsvrc.org/

Prevent Child Abuse America. Retrieved from http://www.preventchildabuse.org

PreventConnect: A National Online Project Dedicated to the Primary Prevention of Sexual Assault and Domestic Violence. Retrieved from http://www.preventconnect.org

Prevention Innovations. Retrieved from http://www.unh.edu/preventioninnovations/

Prevention Institute. Retrieved from http://www.preventioninstitute.org

Prevention, Child Sexual Abuse

Child sexual abuse (CSA) is a serious and complex social challenge that warrants a comprehensive approach to address it. CSA is when a child is coerced or forced to engage in a sexual act by a person who has power or control over them. The abuse can involve noncontact such as exposure to sexual activity or direct contact such as fondling or penetration. According to the World Health Organization (2002), approximately three percent of children in the world experienced sexual abuse with females being twice as likely to experience abuse as males. In the United States, in 2009 it was estimated that 65,194 children experienced sexual abuse, representing 1.5 per 1,000 children. Research indicates that children who have been sexually abused are more likely to experience mental health concerns, such as depression, anxiety, and self-injurious behaviors, as well as academic troubles, physical problems, and interpersonal difficulties. Given the scope and consequences of CSA, prevention efforts are necessary and important.

The National Center for Missing and Exploited Children (1999) notes that effective CSA prevention programs are research based, developmentally appropriate, and sensitive to special-needs children. These programs focus on core concepts and skills, such as teaching children what CSA is and how to avoid, handle, and protect themselves from dangerous situations. These programs also assure victims they are not at fault. Effective programs tend to be more time intensive and provide ample opportunities for active participation and practice. CSA prevention programs can occur in an array of settings, including homes, schools, and communities.

Since research suggests that the majority of CSA perpetrators are individuals known to the child, many child advocates agree that home-based prevention programs would be helpful, as parents are often the closest to a potential victim's environment. While there are few well-established home-based programs, several parent-focused strategies exist that may assist in preventing CSA. First, parents can collaborate with established prevention programs in the school and community and reinforce CSA safety concepts and skills in the home. Second, parents can be coached on discussing sexuality with their children, trained to identify the indicators of abuse, and be instructed on how to handle any disclosures of abuse. With this knowledge and these skills, parents can be better equipped to comfortably discuss CSA. Lastly, since most perpetrators are known by their victims, parents need to become well versed with the profile of typical perpetrators, the ploys perpetrators use to abuse children, and how best to address these topics with their children. The research suggests that family-based programs that are long term (one to three years) and include home visitation are more effective than stand-alone programs. Recruiting and involving parents in CSA prevention efforts is very important, as they are deemed to be key players in the prevention process.

The majority of CSA prevention programs are school based with approximately 88 percent of elementary school districts in the United States offering some form of prevention presentation to their students. These programs typically teach children how to recognize, resist, and report abuse, commonly known as the three R's. Many studies have established that when students participate in school-based programs, they learn important sexual abuse concepts and demonstrate self-protection skills. The programs that produced the largest changes were those used a time-intensive behavioral skills training approach that included modeling, practice, and reinforcement. School-based presentation modes vary and can include videos, theatrical presentations, lectures, discussion, and written material. One well-researched program is the Good-Touch/Bad-Touch program, which has been field-tested with over 250,000 children.

Community-based CSA prevention efforts attempt to change the broader messages that may be associated with CSA. Child advocates assert that the causes of CSA are rooted in the environment and maintained by societal norms. Rigid gender roles, marginalization, and improper sexualized messages are credited with contributing toward CSA. To combat these factors, several communities have established media campaigns that clearly communicate that CSA is wrong, is illegal, and will not be tolerated. While these efforts seem promising, research needs to be conducted to evaluate their effectiveness. Child advocates also suggest that relevant professionals such as teachers, pediatricians, and clinicians be adequately trained in CSA prevention efforts to ensure an intensive, wide-ranging, and pervasive impact. As these above efforts are developed and implemented, the crafters of these initiatives are urged to consider the racial and ethnic demographics of their communities to ensure the prevention efforts are received by the intended audiences.

A tertiary prevention effort that is vital to eliminating CSA involves treating the perpetrators. While perpetrator treatment has enjoyed great controversy since its inception, recent research reviews have revealed more promising findings. This research suggests that psychological treatment can reduce the likelihood of reoffending by 37 percent (Friedrich & Schmucher, 2005). However, since many of the studies did not employ an experimental approach, this finding is often questioned. The treatment that has been found to be most effective involves a cognitive behavioral approach. Fortunately, the research treatment for juvenile offenders is based on more sound experimental designs and has concluded that multisystemic therapy is an effective approach. Also, since about 50 percent of perpetrators have a history of CSA, providing timely and effective sexual abuse treatment to all CSA victims can contribute toward prevention efforts.

A major challenge associated with CSA prevention efforts involves demonstrating whether prevention can actually reduce and stop CSA. However, despite this difficulty, from 1990 to 2004 the research suggests that the number of substantiated CSA cases in the United States had decreased 49 percent (Finkelhor & Jones,

2004). Also, CSA prevention efforts have been found to improve parent-child communication, increase CSA knowledge, and improve self-protections skills—all factors that are associated with CSA prevention. These findings reveal promising trends, providing preliminary support that CSA prevention efforts can decrease the occurrence of sexual abuse.

Milton A. Fuentes and Michelle Marie Truffin

See also Child Sexual Abuse; Grooming the Victim; Reporting, Mandated and Abuse Registries

Further Reading

Finkelhor, D. (2009). The prevention of childhood sexual abuse. *The Future of Children, 19*(2), 169–194.

Finkelhor, D., & Jones, L. M. (2004). *Explanations for the decline in child sexual abuse cases*. Washington, DC: U.S. Department of Justice, Office of Justice Programs, Office of Juvenile Justice and Delinquency Prevention.

Friedrich, L., & Schmucher, M. (2005). The effectiveness of treatment for sexual offenders: A comprehensive meta-analysis. *Journal of Experimental Criminology, 1*(1), 117–146.

Gibson, L. E., & Leitenberg, H. (2000). Child sexual abuse prevention programs: Do they decrease the occurrence of child sexual abuse? *Child Abuse & Neglect, 24*(9), 1115–1125.

Kenny, M. C., Thakkar-Kolar, R., Ryan, E. E., Runyon, M. K., & Capri, V. (2008). Child sexual abuse: From prevention to self-protection. *Child Abuse Review, 17*, 36–54.

Lyles, A., Cohen, L, & Brown, M. (2009). *Transforming communities to prevent child sexual abuse and exploitation: A primary prevention approach*. National Sexual Violence Resource Center. Retrieved from http://www.nsvrc.org/publications/articles/transforming-communities-prevent-child-sexual-abuse-and-exploitation-primary-p

National Center for Missing & Exploited Children (1999). *Guidelines for programs to reduce child victimization: A resource*. Retrieved from http://www.missingkids.com/en_US/publications/NC24.pdf

World Health Organization & International Society for Prevention of Child Abuse and Neglect (2006). *Preventing child maltreatment: A guide to take action and generate evidence*. Geneva, Switzerland: World Health Organization.

Wurtele, S. K. (2009). Child sexual abuse prevention: Preventing sexual abuse of children in the twenty-first century: Preparing for challenges and opportunities. *Journal of Child Sexual Abuse, 18*(1), 1–18.

Selected Websites

Comprehensive listing of resources and links. Stop It Now! Retrieved from http://www.stopitnow.org/resources_comprehensive

Learn about child sexual abuse prevention. Stop It Now! Retrieved from http://www.stopitnow.org/learn

Sexual abuse prevention programs. Child Welfare Information Gateway (U.S. Department of Health and Human Services, Administration for Children and Families). Retrieved from http://www.childwelfare.gov/preventing/programs/types/sexualabuse.cfm

Prevention, Colleges and Universities

All postsecondary institutions under Title IV of the Higher Education Act of 1965 are mandated under the Jeanne Clery Disclosure of Campus Security and Policy and Campus Crime Statistics Act to publish an annual report that includes their sexual offenses statistics and a description of their rape prevention programs. Schools have an obligation under Title IX of the Education Amendments of 1972 to take prompt and effective action to end or prevent rape. Congress allocated monies for the Office of Violence Against Women to annually fund grants to establish education and prevention programs, which are to in collaborate with campus- and community-based victim advocacy organizations. More than 6,500 Title IV postsecondary institutions have implemented rape prevention programs. The handful of published evaluations of campus rape prevention are limited in generalizability because they are largely characterized by a single site with a small convenience sample, and rarely have a before-or-after research design or a comparison group.

From a public health perspective, prevention efforts are considered in terms of primary, secondary, and tertiary. Primary prevention takes place *before* a rape has occurred to prevent initial victimization or perpetration. These programs involve educational presentations about a variety of topics, including but not limited to defining rape and explaining risk factors, challenging sex-role stereotypes and prevailing rape myths and behaviors that support violence toward women, distinguishing between consent and coercion, and teaching bystander behaviors to intervene in risky situations that could lead to rape. Campus administrators typically target these programs to all their students.

The overall effectiveness of primary prevention programs in reducing the incidence of rape is questionable at best. Programs are effective in increasing knowledge about rape and changing rape-supportive attitudes, but the effects diminish over time. Bystander intervention education programs show promise in increasing students' bystander behaviors in risky situations.

Secondary prevention targets at-risk individuals *before* a rape occurs in an effort to decrease the incidence of rape victimization or perpetration by reducing known or suspected risk factors. Conducting acquaintance and date rape prevention programs geared toward groups at high risk for perpetrating sexual violence, such as male athletes and fraternity members, and those who are at risk for rape victimization, such as sorority members or first-term undergraduates, also are common. These types of programs are often directed at reducing risk associated with lifestyles characterized by alcohol, especially binge drinking, and illegal drugs. Another programmatic focus is preventing revictimization among rape victims, who are at high risk for subsequent rapes. To reduce students' risk of stranger rape, many schools have late evening escort and/or shuttle services. Many campuses also promote self-defense training to thwart rape.

The effectiveness of secondary prevention is mixed. Using forceful physical or verbal resistance enhances rape avoidance, whereas nonforceful verbal resistance is ineffective. One evaluation reports that a program with components of self-defense and advice about risky dating behaviors was successful in decreasing rates of sexual assault for females with no prior sexual victimization. Other evaluations of similar types of programs do not report similar results.

Tertiary prevention involves responding to the needs of the victim *after* a rape has occurred to minimize the lasting consequences and harm caused by the experience. Tertiary responses include psychological counseling and mental and physical health support. Title IV schools are required to notify students of existing counseling services. They must inform victims of their rights by providing information about internal disciplinary procedures, and options to notify local and campus law enforcement, as well as changing housing and academic situations. Some campuses have established sexual assault response teams (SARTs) to respond to and coordinate victims' needs, including transportation to a sexual assault nurse examiner (SANE) or doctor who collects forensic evidence for legal proceedings or connections to a victim advocate who provides support during criminal justice procedures.

Armanda Venezia and Bonnie S. Fisher

See also Bringing in the Bystander (Program); Colleges and Universities; The Green Dot (Program); The Men's Program; Prevention, Levels; Prevention, Organizations for; SARTs (Sexual Assault Response Teams); SCREAM Theater (Program)

Further Reading

Banyard, V. L., Moynihan, M. M., & Plante, E. G. (2007). Sexual violence prevention through bystander education: An experimental evaluation. *Journal of Community Psychology, 35*, 463–481.

Fisher, B. S., Daigle L. E., & Cullen F. T. (2010). *Unsafe in the ivory tower: The sexual victimization of college women*. Thousand Oaks, CA: Sage.

Karjane, H. M., Fisher, B. S., & Cullen, F. T. (2005). *Sexual assault on campus: what colleges and universities are doing about it*. National Institute of Justice: Research for Practice. Retrieved from http://www.ncjrs.gov/pdffiles1/nij/205521.pdf

Lonsway, K. A., Banyard, V. L., Berkowitz, A. D., Gidycz, C. A., Katz, J. T., Koss, M. P., . . . Ullman, S. E. (2009). *Rape prevention and risk reduction: Review of the research literature for practitioners*. Harrisburg, PA: National Resource Center on Violence Against Women. Retrieved from http://www.vawnet.org/Assoc_Files_VAWnet/AR_Rape Prevention.pdf

Vladutiu, C. J., Martin, S. L., & Macy, R. J. (2011). College- or university-based sexual assault prevention programs: A review of program outcomes, characteristics, and recommendations. *Trauma, Violence, & Abuse, 12*, 67–86.

Prevention, Dating Violence

A dating relationship can start out with great promise, but it may end up being violent or threatening. Both teens and adults can be involved in violent dating relationships. However, this entry focuses on teen dating violence (TDV). TDV has received increasing attention due to the widespread incidence. Estimates of how common it is vary because of differences in definitions, but about 10 percent of U.S. teens reported experiencing physical TDV (Youth Risk Behavior Surveillance, 2007). When researchers include sexual and psychological abuse, rates of TDV rise to at least 20 percent (Silverman, Raj, Mucci, & Hathaway, 2001). Physical abuse can include hitting, pushing, or holding down, as well as more severe harm, such as beating someone up or using or threatening with a weapon. Psychological abuse includes name-calling, demeaning, and controlling behaviors. Sexual abuse can take the form of using verbal or physical threats or manipulation to force a partner to engage in unwanted sexual acts. The current widespread use of technology is leading to new forms of abuse. It has been reported that one in four teens has been the victim of technologically facilitated abuse (Liz Claiborne, 2007). In today's adolescent dating climate, threatening, manipulation, or coercive control may be exercised through the constant contact that e-mail, instant messaging, social networking, texting, and sexting provide.

Teenage girls and boys report equal levels of perpetration and victimization on surveys, but most experts believe girls are more likely to be seriously injured and to experience fear and intimidation because of TDV. Adult gay and lesbian couples apparently experience similar rates of partner violence compared to rates reported by heterosexual couples, but methodical research about rates of gay and lesbian TDV is nonexistent. Teens with friends who perpetrate or are victimized by TDV are at higher risk for being involved in TDV themselves (Arriaga & Foshee, 2004), and teens with a history of exposure to other types of violence are also at higher risk (O'Keefe & Treister, 1998).

Consequences of TDV can be serious, including health and mental health problems, and it can be the beginning of a pattern of physical violence that continues into adulthood. Not surprisingly, TDV victimization can be associated with depression, anxiety, or trauma symptoms. Teens who are victimized are more likely to use drugs or alcohol and have problems with eating disorders (Ackard, Eisenberg, & Neumark-Sztainer, 2007).

There are many theories about the causes of TDV, but people who work with teens suggest that teens lack information about healthy, respectful relationships and about how to negotiate disagreements. Unfortunately, many teens interpret controlling and jealous behavior as a sign of love, even though this type of behavior is often part of a pattern of violence. Teens may have had few opportunities to see healthy, respectful relationships and may not know how to set limits when relationships start to become uncomfortable or threatening. Norms are often established that give young males the idea that to be truly masculine they should control their partners by any means necessary. Young people also may lack information on how to get help if they are involved in a violent relationship. TDV victims often tell no one about the violence they experience. When they do tell someone, it is likely to be other adolescents, who may not have the knowledge and skills required to give them good advice.

Experts on TDV prevention suggest that it should take place on many levels, including the media, community, family, peer groups, and individuals. Teens need to be exposed to media showing healthy relationships and healthy boundaries to counter pro-violence messages they may receive from music, movies, TV, and video games. Community-wide messages are needed to show teens and adults that TDV is unacceptable and that there is help available. Families and school personnel spend much more time with teens than any staff members from prevention programs could possibly spend on prevention programming. Therefore, it is very important for adults in the teens' communities to understand the dynamics of TDV. Parents may need help in understanding the prevalence, risks, and types of TDV. For example, a recent study undertaken by the Liz Claiborne Foundation showed that parents underestimated the extent and seriousness of technological abuse. Parents can learn to provide support to allow teens appropriate choices in decision making so that teens approach them about risky relationships without fearing that their parents will take over and make decisions for them. It is also important for school personnel to be aware of and approachable about TDV as well as to convey the unacceptability of violence. Increasingly, the Internet can be a source of information about TDV for teens and adults. Legal remedies for TDV victims are scarce. Some states allow teens to seek protective or restraining orders to keep threatening or violent partners away from them, but some states do not allow teens to get these orders, or state law leaves the decision about age limitations up to individual courts.

Increasingly, programs are available across the country to help teens become aware of dating safety issues. Most prevention programs are done in schools, because schools provide access to a wide variety of teens, and these programs are led by teachers, trained peers, or staff members of local violence against women programs. Programs may range from a single session to multiple sessions that extend over months or a whole school year. Prevention educators believe that single sessions are rarely effective in changing entrenched beliefs about dating or gender roles. The best programs enable youths to participate in a great deal of discussion rather than listening to lectures. Discussions enable youths to address the issues that are most relevant and interesting to them. In addition, peer education, often including participatory theater or skits, is a popular way to engage teens in thinking about ways to prevent TDV. Many programs now focus on changing social norms (ideas about what is acceptable) and encouraging bystander intervention so that friends speak up when they become aware of relationships that are psychologically, physically, or sexually abusive. Bystander intervention programs capitalize on the helpful, healthy impulses of teens to establish the belief that friends should speak up and try to stop incidents of violence or patterns of controlling or threatening behavior.

Arlene N. Weisz

See also Bringing in the Bystander (Program); Bystander Intervention; The Green Dot (Program); Intimate Partner Violence; Mentors in Violence Prevention (Program); SCREAM Theater (Program)

Further Reading

Ackard, D. M., Eisenberg, M. E., & Neumark-Sztainer, D. (2007). Long-term impact of adolescent dating violence on the behavioral and psychological health of male and female youth. *The Journal of Pediatrics, 151*(5), 476–481.

Arriaga, X. B., & Foshee, V. A. (2004). Adolescent dating violence: Do adolescents follow in their friends', or their parents', footsteps? *Journal of Interpersonal Violence, 19*(2), 162–184.

Liz Claiborne Foundation (2007). *Tech abuse in teen relationships study.* Retrieved from http://www.loveisrespect.org/wp-content/uploads/2009/03/liz-claiborne-2007-tech-relationship-abuse.pdf

O'Keefe, M., & Treister, L. (1998). Victims of dating violence among high school students: Are the predictors different for males and females. *Violence Against Women, 4*(2), 195–223.

Silverman, J. G., Raj, A., Mucci, L. A., & Hathaway, J. E. (2001). Dating violence against adolescent girls and associated substance use, unhealthy weight control, sexual risk behavior, pregnancy, and suicidality. *JAMA, 286*(5), 572–579.

Weisz, A. N., & Black, B. M. (2009). *Programs to reduce teen dating violence and sexual assault: Perspectives on what works.* New York, NY: Columbia University Press.

Youth Risk Behavior Surveillance (2007). Atlanta, GA: Centers for Disease Control and Prevention.

Selected Websites

Break the Cycle: Empowering Youth to End Domestic Violence. Retrieved from http://www.breakthecycle.org/

That's Not Cool (Site for teens and parents). Retrieved from http://www.thatsnotcool.com

Violence Against Women Online Resources. Retrieved from http://www.vaw.umn.edu/

Prevention, Ecological Model of

Given the complexity of risk factors for and contributors to sexual violence, this problem is increasingly analyzed using ecological frameworks. Ecological frameworks acknowledge that human behavior is shaped by multiple, interrelated influences within and surrounding individuals. These influences include individual traits and experiences, characteristics of families and social networks as well as the structures, social norms, and policies that characterize communities and broad societal environments (see the **Theory, Ecological Approach** entry for an expanded discussion). Acknowledgment that risk for sexual violence perpetration and victimization emerges from multiple levels of individuals' environments has increasingly been accompanied by ecological conceptualizations of sexual violence prevention. Ecological approaches to prevention suggest that prevention interventions need to simultaneously target risk factors for sexual violence at each level surrounding individuals, thereby reducing contributors to sexual violence in families, peer groups, and communities, and within society as a whole. An ecological approach to prevention ensures that positive changes in attitudes, knowledge, or behavior among individuals are reflected and supported by positive, respectful norms and behaviors in the family, peer, and community contexts surrounding those individuals.

The Centers for Disease Control and Prevention (CDC) have been at the forefront of defining sexual violence as a public health problem, and of applying an ecological model to sexual assault prevention. Building on the work of the World Health Organization (2002), who compiled global research regarding ecological risk factors, the CDC proposes that sexual violence prevention approaches need to target risk factors at four levels: individuals, relationships, communities, and society. For the purposes of illustrating an ecological framework for sexual violence prevention, this entry will briefly summarize how prevention initiatives might work in tandem at each of these levels.

Prevention strategies at the *individual* level strive to change individuals' violence-related attitudes, beliefs, knowledge, and behaviors. These strategies often include educational presentations to increase knowledge about sexual assault, to challenge misconceptions about rape and rape victims, and to explore related topics such as consent in sexual situations and gender role socialization. Individual-level prevention also includes opportunities for individuals to practice communication skills, respectful relationship skills, and sexual negotiation skills. In isolation, however, individual-level prevention strategies may be insufficient, as any resulting changes in an individual's attitudes or behaviors may be undermined by entrenched supports for coercive or disrespectful behavior in peer or community environments. Thus the ecological approach to prevention suggests that prevention initiatives should simultaneously work to reduce risk factors and promote nonviolence in these broader contexts.

Prevention at the *relationship* level aims to foster family and peer group norms that support respectful, noncoercive behaviors in sexual and intimate relationships. These strategies might include discussions or educational efforts with specific peer groups such as athletic teams or high school groups to encourage norms of nonviolence and respect for women. Increasingly, relationship-level prevention efforts have included a bystander component, designed to empower individuals to intervene in any disrespectful, exploitive, or aggressive behavior by peers that might lead to a sexual assault. By increasing the number of people in a peer network willing to take a stand against violence, bystander approaches can help to foster positive, respectful group norms.

Prevention at the *community* level endeavors to promote climates of safety and respect in schools, workplaces, neighborhoods, and other community settings. Accompanying strategies include training educators, health care providers, supervisors, and other community members to recognize and respond to risk factors for violence and to implement primary prevention efforts in their settings. Prevention at this level might also involve community organizing that brings coalitions together to identify culturally relevant strategies for undermining community-level risks for violence, such as violence-supportive norms, a lack of economic opportunity, or ineffective responses to perpetrators. Creating, updating, and enforcing antiharassment and abuse policies in institutions such as schools and workplaces can also contribute to community-level prevention.

Societal-level prevention includes policy and legislative advocacy efforts at the local, state, and federal levels. This could include advocacy for the enforcement of gender equity and antidiscrimination laws, for funding for primary prevention, and for policies that support the implementation of prevention efforts in schools, workplaces, and communities.

Ecological frameworks suggest that as prevention strategies are implemented at each of these levels simultaneously, they become reciprocally supportive and reinforcing. For example, shifts in community- and society-wide concern and responsiveness to the issue of sexual violence can both mirror and foster positive attitudinal and behavioral change among individuals and peer groups.

A second framework consistent with an ecological conceptualization of sexual violence prevention is the Prevention Institute's *Spectrum of Prevention* (Davis, Parks, & Cohen, 2006). This model identifies six levels of prevention that work in "synergy" with one another, holding the potential to simultaneously create positive change within individuals and in their surrounding environments. These levels include educating and skill building with individuals, enhancing community education about sexual violence, training community members about prevention, building partnerships and networks within communities, improving policies and procedures in organizations, and policy advocacy.

The strength of an ecological approach to prevention is its flexible and simultaneous attention to multiple levels of influence on the problem of sexual violence. By encouraging the fostering of healthy relationship skills among individuals while building supports for respectful, nonviolent norms in family, peer, and community contexts, an ecological approach increases the likelihood of an enduring reduction in sexual violence. Like ecological models generally, however, an ecological approach to prevention must be augmented with theory and research regarding mechanisms for creating behavioral and social norm change. The ecological model serves as a device for cataloguing possible targets for prevention intervention at multiple levels, but does not prioritize these targets or offer theory-based, tested interventions through which change can be accomplished. When used in conjunction with other theories of behavioral and social change, the ecological framework can offer a powerful tool for conceptualizing and implementing sexual violence prevention efforts.

Erin A. Casey

See also Prevention, Levels of; Theory, Ecological Approach

Further Reading

Casey, E. A., & Lindhorst, T. (2009). Toward a multi-level, ecological approach to the primary prevention of sexual assault: Prevention in peer and community contexts. *Trauma, Violence, and Abuse, 10*, 91–114.

Centers for Disease Control and Prevention (2004). *Sexual violence prevention: beginning the dialogue*. Atlanta, GA: Author.

Davis, R., Parks, L. F., & Cohen, L. (2006). *Sexual violence and the spectrum of prevention: Towards a community solution*. Enola, PA: National Sexual Violence Resource Center.

World Health Organization (2002). Sexual violence. In *World report on violence and health* (pp. 147–181). Geneva, Switzerland: World Health Organization.

Selected Website

The Prevention Institute. Retrieved from http://www.preventioninstitute.org/ (website provides information about the Spectrum of Prevention, as well as resources for conceptualizing prevention across a range of social issues, including sexual violence)

Prevention, Involving Men

In 1983, the self-described "militant feminist" Andrea Dworkin addressed the National Organization for Changing Men. Up until this time, the National Organization for Changing Men's major activity was organizing a yearly conference on Men and Masculinity—this was the extent of men's organized efforts to prevent sexual violence. This speech is often described as the "24-Hour Truce" speech, due to its dramatic crescendo:

And I want one day of respite, one day off, one day in which no new bodies are piled up, one day in which no new agony is added to the old, and

I am asking you to give it to me. And how could I ask you for less—it is so little . . . I want a twenty-four-hour truce during which there is no rape.

Although this speech is historically important for a number of reasons, one particular concept that Dworkin emphasized in the speech still greatly influences in how men approach ending sexual violence today. That is, in order to end sexual assault and stretch the boundaries of hegemonic masculinity, men need to challenge those who do not already share their views and change the system of patriarchy that oppresses women.

One immediate impact of this speech was the way in which men were inspired to form their own groups to directly oppose sexual violence. Organizations like the National Organization for Changing Men became much more active shortly afterward. Additionally, a number of nonhierarchical collectives formed—modeled somewhat on the early feminist consciousness-raising groups. These collectives, such as "Men Stopping Rape" in Madison, Wisconsin, and "Men Can Stop Rape" in Washington, DC, aimed to create a social movement to end men's violence against women; they worked toward changing the patriarchal system that perpetuated sexual violence and directly challenge men on an interpersonal level.

One of the larger challenges facing these collectives is defining what "counts" as a political challenge to patriarchal systems. One of the more popular efforts has been men's participation in "Take Back the Night"—a yearly rally held to protest men's violence against women and to emphasize that women are generally not safe in their own communities. At these events, men will often sit on planning committees, provide speakers emphasizing the importance of men's role in ending men's violence against women, and be responsible for turning out men to come to the event. This provides support to the political goals of antirape lobbying efforts, showing that men also want to see a change to patriarchal systems.

Another relatively frequent effort is to organize boycotts of rape-supportive media and institutions. Corporations and media that satirize and trivialize instances of men's violence against women are targeted; one recent example is Amazon.com, which sold a book titled *The Pedophile's Guide to Love and Pleasure*. The goal of a boycott strategy is to demonstrate that pro-sexual violence messages will harm revenues rather than help, which in turn reduces sexually aggressive models for young boys.

Aside from these two examples, however, it is difficult to identify successful or widespread political efforts to end sexual violence. In fact, today Men Stopping Rape is active only during Sexual Assault Awareness Month, while Men Can Stop Rape focuses far more effort on interpersonal change than political organizing. This can be attributed—at least partially—to the difficulties in identifying appropriate institutional targets that are both receptive to pressure and stimulate broad grassroots participation.

422 | Prevention, Involving Men

Without a doubt, most organized male participation in ending sexual violence focuses on educating individuals. These programs are often: (1) heavily subsidized by federal grants, (2) feature paid staff or peer educators rather than untrained volunteers, and (3) target students in middle school, high school, or college. Depending on the curriculum, these programs may focus on the individuals in the group as either potential bystanders or perpetrators; the desired outcomes are usually that students will increase their willingness and ability to intervene in a scenario where sexual violence is possible, or to reduce the likelihood that participants will commit sexual assault.

Thanks to many of these programs, men have gained new visibility in antirape efforts. Staff or peer educators are commonly all-male to reduce defensiveness, as young men are far more likely to listen to men than women when discussing sexual violence. Another popular model is a combination of male and female facilitators in tandem to model respectful interactions between men and women. However, the prevalence of these programs relative to the politically oriented groups means that there are fewer organized options for ending men's violence against women. Additionally, running an antirape program is extremely expensive, and so only a limited number of men may receive training and/or a paycheck. As a result, those interested men who are not yet ready or capable to facilitate discussion tend not to get involved.

However, structured programming activities also increase the number of men involved in men's sexual violence prevention efforts. Due to the fact that educational efforts may reach entire incoming classes of students at high schools and universities, an unprecedented number of young men are exposed to the idea that they may take an active role in ending sexual violence. As a result, it is entirely possible that these efforts may encourage a greater diversity of young men to become involved, rather than simply recruiting young men already predisposed to profeminist ideals.

Jonathan Horowitz

See also Coaching Boys into Men (Program); The Men's Program; Prevention, Colleges and Universities; Theory, Male Peer Support

Further Reading

Berkowitz, A. D. (2002). Fostering men's responsibility for preventing sexual assault. In P. Schewe (Ed.), *Preventing violence in relationships: Interventions across the life span* (pp. 163–196). Washington DC: American Psychological Association.

Dworkin, Andrea (1993). "I want a twenty-four-hour truce during which there is no rape." In *Letters from a war zone* (pp. 162–171). New York, NY: Lawrence Hill Books.

Katz, J. (2003). *Building a "big tent" approach to ending men's violence.* Building Partners Initiative, Prevention Institute. Retrieved June 22, 2012, from http://thrive.preventioninstitute.org/bpi.html.

Selected Websites

Men Can Stop Rape: Creating Cultures Free from Violence. Retrieved from http://www.mencanstoprape.org

NOMAS: National Organization of Men against Sexism. Retrieved from http://www.nomas.org

Take Back the Night. Retrieved from http://www.takebackthenight.org

Prevention, Levels

Public health discussions of disease prevention have classified prevention efforts into different levels of prevention. These levels describe both the scope of the target audience for intervention and the timing of efforts within the trajectory of a disease or problem acquisition. Definitions of these levels continue to evolve and change and yet serve as a helpful organizing framework for developing and assessing comprehensive community responses to sexual violence. Levels of prevention remind us of the range of possible populations and sites for work to end sexual violence and abuse. A brief summary of some of the more well-known frameworks and their application to the problem of sexual violence follows.

The Committee on Prevention of Mental Disorders of the Institute of Medicine describes prevention levels as universal, selective, and indicated. Universal prevention strategies target whole populations while selected tools target high-risk groups for a particular problem. At the level of indicated strategies, intervention is targeted at individuals in whom aspects of the problem already exist and attempts are made to inhibit the development of a full-blown problem or to decrease the long-term consequences of the problem. Applying this model to sexual violence, universal prevention would be exemplified by large-scale social marketing and public awareness campaigns that highlight the problem of sexual assault for communities. Selected strategies would describe efforts with particularly at-risk groups, especially youth between the ages of 16 and 24 (the age group research indicates is at highest risk for sexual assault). Awareness campaigns and educational programs on college campuses including risk reduction workshops for women would fall under this category. Indicated strategies as applied to sexual violence would seem to encompass the range of support services for survivors (crisis centers and hotlines, advocacy services) as well as treatment and criminal justice responses for offenders.

Other models describe levels of prevention as primary, secondary, and tertiary. A recent publication by the Centers for Disease Control and Prevention (CDC) describes these levels in relation to sexual violence prevention. In this model primary prevention describes efforts to address sexual violence before instances of victimization have taken place. These include broad social marketing campaigns to decrease rape myth acceptance and increase awareness of definitions of sexual assault and of consent (e.g., Potter et al.; Futures without Violence). They also include educational efforts that aim to teach community members and peer groups to not be passive onlookers to risky situations but to step in and take action when risk markers appear. For example, Potter et al. at the University of New Hampshire have developed a campaign entitled "Know Your Power," which uses posters and products to model helpful behaviors that informal helpers can do to prevent sexual assault, such as encouraging friends to seek consent and to not use alcohol when initiating sexual contact with a partner. All campus community members are exposed to these messages, which aim to de-escalate or interrupt potentially risky situations before an assault takes place. A variety of prevention efforts, particularly those with children and young people (e.g., Foshee's Safe Dates Program), may be classified as primary prevention efforts as they focus on teaching ways to form relationships free of coercion and shaped around respect and consent.

Secondary prevention is described in the CDC publication as efforts to immediately respond to an incident of sexual violence. The aim here is to prevent long-term negative consequences for survivors by providing a swift and supportive immediate response to the incident. Using this definition, the use of sexual assault nurse examiners (SANEs) and victim advocates as immediate responders to a victim would be examples since their aim is to minimize negative ongoing consequences of the assault through a supportive and helpful early response. Other definitions of the term "secondary prevention," however, use it to mean efforts targeted at at-risk groups. Using this meaning of the term, risk reduction programs like those developed by Christine Gidycz and colleagues at Ohio University would be an example. These programs aim to teach a high-risk group, college-attending women, protective skills to reduce their risk of victimization.

The tertiary level is defined by the CDC report authors as more long-term responses to sexual assault, including treatment for offenders. Examples at this level include trauma-focused treatment for survivors, crisis center advocacy services, criminal justice responses to prosecute perpetrators, and sexual offender treatment.

An alternate conceptualization of levels of prevention is described by Cohen in his "Spectrum of Prevention," which has been applied to sexual violence. This framework uses an ecological model to describe six levels of intervention efforts to ensure that communities are being as comprehensive as possible in targeting leverage points for creating change. The levels are defined as: (1) individuals' knowledge and skills, (2) promoting community education, (3) educating providers, (4) fostering coalitions and networks, (5) changing organizational practices, and (6) influencing policies and legislation. The main premise of the model is that prevention must occur across all of these levels in order to end sexual violence. Further, the activities of prevention will necessarily differ by level and thus the framework can serve as a template for outlining a broad array of prevention tools and ideas.

The CDC (2004) report integrates both the spectrum of locations for prevention and levels in terms of timing of prevention. Specifically, the authors discuss prevention before an incident and after and describe within each time frame strategies to target intervention with individuals, within relationships, with communities, and with regard to wider societal norms, policies, and influences. The overall aim is to increase the comprehensiveness of sexual violence prevention initiatives. Discussions in the field of sexual violence seem to agree that to date, more resources have been devoted to secondary and tertiary levels of prevention and that innovation and evaluation of primary prevention should be a key piece of future research and practice agendas.

Victoria L. Banyard

See also Bystander Intervention; Prevention, Colleges and Universities; Prevention, Ecological Model of; Prevention, Organizations for

Further Reading

Foshee, V., & Langwick, S. (2010). *Safe dates: An adolescent dating abuse prevention curriculum* (2nd ed.). Center City, MN: Hazelden.

Davis, R., Parks, L. F., & Cohen, L. (2006). Sexual violence and the spectrum of prevention: Towards a community solution. Enola, PA: National Sexual Violence Resource Center. Retrieved from http://www.nsvrc.org/sites/default/files/Publications_NSVRC _Booklets_Sexual-Violence-and-the-Spectrum-of-Prevention_Towards-a-Community -Solution.pdf

Lonsway, K. A, Banyard, V. L., Berkowitz, A. D., Gidycz, C. A., Katz, J., Koss, M. P., . . . & Ullman, S. E. (2009, January). *Rape prevention and risk reduction: Review of the research literature for practitioners*. Retrieved from http://www.vawnet.org/print -document.php?doc_id=1655&find_type=web_desc_AR

Selected Websites

Futures without Violence (formerly Family Violence Prevention Fund. Retrieved from http://www.endabuse.org/section/campaigns/

Institute of Medicine prevention categories. Retrieved from http://www.kitsco.com/ casupport/WebHelp_Prevention101/Institute_of_Medicine_IOM_for_Prevention.htm

Potter, S. J., Moynihan, M. M., Stapleton, J. G., & Banyard, V. L. (2009). Empowering Bystanders to Prevent Campus Violence Against Women. *Violence Against Women*, *15*, 106–121.

Spectrum of prevention. PreventConnect: A National Online Project Dedicated to the Primary Prevention of Sexual Assault and Domestic Violence. Retrieved from http://wiki.preventconnect.org/Spectrum+of+Prevention

Violence prevention. Centers for Disease Control and Prevention. Injury Center. Retrieved from http://www.cdc.gov/ncipc/dvp/SVPrevention.pdf

Prevention, Organizations for

Since sexual violence affects people across the world, organizations have been created to support survivors and victims and educate the broader community about how to prevent sexual violence. These organizations vary in their approach to prevention, but they share a mission of ending sexual violence. The scope of these organizations varies in size with some focusing on local communities and others focusing on the state or national levels. Many are nonprofit organizations, although federal and state governments have information available on standards for prevention. For instance, the Centers for Disease Control and Prevention (CDC) has a website, www.vetoviolence.org, that provides best practices on sexual violence prevention.

Sexual violence prevention organizations work with a range of stakeholders including victims, survivors, offenders, policy makers, schools, parents, and concerned citizens. The population served may be children and/or adults, depending on the organization's mission. Additionally, some organizations exclusively focus on supporting women or men whose lives have been affected by sexual violence, while others provide programming for both genders.

As noted, sexual violence occurs across the world and can be found in countries at war and those at peace. For that reason, prevention organizations operate across the globe. International agencies like the United Nations and the World Health Organization have compiled numerous reports and have standing committees that focus on sexual violence. Private-public partnerships, like the Clinton Global Health Initiative, have also formed teams of experts working to prevent sexual violence.

There are three types of prevention programs including primary, secondary, and tertiary prevention programs. Some organizations focus on one form of prevention, while others incorporate all three.

Primary prevention programs are those that employ strategies to stop violence before it occurs. Such programs allow for a broader community to engage in preventing sexual violence. For example, PreventConnect is an organization that provides online media prevention strategies. Interested agencies and individuals have access to web conferences, Listservs, and podcasts.

Secondary prevention programs focus on the immediate response after an incident has occurred. For that reason, secondary prevention organizations provide services that typically center on the victim and may include medical or emergency services. For example, WOAR (Women Organized against Rape), based in Phila-delphia, Pennsylvania, is the first rape crisis center in the United States, and since then centers have sprung up across the country. They have a number of services for victims that include: a hotline service, WOAR representatives at the hospital during medical exams, and walk-in crisis counseling. These services are available for adults and children. In addition, WOAR provides preventative educational pro-gramming, counseling, and legal services.

Tertiary prevention programs focus on targeting long-term approaches after vio-lence occurs. Services may focus on rehabilitation of the perpetrator or therapeutic services to the victim ("Vetoviolence," n.d.). For example, ChildHelp is a child-centered organization working in five states. Children have access to a range of programs. These include long-term treatment for children who experience abuse, including sexual abuse. Children have access to foster care, group homes, residen-tial treatment, and advocacy centers. All three types of prevention are crucial to providing the services communities need to prevent and heal from sexual violence.

In 1983 Larry Cohen developed the Spectrum of Prevention to be used as a way for practitioners to develop a comprehensive approach to prevent sexual violence. The Spectrum has six levels with each level considered as an intervention. The appeal of this approach is that if used together the Spectrum becomes a more transformational force for individual, community, and societal well-being.

The six areas are described below with examples of organizations:

Strengthening Individual Knowledge and Skills: In this level, programs work to increase individuals' capacity for learning about and preventing sexual violence. For example, Darkness to Light is a national organization that empowers individuals to prevent child abuse. They have developed online training manuals to improve individual knowledge and skills for adults on how to protect children.

Promoting Community Education: In this level, programs work to broaden the engagement of individuals to groups and communities. For example, Green Dot is a national organization that provides primary prevention training to communities and organizations. Agencies then train groups of individuals to spread green dots (saying no to violence) with the goal of eliminating red dots (violence) from our communities.

Educating Providers: In this level, prevention programs focus on educating providers from a wide range of disciplines and professions. For example, CHAMP (Child Abuse Medical Provider Program) offers medical providers in New York training about child sexual abuse and child abuse. The goal is to improve diagnosis, treatment, and reporting of child abuse and neglect.

Fostering Coalitions and Networks: These types of prevention programs encourage individuals to create a critical mass behind a community effort or help groups trust one another. One such example is CALCASA (California Coalition against Sexual Assault), which provides resources to anyone looking to end sexual violence. Primary membership of the coalition includes rape crisis centers and prevention programs within the state.

Changing Organizational Practices: In this level, prevention programs examine practices in schools and organizations and seek ways to reform them to create safer environments for the community. For example, Security on Campus strives to create safer college campus communities. They provide training to higher education institutions on how to implement federal policies around campus security.

Influencing Policy and Legislation: Programs at this level of prevention attempt to influence local, state, and national level policies. One example includes RAINN (Rape, Abuse & Incest National Network), which has a division within the organization focused on national policy. Their policy areas include fighting sexual violence with DNA, campus safety, improving services for victims, and protecting children against sexual predators.

Finally, Futures without Violence (FWV) is an example of an organization integrating all six levels into their work. The mission of FWV is to prevent violence within the home and community.

Sexual violence is preventable. Everyone should have the opportunity to learn how to prevent sexual violence. Organizations across the world are working tirelessly to eliminate this brutal form of violence from our communities. There are a number of approaches organizations can utilize to help them target their audience and become even more effective with their programming.

Melanie Lowe Hoffman

See also Impact, Community; Organizational Response (Overview); Prevention, Levels

Further Reading

Cohen, L., & Swift, S. (1999). The spectrum of prevention: Developing a comprehensive approach to injury prevention. *Injury Prevention, 5,* 203–207.

David, R., Fujie, L., & Cohen, L. (2006). *Sexual violence and the spectrum of prevention: Towards a community solution.* Enola, PA: National Sexual Violence Resource Center.

VetoViolence: Stop Violence Before It Happens. (n.d.). Retrieved from http://www.vetoviolence.org/basics-primary-prevention.html

World Health Organization/London School of Hygiene and Tropical Medicine. 2010. *Preventing intimate partner and sexual violence against women: Taking action and generating evidence.* Geneva, Switzerland: World Health Organization.

Selected Websites

The following websites are mentioned in this entry:

CALCASA (California Coalition Against Sexual Assault). Retrieved from http://calcasa.org/

CHAMP (Child Abuse Medical Provider Program). Retrieved from http://champprogram.com/

Child Help (Prevention and Treatment of Child Abuse). Retrieved from http://www.childhelp.org/

Darkness to Light (End Child Sexual Abuse). Retrieved from http://www.darkness2light.com

Futures without Violence. Retrieved from http://www.endabuse.org/

The Green Dot. Retrieved from http://www.livethegreendot.com

PreventConnect: A National Online Project Dedicated to the Primary Prevention of Sexual Assault and Domestic Violence. Retrieved from http://www.preventconnect.org

Prevention Institute. Retrieved from http://www.preventioninstitute.org

RAINN (Rape, Abuse & Incest National Network). Retrieved from http://www.rainn.org

Security on Campus. Retrieved from http://www.securityoncampus.org

Veto Violence (Initiative of CDC). Retrieved from http://www.vetoviolence.org

WOAR (Women Organized against Rape). Retrieved from http://www.woar.org/

Prevention versus Risk Reduction

Since the beginning of the anti-sexual violence movement, advocates have worked diligently to educate individuals and communities about the problem of sexual violence. Much of this work has included reducing risk through sharing information about the problem and increasing awareness of how to prevent victimization, how to help someone who is victimized, and how communities can respond. Elements of this strategy have become problematic as the field examines the systemic causes of sexual violence and works to implement effective prevention strategies. Integrating principles and practices of the public health approach with the expertise of activists within the field of sexual violence prevention has helped bring forth a newer model that may work more efficiently to prevent sexual violence. Practitioners and researchers in the field continue to explore ways to emphasize the strengths of these two approaches rather than see them at odds with one another.

Beginning in the early part of the twenty-first century, the anti-sexual violence movement shifted from looking at sexual violence as an issue that affects individuals, to looking at it as a symptom of other societal problems. A more intentional and effective approach consists of examining the problem within a larger context, identifying the root causes, developing strategies to combat those causes, and then evaluating various approaches as they are implemented in the field. This shift to the public health model allows opportunities for those in the prevention field to address sexual violence as a continuum of behaviors that affects everyone in some way, either directly or indirectly. It also incorporates analyses of systems of oppression that serve as the root causes of sexual violence. This approach is called primary prevention, and seeks to involve the entire community in the prevention of sexual violence instead of placing that responsibility solely on individuals. Primary prevention efforts seek to address the underlying conditions that exist that allow sexual violence to occur, by addressing risk factors (events, conditions, situations, exposure to influences) and promoting protective factors.

Researchers have identified a number of characteristics of effective prevention implementation: (1) programs should impact social norms in multiple settings; (2) programs should use varied methods to convey information and change; (3) participants should be exposed to messaging in a way that promotes affect; (4) strategies need to be rooted in theory and evidence; (5) programs should be appropriately timed and culturally relevant; (6) staff should be well trained and supported; and (7) a thoughtful outcomes evaluation should be implemented to ensure effectiveness (Nation et al., 2003). These seven elements help provide structure and guidance to program development and evaluation; they also complement the public health model by building in practical strategies and specific areas of focus.

In order begin changing social norms and challenge systems of oppression, the message must be delivered to a larger audience regardless of risk factors. An example of this would be developing and disseminating a student-generated social messaging campaign that addresses gender norms and inequity on a college campus. This message would be received by everyone on campus—from safety officers to health center staff to students and faculty. It is also important to focus efforts on groups that have been identified as higher risk, for either victimization or perpetration. Using the campus prevention universal population example, selecting to work with fraternities where traditionally alcohol-facilitated sexual assaults were seen as acceptable heterosexual male social behavior can reinforce the larger social messaging. By working to change the norms and behaviors around alcohol and sex, as well as gender roles and expectations, programming would create sustainable change.

Where primary prevention efforts focus on shifting discussion away from individual choices and attitudes, risk reduction efforts focus entirely on the individual.

Programs that promote self-defense, "Watch Your Drink" messages, or "No, Go, Tell" child abuse education are typical examples of risk reduction. These types of programs do not work to end oppression or systemic issues that contribute to sexual violence, but focus on decreasing the likelihood of victimization or preventing the completion of an attempted assault. In other words, risk reduction efforts place the responsibility of preventing an assault on the victim or potential victim—not on the perpetrator or the social norms that allow sexual violence to occur.

The potential counterproductive nature of risk reduction rests in its focus on individual responsibility in regard to sexual violence, rather than the community, societal, and/or systemic causes of sexual violence. This approach has had a tremendous impact on the ways in which sexual violence is perceived by society at large. According to a recent study on perceptions of sexual violence, many Americans continue to think of individual character traits or motivations to be the cause of sexual violence; hence, assaults occur because someone did not practice appropriate risk reduction techniques (O'Neil & Morgan, 2010).

Furthermore, research has found that risk reduction strategies and messages such as "Never leave your drink unattended" have been received, but have not reduced or prevented sexual assaults. Indeed, 88 percent of young women in the College Sexual Assault Study did not consume a drink that was left unattended, and 76 percent said they did not accept drinks from people they did not know (Krebs, Lindquist, Warner, Fisher, & Martin, 2007).

Both of the approaches, primary prevention and risk reduction, have a place in anti-sexual violence activism. Because effective prevention is comprehensive and driven by the needs of the community, infusing these two models into every initiative should prove promising when combating sexual violence.

Jennifer Grove and Liz Zadnik

See also Prevention, Levels; Prevention, Colleges and Universities; Theory, Social Norms

Further Reading

Banyard, V. L. (2008). Sexual violence: Current perspectives on prevention and intervention. *Journal of Prevention & Intervention in the Community, 36,* 1–4.

Centers for Disease Control and Prevention (2004). Sexual violence prevention: Beginning the dialogue. Retrieved from http://www.cdc.gov/violenceprevention/pdf/SVPrevention-a.pdf

Curtis, M. J. (n.d.). *Engaging communities in sexual violence prevention: A guidebook for individuals and organizations engaging in collaborative prevention work.* Texas Association against Sexual Assault. Retrieved from http://www.taasa.org/prevention/pdfs/TAASA_ECGuidebook.pdf

Curtis, M. J., & Love, T. (n.d.). *Tools for change: An introduction to the primary prevention of sexual assault.* Texas Association against Sexual Assault. Retrieved from http://www.taasa.org/prevention/pdfs/GuidebookFinal.pdf?utm_source=preventionguidebook&utm_medium=website&utm_campaign=website%3Apdfs

Davis, R., Parks, L., & Cohen, L. (2006). *Sexual violence and the Spectrum of Prevention*. National Sexual Violence Resource Center. Retrieved from http://www.nsvrc.org/sites/default/files/file/Projects_RPE_NSVRC-spectrum.pdf

Fisher, D., Lang, K. S., & Wheaton, J. (2010.) *Training professionals in the primary prevention of sexual and intimate partner violence: A planning guide*. Retrieved from http://www.cdc.gov/violenceprevention/pdf/Training_Practice_Guidelines.pdf

Guy, L. (2006). Re-visioning the sexual violence continuum. In *Partners in Social Change* (pp. 4–7). Olympia, WA: Washington Coalition of Sexual Assault Programs.

Kaufman, K. (Ed.). (2010). *The prevention of sexual violence: A practitioner's sourcebook*. Holyoke, MA: NEARI Press.

Krebs, C. P., Lindquist, C. H., Warner, T. D., Fisher, B. S., & Martin, S. L. (2007). *The Campus Sexual Assault (CSA) Study*. National Institute of Justice. Retrieved from: http://www.ncjrs.gov/pdffiles1/nij/grants/221153.pdf

Lee, D., Guy, L., Perry, B., Sniffen, C., & Alamo-Mixson, S. (2007). Sexual violence prevention. *The Prevention Researcher, 14*, 15–20.

Nation, M., Crusto, C., Wandersman, A., Kumpfer, K. L., Seybolt, D., Morrissey-Kane, E., & Davino, K. (2003). What works in prevention: Principles of effective prevention programs. *American Psychologist, 58*, 449–456.

O'Neil, M., & Morgan, P. (2010). *American perceptions of sexual violence*. Washington, DC: FrameWorks Institute. Retrieved from http://www.frameworksinstitute.org/assets/files/PDF_sexualviolence/AmericanPerceptionsofSexualViolence.pdf

Virginia Sexual and Domestic Violence Action Alliance. (n.d.). Guidelines for the primary prevention of sexual violence and intimate partner violence. Retrieved from http://www.vsdvalliance.org/secPublications/Prevention%20Guidelines%202009%5B1%5D.pdf

Selected Websites

PreventConnect: A National Online Project Dedicated to the Primary Prevention of Sexual Assault and Domestic Violence. Retrieved from http://www.preventconnect.org/display/displaySection.cfm?sectionID=254

Principles of Prevention (POP) online violence prevention course (CDC Veto Violence Project). Retrieved from http://www.vetoviolence.org/pop

Washington Coalition of Sexual Assault Programs Prevention Orientation Online Course. Retrieved from http://www.wcsap.org/prevention-orientation-online-course

Prisons, Rape in Female

Rape in female prisons is a particularly important topic within the subject area of sexual violence and abuse. When rape occurs within prisons, survivors often experience ongoing terror and trauma because they cannot escape the perpetrators.

Rape of female prisoners has been reported since at least the nineteenth century. During this time, women were housed in men's prisons and male correctional officers reportedly raped and forced women prisoners into prostitution. Such treatment, combined with dismal prison conditions and lack of separate facilities for women, set the stage for the creation of the women's prison reform movement of the late nineteenth century. This movement demanded separate female prisons with a focus on rehabilitation.

Over a century later, female prisoners are generally housed in women's prisons, and women now constitute about 56 percent of all guards in such institutions—a percentage that varies by facility (Britton, 2003). However, rape and sexual assault in women's prisons continues to exist. This is even more disconcerting when one takes into consideration that many women in prison have histories of sexual abuse and rape: between 57 and 75 percent of incarcerated women report some form of physical and/or sexual violence before incarceration, and one-third report having been raped (Mauer, Potler, & Wolf, 1999; Browne, Miller, & Maguin, 1999).

Under international law rape of a prisoner is considered torture. Both Amnesty International (1999) and Human Rights Watch (1996) issued reports that document the extent of sexual assault and rape in women's prisons. Both organizations found that male correctional officers subject women prisoners to groping during pat downs, sexual assault, and rape; in some cases, the result has been pregnancy. For example, in California, male guards entered women's cells and raped them, and in New York, a paraplegic prisoner was raped every time she was driven to physical therapy (Human Rights Watch, 1996). More recently, women prisoners at Scott Regional Correctional Facility in Michigan were awarded $15.4 million for the sexual violence they experienced, which included multiple rapes by male guards. In some instances, sexual assault and rape are used as punishment for women who file complaints about prison conditions, self-identify or are viewed as gay, or refuse an officer's sexual advances.

As a result of research on rape in men's prisons, the Prison Rape Elimination Act (PREA) was passed in 2003. This act, which applies to all state and federal prisons and jails, immigrant detention centers, and private prison facilities, states that sexual assault and rape of incarcerated persons can constitute a violation of the cruel and unusual punishment clause of the Eighth Amendment. The Bureau of Justice Statistics now collects and analyzes data about the prevalence of sexual assault and rape behind bars. In addition, the National Prison Rape Elimination Commission was created, which conducts research on sexual abuse behind bars and works to develop national standards to eliminate prison rape.

Under the PREA, sexual assault of women prisoners includes rape, nonconsensual sexual acts, abusive sexual contacts, sexual misconduct, and sexual harassment, both inmate-on-inmate and staff toward inmate. In 2008–9, 4.7 percent of women in prison had experienced sexual assault by another inmate and 2.2 percent had experienced some form of sexual misconduct by a staff member (Beck & Harrison, 2009). Although correctional officers commit rape against women prisoners, some research indicates that it is more common for staff to use their positions of power to coerce sexual activity in exchange for favors or resources (Mangoo, 2011).

In 2006, the U.S. Department of Justice released a report that noted only 37 percent of prison employees who perpetrated sexual abuse, including rape, had faced any type of legal action; when legal action was taken, punishment was often probation rather than prison (Talvi, 2007). As a result of this report, the Board of Prison Terms criminalized sexual contact between guards and prisoners as a felony that carries with it a five-year prison term. However, it is important to note that women must come forward to report the abuse if correctional officers are to be held accountable for their behavior. The numbers of women prisoners who have been raped and sexually assaulted by correctional officers, then, are likely to be higher given that, like women on the outside of prison, many female survivors of sexual abuse and rape do not report it due to feelings of humiliation and, for prisoners, fear of retaliation.

It is also important to take into consideration the threat of sexual assault and rape for transgender women housed in men's prisons. "Transgender women" refers to people who are biologically male but identify as women; some undergo hormonal therapy and/or surgery to align their bodies with their gender identities (and are often referred to as "transsexual"). In *Farmer v. Brennan* (1994), Dee Farmer—a male-to-female transsexual who was housed in the general population of a men's prison in Indiana—sued the state because she was repeatedly raped and beaten by inmates, ultimately contracting HIV. The case went up to the Supreme Court, which ruled that a prison official's "deliberate indifference" to substantial risk of serious harm to a prisoner violates the cruel and unusual punishment clause of the Eighth Amendment. Prison officials now can be held liable for failing to protect an inmate from violence at the hands of other prisoners if they know there is a high risk of serious harm and do not protect that individual. Still, transgender women inmates continue to face high levels of rape and sexual assault. In a study of inmates housed in male prisons in California, 38.2 percent of the transgender inmates surveyed reported an incident of rape (Jenness, Maxson, Matsuda, & Sumner, 2007).

There are a variety of effects of rape and sexual assault in prisons, for both biologically female and transgender women. These include depression, posttraumatic stress disorder, anxiety, and suicidal thoughts. Also, women and transgender prisoners cannot easily escape the abuse, which affects their mental, emotional, and physical well-being.

Jodie M. Lawston

See also Female-on-Female Sexual Violence; Prisons, Rape in Male

Further Reading

Amnesty International (1999). *Not part of my sentence: Violations in the human rights of women in custody*. Retrieved July 26, 2011, from http://www.amnestyusa.org/women/womeninprison.html

Beck, A. J., & Harrison, P. M. (2009). *Sexual victimization in prisons and jails reported by inmates, 2008–2009*. Bureau of Justice Statistics. Retrieved July 25, 2011, from http://bjs.ojp.usdoj.gov/index.cfm?ty=pbdetail&iid=2202

Britton, D. (2003). *At work in the iron cage: The prison as gendered organization*. New York, NY: New York University Press.

Browne, A., Miller, B., & Maguin, E. (1999). Prevalence and severity of lifetime physical and sexual victimization among incarcerated women. *International Journal of Law and Psychiatry, 22*, 3–4, 301–322.

Human Rights Watch (1996). *All too familiar: Sexual abuse of women in U.S. state prisons*. Retrieved from http://hrw.org/reports/1996/Us1.htm#_1_36

Jenness, V., Maxon, C. L., Matsuda, K. N., and Sumner, J. M. (2007). *An empirical examination of sexual assault*. Retrieved July 25, 2011, from http://www.justdetention.org/pdf/VJReport2007.pdf

Manjoo, R. (2011). *Report of the special rapporteur on violence against women, its causes and consequences*. Human Rights Council. Retrieved from http://www.clanstar.org/wp-content/up/2011/06/SRVAW_USA_Rpt.pdf

Mauer, M., Potler, C., & Wolf, R. (1999). *Gender and justice: Women, drugs and sentencing policy*. Washington, DC: The Sentencing Project.

Talvi, S. (2007). *Women behind bars: The crisis of women in the U.S. prison system*. Emeryville, CA: Seal Press.

Selected Website

Just Detention International. Retrieved from http://www.justdetention.org/

Prisons, Rape in Male

Sexually abusive acts can occur in any location, but prisons are fertile grounds for rape for a number of reasons. They hold violence-prone individuals in frustrating environments with little sense of control over their lives. Overcrowded conditions often lead to inadequate supervision, and the atmosphere in these settings is best characterized as a hypermasculine pecking order where the strongest and most violent rule over the weak. We do not know the exact number of sexual offenses that occur in prisons and jails, but recent research suggests that it is a problem that needs to be addressed. Robert Dumond (2003) called this "America's most ignored crime problem."

Released prisoners have long described the sexual assault of inmates, usually (but not exclusively) by other inmates, as a major problem in prisons and jails across the country. Some academic researchers have attempted to study the issue, however success has been limited by their inability to get good information about the problem.

Gathering general information about sexually abusive acts is often difficult, but the circumstances in prisons create a number of unique challenges. The line between consensual homosexual acts (which are prohibited in prison settings) and nonconsensual/coercive acts become blurred to outside observers. Threats and violence are used to obtain victim compliance and maintain victim silence after the act(s). In some cases, the acts occur repeatedly, and after the first attack, victims comply for fear of further physical violence. Investigators gathering information on specific cases are faced with inmate (and staff) noncooperation in obtaining enough information to file criminal complaints. One of the most obvious obstacles to obtaining information about sexual victimization is the shame and stigma that male victims feel about disclosing sexual assaults by other males.

Despite these difficulties, some information has been obtained from the over 2.5 million individuals currently behind bars. If we look at only official reports (made to prison authorities), the numbers are very low. One meta-analysis (grouping together of smaller research studies) arrived at the rate of almost 2 percent of prisoners reporting that they have experienced sexual victimization (Gaes & Goldberg, 2004). In 2001, Human Rights Watch reported that the actual number was closer to three times that estimate. The most recent study published by the U.S. Department of Justice Bureau of Justice Statistics places that number at about 88,500, or about 4 percent of state and federal inmates and 3 percent of county or municipal jail detainees reporting sexually abusive incidents while incarcerated (Beck & Harrison, 2010).

Other researchers have found much higher rates of reported victimization if the information is gathered in a way that guarantees confidentiality to the subjects in the study. The groundbreaking work of Struckman-Johnson and colleagues (Struckman-Johnson, Struckman-Johnson, Rucker, Bumby, & Donaldson, 1996; Struckman-Johnson & Struckman-Johnson, 2000) elicited rates that are considered by most researchers to be more likely representative of the true rate of sexual victimization in incarcerated settings. They found in their studies that about 20 percent of inmates experience sexually abusive acts while incarcerated. Of course, the rates vary according to a number of factors including the security classification at the facility, the average age of the inmates incarcerated, and the staff culture.

Whatever the real number of inmate-on-inmate or staff-on-inmate sexual abuse, the rate of apprehension and prosecution is dismally low. Some states such as Texas have had more success in addressing this problem; it is usually associated with a concerted effort by prison administrations to change the staff culture and to adopt a zero-tolerance policy for this kind of sexual misbehavior. Prisons that turn a blind eye to sexual abuse are harder to manage because they are unsafe for the inmates and unsafe for the staff due to higher levels of nonsexual violence.

The Prison Rape Elimination Act of 2003 (PREA) was heralded as a giant step forward in addressing this problem by recommending standards for administrative transparency and accountability. All states are now required by PREA to gather data on this problem and respond appropriately. Although funding remains a question, public attention is the first step to investigating and addressing this problem.

The effects of sexually abusive acts (whether in a prison setting or not) can be very traumatic and life changing. But most of society does not feel too much concern for those who are in prison for breaking society's rules and victimizing others. The bigger realization is that most of those individuals eventually return to live in the society we all share. Do we want incarcerated individuals to return more damaged, more prone to violence, and possibly infected with sexually transmitted diseases obtained through sexual victimization?

Prisons are designed to hold individuals who break the law. But society also has a responsibility to protect those who are incarcerated, respond appropriately to allegations of unwanted sexual behavior, and bring the perpetrators (inmates or staff) to justice.

We cannot expect to live in a safe society if we turn a blind eye to sexually abusive acts wherever they occur—even among those incarcerated for breaking society's laws.

Jackson Tay Bosley

See also Homophobic Acts; Male-on-Male Sexual Violence; Prisons, Rape in Female

Further Reading
Beck, A. J., & Harrison, P. M. (2010) *Sexual victimization in prisons and jails reported by inmates, 2008–2009*. Washington, DC: U.S. Department of Justice, Bureau of Justice Statistics.

Dumond, R. W. (2003). Confronting America's most ignored crime problem: The prison rape elimination act of 2003. *Journal of the American Academy of Psychiatry and the Law, 31*, 354–360.

Gaes, G. G., & Goldberg, A. L. (2004, March 10). *Prison rape: A critical review of the literature*. Washington, DC: U.S. Department of Justice, National Institute of Justice.

Jones, T. R., & Pratt, T. C. (2008). The prevalence of sexual violence in prison: The state of the knowledge base and implications for evidenced-based correctional policy making. *International Journal of Offender Therapy and Comparative Criminology, 52* (3), 280–295.

Struckman-Johnson, C., Struckman-Johnson, D., Rucker, L., Bumby, K., & Donaldson, S. (1996). Sexual coercion reported by men and women in prison. *Journal of Sex research, 33*, 67–76.

Struckman-Johnson, C. & Struckman-Johnson, D. (2000). Sexual coercion in seven midwestern prison facilities for men. *The Prison Journal, 80*, 379–390.

Selected Websites

Clem, C. (2007). Annotated bibliography on prison rape/inmate sexual assault. Rev. [ed.]. National Institute of Corrections. Retrieved from http://nicic.gov/Library/019764

Male Survivor (for victim support/information). Retrieved from http://www.malesurvivor.org/

Prison rape elimination act. Office of Justice Programs. Retrieved from http://www.ojp.usdoj.gov/programs/prisonrapeelimination.htm

Prostitution

Prostitution is the offering of something of value in exchange for sexual activity. Prostitution is also called "sex work"; this term is preferred by many sex workers and sex worker advocacy groups (Global Network of Sex Work Projects). The research literature uses both terms. Additionally, prostitution is closely associated with trafficking, which is the involuntary recruiting and forcing into prostitution of people (most often women and adolescents). People who use the term "prostitution" tend to believe that sex work is exploitative and harmful to sex workers. People who use the term "sex worker" tend to believe that sex work should be legalized and regulated like any other business. Both camps are fully opposed to trafficking. This entry will use the terms "prostitution" and "sex work" interchangeably. Note that sex workers may be of either sex (or transgender) and may engage in either heterosexual or homosexual activity. While there are no firm numbers on the number of sex workers in the United States, there were approximately 75,000 arrests for prostitution in 2008. Over two-thirds (70%) of those arrested were women (Estimates of arrests in the United States [2001–8]).

Sex work and sexual violence are intertwined at every level. Child sexual abuse is a significant risk factor for entering prostitution. It is worth noting that most prostitutes enter into sex work as minors (average age of entry is 16 for women and 14 for men) (Kotrla, 2010). Some prostitutes are trafficked domestically and forced into sex work through violence, coercion, and intimidation (Kotrla, 2010) (see entry on **Trafficking in Persons**). Others come to prostitution through homelessness, drug addiction, and financial need. Both adolescent and adult sex workers are at much higher risk of physical and sexual violence than the general population. It is likely that female sex workers have the highest rate of occupational death (mostly due to homicide) of any worker group (Potterat et al., 2004).

There is a strong and consistent relationship between child sexual abuse and working as a prostitute. This is true for female, male, and male-to-female transgendered sex workers. Numerous studies estimate that between 55 and 90 percent of all prostitutes were sexually abused as children. Many sex workers report repeated incidents of child sexual abuse, multiple perpetrators, and victimization by family members (Abramovich, 2005; Wilson & Widom, 2008). One study followed a large number of abused children and matched controls (nonabused children) into adulthood. This prospective study found that those abused in childhood are over twice as likely to become prostitutes as compared to those not abused. This was true for both physical and sexual abuse (Wilson & Widom, 2008). Child sexual abuse also affects the current safety of sex workers. Those abused as children enter sex work at a younger age, to engage in unprotected sex, to return to prostitution despite intervention (Roe-Sepowitz, Hickle, Loubert, & Egan, 2011). They are also more likely to be sexually abused by a client.

In general, the path from childhood abuse to involvement in prostitution is not fully understood (Abramovich, 2005; Wilson & Widom, 2008). Child abuse is related other youth problem behaviors such as running away, school problems, and drug use. Each of these problems is related to the other problems and to engaging in prostitution (Wilson & Widom, 2008). The Wilson and Widom study (2008) proposed and tested a model of the path from childhood abuse to prostitution. (See figure from Wilson & Widom, 2008, at http://www.ncbi.nlm.nih.gov/pubmed/20186260.) They hypothesized that child abuse would lead to an increased risk of five problem behaviors (early sexual initiation, running away, juvenile crime, school problems, and drug use) and that these in turn would have a direct effect on engaging in prostitution. The statistical analysis supported this hypothesis and their proposed model.

A qualitative study explored the path to prostitution for girls living in the inner city from their perspective (Dunlap, Golub, & Johnson, 2003). This study conducted interviews over several years with 98 girls and women from severely distressed households in New York City. It found that for many inner-city girls, early and continued experiences of compelled sex with relatives and mothers' boyfriends were part of a pathway leading to prostitution. This pathway also involved teen pregnancy and early motherhood, dropping out of school, drug abuse, and having children by different fathers.

Once a person becomes a sex worker, she or he is at high risk of sexual and physical violence from her or his clients, pimps, gang members, people on the street, and the police. The risk is present for prostitutes who work in both indoor and outdoor venues. Several studies of prostitutes found that, since becoming sex workers, the great majority (roughly 80%) were physically assaulted and almost as many (roughly 70%) had been raped (almost half by customers). Over half of those raped report being raped more than five times (Farley et al., 2004; Raphael & Shapiro, 2004).

Prostitution is sometimes associated with gangs and other criminal activity. Sex workers are at risk of violence from gangs from the risky behavior that simply comes by associating with gang members, the behavior of the gang itself if it is seeking to gain income from prostitution, or the tendency of some gangs to engage in forced prostitution to make money (Knox, 2004). Violence may also come from the police. In a study of New York City sex workers, 14 percent reported violence at the hands of the police and 16 percent reported "sexual situations" with the police (Thukral, Ditmore, & Murphy 2005).

Sex workers have a difficult time obtaining protection from sexual violence. Since they are involved in illegal activities, they are often viewed as offenders rather than as victims. While many cities have services for problems related to sex work (e.g., homelessness, drug abuse), few cities have any collaborative networks of different types of service providers. It is also difficult for sex workers to find help for problems stemming from violence, as professional counselors and shelters are often ill equipped to address their needs. Several recent and proposed models of providing assistance to sex workers include citywide collaborations of agencies, focusing on general harm reduction and involving sex workers in developing resources (Cusick, 2006).

Stacey Plichta

See also Alcohol and Drug Abuse, Victimization; Child Sexual Abuse, Adult Survivors of; Pregnancy; Sex Industry (Overview); Sex Workers; STDs and HIV/AIDS; Trafficking in Persons

Further Reading

Abramovich, E. (2005). Childhood sexual abuse as a risk factor for subsequent involvement in sex work: A review of empirical findings. *Journal of Psychology & Human Sexuality, 17*(1–2), 131–146.

Cusick, L. (2006). Widening the harm reduction agenda: From drug use to sex work. *International Journal of Drug Policy, 17*(1), 3–11

Dunlap, E., Golub, A., Johnson, B.D. (2003). Girls' sexual development in the inner city: from compelled childhood sexual contact to sex-for-things exchanges. *Journal of Child Sexual Abuse, 12*(2), 73–96.

Estimated arrests of all persons in the United States [2001–8]. Easy Access to FBI Arrest Statistics. 1994–2008. http://www.ojjdp.gov/ojstatbb/ezaucr/asp/ucr_display.asp

Farley, M. (2004). "Bad for the body, bad for the heart": prostitution harms women even if legalized or decriminalized. *Violence Against Women, 10*(10), 1087–1125.

Knox, G. W. (2004). Females and gangs: Sexual violence, prostitution, and exploitation. *Journal of Gang Research, 11*(3), 1–15.

Kotrla, K. (2010). Domestic minor sex trafficking in the United States. *Social Work, 55*(2), 181–187.

Potterat, J. J., Brewer, D. D., Muth, S. Q., Rothenburg, R. B., Woodhouse, D. E., Muth, J. B., . . . & Brody, S. (2004). Mortality in a long-term open cohort of prostitute women. *American Journal of Epidemiology, 159*(8), 778–785.

Raphael, J., & Shapiro, D. L. (2004). Violence in indoor and outdoor prostitution venues. *Violence Against Women, 10*(2), 126–139.

Roe-Sepowitz, D. E., Hickle, K. E., Loubert, M. P., & Egan, T. (2011). Adult prostitution recidivism: Risk factors and impact of a diversion program. *Journal of Offender Rehabilitation, 50*(5), 272–285.

Thukral, J., Ditmore, D., & Murphy, A. (2005). *Behind closed doors: An analysis of indoor sex work in New York City.* New York, NY: Sex Workers Project at the Urban Justice Center.

Wilson, H. W., & Widom, C. S. (2010). The role of youth problem behaviors in the path from child abuse and neglect to prostitution: A prospective examination. *Journal of Research on Adolescence, 20*(1), 210–236.

Selected Websites

Bay Area Sex Worker Advocacy Network (San Francisco). Retrieved from http://www.bayswan.org/

Global Network of Sex Work Projects. (NSWP). Retrieved from http://www.nswp.org/

National Institute of Justice. Prostitution: Pathways, Problems and Prevention. Retrieved from http://www.nij.gov/topics/crime/prostitution/welcome.htm

Sex Workers Project: A Project of the Urban Justice Center (New York City). Retrieved from http://www.sexworkersproject.org/

PTSD and Stress

Sexual violence can be an overwhelming and terrifying event when it occurs. For many women, the fear and helplessness lasts far beyond the actual event. Posttraumatic stress disorder, or PTSD, is a psychiatric disorder that gives a name to the symptoms that survivors of sexual violence and abuse may encounter following their traumas.

According to the fourth edition of the American Psychiatric Association's *Diagnostic and Statistical Manual of Mental Disorders* (*DSM-IV-TR*), PTSD may be diagnosed in individuals who have experienced, witnessed, or been confronted with an event that involved actual or threatened death or serious injury, or a threat to the physical integrity of self or others. These individuals must also persistently reexperience this event in one or more ways, including through recurrent and intrusive distressing recollections (including images, thoughts, or perceptions), recurrent distressing dreams of the event, or feeling as though the event is recurring. These thoughts must cause impairment in functioning in the patient for a diagnosis of PTSD to be given.

Symptoms of PTSD usually begin within six months of the incident, but they may take longer than that to appear (delayed-onset subtype). Symptoms must last for at least one month for a diagnosis of PTSD to be considered. Some people are able to recover from the disorder within three months (acute subtype), while it might take others years to recover from it (chronic subtype).

Acute stress disorder (ASD) is a lesser-known disorder, which is similar to PTSD, with a few important distinctions in symptoms. For a diagnosis of ASD, symptoms last for at least two days, but no longer than one month. The *DSM-IV-TR* criteria for ASD put a stronger emphasis on dissociative symptoms than do the criteria for PTSD. There are also some differences in the number of each symptom that must be present.

Prevalence rates of PTSD among survivors of intimate partner violence range from 31 percent to 84.4 percent (Iverson et al., 2011). Nearly one-third of all rape survivors develop PTSD at some point in their lives. The prevalence of PTSD in rape survivors in the first three months after the trauma is around 50 percent (Elklit & Christiansen, 2010). A recent study found that women who were survivors of acquaintance rape (i.e., were raped by someone they had seen or spoken with prior to the assault, including dates, coworkers, and friends) reported more severe PTSD symptoms than woman who were survivors of intimate partner rape (i.e., were raped by current and former boyfriends, husbands, and cohabitants). As well, the amount of fear felt by women during the rape positively predicted PTSD symptom severity. In general, survivors of intimate partner rape experienced less fear during their rape than survivors of stranger rape; it is hypothesized that this is because women who are raped by an intimate partner are more familiar with their attackers and are better able to predict the outcome of the attack.

In 2006, approximately 905,000 children were victims of maltreatment in the United States, and 8.8 percent of those children were sexually abused (U.S. Department of Health and Human Services, 2008). Children suffering from PTSD may demonstrate some different symptoms than their adult counterparts. Children may regress developmentally as evidenced by bed-wetting or thumb sucking, show inappropriate sexual behavior or seductiveness, or have difficulty maintaining boundaries.

If women are sexually abused as children or adolescents, their risk of being abused as adults increases substantially. These women have higher rates of PTSD and depression than women who have been victimized once as adults. A long-term study established that as many as 80 percent of young adults who had been abused as children met criteria for at least one psychiatric disorder, including depression, anxiety, eating disorders, and suicidal ideation, by age 21 (Centers for Disease Control and Prevention, 2011). This may be associated with changes in the brain, including increased reactivity to stress and smaller hippocampi, which are correlated with a biological vulnerability to psychopathology (Glover et al., 2010).

Frequently, children who are abused are threatened by their attackers to not tell anyone about the abuse. Assuming that the person to whom the child is disclosing is a supportive and caring figure, disclosure can be a positive coping mechanism that can buffer against future psychological dysfunction. When a child's disclosure is met with disbelief or blame, the outcome can be as harmful as nondisclosure, a form of avoidant coping, or even more negative than nondisclosure. When children blame themselves for their abuse, they may be at greater risk for psychopathology as adults.

After a traumatic event, it is understandable that a woman would not want to think about, or return to a place that recalls memories of, the event. However, the symptoms of PTSD feed on avoidance; hence seeking professional, therapeutic, and pharmacological help is warranted. Therapeutic help can include cognitive behavioral therapy with an exposure component, which has been shown to be the most effective way to overcome PTSD. Psychopharmacologically, selective serotonin reuptake inhibitors (SSRIs) can be helpful in decreasing some PTSD symptoms, particularly arousal and numbing. At present, only two SSRIs have been approved by the Food and Drug Administration for treatment of PTSD: sertraline (Zoloft) and paroxetine (Paxil). Women may also be prescribed a medication from the benzodiazepine family (Xanax, Ativan, etc.), which can be taken periodically when the anxiety is overpowering; however, these medications do not directly impact core PTSD symptoms (Whealin & Barnett, 2009).

PTSD and other significant psychiatric diagnoses are some of the negative outcomes that survivors of sexual abuse and violence may face long after their traumas have ended, and these are overwhelming and scary in their own way. However, with psychotherapy and medication, survivors of sexual violence can overcome their symptoms so that they may continue on in a more functional and healthy manner.

Beth Lynn Greene Hollander

See also Cognitive Behavioral Therapy; Coping Mechanisms; Eating Disorders; Exposure Therapy; Impact, Brain Functioning; Impact, Work; Sexually Acting Out; Suicidality

Further Reading

Elklit, A., & Christiansen, D. M. (2010). ASD and PTSD in rape victims. *Journal of Interpersonal Violence, 25*, 1470–1488.

Feinstein, B. A., Humphreys, K. L., Bovin, M. J., Marx, B. P., & Resick, P. A. (2011). Victim-offender relationship status moderates the relationships of peritraumatic emotional responses, active resistance, and posttraumatic stress symptomatology in female rape survivors. *Psychological Trauma: Theory, Research, Practice, and Policy, 3*, 192–200.

Glover, D. A., Loeb, T. B., Carmona, J. V., Sciolla, A. S., Zhang, M., Myers, H. F., & Wyatt, G. E. (2010). Child sexual abuse severity and disclosure predict PTSD symptoms and biomarkers in ethnic minority women. *Journal of Trauma & Dissociation, 11*, 152–173.

Iverson, K. M., Gradus, J. L., Resick, P. A., Suvak, M. K., Smith, K. F., & Monson, C. M. (2011). Cognitive-behavioral therapy for PTSD and depression symptoms reduces risk for future intimate partner violence among interpersonal trauma survivors. *Journal of Consulting & Clinical Psychology, 79*, 193–202.

U.S. Department of Health and Human Services, Administration on Children, Youth, and Families. (2008). *Child Maltreatment 2006*. Washington, DC: U.S. Government Printing Office.

Whealin, J., & Barnett, E. (2009, December 17). Child sexual abuse. National Center for PTSD. Retrieved from http://www.ptsd.va.gov/professional/pages/child_sexual_abuse.asp

Selected Websites

Clinician's guide to medications for PTSD. National Center for PTSD. Retrieved from http://www.ptsd.va.gov/professional/pages/clinicians-guide-to-medications-for-ptsd.asp

Intimate partner violence. International Society for Traumatic Stress Studies. Retrieved from http://www.istss.org/AM/Template.cfm?Section=PublicEducationPamphlets&Template=/CM/ContentDisplay.cfm&ContentID=1462

Sexual abuse. National Child Traumatic Stress Network. Retrieved from http://www.nctsn.org/trauma-types/sexual-abuse

Women, trauma, and PTSD. National Center for PTSD. Retrieved from http://www.ptsd.va.gov/public/pages/women-trauma-and-ptsd.asp

R

Racism

Race plays a significant role in sexual violence. Notions of when sexual violence is justified or unjustified often cross stereotypes that are accorded to race. Negative perceptions about black women's sexuality, such as the stereotype of the hypersexualized jezebel or the overly strong superwoman, impact perceptions of women as victims or actors in the violence, needing or not needing services, and able to be helped or unable to be helped. Black women are associated with more negative characteristics, such as being aggressive, and with less positive terms, such as being sincere (Brown & Monahan, 2005). Consequently, they are more likely to experience unwanted sexual attention and sexual coercion as a consequence of these negative stereotypes (Buchanan, Settles, & Woods, 2008). Stereotyping black women creates a generalized acceptance of their victimization.

These negative stereotypes are rooted in the enslavement of African people. Black women were viewed as commodities during slavery. They had no voice over their sexuality and were groped, examined naked on the auction block, routinely raped, and forced to have children. Their sexual victimization was institutionalized whereby there was no legal recourse; black women were viewed as acceptable victims of sexual assault. These negative stereotypes have continued and have contemporary relevance. Societal messages furthering negative images of black women begin early for young people, particularly through music, television, movies, and other venues. These oppressive and negative stereotypes tend to be centered on four myths: (1) the jezebel, (2) the mammy, (3) the superwoman, and (4) the matriarch.

Black women have been labeled as *jezebels*, a term created during slavery in order to justify the rape and impregnation of black women by slave owners. In the Old Testament of the Bible (the Book of Kings), Jezebel is the name of a strong and aggressive queen who dominates her husband, the king, and who also worships false prophets. Later interpretations referred to Jezebel being a painted woman, deceptive, and associated with prostitutes. Jezebels are viewed as hypersexual, promiscuous, and constantly desiring sex, suggesting ultimately that black women want to be victimized. They are viewed as immoral women who have no control over their sexual being and have an insatiable desire for sexual activity regardless of its violent nature. Because the stereotype is centered on the immorality and promiscuous nature of these women, they are not viewed as being able to be raped. The idea is that these women want to be treated in such a fashion and have created lifestyles that promote their being treated in such a way. Thus the man has no control over his actions and could have, in fact, been lured into the violence and forced to have sex with her. The stereotype and myth of the jezebel has been utilized to demerit black women who have experienced sexual violence.

The "mammy" is not viewed as a sexual being. Instead this term, coined during slavery, was reserved for black women forced to work in the slave owner's house and responsible for domestic work and child care. The role of the mammy was placed above the needs of the enslaved woman herself or her children. The mammy is someone who does not complain or try to change her situation. She cares for others and is there to meet others' needs as opposed to taking care of herself. Consequently, if sexual violence occurs at the hands of a slave owner, she is expected to go along with the violence and not raise concerns because her job is to meet others' needs. Thus a woman who associates herself with stereotype may not report experiences of sexual violence due to felt obligations of both loyalty and submissiveness to the perpetrator.

The superwoman stereotype states that black women can withstand anything, including sexual violence. The superwoman, also referred to as the "strong black woman," was manifested during slavery when black women were purported as physically and psychologically suited for enslavement. The superwoman stereotype does not grant black women permission to experience pain or have a weakness. The superwoman is expected to balance life's demands and is celebrated for not complaining or needing help. She may appear to need nothing because she has been taught not to seek help. The provider may view her as aggressive, having it all together, and/or not warranting assistance.

The matriarch, characterized as a female dominating the black household, is viewed as a woman who has emasculated black males. It is assumed that she wants to be and positions herself as the head of the family. She is viewed as stronger or at least equally as strong as black males and thus not warranting of any assistance because she cannot be a victim. This myth is further reinforced when health care providers, judges, and others do not support black women because they assume they are strong and/or do not appear to need help.

The denigration of black women as licentious jezebels, passive mammies, unbreakable superwomen, and domineering matriarchs stems from slavery and persists even today. Legacies of past historical sexual violence against black women continue to foster stereotypical assertions and racism today. It is critical to address the stereotypes to curtail the tide of sexual violence and address the intersection of race and sexual violence.

Tricia B. Bent-Goodley, Noelle M. St. Vil, and Selena T. Rodgers

See also African Americans; Revictimization, Organizations

Further Reading

Brown Givens, S., & Monahan, J. (2005). Priming mammies, jezebels, and other controlling images: An examination of the influence of mediated stereotypes on perceptions of an African American woman. *Media Psychology, 7,* 87–106.

Buchanan, N. T., Settles, I. H., & Woods, K. C. (2008). Comparing sexual harassment subtypes for Black and White women: Double jeopardy, the Jezebel, and the cult of true womanhood. *Psychology of Women Quarterly, 32,* 347–361.

Donovan, R. A. (2007). To blame or not to blame. *Journal of Interpersonal Violence, 22,* 722–736.

Donovan, R. A., & Williams, M. (2002). Living at the intersection: The effects of racism and sexism on black rape survivors. *Women & Therapy, 25,* 95–105.

Hill-Collins, P. (2008). *Black feminist thought: Knowledge, consciousness, and the politics of empowerment* (2nd ed.). New York, NY: Routledge.

Roberts, D. (1998). *Killing the black body: Race, reproduction and the meaning of liberty.* New York, NY: Vintage Press.

White, D. G. (1999). *Ar'n't I a woman?: Female slaves in the plantation South.* New York, NY: Norton.

Selected Websites

Black Women's Health Imperative. Retrieved from http://www.blackwomenshealth.org

Institute on Domestic Violence in the African American Community. Retrieved from http://www.idvaac.org/

Sexual violence: Population-specific approaches (2006). National Online Resource Center on Violence Against Women. Retrieved from http://www.vawnet.org/sexual-violence/population.php?filterby=African%20American

Rape

There is no universal or national definition of rape. Generally, rape is one type of sexual violence. The definition of rape can depend upon the professional perspective or orientation from which rape is being defined. Medical professionals view rape as a medical problem that causes a certain type of injury to the body. Mental health professionals define rape as a mental health issue that impacts the mind and the emotions of the victim. The legal definition of "rape" varies considerably depending on the state or U.S. territory, also known as the jurisdiction, in which the crime occurred. The terminology also varies according to place. It is possible for jurisdictions not to use the term "rape" to refer to acts of sexual violence, but may include types of sexual violence under different terms, such as aggravated sexual abuse, or abusive sexual contact, or criminal sexual conduct. Though terms and definitions vary, in criminal law, many jurisdictions define rape as a type of sexual assault involving sexual intercourse, or other forms of sexual penetration of a person without that person's consent or permission. In short, there are two necessary components for the commission of rape: (1) an act, and (2) lack of consent.

For U.S. jurisdictions, the criminal acts used to define rape vary according to the type of sexual activity (e.g., with or without penile penetration) and who can or cannot be the victim or offender. Some jurisdictions have a broad definition of rape that includes all forced sexual activity. In addition to types of penetration, these forced sexual activities may encompass nonpenetration sexual activity including oral copulation and masturbation. Other jurisdictions define rape in a narrow fashion to cover only acts involving penile penetration of the vagina and/ or anus of a female, treating all other types of nonconsensual activity as sexual assault. In these jurisdictions, rape is sex-specific and can be perpetrated only against a female by a male. Other jurisdictions, however, have expanded the legal definition of rape to include other types of penetration, with or without objects, and a wider variety of activity, e.g., male rape, anal rape, and oral rape. In these jurisdictions, rape is not sex-specific, because penile penetration is not necessary. Penetration can be accomplished by other body parts (including fingers) or objects, and thus includes acts that can be perpetrated by females or males and can have male or female victims.

The second component of rape is lack of consent, meaning the victim did not give his or her permission to be involved in the sexual activity. There are many evidentiary issues concerning consent or the lack thereof that make rape a difficult crime to prosecute. Prosecutions of rape cases usually do not turn on whether or not the sexual activity occurred, but tend to depend on the issue of consent. Previously, victims had to prove with marks and other evidence of bodily injury that he or she was forced into the sexual activity. Some jurisdictions may still have these requirements. Although evidence of force is still highly regarded, proof of force may not be necessary to prove lack of consent.

Consent and lack of consent can be directly expressed and/or indirectly implied from the context, body language, the relationship of the parties, and other actions or factors. However, the absence of an objection does not in and of itself constitute consent. In other words, because a person did not directly say or imply "no" does not mean, unequivocally, that he or she consented to the sexual activity. Similarly, there are no circumstances or factors that without question result in automatic consent. For example, previous sexual relationships, marital relationships (in most jurisdictions), or other circumstances do not provide infallible consent. There are also circumstances under which consent cannot legally be obtained. Generally, consent is deemed invalid if it is obtained from a person who is: (1) under duress (e.g., force, violence, blackmail); (2) judgmentally impaired or incapacitated by alcohol or drugs (legal or illegal); (3) mentally impaired whether by illness or developmental disability; or (4) below the age of consent as defined in that jurisdiction. Such cases are sometimes called statutory rape. It is important to note that consent can be given and then retracted. For example, a person can consent and then change his or her mind before or during the course of the sexual activity. Consent can always be withdrawn at any time, so that any further sexual activity after the withdrawal of consent constitutes rape.

Alexis Jemal

See also Consent; Criminal Sexual Assault or Misconduct; Laws, Rape; Medicalization of Rape; Sexual Assault; Statutory Rape

Further Reading

Cook, S. L., Gidycz, C. A., Koss, M. P., & Murphy, M. (2011). Emerging issues in the measurement of rape victimization. *Violence Against Women, 17*(2), 201–218.

Larcombe, W. (2011). Falling rape conviction rates: (Some) feminist aims and measures for rape law. *Feminist Legal Studies, 19*, 27–45.

Suarez, E., & Gadalla, T. M. (2010). Stop blaming the victim: A meta-analysis on rape myths. *Journal of Interpersonal Violence, 25*(11), 2010–2035.

Selected Website

RAINN (Rape, Abuse & Incest National Network). Retrieved from http://www.rainn.org

Rape, Admitting

Rape is about power, control, dominance, opportunity, and in some cases, emotional relationships—not sex. Rape can happen to men and women and can be perpetrated by men and women of any age. Most agree that a rapist uses force or violence, or the threat of it, to coerce another human being into sexual acts. However, the definition of rape varies from state to state and within research literature. Lack of consensus regarding the definition of rape makes it extremely difficult to produce accurate rape statistics, and in particular, ascertain accurate information about who admits to rape.

Social scientists, criminologists, researchers, and mental health professionals have struggled for decades to understand what motivates one to rape. The last decade in particular has focused on cognitive factors and individual differences. Individual differences such as personality characteristics and temperament, family history, culture, and traditional gender role socialization have been studied and considered but do not explain why most offenders rape, why some women rape men, or why rape occurs in gay and lesbian relationships (Simonson & Subich,1999).

Some theorists and therapists believe that rapists think in distorted ways because they were abused as children and are reenacting their own abuse or that rape is a learned behavior. A prevalent assumption exists that many adult sexual offenders who were sexually abused as children demonstrate cognitive distortions that contribute to sexually abusive behaviors later in life (e.g., McCormack, Rokous, Hazelwood, & Burgess, 1992; Ward, Hudson, Johnston, & Marshall, 1997). This theoretical perspective asserts that cognitive distortions serve to rationalize and maintain offending behavior patterns. In this line of thinking, faulty cognitive processes or cognitive distortions perpetuate sexual offending behavior (Marshall, Marshall, Sachdev, & Kruger, 2003). Defined as "maladaptive beliefs and attitudes, and problematic thinking styles . . . [such] as excusing, blaming, and rationalizing sexually abusive actions" (Ward, 2000, p. 491), many researchers view cognitive distortions to be central to sexual abusive behavior (Ward, Fon, Hudson, & McCormack, 1998). Still others think that rapists lack the ability to empathize with their victims—and thus do not have the ability to put themselves "in another's shoes" and imagine or feel what it would be like to be a victim of rape. For example, a sexual offender may ignore or reject evidence that is contrary to his or her distorted beliefs, such as when a victim pleads, cries, or shouts "stop!" in response to a perpetrator's advances and claims that it was consensual sex. Cognitive distortions may also serve as a defense mechanism, which can be called upon when a perpetrators need to defend themselves against uncomfortable thoughts and feelings of the abusive nature of their behavior or lack of empathy for their victims.

Regardless of underlying theory or individual differences, data tell us that many rapists were abused as children and/or adolescents. What these data do not explain are the large number of people who have been sexually molested or raped who do not go on to become rapists and perpetuate the pattern of abuse. In fact, research has shown that sexual offenders have more often experienced forms of abuse such as emotional and physical abuse rather than sexual abuse. Unfortunately and understandably, what we do know about rapists is limited to studying those who have been caught and are incarcerated. And recent studies show that as little as five percent of rapists are convicted (Bindel, 2007).

The punishment and therapeutic treatment of rapists is controversial. Punishment can include being sentenced to prison, community service, or participation in a restorative justice program, and/or having to attend and participate in a treatment program for sexual offenders. Some believe the answer can be found in a restorative justice model. Restorative justice programs allow victims/survivors to experience of a sense of justice while supporting sexual offenders to understand the consequences and impact of their behavior as well as developing a plan that may address both reparation to the victim and incorporates a treatment plan for the sexual offender. Relative to therapeutic intervention, experts in the field primarily use cognitive behavioral therapy in hopes of decreasing rates of victimization and preventing recidivism by rapists. Most agree that cognitive behavioral models and/or treatment programs that challenge denial or sexual offender's unwillingness to admit to sexual aggression or the act of rape and promote development of victim empathy and relapse prevention have demonstrated modest success. To accurately assess treatment efficacy is problematic, however, due to small numbers, due to individual need, and because the mode of punishment varies widely.

Given that rape is the least reported violent crime in the United States, even more disturbing is that the literature states that only a fraction of known rapes committed actually end in prosecution. And of those caught and prosecuted, only a few rapists ever serve time for their crime (Lisak, 2008). Complicating the issue, offenders who meet the legal definition of rape rarely admit to engaging in activities that could be defined as rape. Of offenders who commit rape, only eight percent will admit to committing rape or attempted rape (http://www.oneinfourusa. org/statistics.php).

Much more work needs to be done regarding rape and victimization/survivor research to answer very important questions of: why do individuals rape, who rapes, and who admits to rape? While steady gains are being made in understanding this violent phenomenon, the answer at present is "we do not know."

Joanne P. Smith-Darden

See also Criminal Justice and Perpetrators; "Justifiable Rape"; Rape, Denial; Rape Justification; Theory, Coercive Control

Further Reading

Bindel, J. (2007). The rapist's enemy. Retrieved July 14, 2011, from http://www .guardian.co.uk/uk/2007/jun/01/ukcrime.law

Lisak, D. (2008). Understanding the predatory nature of sexual violence. Retrieved July 14, 2011, from http://www.innovations.harvard.edu/cache/documents/1348/134841.pdf

Marshall, W. L., Marshall, L. E., Sachdev, S., & Kruger, R. L. (2003). Distorted attitudes and perceptions, and their relationship with self-esteem and coping in child molesters. *Sexual Abuse: A Journal of Research and Treatment, 15*, 171–181.

McCormack, A., Rokous, F. E., Hazelwood, R. R., & Burgess, A. W. (1992). An exploration of incest in the childhood development of serial rapists. *Journal of Family Violence, 7*, 219–228.

Simonson, K., & Subich, L. M. (1999). Rape perceptions as a function of gender-role traditionality and victim-perpetrator association. *Sex Roles: A Journal of Research, 40*(7/8), 617–634.

Ward, T. (2000). Sexual offenders' cognitive distortions as implicit theories. *Aggression and Violent Behavior, 5*(5), 491–50.

Ward, T., Fon, C., Hudson, S. M., & McCormack, J. (1998). A descriptive model of dysfunctional cognitions in child molesters. *Journal of Interpersonal Violence, 14*, 129–143.

Ward, T., Hudson, S. M., Johnston, L., & Marshall, W. L. (1997). Cognitive distortions in sex offenders: An integrative review. *Clinical Psychology Review, 17*, 479–507.

Selected Websites

RAINN (Rape, Abuse & Incest National Network). Retrieved from http://www.rainn.org/

Sexual assault statistics. One in Four. Retrieved from http://www.oneinfourusa.org/statistics.php

Violent crime. Bureau of Justice Statistics (2011). Retrieved from http://bjs.ojp.usdoj.gov/index.cfm?ty=tp&tid=31

Rape, Adult

Rape is a violent crime that affects the health and well-being of many American adult women and men. It is difficult to know exactly how many rapes happen in the United States because so many are not reported. Research has found that about 18 percent of women in our country will experience an attempted or completed rape in their lifetime, with 46 percent of these assaults committed against women age 18 or older. Approximately 3 percent of adult men will also be the target of an attempted or completed rape, 29 percent of whom are assaulted after age 18 (Tjaden & Thoennes, 2006). Most rapes in the United States are committed by someone who knows the victim, and the majority of perpetrators of rape are men. Most adult victims do not report the rape to police. Many risk factors at the individual, group, community, and society levels that are illuminated by the ecological model influence the occurrence of rape in our country.

Legal definitions of rape vary by state. Generally, rape is the penetration of the vagina, mouth, or anus by a penis, finger, or object without the consent of the victim. Victims who are unconscious, have certain disabilities such as developmental delays, or are intoxicated are considered to be unable to give consent for sexual contact. Rape affects victims in many ways. Physical injuries including bruises, sprains, and internal injuries, and broken bones may occur. Victims of rape may experience depression, post-traumatic stress disorder, anxiety, or substance abuse, and may engage in self-harm. Both male and female victims are at risk for contracting a sexually transmitted disease, and female victims may become pregnant as a result of rape. Given that many rape victims know the person who assaulted them, they may have difficulty in their relationships with family and friends and problems with trust. Lost time from work and stress-related health problems due to the effects of the assault may also occur.

Who commits rape in the United States? Research finds that 99.6 percent of women who have been raped were assaulted by a man, while 85.2 percent of male victims were raped by a man (Tjaden & Thoennes, 2006). Most women are raped by current or former husbands or boyfriends, while men are more likely to be raped by acquaintances such as friends, neighbors, or teachers (Tjaden & Thoennes, 2006).

These numbers tell us that rape is usually committed by men who know the victim, and sometimes by those closest to her or him.

Less than 20 percent of rapes are reported to police. Rape victims often do not report because they fear the rapist may retaliate against them, particularly as most know the person who assaulted them. Shame, embarrassment, and the fear of not being believed also affect one's willingness to report. Some victims do not consider the assault to be a crime while others think it is not an issue for police to be involved in. Many victims blame themselves for having been raped.

Why do people commit rape? While there is no one answer, many risk factors that contribute to rape have been identified. The ecological model is a way of thinking about risk factors from four related spheres, or levels, of influence. These four levels are the individual, relationship, community, and societal and each has risk factors that affect the occurrence of rape.

The individual level includes personal and biological risk factors for people that may increase their potential for raping another person. Individuals who have a lower income, were exposed to physical and/or sexual abuse, or witnessed violence between parents are more at risk for committing rape, as are those who have mental illness and who abuse alcohol or drugs. The relationship level includes factors from a person's closest social circle such as family, friends, and dating partners that may influence the occurrence of rape. These factors include relationships in which multiple sex partners, infidelity, and low resistance to peer pressure are common. Community-level factors are found in settings such as neighborhoods, schools, and workplaces where social relationships happen. Community-level risk factors include a lack of community punishment for rape and poverty. The societal level is the level at which social norms, policies, and cultural beliefs operate and influence behavior such as rape. Societal-level risk factors include traditional norms that support violence, belief that males are entitled to sex, and a lack of legal punishment for rape. While no one factor from the individual, relationship, community, or societal level causes rape, these factors contribute to its occurrence and provide a path for designing interventions to prevent rape.

Karen Herman

See also Acquaintance Rape; Date Rape; Drug-Facilitated Rape; Sexual Assault

Further Reading

Brown, J., & Walklate, S. (Eds.). (2011). *Handbook of sexual violence*. London, England: Routledge.

Tjaden, P., & Thoennes, N. (2006). *Extent, nature and consequences of rape victimization: Findings from the national violence against women survey* (NCJ 241036). National Institute of Justice. Washington, DC: U.S. Department of Justice.

World Health Organization (2010). *Preventing intimate partner and sexual violence against women: Taking action and generating evidence.* Geneva, Switzerland: Author.

Selected Websites

National Sexual Violence Resource Center. Retrieved from http://www.nsvrc.org

RAINN (Rape, Abuse, & Incest National Network). Retrieved from http://www.rainn.org

Rape prevention & education (RPE Program). Centers for Disease Control and Prevention. Retrieved from http://www.cdc.gov/violenceprevention/RPE

Rape, Cyber

Cyber rape, also known as virtual rape, has been broadly defined as unsolicited, unwelcome, or assaultive sexual communications taking place in cyberspace. Although some cyber offenses can be clearly identified as criminal acts (e.g., sexual solicitation of a minor), others are less clearly categorized or understood. One such example is cyber rape, in which individuals act out rape fantasies via the Internet. There is considerable disagreement as to whether cyber rape constitutes a criminal act. Although rape has long been understood as an offense with both physical and psychological elements, cyber rape is solely a psychological act and thus fails to meet the conventional legal standard requiring battery. This has resulted in ongoing debate about the meaning of cyber rape within the larger context of sexual assault.

Cyber rape can take several forms, including:

1. Sexual harassment and stalking victims on the Internet, a form of cyberbullying, in which perpetrators send victims threatening messages of a sexually explicit nature. Such communications clearly transgress behavioral norms and are typically seen as psychologically and/or emotionally abusive, as well as predatory. For example, in 2008, a California man was convicted and sentenced to two years in prison after sending threatening messages to his victim via MySpace, demanding phone sex and nude photos. Another example is sexual "extortion," threatening to post nude pictures of the victim on the Internet if she does not agree to have sex (see **Sexting**).

2. Rape enactment in a role-playing game (RPG) employing a user-programmable avatar. Examples include games such as Second Life and The Sims, as well as rape simulations, video games in which the object of the game is to sexually assault the other animated characters. One such game, RapeLay, was released by a Japanese gaming company in 2006 and centers on a male character who stalks and rapes a mother and her two daughters. The game involves realistic simulations of sex acts, such as forced intercourse and bondage. Other games,

such as the Grand Theft Auto series, contain similar themes and objectives. These games have been widely criticized for their graphic imagery and support of sexual brutality.

3. Watching video clips of actual rape with real victims or women acting as victims. The first recorded and perhaps most notorious case of cyber rape occurred in 1993 within a text-based RPG known as LambdaMOO. Using a "voodoo doll," a concept understood by game players to mean that he was controlling their behavior, a participant calling himself Mr. Bungle directed the avatars of two other participants to engage in explicit and involuntary sexual acts. Though many game players protested, Mr. Bungle's behavior continued until the other game players were able to contain him. This incident sparked a debate in which the focal question was, did a rape occur? Could Mr. Bungle's acts be considered actual rape or a portrayal of rape? Some argued that real acts did take place, namely that an actual person directed these events intending to cause an emotional response in his "victims." Others argued that these events constituted no real harm, as no individual was assaulted and all events occurred in virtual, not actual, reality.

Virtual rape has been the subject of intense debate for the better part of the last two decades. Some view cyber rape as a serious violation of boundaries and propriety, going so far as to equate it with actual rape on the basis that the emotional consequences are comparable. Many RPG users who have been the object of unwanted online sexual communications report feeling objectified, violated, and frightened, which are common responses among rape survivors. However, the "perpetrators" see it differently, perceiving cyber rape as a harmless and consequence-free expression of violent fantasies, an acceptable forum in which to release potentially dangerous urges. The result has been renewed dialogue about the meaning of rape: is it a crime against the body alone, or does psychological rape so offend our moral sensibilities that it constitutes a criminal offense? Moreover, there is justifiable concern about whether gratifying rape fantasy increases the intensity of the fantasy, thereby increasing the likelihood that the fantasy will be enacted with a real victim. In addition, what is the larger message for a society that condones the enactment of rape fantasy? Although there are no known empirical studies that address the precise question of whether those who engage in rape RPGs are at increased risk to commit hands-on rape, there are numerous studies that examine the role of sexually violent fantasy in the expression of sexually violent behavior. The gist of this research certainly suggests that sexually violent fantasy is a critical risk factor for such behavior.

Adeena M. Gabriel

See also Sexual Harassment; Video Games; Websites for Perpetrators

Rape, Denial

Denial is a coping mechanism characterized by an individual's refusal to admit or recognize some aspect of reality. The American Psychiatric Association (1987) defines denial as a "defense mechanism in which the person fails to acknowledge some aspects of external reality that would be apparent to others." This type of denial is considered a cognitive distortion or inaccurate mode of thinking. This type of faulty thinking often relates to the severity of the crime, the role that the victim played, or their relapse potential.

There are several different types of denial as it relates to rape and sexual assault offenders. Denial can range from internal to external, and all forms have an unhealthy element. Therapy can help to overcome denial, but the offender has to be willing to see him or herself in the light of reality.

External denial is often the classic "I didn't do it." Offenders know that they committed a sexual assault and for a variety of reasons, they are saying that they did not. The most common reason for this denial is a desire to maintain freedom by avoiding legal repercussions. People on the whole do not want to be arrested or have a legal record of criminal activity, and certainly want to avoid incarceration. Regarding sex offenses specifically, there are the additional repercussions of having to register as a sex offender under Megan's Law and/or have legal monitoring through Parole Supervision for Life.

Another reason for external denial is the desire to maintain social status and family homeostasis; offenders do not want people to know they are capable of sexually offending. When people find out about sex offenses, the offenders often face consequences including the loss of employment and conflict in personal relationships including reactions such as emotional distance, anger, confusion, hurt, embarrassment, and anxiety. Sometimes these relationship problems end up in separation and divorce or other forms of family division. The other side of this is that offenders who have been convicted face additional barriers when entering into new relationships and finding employment.

This type of external denial may show itself in several ways. The offender may say that there was no crime at all. Or the offender may deny involvement in the crime. Another variety of denial would be claiming that the victim was making up the allegations, often claiming motives of revenge. Denying the duration or extent of abuse is another form of denial. This could be regarding the duration of his or her offending behavior regarding the number of victims, for example, claiming there was only one victim and being dishonest about others. This could also relate to the length of time that the abuse occurs, claiming it happened only once and being untruthful about previous sexually abusive incidents.

Some offenders are in such denial that they believe their own lie; ultimately they have told themselves that same thing so often that it is true to them. This is internal denial. As a result of denying the severity of the crime, offenders believe that the effects of the sexual abuse are either nonexistent or not serious. This includes the "they liked it" and the "they will get over it" mentality. This lack of understanding directly relates to the offender's lack of empathy for sexual assault survivors.

One common form of denial is victim blaming in which the offender believes that the victim liked the sexual interaction or even wanted it. Offenders incorrectly interpret that the victim's manner of dress indicates sexual desire and that past sexual interaction indicates a desire for future, more serious sexual interaction. Additionally, offenders may believe that if the victim does not physically fight during the sexual assault, it is a sign that the victim accepted this sexual behavior or even welcomed it. The reality is that many victims do not fight due to fear of serious injury or death or fear of causing the offender to escalate a behavior that is already disrespectful and harmful.

Maintaining denial of inappropriate sexual behaviors often precedes relapse. After an act of abuse offenders often deny that they will ever have sexually deviant thoughts or fantasies again, or they feel they will be able to control them to the extent that they do not act upon them. In reality, they are in denial of their triggers. They also have a lack of healthy, more appropriate responses, as well as a lack of understanding of the repetitive nature of sexual fantasy. People tend to regress in times of stress; they rely, sometimes subconsciously, on things that helped them deal with stress in the past, even if that coping skill was negative in nature. Offenders often convince themselves that they can control their thoughts and behaviors. This may result in an unwillingness to learn to healthy ways of dealing with their sexually inappropriate thinking and behaviors, consequentially leading to high risk for reoffending.

Essentially, denial is a mechanism used to limit cognitive dissonance. Cognitive dissonance is the uncomfortable feeling that people get when they hold opposing thoughts or feelings toward something or someone. In this case, the offender acts in a way that hurts others for self-gain, but still may be caring and considerate toward others. Many offenders do not feel they are wholly defined by their crime, that other parts of them are caring, supportive, and funny. The difference, or cognitive dissonance, between these opposing thoughts and behaviors causes stress for many offenders. Denial is one of the ways that helps to reduce this stress, thereby allowing offenders to maintain the positive image they have of themselves, even while they engage in sexually deviant behavior.

The role of denial is serious and one of the biggest barriers to therapy. Overcoming denial is one of the first important breakthroughs an offender must have if she or he is going to live a healthy, offense-free life.

Larissa Boianelli

See also Megan's Law; Rape, Admitting; Rape Justification; Rape Myths; Sex Offender Registries; Victims, Blaming

Further Reading

Ajzen, I. (2005). *Attitudes, personality, and behavior* (2nd ed.). Milton-Keynes, England: Open University Press.

American Psychiatric Association (1987). *The Diagnostic and Statistical Manual of Mental Disorders, 3rd Edition, Revised.* Washington, DC, pp. 393–395.

Bancroft, J., Janssen, E., Strong, D., Carnes, L., Vukadinovic, Z., & Long, J. S. (2003). The relation between mood and sexuality in heterosexual men. *Archives of Sexual Behavior, 32,* 217–230.

Beech, A. R., & Ward, T. (2004). The integration of etiology and risk in sexual offenders: A theoretical framework. *Aggression and Violent Behavior, 10,* 31–63.

Knight, R. A., & Thornton, D. (2007). *Evaluating and improving risk assessment schemes for sexual recidivism: A long-term follow-up of convicted sexual offenders* (Document No. 217618). Washington, DC: U.S. Department of Justice.

Rape, Older Adult

Despite common misconceptions, advanced age does not protect older adults from sexual violence. Older adults face risks for sexual violence in the forms of exposure to unwanted sexualized behavior, subjection to sexually graphic media, sexual assault, and rape. Given that the population of older adults in this country is growing at unprecedented rates, examination of this issue is both important and timely. Our nation's older adults deserve adequate protection from sexual violence and appropriate services following victimization.

Some type of elder abuse is experienced by 14 percent of older adults living in the community; nearly 20,000 complaints of abuse of older adults living in residential and long-term care facilities were substantiated in 2006 (Administration on Aging, 2006; U.S. General Accountability Office, 2009). More than 60,000 cases of rape of older women (over the age of 50) are reported each year (National Center on Elder Abuse [NCEA], 2005). Older-adult rape is defined as "forced sexual intercourse, including vaginal, anal, or oral penetration" by human anatomy or an object (Rape Abuse and Incest National Network, 2009).

Leading experts agree that even the best estimates of the occurrences of older-adult rape and other forms of older-adult sexual abuse are likely very low. The lack of reporting and underreporting (reporting only some portion of the physical abuse an older adult has experienced) are related to a number of barriers. Older victims may experience shame, concern about social stigma, a lack of awareness about the crime itself and about reporting, overwhelming health concerns, and communication challenges related to cognitive and memory impairments. Furthermore, older adults may fear potential consequences to reporting such as further harm to self or loved ones, not being believed, and the loss of one's sole or primary caregiver, which could result in the need to be moved to a more institutionalized care setting.

In addition to the barriers experienced by the older adult are those that may impede reporting by family members and care providers. Family members may not believe that abuse has occurred or may not recognize the severity of the problem. Complex family dynamics complicate the recognition and reporting of rape. A desire to address the problem without involving authorities may hamper reporting by both families and professional care providers. Administrators of residential and long-term care facilities may focus on addressing older-adult rape internally so as not to damage the reputation of the facility.

Overwhelmingly, victims of older-adult rape are older women. Multiple vulnerabilities, such as having physical disabilities and cognitive impairments, are associated with increased risk for older-adult rape. Older adults who require daily personal care and those who live in institutional care settings also experience increased risk. In essence, increased dependence points to increased risk.

The most prevalent perpetrators of older-adult rape are men. In particular, perpetrators of older-adult rape tend to be male relatives who provide some care to the older adult—most commonly sons and spouses. More formal paid care providers, including those who work in residential and long-term care facilities, also perpetrate older-adult rape. Finally, other nonrelated men are perpetrators of older-adult rape including male residents living in the same care facilities as their victims.

Older adults who have experienced rape present symptoms such as bruising and abrasions to the body, injury to the tissues of the genital area, exacerbation of existing health problems, changes in eating and sleeping patterns, and increased somatic complaints. They may also exhibit psychosocial manifestations of sexual violence—symptoms of trauma. Prevalent psychological problems subsequent to older-adult rape include symptoms of anxiety and depression, memory disturbances, avoidance, and hypervigilance. Changes in social functioning may also occur such as isolating behaviors, difficulty managing natural social rhythms, and disruptions in previously positive relationships.

Sadly, the signs of rape in older adults may be misattributed by doctors, nurses, and other professionals to physical problems associated with aging, common late-life psychosocial changes, or cognitive and memory conditions. Misconceptions and stereotypes about aging may contribute to disbelief of older adults' reports of rape by professionals as well as family members and friends. Ageism may also underpin slow responses from law enforcement, which when coupled with legal complexities add up to few cases of older-adult rape being prosecuted and even fewer convictions of perpetrators of this very serious crime.

The consequences of rape for older adults are far reaching. The experience of rape in older adulthood is associated with increased physical and psychological problems as well as increased mortality. Ultimately, older adult victims of rape experience a lower quality of life than their unharmed counterparts. The costs to society include greater health care expenditures for services to address these co-occurring and interrelated problems.

Older adults who have experienced rape can be best supported with services that reflect sensitivity to age and ageism. Tailored approaches will enhance interviewing techniques and information-gathering procedures of both health care professionals and law enforcement personnel. Helpful interventions that include empowerment-focused groups, policy advocacy, cognitive behavioral and problem-solving therapy, mind-body practices for stress reduction, social support enhancement, and facilitating opportunities for meaningful engagement must be shaped specifically for older adults.

Better estimates of older-adult rape and sexual abuse are critically needed in order to raise national awareness of this important social concern. Public education about risks, prevention, detection of older-adult rape, and appropriate services is of paramount importance with specific training for formal and informal care providers, health care and helping professionals, and key community members who are engaged with older adults. Mechanisms for identification and reporting and timely legal action must be improved at every level. It is essential that older adults be provided culturally responsive interventions at the time of crisis and beyond. Finally, it is critical that policies be developed to ensure the protection and provision of services to our nation's older adults who experience rape, other forms of sexual violence, and all types of elder abuse.

Colleen J. Reed

See also Consent; Nursing Homes

Further Reading

Acierno, R., Lawyer, S. R., Rheingold, A., Kilpatrick, D. G., Resnick, H., & Saunders, B. (2007). Current psychopathology in previously assaulted older adults. *Journal of Interpersonal Violence, 22*, 250–258.

Acierno R, Hernandez-Tejada M, Muzzy W, Steve K. (2009). *Final report: National Elder Mistreatment Study (Document No. 226456)*. Washington, DC: National Institute of Justice.

Administration on Aging. (2006). *National Ombudsman Reporting System Data Tables*. Washington, DC.

Payne, B. (2009). Understanding elder sexual abuse and the criminal justice system's response: Comparison to elder physical abuse. *Justice Quarterly*, 1–19.

Ramsey-Klawsnik, H., Teaster, P., Mendiondo, M., Marcum, J., & Abner, E. (2008). Sexual predators who target elders: Findings from the first national study of sexual abuse in care facilities. *Journal of Elder Abuse & Neglect, 20*, 353–376.

Rape, Abuse & Incest National Network (RAINN): *Types of sexual assault*. Retrieved from http://www.rainn.org/get-information/types-of-sexual-assault/was-it-rape

Roberto, K. A., & Teaster, P. B. (2005). Sexual abuse of vulnerable young and old women: A comparative analysis of circumstances and outcomes. *Violence Against Women, 11*, 473–504.

Sormanti, M., & Shibusawa, T. (2008). Intimate partner violence among midlife and older women: A descriptive analysis of women seeking medical services. *Health & Social Work, 33*(1), 33–40.

U.S. Government Accountability Office. (2011). *Elder justice: Stronger federal leadership could enhance national response to elder abuse.* (GAO Publication No. 11-208). Washington, DC: U.S. Government Printing Office.

Vierthaler, Karla. (2008). Best practices for working with rape crisis centers to address elder sexual abuse. *Journal of Elder Abuse & Neglect, 20*(4), 306–322.

Selected Websites

Elder Justice Now. Retrieved from http://elderjusticenow.org

National Adult Protective Services Association (NAPSA). Retrieved from http://www.apsnetwork.org

National Association of State Long-Term Care Ombudsman Programs. Retrieved from http://www.nasop.org

National Center on Elder Abuse (NCEA). Frequently asked questions. Retrieved from http://www.ncea.aoa.gov/NCEAroot/Main_Site/FAQ/Questions.aspx

National Clearinghouse on Abuse in Later Life. Retrieved from http://www.ncall.us

National Committee for the Prevention of Elder Abuse (NCPEA). Retrieved from http://www.preventelderabuse.org

Senior Law Center: Protecting the Rights of Older Pennsylvanians. Retrieved from http://seniorlawcenter.org

Rape Crisis Centers

In the early 1970s, rape crisis centers (also known as sexual assault programs) were created as a result of the antirape movement to create social change and to provide services to meet the multiple needs of sexual assault survivors and their significant others. Rape crisis centers can be freestanding, independent of other organizations, or they may be housed within domestic violence agencies or other organizations focused on social or health issues (e.g., hospitals, universities, county services, criminal justice organizations, and community mental health organizations). There are 1,265 rape crisis centers in the United States, with 26 percent as freestanding programs and 74 percent affiliated with organizations that focus on multiple social problems (National Sexual Violence Resource Center, personal communication, April 30, 2009).

Many survivors experience psychological distress (e.g., nightmares, fear, anxiety, depression) following a sexual victimization. To meet survivors' emotional needs, many rape crisis centers provide hotlines, crisis intervention, and individualized counseling. In addition, rape crisis centers may offer support groups to decrease survivors' feelings of social isolation, stigma, or shame. These centers tend to be more accessible to survivors than traditional mental health agencies because they typically provide services free of charge.

There have been few studies that have examined the effectiveness of rape crisis centers' services, but the emerging research indicates that they have been responsive to survivors' emotional needs. For example, Zweig and Burt (2007) surveyed survivors who used rape crisis center services in 26 communities and found that the survivors characterized the services as helpful particularly when staff members were being respectful of them, listening to their stories, and allowing them to have a sense of control during their interactions.

Wasco and her colleagues (2004) evaluated the hotline and counseling services of Illinois rape crisis centers and found that the majority of survivors reported feeling satisfied with the services. In addition, this study examined the impact of counseling on survivors by comparing self-reported post-traumatic stress symptoms (e.g., nightmares) before and after they received counseling. The study found that survivor levels of distress and self-blame significantly declined from pre- to postcounseling. In addition, survivors had more social support postcounseling. However, this study did not use a comparison group (i.e., comparing those who received services to those who did not receive services) and thus it is uncertain if the changes in the survivors can be linked to the services.

Because survivors often experience hurtful interactions with those in the medical and legal systems, rape crisis center advocates often accompany survivors to the hospital, police station, or court to provide survivors with crisis intervention and support, as well as intercede on their behalf if they experience poor treatment from other professionals. Wasco and her colleagues (2004) found that most survivors who received advocacy by Illinois rape crisis center advocates were pleased with the service. Emerging research also suggests that advocacy from rape crisis centers may help prevent survivors from being treated poorly by medical and law enforcement personnel. Campbell (2006) compared the experiences of survivors who received a medical forensic exam at two urban hospitals. The two hospitals were very similar in their practices, the number of survivors served, and the demographics of their patients (e.g., race, age). However, one hospital has a policy to page rape crisis center advocates to assist survivors while the other hospital does not utilize advocates. Survivors who received advocacy services were significantly more likely to receive comprehensive medical care than those without advocates. In addition, survivors with advocates were more likely to be treated in a respectful manner by the medical staff and law enforcement (Campbell, 2006).

Finally, many rape crisis centers focus on social change by helping eliminate society's tolerance of sexual violence. This may include raising awareness of sexual assault through public education, protests, holding survivor speak-outs, lobbying for violence against women legislation, and training other professional agencies on how to improve responsiveness to survivors. Rape crisis centers have been successful in their efforts to improve rape laws to afford victims with more legal protection (e.g., rape shield laws, revoking marital exemption laws).

In conclusion, there have been few studies examining the effectiveness of rape crisis centers, but the preliminary findings suggest they are responsive to the needs of survivors and have been successful in improving legislation that affects sexual assault survivors.

Debra Patterson

See also Advocacy; Crisis Counseling; Crisis Intervention; Hotlines; Laws, Victim Shield

Further Reading

Campbell, R. (2006). Rape survivors' experiences with the legal and medical systems: Do rape victim advocates make a difference? *Violence Against Women, 12,* 1–16.

Campbell, R. (2008). The psychological impact of rape victims' experiences with the legal, medical, and mental health systems. *American Psychologist, 63*(8), 702–717.

Matthews, N. A. (1994). *Confronting rape: The feminist anti-rape movement and the state.* New York, NY: Routledge.

Ohio Family Prevention Center (2010). *Excellence in advocacy: A victim-centered approach.* Retrieved from http://www.ocjs.ohio.gov/VictimServicesPublication.pdf

Spousal rape laws: 20 years later (1999/2000, Winter). *Victim Policy Pipeline.* National Center for Victims of Crime. Retrieved from http://www.ncvc.org/ncvc/main.aspx?dbName=DocumentViewer&DocumentID=32701

Wasco, S. M., Campbell, R., Howard, A., Mason, G. E., Staggs, S. L., Schewe, P, A., & Riger, S. (2004). A statewide evaluation of services provided to rape survivors. *Journal of Interpersonal Violence, 19*(2), 252–263.

Zweig, J. M., & Burt, M. R. (2007). Predicting women's perceptions of domestic violence and sexual assault agency helpfulness: What matters to program clients? *Violence Against Women, 13*(11), 1149–1178.

Selected Website

FAQ: Rape Shield Laws. National Center for Victims of Crime. Retrieved from http://www.ncvc.org/ncvc/main.aspx?dbID=DB_FAQ:RapeShieldLaws927

Rape Drugs

A variety of drugs may be used with criminal intent to facilitate rape. The most well known is Rohypnol, known on the street by a variety of names, including rope, ropies, roopies, ruffies, roaches, roach-2, Mexican valium, rib, and

Forget-me Pill. Chemically, Rohypnol is flunitrazepam, a benzodiazepine, produced by Hoffman-La Roche and sold legally in Europe and Latin America as a short-term treatment for insomnia and as a preanesthetic. It is not produced or sold legally in the United States. It is typically smuggled in and can be purchased very inexpensively on the street—for roughly $5.

The physiological effects are similar to Valium (diazepam), but Rohypnol is approximately 10 times stronger than Valium. Rohypnol can cause a drop in blood pressure, drowsiness, visual disturbance, dizziness, and confusion. Users often report feelings similar to intoxication but wake up without a hangover. In sexual assault cases, forensic labs screen for the metabolite of Rohypnol (7-amino-flunitrazepam). Although Rohypnol breaks down quickly, a 2 mg dose can be detected within 72 hours of ingestion.

Why is Rohypnol associated with date rape? A significant side effect of the drug is anterograde amnesia, a condition in which events that occur while under the influence of the drug are not remembered. About 10 minutes after ingesting the drug, the individual may feel dizzy, disoriented, or nauseated, experience difficulty speaking and moving, and eventually pass out. Victims of sexual assault typically have no memory of what happened while under the influence of the drug.

Rohypnol is often slipped into a drink at a party. This is critical, because alcohol enhances the effect of Rohypnol, resulting in an especially dangerous combination. Effects on memory and judgment are greater than the effects of either one alone. Effects begin within about 30 minutes and may persist for up to 8 hours. Intoxication from alcohol and Rohypnol can result in "blackouts" lasting 8 to 24 hours following ingestion.

Rohypnol is not the only drug used in rape. Another drug, GHB (gamma-hydroxy butyrate), is naturally occurring in the cells of all mammals and is found in small amounts in the central nervous system. It has been sold on the street as a euphoric, a sedative, and an anabolic steroid (used in, e.g., bodybuilding) for at least 20 years. GHB is known on the street by numerous names, including liquid Ecstasy, liquid X, liquid E, scoop, Georgia home boy, G-Riffick, somatomax, organic Quaalude, and, most notably, Easy Lay. GHB has been associated with rape in locations throughout the United States.

Similar to Rohypnol, high-dose GHB decreases cardiac output, depresses respiration, and produces seizure-like activity, as well as causing giddiness, dizziness, verbal incoherence, and eventually sleep. A sufficiently large dose will produce "sudden sleep" in about 10 minutes. GHB has a steep dose-response relationship. That is, small increases in the amount taken lead to significant intensification of the effect. Like Rohypnol, GHB results in amnesia, as well as hypotonia (abnormally low muscle resistance to movement). GHB was used in the past as a general anesthetic, and is currently used to treat narcolepsy. Unlike Rohypnol, GHB is regulated and sold in the United States under the trade name Xyrem.

Burundanga or "voodoo powder" comes from a Colombian plant of the nightshade family. It has been used for hundreds of years by natives in religious ceremonies. The Spanish discovered burundanga when they invaded Columbia in the seventeenth century, referring to it as "the tree that drives people mad." Over the past 15 to 20 years, burundanga has become a common drug used in crime. Under the influence of burundanga, individuals have been ordered to disclose passwords, empty bank accounts, and engage in sexual acts. Burundanga is traded as currency in immigrant-criminal and illegal-alien-criminal markets. As noted, burundanga has been increasingly associated with rape. Like the stronger benzodiazepines, burundanga can induce retrograde amnesia, resulting in a loss of will and a loss of memory, sometimes for days. A young American woman visiting Bogatá was raped by seven different men with no memory of the crime.

All three of these substances are functionally different. Rohypnol is a benzodiazepine, a powerful antianxiety drug that acts by enhancing the effects of gamma-aminobutyric acid (GABA) in the brain. GHB is a central nervous system depressant. In burundanga the primary active ingredient is scopolamine, an anticholinergic (cholinergic blocking agent). What all three have in common, however, is the effect of anterograde amnesia. Beyond simply inducing sleep, which can be achieved with sufficient alcohol, these substances induce amnesia for experiences that have occurred while under the influence.

Robert A. Prentky

See also Alcohol to Subdue Victims; Alcohol-Facilitated Sexual Assault; Drug-Facilitated Rape

Further Reading

Britt, G. C., & McCance-Katz, E. F. (2005). A brief overview of the clinical pharmacology of "club drugs." *Substance Use & Misuse, 40*, 1189–1201.

Fitzgerald, N., & Rile, J. K. (2000, April). Drug-facilitated rape: Looking for the missing pieces. *National Institutes of Justice Journal.* Retrieved from http://www.ncjrs.gov/pdffiles1/jr000243c.pdf

Selected Website

Rohypnol. The Partnership for a Drug-Free America. Retrieved from http://www.drugfree.org/drug-guide/rohypnol

"Rape Justification"

"Rape justifications" are reasons given to defend a rape perpetrator's behaviors. Furthermore, these reasons generally suggest that the victim deserved to be raped, and the perpetrator should not be held responsible for the crime. Rape justifications are generally based on rape myths, which are commonly held false attitudes and beliefs that justify sexual aggression. Many of these myths are rooted in gender stereotypes about men and women, or children.

Justifications may be given by perpetrators and victims of rape, and also society at large. When a rape justification is believed by a victim, she or he may internalize the message that she or he was responsible for the rape, and therefore may decline to take action against the perpetrator. This results in lower numbers of victims reporting rapes or assault to law enforcement. When a victim does decide to report a rape to another person, such as a friend, family member, health care professional, or law enforcement, the victim may become victimized again if the justification for rape is used against her or him. Secondary victimization occurs when the victim turns to another for help, including formal and informal sources of help and, in turn, those individuals minimize the rape or blame the victim for the rape. Rape and secondary victimizations can lead to negative consequences for the victim, which includes mental health problems, such as post-traumatic stress disorder, and physical problems, such as the contraction of HIV/AIDS or other sexually transmitted diseases.

Justifications for rape stem from the perpetrator's negative beliefs about women, societal beliefs about sexual relationships, the perpetrator's beliefs about child sexual behaviors, or situational factors involved in the rape. For example, some convicted rapists and individuals who commit rape within a marriage or partnership hold similar views about women, which include the idea that women are manipulative and untrustworthy. The basis of this justification is misogyny, defined as the hatred of women. Thus the perpetrator justifies the rape as a form of justice, in response to the woman's manipulative action(s) against him. In addition to the perpetrator holding negative beliefs about women, society in general holds certain beliefs about sexual relationships. These beliefs are generally based on gender stereotypes. For example, the belief that men are sexually dominant leads to a belief that male sexual aggression is natural. This aggression allows men to be more sexual than women, and thus women should be sexually submissive. When a woman behaves in a sexual way, some may justify rape by suggesting that she was provoking the perpetrator. This justification is vocalized when someone states that the victim was, "asking for it." Another gender stereotype of female sexual behaviors is the belief that women are the gatekeepers of sexual activity and are expected to resist sexual advances from men. The combination of female submissiveness and the expectation of resistance have caused some men to disbelieve women when they refuse sexual activity. They interpret the refusal as "token resistance" and believe that the rape was justified because "no" really meant "yes." In situations where rape occurs within a marital or coupled relationship, there is a false belief that the wife/female partner should always be sexually available to their husband/male partner, and thus the man is entitled to sexual intercourse without regard for the wife/female partner's choice to participate.

In rapes where a child is the victim, perpetrators also have underlying beliefs about sexual behavior in children—called cognitive distortions or implicit theories. One of these distortions or theories suggests that children are sexual beings and pursue sexual contact. The perpetrator believes that sexual contact between adults and children is harmful only if it includes force or verbal threats. Society has made this type of sexual contact illegal because children do not have the developmental maturity to make healthy decisions about sexual activity until a certain age, generally 16 or 18 years old. Age-of-consent laws have been established to prohibit adults from abusing the power they have over children to gain sexual access to a child.

Finally, situational factors have also been used as a way to justify rape. These include the use of alcohol and/or other drugs just before the rape occurred. In this situation victims may feel that they were responsible because they were not in control and did not take precautions to prevent the rape. Additionally, the perpetrator may use substance abuse as a way to deny responsibility for the rape. A rape may also be justified in a situation where the victim chose to go back to the perpetrator's home or if the perpetrator has paid for the date and is thus "owed" sexual activity. Rape has also been justified based on the victim's inappropriate behavior or appearance (e.g., tight clothing or near-visible sexual body parts). Victims may also feel that the rape was justified if they were unable to physically fight off the perpetrator during the rape. In cases where the crime did not include sexual intercourse, classified as a sexual assault, there may be a belief that sexual violence is a crime only if there is penetration.

Rape and sexual assault are crimes that cannot be justified by false beliefs about women and children, by false beliefs about sexual relationships or gender stereotypes, or based on a victim's behavior or appearance. As previously noted, rape justifications can add additional harm to victims; thus it is important that one does not use a justification if they are approached by a victim for information or assistance. Additionally, society must work to remove the gender stereotypes and justifications used in everyday discussions about rape and rape victims.

Erin B. Comartin

See also Alcohol and Drug Abuse (Overview); "Justifiable Rape"; Rape Myths; Unintended Rape; Victims, Blaming

Further Reading

Campbell, R., & Raja, S. (1999). Secondary victimization of rape victims: Insights from mental health professionals who treat survivors of violence. *Violence and Victims, 14*(3), 261–275.

Ryan, K. (2004). Further evidence for a cognitive component of rape. *Aggression and Violent Behavior, 9*, 579–604.

Scully, D., & Marolla, J. (1984). Convicted rapists' vocabulary of motive: Excuses and justifications. *Social Problems, 31*(5), 530–544.

Ward, T., & Keenan, T. (1999). Child molesters' implicit theories. *Journal of Interpersonal Violence, 14*(8), 821–838.

Weiss, K. (2009). "Boys will be boys" and other gendered accounts: An exploration of victims' excuses and justifications for unwanted sexual contact and coercion. *Violence Against Women, 15*(7), 810–834.

Rape Kits

A forensic exam in which evidence is collected from a victim of sexual assault is also known as completion of the rape kit. This exam records any injuries suffered by the victim and allows for the collection of any DNA or other evidence that may have been left by the perpetrator and could be used in a prosecution. The exam does not determine if a sexual assault occurred; it merely collects the physical evidence of a sexual assault. The exam may be performed in a hospital or in another medical facility, depending on the state. Ideally, the exam is performed by a trained forensic nurse, sometimes known as a sexual assault nurse examiner (SANE). Other nurses or doctors can also perform the exam and collect the evidence, though research has shown that trained forensic nurses are the most likely to collect the proper evidence (Du Mont & White, 2007).

A forensic exam must be done within a few days of a sexual assault if biological evidence is being collected. The time varies between states but usually not more than five days in any state. The completion of the forensic exam is usually accompanied by the activation of the sexual assault response team (SART), if there is a local SART. This helps to ensure that a survivor receives all the care he or she needs and to ensure that the survivor does not need to give an account of the assault many times. The victim must consent to the forensic exam and can refuse any portion of the exam at any time.

The collection of evidence from a victim includes a physical exam by the forensic nurse. This involves a complete medical history, including an account of the assault. The forensic nurse will also perform a head-to-toe physical exam, including the victim's genitals. The nurse will also collect blood, urine, hair, and other body secretion samples, and will photograph any visible injuries. The exam usually takes a few hours to allow for careful and thorough evidence collection. The exam may vary depending on the nature of the assault. For example, a forensic nurse would not do an oral swab if the victim says that there was no contact with her or his mouth.

In addition to the collection of evidence, the forensic nurse also takes note of any follow-up needed by the survivor. Prophylaxis for sexually transmitted diseases is usually provided to the survivor, though states vary in the ability to provide HIV prophylaxis and follow-up. Many states also provide emergency contraception to the survivor. If the survivor needs other medical care, the forensic nurse will provide the appropriate referral or the survivor will receive treatment at the facility where the exam has been performed.

Once the exam is complete, all specimens and evidence collected are carefully stored to ensure they are not contaminated and to ensure that the evidence is not compromised. They are then kept until further action by law enforcement is taken. Depending on the state, the evidence in the kits may be processed only by request of the police or prosecutor. Other states, such as Illinois or California, require that all evidence kits be processed and the DNA evidence analyzed. Laws requiring that all kits be processed have been in response to investigations and controversies over large numbers of forensic kits found to have been stored by law enforcement without being processed. In 2009, Human Rights Watch published a report describing the backlog of nearly 13,000 forensic kits where the survivor made a report to law enforcement and evidence was collected but the evidence was never processed, unbeknownst to the survivor (Human Rights Watch, 2009).

Under the Violence Against Women Act of 2005, victims can have an exam done free of charge but not file an official police report. States have different policies regarding how long they will hold a forensic kit while a survivor decides whether to report. California allows kits to be held for 15 years before they are destroyed if the victim did not make a police report. In other states, the time may be much shorter, such as Illinois, where kits are held for two weeks while the victim decides whether to make a report.

The kit itself is usually a small box containing all the tools needed by the examiner for a forensic medical exam. The kit usually includes:

- Instructions
- Bags/containers for evidence—includes clothing/undergarments
- Swabs
- Comb
- Envelopes
- Blood collection devices
- Documentation forms

Much effort has been made over the last several years to make kits smaller to allow for easier storage. This is particularly important as states move toward keeping kits for longer periods of time and require larger storage areas.

Jennifer Nix

See also Forensic Nursing; Medicalization of Rape; SANE (Sexual Assault Nurse Examiner); SARTs (Sexual Assault Response Teams)

Further Reading

Du Mont, J., & White, D. (2007). *The uses and impacts of medico-legal evidence in sexual assault cases: A global review.* Sexual Violence Research Institute. Retrieved from http://www.svri.org/medico.pdf

Human Rights Watch (2009). Testing justice: The rape kit backlog in Los Angeles City and County. Retrieved from http://www.hrw.org/reports/2009/03/31/testing-justice-0

U.S. Department of Justice, Office on Violence Against Women (2004). *A National Protocol for Sexual Assault Medical Forensic Examinations: Adults/Adolescents* (NCJ 206554). Retrieved from https://www.ncjrs.gov/pdffiles1/ovw/206554.pdf

Selected Websites

DNA technology. National Alliance to End Sexual Violence. Retrieved from http://endsexualviolence.org/where-we-stand/dna-technology

What is a rape kit? RAINN (Rape, Abuse & Incest National Network). Retrieved from http://www.rainn.org/get-information/sexual-assault-recovery/rape-kit

Rape Myths

Rape is considered the most widely underreported of all crimes. Given this reality, establishing a clear picture of the prevalence of rape/attempted rape and clearly identifying characteristics of both the offenders and victims in these events is quite challenging. From official data provided in the Uniform Crime Reports (collected by the U.S. Department of Justice), self-report data from the annual National Crime Victimization Survey, and numerous studies conducted by criminology/victimology researchers, however, a sense of the nature and scope of the problem can begin to take form. Collectively, this information makes it clear that the commonly held stereotype of a "real rape"—a stranger forcibly raping an innocent young woman in a public space—is actually the least common of all types of rape/sexual assault. Instead, the majority of rapes/rape attempts involve an acquaintance, date, or a current or former intimate partner who uses physical force, intimidation, and/or coercion to engage in unwanted sexual activity. In fact, research indicates that one in four women will be a victim of rape or attempted rape in her lifetime, and more than 80 percent of these women will experience this sexual assault before they are 25 years of age (Tjaden & Thoennes, 1998). Over

70 percent of all rapes will come at the hands of someone who is known to the victim, a number that increases to nearly 90 percent for rapes that occur on college campuses where date/acquaintance rape often occurs (Fisher, Cullen, & Turner, 2000). Additionally, calling into question the popularly held view that rape and sexual assault occur solely as male-on-female violence, research indicates that approximately three percent of men will experience some form of sexual assault in their lifetime (Tjaden & Thoennes, 2006). Despite these alarming numbers, a variety of social and cultural factors contribute to both the environment that makes such events occur and the responses/perspectives of perpetrators, victims, and others who become aware of the assault. In the 1970s, sociologists and feminist scholars first began to describe these pervasive cultural messages as *rape myths*.

Rape myths are widely views and stereotypes that stem from prevailing cultural norms and messages that are argued to be contributing factors in the perpetuation of rape/sexual assault. Examples of rape myths include the following:

- When women say "no" they really mean "yes."
- Women who are dressed provocatively, flirt with the offender prior to the assault, are out late, and/or are drinking are culpable in their rapes.
- If a woman goes on a date with a man and allows him to pay, she owes him sex.
- If it was really rape, she would have reported it.
- If she did not want it, she would have fought back. The absence of injury is viewed as an indication that the rape was actually consensual sex.
- Women lie about having been raped because they regret their decision to have consensual sex.
- It is not rape when it involves someone with whom the woman has been previously intimate.
- Once men are sexually aroused they cannot be expected to stop.
- Rape is sex.
- Only women get raped.

In each case the idea conveyed by the rape myth reflects a widely held misperception about who gets raped, who should be held accountable (if anyone), and/or what actually constitutes the occurrence of rape. A number of societal and cultural factors contribute to the development and maintenance of these myths. For instance, traditional gender role expectations are evident in many rape myths. Growing up, both boys and girls are exposed to the message that "no" really means "yes," and that women really want to be forced into sex. This shared socialization about gender norms and male-female interactions often means that one or both parties may fail to see forced or coerced sexual activity as rape. Similarly, although laws have been enacted that address the reality of marital/intimate partner rape, many who adhere to tradition views of male-female relationships view any sexual interaction between current or former intimate partners to be sex, not rape. A number of studies involving undergraduate college student samples have demonstrated that a significant minority of both male and female students fail to identify sexual assaults where previous sexual contact may not have occurred as incidents of rape.

For many victims of rape/sexual assault, awareness of rape myths often serves to increase the negative consequences associated with the assault in a number of ways. For instance, given the large number of rapes and sexual assaults that involve someone who is known to the victim, many victims of rape blame themselves, often questioning what they might have done to precipitate the rape or why they did not resist the offender in a more forceful manner. These feelings of accountability often increase the likelihood that the victim will not report the rape to anyone. The problem is often exacerbated by questions and responses from family and/or friends who may ask questions such as why the victim was where she was, whether she was drinking at the time, or what she was wearing when the attack occurred. Implicit in these questions is a suggestion that such actions somehow negate or justify the behavior of the offender. This is referred to as victim blaming.

The reach of the influence of rape myths can be seen throughout society. When rape is reported to the police or other authorities, research indicates that many law enforcement and criminal justice system officials also subscribe to rape myths. Questions about whether the victim was threatened with harm, whether she or he fought back against the advances of the perpetrator, or whether she or he has ever engaged in any type of intimate contact with the perpetrator all speak to subtle and not so subtle endorsements of commonly held myths about what constitutes rape. Research on jury responses to victims in rape cases also underscores the impact of rape myths on jury decision making as well. Since the 1970s all states have passed rape shield laws that preclude the introduction of victim behavior-related information during a rape trial. Despite this policy change, research suggests that rape myths remain pervasive in our culture.

Melanie D. Otis

See also Bias, Police and Prosecution; False Allegations; Laws, Victim Shield; Male-on-Male Sexual Violence; "Real Rape" and Blaming Victims; "Real Rape" and "Real Victims"—Correcting Misinformation; Victims, Blaming

Further Reading

Burt, M. R. (1980). Cultural myths and supports for rape. *Journal of Personality and Social Psychology, 38*(2), 217–230.

Fisher, B. S., Cullen, F. T., & Turner, M. G. (2000). *The sexual victimization of college women.* Washington, DC: U.S. Department of Justice, National Institute of Justice.

Littleton, H. A., & Axsom, D. (2003). Rape and seduction scripts of university students: Implications for rape attributions and unacknowledged rape. *Sex Roles, 49*, 465– 475.

Lonsway, K. A., & Fitzgerald, L. F. (1994). Rape myths. *Psychology of Women Quarterly, 18*, 133–164.

Page, A. D. (2008). Judging women and defining crime: Police officers' attitudes toward women and rape. *Sociological Spectrum, 2*(4), 389–411.

Ryan, K. M. (2011). The relationship between rape myths and sexual scripts: The social construction of rape. *Sex Roles, 65*(11–12), 1–9.

Tjaden, P., & Thoennes, N. (1998). *Prevalence, incidence and consequences of violence against women: Findings from the National Violence Against Women Survey.* Washington, DC: National Institute of Justice, Office of Justice Programs, U.S. Department of Justice.

Tjaden, P., & Thoennes, N. (2006). *Extent, nature, and consequences of rape victimization: Findings from the National Violence Against Women Survey.* Washington, DC: National Institute of Justice, Office of Justice Programs, U.S. Department of Justice.

Selected Websites

Sexual assault-rape myths. Stony Brook University Center for Prevention and Outreach. Retrieved from http://studentaffairs.stonybrook.edu/cpo/rape_myths.shtml

The truth about rape. Medicinenet.com. Retrieved from http://www.medicinenet.com/script/main/art.asp?articlekey=46850

Reactions, Family and Friends

At the same time that sexual assault victimization is a highly traumatic event, there is still a considerable amount of societal and legal system blaming and stigmatizing of these victims (often more so than of the offenders). These troubling reactions result in sexual assaults as one of the most, if not the most, unreported of all crimes. Additionally, victim blaming is more pronounced among sexual assaults where the victim and offender know each other, and these acquaintance sexual assaults are far more common than stranger sexual assaults. Importantly, between 65 percent and 92 percent of sexual assault victims disclose to another person, and the majority of these disclosures include at least one informal source (Ahrens, Cabral, & Abeling, 2009). Indeed, sexual assault survivors are more likely to disclose their victimizations to informal sources, such as their friends, romantic partners, and family members, than to formal sources, such as the police, rape crisis centers, and mental health providers. Thus improving the support for sexual assault survivors must include providing more education for community members to respond more effectively and compassionately when their loved ones report these victimizations to them.

The myriad of reasons rape survivors provide for why they disclose to informal sources include that they feel close to the individual and do not want to keep the assault a secret from loved one(s), they want emotional support and/or advice, they want tangible aid (such as driving them to the hospital or police, staying overnight with them, etc.), and they need to talk. Although most people want to be helpful to loved ones and other acquaintances who disclose rape victimizations to them, they often feel at a loss, even helpless, in terms of how to respond. For example, people worry that their responses to a rape victim's disclosure will make the victim feel even worse, and that that they will not appear sufficiently sensitive or supportive to the victims.

Gender is an important consideration in sexual assault survivors' disclosures. Survivors are more likely to disclose to women than to men, and typically feel more supported by the women than the men to whom they disclose. Related to this, men are more likely than women to report anxiety and helplessness in how to respond to rape survivors who disclose to them. The individual relationship that adult sexual assault survivors are most likely to disclose to (among all informal and formal supporters) is that of friend and typically followed by romantic partners and family members. Sexually assaulted adolescents, like adults, are also most likely to disclose to their friends, unless the assault is by a family member, and then they are most likely to disclose to their mothers. Further, the majority of sexually assaulted children do not disclose until adulthood; however, those who do disclose are most likely to disclose to their mothers.

The research is consistent in identifying what is most helpful to sexual abuse survivors when they disclose to their friends, family, romantic partners, coworkers, and so on. First, rape survivors report that being *believed* and that what they experienced was sexual assault is extremely important to them when they disclose. Second, rape survivors report that it is important that responders not judge them, especially if such judgments suggest that the sexual assault was fully or partly the victims' fault. Instead it is important to communicate that the rapists, not the victims, are entirely responsible and accountable for sexual assaults. Third, sexual assault survivors appreciate friends, family, and others to whom they disclose to being able to *listen* to them. Unfortunately, since most people are uncomfortable talking about sexual assault, survivors often report feeling their loved ones' silence and discouraged their loved ones from talking about what happened and how they felt at the time of the assault, or even when discussing how they feel at a later date after the assault. Understandably, sexual assault survivors feel unsupported, or even angry and/or scared, when loved ones and other acquaintances that they have disclosed to react egocentrically (in a self-centered manner), blame or otherwise judge the survivors, violate the survivors' trust (by telling others when the survivors requested confidentiality about the sexual assault), and interrupt or even stop the survivors from discussing the assault or their feelings during or after the assault.

When informal sources respond positively to sexual assault victims' disclosures, the victims are more likely to feel validated and supported, have higher feelings of self-worth, and be more willing to report to formal sources (e.g., the police). Likewise, when informal sources respond negatively, victims are more likely to experience shame, feelings of isolation, and post-traumatic stress disorder (PTSD). Fortunately, research indicates that many sexual assault survivors report that informal sources tend to provide more positive than negative responses. One potential informal response that receives mixed reactions by survivors, a response most typically involving males (fathers, brothers, boyfriends, and male friends), is acting protectively toward the survivor. Some survivors find this comforting, while others view this as overprotecting, infantilizing, and disempowering.

Belonging to a minority population may hold unique impacts for sexual assault survivors that might be related to legitimate cultural differences and even disparaging stereotypes. For example, some women and girls of color may face different cultural expectations regarding strength/weakness, independence/dependence, and/or varying expectations of privacy around sexual issues in general (even consensual sex, but including nonconsensual sex). Thus it appears that women and girls of color may be less likely to disclose sexual assault to both formal and informal sources. Additionally, sexual assault victims who identify as a sexual minority (i.e., lesbian, gay, bisexual, or transgendered individuals) also have complicated experiences disclosing to their friends and family. When disclosing the details of the assault, sexual minorities have been found to utilize friends and relatives with equal frequency to heterosexually identified victims, although bisexual women have been found to have significantly fewer positive reactions from informal sources. Finally, men who have experienced sexual assault are just as likely as women to disclose their assault to friends and family; however, men are significantly less likely to report the assault to formal support systems, and therefore friends and family form the entirety of the disclosure support.

Elizabeth Whalley and Joanne Belknap

See also Help Seeking, from Family and Friends; Impact, Family; Victims, Blaming; Victims, Disclosure

Further Reading

Ahrens, C. E., Cabral, G., & Abeling, S. (2009). Healing or hurtful: Sexual assault survivors' interpretations of social reactions from support providers. *Psychology of Women Quarterly, 33*(1), 81–94.

Banyard, V. L., Moynihan, M. M., Walsh, W. A., Cohn, E. S., & Ward, S. (2010). Friends of survivors: The community impact of unwanted sexual experiences. *Journal of Interpersonal Violence, 25*(2), 242–256.

Jacques-Tiura, A. J., Tkatch, R., Abbey, A., Wegner, R. (2010). Disclosure of sexual assault: Characteristics and implications for posttraumatic stress symptoms among African American and Caucasian survivors. *Journal of Trauma & Dissociation, 11*(2), 174–192.

Ullman, S. E. (2010). *Talking about sexual assault: Society's responses to survivors.* Washington, DC: American Psychological Association.

Washington, P. A. (2001). Disclosure patterns of black female sexual assault survivors. *Violence Against Women, 7*(11), 1254–1283.

Selected Websites

Reactions of loved ones. Sexual Assault Interagency Council (Denver). Retrieved from http://www.denversaic.org/reactions_lovedones

Self-care for friends and family members. RAINN (Rape, Abuse & Incest National Network). Retrieved from http://www.rainn.org/get-information/sexual-assault-recovery/tips-for-friends-and-family

Reactions, Mothers

Historically, research on nonoffending caregivers of sexually abused children, or the caregiver who did not abuse the child, considered them to be passive, collusive, or mentally ill. The literature on collusive mothers depicts them as deliberately evading detecting sexual abuse and denying that it is transpiring (Johnson, 1992). The theory of collusive mothers is not supported by empirical research and likely emerges from the gender stereotype that "a woman knows," or that women and mothers are exceptionally sensitive to relational betrayal and consequently know when sexual abuse is occurring, and either unconsciously or consciously permit the abuse to continue. Nonoffending mothers have faced lingering perceptions of their collusion, reporting in some research that interactions with the criminal justice and social services systems often involved blame and distrust of the mothers, leading to hostile relationships with those who are intended to offer support. This entry discusses research on maternal responses to disclosures of sexual abuse, the emotional reactions of mothers upon discovery of sexual abuse, and barriers facing mothers' intervention upon and recovery from the discovery of sexual abuse.

Studies employing secondary data, retrospective self-report data from mothers, and information from children regarding their mother's reactions, have found that most mothers believe their children. However, despite the fact that most mothers do believe their children, belief does not universally result in intervention on behalf of or protection of the victim.

In one sample of children victimized by incest, supportive responses by the nonoffending parent ranged from calling the authorities, bringing the child in for medical and psychiatric care, evicting the perpetrator from the home, and pressing charges (Adams-Tucker, 1982). Unsupportive responses included: knowledge of the abuse without action, taking action only when the child displays evident symptoms (i.e., anxiety or adjustment issues), permitting contact between the perpetrator and the victim, and siding with the offender and reproaching the child. Belief and support do not always coincide. Pintello and Zuravin (2001) observed that of a sample of mothers whose children had been sexually abused, 41.8 percent of mothers believed their child's disclosure and protected their child, 30.8 percent did not believe nor protect, 13.3 percent believed and did not protect, and 14 percent did not believe but did elect to protect their child. Various factors influence maternal belief of sexual abuse disclosures and support for their children. Mothers are more likely to believe their children if mothers were not home during the abuse than if they were home, and if their child was preschool or preadolescent age than if their child was an adolescent. Adolescents often face greater disbelief and unsupportive reactions than younger children due to the perception that older children are able to interrupt the abuse and inform an adult about the abuse. Mothers have also been found to be more likely to believe the disclosure if children stated that the perpetrator was not using alcohol versus using alcohol. Belief and protectiveness have also been demonstrated to be related to mothers giving birth to their firstborn in adulthood, not being in a relationship or sharing a home with the offender, not abusing substances, shorter periods of abuse, being unaware of the abuse, and whose children who were not displaying sexual behaviors. The varying reactions of nonoffending mothers to the discovery of sexual abuse may be due to the possibility that denial and acceptance as well as degrees of support rest on continuums, wherein mothers may initially deny the abuse and then believe and take action.

Emotional and psychological responses that mothers experience upon discovery of their child's sexual abuse are diverse. Mothers often follow the Kubler-Ross grief cycle (Johnson, 1992) by first responding with denial, then anger, bargaining, depression, and acceptance. Deblinger, Russell-Hathaway, Lippmann, and Steer (1993) also found that mothers' stress levels after disclosures were similar to that of patients receiving psychiatric care. Mothers who have experienced sexual abuse themselves may experience even greater psychological disturbances. Insomnia, appetite loss, and intermittent crying are common behavioral responses, and feelings of sadness, fear, frustration, inadequacy in parenting, and distrust are common emotional reactions by mothers discovering sexual abuse of their children. Such responses to disclosures mirror trauma symptoms, resulting in these nonoffending parents to be considered "secondary victims" (Strand, 2000). Mothers additionally face system-based, social, and economic stressors that influence their ability to recover in the aftermath of the discovery of sexual abuse. Researchers have suggested the concept of "reporting costs," finding that the nonoffending parent often experiences a range of relational and financial sanctions after reporting the abuse. Such reporting costs can include anger and unfriendliness following disclosures to family and friends. Some mothers confront family members and friends, urging them to permit the perpetrator to stay in the home and to not contact the police. Loss of custody may also occur due to delays in removing the perpetrator from the house or because the nonoffending parent was deemed unable to protect the child. Nonoffending parents also face tension in their relationship with the perpetrator due to being forced to choose between the child or the perpetrator, as well as financial pressure at the possibility of losing the offender's income. The nonoffending parent also may face homelessness and financial loss and an increase in use of government assistance programs such as food stamps, disability, and Social Security. Many lose their job due to the time constraints of therapy, court proceedings, and other time strains due to the disclosure. Reporting costs also vary by race and ethnicity, as a result of racialized property and institutionalized racism, and immigration status may discourage women from reporting due to the risk of deportation. When the sexual abuse is intrafamilial (i.e., abuse that is perpetrated by a family member of the victim), mothers often confront others assigning culpability to them, such as social service agents, friends, and family members. Although historically it was perceived that mothers were complicit in their children's sexual abuse, empirical research has indicated that most mothers are unaware of the abuse, and do believe their children upon disclosures of sexual abuse. Mothers and caregivers face serious trauma and potential job loss and homelessness upon discovering and intervening on sexual abuse in their family, challenging their ability to properly support their children after a disclosure. As a result, it is important to address the serious psychological and economic issues nonoffending mothers face when considering how to properly serve those who seek out public intervention and assistance on behalf of their children.

Elizabeth A. Tomsich and Angela R. Gover

See also Child Sexual Abuse; Help Seeking, from Family and Friends; Impact, Family; Victims, Disclosure

Further Reading

Adams-Tucker, C. (1982). Proximate effects of sexual abuse in childhood: A report on 28 children. *American Journal of Psychiatry, 139*, 1252–1256.

Deblinger, E., Russell-Hathaway, C., Lippmann, J., & Steer, R. (1993). Psychosocial characteristics and correlates of symptom distress in nonoffending mothers of sexually abused children. *Journal of Interpersonal Violence, 8*(2), 155–167.

De Jong, A. R. (1988). Maternal responses to the sexual abuse of their children. *Pediatrics, 81*, 14–21.

Johnson, J. T. (1992). *Mothers of incest survivors: Another side of the story.* Indianapolis, IN: Indiana University Press.

Massat, C. R., & Lundy, M. (1998). "Reporting costs" to nonoffending parents in cases of intrafamilial child sexual abuse. *Child Welfare, 77*(4), 371–388.

Pintello, D., & Zuravin, S. (2001). Intrafamilial child sexual abuse: Predictors of post-disclosure maternal belief and protective action. *Child Maltreatment, 6*, 344–352.

Sirles, E., & Franke, P. (1989). Factors influencing mothers' reactions to intrafamilial sexual abuse. *Child Abuse & Neglect, 13*, 131–139.

Strand, V. C. (2000). *Treating secondary victims: Interventions with the nonoffending mother in the incest family.* Thousand Oaks, CA: Sage.

Reactions, Support Providers

Sexual violence (SV) and child sexual abuse (CSA) are physically and psychologically traumatic experiences for survivors that give them a reason to seek help. Despite the high incidence and grave effects of CSA, empirical studies reveal that CSA survivors either (1) fail to disclose the abuse or (2) delay telling their experiences for years (Ullman, 2003). Survivors often turn to formal and informal providers for support in the aftermath of their victimization experiences. Formal support providers include police, legal prosecutors, mental health personnel, counselors, physicians, rape crisis advocacy agencies, clergy, and other nonprofit organizations. Informal support providers include but are not limited to family, friends, romantic partners, and coworkers. These providers relegate a set of mixed social reactions, both positive and negative, reflective of their mind-set, attitude, perspective, and inherent beliefs toward the issue. The focus of this entry will be on reactions of formal providers.

Reactions of service providers toward disclosures made by sexual assault (SA) and CSA survivors vary. In the case of CSA, one needs to draw from the retrospective studies of adult survivors as they rarely share their victimization experiences when they are children. The reaction of providers to CSA is linked more to factors such as the age of the individual when the disclosure happens (childhood, adolescence, or adulthood), the extent and nature of the disclosure, and the person to whom one discloses. Since secondary literature review has less focus on male survivors, representative samples are primarily based on female survivors of sexual violence. Research shows that one-third of women never disclose their CSA experiences, while the two-thirds who do disclose do so after waiting many years (Ullman, 2003). Evidently, in the aftermath of experiencing an assault, survivors are usually faced with the fear of confronting negative reactions (e.g., blame, doubt), which may cause them to choose not to disclose. They constantly struggle with the dilemma of whether to forgo seeking support to avoid negative reactions or to endure the shame from negative reactions with the hope to receive support, education, and resources. Hence, the role of service providers is perceived to be critical and vital to the survivor's healing process.

Reactions of providers can be positive or negative. Positive social reactions usually are in the form of giving emotional support and tangible aid while negative reactions are often expressed through blaming, doubting, egocentric and controlling behavior, distracting, or differential treatment. Thus it is the helpful or harmful nature of the reaction that greatly influences a survivor's decision to either disclose or pursue the case further. Interestingly, the rates of disclosure and pursuance of cases vary with the specific types of providers. In general, rates of disclosure to informal support providers are related to its higher rate of positive reactions when compared to formal support providers, who are usually associated with negative reactions. A key point to remember is that the reactions of providers do not always follow the same pattern; they are subjected to interpretation by survivors based on the unique identity of both the support provider and the survivor. For example, some survivors consider blaming or doubting reactions from partners, family members, and legal personnel as hurtful in comparison with the same reaction from friends, counselors, and medical personnel. For instance, a survivor may feel that her counselor's focus on her fault was more of a protective measure and had a healing effect as it was intended to save her from future assaults. Whereas her romantic partner's speculation on what she did wrong may be perceived as blaming her for the assault, which was hurtful. Such a reaction by her partner may be dehumanizing, aggravates her guilt, or robs her of the opportunity to regain self-worth and integrity, thereby increasing her vulnerability. This indicates that negative or positive evaluation of the same reaction is a result of the kind of relationship one has with or the identity of the support provider.

Similarly, reactions of providers also differ with regard to the identity of the survivor based on traits such as gender, ethnicity, age, economic background, education, and mental and physical abilities. For example, a survivor discloses her story to a police officer and the officer fails to exhibit an empathetic response. This leads the survivor to interpret that the officer does not believe her because of the way she looked or presented, seemingly as if she had "no credibility." Consequently, her disappointing experience weakens her trust in such formal law enforcement agencies, discourages her from further reporting, and leads her to believe that seeking formal assistance was in vain.

Thus negative reactions have a catalytic effect, aggravating physical and emotional health problems, including post-traumatic stress disorder (PTSD) and depression, in survivors. These problems often impede the healing process and lead to symptoms such as feelings of low self-esteem, suicidal tendency, relationship difficulty, substance abuse, and hyperanxiety. Scholarly research on the interpretation of provider reactions highlights the importance of positive reactions through listening and believing survivor experiences. These findings inspire and reinstate in survivors a sense of power and control over their story and life, gradually empowering them to address the violation of their rights.

Thus the reactions of support providers could be a positive, life-changing process or could have a gross detrimental influence on the recovery of a sexual assault survivor. A critical review of provider reactions emphasizes the provision of both emotional and tangible aid with a positive intent for survivors. A comprehensive approach toward crisis intervention is recommended. This could include immediate crisis support along with empowerment-based advocacy programs and community outreach for raising awareness of the issue among family, friends, neighbors, counseling service providers, and law enforcement, and training other formal support providers to empathize with survivors along with providing tangible assistance.

Sanjukta Chaudhuri and Aimee Sutherlin

See also Help Seeking, Formal and Informal; Organizational Response (Overview); Revictimization, Organizations

Further Reading

Ahrens, C. E., Cabral, G., & Abeling, S. (2009). Healing or hurtful: sexual assault survivors' interpretation of social reactions from support providers. *Psychology of Women Quarterly, 33*, 81.

Filipas, H. H., & Ullman, S. E. (2001). Social reactions to sexual assault victims from various support sources. *Violence and Victims, 16*, 673–692.

Ullman, S. E. (1996). Do social reactions to sexual assault victims vary by support provider? *Violence and Victims, 11*, 143–157.

Ullman, S. E. (2000). Psychometric characteristics of the Social Reactions Questionnaire: A measure of reactions to sexual assault victims. *Psychology of Women Quarterly, 24*, 257–271.

Ullman, S. E. (2003). Social reactions to child sexual abuse disclosures: A critical review. *Journal of Child Sexual Abuse, 12*(1), 89–121.

Ullman, S. E., & Filipas, H. H. (2001). Correlates of formal and informal support seeking in sexual assault victims. *Journal of Interpersonal Violence, 16*, 1028–1047.

"Real Rape" and Blaming Victims

Determining whether a rape is "real" is complicated by the prevalence of widely held rape myths. Commonly held misconceptions about rape are known to be pervasive throughout Western culture, as similar rape stereotypes have been observed by scholars in the United States, UK, Canada, New Zealand, and Germany. The significant influence that rape myths have on the public, the media, jurors, and the criminal legal system makes it very difficult to uncover the truth about whether a rape allegation is "true" or not. As such, rape myths promote the assumption that victims are often making false reports. Such an assumption poses real disadvantages for victims. Research examining rape stereotypes suggests that one of the most prominent myths about rape is the "real rape" myth.

"Real rape" refers to the stereotype that rape involves an unsuspecting woman, attacked by a stranger, in an outdoor location, with an assailant who employs force or threat of force with the use of a weapon. The "real rape" myth not only assumes that the "real victim" of rape will physically resist her assailant during the rape; but it also assumes that, after the rape, she will appear highly traumatized and immediately report the rape to police. Rape victims who have experienced scenarios consistent with the "real rape" myth are generally viewed sympathetically and are not perceived to be at fault or responsible for what has happened to them. However, victims whose experiences deviate from the "real rape" scenario are more likely to be blamed for their assaults and less likely to be treated sympathetically by others. In other words, the less a sexual assault resembles a "real rape," the more likely a defendant will be acquitted (i.e., found not guilty). Common deviations from the "real rape" stereotype include situations in which a victim knew or had a previous sexual relationship with her assailant, situations in which a victim was raped in her own home, or situations in which a victim was under the influence of drugs or alcohol at the time of the rape.

The "real rape" myth prevails despite overwhelming evidence that the "real rape" scenario does not accurately portray experiences of a majority of rape victims. According to recent data from the U.S. Bureau of Justice Statistics, 79 percent of female rape victims in the United States were raped by nonstrangers. The data also revealed that in 85 percent of rape cases, victims indicated that no weapons were used (Truman & Rand, 2010). Thus the stereotype of an assailant who is an armed stranger is actually quite rare and should be considered an exception rather than a rule.

Furthermore, the assumption that a "real rape" victim will fight off her assailant fails to take into account psychological and physiological factors that may prevent a victim from fighting back during a rape. Experts in the trauma field have identified several innate survival responses, which are activated by the nervous system during a traumatic event: fight, flight, freeze, and submit (Ford & Courtois, 2009; Van der Hart, Nijenhuis, & Steele, 2006). Thus the "real rape" myth neglects to consider that the innate response of the brain and nervous system during a traumatic event may often be to prepare both mind and body to freeze or submit.

The myth that a "real rape" victim will appear emotionally distraught and immediately report her experience to the police minimizes the overwhelming emotional challenges that rape victims face. Rape victims may not necessarily appear emotionally distraught immediately after a rape occurs, as it is widely known that a common reaction to psychological trauma is emotional numbing or detachment. Moreover, there are numerous psychological factors that may inhibit a woman from reporting including: shame, guilt, embarrassment, concerns about confidentiality, and fear of being discredited and blamed. Rape victims themselves have been found to endorse the "real rape" myth by questioning whether what happened to them meets the criteria of a legitimate crime. Thus the "real rape" stereotype is believed to have a significant impact on victims' decision to report rape.

Since only a small proportion of rapes actually resemble the features of the "real rape" myth, the "real rape" stereotype effectively prevents many women from being acknowledged as legitimate victims of rape. Scholars examining the impact of the "real rape" myth conclude that broad cultural and legal reform is needed to challenge the myth of "real rape," as it is a stereotype that perpetuates victim blame, undermines the seriousness of sexual assaults, and exonerates perpetrators.

Diana Ali

See also Rape Myths; "Real Rape" and "Real Victims"—Correcting Misinformation; Stranger Rape

Further Reading

Belknap, J. (2010). Rape: Too hard to report and too easy to discredit victims. *Violence Against Women, 16*, 1335–1344.

Estrich, S. (1987). *Real rape*. Cambridge, MA: Harvard University Press.

Ford, J. D., & Courtois, C. A. (2009). Defining and understanding complex trauma and complex traumatic stress disorders. In J. D. Ford & C. A. Courtois (Eds.), *Treating complex traumatic stress disorders* (pp. 13–30). New York: Guilford Press.

Temkin, J., & Krahe, B. (2008). *Sexual assault and the justice gap: A question of attitude*. Portland, OR: Hart.

Truman, J. L., & Rand, M. R. (2010). *Criminal victimization, 2009*. Washington, DC: U.S. Department of Justice, Bureau of Justice Statistics.

van der Hart, O., Nijenhaus, E. R., & Steele, K. (2006). *The haunted self: Structural dissociation and the treatment of chronic traumatization*. New York, NY: Norton.

"Real Rape" and "Real Victims"—Correcting Misinformation

There is a lot misinformation about rape in society, much of which focuses on the actions that are legally considered rape and on the behavior of victims before, during, and after a rape occurs. This misinformation—collectively known as rape myths—holds victims responsible for their rapes while excusing the behavior of the perpetrators of these crimes. What follows is a discussion of some of the erroneous beliefs about sexual victimization and why these beliefs are incorrect.

The word "rape" has a legal and a connotative meaning. Legally, criminal statutes about which actions constitute rape vary from state to state. In addition to forced sexual intercourse, some states include forced anal sex and forced oral sex in their definitions of rape. Many states have laws addressing rape that occurs when a victim is intoxicated or otherwise unable to consent to sexual activity. Other types of sexual victimization are addressed in separate laws. However, for people who have been sexually victimized, the word "rape" may have more of a connotative meaning used to describe the feelings of violation and loss of control that occur after a sexual victimization, whether or not some type of penetration occurred.

Rape myths serve to discredit victims and minimize the seriousness of rape. Some of these myths focus on the characteristics of a "real rape" victim. One of these beliefs is that only certain women can be real rape victims and only certain men can be rapists. Women who are married, sexually inexperienced, or raped by strangers are considered to be real rape victims. Other women—those who are single, sexually experienced, or raped by someone known to them—often have their claims dismissed and are believed to be deserving of any harm that came to them. There also exists a belief that males cannot be rape victims and that those who have been sexually assaulted are homosexual or effeminate. This belief downplays the existence of sexual violence against men and contributes to the difficulty male rape victims have in seeking assistance after a victimization.

A pervasive belief about rape and other forms of sexual assault is that only strangers commit these crimes. Research since the 1980s has consistently refuted this belief, instead finding that people known to the victims are largely responsible for any sexual assaults committed. The most likely offenders are friends, acquaintances, and significant others. People who are raped by known offenders often find themselves being scrutinized for what they were doing and how they were acting, and are often disbelieved.

Further contributing to victim blame is the tendency to believe that people who are raped while drinking alcohol or using drugs deserved what happened to them because they were behaving irresponsibly. In reality, many sexual victimizations occur while the victim is under the influence of alcohol or drugs, which is used by offenders to their advantage to reduce the likelihood of resistance and to discredit victims. Sometimes offenders will purposefully give their victims these substances to facilitate a sexual assault.

Society expects that a real rape victim will engage in certain behavior during an assault. Real rape victims are expected to physically resist their attacker, even if doing so results in injury. While many rape victims make an attempt to verbally and/or physically resist a rape, it is not always possible. The attacker may be physically stronger or make threats against the victim's life, which reduces the likelihood of successful resistance. Sometimes victims cannot resist an assault, as may be the case when alcohol or drugs are involved. It is also expected that real rape victims sustain serious injuries. In reality, most rape victims are often not injured, and injuries that are received are not life threatening. Often, threats of physical violence are enough to gain compliance from a victim who is trying to escape the circumstances with as little injury as possible.

After a rape, victims are expected to call the police immediately. In reality, rape victims frequently wait at least 24 hours to contact the police. There are several possible reasons for a delay in reporting. The victim must process the event and determine whether or not what happened to her is police business. The victim may have been incapacitated by drugs or alcohol at the time of the rape and may be unable to immediately contact the police. Victims may also be afraid of the reporting process, which requires them to recount in some detail what occurred. If the victim has been using drugs or drinking underage, they may be reluctant to report out of fear they will be prosecuted with a crime. More often than not, victims never tell the police because they are afraid of retaliation by the offender, they are afraid they will not be believed, or they believe the police have other things to do that are more important. Victims are also expected to be emotional about what happened to them, but many are calm and unemotional. Rape is a traumatic event, and like others who experience trauma, rape victims may not experience the full emotional impact until a later time.

Victims who do not meet the behavioral expectations as described above may find themselves scrutinized and blamed for their sexual victimization. As a result most rapes are not reported and offenders are never held accountable for their actions, thus perpetuating the cycle of victim blame and excusing perpetrator behavior.

Wendy Perkins Gilbert

See also Bias, Police and Prosecution; Laws, Victim Shield; Rape Myths; "Real Rape" and Blaming Victims; Victims, Blaming

Further Reading

Brownmiller, S. (1975). *Against our will: Men women and rape*. Chicago, IL: Simon & Schuster.

Sanday, P. R. (2007). *Fraternity gang rape: Sex, brotherhood, and privilege on campus* (2nd ed.). New York, NY: New York University Press.

Selected Websites

National Sexual Violence Resource Center. Retrieved from http://www.nsvrc.org

RAINN (Rape, Abuse & Incest National Network). Retrieved from http://www.rainn.org

Reasoned Action Approach

The reasoned action approach is a theory that guides prediction and explanation of individual behavior. This theory has been tested in over 1,000 empirical studies on topics ranging from voting behavior and job performance to condom use and interpersonal violence (Fishbein & Ajzen, 2010). The reasoned action approach originated from the work of Martin Fishbein, a social psychologist who developed the original construct for this theory based on his understanding and adaptation of Dulany's theory of propositional control, emphasizing the importance of intention in predicting behavior.

According to Fishbein, intention to perform a behavior forms immediately before the behavior itself; hence, it is important to understand what constitutes intention to better predict actual behavior. Initially, Fishbein believed that intention was composed of three factors: the person's attitude toward the behavior, a person's normative beliefs (what important others expect from the person's behavior), and how motivated the person is to perform the behavior based on attitude and normative beliefs. In 1975, together with psychologist Icek Ajzen, Fishbein added to his theory the notion of "subjective norms" or perceived social pressure, to further understand and predict whether a person would engage in a given behavior. By 1980, Fishbein and Ajzen referred to this model as the theory of reasoned action, by acknowledging the importance of background factors such as demographics and personality in influencing behavior. Ajzen went on to revise the theory of reasoned action into the theory of planned behavior by adding "perceived behavioral control" or a person's perception of his or her ability to perform a given behavior.

In 1991, Fishbein met with five other theorists to clarify the commonalities in their theories in order to support a unified theory guiding HIV prevention research. Out of this process, Fishbein developed the integrative model, which combined Bandura's idea of *self-efficacy*, (i.e., people's beliefs about their abilities to act for a desired outcome) with the idea that perceived normative pressure is comprised of an individual's thoughts about important others' attitudes as well as perceptions of important others' behavior choices. Beginning in 2001, Fishbein and Ajzen worked to reconcile their respective theories in what is now known as the reasoned action approach. The cumulative work by these two theorists, embodied in this approach, include the following constructs, which are used to predict behavior: (1) beliefs, (2) attitudes, (3) perceived norms, (4) intention, and (5) background factors.

Beliefs include behavioral, normative, and control. Behavioral beliefs are those beliefs that one has about the likely consequences of a behavior. Normative beliefs are beliefs one has about important others' thoughts about whether or not to perform a given behavior, and a person's motivation to comply with those perceived norms. Control beliefs are those beliefs about personal and environmental factors that will support or undermine efforts to perform a given behavior. Control beliefs result in a person's *perceived behavioral control* or sense of self-confidence toward performing a behavior. For example, if a guy wants to have sex with a girl who is drunk, he may first consider the possible consequences of sex with someone who cannot give consent due to intoxication. The person may then consider what his parents, peers, and mentors think about this behavior. Furthermore, he may be in an environment where concerned bystanders have noticed that that girl is impaired by alcohol and prepare to take action to help her get medical attention. As a result, the guy would probably not feel confident about having sex with her, and forgo this behavior.

Attitudes are the result of a person's evaluation of her or his own behavioral beliefs. The key to understanding the role of attitude in predicting behavior is that the attitude must be measured in relation to a very specific behavior. Perceived norms are the pressures a person feels to perform or not perform a given behavior based on social pressure. A behavioral intention is formed as a result of a person's attitude toward a given behavior, his or her perceived norms, and perceived behavioral control. If the intention results in a positive attitude toward a given behavior, the person is more likely to actually engage in the behavior. Once the intention to perform a behavior is formed, the person's decision to act is shaped by *background factors* including individual factors (i.e., personality, mood, emotion, values, stereotypes, and past behavior), social factors (i.e., education, age, gender, income, religion, race, ethnicity, and culture), and information (i.e., knowledge, media, and intervention). Finally, a person's skills and abilities to perform a given behavior, as well as environmental factors, determine actual behavior. For example, if an individual sees a guy at a party put a drug in his date's drink, the individual may intend to intervene to prevent the date from taking a sip of the contaminated drink. However, that individual may not know how to remove the drink while staying safe, possibly because that individual has not had the opportunity to learn prosocial bystander skills. Moreover, the date may drink the drug or leave the room before the individual can locate help, or the police may break up the party before the individual is able to intervene; these are environmental factors beyond the individual's control that may limit her or his opportunities for intervention.

While these theories use the terms "reasoned" and "planned," Fishbein and Ajzen are clear that they do not wish to suggest that they view individuals as rational or taking long periods to plan a given behavior. Rather, their focus is on predicting and explaining behavior based on the notion that individuals' behavioral intentions are derived in a reasonable or consistent way based on beliefs about a given behavior. Because they believed that previous research focused too broadly on the relationship between a general attitude and a behavior, the theory of reasoned action is based on the "principle of correspondence" or compatibility between the intention and a given behavior, measuring at the same level of generality or specificity. For example, a person may have a general belief in the importance of intervening in dangerous situations. However, when this same person is asked about intervening to prevent a potential sexual assault in the context of a party on a college campus, he or she may be reluctant to engage in that specific behavior.

In the field of sexual violence, the reasoned action approach and its prior versions have been used to predict women's intentions to leave abusive relationships, and to measure individuals' intention to participate in dating violence prevention programs.

Sheila McMahon

See also Bystander Intervention; Theories (Overview)

Further Reading

Ajzen, I. (1991). The theory of planned behavior. *Organizational Behavior and Human Decision Processes, 50*(2), 179–211.

Ajzen, I., & Albarracin, D. (Eds.) (2007). *Prediction and change of health behavior: applying the reasoned action approach.* Mahwah, NJ: Erlbaum.

Byrne, C. A., & Arias, I. (2004). Predicting women's intentions to leave abusive relationships: An application of the theory of planned behavior. *Journal of Applied Social Psychology, 34*(12), 2586–2601.

Fishbein, M., & Ajzen, I. (2010). *Predicting and changing behavior: The reasoned action approach.* New York, NY: Psychology Press.

Selected Website

Webpage of Icek Ajzen. Retrieved from http://www.people.umass.edu/aizen/

Recovery

Recovering from rape is different for everyone although there are some commonalities in both how individual people experience the act of rape and how they recover. As people respond to any type of trauma differently, not all rape victims experience the same reactions nor do they experience them in any specific pattern of occurrence (Blimling, 2010).

According to Burgess and Holmstrom (1979) recovery from rape can be seen as a two-phase reaction, an acute phase of disorganization and a long-term process of reorganization. Often referred to as rape trauma syndrome, the immediate reaction can be very different for each person and can range from being very controlled and able to talk about what happened to feeling unable to speak about it at all or feeling totally out of control. Along with the immediate reactions, victims often experience physical reactions described as feeling sore all over; sleeping problems may range from the inability to sleep, waking up with nightmares, to being able to sleep and not do anything else. Generally, the physical reactions can make individuals feel very unhealthy and not themselves.

Victims also describe a strong decrease in their appetite that is sometimes related to the physical reaction and sometimes is just a lack of interest in food, while others can eat almost uncontrollably. Victims may also feel anger, fear, and an overwhelming sense of sadness, as their life has changed. They may also feel dirty and wonder if everything will ever be normal again. The last area in the acute phase is the experience of a broad range of emotional reactions including an intense sense of fear, shame, betrayal, and uncertainty about the future. It is important to note that not all victims experience all of these symptoms or may have their own timeline for recovery especially if they do not receive helpful responses.

The second phase of reorganization can last for a few months to, for some, a lifetime. It includes trying to return to a sense of normalcy such as working on feeling physically and psychologically stronger, developing a postrape social comfort, and making choices about whether and when to become sexually active. This may include a range of feelings such as the fear of being alone, feeling out of control, fear of men who look like the assailant, and even a strong desire to move away or leave their current environment (e.g., school, neighborhood) because they no longer feel safe.. Survivors often are reluctant to tell their family members, even though they need that type of support, and they often do not tell anyone. There are certainly issues that can compound this recovery, and again, not everyone experiences the same symptoms or the same time frame.

Herman (1992) conceptualized the recovery in three stages: safety, remembrance and mourning, and reconnecting. In addition to adult rape, Herman connected these stages to childhood sexual abuse. Because being the victim of rape or other types of trauma takes away the victim's power and control, regaining that sense of safety and control is important. Much of stage 1 is spent regaining some sense of personal safety and developing or recognizing the skills the survivor has to help them through this process. Stage 2 focuses on trying to understand and thereby reduce the negative impact of the trauma and in some instances mourning for the losses experienced. The third and final stage, reconnecting, is an integration of personal activities and people that provide meaning to the survivor's life.

There are some things that will help the survivor recover and feel stronger and better. Calling the local rape crisis center and talking with the trained advocate can provide the victim with important information and support so the victim can decide next steps and who, if anyone, to tell about what happened. Advocates can provide information about going to the hospital or doctor, calling the police, and what will happen if the victim chooses either of those options. The advocate can even go with the victim to get medical care or to report the rape to the police. Advocates also provide confidential counseling, and most rape crisis centers offer both individual and group counseling, sometimes free of charge. Most counseling focuses on helping victims manage some of the problems they are experiencing, problems that were caused by the rape, and then return to their normal lifestyle. There are many things an advocate can provide—perhaps the most important being a safe space to talk about how feelings and someone who will support decisions.

Sometimes recovery is more difficult because of the age of the victim or the initial reactions that someone receives from family, friends, or someone else they trusted and thought would be helpful. For example, the school-age victim who is raped by someone he or she knows or a person in his or her school, may be frightened to return to school. Such close proximity can compound the recovery, especially if the victim chooses not to tell anyone or if he or she feels like everyone knows. Recovery can also be more difficult if this rape is not the first time this has happened or the victim has experienced other types of trauma or loss in his or her life. No matter what has happened, talking with a counselor or advocate can help reduce some of these fears and feelings and help the survivor get back to feeling stronger and more in control.

No matter what happened and how the victim experiences the rape and the process of recovery, it is important to remember that things can and will get better and that what happened is not the victim's fault. Working through some of the issues and feelings will help victims to understand that they did not do anything wrong and that they are not to blame for their own victimization.

Ruth Anne Koenick

See also Remembrance and Mourning; Safety Plans

Further Reading

Blimling, G. (2010). *The resident assistant* (7th ed.). Dubuque, IA: Kendall Hunt.

Burgess, A., & Holmstrom, L. (1979). *Rape crisis and recovery.* Bowie, MD: Robert J. Brady Co.

Herman, J. (1992). *Trauma and recovery.* New York, NY: Basic Books.

Homstrom, L., & Burgess, A. (1985). Rape trauma syndrome and post traumatic stress disorder. In A. Burgess (Ed.), *Rape and sexual assault: A research handbook* (pp. 46–60). New York, NY: Garland.

Warshaw, R. (1988). *I never called it rape.* New York, NY: Harper/Perennial.

Selected Websites

California Coalition against Sexual Assault. Retrieved from http://calcasa.org/

Male Survivor. Retrieved from http://www.malesurvivor.org/

National Sexual Violence Resource Center. Retrieved from http://www.nsvrc.org/

Pennsylvania Coalition against Rape. Retrieved from http://www.pcar.org/

RAINN (Rape, Abuse & Incest National Network). Retrieved from http://www.rainn.org/

Refugee Women in the United States

Each year, tens of thousands of refugees enter the United States for resettlement. A refugee, as defined by Section 101(a)42 of the Immigration and Nationality Act (INA) (based on the United Nations 1951 Convention and 1967 Protocols relating to the Status of Refugees), is a *person who is unable or unwilling to return to the home country because of a "well-founded fear of persecution" due to race, membership in a particular social group, political opinion, religion, or national origin.*

They typically come from conflict-affected nations, where women and girls are at very high risk for sexual violence from soldiers, police, and even neighbors or family. Refugees are commonly transported from these conflict areas to supposedly lower-risk internally displaced persons (IDP) camps, but this environment has also proven to be a high-risk locale for sexual violence, again often from those supporting or surrounding the camps (e.g., border guards, peace officers, as well as camp residents). Consequently, refugee women entering the United States are not uncommonly victims of sexual violence and struggle with the mental and physical health consequences of their experiences. Unfortunately, disclosure and help seeking are not normative in these refugee groups, inhibiting improvement of these health consequences. U.S. refugee health services should offer greater focus than currently provided to ensure assessment of and treatment for the consequences of sexual violence against refugee women and girls.

There are more than 13 million refugees internationally. Over the past five years, the United States has accepted approximately 40,000 to 75,000 refugees annually (Immigration Policy Center [IPC], 2010). Currently, the largest populations of refugees entering into the United States are from Asia and the Near East (e.g., Iraq and Burma). Those prioritized for refugee status are those who are being persecuted in their country of origin and have no recourse to escape the persecution, those coming from "special concern" nations (e.g., Iraq for fiscal years 2010 and 2011), or close relatives of refugees already resettled in the United States (IPC, 2010). Eligible individuals must go through a formal screening process, and if found to be qualified, will be supported to resettle in a specified location. Refugees receive medical screening and health services prior to entering the United States and again at entry, and they are additionally supported in terms of housing and employment via local volunteer agencies.

Refugee populations are disproportionately affected by violence generally and sexual violence in particular, as they typically come from nations struggling with conflict and instability (United Nations High Commissioner for Refugees [UNHCR], 2010; Hynes & Cardozo, 2000). In such contexts, raping of women and girls is too often used as a weapon by soldiers or police to control or destroy populations. Forced migration is typical and can require migration of families to IDP camps, which also brings additional vulnerability to sexual violence against women and girls. Border guards, men residing around or supporting the camp (including peace officers), as well as camp residents, sometimes traumatized by what they experienced or witnessed in countries of origin, have also been known to take advantage of vulnerable women and girls in the camp, victimizing them or revictimizing them in the very camps designed to provide them with security. In these contexts of conflict and displacement, many families will marry off daughters at a young age and sometimes without their consent, as an assumed means of protecting them from such violence (Raj, 2010).

For those victims who eventually make it to the United States for resettlement, they often contend with the physical and mental health consequences of their victimization as well as from other experiences or witnessing of violence to which they were exposed. Shame, stigma, and subsequent lack of disclosure to others, including health providers, about their history of victimization inhibits their capacity to heal. Sadly, those with male partners from these same regions are again at increased risk for sexual violence, as men exposed to such conflict are more likely to perpetrate abuse against female partners (Gupta et al., 2009). Refugee health services have expanded to consider mental health and trauma issues for this population, but only if disclosure of victimization occurs on its own, which is uncommon. These services can better support this population via consistent trauma-sensitive assessment of and intervention for sexual violence among both potential female victims as well as male perpetrators. The United States may have minimal control over sexual violence against refugees outside the United States, but can do better to support our refugees in the United States, in terms of both treatment and prevention.

Anita Raj and Anindita Dasgupta

See also Help Seeking, Barriers to; Victims, Disclosure; Violence Against Women Act (VAWA)

Further Reading

Eckstein, B. (2011). Primary care for refugees. *American Family Physician*, *83*(4), 429–436.

Gupta, J., Acevedo-Garcia, D., Hemenway, D., Decker, M. R., Raj, A., & Silverman, J. G. (2009). Premigration exposure to political violence and perpetration of intimate partner violence among immigrant men in Boston. *American Journal of Public Health*, *99*(3), 462–469.

Hirschfeld, K., Leaning, J., Crosby, S., Piwowarczyk, L., VanRooyen, J., . . . Lanigan, K. (2009). *Nowhere to turn: Failure to protect, support and assure justice for Darfuri women.* Cambridge, MA: Physicians for Human Rights in partnership with the Harvard Humanitarian Initiative.

Hynes, M., & Cardozo, B. L. (2000). Sexual violence against refugee women. *Journal of Women's Health and Gender-Based Medicine, 9*, 819–823.

Immigration Policy Center (2010, October 21). *Refugees: A fact sheet*. Retrieved from http://www.immigrationpolicy.org/just-facts/refugees-fact-sheet

Raj, A. (2010). When the mother is a child: The impact of child marriage on the health and human rights of girls. *Archives of Disease in Childhood, 95*(11), 931–935.

United Nations High Commissioner for Refugees (2001, March 27–29). *Prevention and response to sexual and gender-based violence in refugee situations: Inter-agency lessons learned conference proceedings*. Retrieved from http://www.unhcr.org/cgi-bin/texis/vtx/home/opendocPDFViewer.html?docid=3bb44cd811&query=Prevention%20and%20Response%20to%20Sexual%20and%20Gender-Based%20Violence%20in%20Refugee%20Situations:%20Inter-Agency%20Lessons%20Learned%20Conference%20Proceedings

United Nations High Commissioner for Refugees (2010, June 15). *2009 global trends: Refugees, Asylum seekers, returnees, internally displaced, and stateless persons*. Retrieved from http://www.unhcr.org/cgi-bin/texis/vtx/home/opendocPDFViewer.html?docid=4c11f0be9&query=Global%20Trends%202009

United Nations Population Fund (1999). Sexual and gender-based violence. In *Reproductive health in refugee situations* (chapter 4). Retrieved from http://www.unfpa.org/emergencies/manual/4.htm

U.S. Department of Health and Human Services, Administration of Children and Families, Office of Refugee Resettlement (2009). *Fiscal year 2009 refugee arrivals*. Retrieved from http://www.acf.hhs.gov/programs/orr/data/fy2009RA.htm

Selected Websites

Department of Homeland Security (2010, June 15). *Yearbook of immigration statistics: 2009*. Retrieved from http://www.dhs.gov/files/statistics/publications/YrBk09RA.shtm

Immigration Policy Center (2010, October 21). *Refugees: A fact sheet*. Retrieved from http://www.immigrationpolicy.org/just-facts/refugees-fact-sheet

U.S. Department of Health and Human Services, Administration of Children and Families, Office of Refugee Resettlement (2008, September 18). *Who we serve*. Retrieved from http://www.acf.hhs.gov/programs/orr/about/whoweserve.htm

Religious Groups (Overview)

Religion is a complex and multifaceted issue, including structural norms and expectations, as well as personal faith and religious identity. Any discussion of religion is further complicated by questions of culture. For example, as Das Dasgupta writes about **Islam**, the cultural context in which the religion is embedded strongly impacts the interpretation of that religious tradition's laws and practices. In addition, religions change over time, not only as a result of culture, but also due to events in time that deeply impact the self-understanding of a particular people. When one considers the historical persecution of Jewish people, as Spencer-Linzie notes, the concepts of exile, separation, and loss become salient in interpreting the views and values expressed in **Judaism**. Finally, to add to the complex interplay among religion, culture, and history, religions contain powerful and often conflicting messages about human sexuality and the crimes of sexual violence, which are often conflated in ways that can be damaging to victims of violence, can result in victim blaming, and can leave perpetrators of sexual violence free to continue to wreak havoc on others.

The entries in this overview address questions about the perspectives of a variety of religions on both questions of sexuality and sexual violence, as well as illustrate the ways in which healthy sexuality and sexual violence are sometimes conflated and otherwise confused within religious institutions, resulting in complex and often confusing messages from religions to their adherents about sexual ethics and the role of religion in protecting individuals from sexual victimization. This overview includes entries on five major religions: Hinduism, Buddhism, Judaism, Christianity, and Islam.

In her overview of **Hinduism**, Venketraman emphasizes the importance of text and context within Hinduism as keys to understanding views on gender and sexuality within this rich, ancient, and polytheistic tradition. Some sacred texts within Hinduism portray women as subservient and highly virtuous, as well as powerful, and as full beings complete with sexual identities. While there is a rich literature in Hinduism on sexuality (see the Kama Sutra), sexual matters are considered highly private and public exposure could bring shame to a Hindu family, particularly if the family ascribes to traditional cultural beliefs about gender, sexuality, and sexual violence. Hence, sexual violence is often hidden or minimized.

Similarly, as Williams discusses, **Buddhism** itself is a religion that holds egalitarian views on sexuality and condemns sexual violence, yet sexual exploitation does continue to be a pervasive social issue in many countries in which the majority of citizens identify as Buddhist. Even Buddhist monastic communities are not immune from the patriarchal norms and structures that tend to inform the hierarchies within religious institutions. Like other traditions examined here, there is an ongoing problem of clergy sexually abusing vulnerable children entrusted in their care. The work of feminist and socially engaged Buddhists has brought to light this clash between Buddhist values of nonviolence and the behaviors of some religious leaders by providing a philosophical and practical approach to Buddhist teaching and practice that takes into account structural causes of violence, rather than allowing victim blaming and denial of abuse to continue.

Judaism, the oldest of the three Abrahamic faiths (Judaism, Christianity, and Islam), draws on Jewish law, tradition, and rituals to make sense of many ethical and moral issues that Jewish communities face. However, as Spencer-Linzie points out in her entry on **Judaism**, questions about sexual violence were not highlighted within Judaism until the rise of the modern feminist movement in the twentieth century. Like the other Abrahamic traditions, the Hebrew scriptures address sexuality primarily through the lens of men's experiences, largely because of the role of sex in reproduction and men's control over who constituted legitimate members of the tribe, which in turn represented who was eligible to inherit goods or status, based on bloodlines. Similarly, Hebrew scriptures that depict sexual violence against women were often written within the framework of the impact of these violations on men's status and potential threats to their honor or family status. Feminist Jewish religious scholars have drawn on the view of sex as a mitzvah or blessing, and the commitment to restoring justice, evident throughout Jewish scripture and tradition, to advocate for a collective commitment to fighting rape and other forms of sexual violence.

Not unlike Judaism, in Islam there are laws, referred to as *Shari'a*, intended to guide Muslims and maintain respectful order in Muslim communities. Das Dasgupta touches on some implications of adherence to this law in matters related to sexuality, particularly for women, in her entry on **Islam**. She astutely points out that while Islamic law itself may view any sexual activity outside the confines of marriage as a carnal act, and women are consequently held responsible for consensual sex and sexual assault without distinction, it is the cultures in which Islam is practiced that reinforce women's culpability in any sexual act, whether or not the woman consented. In such cultures of victim blaming, women who are sexually assaulted can be further victimized because they are considered "damaged goods." In some instances, these women who have been victimized can face not only repeated victimization but punishment by death, in the form of "honor killings," for bringing shame to one's family as a result of being sexually violated. The Muslim holy book, the Qur'an, encourages sex education and knowledge for healthy marital relationships, even if sexuality is considered a taboo topic in many Muslim communities. Through the reinterpretation of Qur'an, recognition of the holy book's promises of equality for all, and working to establish safety and justice for sexual assault survivors, feminist Muslim scholars and activists are holding the Islamic tradition accountable to its own highest values, expressed in its holy book.

With nearly 80 percent of U.S. adults identifying as Christian, this is still the largest religious group in the United States. Membership in religious institutions in the United States is characterized by diversity and fluidity. The Pew Forum on Religion and Public Life (http://religions.pewforum.org/reports) estimates that upwards of 28 percent of Americans have left the religious tradition in which they were raised, in favor of either another religious tradition or no affiliation at all. Approximately one in four Americans age 18 to 29 identify as having no current religious affiliation. Nonetheless, 78 percent of adults in their sample of 35,000 individuals identified as "Christian," so while religious affiliations change, and growing numbers of Americans do not affiliate with any religious tradition, religion still plays a role in the lives of the majority of American adults. The pervasive role of religion in American public life raises questions about the potential and actual impact of religions, particularly Christianity, on sexual violence perpetration, prevention, and intervention.

The central text within Christianity, the Bible, has been used to justify slavery, homophobia, and violence against women. As Williams explains in her entry on **Biblical Legacy**, biblical passages that state women ought to be subservient to their husbands or women were created for men's sake, are often used to maintain a patriarchal social structure in which men dominate women. The legacy of this inequality is particularly insidious when one considers the consequences of unbridled dominance of another human being, as what has occurred in the ongoing sexual abuse of children by Catholic priests. As Spencer-Linzie notes in her entry on **Clergy Abuse**, the Catholic Church has received intense public scrutiny as a result of revelations of sexual abuse by clergy. With sexual abuse survivors spanning the globe, here in the United States church leaders have faced lawsuits in criminal and civil courts not only for perpetrating abuse, but also for maintaining silence and complicity in the face of abuse perpetrated by fellow clergy members. The painful realities of these sexual abuse cases raise fundamental questions about religions' role in silencing discussion about healthy sexuality, as well as recognizing that sexual assault and other forms of sexual abuse constitute a form of extreme violence in which sex is the weapon.

Yet as Spencer-Linzie states in her entry **Christianity**, beginning in the mid-twentieth century, feminist, womanist, and mujerista critique of the patriarchal Christian tradition opened up new dialogue on women's and children's status within the church and society. The role of males as leaders of family, church, and society were questioned, as were the Christian biblical and theological traditions that had supported such roles. This opening-up process not only has created space for conversation on women's roles within Christian religious traditions, but also provides an opportunity to address issues of both healthy sexuality and the use of sex as a weapon. Feminist theologians in the Christian tradition, much like their Jewish counterparts, both critique the Bible and also look for ways to reinterpret this sacred text in ways that challenge patriarchy, promote solidarity against violence, and provide healing for victims of all forms of abuse, especially sexual abuse. For example, as Spencer-Linzie discusses, Mary, the mother of Jesus, has traditionally been portrayed as valuable because of her virginal womanhood, but many mujeristas have focused instead on Mary's strength as a mother and a leader in her community. This interpretation has led to a wealth of empowered visual images of Mary and offers women an empowered perspective in which to ground theological discourse. In turn, this sense of empowerment affords the necessary support for challenging patriarchal structures, stories, and traditions within Christianity.

All of the traditions addressed in this overview contain both the limitations and controls of patriarchal structures, as well as stories of creativity and empowerment. These challenges to traditional religious structures by feminist, womanist, and mujerista theologians, activists, and church leaders offer hope that religious views and norms regarding sexuality and sexual violence may grow in sophistication and clarity. Sexuality is a part of human life course development, much like other developmental tasks. This normative development stands in stark contrast to the use of sex as a weapon, which results in sexual violence for which victims should never be blamed. Religions, given their powerful stories, laws, and traditions, make a unique contribution to moral and ethical questions pertaining to sexual violence. Feminist and other socially conscious activists press religions to stay true to their highest values, such as seeking social justice and care within communities, and to the most pressing issues of our time, including the pervasive and insidious problem of sexual violence.

Remembrance and Mourning

Important parts of the healing process are recalling traumatic memories of sexual violence and abuse, and healing the feelings associated with them. A traumatic memory is the recall of an experience in which the person is afraid of being seriously hurt or killed, or afraid that someone she or he cares about is going to be seriously hurt or killed. Memories of traumatic experiences such as sexual violence or abuse are different from most everyday memories. Most memories have details about the time and place of the experience, others who were present, some details about what happened, and feelings associated with the experience. Most memories are easily integrated with other experiences and memories. However, traumatic memories are often not integrated and are not easily remembered.

Traumatic memories are stored in various ways. Some are stored with vivid cognitive detail (flashbulb memories); other memories are disconnected from the emotions experienced; and others come to mind when they are not wanted or expected (intrusive thoughts). A victim may resist remembering (avoidance) because the memory triggers uncomfortable feelings such as anger, fear, sadness, and shame or embarrassment. Traumatic memories can be partially or totally forgotten (suppression) or buried deep in the mind (repression). Memories may come to mind when triggered by a sight, sound, smell, touch, or some other factor that is similar to the traumatic experience. These memories might be viewed as though they were happening to someone else (dissociated) or reexperienced as though the event is happening again (a flashback). Sometimes the connection between the trigger and the traumatic event is evident, but not always. For example, Beth reported having panic attacks in the canned goods aisle of the grocery store. In therapy Beth recalled a childhood incident in which she hid from her abusive step-father in a pantry; the grocery store triggered her feelings of fear and panic. Retrieving and/or processing traumatic memories often require professional help.

Memory recall can be difficult and should not be rushed into without proper preparation. Recalling traumatic memories often releases a flood of emotions that can be overwhelming to victims of any age. Therefore before attempting to retrieve memories, the survivor needs to develop skills to manage emotions, be in a safe environment, and develop a healing relationship with a trusted competent therapist who can guide and pace the recovery process. Bryant-Davis (2005) recommends choosing a therapist who addresses emotions related to the cultural environment in which the trauma occurred. Some cultural areas that may complicate recovery are disability, religion, race, migration status, sexual orientation, and socioeconomic status. Therapists should also be familiar with child development because memory recall and perception are influenced by chronological age and developmental stage of the victim.

Patience is a must when attempting to create a narrative of the traumatic event. It requires allowing time to manage difficult emotions and editing the story as new information is disclosed. Re-creating a traumatic narrative from beginning to end is often like putting together pieces of a puzzle because of the way memories are stored and retrieved. Age and stress are among the reasons that details are remembered without context or not recalled in the order in which they happened. For example, preschool-age children have not yet developed the ability to put events in sequential order, causing their memories to be disjointed. Older victims may have gaps in their recall because the most traumatic details are often the last to surface. Some clinical tools and techniques used to help victims remember the trauma are art therapy, journaling, meditation, exposure therapy, and therapeutic discourse. The therapist's role is to witness the survivor's memories by hearing her or him "speak of the unspeakable" and to become an ally in remembrance (Herman, 1997, p. 175). Creating the narrative of the traumatic experience begins the process of integrating memories and lays the groundwork for mourning losses.

There are many losses related to trauma; some of the most common losses are a sense of safety, ability to trust, a sense of power, faith, health, and relationships. Mourning begins with identifying what has been lost and recognizing the emotions related to the loss such as grief, sadness, depression, and anger/rage. Factors that influence coping with loss are personal traits such as optimism and mastery, social support, being able to make sense of the loss, and identifying some benefit from the loss. Victims may need to let go of fantasies of revenge or forgiveness before they can regain personal power.

Monna Bender Zuckerman

See also Depression and Anxiety; Exposure Therapy; PTSD and Stress; Recovery; Repressed Memories

Further Reading

Bryant-Davis, T. (2005). *Thriving in the wake of trauma: A multicultural guide.* Westport, CT: Praeger.

Herman, J. L. (1997). *Trauma and recovery.* New York, NY: Basic Books.

McNally, R. J. (2003). *Remembering trauma.* Cambridge, MA: Belknap Press of Harvard University Press.

Neimeyer, R. A. (Ed.). (2001). *Meaning reconstruction and the experience of loss.* Washington, DC: American Psychological Association.

Reporting, Blind

Blind reporting is the opportunity for a sexual abuse victim to report the crime anonymously to the police. With blind reporting, a victim may decide to report the crime for the record and possible investigation in the short term without filing an immediate formal complaint for prosecution. In the past, rape victims and their families who filed complaints were frequently retaliated against by perpetrators, harassed by the criminal justice system, and/or further traumatized by loss of privacy and self-determination. It is little wonder that approximately 84 percent of victims did not report the crime to the police. Blind reporting encourages sexual assault victims to provide information immediately, at least for the public good, whether or not a specific complaint on behalf of the victim is filed. The advantages for the victim, the criminal justice system, and society are significant.

For the victim, it means that she or he may take time to consider the option to prosecute without immediate commitment. Many jurisdictions that allow blind reporting investigate the case and gather and protect the evidence whether or not the victim decides to prosecute. Thus she or he can consider whether to risk the publicity of a trial characterized by psychological attacks by defense attorneys, judges, and the media, possible further attacks by the abuser, embarrassment and danger to her family and loved ones, and the risk of extensive emotional and financial investment in an unsuccessful outcome. Historically, the prosecution of rape cases has been said to amount to a "second rape" of the victim by the criminal justice system. If the case is investigated, the authorities and legal counsel may be able to assess the strength of the case and advise as to whether prosecution is worthwhile. The option allows the victim to undergo the forensic medical exam, including the immediate collection of samples of her own skin, hair, and body fluids as well as the assailant's.

For the criminal justice system, it is a valuable opportunity to gain background information on a sexual offender and new data as to local patterns of sexual crimes. Sex offenders tend to be recidivists. Whether or not the victim prosecutes this particular crime, the cases of past and future victims of the same perpetrator may be strengthened by the information gained.

Perhaps society benefits most of all. Information gained in the blind-reporting process allows police not only to gather data but also to notify the community of patterns discovered—locations where rapes are more likely, the method of operation of a specific perpetrator, and generally correlated circumstances like substance abuse, patterns of luring, or methods of home invasion. Successful prosecution of more rape and sexual assault cases sends the message that sexual violence will not be officially tolerated and that perpetrators will be brought to justice. Criticisms of blind reporting primarily focus on the practical difficulties of storage and maintenance of evidence and the additional resources required to implement new blind-reporting policies in local jurisdictions.

Research has revealed patterns in the criminal justice system that have harmed women and undermined the effectiveness of prosecution of sexual crimes. The women's movement has made reform of the criminal justice system a priority. Feminist advocates have developed protocols for the treatment of rape victims and revised court procedure to better reflect the realities of sexual assault. Two landmark events have framed this nationwide reform over the last decade. In 2004, in response to victim advocates within the military, the U.S. Department of Defense created a graduated reporting system for victims of sexual violence that facilitated blind reporting.

Then, a second key reform was achieved with the Violence Against Women Act of 2005. This law rewarded states for complying with the federal directive to offer forensic medical examinations to victims of sexual assault without cost, and without a formal charge to law enforcement. The law provided for immediate medical attention to prevent sexually transmissible diseases and to address the possibility of pregnancy, but also to preserve evidence for a possible future trial. States are not required to comply, but are offered federal grants for instituting the changes indicated in the Violence Against Women Act. Thus blind reporting is now allowed throughout the military and in many civilian jurisdictions in the country.

Louise A. Taylor

See also Disclosure, Seeking Help; Rape Myths; "Real Rape" and "Real Victims"— Correcting Misinformation; Underreporting; Victims, Guilt and Shame

Further Reading

Garcia, S., & Henderson, M. (1999). Blind reporting of sexual violence. *FBI Law Enforcement Bulletin*, June, 12–16.

Options for reporting sexual violence: Developments over the past decade. Retrieved December 23, 2011, from http://www.thefreelibrary.com

Reporting, Mandated and Abuse Registries

All state child protection and social service agencies maintain records that include reports and outcomes of allegations of child abuse and neglect. These records are often filed within a database commonly referred to as a central registry. There are existing laws that determine the type of information that is captured within the database, who has access to the information, and what information can be shared. These central registries include offender/perpetrator data; however, they can also include information about the identified victims.

Each state has a government agency responsible for addressing reports of child abuse and neglect. The names of the agencies vary from state to state, but the primary responsibility is the same. Child protection agencies receive reports of suspected child abuse or neglect from a variety of individuals within the community. Instances of child abuse can be physical, sexual, or emotionally harmful situations. The state agency then investigates the allegation in a variety of ways. Throughout the investigative process, including a final outcome, employees of the agency input information into a database.

Just as each state has a government agency responsible for addressing reports of child abuse and neglect, each state identifies citizens who must report any suspected incidences. In most states, any individual can submit a report through a hotline administered by that state's child protection agencies; however, there are also specific individuals who must report any suspected abuse or neglect based on their role within that child's life. Individuals who must report are called "mandated reporters." Each state/territory of our country determines, through law, who will be identified as a mandated reporter. For instance, in a majority of the states, there are designated professionals who are mandated reporters. This list includes: social workers, teachers and school personnel, health care providers, mental health professionals, child care providers, and law enforcement officers. Additionally, states may include or exclude other professions or individuals to the list of mandated reporters. For example, some states exclude clergy as mandated reporters due to their belief that confidentiality overrides mandatory reporting. In approximately 18 states, any person who suspects child abuse or neglect is a mandated reporter. Due to the discrepancy of mandated reporters from state to state, challenges and controversy regarding accountability or liability of individuals who suspect child abuse or neglect often occurs. Highly publicized events, such as the child abuse scandal at Penn State University in 2011, highlight the challenges of limiting mandated reporting to certain professions. For more information regarding mandated reporting across the county, access the individual state agency or visit the Child Welfare Information Gateway.

Many state agencies utilize two different database systems to follow an individual or family that has entered their system. The first is the registry that is kept, in accordance to law, which includes the names and other information about any person who has a substantiated, or confirmed, incidence of child abuse or neglect against them. The second is more of an internal database that is used to collect information about any report of alleged child abuse or neglect. These databases are different from those maintained by the criminal justice system to keep track of criminal histories and records of convictions.

The registry of confirmed reports of child abuse and neglect often includes information about the perpetrator and the type of abuse or neglect that was committed. It might also include nonidentifying information about the victim, including age and relation to the perpetrator. This registry is accessible in varying levels by a variety of other agencies/entities who are involved in either the accountability of the perpetrator or services for the victim.

The internal database is used by agency staff. Information about any allegation of child abuse or neglect is included within this database. The type of information contained in these databases varies from state to state; however, it includes many details about the alleged perpetrator, incident, victim, and actions taken by the agency, as well as services that have been provided to all those involved. This is a confidential database and is accessed, in varying levels, by agency staff. There are a limited number of others agencies that could access this information with a court order.

There are both benefits and limitations for abuse registries. The registry for substantiated abuse and neglect provides information to a variety of different individuals, entities, or agencies that might interact with an individual on the registry. It gives information about a perpetrator that allows for employment agencies to screen out potential employees or volunteers who would interact with children. It may also be used as a tool for risk reduction by the general public. Because the general public can gain information about how the perpetrator had access to his or her victim and the age of the victim, it may limit the amount of access others give this individual to their child(ren). This may impact further or future perpetration. Abuse and neglect is often committed with little to no evidence of such abuse occurring. Since this is only a registry of substantiated reports, it does not include every instance of abuse and neglect—only those that could be confirmed by the state agency. It is also understood that child abuse and neglect is underreported, so this registry captures only a small percentage of the actual incidents of report and neglect. To gain a further understanding of the impact and magnitude of child abuse and neglect, one should also view other studies, such as the adverse childhood experience report that is conducted as part of Behavioral Risk Factor Surveillance System through state departments of health as this includes self-reporting by adults regarding a variety of adverse childhood experiences (Centers for Disease Control and Prevention, 2010).

The internal database used by Child Protective Services can be helpful in coordinating therapeutic and intervention services. As this internal tool typically includes many more details regarding the reported incident and details about the current situation for the child and family, employees can utilize this tool to make and track recommendations made for the victim, alleged perpetrator, and nonoffending family members. Since all of this information is stored within in the database and a variety of people have access to the system within the agency, monitoring and frequent review of cases will occur. Additionally, this database includes all reported incidences of abuse and neglect, rather than only substantiated cases. So, any situation that is concerning to the agency can be monitored and services can be recommended, regardless of a substantiation. This will help ensure that consistent and appropriate intervention services are provided for victims of child abuse and neglect.

Laura Luciano

See also Child Maltreatment (Neglect and Physical); Child Protective Services; Child Sexual Abuse; Megan's Law; Sex Offender Registries; Substantiation (of Legal Charges)

Further Reading

Anda, R. F., Butchart, A., Felitti, V. J., & Brown, D. W. (2010). Building a framework for global surveillance of the public health implications of adverse childhood experiences. *American Journal of Prevention Medicine, 39*(1), 93–98.

Centers for Disease Control and Prevention (2010). Adverse childhood experiences reported by adults—five states, 2009. *Morbidity & Mortality Weekly Report, 59*, 1609–1613.

Selected Websites

Administration for Children and Families. U.S. Department of Health and Human Services. Retrieved from http://www.acf.hhs.gov/index.html

Adverse childhood experiences (ACE) study. Centers for Disease Control and Prevention. Retrieved from http://www.cdc.gov/ace/index.htm

Child Welfare Information Gateway. Retrieved from http://www.childwelfare.gov/

Reporting Rates

The decision to report a sexual assault can be extremely difficult for any survivor. There are many factors—physical, psychological, emotional, financial, and/or social—that influence a survivor's ability to disclose a sexual assault to another individual. Traditionally, reporting has been defined as alerting a law enforcement authority about the occurrence of a crime, but disclosures can be made to any trusted individual such as a family member, friend, advocate, teacher, or health care professional. Similarly, many survivors choose not to disclose, making the exact number of sexual assaults that occur impossible to determine. In order to fully understand the incidence rate of sexual assault, it is important to understand why a survivor may or may not report a sexual assault and how reporting rates are not indicative of the actual rate of perpetration.

Compelling factors influence a survivor's decision about whether or not to report incidents of sexual abuse. Studies by the U.S. Department of Justice's Bureau of Justice Statistics have consistently found increased reporting in cases involving the following factors: a perpetrator who is a stranger, a serious injury sustained, medical treatment sought, and/or no drugs or alcohol present. It is much more prevalent, however, for sexual assault to occur within a preexisting relationship, without external physical injuries, or involving drugs and/or alcohol use by the survivor—all circumstances that can create a very complicated and confusing situation. Survivors of these types of cases, particularly nonstranger cases, often experience pervasive victim blaming by others, self-guilt, and shame as a result of the sexual assault. These negative attitudes are reinforced by social systems that question rape victims' credibility and motives. The closer the relationship between offender and survivor, the less likely the police are informed and therefore many sexual assaults go unrecorded and unpunished.

Another reason reporting rates do not reflect actual perpetration is because of the conflicting definitions used by various sources. For example, the Uniform Crime Report (UCR) is often cited as the primary source of crime statistics in the United States. Since 1930 the Federal Bureau of Investigation (FBI) has been tasked with collecting, publishing, and archiving those statistics. While all local, county, state, tribal, and federal law enforcement agencies report their statistics to the FBI on a monthly basis, the UCR's classification of sex offenses is extremely problematic. The only sex offense named in the UCR is "forcible rape." The UCR defines forcible rape as "the carnal knowledge of a female forcibly and against her will." The 2004 UCR Handbook defines "carnal knowledge" as "the act of a man having sexual bodily connections with a woman; sexual intercourse" and "against her will" as "instances in which the victim is incapable of giving consent because of her temporary or permanent mental or physical incapacity (or because of her youth)."

This narrow definition is underinclusive of most types of sexual violence. First, crimes are limited to those involving vaginal/penile penetration. This excludes all other forms of penetration into other parts of the body such as inserting objects into the anal area, digital penetration, or forced oral sex. Second, the UCR confines the gender of victims to female and the gender of perpetrators to male even though the rate of male sexual abuse is found at increasingly high rates and females are certainly capable of perpetrating sexual violence. Third, and perhaps most problematic, is the requirement of force to be present in order to be considered rape. It has been well established that nonstranger perpetrators rarely employ physical force or weapons to commit a sexual assault. Rather, more subtle behaviors such as coercion or implicit threats are used to manipulate victims into compliance. As a result, UCR statistics may differ from another source's statistics that uses a more current definition of sexual assault.

Just prior to printing of this publication, Attorney General of the United States Eric Holder announced revisions to the UCR's definition of rape that are more inclusive, better reflect state criminal codes, and focus on various forms of sexual penetration understood to be rape. The new definition is "the penetration, no matter how slight, of the vagina or anus with any body part or object, or oral penetration by a sex organ of another person, without the consent of the victim." The revised definition includes any gender of victim or perpetrator, and includes instances in which the victim is incapable of giving consent because of temporary or permanent mental or physical incapacity, including due to the influence of drugs or alcohol or because of age. Implementing this new definition to be used by the FBI when collecting information from law enforcement agencies is an important step to providing a more accurate understanding of the scope and volume of sex crimes.

Survivors of sexual abuse often experience a multitude of forces that impact their ability to talk about and ultimately report their victimization. While reporting to law enforcement authorities may help hold perpetrators accountable, it often subjects the survivor to more scrutiny and blame than she or he is willing and/or able to undergo. Understanding the barriers to reporting is imperative in order to more fully understand the discrepancies that exist between rates of reporting sexual assault and actual rates of sexual assaults committed. Therefore it is often helpful to consult multiple sources rather than relying on reporting rates alone to paint a complete picture of the prevalence of sexual violence.

Kareen Bar-Akiva

See also Disclosure, Seeking Help; Help Seeking, Barriers to; Rape Myths; "Real Rape" and "Real Victims"—Correcting Misinformation; Underreporting; Victims, Guilt and Shame

Further Reading

Federal Bureau of Investigation (2004). *Uniform Crime Report handbook*. Clarksburg, WV: Uniform Crime Reporting Program.

Rennison, Callie Marie (2002). *Rape and sexual assault: Reporting to police and medical attention, 1992–2000*. Bureau of Justice Statistics Selected Findings (NCJ 194530). Washington, DC: Bureau of Justice Statistics.

Truman, Jennifer L., & Rand, Michael R. (2010). *Criminal victimization, 2009*. Bureau of Justice Statistics National Crime Victimization Survey (NCJ 231327). Washington, DC: Bureau of Justice Statistics.

U.S. Department of Justice (2012). Attorney General Eric Holder announces revisions to the Uniform Crime Report's definition of rape [Press Release]. Retrieved from http://www.fbi.gov/news/pressrel/press-releases/attorney-general-eric-holder-announces-revisions-to-the-uniform-crime-reports-definition-of-rape

Repressed Memories

Repressed memories, also known as motivated forgetting, occur when the experience of an event is not available for recall, meaning an individual cannot access the memory of a specific experience or a series of experiences. Memories are usually repressed when the experience of an event is traumatic for the individual. This can occur with any experience that an individual feels is deeply upsetting; it frequently occurs in cases of child abuse or sexual abuse. The individual experiencing the traumatic event will suppress the memory in order to protect himself or herself from integrating the memory into his or her life experience. This can occur in situations where the individual is reliant on the perpetrator of the abuse, as in a case where a parent sexually abuses his or her child. By repressing the memory of the abuse, the child may continue to accept care without the dissonance of accepting maltreatment.

Memories that were previously repressed may later be recalled; frequently their recall is related to a visual, auditory, kinesthetic, or other stimulus related to the content of the original memory. Memory recall may be spontaneous or elicited on purpose. Recalled repressed memories may be experienced as a complete memory, as a flashback, or through dreams. They may be very specific or they may be more vague. Some repressed memories may manifest only as a feeling or sense the individual experiences.

Symptoms that an individual may have repressed memories may include nightmares, unexplained phobias, or post-traumatic stress disorder-like symptoms. Individuals may experience their repressed memories like a sense of déjà vu they experience when they are in the same location as or surrounded by the same circumstances of their original memory. There are numerous types of therapies and help for individuals experiencing these symptoms or those who suspect they may have repressed memories.

While the concept of repressed memories originated with Freud, who developed theories about the nature of the unconscious, repressed memories became more common in modern culture in the 1980s and 1990s. It was at this time that court cases commonly began to use previously repressed memories in testimony. Juries respond significantly to eyewitnesses, so these testimonies were persuasive and led to a number of criminal convictions.

Because of the importance of the repressed memories of key witnesses, further research was done in the area by Dr. Loftus, resulting in her 1991 book, *The Myth of the Repressed Memory*, a collaboration with Ms. Ketcham. Prior to this research, it was assumed that all recovered repressed memories were true. However, Dr. Loftus's research introduced controversy to the reliance on recovered repressed memories by showing that these memories were not necessarily true. Dr. Loftus introduced the idea of false memories, whereby a memory seems real but is not.

The idea of a memory feeling real but not being true led to the creation of false memory syndrome (FMS). FMS is where individuals feel as though they have recovered a memory but instead their mind has created a pseudo-memory. The pseudo-memory is typically like any other memory. It usually involves people, places, and things about which the individual already has memories. However, this memory is created by the brain and is of an experience that never occurred. The pseudo-memory is not a lie the individual is telling; instead, it is more like a trick the brain is playing on the individual. Unfortunately, at this time, there is no way to tell the difference between a pseudo-memory and a real recovered memory. Corroborating evidence is currently used to determine if something remembered is real or an illusion.

The existence of FMS is part of the reason it is difficult to use therapy to access previously repressed memories. People are frequently persuaded by the power of suggestion, and thus a therapist asking about possible repressed memories might be seen as creating false memories. Law enforcement and child protection officers who might be called in to investigate allegations of physical or sexual abuse are also trained in how to question individuals in a way to avoid creating false memories. Two key elements of this questioning style are to ask open-ended questions that are not leading and to not repeat questions regarding specific events. Having individuals repeat their memory of events may, in itself, modify their memories of that experience.

Although controversy remains over repressed memories, any symptoms or suspicions of repressed memories should be addressed by an individual trained to work with repressed memories. Repressed memory therapy (RMT) was originally developed to help individuals who believed that they had repressed memories. This therapy uses hypnosis, visualization, and trance-like states in patients to encourage them to recover their repressed memories. Due to research in the area of FMS, this therapy is controversial because of the suggestible nature of the individual undergoing treatment and the ability of the therapist to inadvertently create pseudo-memories. Instead, individuals who suspect they may have repressed memories may see a psychotherapist, psychoanalyst, psychologist, or social worker, all of whom may be able to provide counseling specific to this problem.

Judith Leitch

See also Child Sexual Abuse; Child Sexual Abuse, Adult Survivors of; Coping Mechanisms; False Allegations; Sexual Assault

Further Reading

Amicus curiae brief in *Taus v. Loftus* (Supreme Court of California 2006-02-21).

Dixon, S. J. (2008). *The invisible girl: Uncovering repressed memories of childhood sexual abuse*. Blyth, England: Percy House.

Freud, S. (1953). Three essays on the theory of sexuality. In J. Strachey (Ed.), *The standard edition of the complete psychological works of Sigmund Freud* (Vol. 7, pp. 135–243). London, England: Hogarth Press. (Original work published 1905)

Loftus, E. (1993). The reality of repressed memories. *American Psychologist, 48*, 518–537.

Loftus, E., & Ketcham, K. (1994). *The myth of repressed memory*. New York, NY: St. Martin's Press.

van Till, R. (1997). *Lost daughters: Recovered memory therapy and the people it hurts*. Grand Rapids, MI: Eerdmans.

Selected Website

Questions and answers about memories of child abuse. American Psychological Association. Retrieved from http://www.apa.org/topics/trauma/memories.aspx#

Research (Overview)

Researchers from disciplines spanning the social and health sciences have developed a variety of quantitative and qualitative methods to study the extent and nature of sexual violence and abuse. Generating new knowledge and results relies on rigorous research designs characterized by valid and reliable measurement and appropriate sampling and data collection strategies to estimate incidence and prevalence, test theories, inform intervention development and prevention strategies, and evaluate their effectiveness. No single method can answer all research questions nor provide the most accurate estimates or best results. Rather, a combination of methods coupled with ethical considerations for both participants and researchers is needed from planning the research to disseminating its findings.

Different theoretical frameworks have shaped methodological and ethical considerations over time. Social science researchers from the fields of criminology, victimology, sociology, and psychology have identified factors that increase individual's risks of sexual violence and abuse. Public health, clinical, and medical researchers have examined the impact of sexual violence and abuse on individuals' health and well-being and the associated financial costs. Researchers, service providers, advocates, and policy makers have long supported the development and evaluation of primary, secondary, and tertiary prevention programs and interventions that address risk factors associated with sexual violence and abuse and evidence-informed services to address the economic, legal, psychological, and medical needs of victims.

Defining Sexual Violence and Abuse

Researching sexual violence and abuse involves many methodological decisions, including how to define and operationalize the prevalence (those who experienced at least one act during lifetime or childhood) or incidence (number of incidents in a given time period) of sexual violence or abuse.

Defining any concept is essential to obtaining valid and reliable measurement. From a legal perspective, the definitions of sexual violence and abuse are found in the penal code that defines each term, and there is variation in these codes across countries and from state to state in the United States. Medical and social service providers also have a set of definitions for sexual violence and abuse, many of which are grounded in legal statutes due to mandatory reporting of child and elder abuse. There also are numerous definitions of sexual violence across disciplinary fields (e.g., criminal justice, psychological, medicine, public health) and theoretical perspectives (e.g., legal, feminist, humanist).

Definitions vary in the acts and circumstances they include or cover. Sexual abuse is usually used in reference to a childhood or elder-adult experience, whereas sexual violence is used to refer to an adulthood experience. Childhood sexual abuse refers to the use of a child for the sexual gratification of an adult or older child either intrafamilial (e.g., blood relative) or extrafamilial (e.g., outside family members). Examples include fondling a child's genitals, making a child touch adult sexual organs, attempted or completed penetration of the child's vagina or anus, oral sex, or exposing the child to pornographic material. Sexual violence involves adult physically or psychologically coercing another adult into sexual acts against her or his will or without his or her consent. Examples include attempted or completed penetration of one's vagina or anus, oral sex, or touching of one's genitals. When these sexual acts are committed against an elder adult, the term elder sexual abuse may be used. Victims and perpetrators can be male, female, or transgender; their sexual orientation can be heterosexual, lesbian, homosexual/gay, bisexual, transgender, or queer (LGBTQ).

There is no strong consensus among scholars as to the definition and, therefore, the acts that constitute either sexual violence or abuse. Some would agree that the definition at minimum needs to be grounded in the legal statutes of a country or state. Others argue that these legal statutes are too narrow and exclude acts that constitute sexual violence or abuse. Another definition issue involves the age of the victim and offender. If both are under the age of 18 years old, some would define this as child abuse while others would not.

Data Sources on Sexual Violence and Abuse

Data can be quantitative, qualitative, or a mixture. Quantitative data are empirical—such as the number of times different types of sexual violence or abuse occurred—whereas qualitative data are useful to obtain rich descriptive information in the victims' own words about the nature of experience and the meanings and feelings victims associate with these experiences.

There are different sources of sexual violence and abuse quantitative data that are generated from government and nongovernment entities. "Official" crime statistics, such as the Federal Bureau of Investigation's Uniform Crime Report (e.g., forcible rape) or National Incident-Based Reporting System (e.g., forcible rape, sexual assault with an object, forcible sodomy, statutory rape), allow researchers to examine specific types of sexual violence recorded by law enforcement. State protection or welfare agencies also collect data on the reported number of child or elder sexual abuse cases. These official sources of data, as well as other criminal justice data, such as prosecution or court statistics, are limited. Research repeatedly has shown that many cases of sexual abuse or violence never get reported to officials so both law enforcement and welfare agency data usually underestimate the number of victims. Public health and medical data (e.g., hospital records, trauma registry) provide information on the number and nature of victims who present to health agencies or the type of injuries sustained. These data also are limited given that not all victims seek services from health agencies (see **Underreporting** entry). One example of a large-scale self-report victimization survey under the auspices of the United States Department of Justice/Bureau of Justice is the National Crime Victimization Survey (NCVS), which is administered to all members 12 and older in selected housing units for three and half years. The NCVS provides annual rape and sexual assault estimates; estimates are based on incidents reported and not reported to law enforcement. These data are limited due, in part, to recall bias.

Another source of sexual violence and abuse data comes from large-scale crossnational (e.g., International Violence Against Women Survey) or national population studies (e.g., National Violence Against Women Study, National Intimate Partner and Sexual Violence Survey) or specific populations (e.g., National College Women Sexual Victimization Study, National Elder Mistreatment Study) and smaller-scale ones (e.g., city, college campus) that collect information directly from adult respondents or minors (e.g., the Developmental Victimization Survey interviewed primary caregiver for those respondents age 2 to 9 and interviewed child for those age 10 to 17). Some surveys are administered to samples of respondents (e.g., college students, adults) who answer questions about their sexual violence and/or abuse experiences. Others surveys use samples—usually convenience samples—from a variety of settings where sexual violence or abuse victims are likely to congregate, including crisis centers, homeless or battered women's shelters, or prisons (see **Sampling** and **Research, Interviewing** entries). Although such settings provide a good source of victimized respondents, one shortcoming is that the generalizability of the findings is compromised.

Methodological Challenges to Measuring Sexual Violence and Abuse

There is a wide variation among estimates of the number of children and elder adults who have experienced sexual abuse and the number of adults who have experienced sexual violence. This is largely because measuring the extent of sexual violence and abuse is fraught with methodological challenges (see **Research, Measurement** entry). Even when two studies adopt the same definition, they might produce different estimates depending on the types of behaviors used to measure sexual violence or abuse, the time period the studies cover, or their sampling design.

Operationalization is the process of transforming an abstract concept into an empirical measure of its different attributes (e.g., type of acts experienced, number of times occurred). Typically, the broader the definition and the operationalization, the larger the number of sexually violent acts recorded. Survey questions are one means used to operationalize sexual violence. Study participants are asked, for example, whether they had experienced different acts used to define sexual violence (e.g., penile-vaginal penetration, anal penetration, unwanted fondling of breasts or penis).

Among the most controversial issues underlying researching sexual violence and abuse is whether a valid and reliable measure exists. In particular, the wording of questions used to operationalize sexual victimization has been criticized. Survey research has shown that question wording influences respondents' answers. A consensus among researchers is that behaviorally specific questions—use of terms or words that graphically describe exactly which act(s) or behavior(s) are included—are preferred because they reduce the possibility of measurement error by facilitating women's recall and disclosure and reducing nonreporting (see **Research, Measurement** and **Underreporting** entries). Colloquial terms such as "rape" or "sexual assault" are usually avoided because they most likely introduce measurement error (i.e., respondents will include or exclude different sexual acts under the ambiguous term) and lead to biased estimates of sexual violence. Using multiple items to measure sexual violence usually produces higher estimates than the use of a single item because the former captures a larger number of different types of violent or abusive experiences. For example, the multi-item Sexual Experiences Survey was recently revised to more accurately capture the diversity of sexual violence experiences. Rape and attempted rape each are now measured with three different questions, and subquestions have been introduced to distinguish between forms of sexual coercion (e.g., lies, verbal pressure) and rape (e.g., use of threats, force, or while intoxicated). The Juvenile Victimization Survey comprised seven questions about different types of sexual victimization, including completed and attempted rape, sexual touching, and flashing or sexual exposure.

Asking participants about their abusive sexual experiences is a sensitive challenge, in particular when asking about childhood sexual abuse (see **Research, Interviewing** entry). Because of the difficulties and risks inherent to conducting research with children (e.g., comprehension, secondary victimization), many researchers choose to ask retrospective questions to adult respondents, which, in turn, is limited by recall bias (e.g., forgetting; see **Data Collection** and **Sampling** entries). Research involving elder abuse might also be challenging when elder people display memory loss problems or limited mental capacities, or when residing in assisted-living housing or a nursing home.

With the goal of assessing the true extent of sexual violence and abuse, researchers have put tremendous efforts into developing, revising, and assessing instruments. Yet no single instrument has been established as a "gold standard." Rather, instruments that are most "appropriate" to answer specific research or evaluation questions must be selected, explained, and ultimately justified and defended by the investigators.

Research Design

Researchers select a research design according to the objectives of their study (see **Sampling**, **Research, Measurement**, and **Statistics** entries). Research designs can be *cross-sectional* or *longitudinal*. In a cross-sectional design, data are collected from sample units at one point in time, whereas data are collected over time in longitudinal design. Longitudinal designs include *trend studies* (i.e., data are collected at different points in time from different samples representing the same population), *panel studies* (i.e., data are collected from the same sample units at different points in time), and *cohort studies* (i.e., data are collected at different points in time from sample units comprising the cohort). For example, LONG-SCAN is a consortium of cohort studies on child abuse and neglect conducted across multiple sites in which researchers have been following children and families over time. Data are collected from multiple sources at least every two years and yearly telephone interviews allow the sites to assess yearly service utilization and life events.

Each study design has its strengths and weaknesses. Cross-section designs are not adequate to examine causal relationships, even when including retrospective questions (e.g., child and/or adolescent abuse items in a survey administered to adults) and employing statistical analyses such as structural equation modeling. Panel and cohort designs are suitable to examine causal relationships but are costly and take time to collect data over multiple waves. These studies are subject to the attrition of sample units (e.g., respondents drop out, cannot be traced) and other threats (e.g., historical event, a change in the measuring instrument) that if not addressed statistically could compromise the validity of the results.

Data Collection

Different data collection strategies have been used to research sexual violence and abuse (see **Data Collection** entry). Interviews and surveys are the most common approaches and can take multiple forms, including face-to-face, self-administered in person or via mail/e-mail, web-based, computer-assisted, or telephone. A case study is common in qualitative research as it provides readers with in-depth illustration of typical phenomena. More recently, physical examination has also been used in the form of sexual assault exams or autopsy reports to collect forensic evidence. Self-reports typically are not a feasible method of data collection with children. Alternative methods have been developed from self-reporting instruments administered to parents or caregivers about a child's behaviors (e.g., seductive behavior not appropriate for child's age, nightmares) to observations by parents, teachers, or health care and social work professionals of physical signs (e.g., difficulty walking, swollen penis, redness around genitals, underwear containing semen).

No single data collection strategy is sufficient as such to capture the various dimensions relevant to the understanding of the scope and nature of sexual violence and abuse. The choice of data collection strategy stems from which type of data is needed to answer the research question, balanced by the strengths and weaknesses of the strategy. Survey research is relatively cost effective to collect a wide range of information from a large sample of individuals, yet is subject to inherent limitations including recall bias, social desirability bias, or survey item wording effects that influence sexual violence estimates. By using multiple data collection strategy (i.e., triangulation), researchers may balance the weaknesses of a specific strategy.

Ethical Considerations in Researching Sexual Violence and Abuse

Ethical considerations in researching sexual violence and abuse are drawn from standard ethical guidelines in social science. Researchers are required to minimize risks and maximize benefits of participation, ensure anonymity and confidentiality, ensure free and informed consent to participate, and ensure that the benefits of research are fairly distributed. Each of the following principles should be built into research designs to ensure that the study is conducted in a safe and ethical manner. Safety considerations include minimizing and responding to emotional distress of both respondents and interviewers (see **Research, Interviewing** and **Research Subjects, Protecting Rights** entries)

Safety of Participants and Researchers

Guidelines produced by the World Health Organization (WHO) to minimize risk to respondents recommend interviewing only one woman per household to reduce the number of people who are aware of the nature of the study, not broadcasting the nature of the study to the wider community, and not conducting research on violence with men in the same areas where women have been interviewed. Studies are to be introduced under a general topic such as women's health and life experiences so as not to alert an abusive family member. Study material including letter or telephone messages must be framed in a neutral language so as not to jeopardize participants' safety. Interviewers must be trained to ensure that they are attuned to safety issues, place a priority on conducting interviews in private, and are skilled at adjusting the timing and location of interviews in response to respondents' concerns. The safety of interviewers comes into play when studies are conducted in face-to-face settings and interviewers must travel to unsafe locations; a common practice is to provide interviewers with escorts as they conduct their work.

Informed Consent, Assent, and Confidentiality

Free and informed consent means ensuring that respondents have sufficient knowledge about the purpose of the research early on in the research process, what their participation will involve, and possible risks or costs entailed in their partici-pation. Research involving children is strictly regulated by funding institutions (e.g., National Institutes of Health) and strict guidelines have been developed. Children are not legally capable to consent to participating in research, yet in some cases they can give their assent. Assent is the active affirmation by a minor of the desire to participate. Even very young children or those with limited cogni-tive ability can assent and they can certainly indicate a desire not to participate, which must be honored. For consent and assent to be given freely, researchers must not use their authority to coerce anyone into participating, as might be the case when the interviews take place in a shelter or other service setting. Anonym-ity has to be guaranteed and access to and control of all personal information must be rigorously protected against breaches of confidentiality. All data must be pre-sented in a format that is sufficiently aggregated so that no individual can be iden-tified (see **Research Subjects, Protecting Rights** entry).

Minimizing and Reacting to Emotional Distress

Emotional distress is a natural reaction to sexual violence experiences and it is likely that for some reliving experiences of violence through participation in a research project can be upsetting. The need to guard against emotional distress must inform the design of survey questions and the training of interviewers. Sex-ual violence and abuse being highly stigmatized, it is important that questions are framed in a nonjudgmental language and that interviewers are trained to con-duct interviews with sensitivity. Researchers have an ethical obligation to provide information to respondents about sources of support in the local community who are available to respond to emotional distress. Further, emotional trauma is not uncommon among interviewers after hearing about children's and women's experiences over the course of the research study, particularly if interviews trigger memories of their own violent or abusive experiences. Principal investigators have an ethical obligation to provide regular opportunities for interviewers to debrief with supervisors and with one another, and to stimulate discussion about stress-reducing activities. In addition to physical and emotional harm, others that might accompany participation in a research study include economic harm (if the participant separates from the abuser), social harm (damage to the reputation of the participant or his or her family), or political harm (if participation is seen as a betrayal of one's cultural community). These risks can be minimized by planning in advance and consulting with the local community.

Disseminating Findings

The accurate interpretation of research results and the maximization of the benefits are part of the ethical conduct of research. Researchers must ensure that the benefits to be realized from the research study are fairly distributed across society. This requires that groups are equally represented, or that underinclusion does not deny them access to the benefits of the research. Researchers also must strive to minimize underreporting of violence. Experiences of sexual violence and abuse are likely to be underreported unless special attempts are made to build rapport with respondents, incorporate behaviorally specific and sensitive question wording, and ensure privacy and safety. Maximizing the benefits of the research also means reporting results accurately, disseminating results widely to advocates and policy makers, providing access to the data to other researchers, and making the shortcomings of the research known.

Bonnie S. Fisher and Véronique Jaquier

Further Reading

Campbell, R. (2001). *Emotionally involved: The impact of researching rape.* New York, NY: Routledge.

Ellsberg, M., & Heise, L. (2005). *Researching violence against women: A practical guide for researchers and activists.* Geneva, Switzerland: World Health Organization.

Finkelhor, D., Ormrod, R., Turner, H., & Hamby, S. L. (2005). The victimization of children and youth: A comprehensive, national survey. *Child Maltreatment, 10*(1), 5–25.

Fisher, B. S., & Cullen, F. J. (2000). Measuring the sexual victimization of women: Evolution, current controversies, and future research. In D. Duffee (Ed.), *Criminal justice 2000: Measurement and analysis of crime and justice* (pp. 317–390). Washington, DC: U.S. Department of Justice, National Institute of Justice.

Fontes, L. A. (2004). Ethics in violence against women research: The sensitive, the dangerous, and the overlooked. *Ethics and Behavior, 14*(2), 131–174.

Jaquier, V., Johnson, H., & Fisher, B. S. (2010). Research methods, measures and ethics. In C. M. Renzetti, J. Edleson, & R. Kennedy Bergen (Eds.), *Sourcebook on violence against women* (2nd ed., pp. 23–48). Thousand Oaks, CA: Sage.

Koss, M. P., Abbey, A., Campbell, R., Cook, S., Norris, J., Testa, M., ... White, J. (2007). Revising the SES: A collaborative process to improve assessment of sexual aggression and victimization. *Psychology of Women Quarterly, 31*(4), 357–370.

Selected Websites

Child Welfare Information Gateway. U.S. Department of Health and Human Services. Retrieved from http://www.childwelfare.gov

Crimes against Children Research Center. University of New Hampshire. Retrieved from http://www.unh.edu/ccrc/about/index.html

Injury center: Violence prevention. Centers for Disease Control and Prevention. Retrieved from http://www.cdc.gov/ViolencePrevention/overview/index.html

National Sexual Violence Resource Center. Retrieved from http://www.nsvrc.org

Sexual abuse. National Committee on the Prevention of Elder Abuse. Retrieved from http://www.preventelderabuse.org/elderabuse/s_abuse.html

Research, Interviewing

Applied and academic researchers use interviews to gain in-depth information about participants' life experiences. Sexual violence researchers may use interviews, for example, to better understand what happens when survivors turn to their community for help after their assault. When conducting interviews with rape survivors, the researcher must balance two issues. First, the interviews must generate data that meet scientific standards of merit and can be used, for example, to develop rape intervention and sexual violence prevention programs. Equally importantly, the interview must respect individual rape survivors' safety, privacy, and recovery process. Interviews for rape survivors must be developed as part of a rigorous research design. Well-designed and skillfully implemented interview protocols can both facilitate the sharing of deeply personal life stories *and* record those stories as scientific knowledge. Interviewers must be carefully selected, trained, and supported in rape research work. In addition to possessing interpersonal skills for discussing sensitive topics, rape research interviewers must be culturally sensitive, have a working knowledge of research methods, and be trained in rape crisis intervention and self-care strategies.

Sexual assault research poses measurement issues that can be handled more easily in an interview than in a survey, but require careful thought and practice. Open-ended questions such as "describe what happened" or "tell me your story" can establish rapport and flow in the interview, but follow-up probing will be required to clarify any words that could have multiple meanings and assure that experiences are recorded in terms of standardized, behavioral definitions of sexual violence. Effective follow-up questions can provide a series of prompts, for example, "Would you say your first disclosure took place within 24 hours of the assault, within a week, within a month, or longer than a month after the assault?" When designing interview questions, it is important to consider that some participants will have multiple sexual victimization experiences. Rape is not always experienced as a single isolated event. For example, some survivors report that postassault reactions from others can be as traumatic as the assault itself. Because it may be difficult to compartmentalize these traumatic experiences, the interview protocol and interviewer must be able to accommodate this kind of complexity.

Participation in a research interview should not compromise survivors' safety or psychological well-being. Because research participants may not have disclosed their victimization to their friends, family members, or intimate partners (any of whom could possibly be the perpetrator), it is especially important to protect the privacy and confidentiality of research participants in all research activities including recruitment and follow-up. The entire research team must work to foster a healthy interviewing environment for rape survivors. Establishing interpersonal rapport may be the most important part of creating a safe space for talking about sexual violence, but creating a homelike setting with comfortable seating and access to bathrooms can help. Interviewers should give survivors choices and opportunities to exercise control when possible; for example, allowing the survivor to pick the location, or allowing the participant to set the pace of the questioning and take breaks.

Because reactions from others play a major role in a rape survivor's recovery, the interviewer has a great responsibility to conduct the interview in a nonjudgmental and supportive manner. A critical part of supporting rape survivors in research interviews, which is beyond the scope of this entry, is respecting participants' cultural backgrounds. Virtually all rape survivors feel some guilt or shame, even long after the assault. Interviewers must take care to use language and tone that do not suggest blame when clarifying specific details required for the study. Talking about the assault may be an emotionally cathartic experience for the survivor, for better or for worse. Interviewers must be prepared for symptoms of trauma, ranging from flat affect to "flashbacks," as well as expressions of relief, gratitude, or enthusiasm. Interviewers should provide a resource guide to every participant, connecting them to information about rape and other community resources.

Finally, it is important to safeguard research interviewers' well-being throughout the course of the research project. It can be difficult to repeatedly bear witness to stories of horrific interpersonal violence; interviewers may experience symptoms similar to those of victims, which have been termed vicarious trauma or compassion fatigue. If possible, research projects that interview many rape survivors should employ a team of trained interviewers that reflects the diversity of research participants included in the study. The research team can meet regularly to check in on and debrief various aspects of the research project and provide support to one another.

Sharon M. Wasco and Ashley Nolan

See also Data Collection; Research Subjects, Protecting Rights; Underreporting; Victims, Disclosure

Further Reading

Ahrens, C. A., Isias, L., & Viveros, M. (2011). Enhancing Latinas' participation in research on sexual assault: Cultural considerations in the design and implementation of research in the Latino community. *Violence Against Women, 17,* 177–188.

Basile, K. C., & Saltzman, L. E. (2002). *Sexual violence surveillance: Uniform defini-tions and recommended data elements.* Atlanta, GA: National Center for Injury Prevention and Control, Centers for Disease Control and Prevention.

Campbell, R. (2002). *Emotionally involved: The impact of researching rape.* New York, NY: Routledge.

Draucker, C. B., Martsolf, D. S., & Poole, C. (2009). Developing distress protocols for research on sensitive topics. *Archives of Psychiatric Nursing, 23,* 343–350.

Renzetti, C. M., & Lee, R. M. (1993). *Researching sensitive topics.* Newbury Park, CA: Sage.

Selected Websites

Interviews. Research Methods Knowledge Base. Retrieved from http://www.socialresearchmethods.net/kb/intrview.php

Research: Guidelines and Recommendations for Conducting Research. The National Online Resource Center on Violence Against Women. Retrieved from http://www.vawnet.org/research/guidelines.php

Sexual Violence Research Initiative. Retrieved from http://www.svri.org/tools.htm

Toolkit for the Impact of Digitised Scholarly Resources (TIDSR). Retrieved from http://microsites.oii.ox.ac.uk/tidsr/kb/40/interviews-short-bibliography

Research, Measurement

The measurement of sexual violence and abuse is both an important and challeng-ing task. Researchers have attempted to gain a better understanding of the extent and nature of sexual violence, but have found it difficult to accurately measure due to differences in survey methodology and how sexual violence and abuse is defined. Every decision a researcher makes, from creating a survey instrument to data analysis, will potentially affect sexual violence estimates. It is important to understand that the final estimates of sexual violence and abuse obtained by a researcher must be interpreted with great attention paid to the research methodology employed.

One of the most important decisions a research must consider is which definition they will use in their survey instrument. There are many types of definitions to choose from, including legal definitions and more graphic and detailed definitions utilized in previous research on the topic. The definition the researcher chooses to use will ultimately affect the estimates that are derived. For example, choosing a definition of sexual violence and abuse that is broad would potentially lead to higher estimates, because more acts would fall under what would be considered sexual violence. Conversely, choosing to use a strict legal definition may lead to lower estimates of sexual violence, because the criteria for meeting the legal definition are more stringent. It is extremely difficult to compare estimates of sexual violence and abuse across research studies because of the lack of a standardized definition.

How questions are worded in a survey instrument may also affect measurement. If individuals are unsure as to what is being asked of them, then they may not respond accurately. Typically, researchers test a survey instrument prior to going out in the field to collect data. This helps to ensure that the questions being asked are understood by research participants, and that the question what it was intended to ask. Previous studies have also shown that using behaviorally specific or graphic questions that specifically provide examples of what is being asked help achieve more accurate measurement.

Researchers who choose to use secondary data sets must also consider how the data set they choose will affect measurement. If one uses data from the Uniform Crime Reports (UCR), one would expect lower estimates of sexual violence and abuse because UCR data are comprised of only incidents reported to police. However, if one uses data from the National Crime Victimization Survey (NCVS), which surveys individuals who have both reported and not reported violence to law enforcement, one would expect to find higher estimates of sexual violence and abuse than those obtained from the UCR.

Another important factor that will affect measurement is data analysis. Different steps in data analysis will affect estimates, such as how the data are cleaned, which cases are included or excluded from the analysis, and which statistical procedure is used. For example, the decision to include cases with missing data will have an effect on the final estimates. Also, different statistical procedures may yield potentially different results. Each decision a researcher makes will affect measurement, and it is important for a researcher to be mindful of this during each step of data analysis.

To better understand the problem of sexual violence and abuse, one must determine the extent and nature of the problem. A researcher must be aware that measurement is affected by numerous factors—from definitions to data analysis—and that each decision made must be carefully thought through. The individual reading the research studies must also consider the research methodology of each study to fully understand how it will affect measurement. In the end, measurement is a complicated issue, one that requires close scrutiny and careful consideration on the part of both the researcher and the reader.

Megan Stewart

See also Data Collection; Research, Interviewing

Further Reading

Fisher, B. S., & Cullen, F. T. (2000). Measuring the sexual victimization of women: Evolution, current controversies and future research. In D. Duffee (Ed.). *Criminal justice 2000: Vol. 4. Measurement and Analysis of Crime*. Washington, DC: U.S. Department of Justice, National Institute of Justice.

Jaquier, V., Johnson, H., & Fisher, B. S. (2011). Research methods, measures, and ethics. In C. M. Renzetti, J. L. Eddleson, & R. K. Bergen (Eds.), *Sourcebook on violence against women* (2nd ed., pp. 23–48). Thousand Oaks, CA: Sage.

Research Subjects, Protecting Rights

Research that investigates sexual violence falls under the umbrella of sensitive research topics, so it is important to protect a subject's rights. For example, violent perpetrators may react violently if they discover their victim has talked with an interviewer. Also, recalling violent past victimizations may harm or cause distress to a subject. In order to ensure that a research participant's rights are protected by researchers, there is an Institutional Review Board (IRB) set up to review and approve all research involving human subjects prior to the research beginning. Subjects' rights include receiving complete information on the study to allow for an informed consent, respect of privacy, confidentiality, protection of physical and psychological well-being, and providing resources for ongoing support if necessary.

Informed consent is an individual's voluntary agreement to participate in research, based upon the respondent having been: (1) provided adequate information about the purpose of the research study, (2) told what his or her participation will require, (3) notified of any potential risks or harm. The subject cannot be coerced in any way to participate in the research, and must be given the option not to participate. If a study offers some type of incentive for participation, the researchers cannot take the incentive away if the participate decides not to finish.

A subject also has the right to safety, privacy, and confidentiality. Sexual violence and abuse is often perpetrated by someone known to the victim, so it is important that the subject not suffer negative consequences as a result of participating in the research. Safeguards are often put into place to try to ensure a subject's safety. Such safeguards would include: (1) interviewing only one person per household to avoid alerting others in the home as to the nature of study, (2) conducting interviews in complete privacy, (3) using dummy questionnaires if someone else enters the room, and (4) not informing the wider community that the survey includes questions on violence. Subject privacy is also important to maintain in order to ensure subject safety. However, privacy can often be difficult to achieve, especially if young children or other household members are present. Confidentiality is promised to subjects, and researchers must work hard to protect against breeches in confidentiality. All personal information that can link responses to a participant must be removed, and any individual case information should be presented anonymously so that there is no way of tracing a specific response or answer back to any one participant.

One of the major concerns of research utilizing human subjects is minimizing participant harm and psychological distress. Sensitive topics, such as sexual victimization, can often bring the subject to relive the victimization or become upset. Recalling the violence can also be humiliating, and make the respondent feel guilt or shame. It is the job of the researcher to minimize all potential risks to the participant. To ensure that a subject experiences minimal distress during the research process, it is the researcher's duty to carefully word questions she or he will ask, approach a subject with sensitivity and respect, and provide proper referrals for support and care. Recent empirical evidence suggests that although trauma or sex surveys may seem more risky to participants than cognitive measures, participants report minimal problems and distress (Yeater, Miller, Rinehart, & Nason, 2012).

While the pursuit of knowledge is important, acquiring that knowledge must be weighed against the potential negative consequences to an individual participating in that research. A research subject has rights, and a researcher has the responsibility to protect those rights. The role of the IRB is to review research before it begins, in order to ensure that subjects' rights are being protected by the researchers. It is important to note that gaining IRB approval is not an easy task, and researchers face many challenges in continually meeting IRB standards. One example of such a challenge is researchers must provide IRB with the questions they are going to ask participants prior to going out in the field; however, questions are often changed, which means having to have IRB reapprove the new questions. Also, if a participant signs a consent form to participate, and then the requirements of her or his participation change, the IRB requires that a new consent form be filled out. Overall, protecting human subjects is a complex yet vital part of conducting ethical research that must remain a top consideration during all points in a research study.

Megan Stewart

See also Data Collection; Research, Interviewing; Revictimization, Organizations; Victims, Disclosure

Further Reading

Ellsberg, M., & Heise, L. (2005). *Researching violence against women: A practical guide for researchers and activists*. Geneva, Switzerland: World Health Organization.

Fontes, L. A. (2004). Ethics in violence against women research: The sensitive, the dangerous, and the overlooked. *Ethics and Behavior, 14*, 131–174.

Jaquier, V., Johnson, H., & Fisher, B. S. (2011). Research methods, measures, and ethics. In C. M. Renzetti, J. L. Eddleson, & R. K. Bergen (Eds.), *Sourcebook on violence against women* (2nd ed., pp. 23–48). Thousand Oaks, CA: Sage.

Schneider, William H. (n.d.). *The history of institutional review boards in the U.S. Indiana University-Purdue University Indianapolis*. Retrieved from http://www.iupui.edu/~histwhs/G504.dir/irbhist.html

Yeater, E., Miller, G., Rinehart, J., & Nason, E. (2012). Trauma and sex surveys meet minimal risk standards: Implications for Institutional Review Boards. *Psychological Science, 23*(7), 780–87.

Selected Website

Ethical standards and procedures for research with human beings. World Health Organization. Retrieved from http://www.who.int/ethics/research/en/

Response, Schools and Colleges

Sexual violence is a widespread problem on college campuses, with research indicating that 3 percent of college women experience either a completed or attempted rape in an academic year (Karjane, Fisher, & Cullen, 2005). High school students are also impacted by sexual violence, as a study on school crime and student safety found reports of 800 rapes or attempted rapes among public high school students during the 2007–8 school year (Robers, Zhang, Truman, & Snyder, 2010). In recent years, schools have been called to take action against the occurrence of sexual violence on campus by implementing policies and protocols for responding to reports of sexual violence on campus, as well as prevention programming.

Pursuant to Title IX (federal civil rights law prohibiting discrimination on the basis of sex in educational programs or activities that receive federal funding), schools have an obligation to respond to sexual violence. Under Title IX, sexual violence is viewed as a form of sexual harassment and as contributing to a hostile environment. When schools are aware of acts that contribute to creating a hostile environment, such as sexual assault among students, Title IX requires institutions to act immediately in order to eliminate the violence, prevent it from happening again, and address the effects of the incident. In addition, schools are required to make available a notice of nondiscrimination and adopt and publish grievance procedures; however, it should be noted that Title IX does not require schools to have policies specifically prohibiting sexual violence. In order to comply with these requirements and ensure a proper response, schools must take measures to educate faculty and staff so they know how to report and who to report an incident to, as well as how to identify sexual violence. All schools must designate one employee responsible to coordinate compliance of Title IX.

The Clery Act, passed in 1990 (as the Crime Awareness and Campus Security Act), is currently the only standardized guidelines used to collect statistical information on the occurrence of sexual violence on college campuses. Under the Clery Act, institutions are required to publish annual reports disclosing crime statistics and security policies and they must make the campus community aware of crimes that may pose a threat to students and employees through timely notifications and a public crime log. While the Clery Act has raised awareness of safety on college campuses, criticisms do exist regarding the logistics of the act, including confusion about how to report statistics, who on campus is responsible for reporting, when to report an incident, misclassifying certain crimes (sexual assault is narrowly focused on criminal sexual assault, leaving out such incidents as dating violence, stalking, sexual harassment, or child sexual abuse), and lack of knowledge about the act itself by faculty, staff, and students. For example, recent incidents involving allegations of child sexual abuse by former coaches at Penn State have questioned whether or not the incidents should have been reported by the athletic department as violations of the Clery Act.

The Clery Act also includes the "Campus Sexual Assault Victims' Bill of Rights," which requires that all colleges and universities provide victims of sexual assault with certain rights. The Campus Sexual Assault Victims' Bill of Rights (1992) provides that both the survivor and perpetrator are given the same opportunities to have others present during disciplinary proceedings; both the survivor and perpetrator will be informed of the outcome of any disciplinary actions; survivors are given information about counseling services; survivors are notified that they can report the incident to the proper law enforcement authorities; and survivors will be given options for changing academic schedules and residency. Currently, legislators are seeking to update the Campus Sexual Assault Victims' Bill of Rights, with the Sexual Violence Elimination Act (SaVE Act), which will include broadening the response to include sexual assault, domestic violence, dating violence, and stalking.

The response a student receives to an incident of sexual violence often varies depending on the actual college and university. When a college student seeks to report an incident of sexual violence, many barriers may exist within the college or university that inhibits the reporting process. Survivors of sexual violence rarely report assaults, with research indicating only five percent of on-campus incidents of sexual assault reported to the police or campus authorities (Fisher, Daigle, Cullen, & Turner, 2003). Institutional-level barriers to reporting sexual violence include inconsistent definitions of what constitutes sexual assault and ambiguous policies and procedures about what to do after an incident occurs (i.e., who to report to, what information to report). If both a student and the information provided by the university are unclear in their own definitions of what constitutes sexual assault, it is likely that the act will go unreported, as the student may not know how to classify the incident. The response a student receives from formal sources of support on campus also plays a role in whether or not the student decides to come forward. Those campus administrators who hold victim-blaming beliefs or attitudes, or who express disbelief or blame the survivor over a report of sexual violence, risk revictimizing the student and creating an atmosphere where students do not feel safe and supported in reporting incidents of sexual violence.

Policies and procedures also may vary, depending on the institution. Some schools may have statements within a student code of conduct prohibiting sexual violence on campus, while others may have more detailed policies, including clear definitions of sexual assault, information for faculty, staff, and other students about what to do if a survivor discloses, contact information for on- and off-campus resources, guidelines for reporting an incident, and disciplinary procedures for perpetrators. Reporting procedures may differ depending on the school; common reporting options include calling a hotline, anonymous reporting, contacting a specific office or department on campus, or off-campus resources. Anonymous reporting tools allow colleges and universities to have a greater idea of the number of incidents on campus, and may encourage faculty, staff, and students to disclose incidents of sexual violence.

Collaboration between departments on campus is essential to providing a comprehensive response to survivors of sexual violence, and many institutions have a centralized department providing specific services for those impacted by sexual violence, including crisis intervention and counseling services. Schools may also have sexual assault response teams (SARTs) or other task forces with designated faculty, staff, or students who respond to incidents. Departments that focus on sexual violence also collaborate with and provide access and assistance to students seeking medical care, judicial/legal support, and academic support. In addition, such departments may also provide prevention, education, and awareness programming about sexual violence on campus.

Some states also have coalitions made up of representatives from universities and community organizations who work with campuses to improve the response to sexual violence. Statewide coalitions provide a forum for campus administrators, faculty, staff, students, and community members to share resources, and support and develop best practices to enhance policies, procedures, programming, and services related to sexual violence on campus.

Rachel Schwartz

See also Bias, Police and Prosecution; Prevention, Colleges and Universities; Reactions, Support Providers; SARTs (Sexual Assault Response Teams); Victims, Blaming

Further Reading

Crossing the line: Sexual harassment at school. (2011). American Association of University Women (AAUW) Educational Fund. Retrieved from http://www.aauw.org/learn/research

Fisher, B. S., Daigle, L. E., Cullen, F. T. & Turner, M. G. (2003). Reporting sexual victimization to the police and others: Results from a national-level study of college women. *Criminal Justice and Behavior, 30*(1), 6–38.

Karjane, H. M., Fisher, B. S., & Cullen, F. T. (2002). *Campus sexual assault: How America's institutions of higher education respond* (Final Report, NIJ Grant #1999-WA-VX-0008). Newton, MA: Education Development Center. Retrieved from http://www.ncjrs.gov/pdffiles1/nij/grants/196676.pdf

Karjane, H. M, Fisher, B. S. & Cullen, F. T. (2005). Sexual assault on campus: *What colleges and universities are doing about it.* Washington, DC: U.S. Department of Justice, Office of Justice Programs, National Institute of Justice. Retrieved from http://www.ncjrs.gov/pdffiles1/nij/205521.pdf

Lichty, L. F., Campbell, R. & Schuiteman, J. (2008). Developing a university-wide institutional response to sexual assault and relationship violence. *Journal of Prevention & Intervention in the Community, 36*(1/2), 5–22.

Payne, B. K. (2008). Challenges responding to sexual violence: Differences between college campuses and communities. *Journal of Criminal Justice, 36*, 224–230.

Robers, S., Zhang, J., & Truman, J. (2010). *Indicators of school crime and safety: 2010.* National Center for Education Statistics, U.S. Department of Education, and Bureau of Justice Statistics, Office of Justice Programs, U.S. Department of Justice. Retrieved from http://nces.ed.gov/pubs2011/2011002.pdf

Selected Websites

Campus Sexual Violence Resource List. National Sexual Violence Resource Center. Retrieved from http://www.nsvrc.org/saam/campus-resource-list (a listing of resources related to campus sexual violence, including policy information, prevention on campus, statistics, training tools, and information for administrators, student activists, and law enforcement)

SAFER (Students Active for Ending Rape). Retrieved from http://safercampus.org/ (provides information about campus sexual assault policies and programming)

Security on Campus, Inc. Retrieved from http://www.securityoncampus.org/ (information about the Clery Act and other legislation regarding reporting sexual violence on campus)

U.S. Department of Education, Office for Civil Rights. Retrieved from http://www2.ed.gov/about/offices/list/ocr/letters/colleague-201104.html

Revictimization, Individuals

The phenomenon of sexual revictimization refers to being sexually victimized in either childhood or adolescence and then experiencing a subsequent physical or sexual assault(s) in adulthood. It is generally thought that there are factors related to the earlier sexual assault experience that are strongly associated with the secondary experience. While there is no one pathway leading to revictimization experiences in adulthood, many recognize that there are multiple environmental, family, and personal factors involved that may exacerbate the childhood abuse experience; these factors, alone or in combination with one another, could create vulnerabilities to later revictimization. This entry will discuss the most salient of these factors, issues, and pathways, as well as other theoretical and clinical elements relevant to understanding how sexual victimization can repeatedly happen. It is important to note that while sexual revictimization can occur in both males and females, it is far more prevalent in females, and therefore garners much more clinical attention and research examination than does revictimization in males. Therefore this entry will solely focus on reviewing the current empirical literature on the sexual revictimization experiences of females.

While several studies have demonstrated a strong link between childhood sexual abuse and later sexual victimization (for reviews see, Classen, Palesh, & Aggarwal, 2005; Fargo, 2009), it is very difficult to tease apart what the specific factors of these earlier experiences are that may lead to later vulnerabilities. Certainly not every individual who is sexually abused in childhood will go on to experience later sexual trauma. Yet compared to those who were never sexually abused in childhood at all, having a history of abuse is a substantial risk factor. Therefore this begs the question about what it is about former victims that makes them susceptible to later victimization, particularly since the second experience may happen several years following the earlier one. For instance, does it have something to do with being victimized at a young age or at a relatively older age, in adolescence perhaps? Or perhaps it is not the age at which the childhood sexual abuse begins, but more the duration of the abuse that has critical influence on later experiences. Additionally, is the significance between the two victimization experiences connected to whom the perpetrator is and what the victim's relationship is to him?

Researchers have attempted to investigate these and other relevant questions that may shed light on risk factors linking these two sets of traumatic experiences.

Risk factors such as *age* of the initial victimization in childhood is a key starting place, yet it is not easy to isolate the age of the victim from other attributes that may coincide with age. For example, along with the younger age of the child is the likelihood that the earlier the abuse begins, the longer the duration—and perhaps the escalating severity—is of the abuse (Messman & Long, 1996). On the other hand, if the childhood sexual abuse begins in adolescence, it may also be linked with pronounced use of physical force, which may cultivate more chronic emotional injuries to an adolescent than solely the age at which it happened.

In addition, there are no known demographic differences to explain why some women reexperience sexual trauma in adulthood. In other words, women from all ethnic and socioeconomic backgrounds who have histories of childhood sexual abuse are at equal risk for later sexual victimization.

Many have advanced the notion that there are multiple pathways—and numerous mediating factors—from child and adolescent victimization to revictimization in adulthood (Classen, Palesh, & Aggarwal, 2005). When childhood abuse occurs, it is frequently present in the context of numerous associated difficulties in the child's family, home, and possibly the neighborhood community too. Some researchers have examined risk factors pertinent to the child's *home environment* during her childhood. In one study of adult, predominantly African American women who had experienced revictimization, the study author noted that the level of chaotic home environments was significantly related to their adult victimization experiences. Chaotic home environments were characterized by living with multiple different caregivers, witnessing domestic violence between their caregivers, maternal substance abuse and/or mental health difficulties, and potential instances of neglect and physical abuse or harsh discipline (Fargo, 2009).

For many young women, when adolescent conduct is examined, there are multiple patterns that may emerge. First, it has been theorized that sexually abused girls may be at risk for *early onset of consensual sex* as young adolescents, which may engender a causal chain of subsequent risky sexual encounters (Fergusson, Horwood, & Lynskey, 1997). Indeed, some research has shown that this pattern may continue into adulthood (Fargo, 2009). Second, a component of risky adolescent conduct is the presence of *substance use* and *delinquent activity*, which may precipitate involvement in risky sexual behaviors, or at least put one at risk for such involvement (Fargo, 2009). Finally, recent research, in large samples of female college students, also found a significant association between personal characteristics of child sexual abuse survivors such as *social isolation*, *self-blame*, and mental health difficulties such as the presence of *PTSD* or *dissociative symptoms* during and/or following the abuse (Filipas & Ullman, 2006). Many of these risk factors can work in concert with one another by exposing young women to potentially dangerous situations and/or leaving them ill equipped to critically perceive potential danger.

When examining pathways between these two traumatic events in childhood and adulthood, caution must be used not to "blame the victim" for the subsequent set of traumatic circumstances. Many researchers, theorists, and clinicians have advocated for a perspective that recognizes risk factors unique to survivors of childhood sexual abuse, yet does not also engage in victim blaming when the weight of these risks results in subsequent victimization. Such a perspective would be comprehensive in nature and would appreciate the interdependence of psychological, social, and community factors, as well as perpetrators' roles in identifying potential victims. As a final note, understanding the confluence of risk elements in victimized women's lives is important so that accurate and effective interventions, at both interpersonal and legal levels, are developed and enhanced. Whereas it was once commonly assumed that survivors of childhood sexual abuse and/or adulthood sexual violence were perhaps "damaged goods," we now know that many former victims can lead productive, healthy, and stable lives.

Cassandra Simmel

See also Child Sexual Abuse; Child Sexual Abuse, Adult Survivors of; Revictimization, Organizations; Risk for Future Violence

Further Reading

Classen, C. C., Palesh, O. G.. & Aggarwal, R. (2005). Sexual revictimization: A review of the empirical literature. *Trauma, Violence, & Abuse, 6*(2),103–129.

Fargo, J. D. (2009). Pathways to adult sexual revictimization. *Journal of Interpersonal Violence, 24*(11), 1771–1791.

Fergusson, D. M., Horwood, L. J., & Lynskey, M. T. (1997). Childhood sexual abuse, adolescent sexual behaviors and sexual revictimization. *Child Abuse and Neglect, 21*, 789–803.

Filipas, H. H. & Ullman, S. E. (2006). Child sexual abuse, coping responses, self-blame, posttraumatic stress disorder, and adult sexual revictimization. *Journal of Interpersonal Violence, 21*(5), 652–672.

Messman, T. L., & Long, P. J. (1996). Child sexual abuse and its relationship to revictimization in adult women: A review. *Clinical Psychology Review, 16*(5), 397–420.

Revictimization, Organizations

Sexual assault victims may seek help from multiple types of organizations, including the criminal justice, medical, and mental health systems. Unfortunately, many victims have negative experiences when they seek help from professionals within these organizations. In fact, many victims who seek help from such professionals report receiving more negative reactions than those seeking support from friends and family. Negative interactions with professionals have been termed "revictimization" or "secondary victimization," because victims often report that the hurtful experience feels like a "second rape." Contrary to some television programs that present sensitive treatment of sexual assault victims, recent research suggests that law enforcement continue to treat many victims in a hurtful manner. Research suggests that poor treatment of many victims by law enforcement and health care professionals continues (Campbell & Raja, 2005; Patterson, 2011).

Studies suggest the criminal justice system treats almost half of sexual assault victims who make a police report in ways they experience as upsetting (Filipas & Ullman, 2001). For example, many victims describe being told their stories are unbelievable or that their cases are not serious enough to investigate (Campbell et al., 1999). Many victims state the criminal justice personnel lack compassion, and blame them for their victimization (Logan, Evans, Stevenson, & Jordan, 2005). A recent study suggests the criminal justice system may treat victims poorly when they do not believe the victim's account of the assault (Patterson, 2011). Negative experiences with the criminal justice system are associated with higher psychological and physical health distress (Campbell et al., 1999). In addition, victims may feel dehumanized or blame themselves as a result of these negative interactions.

Traditionally, sexual assault victims have sought medical care for the assault from emergency departments because their services are available 24 hours a day. Unfortunately, emergency department personnel (e.g., doctors, nurses) often do not receive adequate training on how to respond appropriately to sexual assault victims. As with the criminal justice system, research has found that some victims have negative experiences in emergency departments. For example, only five percent of victims in Ullman's (1996) study rated physicians as a helpful source of support. Victims have multiple physical and emotional health needs when seeking medical care, including treating injuries, receiving medication to prevent sexually transmitted infections and pregnancy, receiving a medical forensic exam, and receiving information and help to cope with the victimization. Despite these complex needs, Campbell and Raja (2005) found that one-third of the victims who sought medical attention expressed feeling rushed throughout their medical care, and felt that medical staff were not attentive to their emotional needs.

Research has also shown that many victims who seek medical care describe their experience with medical professionals as hurtful. Victims in these studies report feeling blamed for their sexual victimization when asked about their prior sexual history, being told their stories are unbelievable, and not being offered choices about their medical care (Campbell & Raja, 2005). Experiencing negative reactions by medical professionals is associated with increased psychological distress (Filipas & Ullman, 2001). For example, Campbell and Raja (2005) found that most victims reported they felt depressed, distrustful of others, bad about themselves, and reluctant to seek additional help as a result of their negative interactions with medical professionals.

Fortunately, many communities are developing sexual assault nurse examiner (SANE) programs, whereby nurses or health care clinicians receive extensive training in responding compassionately to victims, while providing an accurate and thorough medical forensic evidence examination.

Few studies have explored victims' experiences with mental health professionals. Overall, many victims describe their experiences with mental health professionals as positive and find these services as helpful and healing (Campbell et al., 1999). However, some mental health practitioners have questioned whether their own profession works effectively with sexual assault victims. For example, Campbell and Raja (2005) conducted a statewide survey and found that 58 percent of practitioners feel mental health providers engage in counseling practices that could further traumatize victims and questioned the degree to which victims benefit from these services. Further research is needed to understand how mental health services can help or hinder victims' emotional recovery. Despite this concern, research has found that mental health services can be particularly helpful for victims who have had revictimizing experiences with legal and/or medical professionals (Campbell et al., 1999). Specifically, receiving mental health services after negative experiences with professionals was related to a significant decrease in post-traumatic stress symptoms (e.g., nightmares).

Debra Patterson

See also Bias, Police and Prosecution; Emergency Rooms and Medical Settings; Reactions, Support Providers; SANE (Sexual Assault Nurse Examiner); SARTs (Sexual Assault Response Teams)

Further Reading

Campbell, R., & Raja, S. (2005). The sexual assault and secondary victimization of female veterans: Help-seeking experiences with military and civilian social systems. *Psychology of Women Quarterly, 29,* 97–106.

Campbell, R., Sefl, T., Barnes, H. E., Ahrens, C. E., Wasco, S. M., & Zaragoza-Diesfeld, Y. (1999). Community services for rape survivors: Enhancing psychological well-being or increasing trauma? *Journal of Consulting and Clinical Psychology, 67,* 847–858.

Filipas, H. H., & Ullman, S. E. (2001). Social reactions to sexual assault victims from various support sources. *Violence and Victims, 16*(6), 673–692.

Handbook on justice for victims (1999). Office of Victims of Crime. Retrieved from http://www.uncjin.org/Standards/9857854.pdf

Logan, T., Evans, L., Stevenson, E., & Jordan, C. E. (2005). Barriers to services for rural and urban survivors of rape. *Journal of Interpersonal Violence, 20*(5), 591–616.

Martin, P. Y. (2005). *Rape work: Victims, gender, and emotions in organization and community context.* New York, Routledge

Patterson, D. (2011). The impact of detectives' manner of questioning on rape victims' disclosure. *Violence Against Women, 26*(18), 3618–3639.

Tomz, J. E., & McGillis, D. (1997). *Serving crime victims and witnesses* (2nd ed.). (1997). National Crime Justice Reference Services. Retrieved from http://www.ncjrs.gov/pdffiles/163174.pdf

Ullman, S. E. (1996). Correlates and consequences of adult sexual assault disclosure. *Journal of Interpersonal Violence, 11*(4), 554–571.

Ullman, S. E. (2010). *Talking about sexual assault: Society's response to survivors.* Washington, DC: American Psychological Association.

Selected Website

Landmark in Victims' Rights and Services. Office of Victims of Crime. Retrieved from http://ovc.ncjrs.gov/ncvrw2011/pdf/landmarks.pdf

Risk Assessments

Risk assessments are conducted in order to predict if and when a violent act is likely to occur. The ultimate goal is to use this information to help prevent a future act of violence from being committed. There are three common methods of risk assessment, each with specialized tools that have been developed to assist with the prediction and management of violence. Although risk assessments continue to raise legal and ethical concerns, valuable information can be gleaned when conducted by a trained clinician. This information can be used to develop appropriate intervention strategies, including providing support and education to victims of intimate partner violence.

Information gathered during risk assessments can be provided by the offender, victim, or other close individuals like family members, friends, or health care professionals. Offenders may deny previous acts of violence or minimize the consequences of their violent behavior. The level of risk should therefore not be determined solely on information provided by the offender. Instead, most risk assessments are based on information given by the victim. Clinicians should be aware, however, that victims may also minimize the past history of violence or current level of risk. This can occur for several reasons, including fear or safety concerns, denial, not wanting to participate in criminal or civil matters, or a lack of understanding about the factors that increase risk of violence.

There are three methods to conduct a violence risk assessment including (1) actuarial decision making, (2) unstructured clinical decision making, and (3) structured professional judgment. The actuarial method uses specialized tools to measure various factors that are correlated with an increased level of risk. This approach is considered the most effective way to predict future acts of violence (Yang, Wong, & Coid, 2010). Unstructured clinical decision making, on the other hand, does not follow a standardized procedure. This approach allows the flexibility to modify the assessment and intervention depending on the unique characteristics of each situation. Although still widely used and considered to be the most practical, this method is not recommended because decisions are not based on empirical evidence. Finally, structured professional judgment combines the advantages of both, using standardized tools to identify risks and the clinician's professional judgment to determine the level of risk at a particular time.

When conducting assessments, clinicians should consider a combination of static and dynamic factors. Static factors are fixed or unchanging characteristics about the offender, including past history of violent behaviors, prior involvement with law enforcement, and antisocial personality traits. Dynamic factors, which are more likely to change over time, include an escalation in the severity and frequency of violence, violation of court orders or restraining orders, use of alcohol or other substances, and social stressors such as employment problems. Violence is also likely to escalate when a victim attempts to or has recently left an abusive relationship (Kress, Protivnak, & Sadlak, 2008).

Many assessment tools have been designed to assess risk relating to sexual and domestic violence. Despite similarities, they differ in their method of data collection and measurement of static and dynamic risk factors. Tools that have been developed to assess risk of sexual violence include the Static 99, Sexual Violence Risk-20, and the Violence Risk Scale-Sexual Offender version (Yang, Wong, & Coid, 2010). Tools that are commonly used to assess risk of intimate partner violence include the Danger Assessment, Domestic Violence Screening Inventory, Ontario Domestic Assault Risk Assessment, and the Spousal Assault Risk Assessment Guide. Researchers have validated each of these assessment tools for their ability to predict risk, but have not identified any one tool that seems to be more accurate than the others (Kropp, 2008).

The process of monitoring involves repeating the risk assessment regularly in order to determine if the dynamic factors have changed and the level of risk has increased. The higher the level of risk that is identified, the more important it is to provide immediate intervention strategies with the victim and/or offender. Appropriate interventions with offenders can serve to improve daily functioning thereby preventing a future act of violence from being committed. When working with victims, it is important for the clinician to provide education about each risk factor that was identified in the assessment. A safety plan can also be created and revised as needed to help reduce the negative impact that these potential acts of violence may have. The goal is to support and empower the victim to take safety precautions while being careful not to infer that the victim has the ability to control the offender's behavior.

Although risk assessments are beginning to become more widely utilized, they raise several legal and ethical concerns. Currently, there are no professional standards or required credentials in order to be able to conduct a risk assessment.

A lack of training in the area of intimate partner violence and/or risk assessments can cause serious danger to the victim. Even properly trained or experienced clinicians may make errors in predictions if they are given inaccurate or incomplete information. Risk assessments are likely to remain controversial because they will not be able to predict a violent act from being committed every time.

Sophia Marandino

See also Intimate Partner Violence; Safety Plans

Further Reading

Carroll, A. (2007). Are violence risk assessment tools clinically useful? *The Royal Australian and New Zealand College of Psychiatry, 41*(4), 301–307.

Kress, V. E., Protivnak, J. J., & Sadlak, L. (2008). Counseling clients involved with

violent intimate partners: The mental health counselor's role in promoting client Safety. *Journal of Mental Health Counseling, 30* (3), 200–210.

Kropp, P. R. (2008). Intimate partner violence risk assessment and management. *Violence and Victims, 23*(2), 202–220. doi:10.1891/0886-6708.23.2.202

Yang, M., Wong, S. C. P., & Coid, J. (2010). The efficacy of violence prediction: A meta-analytic comparison of Nine risk assessment tools. *Psychological Bulletin, 136*(5), 740–767. doi:10.1037/a0020473

Risk for Future Violence

The majority of victims of childhood sexual abuse (CSA) grow up to be nonviolent adults. Only about 9 percent end up being arrested for violent crimes (Widom & Maxfield, 2001). This may be partially explained because women make up a substantially higher percentage of sexual abuse victims than men, and women are at much lower risk of committing violent crimes. However, regardless of gender CSA does increase the risk that the victims will perpetrate sexual violence, intimate partner violence, and physical violence in later years. In addition those who experience CSA are more likely to engage in bullying and cruelty to animals. Family relationships and income, education, and religion are protective factors.

Among those men who experience CSA, engaging in the cycle of violence by sexually abusing others in adolescence and adulthood is a serious risk. Sexually abused adult males are six times more likely to perpetrate sexual violence than adults who were not abused (Loh & Gidycz, 2006). Men who resolve conflict aggressively are at particularly high risk of perpetrating, compared to those who use nonviolent means of resolving conflict. Studies of adolescents have found that CSA increases the risk of perpetrating sexual coercion by 4 to 21 times (Banyard, Cross, & Modecki, 2006). Substantial percentages of sexually violent females have been victims of sexual abuse themselves; between 38 to 67 percent report being sexually abused (Elliott, Eldridge, Ashfield, & Beech, 2010). However, studies have found that CSA does not significantly increase a female's risk of perpetrating sexual violence.

Children with history of sexual abuse are more likely to perpetrate physical violence in dating relationships in adolescence and adulthood. One study found that CSA explained over 11 percent of the risk for physical dating violence (Miller et al., 2011). Male adolescents who have been sexually abused are 26 to 44 times more likely to perpetrate dating violence than those who have not been sexually abused (Duke, Pettingell, McMorris, & Borowsky, 2010). Females victims of CSA are three times more likely to engage in dating violence than those who have not been victimized (Duke, Pettingell, McMorris, & Borowsky, 2010). However, other studies have found that CSA increases risk of perpetrating intimate partner violence for males, but not for females, so more research is needed to better understand possible gender differences in intimate partner violence among survivors of childhood sexual abuse. The evidence on whether victims of CSA are more likely to bully their peers is mixed. Studies have found that both males and females who were sexually abused are about twice as likely to bully others in adolescence than their non-sexually abused peers (Duke, Pettingell, McMorris, & Borowsky, 2010). However, other studies have found no relationship between CSA and bullying for either gender when demographic, socioeconomic, and behavioral disorders are taken into consideration.

Victims of CSA are also at increased risk of harming animals. Children whose parents report a history of cruelty to animals are nearly three times more likely to have been sexually abused (Boat et al., 2011). Sexual abuse in the form of sexual touching and fondling has also been found to increase the risk of cruelty to animals.

Sexually abused females are about two times more likely to be arrested for a violent crime in both adolescence and adulthood (Siegel & Williams, 2003). Their risk of engaging in violent behaviors in adolescence such as threatening to use or actually using weapons, serious physical fights, and gang fights is substantially higher than nonabused females. Girls who were abused are about two times more likely to engage in physical fights than those who were not abused; abused boys are about four times more likely (Duke, Pettingell, McMorris, & Borowsky, 2010). The risk of carrying a weapon is increased even more. Abused girls are four times more likely to carry a weapon; abused boys over six times more likely (Duke, Pettingell, McMorris, & Borowsky, 2010).

In addition to the increased risk of harming others, children who were sexually abused are at significantly higher risk of hurting themselves in adolescence. Female adolescents with a history of CSA are at three to four times higher risk of engaging in self-harming behaviors than their nonabused peers and at four to five times higher risk of attempting suicide (Duke, Pettingell, McMorris, &

Borowsky, 2010). Abused males are five to six times more likely to have self-harming behaviors and at 11 to 15 times higher risk of attempting suicide (Duke, Pettingell, McMorris, & Borowsky, 2010).

Although clearly at increased risk of perpetrating multiple types of violence in adolescence and adulthood, being female is also a protective factor as compared to being male in decreasing the risk of violence perpetration. Other protective factors include higher family income and family stability; educational achievement; and stronger feelings of the importance of religion in one's life and more frequent praying (Vaughn et al., 2011; Yun, Ball, & Lim, 2011).

Karen M. Matta Oshima

See also Child Sexual Abuse; Intimate Partner Violence; Prevention, Dating Violence; Sexually Acting Out

Further Reading

Banyard, V. L., Cross, C., & Modecki, K. L. (2006). Interpersonal violence in adolescence: Ecological correlates of self-reported perpetration. *Journal of Interpersonal Violence, 21*(10), 1314–1332. doi:10.1177/0886260506291657

Boat, B., Pearl, E., Barnes, J., Richey, L., Crouch, D., Barzman, D., & Putnam, F. (2011). Childhood cruelty to animals: Psychiatric and demographic correlates. *Journal of Aggression, Maltreatment & Trauma, 20*(7), 812–819. doi:10.1080/10926771.2011.610773

Duke, N., Pettingell, S., McMorris, B., & Borowsky, I. (2010). Adolescent violence perpetration: Associations with multiple types of adverse childhood experiences. *Pediatrics, 125*(4), e778–786. doi:10.1542/peds.2009-0597

Elliott, I. A., Eldridge, H. J., Ashfield, S., & Beech, A. R. (2010). Exploring risk: Potential static, dynamic, protective and treatment factors in the clinical histories of female sex offenders. *Journal of Family Violence, 25*(6), 595–602. doi:10.1007/s10896-010-9322-8

Loh, C., & Gidycz, C. (2006). A prospective analysis of the relationship between childhood sexual victimization and perpetration of dating violence and sexual assault in adulthood. *Journal of Interpersonal Violence, 21*(6), 732–749.

Miller, E., Breslau, J., Chung, W.-J. J., Green, J. G., McLaughlin, K. A., & Kessler, R. C. (2011). Adverse childhood experiences and risk of physical violence in adolescent dating relationships. *Journal of Epidemiology & Community Health, 65*(11), 1006–1013. doi:10.1136/jech.2009.105429

Siegel, J. A., & Williams, L. M. (2003). The relationship between child sexual abuse and female delinquency and crime: A prospective study. *Journal of Research in Crime & Delinquency, 40*(1), 71–94. doi:10.1177/0022427802239254

Vaughn, M. G., Fu, Q., Beaver, K. M., DeLisi, M., Perron, B. E., & Howard, M. O. (2011). Effects of childhood adversity on bullying and cruelty to animals in the United States: Findings from a national sample. *Journal of Interpersonal Violence, 26*(17), 3509–3525. doi:10.1177/0886260511403763

Widom, C. S., & Maxfield, M. G. (2001). *An update on the "cycle of violence"* (Research Brief) (pp. 1–8). Washington, DC: National Institute of Justice.

Yun, I., Ball, J. D., & Lim, H. (2011). Disentangling the relationship between child mal-treatment and violent delinquency: Using a nationally representative sample. *Journal of Interpersonal Violence, 26*(1), 88–110. doi:10.1177/0886260510362886

Runaway and Throwaway Youth

There are a variety of definitions of runaway and throwaway youth. In general, a runaway youth is a minor who left the custody of his or her parent or legal guardian voluntarily and without permission. A throwaway youth is one who is told to leave home (or not allowed to return home) by a parent or legal guardian without any alternative care being arranged for them. The group of youth we typically think of as runaways is comprised of both runaway and throwaway children. These youth are more likely to be victims of child abuse than those that do not run away. They are also at high risk of homelessness, drug abuse, sexual violence, and intimate partner violence. Additionally, they are at high risk of being domes-tically trafficked into sex work. Note that the research literature generally uses the term runaway to refer to any youth who has left home, regardless of whether or not they were thrown away or ran away.

There are many more runaway youth than most people realize. Overall, between 7 and 10 percent of youth will run away at least once before turning 18 (Benoit-Bryan, 2011). Each year, between 1.4 and 2.8 million youth run away or are thrown away from home, and it is estimated that 71 percent of these youth are endangered. However, only 21 percent of runaways are reported to the police. In one study of shelter youth, over 50 percent of the teen shelter residents said that their parents either told them to leave or did not care that they were leaving (Pergamit & Ernst, 2010). Even so, the great majority of runaway youth eventually return home, although over 4,000 children a year neither return home nor are located (Hammer, Finkelhor, & Sedlak, 2002).

Sexual violence is a serious threat to the health and well-being of runaway youth. Child sexual abuse (as well as child physical abuse and neglect) is a key risk factor for running away. Once a youth has run away, he or she at significant risk for rape, sexual assault and for becoming a sex worker (often through domes-tic trafficking). These threats are largely mediated through the associated high risks of housing instability, homelessness, and substance abuse that runaway youth face. While services and hotlines are available for runaway youth, the majority of youth are not reached by such professional organizations.

There is a strong and consistent relationship between child sexual abuse and running away; this is true for both males and females. Those youth sexually abused as children are two to three times as likely to be runaways than are nonabused children (Benoit-Bryan, 2011; McIntyre & Widom, 2011). Studies of runaway youth estimate that around one-quarter were sexually abused as children (Hammer, Finkelhor, & Sedlak, 2002; Tyler & Johnson, 2006). Many sexually abused runaway youth report repeated incidents, multiple perpetrators, and victimization by family members. A history of child physical abuse and neglect is also common in runaway youth (Tyler & Johnson, 2006).

Runaway youth who were sexually abused are at even higher risk of the negative impact of running away than other (nonabused) runaways. They have significantly more arrests (Chapple, Johnson, & Whitbeck, 2004). They are also more likely to engage in sex work and to engage in risky sexual behaviors as well as to use drugs (Chen, Tyler, &Whitbeck, 2004) and to have mental health problems than other runaways (Whitbeck, Hoyt, Johnson, & Chen, 2007).

Runaway youth are at significantly higher risk for sexual assault and rape than other youth (Tyler & Johnson, 2006). Studies of female runaways report rates of forced sexual activity and rape of between 25 and 43 percent (Thrane, Yoder, & Chen, 2011). This risk remains even after the runaways return home; one study used a nationally representative data set to compare runaway girls with other girls and found that 8 percent were assaulted in the year that they came back home (Thrane, Yoder, & Chen, 2011). Runaways are also at high risk of being domestically trafficked and engaging in sex work and early entry into prostitution). The risks of sexual violence from trafficking and prostitution are significant.

There are services for runaway and homeless youth, although availability varies greatly by region of the country. It appears that the majority of runaway youth do not take advantage of the services available and over half may not even know where to go for help (Levin, Bax, McKean, & Schoggen, 2005). Although at least 1.4 million youth run away each year, the national runaway switchboard only gets about 100,000 calls a year for help (http://www.1800runaway.org/).

A review of services for runaway youth found that comprehensive interventions which target a variety of service needs of the youth and their families are promising (Slesnick et al., 2009). One study reported that positive outcomes from the use of emergency shelter and crisis services was seen at six weeks post shelter, but that some of these effects did not last long term (Pollio, Thompson, & Tobias, 2006). The Runaway Intervention Program reported sustained success over a one-year period with sexually exploited young runaway girls. This intervention involved home visiting, case management, and group support and was staffed by advanced practice nurses (Saewyc & Edinburgh, 2010). Overall, however, challenges remain in the prevention of running away, the intervention with runaway youth and the connection of runaway youth to programs.

Stacey Plichta

See also Alcohol and Drug Abuse, Victimization; Child Maltreatment (Neglect and Physical); Child Sexual Abuse; Crisis Counseling; Prostitution; Sex Workers; Trafficking in Persons

Further Reading

Benoit-Bryan, J. (2011). *National Runaway Switchboard 2011 reporter's source book on runaway and homeless youth*. Chicago, IL: National Runaway Switchboard.

Chen, X., Tyler, K., Whitbeck, L. B., & Hoyt, D. R. (2004). Early sexual abuse, street adversity, and drug use among female homeless and runaway adolescent in the Midwest. *Journal of Drug Issues, 22,* 1–22.

Greene, J. M, Sanchez, R., Harris, J., Cignetti, C., Arkin, D., & Wheeless, S. (2003). *Incidence and prevalence of homeless and runaway youth*. Final report to the U.S. Department of Health and Human Services. Research Triangle Park, NC: RTI International.

Hammer, H., Finkelhor, D., & Sedlak, A. J. (2002). Runaway/thrownaway children: National estimates and characteristics. NISMART Bulletin, Office of Juvenile Justice and Delinquency Prevention. Washington, DC: U.S. Department of Justice.

Levin, R., Bax, E., McKean, L., & Schoggen, L. (2005) *Wherever I can lay my head: Homeless youth on homelessness*. Center for Impact Research. Retrieved from http://www.thenightministry.org/070_facts_figures/030_research_links/060_homeless_youth/Wherever%20I%20Can%20Lay%20My%20Head%20March%202005.pdf

McIntyre, J. K., &Widom, C. S. (2011). Childhood victimization and crime victimization. *Journal of Interpersonal Violence, 26,* 640–663.

Pergamit, M. R., & Ernst, M. (2010). *Runaway Youth's Knowledge and Access of Services*. Retrieved from http://www.nrscrisisline.org/media/documents/NORC_Final_Report_4_22_10.pdf

Pollio, D. E., Thompson, S. J., & Tobias, L. (2006). Longitudinal outcomes for youth receiving runaway/homeless shelter services. *Journal of Youth and Adolescence, 35*(5), 859–866.

Saewyc, E. M., & Edinburgh, L. D. (2010). Restoring healthy developmental trajectories for sexually exploited young runaway girls: Fostering protective factors and reducing risk behaviors. *Journal of Adolescent Health, 46*(2): 180–188.

Slesnick, N., Dashora, P., Letcher, A., Erdem, G. & Serovich, J. M. (2009). A review of interventions for runaway and homeless youth: Moving forward. *Children and Youth Services Review, 31,* 732–742.

Thrane L.E., Yoder Y.A., & Chen, X. (2011). The influence of running away on the risk of female sexual assault in the subsequent year. *Violence and Victims, 26*(6), 816–829.

Tyler, K. A., & Johnson, K. A. (2006). A longitudinal study of the effects of early abuse on later victimization among high-risk adolescents. *Violence and Victims, 21,* 287–306.

Whitbeck, L. B., Hoyt, D. R., Johnson, K. D., & Chen, X. (2007). Victimization and posttraumatic stress disorder among runaway and homeless adolescents. *Violence and Victims, 22*(6), 721–734.

Immediate Help

If you are in a crisis and need help right away or know someone who needs immediate help, call the National Runaway Switchboard at 1-800-RUNAWAY. This hotline is open 24/7, and you will be able to talk to a live person.

Selected Websites

National Incidence Studies of Missing, Abducted Runaway, and Throwaway Children. National Estimates and Characteristics. Retrieved from https://www.ncjrs.gov/html/ojjdp/nismart/04/

National Runaway Switchboard. Retrieved from http://www.1800runaway.org/

Runaway & Homeless Youth and Relationship Violence Toolkit. Retrieved from http://www.nrcdv.org/rhydvtoolkit/index.html

Rural Communities

Sexual assault that occurs in rural areas of the United States is often a hidden crime with dynamics unique to rural communities. Many different aspects of geography, culture, and economics shape how sexual violence is experienced and addressed in these communities. More research is needed to examine the prevalence of sexual assault in rural areas and effective strategies for responding to it.

Defining "rural" can be challenging, and much diversity exists between rural communities in the United States. Rural is generally understood to mean low population density, or a limited number of people, in a particular area. A designation of rural may also take into account a community's distance to the nearest city or an economy that is based on agriculture instead of industry. These kinds of differences affect how victims of sexual assault are treated and the services available to them.

Currently, the rate of sexual assault that is happening in rural communities is not well understood. Past research indicated that compared to urban communities, sexual violence occurred less often in rural places (Lewis, 2003). Recent research examining rates of sexual assault in rural versus urban communities in the states of Pennsylvania, Alaska, Oklahoma, and Mississippi has found that some of the highest rates occurred in the most rural communities (Lewis, 2003). While research from four states cannot be used to draw conclusions about the entire country, these results raise important questions about the frequency of sexual assault and the needs of those living in rural places with respect to sexual violence.

The geography of rural areas of the United States affects sexual assault victims in many ways. Rural communities are isolated, meaning that going to a rape crisis center or hospital for care often requires travel over long distances and sometimes on very rough roads. In some states such as Alaska, access to and from many rural areas requires travel by airplane and may take several days. Many victims lack access to their own transportation, which makes getting to services difficult. Reaching help by phone is often challenging as cell phone coverage is lacking in many rural areas. For victims who choose to report sexual assault, response times for law enforcement are often long due to the distance law enforcement must travel and the limited number of officers in many rural areas.

The economic conditions of many rural communities also factor into the response to sexual assault victims in these communities. Poverty is higher in most rural areas as compared to cities. Less funding is available for services to address sexual violence, including direct services for victims and outreach and education to make community members aware of services that are available. Higher poverty in rural areas also affects victims' options for reporting sexual violence, particularly when it is perpetrated by someone within the family. Many rural families need income provided by all family members, including those who are committing sexual violence, for basic needs such as food and housing. Reporting sexual assault in these circumstances may not be an option.

Social conditions and cultures in rural areas of the United States are unique, and much diversity exists between cultures in rural communities. For example, the remote areas of Appalachia in Virginia have their own dialect and values that are very distinct from Native American tribal communities in the rural Southwest or small towns in the Midwest. Along with this diversity, some common aspects of rural social and cultural environments that affect sexual assault victims have been found (Logan, Evans, Stevenson, & Jordan, 2005). Given the smaller numbers of people residing in rural areas and their isolation from cities, people tend to know each other. This high degree of familiarity between community members can make addressing sexual violence difficult in several ways. Often, victims are more reluctant to report a sexual assault when it was committed by someone they know. They may fear blame, and a lack of confidentiality since everyone in their community seems to know everyone else. The offender who committed the assault may be related to law enforcement, medical providers, or the advocate providing sexual assault services. This can increase victims' fears that they will not receive fair treatment and have their story kept private. Victims may see the offender regularly in their small community and fear retaliation if they seek services or report the assault.

The culture of many rural communities includes social expectations and controls that further shape the response to sexual assault. Distrust of outsiders and a reluctance to ask for help are two aspects of rural culture that affect victims' help-seeking behavior and the pressure on many victims to stay quiet about their assault. Emphasis on maintaining the family reputation and social position may also be used to silence victims. In some rural communities, traditional gender roles make male control over women and entitlement to sex normal. These attitudes can affect how sexual assault is defined, and it may not be seen as a "real crime," particularly when it is committed by a family member or someone else known to the victim. Child sexual abuse is often met with denial and the belief that such abuse of children does not happen in small, close-knit communities.

Rural communities also possess strengths that can be tapped to challenge sexual violence and develop services that meet victims' and community needs. Self-reliance and creative problem solving are often a part of life in communities that are far from the types of resources found in metro areas, as is a strong ethic of connection and care among community members. With education and training on sexual violence, how to create services that promote healing for victims, and prevention, these types of strengths can be used to create a positive community response to sexual assault.

Our understanding of sexual assault in rural communities in the United States is in the early stages. Once thought to be a phenomenon that occurred with less frequency than in urban areas, more research is needed to examine prevalence rates of sexual assault and other aspects of sexual violence that are unique to rural places.

Karen Herman

See also Help Seeking, Barriers to; Rape Myths

Further Reading

Lewis, S. (2003). *Unspoken crimes: Sexual assault in rural America*. Enola, PA: National Sexual Violence Resource Center.

Logan, T., Evans, L., Stevenson, E., & Jordan, C. (2005). Barriers to service for rural and urban survivors of rape. *Journal of Interpersonal Violence, 20*(5), 591–616.

Selected Websites

National Online Resource Center on Violence Against Women. Retrieved from http://www.vawnet.org

National Sexual Assault Coalition Resource Sharing Project. Retrieved from http://www.resourcesharingproject.org

S

Safety Plans

Many people use safety planning without conscious thought. Parking a car in a well-lit area, making sure to have a cell phone handy, and being aware of one's surroundings are all parts of a safety plan. In cases such as these, people are trying to protect themselves from a stranger who might bring them harm. In many cases, safety planning is a process used with someone who is in an abusive or violent relationship. The plan seeks to increase the person's safety and/or lower her or his risk for future abuse or violence. Ideally, safety plans are developed prior to an abusive or violence incident occurring.

Safety planning in the area of sexual violence is often confused with prevention. Safety planning is actually risk reduction. Most experts view prevention as a societal issue. For example, we seek to *prevent* sexual violence by enacting laws that hold assailants accountable.

Safety planning in the realm of sexual violence seeks to reduce a person's risk from assault. In the past women were told "don't walk alone" or "carry pepper spray or mace." These may be valid strategies against stranger violence, but since the majority of victims of sexual assault know their perpetrator, a variety of strategies must be used.

The Rape, Abuse & Incest National Network (RAINN) suggests the following to help reduce the risk of sexual assault:

- Be aware of your surroundings. Knowing where you are and who is around you may help you to find a way to get out of a bad situation.
- Try to avoid isolated areas. It is more difficult to get help if no one is around.
- Walk with purpose. Even if you do not know where you are going, act like you do.
- Trust your instincts. If a situation or location feels unsafe or uncomfortable, it probably is not the best place to be.
- Try not to load yourself down with packages or bags as this can make you appear more vulnerable.
- Make sure your cell phone is with you and charged and that you have cab money.

- Do not allow yourself to be isolated with someone you do not trust or someone you don't know.
- Avoid putting music headphone in both ears so that you can be more aware of your surroundings, especially if you are walking alone.

As you can see, these suggestions are focused more on reducing risk from a stranger. RAINN has an additional list of strategies when a person is in a social situation:

- When you go to a social gathering, go with a group of friends. Arrive together, check in with each other throughout the evening, and leave together. Knowing where you are and who is around you may help you to find a way out of a bad situation.
- Trust your instincts. If you feel unsafe in any situation, go with your gut. If you see something suspicious, contact law enforcement immediately.
- Do not leave your drink unattended while talking, dancing, using the restroom, or making a phone call. If you have left your drink alone, just get a new one.
- Do not accept drinks from people you do not know or trust. If you choose to accept a drink, go with the person to the bar to order, watch it being poured, and carry it yourself. At parties, do not drink from the punch bowls or other large, common open container.
- Watch out for your friends and vice versa. If a friend seems out of it, is way too intoxicated for the amount of alcohol he or she has had, or is acting out of character, get him or her to a safe place immediately.

Sexual assault may also be a part of domestic violence. Safety planning may be used with someone who is in an abusive or violent relationship and/or someone who is planning to leave such a relationship. Ideally, the plan should cover all of the areas in which the person may be vulnerable: home, work, school, in or around town, etc. A safety plan should include children or other family members when appropriate.

What makes safety planning different in the case of domestic violence is that the victim is trying to protect her or himself from a known individual. The abuser has greater knowledge of the victim and often greater access to that victim. The abuser may know not only where the victim lives but also where her or his family and friends live. The abuser may know the victim's routine or usual schedule. All of these things, and more, must be taken into account when developing a safety plan.

As most experts agree, the most dangerous time for victims of domestic violence is when they are in the process of leaving that abusive relationship. At its core, domestic violence is about power and control in which the abuser uses a variety of tactics, including sexual violence, to maintain control over the victim.

When the victim tries to leave the abusive relationship, the abuser will often increase the control by abusive or violent means in order to keep the victim in the relationship. The abuse or violence can escalate, sometimes to life-threatening levels. This makes careful planning essential.

One way to begin a safety plan is for the victim to think about a typical week. Does the victim work outside the home? If she or he has children, are they in day care and/or school? Are the children involved in regular activities? One of the basic suggestions to a victim of domestic violence is to vary the routine. Change their work schedule; use a different route to get there. This is assuming the abuser is aware of the victim's schedule. Is it possible to take the abuser off of the "okay to pick from day care or school list"? If the abuser is a parent of the child, this may not be possible without some sort of court order.

Once the areas of vulnerability are identified, the risks associated with that location must be considered and a plan constructed to reduce the risk(s). For example, a victim may be vulnerable when at work. The victim's abuser may have stopped by the office on several occasions and has always been able to walk right in. One plan might include the victim letting the receptionist at work know that the abuser should no longer be given access to the building.

Risks associated with the home are usually more complicated and potentially more dangerous. Even if the victim has received an order of protection, there may be risks. Changing the locks may be only the first step of the plan. The victim needs to think about all of the risks associated with the house or apartment. The victim also needs to keep all the major types of abuse or violence, including sexual assault in mind. It is often possible to include others in the implementation of the plan. In the case of the house or apartment, neighbors may be of assistance. The planning continues until all areas of vulnerability and the risks associated with those areas are covered.

Lisa J. Smith

See also Intimate Partner Violence; Recovery; Remembrance and Mourning; Risk Assessments; Stalking; Teen Dating Abuse

Further Reading

Davies, Jill (1998). *Safety planning with battered women.* Thousand Oaks, CA: Sage.

Selected Websites

Domestic Violence Safety Plan Guidelines. National Center for Victims of Crime. Retrieved from http://www.ncvc.org/ncvc/main.aspx?dbName=DocumentViewer&DocumentID=41374

National Center on Domestic and Sexual Violence. Retrieved from http://www.ncdsv.org

RAINN (Rape, Abuse & Incest National Network). Retrieved from http://www.rainn.org/

Sampling

Sampling is the process of selecting units (e.g., individuals, court cases, medical records) from a definable population. Given the resources needed to access all the units in a population, drawing a sample—a smaller subset of units—allows researchers with some degree of confidence to make inferences from the sample results to the population. To make valid inferences, a sample must be representative of the population from which it was drawn. Generalizability is an important issue given that most studies rely on data from a sample to estimate the extent of a phenomenon, describe its characteristics, and test hypotheses.

Sampling designs are grouped into two main categories: probability or nonprobability. In *probability sampling* designs, units are randomly selected and every unit in the population has a known and nonzero probability of selection. One advantage of probability samples is that they allow researchers to use probability theory to calculate measurement error associated with the results obtained from the sample. *Nonprobability sampling* relies on a nonrandom selection of units. Nonrandom selection means that some units have a greater, but unknown, probability than others of selection. Generally speaking, nonprobability sampling is more frequently employed in qualitative research, whereas probability sampling is more widely used in quantitative research.

Probability sampling designs rely on identifying the population of interest and creating a sampling frame—a list of all units to be sampled—to ensure representativeness. In *simple random sampling*, units are randomly selected from the population of interest, with each unit having the same probability as any other unit of selection. *Systematic random sampling* is less time consuming and involves randomly selecting the kth unit of the population from the sampling frame and then systematically selecting the kth unit of the remaining nonordered units. *Stratified random sampling* involves dividing the population into mutually exclusive strata—homogeneous groups based on some characteristic(s) (e.g., sex, geographical location)—before sampling, and, then randomly selecting units within each stratum to reduce the sampling error on the characteristic(s) that defined strata. *Cluster sampling* requires that the entire population be divided into mutually exclusive groups—clusters. A random sample of these clusters is selected and then all units within the clusters are selected. No units are observed in nonselected cluster; this differs from stratified sampling, in which some units are selected from *each* stratum. If a subset of units is randomly selected from each selected cluster, then it is referred to as two-stage cluster sampling (e.g., all sexual trauma patients from selected emergency departments in selected cities); when three or more stages of selecting units are used, then it is referred to as multistage cluster sampling (e.g., selected sexual trauma patients from selected emergency departments in selected in cities).

Nonprobability sampling designs are used for a variety of reasons, including when there are budgetary constraints, no sampling frame exists, an exploratory study is being conducted, or it is convenient to access a specific sample (e.g., women residing in a local battered women's shelter, survivors/victims receiving services at a rape crisis center). Using nonprobability sampling does not guarantee that the sample is representative of the population from which it was drawn so generalizability is compromised and results most likely are biased.

Many sexual violence and abuse studies have relied on *convenience samples*—units that are currently available—derived from variety of settings such as a victim/survivor support group, hospital emergency department, or victim service agency. *Quota sampling* involves setting the percentage of a given characteristics (e.g., race, age) in the sample so that it mirrors the percentage in the population of interest. *Purposive or judgment sampling* is a design in which the sample is selected by the researcher subjectively in an attempt to obtain a sample that appears to be representative of the population. *Snowball sampling* refers to an approach in which initial respondents are asked whether they can suggest others to participate in the study who have the desired characteristic(s) that the researchers are studying. For example, a researcher who interviewed women with physical disabilities about adolescent sexual violence asks each one at the end of the interview to suggest other women who have physical disabilities who might be willing to participate in the study.

When there is either overcoverage or undercoverage in the sampling frame, or substantial nonresponse from the selected sample, selection bias most likely occurs. Additional sampling issues inherent to sexual violence and abuse research are not different from sampling challenges in other fields where the phenomenon under study is a rare occurrence in the population. Under these conditions, it is necessary to select a large enough sample to produce reliable estimates of the prevalence or incidence of sexual violence and abuse. To undertake studies of this scale requires many resources (e.g., financial). Due to this constraint, many studies on sexual violence and abuse have been conducted using a nonprobability sample, in particular, a convenience or purposive sample. For example, conducting a study on the long-term consequences of childhood sexual abuse or repeat sexual violence might be done by recruiting participants through a crisis center or psychological service agency rather than by using a large probability sample of women. Studying the extent and nature of sexual violence and abuse among vulnerable and marginalized populations, such as drug users, LGBTQ individuals, runaway teenagers, or prostitutes, may also be best suited for nonprobability samples.

Véronique Jaquier and Bonnie S. Fisher

See also Data Collection; Research, Interviewing

Further Reading

Kish, L. (1965). *Survey sampling*. New York, NY: Wiley.

Lohr, S. (2010). *Sampling: Design and analysis* (2nd ed.). Boston, MA: Brooks/Cole.

Selected Websites

American Association for Public Opinion Research. Retrieved from http://www.aapor.org

Web Center for Social Research Methods. Retrieved from http://www.socialresearch methods.net

SANE (Sexual Assault Nurse Examiner)

Sexual assault nurse examiner (SANE) programs were created in the 1970s by the nursing profession, in collaboration with rape crisis centers/victim advocacy organizations, and grew in rapid numbers during the 1990s. These programs were designed to circumvent problems with traditional hospital emergency department care by having specially trained nurses, rather than doctors, provide 24-hour, first-response psychological, medical, and forensic care to sexual assault victims/survivors. Though physicians can and still do perform sexual assault exams, SANE programs provided new professional opportunities for practitioners who wanted to specialize in forensics. SANE programs are staffed by registered nurses or nurse practitioners who have completed a minimum of 40 hours of classroom training and 40–96 hours of clinical training, which includes instruction in evidence collection techniques, use of specialized equipment (e.g., colposcope), injury detection methods, pregnancy and sexually transmitted infections (STIs) screening and treatment, chain-of-evidence requirements, expert testimony, and sexual assault trauma response. Most SANE programs are hospital based (e.g., emergency departments) (75–90%), but some are located in community settings (e.g., clinics or rape crisis centers) (10–25%). Nearly all programs serve adolescents and adults, and approximately half serve pediatric victims/survivors as well.

To address victims/survivors' psychological needs, SANEs focus on treating victims with dignity and respect to ensure that they are not retraumatized by the exam. Many SANE programs work with their local rape crisis centers so victim advocates can provide emotional support. This delineation of roles is critical because rape victim advocates can offer victims/survivors confidentiality whereas SANEs may have to testify in court about their communications with survivors. To attend to victims/survivors' physical health needs, SANEs treat victims' injuries, offer emergency contraception for those at risk of becoming pregnant, and provide prophylactic antibiotics to treat STIs that may have been contracted in the assault.

For the forensic evidence collection itself, most SANE programs utilize specialized equipment, such as a colposcope, which is a noninvasive, lighted magnifying instrument used for examining the anogenital area for the detection of microlacerations, bruises, and other injuries. A camera is attached to the colposcope to document anogenital injuries. The forensic evidence collected by the SANEs is typically sent to the state crime lab for analysis. If a case is prosecuted, SANEs may provide expert witness testimony in court.

Although there are well over 700 SANE programs in existence in the United States, Canada, and other countries, there is limited research on the effectiveness of SANE programs with respect to victim health outcomes and legal prosecution outcomes (see Campbell, Patterson, & Lichty, 2005, for a comprehensive review). No national-scale studies have examined how SANE programs may improve patients' psychological well-being, but program-specific evaluations have found that the care provided by SANEs decreases victims' distress and increases their feelings of control and empowerment (Campbell, Bybee, Ford, Patterson, & Ferrell, 2009). National-scale studies have found that SANE programs provide significantly more comprehensive postassault health care services than do traditional hospital emergency departments (Campbell et al., 2006). With respect to forensic evidence collection, regional studies have found that the evidence collected by SANEs is of superior quality than that obtained by non-SANE medical personal (Sievers, Murphy, & Miller, 2003). Turning to legal prosecution outcomes, numerous case studies suggest that SANEs are a vital resource to police and prosecutors and that implementation of these programs can contribute to increased prosecution rates. To date, only two quasi-experimental have tested this hypothesis explicitly. Both studies were regional in scale, but found consistent findings such that prosecution rates significantly increased after the implementation of SANE programs and that these increases can be reasonably attributed to the services provided by the SANE program to both victims and members of the legal community (Campbell, Bybee, Ford, Patterson, & Ferrell, 2009; Crandall & Helitzer, 2003). It is important to note that the Campbell, Bybee, Ford, Patterson, and Ferrell (2009) study found that not pressuring victims to participate in the criminal justice system was critical for program success; empowering survivors' choices was important for victims' emotional well-being and had an indirect positive effect on their participation in the criminal justice system. These results suggest SANE programs may be an effective intervention for addressing the long-standing problem of sexual assault underprosecution. However promising these findings may be, they need to be interpreted with caution because SANE programs have proliferated much faster than evaluative data have been generated to guide practice.

Rebecca Campbell

See also Emergency Rooms and Medical Settings; Forensic Nursing; Medicalization of Rape; Rape Kits

Further Reading

Campbell, R., Bybee, D., Ford, J. K., Patterson, D., & Ferrell, J. (2009). *A systems change analysis of SANE programs: Identifying mediating mechanisms of criminal justice system impact.* Washington, DC: National Institute of Justice.

Campbell, R., Townsend, S.M., Long, S.M., Kinnison, K.E., Pulley, E.M., Adams, S.B., & Wasco, S.M. (2006). Responding to sexual assault victims' medical and emotional needs: A national study of the services provided by SANE programs. *Research in Nursing and Health, 29,* 384–398.

Campbell, R., Patterson, D., & Lichty, L. F. (2005). The effectiveness of sexual assault nurse examiner (SANE) program: A review of psychological, medical, legal, and community outcomes, *Trauma, Violence, & Abuse, 6,* 313–329.

Crandall, C., & Helitzer, D. (2003). *Impact evaluation of a sexual assault nurse examiner (SANE) program* (NIJ Document No. 203276; Award Number 98-WT-VX-0027).

Ledray, L. (1999). *Sexual assault nurse examiner (SANE) development & operations guide.* Washington, DC: Office for Victims of Crime, U.S. Department of Justice.

Sievers, V., Murphy, S., & Miller, J. (2003). Sexual assault evidence collection more accurate when completed by sexual assault nurse examiners: Colorado's experience. *Journal of Emergency Nursing, 29,* 511–514.

U.S. Department of Justice (2004). *A national protocol for sexual assault medical forensic examinations: Adults/adolescents.* Washington, DC: Author.

Selected Websites

International Association of Forensic Nurses. Retrieved from http://www.iafn.org/

Sexual Assault Nurse Examiner; Sexual Assault Response Team. Retrieved from http://www.sane-sart.com/

SARTs (Sexual Assault Response Teams)

A sexual assault response team (SART) is a coordinated, multidisciplinary community effort to respond to sexual assault victims' postassault needs, such as injury treatment, forensic medical exams, pregnancy evaluation, sexually transmitted infection screening, police reporting, and psychological crisis intervention. SARTs bring together key stakeholders, such as rape victim advocates, medical personnel (including sexual assault nurse examiners [SANEs]), law enforcement personnel, and prosecutors to work together as a team to promote survivors' well-being and community change. Typically, SARTs meet regularly as a team to address problems with their community's response to sexual assault, delineate the desired response, institutionalize this response through policies and procedures, and hold stakeholders accountable through monitoring of individual cases. In addition, many SARTs facilitate cross-disciplinary trainings to foster understanding of others' roles and share specialized knowledge.

SARTs have been widely implemented throughout the United States and Canada, and, although there are no national or international registries of these programs, practitioner organizations estimate there may be at least 500 SARTs currently in operation. Most of what is known about SARTs comes from practitioner-oriented manuals and descriptive social science research studies. From these sources, it is clear there is tremendous variability in SARTs' real-world practice. SARTs often vary with respect to their membership, goals, structure, and the activities they engage in to promote change. Most often, SARTs' *membership* includes victim advocates, medical personnel, police, and prosecutors; however, some SARTs may not be able to engage each of these groups, and other SARTs bring together even more stakeholder groups, such as representatives of the faith community, agencies serving marginalized populations (e.g., people with disabilities), and other social service agencies (such as drug treatment programs). SARTs' *goals* can be organized into three broad themes: (1) promoting offender accountability through increasing reporting and prosecution rates; (2) enhancing victim recovery by addressing barriers to help seeking and gaps in services delivery, as well as improving how system personnel treat victims; and (3) community-wide education to prevent and increase awareness of sexual assault. Although these are commonly cited goals across SARTs, some SARTs may prioritize one or two goals over others, while others may focus on all three equally. SARTs also vary in how they are *structured*. Some SARTs may have a variety of formalized structures in place, such as a leadership or coordinator role, a defined mission statement, and policies and procedures of operation, but some SARTs forgo such structures and instead rely on informal collaboration among members. Finally, different *activities* are utilized by SARTs to pursue changes in their community, including, but not limited to: (1) regular review of cases to assess progress through the legal system and ensure cases do not "fall through the cracks"; (2) cross-trainings during which stakeholders educate one another about issues related to their roles and areas of expertise; (3) team construction of written policies, protocols, and/or guidelines specifying the desired response to survivors by each system; and (4) development of resources for responders (e.g., checklists) and victims (e.g., pamphlets on community resources). Individual SARTs may engage in some or all of these activities.

Although SARTs have spread rapidly, and are widely espoused as best practice, there is minimal research on the effectiveness of these interventions and the findings have been mixed. For example, in a national-scale study, Campbell and Ahrens (1998) found that sexual assault victims who lived in communities with coordinated response teams were significantly more likely to have their cases successfully prosecuted. In a regional-scale quasi-experimental study, Nugent-Borakove and colleagues (2006) found that in communities with joint SANE-SART Programs (compared to SANE/no-SART and no-SANE/no-SART cases) victims were significantly more likely to participate in criminal justice prosecution proceedings. However, SANE-SART cases were not significantly more likely to result in conviction of offenders. Similarly, Wilson and Klein's (2005) study of a Rhode Island SART found no differences in the prosecution rates between SART and non-SART cases. It is important to note there were methodological limitations with all of these studies—which is not uncommon in developing literatures on new, innovative community interventions—and as such, it is premature to conclude whether SARTs are or are not effective in promoting their goals. Further research is needed on SARTs structure and functions and how different implementation practices may affect victims' services and criminal justice outcomes.

Rebecca Campbell

See also Advocacy; Advocates; Crisis Intervention; SANE (Sexual Assault Nurse Examiner)

Further Reading

Campbell, R., & Ahrens, C. (1998). Innovative community services for rape victims: An application of multiple case study methodology. *American Journal of Community Psychology, 26*, 537–571.

Nugent-Borakove, M.E., Fanfilk, P., Troutman, D., Johnson, N., Burgess, A., & O'Connor, A. L. (2006). *Testing the efficacy of SANE/SART programs: So they make a difference in sexual assault arrest and prosecution outcomes?* (NIJ Award Number 2003-WG-BX-1003). Washington, DC: National Institute of Justice.

Oregon Attorney General's Sexual Assault Task Force. (2009). *SART handbook version III*. Salem, OR: Author.

Peterson, M. S., Green, W., & Allison, B. (2009). *California SART report: Taking sexual assault response teams to the next level.* Davis, CA: University of California.

U.S. Department of Justice. (2004). *A national protocol for sexual assault medical forensic examinations: Adults/adolescents.* Washington, DC: Author.

Wilson, D., & Klein, A. (2005). *An evaluation of the Rhode Island sexual assault response team (sart)* (NIJ Award No. 2002-WG-BX-0007). Washington, DC: National Institute of Justice.

Selected Websites

International Association of Forensic Nurses. Retrieved from http://www.iafn.org/

Sexual Assault Nurse Examiner Sexual Assault Response Team. Retrieved from http://www.sane-sart.com/

SCREAM Theater (Program)

SCREAM (Students Challenging Realities and Educating against Myths) Theater is a student-based peer educational, interactive theater program at Rutgers, the State University of New Jersey. The group performs nationwide to universities, high schools, middle schools, community groups, and professional organizations through the Rutgers Office for Violence Prevention and Victim Assistance. The goal of SCREAM Theater is to use a theatrical performance and an in-character question/answer session with the audience to address issues of sexual violence, domestic violence, stalking, sexual harassment, and bullying.

The use of a peer education theater group to educate on issues of interpersonal violence is supported by the theory of entertainment education, which maintains that it is engaging and entertaining while also delivering educational information to the audience. It is also based in the theory of diffusion of innovations in which opinion leaders spread knowledge and ideas to others and hence diffuse the information throughout the community. SCREAM Theater skits are engaging, realistic, and often humorous, providing a unique and interesting way for audience members to learn about potentially difficult topics.

The SCREAM Theater primary prevention program highlights bystander intervention as an effective strategy in eliminating sexual violence. SCREAM Theater's expanded primary prevention program is called *SCREAMing to Prevent Violence (STPV)* and it includes four interactive sessions on positive active bystander intervention. The *STPV* curriculum would be used when there is access granted to a specific population for more than a onetime program. The three sessions are outlined as follows:

1. *STPV—Performance* (also known as the original SCREAM Theater) provides an introduction to sexual violence, including the basics of sexual violence, including but not limited to consent, the role of alcohol as a weapon in facilitating sexual assault, how to support a victim of sexual violence, how to confront a perpetrator, and the importance of being a positive active bystander.

2. *STPV—You Choose* includes an introduction to positive active bystander intervention. SCREAM actors re-create scenes from the previous performance and, at points of potential bystander intervention, the audience votes on what the characters should do next. The SCREAM actors then act out the intervention that received the most votes.

3. *STPV—Acting Makes a Difference* builds on the previous sessions. Audience members work in small groups to come up with new bystander interventions for the same scenes previously viewed in *Performance* and *You Choose*. The group chooses one intervention to act out for the rest of the audience.

4. *STPV—What Would RU Do?* allows participants to view several short vignettes performed by SCREAM Theater actors. Participants are asked to view the scene, and then decide if they would intervene or not. The goal of the session is to challenge ideas around gender norms and bystander intervention.

In addition to SCREAM Theater and the SCREAMing to Prevent Violence prevention curriculum, the Office for Violence Prevention and Victim Assistance also utilizes SCREAM Athletes in the prevention of sexual violence within the athletic community. Because of the unique challenges that student-athletes face, the SCREAM Athletes program uses student-athletes to provide peer education to other athletes on issues of interpersonal violence. These student-athletes are leaders in their community, and are best able to convey attitudes and beliefs that are specific to the athletic community.

Sharon Zucker

See also Bringing in the Bystander (Program); Bystander Intervention; The Green Dot (Program); Prevention, Colleges and Universities; Sports Teams; Theory, Diffusion of Innovations

Further Reading

McMahon, S. & Salerno, N. (2002, August). *Quantitative research project: Assessing the effectiveness of SCREAM Theater* (Executive Summary). Retrieved from http://vpva .rutgers.edu/scream.htm

Sex Industry (Overview)

The sexually exploitative industry, including pornography (Internet, film, print), strip clubs, prostitution, and sex work, is a multi-billion-dollar industry worldwide. The sexually exploitative industry has been theorized as being connected to sexual violence in both direct and indirect ways and impacts individuals, communities, and society as a whole. Opposition to the sexually exploitative industry is largely based in the antipornography feminist movement, which argues that the industry degrades women and contributes to the escalation of gender violence. Andrea Dworkin and Catherine MacKinnon are widely cited within this movement and assert that pornography sexualizes the inequality between men and women and encourages the subordination of women through its construct of women as sexual objects. This theory views male dominance and submission as being eroticized and thus legitimizes sexual violence of women through various forms of entertainment.

Several entries in the encyclopedia specifically discuss the relationship between sexual violence and the sexually exploitative industry. This entry begins with a general discussion about pornography, and how the content of pornography in various forms (print, Internet, videos) may influence attitudes and behaviors related to sexual violence. Child pornography is also discussed, including differences in definitions and legality of materials. This entry will conclude with information about commercial sex workers, including prostitution and strip clubs.

All entries referenced here highlight the impact the sexually exploitative industry has on potential perpetrators and victims of sexual violence.

Pornography

In his entry on **Pornography**, Robert Jensen notes that the term "pornography" is often used to describe all sexually explicit books, magazines, movies, and websites, with a distinction made between soft-core and hard-core images. In addition, pornography is also distinguished between erotica, material that depicts sexual behavior with mutuality and respect, and pornography as the term for materials depicting sex with domination or degradation. Pornography comes in many forms, including Internet, photographs, film, telephones, video, DVD, and print.

Analysis of the content of pornography has found pornography to hold recurrent themes related to the degradation of women, including male dominance, female pain, and the use of violence to obtain sex. Such themes are found in hard-core pornography, but also among what is considered as mainstream, or popular pornography. Reviews of mainstream pornography typically include best-sellers, or most commonly purchased titles. In a review of mainstream pornographic videos and novels, Jensen and Dines (1998) found male dominance to be a major theme, as men took control of sex by physically forcing or ordering women to engage in specific acts. Physical aggression in pornography often includes spanking, hair pulling, choking, slapping and gagging. Verbal aggression is also frequent, and includes name calling, threats of physical harm, and coercive language.

Pornographic novels have been found to use rape-fantasy scenarios, in which women initially resist sex, but after some level of force and pain inflicted by the male, the women give up and become a willing participant in the sexual relationship, and are often depicted as gaining pleasure from being raped (Jensen & Dines, 1998). Other forms of print pornography, including magazines, may include violent images in the form of cartoons and pictorials.

The Internet also offers consumers numerous options of types of pornography to view, many of which are easily accessed from a computer, often at no charge. As pornography has progressed from print/magazines to videos to the Internet it has been found to have become increasingly violent (Baron & Kimmel, 2000). Internet pornography, or cyber pornography, allows users more freedom to view different scenarios and situations, including rape-fantasy scenarios. In an analysis of violent Internet pornography, Gossett and Byrne (2002) found that of all the websites they reviewed, all contained some text about rape (in the title or web address) or visual rape images. Dominance is also a prevalent theme in Internet pornography, as viewers can often take control of creating their own rape-fantasy scenarios, through programs such as "cyber-slave" or controlling the setting in which a woman can be sexually victimized (Gossett & Byrne, 2002).

The recurring themes of male dominance, physical and sexual violence, female pain, and other degrading behaviors toward women are common in all forms of pornography. While some might argue that the content of pornography itself does not cause sexual violence, it may influence attitudes and behaviors that support sexual violence. Researchers have found that pornography is used to develop attitudes about sex, sexuality, and women that are degrading, and that those who use pornography have increased acceptance of attitudes that support or tolerate sexual violence (Hald, Malamuth, & Yuen, 2010). Pornography is often used as a source of information about sexual behavior, and while there may not be anything wrong with learning about sex through the Internet, media, or other publications, the depiction of sexual behaviors that may be humiliating, degrading, and painful to women and that are constructed within a theme of male dominance is problematic. Pornography may teach its viewers that what they are viewing is "normal" and that they should expect certain behaviors and appearances from women, as well as behavior for males that accepts the objectification of women (Oddone-Paolucci, Genuis, & Violato, 2000). Research has also found links between exposure to pornography and an increased acceptance of rape myths (Oddone-Paolucci et al., 2000).

The use of pornography has also been linked to having a direct impact on behavior related to sexual violence, including the increased likelihood of aggression and dominance. Studies have found a relationship between frequent pornography use and sexually aggressive behaviors (Malamuth, Addison, & Koss, 2000). In addition, research has looked at behaviors of abuse partners who use the sex industry and how pornography may impact abuse. One study found that pornography may often play a role during the abuse of women, and can include use of pornography before or during an abusive act, forcing a partner to participate in the making of pornography, or photographing and videotaping sexually violent acts (Bergen & Bogle, 2000).

Child Pornography

Another form of pornography is child pornography. In her entry, Poco Donna Kernsmith defines **Child Pornography** as the depiction of a minor in a sexually explicit manner, including nudity or partial nudity of children, or children engaged in sexual activities. Child pornography can include photographs, video, artwork, or computer-generated images that actually depict a minor or are altered to appear to depict a minor. Unlike the forms of pornography described above, in the United States it is a federal crime to create, possess, or distribute child pornography. As with mainstream pornography, the Internet is commonly used to distribute child pornography. Kernsmith discusses that while research on the content of child pornography is limited, the average age of children depicted in child pornography is 13 years old, and one national study of convicted Internet child pornography cases found that females were depicted in 87 percent of the cases (Wolak, Finkelhor, Mitchell, & Jones, 2011). Kernsmith states that children are commonly coerced, manipulated, or forced into pornography, and images may be produced without the knowledge of the victim.

Sex Workers

Commercial sex work, in which materials such as money, food, and/or drugs are exchanged for sexual services or sexually graphic behaviors or products, is another area of the sexually exploitative industry. Forms of commercial sexual exploitation may include prostitution, stripping, live sex shows, and peep shows. In her entry on **Sex Workers**, Stéphanie Wahab describes sex work as including such venues as street work, escort agencies, brothels, exotic dance clubs, paid domination, phone sex, and sexual massage. Some of these venues (escort agencies and exotic dance clubs) are legal, while others (street work) are not. Commercial sex work is criminalized throughout the United States, except in Nevada, where brothels can be licensed. Wahab discusses that sex workers experience violence both within and outside the context of sex work. Sexual violence experiences by sex workers may include sexual, verbal and physical humiliation, rape, hate crimes, extortion, and blackmail. Perpetrators of sexual violence against sex workers include clients, strangers, pimps, managers, and in some instances, the police.

Strip Clubs

Strip clubs, also known as exotic dance clubs, are another part of the sex industry. Strip clubs provide a range of options to patrons, including the traditional practice of watching women remove their clothing and dance, as well as purchasing lap dances and receiving private dances in booths or other areas of clubs. Private dance options may include peep shows or live sex shows, in which sexual acts are either simulated or acted out in front of customers who participate by masturbating in private booths. In her entry on **Strip Clubs**, Melissa Lavin defines strippers as another type of sex worker and discusses ways in which strippers are at high risk for sexual violence, from clients, club owners, and managers. Workers may be subject to physical and sexual abuse, verbal harassment, stalking, as well as being sexually exploited (Barton, 2006).

Male dominance can also be seen as a key feature in strip clubs, as male customers, managers, owners, and staff retain a position of power and control over female strippers who serve and perform for males (Price, 2008). The male-dominated atmosphere of strip clubs may lead to the objectification of women and contribute to attitudes and beliefs that support sexual violence. Attitudes toward strippers are typically negative, and strippers have been regarded by clients as hookers, whores, sexually promiscuous, drug and alcohol abusers, lazy, and overall "bad" women (Barton, 2006; Price, 2008). These attitudes often follow women who work in the sex industry, and create a "whore-stigma," which may impact how they are treated outside of the strip club (Barton, 2006).

In conclusion, the sexually exploitative industry contributes to sexual violence through the depiction of sexually degrading and violent images in pornography, child pornography, the abusive treatment of those who work in the sex industry, reinforcement of attitudes and beliefs that support sexual violence, and attitudes that support or legitimize violent behaviors toward sex workers.

Rachel Schwartz

Further Reading

Baron, M., & Kimmel, M. (2000). Sexual violence in three pornographic media: Toward a sociological explanation. *Journal of Sex Research, 37*(2), 161–168.

Barton, B. (2006). *Stripped: Inside the lives of exotic dancers.* New York, NY: New York University Press.

Bergen, R. K., & Bogle, K. A. (2000). Exploring the connection between pornography and sexual violence. *Violence and Victims, 15*(3), 227–234.

Gossett, J. L., & Byrne, S. (2002). "Click here": A content analysis of Internet rape sites. *Gender and Society, 16*(5), 689–709.

Hald, G. M., Malamuth, N. M., & Yuen, C. (2010). Pornography and attitudes supporting violence against women: Revisiting the relationship in nonexperimental studies. *Aggressive Behavior, 36*, 14–20.

Jensen, R., & Dines, G. (1998). The content of mass-marketed pornography. In G. Dines, R. Jensen, & A. Russo (Eds.), *Pornography: The production and consumption of inequality* (pp. 66–100). New York, NY: Routledge.

Malamuth, N. M., Addison, T., & Koss, M. (2000). Pornography and sexual aggression: Are there reliable effects and can we understand them? *Annual Review of Sex Research, 11*, 26.

Oddone-Paolucci, E., Genuis, M., & Violato, C. (2000). A meta-analysis of the published research on the effects of pornography. In C. Violato, E. Oddone-Paolucci, & M. Genuis (Eds.), *The changing family and child development* (pp. 48–59). Burlington, VT: Ashgate.

Price, K. (2008). "Keeping the dancers in check": The gendered organization of stripping work in The Lion's Den. *Gender & Society, 22*(3), 367–389.

Wolak, J., Finkelhor, D., Mitchell, K. J., & Jones, L. M. (2011). Arrests for child pornography production: Data at two time points from a national sample of U.S. law enforcement agencies. *Child Maltreatment, 16*(3), 184–195. doi:10.1177/1077559511415837

Selected Websites

Prostitution Research and Education. Retrieved from http://www.prostitutionresearch.com/

Sex Workers Outreach Project. Retrieved from http://www.swopusa.org

Sex Workers Project at the Urban Justice Center. Retrieved from http://www
.sexworkersproject.org

Stop Porn Culture. Retrieved from http://stoppornculture.org/home/

Sex Offender Registries

Sex offender registries (SORs) are databases of criminal, residential, and personal information collected on individuals convicted of perpetrating a criminal sex offense. They are most often collected and maintained by government divisions at multiple levels (national, state/province, local) under legislative mandate for public protection. These systems for monitoring and controlling sex offenders are currently being utilized in the United Kingdom, Canada, and the United Sates. As of 2010, the United States had nearly 730,000 registered sex offenders.

In 1994, the United States passed the Jacob Wetterling Crimes against Children and Sexually Violent Offender Registration Act (also informally referred to as Megan's Law), which required each state to create and maintain sex offender registries as well as to make those data easily available to the general public. The style of information dissemination is the choice of individual states and includes community notification letters to residents when an offender moves into a neighborhood, searchable websites, and published lists made available at local law enforcement offices. For example, California's notification system originally required residents to visit local law enforcement offices in person or dial a "900" toll telephone number to access SOR information. A bill that was passed by the state legislature in 2004 now requires the creation and maintenance of a public SOR website that provides online access to about 75 percent of their registrant records. States also exercise discretion regarding the exact type of information stored on the registry. In the UK and Canada, registry data can be accessed only by law enforcement agencies. In the United States, states also have flexibility in the offenses they choose to be eligible for inclusion on the registry and whether juveniles are included on the public registry. In 2006, the Adam Walsh Child Protection and Safety Act was signed into law. This legislation requires states to create a three-tiered system of offense severity ranking and sets minimum registration terms to 15 years, 25 years, or life based on offense severity tier.

The expressed goal of these registry efforts is to reduce the risk of reoffending among convicted sex offenders though the public identification and monitoring of offenders. Public availability of this information is intended to help families keep their children safe from predatory violent pedophiles by allowing parents to be aware of threats in their neighborhoods and to supervise their children accordingly. The justification for the need for continued long-term governmental supervision of sex offenders beyond the term of prison sentences or supervised release rests on the belief that pedophiles are very resistant to rehabilitation and have high rates of recidivism.

However, the empirical data do not bear out the assumptions underlying these sex offender registry policy efforts. Despite popular media caricatures, children are far more likely to be abused by family members or other acquaintances, not strangers. The U.S. Department of Justice reports that only seven percent of reported sexual assaults on juveniles between 1991 and 1996 were perpetrated by a stranger (Snyder, 2000). Also, sex offenders convicted of perpetrating against children have been found to have a three-year rearrest rate for sex crimes against children of about six percent (Langan, Schmitt, & Durose, 2003). With regard to treatment, an examination of the results of more than 20 evaluation studies shows a great deal of inconsistency in the effectiveness of intervention. In a review of prison-based research, it was found that offenders who participated in cognitive behavioral treatment while in prison had significantly lower recidivism rates for sexual offenses (Polizzi, MacKenzie, & Hickman, 1999). These findings suggest that sex offender registries may lead families to a false sense of security by emphasizing "stranger danger" while offering an official list of sex offenders. Most parents may be unaware that most offenders do not come to the attention of law enforcement, and that threats to their children are more likely to loom in their own circle of family and acquaintances.

In addition to being a policy based on empirically unfounded assertions, sex offender registry policies, when put into practice, have not demonstrated effectiveness in reducing offender recidivism. In a systematic review of research, Drake and Aos (2009) found that the implementation of registry laws generally had little significant effect on sex offender recidivism. However, there is consistent research demonstrating that registration has significant unintended negative consequences. Tewksbury (2005) has shown that registration has serious negative impacts on offenders' reintegration in to society due to difficulty finding housing, inability to find employment, neighborhood harassment, and other varieties of public social stigmas.

Roger Kernsmith

See also Megan's Law; Rape Myths; Stranger Rape

Further Reading

Drake, E. K., & Aos, S. (2009). *Does sex offender registration and notification reduce crime? A systematic review of the research literature* (Document No. 09-06-1101). Olympia, WA: Washington State Institute for Public Policy.

Langan, P., & Schmitt, E., & Durose, M. (2003). *Recidivism of sex offenders released from prison in 1994*. Washington, DC: Bureau of Justice Statistics, U.S. Department of Justice.

National Center for Missing and Exploited Children (2010). Map of registered sex offenders in the United States. Retrieved from http://www.missingkids.com/en_US/documents/sex-offender-map.pdf

Polizzi, D., Mackenzie D., & Hickman, L. (1999). What works in adult sex offender treatment? A review of prison- and non-prison-based treatment programs. *International Journal of Offender Therapy and Comparative Criminology, 43*, 357–374.

Prescott, J., & Rockoff, Jonah E. (2008). *Do sex offender registration and notification laws affect criminal behavior?* (NBER Working Paper No. 13803; third annual conference on Empirical Legal Studies Papers; University of Michigan Law & Economics, Olin Working Paper No. 08-006). Retrieved from http://ssrn.com/abstract=1100663

Snyder, H. (2000). *Sexual assault of young children as reported to law enforcement: victim, incident, and offender characteristics.* Washington, DC: Bureau of Justice Statistics.

Tewksbury, R. (2005). Collateral consequences of sex offender registration. *Journal of Contemporary Criminal Justice, 21*(1), 67–82.

Selected Website

Association for the Treatment of Sexual Abusers. Retrieved from http://www.atsa.com

Sex Workers

Despite numerous studies that report significant rates of sexual violence within the lives of commercial sex workers (CSWs), not all sex workers experience sexual violence while engaged in sexual commerce. Like non-sex workers, CSWs also experience sexual violence outside of the sex industry (e.g., within their families, intimate partnerships, and friendships; by coworkers and friends). Drug and immigration laws, combined with the criminalization of prostitution contribute to an environment where sexual violence against sex workers is both facilitated and tolerated by many.

Language and definitions are central to the multiple narratives and discourses associated with sex work. Commercial sex work is often defined as the exchange of material goods such as money, food, drugs, transportation, housing, etc., for sexual services. Other common terms include prostitution, sex trade, and sexual commerce. People engaged in sex work identify as women, men, transgender, gender queer, and gender neutral. Some involved in sex commerce identify as sex workers while others, engaged in either informal and/or occasional sexual transactions (where material goods and sexual services are exchanged), do not. Whether someone identifies as engaging in sexual commerce or not is often influenced by how protected from arrest, punishment, deportation, stigma, and judgment they may feel in a given context. Those involved in sexual commerce without trading sexual services themselves include (but are not limited to) those who may work as managers, property owners, drivers, telephone and camera operators. Sex work is generally understood to include but is not limited to street work, escort work, work in brothels, exotic dance clubs, paid domination, phone sex, web cam sex, and sexual massage.

Sex work (or prostitution) is systematically conflated with human trafficking (a serious human rights abuse acknowledged by the U.S. government under the Trafficking Victims Protection Act of 2000 and subsequent reauthorizations) across various legal, cultural, social service, and feminist discourses. Many have discussed the multiple harms associated with conflating sex work and trafficking (e.g., Best Practices Policy Project, 2010; Center for Health and Gender Equity, 2010; Lerum, McCurtis, Saunders, Wahab, 2012; Sex Workers Project at the Urban Justice Center, 2007) and differences and tensions are significant among those who wish to untangle sex work and trafficking (sex workers' and human rights advocates) and those who wish to equate one with the other (abolitionists—those who would like to see sex work abolished all together).

Some venues and aspects of CSW are legal in the United States (for example, escort agencies, exotic dance clubs, and pornography) while others are not (for example, street work). Prostitution is criminalized in virtually all jurisdictions in the United States, except the state of Nevada, which allows certain houses known as brothels to obtain licenses.

Some of the violence, including sexual violence, experienced by CSWs often includes experiences of violence perpetrated by the state through policing and legislation of prostitution, drug, and immigration laws. Brents and Hausbeck (2001; 2005) have examined sex workers' perceptions of safety and risk, and managerial brothel practices designed to mitigate violence in the context of legalized brothel prostitution in Nevada. Their findings with respect to violence suggest that the legalization of prostitution brings a level of "public scrutiny, official regulation, and bureaucratization to brothels" (271) that de facto promote greater safety and less risk of systematic violence than illegal prostitution.

Those engaged in sexual commerce on the streets tend to bear the brunt of policing efforts and activities because they tend to be the most visible of those engaged in sexual commerce. This means that low-income communities, immigrants, people of color, and gay, lesbian, bisexual, and transgender people tend to be greater targets for policing and consequently harassment by law enforcement.

In many jurisdictions in the United States, police have been accused of and reprimanded for extortion of sexual favors from sex workers to avoid arrest. Police also illegally engage in sexual acts with individuals to provide evidence that prostitution occurred (Sullivan & Schwarzen, 2005). In a New York City-based study, 27 percent of sex workers surveyed had experienced violence at the hands of law enforcement (Sex Workers Project at the Urban Justice Center, 2003). Another study in Washington, DC, found that more than 50 percent of CSWs who went to the police for assistance were either ignored or further abused by officers (Alliance for a Safe & Diverse DC, 2008). Sexual violence is not only potentially traumatizing to workers but it also threatens their physical, emotional, and psychological health, overall well-being, and livelihoods as rape almost always takes place without the protection of condoms.

Cooper, Moore, Gruskin, and Krieger (2004) reported that women who inject drugs, particularly sex workers, bore the brunt of police abuse. From their interviews with CSWs who also inject drugs, they found that 33 percent of injectors compared to 12 percent of nonusers reported experiencing or witnessing police-perpetrated sexual violence.

Violence and other forms of human rights abuses against CSWs are endemic in the United States (Best Practices Policy Project, 2010). Sex workers experience violence within and outside of the context of sex work. It is important to note that not all sex workers experience violence within the sex industry; however, among those who do, sexual, verbal, and physical humiliation and abuse, rape (date, partner, stranger, and gang), hate crimes, extortion or blackmailing, and murder are common. One of the limitations in our understanding of sexual violence in the lives of CSWs is that most of the studies have involved street-based female sex workers (Wahab, 2005), which means that poor women are overrepresented in the research while male, transgender, and middle-class sex workers are absent or obscured in our knowledge base. Ultimately, researchers know very little about the prevalence of sexual violence experienced by more privileged sex workers engaged in more private forms of sexual commerce.

All forms of violence against sex works occur within social and political contexts informed by social inequalities and political-economic stratifications. That is to say, CSW does not occur in a vacuum, but rather takes place similarly to other forms of work within systems of domination including racism, classism, sexism, homophobia, and xenophobia. Many have argued that the criminalization of prostitution contributes to an environment where sexual violence against sex workers is tolerated. Criminalization and human rights' abuses coupled with the lack of legal, social, and physical protection afforded to sex workers places those with the least access to white, middle class, heterosexual, able bodied, U.S. citizenship privileges at the greatest risk for all forms of violence. Sexual violence against sex workers cannot be understood without considering these broader social, political, cultural and economic realities.

Stéphanie Wahab

See also Pornography; Pornography, Internet; Prostitution; Strip Clubs

Further Reading

Alliance for a Safe and Diverse DC (2008). *Move Along: Policing sex work in Washington, DC*, Different Avenues, retrieved September 2011, http://dctranscoalition.files.wordpress.com/2010/05/movealongreport.pdf

Best Practices Policy Project, Desiree Alliance, Sexual Rights Initiative (2010). *Report on the United States of America: 9th Round of the Universal Periodic Review*, retrieved September 2011, http://www.bestpracticespolicy.org/downloads/FinalUPRBPPP_Formatted.pdf.

Brents, B., & Hausbeck, K. (2001). State-sanctioned sex: Negotiating formal and Informal regulatory practices in Nevada brothels. *Sociological Perspectives*, 44(3), 307–332.

Brents, B., & Hausbeck, K. (2005). Violence and legalized brothel prostitution in Nevada. *Journal of Interpersonal Violence*, 20(3), 270–295.

Center for Health and Gender Equity (CHANGE) and Center for Human Rights and Humanitarian Law at American University Washington College of Law. (2010). *Human trafficking, HIV/AIDS, and the sex sector: Human rights for all*. Retrieved from http://www.genderhealth.org/files/uploads/change/publications/Human_Trafficking_HIVAIDS_and_the_Sex_Sector_12_3_2 010_FINAL.pdf

Cooper, H., Moore, L., Gruskin, S., & Krieger, N. (2004). Characterizing perceived police violence: Public health implications. *American Journal of Public Health, 94*(7), 1109–1118.

Different Avenues (2008). *Move along: Policing sex work in Washington, D.C.* A report prepared by the Alliance for a Safe and Diverse, Washington, DC. Retrieved from http://dctranscoalition.files.wordpress.com/2010/05/movealongreport.pdf

Lerum, K., McCurtis, K., Saunders, P., Wahab, S. (In press). Using human rights to hold the US accountable for its anti-sex trafficking agenda: The Universal Periodic Review and new directions for US policy. *The Anti-Trafficking Review Journal*.

Sex Workers Project at the Urban Justice Center (2003). Revolving door: An analysis of street-based prostitution in New York: Fact Sheet. Retrieved from http://www.sexworkersproject.org/downloads/RevolvingDoorFS.html

Sex Workers Project at the Urban Justice Center (2007). *The danger of conflating trafficking and sex work: A position paper from the Sex Workers Project of the Urban Justice Center*. Retrieved from http://www.sexworkersproject.org/media-toolkit/downloads/20070330-BriefingPaperOnConflationOfTraffickingAndSexWork.pdf

Sullivan, J., & Schwarzen, C. (2005, October 7). Did local vice cops cross the line? *Seattle Times*. Retrieved from http://seattletimes.nwsource.com/html/localnews/2002545187_prostitutes07m.html

Wahab, S. (2005). Introduction to the special edition on sex work. *Journal of Interpersonal Violence*, 20(3), 263–269.

Selected Websites

Best Practices and Policy Project. Retrieved from http://www.bestpracticespolicy.org/

December 16th, International Day to End Violence Against Sex Workers. Retrieved from http://www.swopusa.org/dec17/

Human Rights for All. Retrieved from http://www.humanrightsforall.info

Sex Workers Project at the Urban Justice Center. Retrieved from http://www.sexworkersproject.org/

Young Women's Empowerment Project. Retrieved from http://ywepchicago.wordpress.com/

Sexting

Sexting, a term derived from the combination of the words "sex" and "texting," is used to describe the act of sending sexually explicit images or messages to others by means of a cellular phone. Sexting generally involves the exchange or distribution of nude and/or seminude pictures, videos, or a sexually provocative depiction of another person from one cell phone to another, or to a social networking website. Sexting has become a complex legal issue, mainly because many of those who "sext" are adolescents and legally considered minors. Transmitting or receiving nude images of a minor, even if the minor is sending images of herself or himself to a friend violates laws governing transmission and possession of child pornography. Teenagers have found themselves arrested and charged under the prevailing child pornography statutes for engaging in behavior that, in their mind, is innocuous and not even remotely "criminal."

Approximately one in five teenagers (22% girls, 18% boys) state they have either sent or posted pictures or videos of themselves in which they are nude or partially clothed (Chalfen, 2009). Although most teens who send these images or messages are sending them to boyfriends/girlfriends, others admit sending the images/messages to someone they wanted to date or hook up with or to someone they knew only online. Most teenagers report sexting to be "fun and flirtatious," citing it as a great way to communicate with the opposite sex. Other reasons include (1) peer pressure, where boys are asking for these pictures, whether it be for personal enjoyment (a "sexy" present) or as a sign of endearment; (2) a response to a sexual image of similar content they received; or (3) a way to receive attention or peer approval, to feel sexy, or as a joke.

As noted, because teenage-content "sexts" are frequently sexually explicit images of minors, they fall within the purview of both state and federal child pornography laws. Thus teenagers can find themselves with serious criminal charges, whether it be a felony or a misdemeanor, occasionally requiring registration as a sex offender. In one such case, an 18-year-old distributed nude photographs of his former 16-year-old girlfriend to dozens of friends and family. He was convicted of distributing child pornography, placed on probation for five years, and required to spend 25 years on Florida's sex offender registry list (Feyerick & Steffen, 2009).

Recent legislative attempts have focused on finding less punitive responses. Although teenagers who sext are heterogeneous in their motives, and some may be driven by clearly unhealthy wishes (e.g., to embarrass or humiliate, to get revenge, to bolster a "macho" or hypermasculine image), most teen sexters are naïve children engaging in what they regard to be flirting. Legislators are currently working on changing the penalties associated with sexting. Many states are opting to reduce penalties for sexting so that the offenders are not prosecuted under the same laws as child pornographers and pedophiles. Some states are choosing to implement educational programs instead of criminal charges, while others advocate for federal legislation to standardize penalties for minors engaging in sexting.

Sexting appears to be only one of many expressions of the complex, poorly navigated interface between (1) rapidly changing technology, (2) laws that have failed to keep up with changes in technology, and (3) the changing sexual mores and values of modern Western society. In summary, sexting is not merely a benign expression of adolescent flirtatiousness. Sexting can carry with it a host of negative outcomes, ranging from mild (e.g., embarrassment) to moderate (e.g., feeling humiliated when revealing images of oneself are seen by unintended people, including one's parents, one's teachers, the school principal, and the police) to severe. Severe outcomes can include sexual harassment, bullying, sexual extortion (e.g., "have sex with me or I will put those images I have of you up on the web"), or victimization by criminals who have access to the naked images. Given that the vast majority of teenagers nationwide have their own cell phone with a built-in camera and that roughly 20 percent report some experience with sexting (http://www.TheNationaCampaign.org), the magnitude of the potential problems is considerable. Most importantly, once an image is on the Internet, unrestricted access makes the image instantly and permanently available to *everyone*, not just a boyfriend or girlfriend. This is one outcome that most youngsters do not contemplate.

Kimberly Haller, Jarell Myers, and Kei Okada

See also Stalking; Teen Dating Abuse

Further Reading

Chalfen, R. (2009). New media review. *Visual Studies, 24*(3), 258–268.

Feyerick, D., & Steffen, S. (2009). "Sexting" lands teen on sex offender list. Retrieved from http://www.cnn.com/2009/CRIME/04/07/sexting.busts

The National Campaign to Prevent Teen and Unplanned Pregnancy (2008). *Sex and tech: Results from a survey of teens and young adults*. Retrieved from http://www.thenationalcampaign.org.sextech/PDF/SexTech_Summary.pdf

Sexual Assault

Sexual assault occurs when one person touches another person's body in a sexual way, even through clothing, without that person's consent. The term "sexual assault" includes attempted rape, sexual intercourse (rape), oral or anal sexual acts (sodomy), fondling, child molestation, and incest. Any nonconsensual sexual behavior that causes a person to feel uncomfortable, intimidated, or scared qualifies as sexual assault. Perpetrators commit sexual assault through tactics such as coercion, manipulation, pressure, threats, and violence. Sexual assault occurs in heterosexual and nonheterosexual contexts. The sexual orientation of the perpetrator may differ from that of the victim. Perpetrators can be strangers, acquaintances, friends, relatives, intimate partners, or spouses. Not all incidents of sexual assault are reported, prosecuted, or result in conviction.

Legal definitions of sexual assault, the terms used in statutes (e.g., criminal sexual contact, sexual assault, indecent contact, rape) and the definitions of those terms are not always consistent across states. Many states have replaced the term "rape" with the term "sexual assault" in order to make statutes more gender-neutral and to cover various types of sexual victimization and coercion. Historically, the common-law definition of rape required the sexual act to be intercourse, the rapist to be male, and the victim to be female. In addition, the act had to be committed as a result of force or the threat of force and the victim and perpetrator could not be married. Most current sexual assault statutes cover rape along with other forms of sexual violence, making them applicable in heterosexual and nonheterosexual contexts regardless of the gender identity of the victim or the perpetrator.

Researchers have documented that sexual assault is one of the most underreported crimes in the United States, that perpetrators of sex offenses are found throughout the social spectrum, and that the majority of sexual assaults are attempted or committed by someone that the victim knows. According to the U.S. Department of Justice (2005) 60 percent of rapes are unreported. Despite underreporting, researchers agree that the majority of sexual assault victims are female and most perpetrators are male. Using a definition of rape that includes forced vaginal, anal, or oral sex, the National Violence Against Women Survey found that 1 in 6 U.S. women and 1 in 33 U.S. men have experienced an attempted or completed rape (National Institute of Justice & Centers for Disease Control and Prevention, 1998).

Many survivors struggle with whether or not to report their experiences. The decision is a personal one and there are a number of factors survivors must consider. Survivors may have concerns about: being believed or being judged by family, friends, and authorities; treatment from law enforcement and other systems; or the impact that reporting may have on their families and communities. Issues with the legal system may be additionally complicated if the survivor is a member of an oppressed population. Survivors who report sexual assault may experience negative reactions from society and support systems. Negative reactions may include blaming survivors or minimizing their experiences and can serve a silencing function.

Following a sexual assault it is normal for survivors to feel embarrassed or scared. These feelings may prevent the survivor from wanting to report the assault right away. While there is no time limit for survivors to report a sexual assault, they are encouraged to seek medical care. Since certain types of evidence that may be present following an assault disappear over time, survivors may elect to have a forensic exam even if they are not making a formal report. In some states, a forensic kit (sometimes called a "rape kit") is collected only within 72 hours of the incident. In cases where survivors report their experiences, they may or may not wish to proceed with an investigation. Regardless of whether or not there has been an official report, survivors are eligible for free and confidential services from sexual assault programs, can receive medical treatment, and can elect to have a forensic exam.

The experience of sexual assault has different meanings for each person. There is no way to know how a person will react to a severe emotional and physical violation. Survivors often experience depression, fear, and/or anxiety. They may become dependent on alcohol or use illicit substances. Survivors may also experience suicidal thoughts. Many survivors exhibit symptoms of rape trauma syndrome, a form of post-traumatic stress disorder (PTSD). Trauma can result in feelings of helplessness and powerlessness, as well as physical symptoms such as difficulty breathing, vomiting, trembling, outbursts of anger, nightmares, and the inability to remember events. Anxiety and fear may result in the survivor attempting to avoid any situation that could trigger memories.

Rachael White

See also Criminal Sexual Assault or Misconduct; Impact and Consequences (Overview); Laws, Rape; Rape; Rape, Adult

Further Reading

National Institute of Justice & Centers for Disease Control and Prevention (1998). *Prevalence, incidence and consequences of Violence Against Women Survey.* Washington, DC: National Institute of Justice.

U.S. Department of Justice (2005). National Crime Victimization Survey. Washington, DC: Bureau of Justice Statistics.

Selected Websites

National Sexual Violence Resource Center. Retrieved from http://www.nsvrc.org

RAINN (Rape, Abuse & Incest National Network). Retrieved from http://www.rainn.org

Sexual Coercion

Sexual coercion is found on the continuum of sexual violence, which includes more overtly sexually aggressive behaviors such as rape, sexual assault, and sexual abuse.

Sexual coercion, which occurs in heterosexual or nonheterosexual contexts, can be challenging to define because the term covers a variety of covert or subtle tactics and most often occurs in intimate relationships, such as friendships, dating relationships, or marriages. Simply defined, sexual coercion occurs when a person initiates unwanted sexual contact with another person, without that person's consent.

Consent is a clear, voluntary, active, enthusiastic, sober, informed, mutual, honest, and verbal agreement prior to, and during, sexual activity. Consent cannot be coerced and is necessary at every stage of sexual activity, even when partners have been dating, are committed, are married, or have given consent to other forms of sexual contact. Consent cannot be implied and cannot be assumed. Silence and passivity do not equal consent. The absence of clear communication and consent means any sexual contact is nonconsensual.

Sexual coercion occurs when a person uses psychological pressure or physical force to initiate unwanted sexual contact or convince another person to engage in sexual activity when consent has not been given or has been withdrawn. Sexual contact is defined as intentional touching of any person in order to "abuse, humiliate, harass, degrade, or arouse or gratify the sexual desire of any person" (United States Code 18). Sexual activities range from kissing and touching to oral, anal, or vaginal intercourse.

Although there is some overlap, coercive tactics are generally separated into two categories: psychological and physical. Physical coercion includes intimidation, threats, continuing with sexual contact after a person pulls away or indicates that he or she does not consent, holding a person down, using weapons, beating, kicking, and choking. Psychological coercion can be more subtle and includes verbal or emotional manipulation such as threats to leave or withhold love, threats of physical force, threats of harm to oneself, bribery, yelling, tricking, lying, blackmailing, use of guilt, use of authority, and use of intoxication. It is important to clarify that the use of substances to gain sexual access by incapacitating an individual is sexual assault or rape, not coercion. When one provides substances, such as alcohol or drugs, in order to lower inhibitions or takes advantage of a situation in which a person is intoxicated and has lowered inhibitions, it is coercion.

Both males and females can be coercive, although the tactics used to gain sexual access may differ based on the gender of the coercer, the relationship between the individuals, and other factors. Intoxication and verbal coercion are the most common forms of coercion used by both males and females. Evidence suggests that the incidence of sexual coercion depends on situational factors such as opportunity and the risk of being caught or criticized. Some research shows that individuals with antisocial traits may be more likely to be aggressive and therefore more likely to be sexually aggressive.

Regardless of any other factors, researchers agree that social messages influence the coercer as well as the individual who is coerced. Social messages contribute to an environment where both males and females may not be believed when they do not consent to sexual activity, may feel obligated to participate in sexual activity, may feel that sexual activity is something that is required in exchange for other sexual or nonsexual favors, may feel that sexual activity or a particular sex act is the "next step" in a relationship, or may feel as if consent cannot be withdrawn once it has been given. Traditional gender roles are one example of social messages that affect males and females. These gender roles often promote the belief that males initiate sexual activity, always want sex, or are always ready to engage in sexual activity and that females are supposed to resist sexual advances or control male access to sex. These gender roles may support the notion that males are "supposed to" convince females to engage in sexual activities and may cause males to feel guilty or less masculine when they do not want to engage in, or consent to, sexual activity.

It is the responsibility of the person initiating a sexual act to obtain clear consent without coercion. Once consent has been given, a person has the right to change his or her mind without providing an explanation. If a person initiates sexual contact without consent or coerces another person, the act is nonconsensual and may result in sexual assault.

Rachael White

See also Acquaintance Rape; Date Rape; Drug-Facilitated Rape; Intimate Partner Violence; Theory, Continuum of Violence

Further Reading

Bartolucci, A. D., Zeichner, A., & Miller, J. D. (2009). Alcohol consumption and perceived sexual coercion: Effects of gender and personality determinants. *Substance Use & Misuse, 44*(9/10), 1399–1414.

Donovan, B. (2005). Gender inequality and criminal seduction: Prosecuting sexual coercion in the early-20th century. *Law & Social Inquiry, 30*(1), 61–88.

Hartwick, C., Desmarais, S., & Hennig, K. (2007). Characteristics of male and female victims of sexual coercion. *Canadian Journal of Human Sexuality, 16*(1/2), 31–44.

O'Sullivan, L. (2005). Sexual coercion in dating relationships: Conceptual and methodological issues. *Sexual & Relationship Therapy, 20*(1), 3–11.

Platt, J. J., & Busby, D. M. (2009). Male victims: The nature and meaning of sexual coercion. *American Journal of Family Therapy, 37*(3), 217–226.

Struckman-Johnson, C., Struckman-Johnson, D., & Anderson, P. B. (2003). Tactics of sexual coercion: When men and women won't take no for an answer. *Journal of Sex Research, 40*(1), 76.

Selected Websites

Sexual coercion awareness and prevention. Florida Institute of Technology. Retrieved from http://www.fit.edu/caps/documents/SexualCoercion_000.pdf

Shifting the paradigm: Primary prevention of sexual violence toolkit. American College Health Association. Retrieved from http://www.acha.org/SexualViolence

Sexual Freedom

Sexual freedom is the inherent sexual rights as humans to develop and express their sexuality, and includes: (1) the freedom of any sexual thought, fantasy, or desire; (2) the right to engage in sexual acts or activities of any kind whatsoever, providing they do not involve nonconsensual acts, violence, constraint, coercion, or fraud; (3) the right to be free of persecution, condemnation, or discrimination in private sexual behavior; (4) the right to pursue a satisfying consensual sexual life; and (5) the right to control conception (see http://www.iashs.edu/rights .html). These rights are closely tied to women's rights and are sometimes referred to as nonrestrictive sexual norms, sexual liberation, and free love. In addition to providing sexual rights to women, sexual freedom also grants sexual rights to minority groups like homosexuals and transgender individuals.

Historically, women, homosexuals, and transgender individuals were not allowed sexual freedom. Women were traditionally seen as sexually innocent and incapable of enjoying sexually explicit images, casual sex, or sex outside of a romantic relationship. The sexual regulation women experienced was rooted in religious beliefs and practices wherein marriage was viewed as the key to sexual freedom. However, even though society called for sexual restriction, many young adults did not follow that social order. One-third of all eighteenth-century brides in New England were already pregnant at the time of their wedding, demonstrating that although premarital sex was seen as immoral, it was also commonplace.

Additionally, throughout history individuals who partook in same sex relationships were viewed as mentally ill and were often ostracized and "treated" by means of castration, lobotomies, and electroshock therapy. Homosexual relationships were defined as a mental illness until the sexual liberation movement of the 1960s.

In the 1960s and 1970s, the discussion of sexual freedom turned into a movement (sexual liberation movement) that was paired with the women's rights movement and the lesbian and gay rights movements of the time. For those involved in these movements, sexuality was seen as something that individuals had possession of for themselves, and that women should be seen as sexually aware, competent humans who are able to chase their fantasies and seek satisfaction. Additionally, they believed that sexual freedom was a basic human right that needed to be protected by the law, not restricted as it had been in the past. Such ideas about women and sexuality were, and are, revolutionary, challenging the perceived social norms.

The sexual liberation movement sought to challenge sexual double standards, separate sex from procreation and marriage, and help couples understand that sexual pleasure is a critical component of personal happiness and success in marriage. The movement advocated for individuals to explore their sexuality in safe ways by encouraging contraception and practicing safe sex, and advocated for legal sexual rights in the courts. The movement amplified fears of immorality, the link between sex and crime, and what sexual freedom would stand for rape perpetrators.

Although many would argue that the sexual liberation movement is still active, there have been clear victories in the name of sexual freedom thanks to the movement. Generally speaking, women in contemporary Western societies are now able to enjoy the same degree of sexual freedom as men have been able to for years. This is due to a change in attitudes and access to birth control. Many of these changes are also due to the support of the U.S. Supreme Court and their rulings in favor of sexual rights and sexual freedom. Such decisions include *Griswold v. Connecticut* in 1965, which struck down state laws that banned the use of birth control by married couples. In 1972 this decision was expanded to include couples who were not married with the case of *Eisenstadt v. Baird*. In 1967 the court ruled that state laws banning interracial marriage were unconstitutional (*Loving v. Virginia*); and in 1969, the court ruled that the possession of obscene materials in one's home was decided to not be a criminal offense (*Stanley v. Georgia*). The most well-known legal case for sexual rights was the case of *Roe v. Wade* in 1973, which overruled states' restrictions on abortion.

Sexual freedom is a basic human right that allows all people the right to explore their sexuality in a safe way. This right has been carved out in the United States through the liberation movements of the 1960s and the subsequent U.S. Supreme Court cases that supported sexual freedom. Prior to this movement "abnormal" sexual thoughts and behaviors were criminalized, stigmatized, and often diagnosed as a mental illness.

Jennifer A. Martinez

See also Feminism, Influence of

Further Reading

Godbeer, R. (2004). Courtship and sexual freedom in eighteenth-century America. *OAH Magazine of History, 18*(4), 9–11.

Milnes, K. (2004). What lies between romance and sexual equality? A narrative study of young women's sexual experiences. *Sexualities, Evolution & Gender, 6*(2/3), 151–170.

Petersen, P. (1997). Female sexuality: A different position. *Social Alternatives, 16*(1), 43–44.

Self, R. O. (2008). Sex in the city: The politics of sexual liberalism in Los Angeles, 1963–79. *Gender & History, 20*(2), 288–311.

Selected Websites

The Institute for Advanced Study of Human Sexuality. Retrieved from http://www .iashs.edu/rights.html

Woodhull Sexual Freedom Alliance. Retrieved from http://www.woodhullalliance.org/

Sexual Harassment

Sexual harassment is a serious form of violence that is often initiated by boys and men that primarily targets girls and women. Although boys and men may also encounter harassment, it is more probable that girls and women will become the victims of sexual harassment. Patriarchal belief systems support male superiority and entitlement. Such beliefs likely influence communities to tolerate sexual harassment, which, in turn, can result in increased violence that primarily targets girls and women.

The Centers for Disease Control and Prevention (CDC) report that sexual harassment may be either intentional or unintentional, and includes unwanted physical, verbal or nonverbal intimidation. The Collins English dictionary defines sexual harassment as "the persistent unwelcome directing of sexual remarks and looks, and unnecessary physical contact at a person, usually a woman, especially in the workplace." The Equal Employment Opportunity Commission (EEOC) reports that the word "unwelcome" is critical. For complex and multifaceted reasons, victims of sexual harassment may be coerced into actively participating with perpetrators of sexual harassment. In part this may be because victims functioning within their regular and commonplace social environments are perhaps surprised or embarrassed by harassment. Commonplace social environments likely include the home, school, workplace, and public places. Victims who are surprised or embarrassed by sexual harassment will likely internalize feelings as demeaning, fearful, humiliating, or perhaps with indignation. However, onlookers may observe victims who appear to consent, and go along with the perpetrators of sexual harassment perhaps because of feelings that may include shame and embarrassment.

Sexual harassment comprises unwanted physical, verbal or nonverbal, intimidation. Examples that encompass physical intimidation may include unnecessary and deliberate physical contact including actual or attempted rape or sexual assault, and sexual touching. Harassment may include standing too close, touching or rubbing oneself sexually against another person, deliberately brushing up against another, intense staring, or looking at another person up and down, that is, "elevator eyes." Other examples include touching another's clothing, hair, or body, including neck massage, stroking, hugging, kissing, or patting. Deliberately blocking another's path, which may prevent another from exiting, and purposefully following another are additional examples of sexual harassment with physical contact. Sexual harassment can also be evidenced through facial expressions that include winking and leering. Finally, sexually graphic signaling that includes sexually explicit gestures through body movements and with hands is another example of harassment.

Additionally, sexual harassment may include unwelcome sexually explicit verbal communications. Examples of verbal communications may include requests for dates, sexual favors, or sexual intercourse. Similarly, personal questions may be asked targeting daily living that incorporate sexual innuendos or stories, along with requests for sexual fantasies, sexual preferences, or sexual history. Likewise, examples of harassment may include sexual comments directed at clothing, anatomy, or looks. Correspondingly, harassment likely includes sexually explicit teasing and jokes. In addition harassment may include misleading remarks that spread rumors and lie about victims' private sex lives. Verbal harassment may also include work-related discussions that are turned into sexual topics. Further examples may include uninvited telephone calls, voice mails, songs, and jokes. Moreover, examples of unwanted verbal harassment likely also incorporate "wolf" whistles, howling, catcalls, kissing sounds, and smacking lips. Also included with verbal sexual harassment is addressing women as girls, honeys, babes, and dolls, and addressing men as hunks. Furthermore, verbal sexual harassment may include invitation to participate in graphic, tawdry gender-typed video games, watching pornographic movies, or discussion of pornographic photographs.

Alternatively, nonverbal sexual harassment may include a variety of sexually suggestive visuals. Examples of nonverbal suggestive visuals may include electronic e-mails, tweeting, and texting. Sexual harassment may also include nonverbal aggression that includes sexual looks and gestures. Finally, sexual harassment may include loitering, or giving unwanted personal gifts.

According to the EEOC, even though there are no laws that protect victims from isolated instances of inappropriate physical, verbal or nonverbal sexual harassment there are laws that do protect individuals from frequent and prolonged sexual harassment. Included among the protective laws are Title VII of the Civil Rights Act of 1964, and Title 29, Labor Chapter XIV, Part 1604.11 sexual harassment. Correspondingly, even though legal prosecution may not be possible for victims with sexual harassment there are appropriate steps that are advisable. For some victims of harassment the first step is acknowledging the reality that sexual harassment is occurring. Admission of harassment may be difficult because of feelings already mentioned that include embarrassment, shame, and guilt. Also, some victims may believe that they are to blame or somehow deserve the harassment. However, keeping sexual harassment a secret will almost certainly prolong unwanted and offensive behaviors. Consequently, it is important to recognize that no one deserves sexual harassment and that finding *professional* help is critical.

Individuals who attempt ending sexual harassment on their own are likely at risk. Consequently, professional advocacy is safer and the preferable choice for solving the serious problems of sexual harassment.

Conclusively, sexual harassment incorporates unwanted physical, verbal or nonverbal, intimidation. Included among the laws that protect individuals from sexual harassment are Title VII of the Civil Rights Act of 1964, and Title 29, Labor Chapter XIV, Part 1604.11 sexual harassment. Sexual harassment likely increases when individuals and communities tolerate harassment. Finding *professional* help and taking collective actions that stop sexual harassment are critical for resolution of this serious issue.

Hazel Jamieson

See also Laws, Rape; Sexual Harassment at Work; Theory, Continuum of Violence

Further Reading

Centers for Disease Control and Prevention (n.d.). Sexual violence. Retrieved from http://www.cdc.gov/ViolencePrevention/sexualviolence/

Equal Employment Opportunity Commission (n.d.). Sexual harrassment. Retrieved from http://www.eeoc.gov/laws/types/sexual_harassment.cfm

Equal Employment Opportunity Commission (n.d.). Title VII of the Civil Rights Act of 1964. Retrieved from http://www.eeoc.gov/laws/statutes/titlevii.cfm

Equal Employment Opportunity Commission (n.d.). Title 29—Labor Chapter XIV—Equal Employment Opportunity Commission Part 1604.11 Guidelines on Discrimination Because of Sex. Retrieved from http://www.access.gpo.gov/nara/cfr/waisidx_09/29cfr1604_09.html

Sexual Harassment at Work

Sexual harassment in the workplace refers to unwanted sexual attention by a coworker, a supervisor, or other individuals who enter the workplace (such as customers, vendors). Workplace sexual harassment includes a work environment that is hostile or discriminatory toward one gender over another. In October 1991, a historic complaint of workplace sexual harassment was made by Anita Hill in testimony to the U.S. Senate Judiciary Committee against the nomination of Clarence Thomas to the U.S. Supreme Court. Following the nationally televised hearings, public awareness on workplace sexual harassment increased as did complaints of sexual harassment.

Workplace sexual harassment occurs between individuals of the same sex or of the opposite sex, although the predominantly reported incidents involve a male harassing a female. A survey of active-duty members in the U.S. armed forces that found 24 percent of the women and 3 percent of the men reported sexual harassment while at work (Lipari & Lancaster, 2003). Sexual harassment in the general population has been reported by 42 percent of women and 15 percent of men in work settings (Charney & Russel, 1994). Sexual harassment has been reported as a common experience for adolescent girls (63%) and for boys (37%) who are working part-time while in school (Fineran, 2002).

Sexual harassment at work falls under specific federal and state laws covering the workplace. Sexual harassment in the workplace is a form of discrimination based on sex as defined in federal law, Title VII of the Civil Rights Act of 1964. Title VII prohibits employment discrimination based on race, color, religion, sex, and national origin in workplaces with at least 15 employees. Workplace discrimination laws relate to youth who are in the workforce as well as adults. In conjunction with federal law, states address employment discrimination in its two forms of quid pro quo and hostile environment.

The quid pro quo form of sexual harassment refers to unwelcomed sexual advances or demands for sexual favors as a condition of employment or benefits. Other characteristics of the quid pro quo form of sexual harassment include severe or pervasive conduct that has a negative effect on the employee's work performance; the harassment is known or should have been known to the supervisor or employer; and the targeted employee experiences some form of jeopardy to her or his employment if and when she or he refuses.

The hostile-environment form of sexual harassment refers to unwelcomed sexual conduct that is so severe or widespread that the targeted employee's work environment is negatively affected, detracting the employee from his or her work and jeopardizing his or her performance. A hostile environment can be experienced by a targeted individual or by others who witness or experience the ongoing intimidation that makes up the sexual harassment.

Employers experience financial consequences from workplace sexual harassment due to the employee's increased health needs, his or her absence, and low productivity. The workplace may experience low morale particularly in incidents of bystander knowledge and witness of the harassment. An employer's company policies and state or federal laws hold employers accountable for the actions of their employees and for any response or lack of response to sexual harassment complaints.

The consequences of sexual harassment vary for adults and adolescents in the workplace. Adult women who were targets of workplace sexual harassment have reported health effects such as loss of sleep, low self-esteem, chronic physical symptoms, work stress, less satisfaction with work, and depression. Beyond the impact on health and well-being, economic consequences for the harassed worker include job loss or job departure and loss of promotions or benefits. Adult employees have reported sexual harassment by their peers, supervisors, clients/patients, and vendors who frequent the workplace. Experiences of sexual harassment on the job include unwanted sexual jokes, whistles, staring, fondling, unwanted touching, being asked out on a date when unwanted, insulting attitudes toward one's gender, sexual coercion (quid pro quo), and sexual assault to name a few.

Adolescents working while in school report sexual harassment by coworkers and adult supervisors impacting their academic performance and interest in school and their education. Girls report work stress and experiences such as groping, sexual remarks, and text messaging of sexual content. In addition, sexual coercion and sexual assault have been the experience of adolescent girls and boys in the workplace.

The remedies for sexual harassment include personal response, employer response, and legal response. The individual being targeted with sexual harassment can inform the harasser to stop the unwelcomed conduct and then document the incidents of harassment according to her or his employer's procedures for filing a complaint of workplace sexual harassment. Support for victims of sexual harassment is available through sexual assault counselors based in the community and employee assistance programs. Deadlines for filing of formal complaints under the federal and state laws vary and need to be taken into consideration by the victim if legal action is desired. The law and subsequent rulings by the courts have provided guidance to employers in developing appropriate sexual harassment policies and procedures to respond to complaints, and to lessen the support for hostile work environments.

Filing a complaint with the EEOC does not preclude a victim from reporting the incident to the proper law enforcement officials. A small percentage of the victims of sexual harassment file a formal complaint with their employer and even fewer file with the EEOC. Victims of sexual harassment more often choose to dismiss the incidents, cope with the harassment, or distance themselves by leaving their employment, or transferring to another work site or department. Leaving employment or transferring departments is less feasible for victims of sexual harassment who have less opportunity for a comparable job, limited education or training to change careers, and are reliant on benefits the employment provides for themselves and their family, such as health care or child care.

Education and behavior reinforcements that lessen workplace sexual harassment and increase civility and nondiscrimination are common components of workplace prevention programs. A combination of efforts by an employer such as policy, procedures, training, and quick response to complaints builds a stronger workplace response to sexual harassment.

Deborah V. Svoboda

See also Rape Justification; Sexual Harassment; Theory, Feminist; Theory, Male Peer Support; Theory, Masculinity

Further Reading

Charney, D. A., & Russel, R. C. (1994). An overview of sexual harassment. *The American Journal of Psychiatry, 151*(1), 10–17.

Crossing the line: Sexual harassment at school (2011). American Association of University Women (Educational Fund). Retrieved from http://www.aauw.org/learn/research

Fineran, S. (2002). Adolescents at work: Gender issues and sexual harassment. *Violence Against Women, 8*, 953–967.

Lipari, R. N., & Lancaster, A. R. (2003). *Armed forces 2002 sexual harassment survey* (DMDC Rep. No. 2003-026). Arlington, VA: Defense Manpower Data Center.

Selected Websites

Legal Momentum (n.d.). Women at work. The Women's Legal Defense and Education Fund. Retrieved from http://www.legalmomentum.org/our-work/women-at-work/

U.S. Equal Employment Opportunity Commission (n.d.). Sexual harassment. Retrieved from http://www.eeoc.gov/laws/types/sexual_harassment.cfm

Sexually Acting Out

Following an experience of sexually violent victimization (i.e., child sexual abuse or adult sexual victimization), a person might experience emotional problems and behavioral difficulties, including sexually acting-out behaviors. Such behaviors can be detrimental to the victim and may involve hurting others. Even though adolescents and adults might also manifest sexually acting-out or inappropriate behaviors, sexually acting out is primarily recognized in children. Thus this entry also reflects this recognition. Readers should also be mindful that not all victims of child sexual abuse or adult sexual violence exhibit sexually acting-out behaviors. In addition, not all persons who have these behaviors have been sexually victimized.

Sexually acting out can be defined as a set of sexualized behaviors that are not developmentally appropriate or that are not within the normally accepted range of behaviors. In children, these behaviors often include age-inappropriate sexual knowledge, making sexually explicit drawings, sexual aggression toward peers or younger children, and excessive masturbation or masturbation to the point of injury. Among adolescents and adults, sexually acting out often manifests as high-risk sexual behaviors, such as impulsive sex or prostitution. Sexually acting out typically involves compulsion, coercion or force with another person, or lack of response to external corrective actions, such as a child who masturbates frequently in the classroom despite redirection from caregivers and teachers. It is important to distinguish sexually acting-out behaviors, such as sex play with children of different ages and/or sizes that may involve coercion or force (e.g., an older child who is larger in size forcing a younger and smaller child to be touched in the genitals), from those that are considered culturally and developmentally appropriate, such as play with same-age peers revolving around sexual curiosity and exploration (e.g., the game of "doctor" in which both children are exploring the human body with curiosity and joy).

Sexually acting-out behaviors have generally been recognized as a reaction to child sexual or physical abuse. One study found that among a sample of 37 young children with sexual behavior problems, 38 percent had histories of substantiated sexual abuse, 47 percent had experienced physical abuse, and 58 percent had witnessed interparental violence, with 11 percent having none of these histories (Silovsky & Niec, 2002). Other potential contributing factors include family dynamics and parenting practices, such as the parents' attitudes toward sexuality and nudity or use of sexual expressions in anger, exposure to traumatic events, and media exposure, such as movies or music videos with developmentally inappropriate sexual content. Sexually acting-out behaviors may also present in persons with cognitive or developmental disabilities and are often related to problems with impulse control, communication skills, or socialization. Persons with such disabilities might receive reduced or no information or exposure to sexual education and social norms regarding sexuality, which might contribute to inappropriate behaviors. In sum, sexually acting-out behaviors occur in response to various contributing factors.

Little is known about the actual prevalence of sexually acting out among children, which is in part due to the varying definitions for these behaviors and difficulty collecting data on sexually acting-out behaviors. Though sexually acting out among children is associated with different forms of child maltreatment, children who have been sexually abused are more likely to exhibit sexual behavior problems than their peers who have not been sexually abused (Kendall-Tackett, Williams, & Finkelhor, 1993). In addition and in comparison to boys, girls with sexual behavior problems were more likely to have been sexually abused (Silovksy & Niec, 2002).

Although child sexual abuse victimization is higher among adult sexual offenders than nonsexual offenders, most persons who were victims of child sexual abuse will not become adult sexual offenders. Children who engage in sexual behavior problems typically respond well to treatment. After successful completion of treatment, these children do not have higher risk of sexual offenses than their non-sexually acting-out peers (Chaffin et al., 2008).

Professionals with expertise in child development, sexuality, and victimization should assess sexually acting-out behaviors to determine if the behaviors are within the normal range or if they are of concern. One assessment tool for sexually acting-out behaviors is the Child Sexual Behavior Inventory (Friedrich, n.d.). This tool may be used with children between 2 and 12 years of age to assess the types and frequency of sexualized behaviors and interests. The results can be compared to developmental and gender norms to distinguish inappropriate or concerning behaviors from typical or normal behaviors. As stated above, sexually acting-out behaviors among children do not necessarily indicate child sexual abuse. Thus assessments should consider but not assume that child sexual abuse has occurred when assessing children who are sexually acting out. Professionals and mandated reporters should follow their community's child maltreatment reporting guidelines, including contacting Child Protective Services to assess for child maltreatment.

Professionals with expertise in child development, sexuality, and victimization should also conduct the treatment of sexually acting-out behaviors. Most sexually acting-out behaviors can be addressed with behavior management techniques. Before such treatment techniques are used however, trust should be established between the professional and victim before any discussion of violence, victimization, and trauma. Common reactions to child sexual abuse can include self-blame or guilt, and these issues should be addressed first. One effective treatment that addresses sexually acting-out behaviors with child sexual abuse victims is trauma-focused cognitive behavioral therapy (see National Child Traumatic Stress Network website listed at the end of this entry for more information).

Sexually acting out is commonly found in children who have experienced some form of trauma, most often sexual or physical abuse. This set of behaviors can be treated through mental health interventions that address the specific behaviors as well as any underlying trauma, and with appropriate treatment, most children who sexually act out will not continue these behaviors into adolescence and adulthood. However, many adolescent and adult sexual offenders do report sexual behavior problems in childhood and adolescence. Further, children who exhibit sexually acting-out behaviors may experience developmental and socialization difficulties related or in addition to the sexualized behaviors. Thus there is a critical need to address sexually acting-out behaviors as they arise in childhood.

McLean D. Pollock

See also Child Sexual Abuse; Prostitution; Reporting, Mandated; Sexual Coercion

Further Reading

Chaffin, M., Berliner, L., Block, R., Johnson, T. C., Friedrich, W. N., Louis, D. G., . . . Madden, C. (2008). Report of the ATSA task force on children with sexual behavior problems. *Child Maltreatment, 13*(2), 199–218. doi:10.1177/1077559507306718

Faller, K. C. (1993) *Child sexual abuse: Intervention and treatment issues.* Retrieved from http://www.childwelfare.gov/pubs/usermanuals/sexabuse/sexabusec.cfm

Friedrich, W. N. (n.d.). Child Sexual Behavior Inventory (CSBI). PAR, Inc. Retrieved from http://www4.parinc.com/Products/Product.aspx?ProductID=CSBI

Gil, E., & Johnson, T. C. (1993). *Sexualized children: Assessment and treatment of sexualized children and children who molest.* Rockville, MD: Launch Press.

Kendall-Tackett, K. A., Williams, L. M., & Finkelhor, D. (1993). Impact of sexual abuse on children: A review and synthesis of recent empirical studies. *Psychological Bulletin, 113*(1), 164–180. Retrieved from http://www.ipce.info/library_3/pdf/impact.pdf

Lamb, S. (2006). *Sex, therapy, and kids: Addressing their concerns through talk and play.* New York, NY: Norton.

Silovsky, J. F., & Niec, L. (2002). Characteristics of young children with sexual behavior problems: A pilot study. *Child Maltreatment, 7*(3), 187–197. doi:10.1177/1077559502007003002

Selected Websites

Association for the Treatment of Sexual Abusers (ATSA). Retrieved from http://www.atsa.com

Child sexual abuse. The Canadian Child Welfare Research Portal. Retrieved from http://www.cwrp.ca/child-abuse-neglect/sexual-abuse

National Center on Sexual Behavior of Youth (NCSBY). Retrieved from http://www.ncsby.org

National Child Traumatic Stress Network (NCTSN). Retrieved from http://www.nctsnet.org

Sibling Abuse, Defining

Sibling abuse is defined as a repeated pattern of aggression toward a sibling with the intent to inflict harm, motivated by an internal emotional need for power and control (Caffaro & Conn Caffaro, 1998.) Sibling abuse is said to be the most common form of family violence, more common than child abuse by parents or abuse between adults. One current study reports that 42 percent of children interviewed had experienced some form of sibling abuse in the past month (Button & Gealt, 2010). However, previous studies suggest higher rates of sibling abuse. Past findings show that approximately 65 percent of children between the ages of 9 and 18 experience some form of sibling aggression (Button & Gealt, 2010). Acts of abuse between siblings may be physical, psychological, or sexual in nature. Psychological abuse may be present in both spoken and unspoken forms, may be used alone, or may accompany physically and sexually abusive behaviors. The discrepancy over what constitutes sibling abuse stems from the mind-set that sibling conflict is a normal part of development. As a result, abusive relationships between siblings are often overlooked. To determine the difference between a developmentally normal sibling conflict and an abusive situation, the emotional and physical impact, severity, and intent of the interaction must be taken into consideration.

Common and recurrent forms of physical abuse among siblings involve actions such as pushing, shoving, hitting, slapping, biting, pinching, hair pulling, scratching, and kicking. Less common forms of physical abuse include the use of objects such as hoses, hangers, and brushes, or weapons such as knives, guns, and razor blades to inflict harm. Some abused siblings have also been subject to drowning, suffocating with a pillow, and being hit in the stomach until they lose their breath.

Psychological abuse among siblings includes ridicule through words and actions, belittling, intimidation, scorn, provocation, verbal abuse, threats, destroying possessions, and torturing or killing pets. The abusive actions involve feelings of contempt and the use of fear on the part of the perpetrator and result in a feeling of degradation on the part of the sibling being abused.

Sexual abuse within sibling relationships, or sibling incest, may be the most common form of sexual abuse within the immediate family. Cases of sibling incest are often seen as a mistake or as part of normal childhood and adolescent development. However, sexually abusive behaviors go beyond developmentally normal mutual sex play, which is based on curiosity and self-exploration with increasing levels of exploration, experimentation, and peer contact over time. Sexual abuse is impulsive, compulsive, and aggressive, lacks consent and equality, and results in feelings of anger, sadness, fear, shame, humiliation, and guilt in the child who did not initiate the behavior. Sexual abuse is not limited to intercourse and may include unwanted sexual advances, sexual leers, or forcing a sibling to view pornographic material. Perpetrators may use physical force, coercion, manipulation, pressure, threats, and/or secrecy to maintain the sexually abusive relationship.

Abusive sibling relationships most commonly involve dyads of younger aged siblings, with the occurrence of sibling abuse decreasing as children get older. Most common are situations in which an older sibling is abusing a younger sibling. Although the abused sibling may be a boy or a girl, the perpetrator is more likely to be a boy. Abusive dyads involving two brothers as well as an older sibling-younger sibling dynamic are found to be most violent. Sexual abuse among siblings most often occurs between an older brother and younger sister, with the brother as perpetrator. Male-male sibling sexual abuse is thought to be the least commonly occurring. However, the level of shame and embarrassment felt by the abused male child may outweigh his desire to disclose the occurrence of abuse, leaving the possibility that male-male sibling sexual abuse occurs more commonly than believed.

These children often develop issues with trust and openness and may have difficulty understanding family relationships. Physical violence has been linked to feelings of insecurity and incompetence in abused children. Children who have been abused by siblings may experience negative health and behavioral outcomes later in life, including habit disorders, conduct disorders, neurotic traits, sexual problems, and increased likelihood for involvement in violent relationships.

Both the perpetrator and victim of sibling abuse are likely to act out, have nightmares and phobias, do poorly in school, and experience depression, aggressiveness, apathy, confusion, isolation, and low self-esteem, which may lead to an increased risk of suicide. The presence of abusive sibling relationships has also been linked to increased substance use, aggression, and delinquency. Abusive sibling relationships may also be linked to the presence of school violence, dating violence, intimate partner violence, and family violence in adulthood.

Sibling abuse most often takes place within families where high levels of disorganization and chaos exist, or where intimate partner violence and other forms of child abuse are already present. Low socioeconomic status, lack of employment, volatile marital status among parents, and a lack of community and family support systems have been associated with an increase in the prevalence of sibling abuse in families. Isolation, secrecy, strict gender roles, power imbalances, poor communication, unclear family roles, and normalization of abusive behaviors within the family structure also affect the frequency and intensity of sibling abuse.

Ignoring abusive behaviors, failure to intervene to stop abusive behaviors, and blaming the abused child for the behavior taking place create a prime environment for abusive relationships to continue. However, families can play a large role in the prevention of abuse if they believe the reporting child, provide adequate supervision for their children when they are not able to be present, provide appropriate-level sexual education and information about sexual relationships, teach children that they own their own bodies, and ensure a violence-free home setting.

Gretchen L. Hoge

See also Impact, Family; Incest; Sexually Acting Out; Sibling Abuse, Identifying and Impact of

Further Reading

Bass, L. B., Taylor, B. A., Knudson-Martin, C., & Huenergardt, D. (2010). *Making sense of abuse: Cases studies of sibling incest. Contemporary Family Therapy, 28*(1), 87–109.

Button, D. M., & Gealt, R. (2010). *High risk behaviors among victims of sibling violence. Journal of Family Violence, 25,* 131–140.

Caffaro, J. V., & Conn-Caffaro, A. (1998). *Sibling abuse trauma: Assessment and intervention strategies for children, families, and adults.* New York, NY: Haworth Press.

Eriksen, S., & Jensen, V. (2006). *All in the family? Family environment factors in sibling violence. Journal of Family Violence, 21,* 497–507.

Kiselica, M. S., & Morrill-Richards, M. (2007). *Sibling maltreatment: The Forgotten abuse. Journal of Counseling & Development, 85,* 148–160.

Straus, M. A., Gelles, R. J., & Steinmetz, S. K. (1980). *Behind closed doors: Violence in the American family.* Garden City, NY: Doubleday.

Selected Websites

Sibling abuse. Out of the FOG. Retrieved from http://www.outofthefog.net/Relationships/SiblingAbuse.html

Sibling abuse. YourChild: Development & Behavior Resources: A Guide to Information & Support for Parents. University of Michigan Health System. Retrieved from http://www.med.umich.edu/yourchild/topics/sibabuse.htm

Sibling rivalry or abuse. A-Better-Child.org. Retrieved from http://www.a-better-child.org/page/873183

Sibling Abuse, Identifying and Impact of

Sibling abuse is the physical, emotional, or sexual abuse of one sibling by another. Some level of sibling rivalry is expected, which is why abuse of a sibling often goes undetected or is misunderstood by parents and other adults. Sibling abuse typically involves multiple types of abuse. Sexual abuse and emotional abuse go hand in hand, as emotional abuse is often used to bully the victim into the sexual act. It has been estimated that over 29 million children commit an act of violence against a sibling each year (Straus & Gelles, 1988), making sibling abuse the most common form of family violence. Abuse can happen between any sibling groups, such as biological siblings, foster siblings, or step-siblings.

Fights between siblings are inevitable, making it important, yet difficult, to distinguish between fights and abuse. Abuse is a pattern of controlling behavior from one sibling to another. While this could be over a short period such as a few months, often the abuse lasts for months, years, or even throughout the life span of the siblings. Emotional abuse may be characterized by name-calling, belittling, or provoking the victim into reacting physically or verbally. Physical abuse includes hitting, slapping, biting, or more violent forms of abuse such as choking or using objects such as a bat or knife. Sexual abuse is also present in some cases, including indecent exposure, sodomy, molestation, or rape.

Identifying sibling abuse can be extremely difficult as the behaviors are usually hidden by the perpetrator and the victim is threatened if he or she reveals what is happening. The result is that abuse can appear to be sibling rivalry. Factors that help distinguish between normal behaviors and abuse include the duration of the abuse and any behavioral patterns. Typically, the abusive behaviors will last for years, or indefinitely without intervention. The abusive sibling will exhibit a pattern of control over the victimized sibling, while the victim may fight back or submit to the abuse. Though it can be difficult to identify abuse because the behaviors are typically hidden, sometimes the abuse becomes evident by the reaction of the victim sibling. The victim may internalize the abuse, becoming depressed or anxious. When the victim fights back, it may look like sibling rivalry; with abuse, the perpetrator will consistently be the instigator and antagonist, though these behaviors may be committed when no adults are observing. Sometimes, as a result of the abuse, the victim will begin using abusive behaviors toward a different, younger sibling.

Sexual abuse does not happen alone, but usually in combination with emotional abuse and sometimes physical abuse. Sexual abuse includes various forms of touching, from fondling or molestation to penetration or rape. Alternatively, the abuse may not involve any touching, but can happen when one sibling forces another to watch pornography or when the sibling watches the other undressing or showering. Victims are often coerced into action through threats, or by using emotional manipulation. Frequently, victims are belittled and made to feel bad about themselves, making them vulnerable to the abuser. After the sexual abuse occurs, the abuser might threaten to harm the victim if he or she tells an adult, or the abuser might convince the victim that he or she is responsible for what happened. Most victims do not tell anyone about the abuse.

Some sexual exploration is normal between siblings. The key to normal behavior is whether it is age appropriate. Normal behavior may include a preschooler who is curious about a baby sibling's genitals or wants to play doctor with other children. Concerning behavior might be when an elementary school-age child pretends to have intercourse or wants to watch adults in the bathroom, as this may be a sign that a child has been victimized. Many child victims of sexual abuse will exhibit an advanced knowledge of sexual behaviors relative to their age, and they may try to act on some of these behaviors with other siblings or peers. Furthermore, while some sexual behavior is normal between siblings, the behavior must be consensual. If one sibling is threatening, manipulating, pressuring, or otherwise coercing the other sibling into any sexual act, the behavior is abusive.

Sibling abuse, including sexual abuse, can have lasting effects on the survivors. Survivors have been shown to exhibit problems of low self-esteem, depression, and anxiety. Some experience more serious mental illness such as post-traumatic stress disorder, dissociative identity disorder, and suicidal thoughts. Furthermore, survivors often struggle in intimate relationships, characterized by difficulties with trust. In some cases survivors develop problems with alcohol and drug addiction or eating disorders. Many survivors feel a deep sense of shame and even blame themselves for the abuse.

Adult survivors of sibling abuse may continue to experience difficulties either in their marriage and parenting or with their family of origin. As child survivors grow up and become parents themselves, they may experience difficulty and anxiety in parenting their own children. While some survivors are able to maintain some level of contact with the offending family member, many struggle with this and other family relationships. In some cases the abuse goes undisclosed, which can further resentment toward adults who did not intervene or cause discomfort when interacting with the abuser at family events. Individual therapy and support groups for survivors can be helpful in assisting survivors to process the abuse and move toward a healthy adult life.

Sibling abuse has not had the same focus as abuse perpetrated by an adult in child protection, in the legal arena, or in research. Police may advise against using the child protection system, the parents may be unwilling to press charges against one of their children, and the response taken by child protective systems varies by state and by their understanding of such behaviors. Of the few states with policies to allow investigations of sibling abuse, many consider sibling abuse to be less serious than child abuse perpetrated by parents. Only a small percentage of research on child sexual abuse includes information on sibling perpetrators; however, sibling abusers often commit a great number of offenses toward a sibling because he or she has ready access to the victim.

Corinne D. Warrener

See also Child Sexual Abuse; Child Sexual Abuse, Adult Survivors of; Incest; Sexually Acting Out Sibling Abuse, Defining

Further Reading

Butler, K. (2006, February 28). Beyond rivalry, a hidden world of sibling violence. *New York Times.*

Caffaro, J. V., & Conn-Caffaro, A. (1998). *Sibling abuse trauma: Assessment and intervention strategies for children, families, and adults.* Binghamton, NY: Haworth Press.

Straus, M., & Gelles, R. (1988). How violent are American families: Estimates from the national family violence survey and other studies. In G. T. Hotaling, D. Finkelhor, M. A. Straus, & J. T. Kirkpatrick (Eds.), *Family abuse and its consequences: New directions in research* (pp. 14–36). Beverly Hills, CA: Sage.

Wiehe, V. R. (1997). *Sibling abuse: Hidden physical, emotional, and sexual trauma* (2nd ed.). Thousand Oaks, CA: Sage.

Selected Websites

Sibling abuse. Your Child: Development & Behavior Resources: A Guide to Information & Support for Parents. University of Michigan Health System. Retrieved from http://www.med.umich.edu/yourchild/topics/sibabuse.htm

Sibling sexual abuse and incest during childhood. Pandora's Project. Retrieved from http://www.pandys.org/articles/siblingsexualabuse.html

Simple Rape

Simple rape is a term commonly used to describe a rape or sexual assault by a lone acquaintance with no weapon, resulting in no clearly visible evidence of physical injury. None of the features that are present in aggravated rape—extrinsic violence, multiple offenders, or offenders who are strangers to the victim—are present in cases of simple rape. The distinction between simple rape and aggravated rape is not defined in modern law. Evidence suggests, however, that simple rape is viewed differently than other forms of rape by the public and is treated differently in the court of law. Victims of simple rape are less likely to report the crime, the character of victims is thought to be scrutinized more, and offenders are considered less likely to be convicted or receive as severe of a conviction in the court of law.

Most sexual assaults can be classified as simple rapes; few cases of rape involve the use weapons by an offender or result in clearly visible physical injury. Also, most rapes are carried out by nonstrangers, such as former or current intimate partner, coworker, neighbor, acquaintance, or relative. Among college women who are victims of rape or attempted rape, over 90 percent of victims know the offender, commonly a classmate, friend, boyfriend, ex-boyfriend, or other acquaintance (Fisher, Cullen, & Turner, 2000). Over 80 percent of these college rape victims experience no additional injuries commonly reported in aggravated rape, such as bruises, black eyes, cuts, swelling, or a chipped tooth. A rape victim's condition or behavior does not cause simple rape, but certain factors appear to increase a victim's vulnerability to it, including excessive drinking, being single, socialization with sexually predatory men, presence at an isolated site, miscommunication about sex, or holding less conservative views about sex. Studies using crime data over several decades find that cases of simple rape where the offender is known to the victim are less likely to be reported to the police than are rape cases committed by strangers. Recent studies have found that women who are victims of simple rape are up to seven times less likely to report the crime than are victims of other forms of rape (Clay-Warner & Burt, 2005).

The concept of simple rape was first introduced when studying jury behavior. Jurors in rape cases were found to blame offenders less when the victim had engaged in "contributory behavior," such as hitchhiking, dating, or talking during a party (Kalven & Zeisel, 1966). These researchers proposed the liberation hypothesis, which states that when jurors are presented with cases of ambiguous evidence they are liberated from legal objectivity and become influenced by their personal biases about gender expectations and sexual assault. Several decades later, researchers asserted that outcomes of simple rape, unlike other forms of rape, would greatly depend on characteristics of the victim. Because simple rapes are not considered by many as "real rapes," the credibility and trustworthiness of the victim play an especially important role in sentencing and determining guilt. For example, if a woman was raped by her boyfriend without a weapon and resulting in no visible injury, her behavior, character, and background may unfairly bias the outcome of the case. Blaming the victim in cases of simple rape is known in social psychology as "the rape perception framework." Recent experimental studies have confirmed that factors such as victim's respectability, physical attractiveness, previous sexual activity, victim resistance, victim intoxication, and victim clothing, all influence the tendency to blame the victim and that victims who are acquainted with their attacker tend to be assigned more responsibility for their rape (Grubb & Harrower, 2008).

In the late 1960s, a coalition of feminists and other concerned citizens pushed to increase the reporting and conviction of rapes, particularly simple rapes, through the passing of rape reform laws. The reforms explicitly intended to reduce the distinction between simple rape and other forms of rape and address the discriminatory legal treatment of victims of rape uncovered during the studying of simple rape. These reforms expanded the definition of rape, eliminated the requirement that the victim prove resistance, and created the rape shield laws that prohibited the victim's entering past sexual conduct and evidence of character and reputation into cross-examination. These reforms are credited for the increase in total rape reporting; however, when compared to other forms of rape, cases of simple rape remain underreported and both victims and offenders continue to be perceived differently by the public and criminal court (Clay-Warner & Burt, 2005).

Louis Donnelly

See also Acquaintance Rape; Date Rape; Laws, Rape; Rape Myths; "Real Rape" and Blaming Victims; "Real Rape" and "Real Victims"—Correcting Misinformation

Further Reading

Clay-Warner, J., & Burt, C. H. (2005). Rape reporting after reforms: Have times really changed? *Violence Against Women, 11*(2), 150–176.

Estrich, S. (1987). *Real rape: How the legal system victimizes women who say no.* Cambridge, MA: Harvard University Press.

Fisher, B. S., Cullen, F. T., & Turner, M. G. (2000). *The sexual victimization of college women.* Washington, DC: U.S. Department of Justice, National Institute of Justice and Bureau of Justice Statistics.

Grubb, A., & Harrower, J. (2008). Attribution of blame in cases of simple rape: An analysis of participant gender, type of rape, and perceived similarity to the victim. *Aggression and Violent Behavior, 13*(5), 396–405.

Kalven, H., & Zeisel, H. (1966). *The American jury.* Boston, MA: Little, Brown.

Tellis, K. M., & Spohn, C. C. (2008). The sexual stratification hypothesis revisited: Testing assumptions about simple versus aggravated rape. *Journal of Criminal Justice, 36*(3), 252–261.

Social Norms Approach

The social norms model is an emerging approach to violence prevention showing promise in reducing men's violence and supported by extensive research

(Berkowitz, 2010). This research suggests that most males are uncomfortable with the language and behaviors of the minority of men who commit sexual violence but do not act on these beliefs or express their discomfort because of the false perception that they are in the minority. Thus men overestimate both the extent to which other men are sexually active and other men's adherence to rape myths, as well as other men's willingness to intervene to prevent a sexual assault.

A characteristic finding was reported in Loh, Gidycz, Lobo, & Luthra (2005):

> Compared to themselves, participants believed that the average college man demonstrated more rape-myth acceptance, was less likely to intervene in situations where a woman was being mistreated, and was more comfortable in situations where women are being mistreated. (p. 1334)

A consequence of these misperceptions is that men and boys keep their true feelings to themselves and do not act on them, becoming bystanders and passive observers of other men's problem behaviors. A parallel phenomenon is that men who engage abusive behaviors toward women overestimate the extent of other men's violence, a misperception that allows them in turn to justify their own abusive behavior.

The social norms approach has been used in health media campaigns and in small-group workshop settings, resulting in positive changes in men's attitudes, willingness to act on antiviolence norms, and increased discomfort with other men's sexism. As predicted by the model, the correction of men's misperceptions of other men is correlated with positive outcomes. In one study in which college men were taught bystander intervention skills and given feedback about accurate group norms, sexual assaults were reduced at four-month follow-up in comparison with a control group (Gidycz, Orchowski, & Berkowitz, 2012).

Social norms interventions require that data be collected about actual and perceived norms. The actual norms are then reported back to the target population. By informing the positive majority that they are not alone in their beliefs and desired actions, permission is given to act on them. Thus men and boys are provided with an incentive to censor and express discomfort with the attitudes and behaviors of other males that embody "rape culture."

The process of asking the right questions, collecting data, presenting it in a manner that is believable and relevant, and addressing skepticism that arises when accurate norms are disseminated require training and familiarity with social norms theory and with common implementation failures. With this in mind, the social norms approach can be a powerful tool for fostering male ally behavior and can be used to design effective interventions to end men's violence that complement other violence prevention strategies.

Alan D. Berkowitz

See also Coaching Boys into Men (Program); The Men's Program; Prevention, Involving Men; Rape Myths

Further Reading

Berkowitz, A. D. (2010). Fostering health norms to prevent violence and abuse: The social norms approach. In K. Kaufman (Ed.), *The prevention of sexual violence: A practitioner's sourcebook* (pp. 147–171). Holyoke, MA: NEARI Press.

Berkowitz, A. D. (2011). Using how college men feel about being men and "doing the right thing" to promote men's development. In T. L. Davis & J. Laker (Eds.), *Masculinities in higher education: Theoretical and practical implications* (pp. 161–176). New York, NY: Routledge.

Brown, A. L., & Messman-Moore, T. L. (2009). Personal and perceived peer attitudes supporting sexual aggression as predictors of male college students' willingness to intervene against sexual aggression. *Journal of Interpersonal Violence, 25*(3), 503–517.

Eyssel, F., Bohner, G., & Seibler, F. (2006). Perceived rape myth acceptance of others predicts rape proclivity: Social norms or judgmental anchoring? *Swiss Journal of Psychology, 65*(2), 93–99.

Gidycz, C. A., Orchowski, L. M., & Berkowitz, A. D. (2012). Preventing sexual aggression among college men: An evaluation of a social norms and bystander intervention program. *Violence Against Women, 18*, 264–288.

Hillebrand-Gun, T., Heppner, M. J., Mauch, P. A., & Park, H. J. (2010). Men as allies: The efficacy of a high school rape prevention intervention. *Journal of Counseling and Development, 88*, 43–51.

Kilmartin, C. T., Smith, T., Green, A., Heinzen, H., Kuchler, M., & Kolar, D. (2008). A real-time social norms intervention to reduce college male sexism. *Sex Roles, 59*, 264–273.

Loh, C., Gidycz, C. A., Lobo, T. R., & Luthra, R. (2005). A prospective analysis of sexual assault perpetration: Risk factor related to perpetrator characteristics. *Journal of Interpersonal Violence, 20*(10), 1385–1348.

Solution-Focused Brief Therapy

Solution-focused brief therapy (SFBT) is a form of brief therapy developed by Insoo Kim and Steve de Shazer in the 1980s. As the name suggests, solution-focused brief therapy is focused on the future, goal oriented, and centered on the solutions that clients want, not on the problems. SFBT can be helpful in working with survivors of sexual violence in achieving the change in their lives that they are seeking.

Solution-focused brief therapy, also called solution-focused therapy, can typically last from 4 to 12 sessions. There are several characteristics of SFBT including: (1) an emphasis on clear and realistic goals; (2) the assumption that clients possesses the knowledge of what will make their life better; and (3) a clear vision of solutions and what it will look like once the goals are achieved. The worker learns from clients how they have solved problems in their past to develop solutions to the problem they are currently struggling with. The focus is on the positive parts of the client's personality, as well as the client's strengths.

In searching for previous solutions, the worker will also help the client determine what some exceptions have been. An exception is when the problem could have occurred but does not. For example, the worker may ask the client "What was different about this one time when this was less of a problem for you?" This helps the client to again focus on what has worked, as opposed to staying in the problem. The worker is strategic in avoiding discussions that stay in the past and instead helps the client to envision what his or her future could be like.

Validation and feedback are another essential part of SFBT. This helps to build rapport and trust between worker and client while also acknowledging the struggle on behalf of the client, as well as the encouragement through the change process. The client is also invited to give self-praise when discussing what has been working well. When acknowledging with the client what has been working, the worker then encourages the client to do more of what has been successful. Additionally, the worker also invites the client to try changes previously identified, termed an "experiment" in sessions.

Another hallmark of SFBT is the "miracle question." The miracle question is proposed to the client in this way: "Imagine tomorrow you wake up and realize that overnight, a miracle has occurred while you slept that fixed the problem you came here seeking to change. All is solved. When you awake, what small signs would you see that would make you realize that your problem has been solved?" The therapist then asks questions to help obtain more detail and help the client describe more fully what life would be like without his or her problem. By doing so, the client focuses on what he or she can do to make the changes he or she needs, as well as identifying what other changes may need to occur.

When time is limited, the worker can also use scaling questions to help clients assess their situation, track progress, and imagine how others might rate them on a scale. This can be especially helpful with clients who are not as verbal and may not be able to follow along with the miracle question. The client's motivation, hopefulness, progress, or other topics can be tracked using a scale such as this.

The worker also integrates coping questions into sessions to help clients develop healthy coping skills, realize that they already possess healthy coping skills, and continue to utilize these for the future. This is again another example of focusing on what works well rather than what has not.

Research has shown that SFBT is useful with a variety of presenting problems, in a variety of settings, and with many different client populations. For survivors of sexual violence, it can be incredibly empowering to clients to be able to identify their internal strengths and play an active role in identifying what has worked in the past. In addition, viewing clients as the expert gives a sense of power and control back. Furthermore, clients can commit to small amounts of time as opposed to staying in therapy for months and years. Provided that the relationship established between workers and clients is safe and respectful, clients are able to tap into their own resources and learn to trust themselves.

The resolution of past trauma can occur with SFBT, and clients can develop more functional behaviors and perceptions that can replace those based in their trauma. By focusing on solutions and working toward them, survivors can look forward to a more positive and fulfilling life.

Chrisula Tasiopoulos

See also Coping Mechanisms; Empowerment; Narrative Therapy; Recovery

Further Reading

Bannink, F. P. (2007). Solution-focused brief therapy. *Journal of Contemporary Psychotherapy, 37*, 87–94.

Bannink, F. P. (2008). Posttraumatic success: Solution-focused brief therapy. *Brief Treatment Crisis Intervention, 8*(3), 215–225.

Dewan, M., Steenbarger, B., & Greenberg, R. (Eds.). (2004). *The art and science of brief psychotherapy: A practitioner's guide.* Arlington, VA: American Psychiatric Publishing.

Iveson, C. (2002). Solution-focused brief therapy. *Advances in Psychiatric Treatment, 8*, 149–156.

Kruczek, T., & Vitanza, S. (1999). Treatment effects with an adolescent abuse survivor's group. *Child Abuse & Neglect, 23*(5), 477–485.

Nelson, T., & Thomas, F. (Eds.). (2007). *Handbook of solution-focused brief therapy: Clinical applications.* New York, NY: Haworth Press.

South Asians in the United States

The South Asian community in the United States is resplendent in diversity, which includes language, religion, socioeconomic status, generation, political engagement, and history of immigration. (South Asians are defined here as individuals who trace their heritage to Bangladesh, India, Nepal, Pakistan, and Sri Lanka. Some include Bhutan and Afghanistan in this list of countries.) While the groups may be distinct in their immigration histories to the United States, they share various cultural traditions and a past of common British colonization. Over the years, the South Asian community has attempted to present its image in the United States as a "model minority" and thereby suppress any chinks in that portrayal by suppressing reports of disease, domestic violence, sexual assault, drug abuse, poverty, unemployment, intergenerational conflict, etc. A fallout of this stance is that the community has often deliberately silenced victims of sexual assault and cloaked incidents of sexual violence in denial.

Public discourse on sexuality and sexual conduct remains a taboo in most South Asian cultures, which has rendered open discussions on sexual abuse/violence extremely difficult. Although immigration to the United States has changed some of the conventional beliefs and conducts in the community, violence against women and girls continues to be considered private and therefore must be concealed from public scrutiny. Nonetheless, a number of high-profile cases and research studies have forced the South Asian community in the United States to confront the problem of sexual assault, however reluctantly.

In 2009, the community was shocked as celebrity South Asian fashion designer Anand Jon was convicted of several counts of rape in California. In 2011, the Indian Consul General in New York was charged with sexually assaulting a domestic worker in his home. In addition, several South Asian physicians, airline passengers, pastors, religious gurus, students, diplomats, motel employees, caregivers, and others have faced criminal charges of sexual assault in the United States. South Asian American women's organizations in the country bear witness to many cases of incest, child sexual abuse, and date/acquaintance rapes in the community. In a study conducted in Boston with 160 highly educated professional women, Dr. Anita Raj and her colleague, Jay Silverman, (2002) found that 19 percent of women had been sexually abused by their current male partners at least once during their time together, while 15 percent claimed that they had been abused within the past year. Professor Margaret Abraham (1999) discovered in her study of South Asian married women in the United States that 60 percent had been coerced by their husbands to have sex against their wills.

South Asian cultures place high value on women's virtues, which is most often equated to virginity, chastity, and sexual fidelity. Women and girls are expected to enter marriage as virgins and remain faithful to their spouses. Thus girls' and women's behaviors are monitored strictly by their families and unrestricted dating by even adult women is frowned upon. This frequently lands girls and women in difficult situations if they have not only to defend themselves against date rapes and sexual assaults by acquaintances but also to find support from family or community if such abuse occurs.

Since sexual purity is considered the crowning female asset, South Asians tend to highlight "sex" in the context of sexual assault rather than the violence that instigates it. The prevalent attitude of South Asians toward sexual assault and rape is that of victim blaming, and many believe a woman must have done something to deserve it. Victims, even young girls, frequently find themselves held responsible for the sexual violence they have suffered. At the least, victims of sexual assault find their reputations ruthlessly sullied in the community. Consequently, parents tend to closely guard the secrets of their daughters' "sexual ruin" to protect their standing in society and often forgo any legal recourse to hold perpetrators accountable. This attitude is more prevalent among first-generation immigrants and has undergone considerable shift among second-generation South Asians. Nonetheless, South Asian Americans are still skeptical about marital rape concurrent to the belief that marriage guarantees men sexual rights to their wives' bodies.

South Asian women who work as nannies, housekeepers, domestic workers, and caregivers to the elderly are especially vulnerable to sexual assault, particularly if they live in their employers' homes. This defenselessness is exacerbated if the women are poor, recent immigrants, undocumented, and fearful of police involvement. When such employees' visas are dependent on their employers' sponsorships, they are precluded from changing jobs to escape abuse lest they become deportable. Women who are placed in detention centers awaiting deportation are also exposed to sexual assault in custody. A 2010 report by Human Rights Watch documents the rampant sexual assaults and rapes of women detainees in such centers. Victims who lack family or support systems in this country and are not fluent in English may be extra susceptible to sexual violence by various people on whom they have to depend to survive. Families of female victims who may be reliant on their incomes may also discourage them to seek justice if violated.

The traditional family structures of South Asia, which are slowly being reconfigured in this country, also place girls and women at high risk of sexual assault. Joint-family living customs and close friendship ties allow many men, related and unrelated, easy access to girls and women in South Asian homes. The stringent monitoring of girls and women that is utilized in the home country by older women in the family is usually absent in immigrant families due to the requirements of wage earning by supervising adults. Frequently, first-generation immigrants establish kinship relations with others in the community to replace the relatives they have left behind. The loyalty and interdependency that ensues from these relationships leads to child care exchanges as well as help with various everyday tasks. Such close associations based on necessity often endanger children's and women's safety and make it highly complicated to speak out if trusted individuals perpetrate sexual violence.

Like many immigrant communities, South Asians are reluctant to seek law enforcement assistance and opt for available legal recourses in the United States. This disinclination is intensified when it comes to intervention in the family and what are regarded as "confidential" matters such as rape and sexual assault. Additionally, with the passing of anti-immigrant measures such as Arizona's S.B. 1070 (but stalled by federal court), Alabama's H.B. 56, Section 287(g) of the federal Immigration and Nationality Act, and the proposed Georgia H.B. 87 legislation, which allow racial profiling and random checks of immigration papers, it is even more unlikely that immigrants, legal or undocumented, will be encouraged to seek legal justice in cases of rape and/or sexual assault.

Shamita Das Dasgupta

See also Forced Marriage; Victims, Guilt and Shame

Further Reading

Abraham, M. (1999). Sexual abuse in South Asian immigrant marriages. *Violence Against Women, 5*, 591–618.

Devdas, N. R., & Rubin, L. J. (2007). Rape myth acceptance among first- and second-generation South Asian American women. *Sex Roles, 56*, 701–705.

Human Rights Watch. (2010). *Detained at risk: Sexual abuse and harassment in United States immigration detention.* New York, NY: Author.

Hunjan, S., & Towson, S. (2007). Virginity is everything: Sexuality in the context of intimate partner violence in the South Asian community. In S. D. Dasgupta (Ed.), *Body evidence: Intimate violence against South Asian women in America* (pp. 53–67). New Brunswick, NJ: Rutgers University Press.

Raj, A., & Silverman, J. (2002). Intimate partner violence against South-Asian women in greater Boston. *JAMWA, 57*, 111–114.

Specialized Victims Units (Police)

Law enforcement detectives are responsible for collecting evidence from sex crime scenes and interviewing the victim and the suspect (if identified). In addition, detectives assess the validity of victims stories and decide whether to treat the incident as a crime and, if so, how to classify the crime. If the detective decides that there is probable cause that a rape occurred, the case is submitted to the prosecuting attorney. Prosecutors determine whether the charge filed by the detectives accurately reflects the facts in the case and whether a conviction seems probable. If the detective decides probable cause is not warranted, the case is reclassified as unfounded and ceases to move forward through the system.

Detectives have a critical role in the earlier stages of the criminal justice system that requires expertise in investigating sexual assault crimes. For example, detectives need to understand how forensic evidence can suggest additional investigational leads. Furthermore, detectives need to obtain information from victims in a sensitive manner. If victims perceive the detective as insensitive, they may be reluctant to share embarrassing information. Therefore detectives who investigate sex crimes require a high level of investigational and interviewing skills.

Because of this critical expertise, some police departments have developed specialized police units for sex crimes. Specialized sex crimes units (SSCUs) are primarily responsible to handle all sex crimes reported to the police. These units have become better known in the public through television shows such as *Law & Order SVU* (specialized victim unit). In larger police departments, an SSCU may have multiple detectives who investigate sex crimes, while smaller departments may have a single detective primarily responsible for investigating sex crimes. Currently, it is unknown how many police departments within the United States have SSCUs.

SSCUs may have some advantages over police departments that assign sex crimes randomly to detectives. First, this structure encourages detectives to develop expertise in sex crimes investigation because that is their primary role. By investigating the majority of sex crimes within a jurisdiction, detectives may be able to hone their investigational skills. However, research is needed to examine whether detectives within SSCUs have a higher level of skills than detectives who do not belong to SSCUs. For example, do detectives within SSCUs investigate cases more thoroughly or interview traumatized victims with more sensitivity?

Second, SSCUs may be more likely to have written investigative procedures for detectives. In a sample of police departments in nine counties in North Carolina, Lord and Rassel (2000) found that SSCU s were more likely to have written procedures for investigating sex crimes than police departments without SSCUs. Written procedures are important because they provide consistency in how sex crimes are handled.

Third, SSCUs may be more likely to have collaborative relationships with other organizations that work with victims, such as rape crisis centers. Lord and Rassel (2000) found that SSCUs were more likely to have a collaborative relationship with rape crisis centers than police departments without SSCUs. For example, detectives from SSCUs consistently invited advocates from rape crisis centers to come to their department to provide emotional support for victims. This is particularly important because emotional support provided to victims immediately after an assault can help victims to recover more quickly.

Finally, SSCUs were originally developed because it was believed that they would increase sex crime arrest rates. However, there has been limited research to determine if this is occurring. The only existing study was conducted 30 years ago. Through observations and interviews, LaFree (1981) found no differences in the arrest rates between police departments with SSCUs and those without SSCUs. LaFree found that the police departments in the sample based their arrest decisions primarily on factors related to victims' behavior, rather than solely evidentiary factors. For example, detectives were less likely to arrest a suspect if the victim had been drinking alcohol or if the victim delayed reporting the crime (see **Substantiation [of Legal Charges]** for additional information about the factors related to cases being dropped or prosecuted). In the past 30 years, there have been advancements in the investigation of sex crimes, particularly in the areas of forensic evidence testing and victim-interviewing techniques, which now may be being employed by SSCUs. Thus further research is needed to understand what influence, if any, SSCUs have on arrest rates for these crimes.

Debra Patterson

See also Bias, Police and Prosecution; Discretion, Law Enforcement; Rape Crisis Centers; SARTs (Sexual Assault Response Teams); Substantiation (of Legal Charges)

Further Reading

Collins, R., Lincoln, R., & Frank, M. (2002). The effect of rapport in forensic interviewing. *Psychiatry, Psychology and Law, 9*(1), 69–78.

Epstein, J., & Langenbahn, S. (1994). *The criminal justice and the community response to rape* (Contract No. OJP-89-C-009). Washington DC: National Institute of Justice.

LaFree, G. (1981). Official reactions to social problems: Police decisions in sexual assault cases. *Social problems, 28*(5), 582–594.

Lord, V. B., & Rassel, G. (2000). Law enforcement's response to sexual assault: A comparative study of nine counties in North Carolina. *Women & Criminal Justice, 11*(1), 67–87.

Martin, P. Y. (2005). *Rape work: Victims, gender, and emotions in organization and community context.* New York, NY: Routledge.

Selected Websites

Examples of Police Specialized Victim Units

Hampton (Virginia) Police Department. Retrieved from http://www.hampton.gov/police/about_us/sex_crimes.html

Nashville (Tennessee) Police Department. Retrieved from http://www.police.nashville.org/bureaus/investigative/sexabuse.asp

Spirituality

Each person is personally influenced by many different factors, including culture, family of origin, and spirituality. So when considering any therapeutic strategy, one must consider the whole person and not merely the fact that he or she has survived an act(s) of sexual violence. Individuals' own spirituality can have a significant impact in the healing process for many clients. Research indicates that religion and spirituality may be an especially important factor for dealing with deaths or other devastating uncontrollable events, such as sexual violence. Whether a person is connected to an organized religion or he or she identifies a personal spirituality, it is important for clinicians and survivors to consider the role that spirituality plays in treatment.

If religion or spirituality does play a role in a victim's life, it is important to focus some attention on it in therapy for many reasons. First, individuals are each a whole person with many characteristics and factors that impact how they view themselves, others, their experiences, the healing process, and therapeutic interventions. Second, religious faith can enhance a person's ability to cope with negative life experiences and therefore act as a positive coping mechanism.

Within sexual assault therapy, clinicians work to empower victims to move through the healing process by reinforcing positive coping mechanisms and individuals' strengths. The practitioner explores with clients positive ways they have worked through difficulties in the past in order to support themselves through the complex process of healing from the act of sexual violence. One study found that sexual assault survivors do engage in spirituality based coping strategies to facilitate healing (Ahrens, Abeling, Ahmand, & Hinman, 2010). This type of coping could involve prayer or allowing their belief in a higher power to help them cope with the trauma. These coping strategies should be viewed as a strength that assists the individual during his or her healing process. One's belief in God or a higher power can also help process feelings of loneliness and shame and be a sense of support for the client.

Practitioners who are working with a client should explore the role of spirituality and, if a client does identify as being spiritual or religious, the use of the client's spirituality based coping methods should be explored. Spirituality needs to be addressed in sexual violence therapy because there is also a possibility clients may have conflict regarding their spirituality and their experience with sexual violence. This conflict can be internal (struggle with God) or influenced by external sources (spiritual community). Studies have found that some sexual assault victims feel a religious disconnect following the assault. They may feel abandoned by God, question how and why God would allow this to happen to them, and even doubt the existence of a higher being (Ahrens, Abeling, Ahmand, & Hinman, 2010). If the survivor has an internal conflict arising from his or her spirituality, the therapist may work with the survivor to address this as a negative coping mechanism that is being used by the client. This should become a focus of reframing within therapy.

Clients may also experience conflicts with members from their religious community. This may be particularly true for survivors of sexual assault who may face high levels of rape myth acceptance from clergy and church members. Research indicates that clergy have been found to instruct sexual assault survivors to ask for forgiveness, try to be less sinful, or change behavior that is perceived as the cause of violence. These beliefs that others may hold can increase the likelihood that victims may start to engage in self-blame and question what they did wrong, or believe that they deserved the abuse. In this situation, a survivor's spirituality and faith may cause more distress for the survivor, rather than positively influencing the healing process. Clinicians should be mindful of the social influences, such as spirituality, that could be contributing to the client's feelings of self-blame and shame surrounding his or her experience. Additionally, rape myths that evolve from the context of one's religious or spiritual beliefs should be addressed as such within the therapeutic process.

Although spirituality may be seen as a personal and sometimes controversial issue, clinicians cannot ignore the role it may play in some clients' healing process from a sexual trauma. If a client presents spirituality as a having an important role in his or her life, it is a clinician's responsibility to explore it as it may have the possibility to assist in the healing process or hamper the client's ability to heal.

Deidre Evans and Laura Luciano

See also Coping Mechanisms; Recovery; Religious Groups (Overview); Victims, Guilt and Shame

Further Reading

Ahrens, C. E., Abeling, S., Ahmad, S., & Hinman, J. (2010). Spirituality and well-being: The relationship between religious coping and recovery from sexual assault. *Journal of Interpersonal Violence, 25*(7), 1242–1263.

Kennedy, J. E., Davis, R. C., & Taylor, B. G. (1998). Changes in spirituality and well-being among victims of sexual assault. *Journal for the Scientific Study of Religion, 37*, 322–328.

Selected Websites

Faith Trust Institute. Retrieved from http://www.faithtrustinstitute.org

Gift from Within: An International Nonprofit Organization for Survivors of Trauma and Victimization. Retrieved from http://www.giftfromwithin.org

Rape Recovery Help and Information. Retrieved from http://www.hopeforhealing.org

Sports Teams

Nearly 20 percent of all females and 4 percent of all males are raped during high school and college (Tjaden & Thoennes, 1998). Sexual aggression and sexual violence are perpetrated more often by people who participate in sports teams (Moynihan & Banyard, 2008; Boeringer, 1999). One explanation for the increase in sexual violence among athletes is that the sports culture often tolerates or promotes violence against others but particularly women.

A rape culture, a term coined by Sanday in 1990, is a culture that contains attitudes, beliefs, rituals, norms, and practices that condone, normalize, excuse, or tolerate or promote sexual violence. In a rape culture, the victims perceive a continuum of threatened violence that ranges from sexual remarks to sexual touching to rape itself. The more that behaviors on the continuum are allowed and promoted the more likely that a culture is created and maintained where sexual violence and rapes occur.

One such culture that may be considered as promoting a rape culture is athletic teams. Many male athletes and coaches report that they use negative or derogatory words to talk about women (McMahon, 2004). Furthermore, when male athletes are among other male athletes, they are more likely to use negative slang words regarding women. Often, the athletes and coaches use derogatory terminology to be funny without understanding the impact of their words. For example, coaches may refer to a player as a "girl" or a "bitch" to imply he is failing to play well (McMahon, 2004). By referring to women with derogatory terms, a culture that tolerates and supports violence against women is created. Examples of behaviors associated with rape culture include victim blaming, sexual objectification, and rape apologism. Such a culture of rape affects women, men, and children.

Athletes and coaches also believe more myths about rape and have more supportive attitudes about rape than other groups of people (Boeringer, 1999). Examples of rape myths are that men cannot be raped, victims make false reports, victims "asked" to be raped by the way that they dress, and all rapists are strangers (see **Rape Myths** for further information). In one study, the athletes who believed more rape myths were male, did not know someone who was raped, and played an individual contact sport for males only (McMahon, 2004).

Some athletes or coaches who rape are not arrested because the players, coaches, or administrators do not report the rape to the police or hide the incident in order to protect the athlete. In 2001 two students, Lisa Simpson and Anne Gilmore, were gang-raped by a college football team in Colorado. Yet the football players were never charged with rape. However, the women sued the university under Title IX, a federal law that prohibits gender harassment and discrimination against women in education programs. The women alleged that the university created a culture that harassed and discriminated against women. The lawsuit specifically brought to light the hiring of strippers to entertain football recruits at parties and included allegations that some women were paid to have sex with football players and high school recruits. The women won the lawsuit against the university; Lisa Simpson received $2.5 million, and Anne Gilmore received $350,000.

A more recent example surfaced at Pennsylvania State University in which the assistant football coach, Jerry Sandusky, allegedly sexually assaulted or had inappropriate contact with at least eight underage boys. Many complained that the witnesses and the university did not do enough to protect the children and actually prevented anyone from reporting Sandusky to the police. Several high-level school officials including the school president, Graham Spanier, and the head football coach, Joe Paterno, were forced to resign because they were accused of covering up the incidents or failing to notify authorities. On November 4, 2011, after a three-year grand jury investigation, the Pennsylvania attorney general, Linda Kelly, indicted Sandusky on 42 counts of child molestation dating from 1994 to 2009, though the abuse may date as far back as the 1970s.

In addition to sexual language and belief in rape myths creating a culture of sexual violence, athletic norms may contribute to such a culture. For example, male athletes are trained to be aggressive and tough while playing sports.

Such aggressiveness and use of violence in athletic games is highly valued in our society. However, many male athletes report the expectation that they "turn it off" when they are not playing sports. Sometimes this switch is hard to make and athletes continue to act aggressive even when they are off the field (McMahon, 2004). For example, in football, players are required to tackle and sack their opponents hard and repeatedly. Players and coaches value intimidation and threatening attitudes and looks. Players are required to take what they want (the football) at all costs; such behavior may spill over to other parts of the players' lives.

Many colleges and sport teams have tried to change the sports culture that allows discrimination, gender harassment, sexual harassment, and rape. For example, some programs have tried to encourage players or team members to prevent and stop sexual assault. One program, Mentors in Violence Prevention (MVP), is a leadership program that motivates both men and women to play a central role in solving problems that historically have been considered "women's issues" such as rape, battery, and sexual harassment. (See **Mentors in Violence Prevention [Program]** entry for more information.) Another example includes SCREAM Athletes, which uses student-athletes as peer educators to explore attitudes, beliefs, community standards, and aspects of the athletic culture that support the occurrence of interpersonal violence, as well as the strengths of the community that can be used to create social change (see **SCREAM Theater [Program]** entry for more information).

Alexandra Redcay

See also Coaching Boys into Men (Program); Colleges and Universities; Fraternities and Sororities; Mentors in Violence Prevention (Program); Rape Myths; SCREAM Theater (Program)

Further Reading

Boeringer, S. (1999). Associations of rape-supportive attitudes with fraternal and athletic participation. *Violence Against Women, 5*(1), 81–90.

Gershman, Bennett L. (2011, November 15). Campus "justice" shows a culture of complacency. Huffington Post. Retrieved from www.huffingtonpost.com/bennett-l-gershman/campus-culture-complacency_b_1095510.html

Martin, P. Y., & Hummer, R. A. (1989) Fraternities and rape on campus. *Gender and Society, 3*, 457–473.

McMahon, S. (2004). Student-athletes, rape-supportive culture, and social change. Department of Sexual Assault Services and Crime Victim Assistance. Unpublished manuscript.

Moynihan, M. M., & Banyard, V. L. (2008). Community responsibility for preventing sexual violence: A pilot study with campus Greeks and intercollegiate athletes. *Journal of Prevention & Intervention in the Community, 36*(1–2), 23–38.

Sanday, P. R. (1990). *Fraternity gang rape.* New York, NY: New York University Press.

Sanday, P. R. (2007). *Fraternity gang rape: Sex, brotherhood, and privilege on campus* (2nd ed.). New York, NY: New York University Press.

Tjaden, P., & Thoennes, N. (1998). *Prevalence, incidence, and consequences of violence against women: Findings from the National Violence Against Women Survey.* Washington, DC: National Institute of Justice, U.S. Department of Justice.

Weir, T., & Brady, T. (2003, December 23). In sexual assault cases, athletes usually walk. *USA Today.* Retrieved from http://www.usatoday.com/sports/2003-12-21-athletes-sexual-assault_x.htm

Selected Websites

Mentors in Violence Prevention. Retrieved from http://www.jacksonkatz.com/mvp.html

Sexual assault statistics. One in Four USA. Retrieved from http://www.oneinfourusa.org/statistics.php

SCREAM Athletes, SCREAM Theater. Retrieved from http://sexualassault.rutgers.edu/screamathletes.htm

Stalking

Stalking is a pattern of behavior that involves following or maintaining close proximity to someone, repeated communication, implicit or explicit threats, or some combination of these behaviors, thereby causing fear in the victim. Technical definitions vary by state. About eight percent of women and two percent of men report having been stalked during their lifetime (Tjaden & Thoennes, 1998). Most victims are in the 18–30 age range. Women are more likely to be victims of stalking than men. Female victims are more likely to be stalked by men, and male victims have similar rates of perpetration by men and women. Stalking can be perpetrated by a stranger, an acquaintance, or an intimate partner such as a boyfriend, girlfriend, husband, or wife; however, most victims have some kind of previous relationship with the perpetrator.

Stalking can escalate over time and become physically or sexually violent. About 2 percent of stalking victims are sexually assaulted by the perpetrator, and about 31 percent of women who are stalked by an intimate partner are also sexually assaulted by the partner (Baum, Catalano, Rand, & Rose, 2009). Sexual assault can include rape (vaginal or anal intercourse) or acts such as kissing, fondling, or oral sex. Of all stalking victims who sustain some sort of injury, about 14 percent are raped/sexually assaulted (Baum, Catalano, Rand, & Rose, 2009).

Stalking behaviors can include following the victim, damaging personal property, or harassing the victim. Threats may be about harming the victim or someone she or he knows. Some stalkers leave gifts for the victim or steal items from the victim. In some cases, the perpetrator will enlist a third party such as a mutual friend or family member to contact the victim. Stalking can go on for years and the perpetrator may have some kind of contact with the victim on a daily, weekly, or monthly basis. The stalker often intimidates the victim through behaviors that appear threatening without using actual verbal threats, for example by following a victim, or sending unwanted gifts or messages. Stalking behaviors are similar to domestic violence in that they involve a pattern of power and control. As the stalker attempts to exert power over the victim, if rejected, the stalker may become aggravated and escalate the stalking since it threatens his or her control.

Stalking can also include technology, called cyberstalking, where the perpetrator sends frequent messages via e-mail or social networking sites, or personal information or rumors are spread via the Internet. Cyberstalking may also include cameras, phones, GPS, computer spyware, or any other form of technology. An example of cyberstalking could be an ex-husband hiding a GPS in a car to track the woman's movements. The use of technology has become increasingly common in stalking, with as many as one in four victims citing some use of technology in the stalking behaviors (Baum, Catalano, Rand, & Rose 2009). Cyberstalking can also intersect with sexual violence if pictures are sent or taken using cell phones, cameras, video cameras, e-mail, or other technology.

Legal definitions of stalking vary by state, as do the options for victims. Some states specifically cite the use of technology as a form of stalking in their statutes, while others do not. The requirements for a victim to obtain a protective order (also called a restraining order) also vary by state, requiring different levels of threat, fear, or behaviors in order to get legal protection. Once obtained, a restraining order can make it easier for the police to take action against a stalker who violates the order by continuing to harass, stalk, or contact the victim. Some states classify stalking as a felony at the first offense, and even more classify it as such at a repeated offense or when special conditions apply, such as possession of a deadly weapon or when the victim is under age 16.

There is no "typical" stalker or typology to help predict or identify when someone might become a stalker. Perpetrators may or may not have a criminal record; those with a criminal record may or may not have a violent history. In about one-third of stalking cases, the victim and perpetrator have a history of domestic violence prior to the stalking behavior (Mohandie, Meloy, McGowan, & Williams, 2006). Fewer than half of perpetrators have a diagnosable mental illness, and about one-third have problems with substance abuse. While about half of perpetrators are single, many are married, dating, living with a partner, or divorced/separated. The victim is most often of the same ethnic background as the perpetrator.

Victims often have fears about when the next incident will happen and whether the stalking will ever stop. Some victims will miss time at work as a result of the stalking. Many victims suffer from anxiety, insomnia, and depression and have difficulty in social functioning. Victims often have to change their behavior to avoid being stalked; they might change the routes that they commonly drive, change phone numbers, or even move. It is recommended that victims keep a record of the stalking, including dates, times, notes about the incidents, and pictures if possible; this can be useful if legal action is necessary. If a stalker does not listen when asked to stop, it is vital to use resources such as local police and advice from an agency dealing with victim's rights, as the behavior may not cease without intervention from an official body.

There is nothing definitive about what will make a stalker stop his or her behavior because every case is different. Use of the criminal justice system is sometimes, but not always, effective. The longer stalking goes on, the less likely it is to stop; therefore the best option is to intervene as early as possible by using legal and local agency support systems.

Corinne D. Warrener

See also Impact, Work; Intimate Partner Violence; Safety Plans; Sexting

Further Reading

Baum, K., Catalano, S. M., Rand, M. R., & Rose, K. (2009). *Stalking victimization in the United States*. Washington, DC: U.S. Office of Justice Programs, Bureau of Justice Statistics.

Mohandie, K., Meloy, J. R., McGowan, M. G., & Williams, J. (2006). The RECON typology of stalking: Reliability and validity based upon a large sample of North American stalkers. *Journal of Forensic Science, 51*(1), 147–155.

Tjaden, P., & Thoennes, N. (1998). *Stalking in America: Findings from the National Violence Against Women Survey*. Washington, DC: U.S. Department of Justice, National Institute of Justice.

Selected Websites

Stalking. RAINN (Rape, Abuse & Incest National Network). Retrieved from http://www.rainn.org/public-policy/sexual-assault-issues/stalking

Stalking resource center. National Center for Victims of Crime: Information, resources. Retrieved from http://www.ncvc.org/SRC/main.aspx?dbID=dash_Home

Violence against women: Stalking. Women's Web. Retrieved from http://www.womensweb.ca/violence/stalking.php

Statistics

Researching sexual violence and abuse is a social science; that is, the content of the research is about a societal issue. To find out more about sexual violence and abuse, social scientists sometimes use quantitative research methods. Quantitative research involves gathering information that can be converted into numbers for statistical analysis, which helps social scientists describe and model life events.

To develop models of life events, researchers gather information and then convert that information into numbers. These numbers are analyzed using statistical tests, the results of which tell us how the independent and the dependent variables are related to each other. These results can be compared to other studies and used to inform policy and practice, and to develop other research studies.

To conduct a study, social scientists begin by reviewing other studies related to their topic. Then, they make an educated guess about what their study might reveal. This educated guess is called a hypothesis. To test a hypothesis, researchers must gather information, called data. When social scientists collect data, they have to use a sample of the available sources of information because using all of the possible sources (called the population) is too expensive and too time consuming.

Data can be classified into two types of variables: independent variables and dependent variables. Dependent variables are the events researchers are interested in learning more about, such as the likelihood a person will experience sexual abuse. An independent variable is something that might impact a dependent variable such as, in this example, a person's age. To determine how an independent variable impacts a dependent variable, researchers use statistics.

After the statistical testing is complete, researchers report their findings using descriptive statistics and test statistics. Descriptive statistics provide general information about a study. For example, if a study reports that the mean age of women in the study is 22, we know that on average, women who participated in study are 22 years old. Other descriptive statistics include the mode (the most frequent value) and the median (the value that falls in the middle). Another frequently reported statistic is the standard deviation, which gives us an idea about how different a single case is from the typical case in the sample.

Test statistics help researchers determine the relationship between the independent and dependent variables. A positive relationship means that as the independent variable increases in value, the dependent variable also increases in value. A negative relationship means that as the independent variable increases in value, the dependent variable decreases in value. Sometimes there is no relationship between the variables.

One of the simplest statistical tests is a bivariate correlation, which tells researchers the strength of the relationship between two variables. Some statistical tests, such as linear regression, help researchers predict the value of the independent variable at a given value of the dependent variable. These tests are used to help predict a person's risk of victimization, or an offender's risk of committing another crime.

When researchers report their findings, they often mention statistical significance, also known as a p-value. When a p-value is low (.10 or lower), the test result is not due to chance alone. When the p-value is high (.11 or above), the findings are likely due to chance and the findings are not statistically significant. The researcher determines what p-value he or she will use, however, it is a general rule that p-values should be .10 or lower to reduce the likelihood of a finding being due to chance alone. However, it is important to focus on the findings as a whole, not just on what is statistically significant.

Several quantitative sources about sexual violence exist. The federal government and academic researchers are the primary providers of this information. All of the sources offer insight into the extent of sexual violence, but many have been criticized by researchers for underestimating its prevalence and incidence. Improvements in methodology have provided a better view of the extent of sexual violence in the United States in recent years.

There are two major national sources of sexual victimization statistics with information gathered by the federal government. The first is the National Crime Victimization Survey (NCVS), which gathers information about criminal victimization from household residents who are over the age of 12. This survey asks participants about a variety of crimes, one of which is rape. The second major source of information gathered by the federal government is the FBI Uniform Crime Report (UCR). These data are collected from police and sheriff's departments on a voluntary basis.

While statistics about sexual violence have been subjected to criticism that asserts that the methods used to gather information likely result in an overinflation of rape prevalence and incidence, it is more likely that the extent of sexual victimization is underestimated. The NCVS uses questions that rely on the participant's subjective definition of rape or sexual violence. If a participant does not believe what happened is rape, then that assault is not included in the count, thus underestimating the number of rapes occurring during the six months prior to the survey. The UCR includes only cases that are reported to the police and resulted in an arrest or another type of clearance, which means that cases with suspects who were not arrested after being investigated are not included. Since most rapes and other sexual victimizations are never reported to the police, the UCR likely underestimates the extent of sexual violence. The UCR also includes only those acts using physical force to obtain sexual intercourse, oral sex, or anal sex, which means that rape occurring as the result of a victim being under the influence of drugs or alcohol, or rapes that are coerced in other ways, are not included. Fortunately, the definition used by the UCR has been modified to focus on multiple forms of penetration without consent including penetration of the vagina, anus, or other body part; oral penetration is also included.

There have been many efforts by academic researchers to more accurately estimate the extent of sexual victimization. Mary Koss and colleagues led research in the 1980s that revealed that sexual violence was more common than believed at that time. This study produced the oft-cited "one in four" statistic, revealing that at least 25 percent of women had been raped while at college, and many more had experienced other forms of sexual victimization. More studies followed with similar findings strengthening the assertion that the federal sources of rape statistics underestimated its prevalence.

Research findings are often used to inform policy and practice in the fields of criminal justice and human services. Studies can provide information about how to reduce the risk of sexual violence and abuse, and how to best help victims of these crimes. Studies can also be used to determine the best course of treatment for offenders to reduce the chances of them committing another act of sexual violence or abuse. The combination of federal statistics and academic research provide necessary information for prevention of this crime.

Wendy Perkins Gilbert

See also Data Collection; Underreporting

Further Reading

Atchley, W. D. (2008). *Beginning statistics*. Mt. Pleasant, SC: Hawks Learning Systems.

Diamond, I., & Jefferies, J. (2001). *Beginning statistics: An introduction for social scientists*. Thousand Oaks, CA: Sage.

Fisher, B. S., Cullen, F. T., & Turner, M. G. (2000). *The sexual victimization of college women* (NCJ 182369). Washington, DC: U.S. Department of Justice.

Koss, M. P., Gidycz, C. A., & Wisniewski, N. (1987). The scope of rape: Incidence and prevalence of sexual aggression and victimization in a national sample of higher education students. *Journal of Consulting and Clinical Psychology, 55*, 162–170.

Tjaden, P., & Thoennes, N. (2006). *Extent, nature, and consequences of rape victimization: Findings from the National Violence Against Women Survey* (NCJ 210346). Washington, DC: U.S. Department of Justice.

Truman, J. L. (2011). Criminal victimization, 2010. National Crime Victimization Survey. U.S. Department of Justice, Office of Justice Programs. Washington, DC: U.S. Department of Justice.

Selected Website

Statsoft Electronic Statistics Textbook. Retrieved from http://www.statsoft.com/textbook/

Statutory Rape

According to the U.S. Federal Bureau of Investigation (FBI), statutory rape is defined as a "non-forcible type of sexual intercourse or contact with a person who is younger than the state's statutory age of consent." This term refers to an act of sexual intercourse, penetration, or other sexual contact between two persons where one of the two people is considered by state law to be legally too young to consent to sexual contact. Typically, the other person is an adult (18 or older) or is older than the victim by at least two to three years, depending upon the age of the younger person.

Laws about the legal age of consent for sexual activity are passed at the state level, so each state has different legal definitions of what is considered "statutory rape." The main issue with statutory rape is not the consent of the victim per se, but the difference in age and thus legal responsibility of the perpetrator. Most often laws on this type of sexual contact do not apply only to sexual intercourse, but may also apply to other forms of sexual contact. The age of consent used in these laws differ from state to state as do the possible penalties for those offenders found guilty.

A research report from Connecticut (Norman-Eady, Reinhart, & Martino, 2003) notes that most state statutes do not use the term "statutory rape," but instead refer to it in their criminal codes as a form of criminal sexual contact, sexual abuse, or sexual assault. These laws assert that until a person reaches legal adulthood (majority) or another legally specified age, they are not able to legally consent to sexual intercourse. In such cases, it is considered illegal activity for an older person (usually 16 years or older) to have sexual contact with a younger person (often 13 to 14 years or younger) who meets that state's definition of "too young to give consent." Force or coercion is not necessary to prove in such sexual assault cases, as the difference in age of the people involved and lack of legal consent are important elements.

In most cases, the penalties for "statutory rape" are related to the difference in age between the two people, and if the older person is an adult. Penalties are generally higher when the age difference is greater or the older person involved is 20 years or older. This does not, however, mean that someone has to be an adult (18 or over) to be charged with a form of statutory rape. For example, in the state of Minnesota the criminal code specifies that a person may be charged with first-degree criminal sexual conduct (the most severe charge) if they engage in sexual contact with a person less than 13 years of age and the alleged perpetrator is more than 3 years older than the complainant, so 16 years old. In such cases, the person being accused or charged cannot claim as a defense that they did not know the younger person's age or that the younger person gave consent. While defined by each state, in the majority of states, the age of consent is 16 years of age.

A person who is found guilty of a sexual offense such as statutory rape may be required to register as a sex offender. Such registrations are also determined at the state level. This means that a juvenile convicted of this type of offense will have a criminal record that may be maintained even after the person is an adult. Sexually based offenses revealed on a criminal background check may restrict the types of jobs and work settings in which the convicted person is allowed to be employed.

While all sorts of sexual assault are underreported to law enforcement, some types of rape and sexual assaults such as "statutory rape" and "acquaintance rape" are even less likely to be reported. Often these sorts of assaults happen between two people who know each other and there is often little or no force or violent behavior used in the sexual act. It has been estimated that approximately one in three sexual assaults fall under that standard of "statutory rape."

Annelies K. Hagemeister

See also Acquaintance Rape; Consent; Laws, Rape; Sexual Assault; Sexual Coercion

Further Reading

Davis, N. S. & Twombly, J. (2000). State legislator's handbook for statutory rape issues. American Bar Association, Center on Children and the Law, OJP. Retrieved from http://www.ojp.usdoj.gov/ovc/publications/infores/statutoryrape/handbook/statrape.pdf

Glosser, A., Gardiner, K., & Fishman, M. (2004, December 15). *Statutory rape: A guide to state laws and reporting requirements.* Retrieved from http://aspe.hhs.gov/hsp/08/sr/statelaws/index.shtml

Leitenberg, H., & Saltzman, H. (2003). College women who had sexual intercourse when they were underage minors (13–15): Age of their male partners, relation to current adjustment, and statutory rape implications. *Sexual Abuse: A Journal of Research and Treatment, 15*(2), 135–147.

Norman-Eady, S., Reinhart, S., & Martino, C. (2003). *Statutory rape laws by state.* Retrieved from http://www.cga.ct.gov/2003/olrdata/jud/rpt/2003-r-0376.htm

Smette, I., Stefansen, K., & Mossige, S. (2009). Responsible victims? Young people's understandings of agency and responsibility in sexual situations involving underage girls. *Young, 17*(4), 351–373.

Troup-Leasure, K., & Snyder, H. N. (2005). *Statutory rape known to law enforcement.* Office of Justice Programs, Office of Juvenile Justice and Delinquency Prevention. Retrieved from https://www.ncjrs.gov/pdffiles1/ojjdp/208803.pdf

STDs and HIV/AIDS

Sexually transmitted diseases (STDs) are infections passed between individuals through infected blood, semen, vaginal, or other bodily fluids, generally through sexual contact. STDs can also be acquired without sexual contact through pregnancy/childbirth or using shared needles for drug use. Commonly diagnosed STDs include chlamydia, genital herpes, gonorrhea, and syphilis. Individuals infected with an STD are at risk for many negative health issues, including being more susceptible to contracting HIV. The Centers for Disease Control and Prevention (CDC) estimate that approximately 50,000 people are infected with HIV each year in the United States, with over 1 million adults and adolescents (over age 13) living with HIV (CDC, 2011b). Of those individuals living with HIV, 25 percent are estimated to be females (CDC, 2011a). The most common methods of HIV transmission for women living with HIV are high-risk heterosexual contact and injection drug use (CDC, 2011a). Women face many factors that may contribute to their risk of being infected with an STD or HIV, including current or past violent relationships, history of trauma, and substance abuse.

Women in abusive relationships may be at higher risk for contracting HIV or other STDs due to power dynamics within the relationship that may not allow them to negotiate safe sex practices, such as condom use. For example, one study found that men's use of violence increased when his partner asked about using a condom; such a request was seen as a sign of distrust or infidelity and a challenge to his power (El-Bassel, Gilbert, Rajah, Foleno, & Frye, 2000). Women are at increased risk for contracting HIV or STDs in relationships in which gender-based power imbalances exist, as they lack control to protect themselves against a partner's risky sexual behavior (Ulibarri, Sumner, & Amaro, 2010). In addition, victims who have been raped by a stranger are also at risk to contract HIV or another STD. Research has shown that men who are perpetrators of partner violence are likely to engage in high-risk sexual behaviors, such as unprotected anal sex, sex with partners who use injection drugs, and sex with multiple partners (without a condom), which also puts them at higher risk for STD or HIV infection and transmission (El-Bassel, Gilbert, Rajah, Foleno, & Frye, 2001). These behaviors impact the victim by putting her at risk of being infected with an STD or HIV.

Adolescents impacted by dating violence are also at risk. One study of sexually active young women found that more than half of high school girls diagnosed with an STD/HIV reported experiencing dating violence; those who reported physical and sexual violence were more likely to have been diagnosed with a sexually transmitted disease than those who experienced no dating violence (Decker, Silverman, & Raj, 2005). Some of the ways that teenage girls may lack control in their relationships is by being afraid to say no to sex, scared to insist their partner use a condom, unable to talk to their partner about abstinence, faithfulness or using protection, and unaware if their partner is doing things that may be putting them both at risk for HIV, such as drug use or having unprotected sex with other partners (CDC, 2007).

A history of trauma may also impact a victim's likelihood of becoming infected with an STD or HIV. History of childhood sexual abuse has been linked to higher rates of risky sexual behaviors for both males and females, including having multiple sexual partners, earlier age of first sexual encounter, becoming a sex worker or buying sex, and to greater probability of contracting an STD or HIV (Senn, Carey, & Vanable, 2008). Therefore the impact of childhood sexual abuse may relate to higher risk-taking sexual behaviors, resulting in transmission of HIV or STDs.

Substance abuse, including intravenous drug use, is also related to increased HIV-related sexual risk behaviors. Individuals using drugs and/or alcohol may be more vulnerable while under the influence, interfering with their ability to engage in safe sex practices. Substance use may also impact the likelihood of the occurrence of sexual violence, as a partner may become sexually violent while using drugs or alcohol (El-Bassel, Gilbert, Rajah, Foleno, & Frye, 2000). Victims of sexual violence who utilize substances are also at risk of contracting HIV or STDs as they may be abused while under the influence and unable to negotiate use of condoms (El-Bassel, Gilbert, Rajah, Foleno, & Frye, 2000).

A consequence of sexual violence is being infected with an STD or HIV. Factors that limit the ability to negotiate for safe sex, such as condom use, are prevalent in relationships and situations where sexual violence exists. In addition to potentially contracting a disease, victims of sexual violence may also be impacted by the stigma associated with having an STD or HIV, as well as stigma attached to being a victim of sexual violence.

Rachel Schwartz

See also Abortion; Alcohol and Drug Abuse, Perpetration; Child Sexual Abuse; Pregnancy; Prevention, Dating Violence

Further Reading

Centers for Disease Control and Prevention (2007). *Prevention challenges*. Retrieved from http://www.cdc.gov/hiv/topics/women/challenges.htm

Centers for Disease Control and Prevention (2011a). *HIV among women*. Retrieved from: http://www.cdc.gov/hiv/topics/women/index.htm

Centers for Disease Control and Prevention (2011b). *HIV in the United States: An overview*. Retrieved from http://www.cdc.gov/hiv/topics/surveillance/resources/factsheets/incidence-overview.htm

Decker, M. R., Silverman, J. G., & Raj, A. (2005). Dating violence and sexually transmitted disease/HIV testing and diagnosis among adolescent females. *Pediatrics, 116*(2), 272.

El-Bassel, N., Fontdevila, J., Gilbert, L., Voisin, D., Richman, B. L., & Pitchell, P. (2001). HIV risks of men in methadone maintenance treatment programs who abuse their intimate partners: A forgotten issue. *Journal of Substance Abuse, 13*, 29–43.

El-Bassel, N., Gilbert, L., Rajah, V., Foleno, A., & Frye, V. (2000). Fear and violence: Raising the HIV stakes. *AIDS Education and Prevention, 12*(2), 154–170.

Resnick, H., Monnier, J, Seals, B., Holmes, M., Nayak, M., Walsh, J., Weaver, T. L., . . . Kilpatrick, D. G. (2002). Rape-related HIV risk concerns among recent rape victims. *Journal of Interpersonal Violence, 17*(7), 746–759.

Senn, T. E., Carey, M. P., & Vanable, P. A. (2008). Childhood and adolescent sexual abuse and subsequent sexual risk behavior: Evidence from controlled studies, methodological critique, and suggestions for research. *Clinical Psychology Review, 28*, 711–735.

Ulibarri, M. D., Sumner, L. A., Cyriac, A., & Amaro, H. (2010). Power, violence, and HIV risk in women. In M. Paludi & F. L. Denmark (Eds.), *Victims of sexual assault and abuse: Resources and responses for individuals and families: Vol. 1. Incidence and psychological dimensions* (pp. 211–236). Santa Barbara, CA: Praeger, ABC-CLIO.

Selected Website

AVERT: Women, HIV and AIDS. Retrieved from http://www.avert.org/women-hiv-aids.htm

Stranger Rape

Stranger rape occurs when someone is forced into nonconsensual sexual intercourse by an unknown perpetrator. In stranger rape, victims are coerced into sexual activity through threats, violence, and physical force. Contrary to popular belief, the majority of rapes are committed by acquaintances of the victim rather than by strangers with 33 percent of rapes being committed by strangers and 77 percent being committed by someone known to the victim (Bureau of Justice Statistics, 1997). Rape is considered to be a crime occurring at the personal, physical, and sexual levels; as each level is reached the level of violation increases (Canter, Bennel, Alison, & Reddy, 2003). Thirty-six percent of rapes are reported to the police, the majority in which the attacker is unknown to the victim (Rennison, 2002). Stranger rape is more likely to be identified as rape based on societal standards and views, increasing victims' credibility as well as the chances for legal ramifications.

While all rapes occur as a result of force and coercion, they have different motivating factors. These behavioral themes include hostility, control, theft, and involvement. When hostility serves as the motivating factor, the sexual act of rape serves as a destructive expression of aggression. Control is involved when the perpetrator is looking for power and sees the victim as an object. Theft can be a motivator when the perpetrator is looking to gain something of value, rather than just sexual gratification, out of the rape. Involvement as motivation is the idea that the perpetrator rapes the victim for the purpose of social contact during which the perpetrator may treat the victim more personably as if in a normal social interaction (Canter, Bennel, Alison, & Reddy, 2003).

There are three major categories of stranger rape: blitz sexual assault, contact sexual assault, and home invasion sexual assault. Blitz sexual assaults occur when the perpetrator rapes the victim quickly and ruthlessly without any prior encounter. These types of rapes are more likely to occur in public places at night. Contact sexual assault occurs when the perpetrator contacts the victim prior to the rape in order to gain her trust. These situations typically occur in bars or other social locations when the perpetrator will lure the victim away from others to his car or other isolated location before the rape. Home invasion sexual assault occurs when the perpetrator breaks into the victim's house and rapes her (RAINN, 2009).

Women fear rape more than they fear other types of violent crimes, including murder and robbery. Contributing to this fear is worry about the immediate consequence of a rape, including physical issues such as sexually transmitted diseases, pregnancy, injury, and death. Additionally, psychological and emotional factors play a role as many women experience flashbacks, nightmares, mistrust of men, and feelings of powerlessness. Perceived risk and lack of control also play a role in the development and strength of women's fear of rape. These ideas about rape are communicated through the media, including movies and television shows that emphasize the brutality and seemingly random quality of stranger rape.

Stranger rape is an incredibly traumatic experience that leaves the victim reeling in its aftermath. Some common reactions that are experienced by victims both during and after the rape include feelings of weakness, shock, fear, vulnerability, numbness, disorientation, helplessness, and loss of control. Many victims experience self-blame for letting the assault happen. Additionally, victims of rape are 3 times more likely to suffer from depression, 6 times more likely to suffer from post-traumatic stress disorder, 13 times more likely to abuse alcohol, 26 times more likely to abuse drugs, and 4 times more likely to contemplate suicide (World Health Organization, 2002). Victims of stranger rape are more likely to reach out to a friend, loved one, or professional for help after the assault than are victims of acquaintance rape.

You can reduce your risk of stranger rape by taking a few safety precautions. Avoid potentially risky situations by being aware of what is going on around you, staying away from isolated areas where you are alone or with someone you do not know, trusting your gut feelings, having a cell phone available, and walking without distractions and with purpose.

Sabrina Starkman

See also Impact and Consequences (Overview); Rape Myths; "Real Rape" and Blaming Victims; Victims, Credibility

Further Reading

Bureau of Justice Statistics (1997). *Criminal victimization in the United States.* U.S. Department of Justice. Retrieved from http://bjs.ojp.usdoj.gov/content/pub/pdf/cvus9701.pdf

Canter, D. V., Bennel, C., Alison, L. J., & Reddy, S. (2003). Differentiation sex offences: A behaviorally based thematic classification of stranger rapes. *Behavioral Sciences and the Law, 21,* 157–174.

Paludi, M. A. (Ed.). 1999. *The psychology of sexual victimization: A handbook.* Westport, CT: Greenwood Press.

Rennison, C. M. (2002). *Rape and sexual assault: Reporting to police and medical attention, 1992–2000* (NCJ 194530). Washington, DC: U.S. Department of Justice, Bureau of Justice Statistics.

Stranger rape (2009). RAINN (Rape, Abuse & Incest National Network). Retrieved from http://www.rainn.org/get-information/types-of-sexual-assault/stranger-rape

World Health Organization (2002). The World Health Report. Retrieved from http://www.who.int/whr/2002/en/

Selected Websites

Avoiding dangerous situations. RAINN (Rape, Abuse & Incest National Network). Retrieved from http://www.rainn.org/get-information/sexual-assault-prevention/avoiding-dangerous-situations

Stranger rape. RAINN (Rape, Abuse & Incest National Network). Retrieved from http://www.rainn.org/get-information/types-of-sexual-assault/stranger-rape

Strengths Perspective

The strengths perspective, more commonly associated with the social work arena, takes the approach that all people have the capacity to decide what is best for themselves, that they are able to act in the best way possible as they are experts in their own lives, and that they have a wide range of skills, knowledge, experience, resources, and gifts that can be tapped to overcome whatever challenge brought them into therapy. Originally identified and developed in the 1980s by Dr. Dennis Saleebey, a professor at the University of Kansas, the fundamental belief and assumption of the strengths perspective is that abuse victims who can survive must possess some strengths and resources, and have the potential to learn, grow, and change.

The strengths perspective sometimes overlaps with solution-focused therapy and positive psychology, developed by Martin Seligman, in that it stands in contrast to the typical medical or deficit model of approaching a client's problem. Simply put, rather than focusing on what is wrong and a client's vulnerabilities, the strengths perspective focuses on utilizing the client's strengths and resources.

Research involving the application of the strengths perspective to providing services to those with mental illness, treatment of emotionally disturbed youth or the elderly, and adults in protective services showed positive outcomes regarding the quality of life, a reduction in hospitalizations, and increase in social functioning (Marty, Rapp, & Carlson, 2001).

Frequently, those who have suffered sexual violence and abuse develop low self-esteem and high levels of shame and self-blame. Conversely, prevention programs that make the greatest strides are successful largely by building on the strengths of individuals or groups. Consequently, the strengths perspective blends the challenge presented by the survivor with what has shown to be successful in altering public consciousness. In a strengths perspective, the making of possibilities is one of the core tenets.

There are 10 significant principles that define the strengths perspective. They are: (1) a person is defined as unique, and traits, talents, and resources add up to strengths; (2) therapy is possibility focused; (3) personal accounts are the essential route to knowing and appreciating the person; (4) the practitioner knows the person from the inside out; (5) childhood trauma is not predictive and it may weaken or strengthen the individual; (6) the centerpiece of work is the aspirations of family, individual, or community; (7) individuals, family, or community are the experts; (8) possibilities for choice, control, commitment, and personal development are open; (9) resources for work are the strengths, capacities, and adaptive skills of the individual, family, or community; and (10) help is centered on getting on with one's life, affirming and developing values and commitments, and making and finding membership in or as a community (Saleebey, 2006).

Assessment of the client is a key phase during which the strengths perspective can be formulated. For example, if the majority of the assessment is focused on the client's problems, then the interventions formulated will lean heavily on the client's deficits and vulnerabilities. From a strengths perspective, a complete assessment will also focus on a utilization of the client's strengths and resources.

In order to assess those strengths, Saleebey developed five types of questions:

1. Survival Questions: Given all the challenges you have had to contend with, how have you managed to survivor thus far? What was your mind-set as you faced these difficulties? What are the special qualities on which you can rely?

2. Support Questions: What people have given you special understanding, support, or guidance? Who are the people on whom you can depend? What is it that these people give you that is exceptional?

3. Exception Questions: When things were going well in life, what was different? What parts of your world and your being would you like to recapture, reinvent, or relive? What moments or incidents in your life have given you special understanding, resilience, and guidance?

4. Possibility Questions: What are your hopes, visions, and aspirations? How far along are you toward achieving these? What do you like to do? What fantasies and dreams have given you special hope and guidance?

5. Esteem Questions: When people say good things about you, what are they likely to say? What is it about your life, yourself, and your accomplishments that give you pride? How will you know when things are going well in your

life; what will you be doing? Who will you be with? How will you be thinking, feeling, and acting?

Sexual abuse in any form can be a devastating, demoralizing experience. Therapy from a strengths perspective not only helps stem the flow of negativity that has infiltrated the fabric of the survivor's life, but also helps to empower him or her by identifying and showcasing the strengths that made him or her a true survivor in the first place—and that is a healing place to start.

Denise Lang-Grant

See also Advocacy; Empowerment

Further Reading

Marty D., Rapp, C., & Carlson, L. (2001). The experts speak: The critical ingredients of strengths model case management. *Psychiatric Rehabilitation Journal, 24,* 214–221.

Saleebey, Dennis. (2006). *The strengths perspective in social work.* Boston, MA: Allyn & Bacon.

Seligman, M. E. P., Park, N., Steen, T. A., & Peterson, C. (2005). Positive psychology progress: Empirical validation of interventions. *American Psychologist, 60,* 410–421.

Tong, Min. (2011). The client-centered integrative strengths-based approach: Ending longstanding conflict between social work values and practice. *Canadian Social Science, 7*(2), 15–22.

Selected Websites

This Emotional Life. A PBS Series. Embracing a Strengths Perspective. Retrieved from http://www.pbs.org/thisemotionallife/blogs/embracing-strengths-perspective

University of Kansas, School of Social Welfare, Strengths Institute. Retrieved from http://www.socwel.ku.edu/strengths/about/index.shtml

University of Pennsylvania, Positive Psychology Center. Retrieved from http://www.ppc.sas.upenn.edu/faqs.htm

Stress Inoculation Training

Stress inoculation training (SIT) is a flexible and individually tailored form of therapy developed by Donald Meichenbaum, PhD, that has proven to be one of the more effective ways in which victims of sexual violence can reduce and manage the anxiety, fear, and physiological symptoms of post-traumatic stress resulting from their assault or abuse.

A sexual assault is the most invasive, personal attack a person can suffer without being murdered. When an assault happens to a person, the mind continues to hold onto the event in a way that includes the original sights, sounds, smells, sensations, and thoughts. The trauma can then be locked inside the memory and "triggered" at any time of day or night, by any of the associated people, sights, or sensations, throwing survivors into a flashback that transports them mentally and physically right into the assault or abuse. The disabling emotional symptoms of this trauma can be experienced for years in the form of depression, anxiety, phobias, and disassociation—or being out of touch with reality—and can impact every aspect of a sexual violence survivor's life. Stress inoculation training teaches sexual abuse survivors how to cope with the hypersensitivity and anxiety that arises from these flashbacks using techniques ranging from muscle relaxation, deep breathing, grounding, and thought stopping, to positive self-talk.

In order to enhance survivors' coping skills and to empower them to use already existing strengths and coping skills, SIT consists of three overlapping phases: (1) conceptualization and education; (2) skill building and rehearsal; and (3) application and follow-through.

In the conceptualization and education phase, a collaborative relationship is developed between the client (survivor) and the therapist (trainer). Survivors learn how fear develops as a learned response to trauma, how to identify those cues in the environment that trigger their fears (i.e., a car that looks like the perpetrator's or the smell of a cologne the perpetrator wore), and relaxation exercises such as progressive muscle relaxation. They also learn to view their triggers as problems-to-be-solved and to identify those hypersensitive reactions as potentially changeable, breaking down stressors into specific short- and long-term coping goals.

The second phase of SIT flows naturally from the first and focuses on helping the survivor acquire coping skills and practicing them. Since every individual is unique and experiences and responds to trauma in a way unique to her or him, the coping skills that are taught are tailored to the specific stressors (triggers) being experienced by the survivor. Some of the specific coping skills can include self-soothing and acceptance, relaxation training, diaphragmatic (or deep) breathing, thought stopping, guided self-talk, and attention diversion procedures such as grounding (sometimes called "centering"). Such skills put distance between the survivor and emotional pain and flashbacks, and using social support systems.

The final phase of SIT, application and follow-through, provides opportunities for the survivor to practice the coping skills that have been learned through increased levels of stressors. This is where the "inoculation" concept is most clearly observed. In medical arenas an inoculation is designed to immunize the patient from a disease. SIT is designed to inoculate the survivor against the impact of the triggers and flashbacks that are experienced as a result of the sexual assault or abuse. Such techniques as role playing, guided imagery, or gradual exposure to those triggers may be utilized. During this phase, survivors also identify high-risk situations that could result in a "relapse" and are encouraged to take ownership of, and reward themselves, for their progress.

Typically, a complete SIT usually takes 7 to 10 sessions. The first phase can take two sessions, phase two may take up to six sessions, and the final phase two to three sessions depending upon the layers and severity of the trauma experienced.

There have been a number of studies performed to examine the validity and success in using SIT for rape victims and sexual abuse survivors. In studies comparing several popular cognitive behavioral therapies including prolonged exposure (PE) and supportive counseling, SIT was the most effective treatment in reducing PTSD symptomatology immediately after treatment, measuring a 55 percent reduction (Foa et al., 1999). SIT is sometimes used in conjunction with PE therapy for an even higher, long-term effective treatment.

Through the use of SIT, sexual assault survivors are successfully learning not only how to identify triggers and confront some of the more devastating residual effects of sexual violence but also how to practice healthy coping and self-soothing skills that mitigate those effects, which, ultimately, allows them to move on with their lives.

Denise Lang-Grant

See also Coping Mechanisms; Depression and Anxiety; Exposure Therapy; PTSD and Stress

Further Reading

Curie, C. G., & Arons, B. S. (2002). *Dealing with the effects of trauma: A self-help guide*. Rockville, MD: U.S. Department of Health and Human Services, Center for Mental Health Services.

Falsetti, S. A., & Bernat, J. A. (n.d.). *Practice guidelines: Rape and sexual assault—empirical treatments for PTSD related to rape and sexual assault*. Retrieved on July 10, 2011, from http://www.musc.edu/vawprevention/advocacy/rape.shtml

Foa, E. B., & Rothbaum, B. O. (1998) *Treating the trauma of rape: Cognitive behavioral therapy for PTSD*. New York, NY: Guilford Press.

Foa, E.B., et al. (1999) *A comparison of exposure therapy, stress inoculation training, and their combination for reducing posttraumatic stress disorder in female assault victims*. Center for the Treatment and Study of Anxiety, Medical College of Pennsylvania-Hahnemann University.

Meichenbaum, D. (1985). *Stress inoculation training*. New York, NY: Pergamon Press.

Mental health and mass violence: Evidence-based early psychological intervention for victims of mass violence. (2002). National Institute of Mental Health. Retrieved from http://www.nimh.nih.gov/health/publications/massviolence.pdf

Najavits, L. M. (2002). *Seeking safety*. New York, NY: Guilford Press.

Veronen, L. J., & Kilpatrick, D. G. (1983). Stress management for rape victims. In D. Meichenbaum & M. E. Jaremko (Eds.), *Stress reduction and prevention* (pp. 341–374). New York, NY: Plenum Press.

Selected Websites

Bay Pines VA Health System: Post Traumatic Stress Disorder Programs. U.S. Department of Veterans Affairs. Retrieved from http://www.baypines.va.gov/BAYPINES/services/Stress.asp

Post Traumatic Stress Disorder Fact Sheet. The National Institute of Mental Health: Stress Inoculation Training: Retrieved from http://www.nimh.nih.gov/health/publications/post-traumatic-stress-disorder-research-fact-sheet/index.shtml

Strip Clubs

Sexual violence and abuse are widespread social problems that span contexts, time periods, and cultures. People who enact violence do so in order to wield power over their victims and, sometimes, what those victims represent. Media depictions of crime and violence shape public perceptions regarding danger. Television and cinema images erroneously suggest that strangers are most likely to pose danger. In fact, we are far more likely to be victimized by friends and acquaintances, coworkers, or family members. Perpetrators of sexual violence defy race, class, and status boundaries, since abusers come from all corners of society.

Women who work in the sex industry also face violence. Sex workers face sexual, physical, and psychological violence in the course of their workday. Places in which sex workers labor include but are not limited to city streets, massage parlors, brothels, and even strip clubs. "Strippers" are a type of sex worker whose sexualized performance is typically confined to an entertainment and bar space called a "strip club."

"Strippers," known by those outside of the trade as "exotic dancers," at times endure high rates of violence. They experience greater threats to their safety and well-being in clubs with poor organizational or working conditions. Perpetrators include men for and with whom strippers work, including club owners, managers, and doormen. They are also sexually and verbally victimized by clients, and are often subject to the harassment and control of the police.

Since we know that sexual violence and abuse expresses power and domination, downtrodden groups like strippers are easy targets. This is because the way in which they earn money is taboo and illegal. Since the U.S. culture frame sex workers as low, despicable women who deserve to be victimized, this makes them more vulnerable to being victimized (Chapkis, 1997; Miller & Schwartz, 1995) and with very little legal or social recourse. Another dangerous stereotype suggests that strippers sell "sex" and therefore cannot be victims of violence or abuse. Alcohol and other drugs sometimes play a part in violence and abuse in strip clubs.

U.S. medical and cultural norms teach us to associate different drugs with inducing certain behaviors when ingested. As an example, it is a common idea that drinking can make people more emotional or violent. Despite other factors being at work, like sexism, patriarchy, and unequal power, strippers and prostitutes view alcohol and other drugs as at times causing violent, aggressive behavior in their clients.

Because we perceive alcohol and other drugs as agents that lower inhibitions and impair judgment, intoxicated strippers become ready victims. Because of their perceived vulnerability when intoxicated, patrons take sexual advantage of them. This is not unique to strippers and other sex workers. Indeed, studies show that male college students target intoxicated women for sexual predation on college campuses. Moreover, with lowered inhibitions themselves, some strip club customers become more sexually and physically aggressive.

In short, many girls and women experience violence and abuse. Strippers and other sex workers are groups at especially high risk to experience such violence. Strippers implicate alcohol and other drugs in order to understand the physical, sexual, and psychological violence that they endure by men in their occupational setting.

Melissa F. Lavin

See also Pornography; Pornography, Internet; Prostitution; Sex Workers

Further Reading

Bernstein, Elizabeth. (2007). *Temporarily yours: Intimacy, authenticity, and the commerce of sex.* Chicago, IL: Chicago University Press.

Chapkis, Wendy. (1997). *Live sex acts: Women performing erotic labor.* New York, NY: Routledge.

Miller, J., & Schwartz, M. D. (1995). Rape myths and violence against street prostitutes. *Deviant Behavior, 16,* 1–23.

Price-Glynn, Kim. (2010). *Strip club: Gender, power and sex work.* New York, NY: New York University Press.

Surratt, Hilary L., Inciardi, James A., Kurtz, Steven P., & Kiley, Marion C. (2004). Sex work and drug use in a subculture of violence. *Crime & Delinquency, 50*(1), 43–59.

Wesely, Jennifer K. (2002). Growing up sexualized: Issues of power and violence in the lives of female exotic dancers. *Violence Against Women, 8*(10), 1182–1207.

Selected Websites

Sex Workers Outreach Project. Retrieved from http://www.spop.org.au

United Nations Women. Retrieved from http://www.unwomen.org

Substance Abuse as a Consequence

The relationship between substance abuse and sexual violence has long been established. Still, this remains a particularly difficult problem to identify, evaluate, or fix because the sexual violence may not have physically observable consequences. The violence may portray the victim in a negative manner such that the victim may not wish to make the abuse public. Complicating this is the vast range of substance abuse that may be involved. Moreover, this is an issue involving multiple people and systems. Victims of sexual violence may end up in an emergency room or in a police department; perpetrators may be incarcerated or institutionalized, or may go to a living situation, leaving the victim, perhaps, more vulnerable. In epidemiological terms, the relationship between these two deviant behaviors questions temporal association. Did the sexual violence precede the substance abuse, did the substance abuse precede the sexual violence, or did they occur simultaneously? The risk of sexual violence, according to most research, is highest when both partners are substance users.

The majority of published research on sexual violence and substance abuse has focused on alcohol abuse. That relationship is clearly established and years of study have concluded that alcohol abuse is common in male perpetrators. The more scant research on illicit drug abuse is less directional. Cocaine increases the likelihood of sexual violence in most studies (Gilbert, El-Bassel, Chang, Wu, & Roy, 2011). The relationship between cannabis or marijuana is less clear and does not appear to follow what in epidemiology is called a dose-response relationship. That is, more cannabis use does not predict greater violence. When drug abuse occurs with alcohol abuse, there is also evidence there is a higher risk of sexual violence.

The relationship between illicit-drug use is harder to evaluate because of the wide range of substances and their different effects on behavior. However, what is certain is that the nature and culture of illicit drugs presents dangers related to the transactions involved in obtaining drugs. These vary greatly but all represent criminal behavior. Moreover, because of the illegal nature of obtaining, possessing, and using illegal drugs, victims may be less likely to report sexual violence incidents. If this is true, the best rates we can use are those derived from medical records and the justice system.

Several theories have been developed attempting to explain which factors contribute to sexual violence in substance abusers. The deviance theory states that substance abuse does not cause sexual violence or the inverse but rather that both are deviant behaviors. Individuals involved in one deviant behavior are likely to be involved in others. An extension of this theory proposes that both these deviant behaviors are linked to antisocial personality disorders. Some studies suggest that drugs interact with neurotransmitters, such as dopamine and serotonin, and this increases the likelihood of aggression. The biopsychosocial model combines elements of previous models and differentiates between proximal causes, or what has occurred recently, versus distal causes, such as childhood trauma. Distal factors may also include previous drug use, which makes a person more vulnerable to recidivism. These multifactor theories make treatment options difficult as it is unclear which deviant behavior or psychosocial problem should be prioritized.

Many women in substance abuse treatment programs are likely to have been sexually assaulted (Schneider, Burnette, & Timko, 2008). Unlike men, they tend to have broader needs often related to caring for children. Treatment that incorporates reducing structural barriers to housing and health care, and factors in children's needs may be more appropriate for younger and minority women. In 1994 Congress passed the Violence Against Women Act, which acknowledged the need for research on violence against women with special needs. This Act was reauthorized a few times since 1994 and is in process now of being reauthorized again. Perhaps because problems related to illicit-drug use seem so urgent, it is more difficult to plan for long-term solutions. Policy makers may, for future populations, examine the role of education in reducing the risk of substance abuse and sexual violence.

Griselda Chapa

See also Alcohol and Drug Abuse, Perpetration; Alcohol and Drug Abuse, Victimization; Child Sexual Abuse; Coping Mechanisms; Underreporting

Further Reading

Andrews, C. M., Cao, D., & Shin, H. C. (2011). The impact of comprehensive services in substance abuse treatment for women with a history of intimate partner violence. *Violence Against Women, 17*(5), 550–567.

Gilbert, L., El-Bassel, N., Chang, M., Wu, E., & Roy, L. (2011, October 24). Substance use and partner violence among urban women seeking emergency care. *Psychological Addictive Behavior.*

Golinelli, D., Longshore, D., & Wenzel, S. L. (2009). Substance use and intimate partner violence: Clarifying the relevance of women's use and partners' use. *Journal of Behavioral Health Services & Research, 36*(2), 199–211.

Moore, T. M., Stuart, G. L., Meehan, J. C., Rhatigan, D. L., Hellmuth, J. C., & Keen, S. M. (2008). Drug abuse and aggression between intimate partners: A meta-analytic review. *Clinical Psychology Review, 28*, 247–274.

Schnitzer, P. G., Slusher, P. L., Kruse, R. L., & Tarleton, M. M. (2011). Identification of ICD codes suggestive of child maltreatment. *Child Abuse & Neglect, 35*(1), 3–17.

Schneider, R., Burnette, M., & Timko, C. (2008). History of physical or sexual abuse and participation in 12-step self-help groups. *American Journal of Drug and Alcohol Abuse, 34*(5), 617–625.

Stuart, G. L., O'Farrell, T. J., & Temple, J. R. (2009). Review of the association between treatment for substance misuse and reductions in intimate partner violence. *Substance Use & Misuse, 44*(9/10), 1298–1317.

Swartout, K. M., & White, J. W. (2010). The relationship between drug use and sexual aggression in men across time. *Journal of Interpersonal Violence, 25*(9), 1716–1735.

Temple, J. R., Stuart, G. L., & O'Farrell, T. J. (2009). Prevention of intimate partner violence in substance-using populations. *Substance Use & Misuse, 44*(9/10), 1318–1328.

Selected Website

Violence prevention. Centers for Disease Control and Prevention. Retrieved from http://www.cdc.gov/ViolencePrevention/index.html (addresses injuries with links to dating violence and other aggression)

Substantiation (of Legal Charges)

Only 14 to 18 percent of all reported sexual assaults are prosecuted (Campbell, 2008). Given this low prosecution rate, researchers examine the factors predicting the prosecution of sexual assault cases by the criminal justice system (CJS). Research suggests that the CJS forwards cases for prosecution only if they are perceived as credible (i.e., believable) or "winnable." For example, many judges and jurors still view a victim's injuries as necessary proof that the victim did not consent even though the law no longer requires physical proof of resistance. As such, most studies suggest that cases in which the victim endures injuries are more likely to be moved forward by CJ personnel.

In addition to injury, the CJS often prosecutes cases in which they believe the victim will make a credible witness. A case might not be prosecuted if officials do not think that the victim will make a credible witness even if CJ personnel believe that a sexual assault occurred. The perception that a victim will make a credible witness may be influenced by characteristics of the victim such as age, race, and alcohol use. For example, middle-aged and white victims are more likely to have their cases prosecuted because CJS personnel believe that jurors will perceive these victims as credible (Campbell, Wasco, Ahrens, Sefl, & Barnes, 2001).

Alcohol and drug use by the victim is another element that significantly influences the CJS system dropping cases (Campbell, Patterson, Bybee, & Dworkin, 2009). For example, Campbell (1998) reported that victims who were drinking at the time of the assault were four times more likely to have their cases dropped. Alcohol or drug use may diminish the victim's credibility in the eyes of the CJS (Spears & Spohn, 1996).

Studies also suggest that lack of victim engagement with the prosecution process significantly influences cases being dropped for prosecution (Kerstetter & Van Winkle 1990). A delay in reporting by victims is also related to cases not being prosecuted. Victims who wait even a day to report their assault may be viewed as less credible or uncertain about prosecuting. Additionally, prosecutors tend to drop cases if there is anything that is inconsistent in the victim's story regarding key aspects of the sexual assault. The discrepancies in the victims' accounts of the assault are used as indicators that the victims lacked credibility. However, prosecutors assumed that the victims' inconsistencies could not be attributed to error of law enforcement.

Research has also established that characteristics of the assault influence prosecution. Studies exploring the role of the victim-offender relationship in prosecution have shown mixed results. Research suggests that sexual assault cases involving acquaintances (i.e., suspects known to the victim) may be assessed and treated differently than incidents involving strangers. The major investigative concern in stranger cases is identifying the offender. Conversely, decisions to warrant acquaintance cases are determined largely by assessing the lack of consent by, and the credibility of, the victim (Kerstetter & Van Winkle, 1990). Earlier studies suggest that if the offender is a stranger to the victim, there is a greater chance that the case will be prosecuted than if the victim knows the offender (Bradmiller & Walters, 1985; Rose and Randall, 1982).. In contrast, more recent studies have shown that the victim-offender relationship has no effect on legal outcomes (Spears & Spohn, 1997). For example, Spohn, Beichner, and Davis-Fernzel (2001) found that prosecutors did not prosecute stranger cases more often than acquaintance cases. They noted that most of the victims of stranger sexual assaults in the study engaged in behavior likely to be questioned by the prosecutors such as delayed reporting.

Finally, offender tactics may influence whether the case is prosecuted. Sex offenders use various types of tactics to control victims such as weapons or force. Several studies have shown that the presence of a weapon or the use of force increased the probability that a case will move forward in the CJS (Campbell, Wasco, Ahrens, Sefl, & Barnes, 2001; Martin, 2005). Weapon use was particularly important in cases where the offender claimed that the victim consented to sexual activity. However, some studies have suggested that weapon use has no effect on the prosecution of sexual assault cases (Spears & Spohn, 1997).

Debra Patterson

See also Alcohol and Drug Abuse, Victimization; Bias, Police and Prosecution; Reporting Rates; Victims, Credibility

Further Reading

Bradmiller, L. L. & Walters, W. S. (1985). Seriousness of sexual assault charges: Influence factors. *Criminal Justice and Behavior*, *12*(4), 463–484.

Bulman, P. (2009). Increasing sexual assault prosecution rates. *National Institute of Justice Journal*. Retrieved from http://www.ojp.usdoj.gov/nij/journals/264/SANE.htm

Campbell, R. (2008). The psychological impact of rape victims' experiences with the legal, medical, and mental health systems. *American Psychologist, 63*(8), 702–717.

Campbell, R., Patterson, D., Bybee, D., & Dworkin, E. R. (2009). Predicting sexual assault prosecution outcomes: The role of medical forensic evidence collected by sexual assault nurse examiners (SANEs). *Criminal Justice and Behavior, 36*(7), 712–727.

Campbell, R., Wasco, S., Ahrens, C., Sefl, T., & Barnes, H. (2001). Preventing the "second rape": Rape survivors' experiences with community service providers. *Journal of Interpersonal Violence, 16*(12), 1239–1259.

Kerstetter, W., & Van Winkle, B. (1990). Who decides? A study of the complainant's decision to prosecute in rape cases. *Criminal Justice and Behavior, 17*(3), 268–283.

Konradi, A. (2007). *Taking the stand: Rape survivors and the prosecution of rapists.* Westport, CT: Praeger.

Martin, P. Y. (2005). *Rape work: Victims, gender, and emotions in organization and community context.* New York, NY: Routledge. Rose, V. & Randall, S. (1982). The impact of investigator perceptions of victim legitimacy on the processing of rape/sexual assault cases. *Symbolic Interaction, 5*, 23–36.

Spears, J., & Spohn, C. (1996). The genuine victim and prosecutors' charging decisions in sexual assault cases. *American Journal of Criminal Justice, 20*(2), 183–205.

Spears, J. & Spohn, C. (1997). The effect of evidence factors and victim characteristics on prosecutors' charging decisions in sexual assault cases. *Justice Quarterly, 14* (3), 501–524.

Spohn, C., Beichner, D., & Davis-Frenzel, E. (2001). Prosecutorial justifications for sexual assault case rejection: Guarding the "gateway to justice." *Social Problems, 48*(2), 206–235.

Spohn, C. C., & Hemmens, C. (2009). *Courts: A text/reader.* Thousand Oaks, CA: Sage.

Selected Website

Criminal Justice for Rape & Sexual Abuse Survivors: A Chat Transcript with Joanne Archambault. Pandora's Project. Retrieved from http://www.pandorasproject.org/criminaljustice.html

Suicidality

Suicidality is suicidal thinking or behavior; it includes completed suicide, attempted suicide, planning suicide, and thoughts of suicide. Experiencing sexual violence is a key risk factor for suicidality. Suicide is the 11th leading cause of death in the United (Centers for Disease Control and Prevention [CDC], 2011). Approximately 36,000 people committed suicide in 2008 (Crosby, Han, Ortega, Parks, & Groerer, 2011). This is just the tip of the iceberg. Each year, many more people are admitted to the hospital with at least an overnight stay for self-injury (197,838 people in 2008), seek care for nonfatal self-injury at emergency departments (323,342 people in 2008), or attempt suicide (estimated 1 million people in 2008) (Crosby, Han, Ortega, Parks, & Groerer, 2011) (see figure from Crosby et al. at http://www.cdc.gov/mmwr/preview/mmwrhtml/ss6013a1.htm). An even greater number plan a suicide or think seriously about committing suicide. The CDC estimates that in 2009, 2.2 million adults made suicide plans and 8.3 million adults had serious thoughts of suicide. Additionally, between 12 and 15 percent of adolescents may experience some form of thoughts about suicide. Key risk factors for suicidality in both adolescents and adults are experiencing child sexual abuse (CSA) and/or experiencing sexual violence as an adolescent or adult.

Many studies report that child sexual abuse (CSA) is a nonspecific risk factor for a range of different mental health problems, including suicide ideation and attempts. One meta-analysis statistically combined the results of over 37 different studies and found that those sexually abused as children were 4.14 times as likely to attempt suicide as those who were not sexually abused as children (Chen et al., 2010). There are mixed data on the effect of age, gender, and specific types of CSA on suicidality. Some studies find that boys, those who were younger when sexually assaulted, those who experienced more severe sexual assaults, and those assaulted by family members are at even higher risk of suicidality. Other studies find limited or no effect by these factors (Maniglio, 2011). Several reviews noted that there are problems with the current literature, including inconsistent or single item definitions of CSA and a lack of control for other factors related to suicidality (e.g. mental health issues, family circumstances) (Maniglio, 2011).

Experiencing sexual violence (dating violence or rape) in adolescence and during young adulthood is a risk factor for suicidality in girls. This relationship is found in nationally representative studies, state-level studies, and studies of specific subpopulations (such as college students and inner-city Latino youth). It is also a risk factor for problem behaviors that are related to suicidality such as binge drinking, substance abuse, and risky sexual behaviors. Studies find that the relationship between suicidality and sexual violence remains even when these behaviors and other factors are accounted for (Olshen, McVeigh, Wunsch-Hitzig, & Rickert, 2007).

Rape and sexual assault in adulthood is an established risk factor for suicidality. One population based study found the risk of suicide ideation was almost six times higher among those sexually assaulted in adulthood than for those not sexually assaulted, even after accounting for other factors related to suicidality such as CSA and sociodemographic factors (age, gender, ethnicity, marital status, employment) (Calder, McVean, & Yang, 2009). Those raped in prison are also at increased risk of suicidality. Other factors that put adult sexual violence victims at an even increased risk of suicidality include being younger, ethnic minority and experiencing repeated violence, multiple perpetrators, or more severe sexual violence (Ullman & Najdowski, 2009).

The risk of suicidality from CSA, adolescent violence, and adult sexual violence is persistent. One study of older women in psychiatric care found that those with suicidality issues were much more likely to have experienced some form of sexual violence in the past (even if the event[s] were many years ago) (Osgood & Manetta, 2000–2001). The risk of suicidality from sexual violence in adulthood remains even among those at elevated risk of suicidality from other factors such as being in the military (Lemaire & Graham, 2011) or experiencing intimate partner violence (Weaver et al., 2007).

In understanding the link between sexual violence and suicidality, it is important to note that sexual violence is both a direct and indirect cause of suicidality. Child sexual abuse, adolescent dating violence, rape, and other sexual violence experienced in adulthood are all associated with increased rates of depression, post-traumatic stress disorder, substance use and abuse, binge drinking, and risky sexual behaviors. These mental health and behavioral issues are also associated with suicidality. However, a number of studies have found that the effect of sexual violence on suicidality persists even when these other factors are taken into account. Experiencing sexual violence may directly increase the risk of suicidality through decreasing a person's perceived reasons for living. One study of college women reveals that those who experience sexual coercion or rape score significantly lower on a validated "Reasons for Living" test (Segal, 2009).

The very limited data available on treatment and intervention for suicidality indicate that it can lessen the risk of suicidality. One study finds that those who felt they had control over their assault recovery were somewhat less likely to have attempted suicide (Ullman & Najdowski, 2009). Additionally, a study of male rape victims finds those who did not receive any treatment or intervention are more likely to attempt suicide than those who do receive some treatment (Walker, Archer, & Davies, 2005).

Stacey Plichta

See also Child Sexual Abuse; Depression and Anxiety; Intimate Partner Violence; PTSD and Stress; Substance Abuse as a Consequence

Further Reading

Calder, J., McVean, A., & Yang, W. (2009). History of abuse and current suicidal ideation: Results from a population based survey. *Journal of Family Violence, 25*, 205–214.

Chen, L. P., Murad, M. H., Paras, M. L., Colbenson, K. M., Sattler, A. L., Goranson, E. N., ... Zirakzadeh, A. (2010). Sexual abuse and lifetime diagnosis of psychiatric disorders: Systematic review and meta-analysis. *Mayo Clinic Proceedings, 85*(7), 618–629.

Crosby, A. E., Han, B., Ortega, L. A. G., Parks, S. E., & Groerer, J. (2011). Suicidal thoughts and behaviors among adults aged $\geq$ 18 years. Surveillance Summaries. *Morbidity and Mortality Weekly Report, 60*(SS13), 1–22. Retrieved from http://www.cdc.gov/mmwr/preview/mmwrhtml/ss6013a1.htm

Lemaire, C. M., & Graham, D. P. (2011). Factors associated with suicidal ideation in OEF/OIF veterans. *Journal of Affective Disorders, 130*(1–2), 231–238.

Maniglio, R. (2011). The role of child sexual abuse in the etiology of suicide and non-suicidal self-injury. *Acta Psychiatrica Scandanavia, 124*, 30–41.

Olshen, E., McVeigh, K. H., Wunsch-Hitzig, R. A., & Rickert, V. I. (2007). Dating violence, sexual assault and suicide attempts among urban teenagers. *Archives of Pediatric & Adolescent Medicine, 161*(6), 539–545.

Osgood, N. J., & Manetta, A. A. (2000–2001). Abuse and suicidal issues in older women. *Omega: Journal of Death and Dying, 42*(1), 71–81.

Segal, D. L. (2009). Self-reported history of sexual coercion and rape negatively impacts resilience to suicide among women students. *Death Studies, 33*, 848–855.

Ullman, S. E., & Najdowski, C. J. (2009). Correlates of serious suicidal ideation and attempts in female adult sexual assault survivors. *Suicide and Life-Threatening Behavior, 39*(1), 47–57.

Walker, J., Archer, J., & Davies, M. (2005). Effects of male rape on psychological functioning. *British Journal of Clinical Psychology, 44*(Pt. 3), 445–451.

Weaver, T. L., Allen, J. A., Hopper, E., Maglione, M. L. K., McCullough, M. A., Jackson, M. K., & Brewer, T. (2007). Mediators of suicidal ideation within a sheltered sample of raped and battered women. *Health Care for Women International, 28*(5), 478–489.

Immediate Help

If you are in a crisis and need help right away or know someone who does need immediate help, call the National Suicide Prevention Lifeline at 1-800-273-TALK (8255). This hotline is open 24/7 and you will be able to talk to a live person.

Selected Websites

Centers for Disease Control and Prevention, National Center for Injury Prevention and Control. (2011). Web-based Injury Statistics Query and Reporting System (WISQARS). Retrieved from http://www.cdc.gov/ncipc/wisqars.

MaleSurvivor. Overcoming Sexual Victimization of Men and Boys. Retrieved from http://www.malesurvivor.org/default.html

National Sexual Assault Online Hotline. RAINN (Rape, Abuse & Incest National Network). Retrieved from http://apps.rainn.org/ohl-bridge/

Suicide in the United States: Statistics and prevention. National Institute of Mental Health. Retrieved from http://www.nimh.nih.gov/health/publications/suicide-in-the-us -statistics-and-prevention/index.shtml

Support Groups

Support groups for survivors of sexual violence and abuse consist of in-person or online professionally led meetings in which survivors share their experiences of sexual abuse and learn from one another. Many support groups also include a group therapy component in which a professional provides therapy to the group based on a specific protocol or manual. In addition to being cost-effective for agencies and participants, support groups decrease isolation and recognize the shared experiences of the group members. Support groups are an effective treatment for many survivors of sexual abuse, and these benefits have been shown to persist after the support group ends. However, support groups may not be beneficial for all survivors of sexual violence. It is critical for practitioners and clinicians to consider the individual needs and state of recovery of each client before referring him or her to a support group.

Support groups are one type of treatment that may be used independent of other treatments, before or after individual therapy, or simultaneously with other types of therapy. By providing treatment to more than one individual at a time, support groups are a cost-effective treatment modality for agencies. Overlapping with self-help groups in many ways, supports groups are professionally led meetings in which members learn from one another, provide reciprocal support, and discuss their individual experiences of sexual abuse while receiving guidance and support from a professional mental health counselor or social worker as needed. Additionally, support groups help survivors recognize the "universality" of their shared sexual violence experience and decrease the social isolation associated with experiences of sexual victimization. Giving and receiving help within the group creates a bond with other group members and allows each member to recognize personal strengths and increase his or her confidence.

Sexual assault and abuse support groups can take a number of different forms. Often these groups are divided into support groups for survivors of rape or sexual assault and support groups for survivors of childhood sexual abuse. Support groups specific to survivors of incest also exist. However, survivors of different types of sexual violence may benefit from involvement in the same support group in smaller communities or agencies. To address specific developmental needs, separate support groups are typically provided to children and to adults. Support groups are also available for parents of children who have been sexually abused. Although support groups vary greatly in their structure and length, time-limited support groups of 15 weekly sessions or fewer have been found to be successful in improving mood and self-esteem levels (De Jong & Gorey, 1996). Each support group develops its own pattern and way of relating. However, developing a sense of group unity is a key component of effective groups (Knight, 1990).

Although goals differ between support groups, Knight (1990) provided five general goals present in many adult support groups. First, support groups help each adult survivor acknowledge that he or she was sexually abused and recognize the feelings he or she associates with the experience. Next, support groups help survivors work through any associated denial or negative emotions and "accept the extent to which they were victimized" (p. 204). Third, support groups help survivors stop blaming themselves for the abuse and shift these feelings to the abuser or assailant. Fourth, support groups aim to decrease the isolating experience of sexual assault. Fifth, support groups help members determine the next step to take to aid in healing from the sexual violence of abuse experienced.

Research comparing survivors who attended group therapy for sexual assault or abuse to control groups of survivors who do not attend group therapy indicates that group therapy is an effective treatment with long-term improvements for many survivors. In a study of 57 women, Bagley and Young (1998) found that female sexual abuse survivors who attended a group therapy program five years earlier were still experiencing higher self-esteem, lower depression, and fewer suicidal ideas or attempts compared to the control group of women who were only referred to a psychiatrist and who did not attend group therapy. In a study of 40 adult female survivors of childhood sexual abuse completed by Morgan and Cummings (1999), women who attended the 20-week group therapy intervention were found to have lower levels of depression, higher levels of social support, and lower levels of guilt related to the sexual abuse when compared to a group of sexual abuse survivors who did not attend group therapy. However, a review of therapeutic interventions for survivors of sexual assault found individual therapy to be more effective than group therapy at improving outcomes for participants (Taylor & Harvey, 2009). Additional research is needed to evaluate the effectiveness of support groups that do not include a group therapy component and support groups for men.

Although sexual abuse support groups are beneficial to many survivors of sexual violence, they should not be a universal treatment for all sexual assault and abuse survivors. Some survivors may experience vicarious traumatization due to participating in a sexual abuse or assault support group. Vicarious traumatization involves experiencing high levels of distress due to listening to the traumatic experiences of another person. Palmer, Stalker, Harper, and Gadbois (2007) found that 20 percent of participants who received a group treatment for women reported symptoms consistent with experiencing vicarious traumatization due to participation in this group. Individuals who have more severe histories of sexual trauma and who are not yet prepared to address these issues or discuss them with other group members may not benefit from support groups. These individuals may require individual therapy or specialized group treatments to specifically address these needs.

In summary, support groups are one form of treatment for survivors of sexual violence and abuse that may aid in recovery. Support groups involving professionally led therapy have been found to improve self-esteem, lower depression, improve social support, decrease feelings of guilt, and decrease suicidal ideation and attempts in female survivors of childhood sexual abuse. Many of these benefits may persist long after the conclusion of the group.

Kristen D. Seay

See also Depression and Anxiety; Group Therapy; Vicarious Traumatization; Victims, Guilt and Shame

Further Reading

Bagley, C., & Young, L. (1998). Long-term evaluation of group counseling for women with a history of child sexual abuse: focus on depression, self-esteem, suicidal behaviors and social support. *Social Work with Groups, 21*(3), 63–73.

De Jong, T., & Gorey, K. (1996). Short-term versus long-term work with female survivors of childhood sexual abuse: A brief meta-analytic review. *Social Work with Groups, 19*, 19–27.

Knight, C. (2005). From victim to survivor: Group work with men and women who were sexually abused. In A. Gitterman & L. Shulman (Eds.), *Mutual aid groups, vulnerable and resilient populations, and the life cycle* (pp. 320–351). New York, NY: Columbia University Press.

Knight, C. (1990). Use of support groups with adult female survivors of child sexual abuse. *Social Work, 35*(3), 202–206.

Morgan, T., & Cummings, A. L (1999). Change experienced during group therapy by female survivors of childhood sexual abuse. *Journal of Consulting and Clinical Psychology, 6*(1), 28–36.

Palmer, S., Stalker, C.A., Harper, K., & Gadbois, S. (2007). Balancing positive outcomes with vicarious traumatization: Participants' experiences with group treatment for long-term effects of childhood abuse. *Social Work with Groups, 30*(4), 59–77. doi:10.1300/J009v30n04_05

Taylor, J. E., & Harvey, S. T. (2009). Effects of psychotherapy with people who have been sexually assaulted: A meta-analysis. *Aggression and Violent Behavior, 14*, 273–285. doi:10.1016/j.avb.2009.03.006

Yalom, I. D., & Leszcz, M. (2005). *The theory and practice of group psychotherapy.* New York, NY: Basic Books.

Selected Websites

RAINN (Rape, Abuse & Incest National Network). Retrieved from http://centers.rainn.org/ (A national hotline for survivors of sexual abuse and assault, this link to RAINN can be used to find an agency providing group counseling for survivors in the United States.)

Pandora's Project. Retrieved from http://www.pandorasaquarium.org (This nonprofit runs an online support group for survivors of sexual violence with a message board and educational resources.)

T

Technology, Use of (Overview)

Sexual violence is a broad category with various definitions from legal, social, and scientific perspectives that have become further complicated over the past 20 years as availability and use of new technology has become mainstream worldwide. "Sexual violence" is an all-encompassing, colloquial term used to describe a wide of range of sexually aggressive and inappropriate behavior, from *sexual battery (assault)* to unwanted paraphilic incidents such as indecent exposure. Classification as *sexual assault* requires that that the act occurred without victim consent. Legal definitions and classification of sexual assault vary by state and are typically defined in varying degrees of severity. Legal definitions typically consider the type of sexual act (penetration, touching, etc.), the ages of the victim and perpetrator, and the use of force or coercion.

From a *social* perspective, sexual assault includes any unwanted sexual contact (including fondling, groping) against a victim without their consent. Sexual assault may be perpetrated by a family member, stranger, or acquaintance (e.g., date rape), against a child, adolescent, or adult. Sometimes, perpetrators use substances that disinhibit or impair judgment (e.g., alcohol) or create a loss of consciousness to reduce resistance (e.g., rape drugs) (see entry on **Rape Drugs**).

The advent of the Internet and its subsequent evolution into a ubiquitous communication medium provides a variety of new ways for sexual violence to be manifested. There are two main manifestations of victimization in cyberspace. The first includes the development of new types of sexual (e.g., cyber rape, cyber sexual harassment) and nonsexual (e.g., cyberbullying) victimization. The other consequence is that cyberspace is used as a gateway to hands-on offenses by meeting and grooming potential victims.

Interpersonal Interactions and the Internet

According to the U.S. Census Bureau (2012), in 2011, 78 percent of American adults currently use the Internet at least occasionally. Among those adults, the two most popular functions of the Internet are communication and information seeking: 94 percent use the Internet for e-mail and 87 percent for accessing search engines. Other common uses include online shopping, social networking, and entertainment (e.g., watching videos). Internet use is widespread among children as well, with 59 percent of children ages 3 through 17 going online at least occasionally (National Center for Education Statistics, 2006). Use begins early: 23 percent of children in nursery school use the Internet. This number increases to 50 percent by third grade and 79 percent by grades 9 through 12. Just as among adults, communication and information gathering are the most common uses for children, with 38 percent reporting that they use the Internet for e-mail and instant messaging and 46 percent to work on school assignments.

As the Internet has grown in popularity and breadth over the last two decades, it has changed the way people communicate. No longer must one either patiently wait for the postal service to deliver a letter, or accumulate expensive long-distance phone charges. The Internet has dramatically increased the speed of global communication, as well as reducing—often eliminating—the costs. Tools such as e-mail, instant messaging, and video chatting make it easier for people to connect almost instantly across great distances. As this technology becomes increasingly more portable, the Internet makes rapid communication possible regardless of location, allowing for communication in places and in ways previously unimaginable.

Communication via the Internet occurs in a variety of formats, most notably through the exchange of text (e-mail, instant messaging, text messaging), images (e-mail, picture messaging), and video (prerecorded such as those found on sites like YouTube and real-time video exchanges using programs such as Skype).

The Internet is accessible through a number of means, the most popular being computers (desktop and laptop), cell phones, "smartphones," such as the Black-Berry and iPhone, and tablet computers, such as the iPad. Using these different formats, cyber interactions take place in a variety of contexts. The following section will describe several such contexts, including phones, websites, and video games.

Phones

The introduction of text messaging and Internet access took wireless phones from simple conversational devices to multipurpose, multifunctional tools. Cell phones now allow for communication in a variety of ways, including voice, e-mail, instant messaging, text messaging, and video calling. A side effect of this enhanced communication is that additional means of engaging in sexual communications have developed as well.

Sexting. (See **Sexting** entry by Haller, Myers, and Okada.) A combination of the words "sex" and "texting," it is the act of sending sexually explicit images or sexually provocative remarks or statements via cell phone. This is a popular practice among teens, with 71 percent of adolescent girls and 67 percent of adolescent boys reporting that they have exchanged sexually suggestive content with another individual, in the form of either text or imagery (National Campaign, 2008). Most individuals in those age groups own cell phones, and most cell phones currently on the market are equipped with cameras, allowing the creation and sharing of sexual imagery to be achieved fairly easily. Young adults participate as well, though at lower rates than adolescents: 36 percent of women and 31 percent of men between the ages of 20 and 26 report that they have exchanged sext messages (Family Research Council, 2009).

Sexting raises a combination of social, emotional, and legal issues. Three-quarters of adolescents and young adults acknowledge that there can be negative emotional consequences of sharing intimate photos and messages, such as embarrassment, shame, humiliation, bad reputation, and disappointing family (Family Research Council, 2009). However, it appears that these consequences are not inhibiting behavior (i.e., are not being taken into consideration when the messages are being composed and sent). In the moment, most sexters give little thought to where these images might end up once they have been released. Consequently, a great deal of media attention has been paid to what can go wrong, particularly when images fall into the hands of parents or when partners naïvely send the images to their friends who, in turn, send them to others, or when ex-partners distribute images out of anger or malice. Furthermore, adolescent sexting practices can result in serious legal issues, since it is a criminal offense in the United States to produce and transmit sexually explicit imagery of those legally defined as children, typically any individual below the age of 17. Despite the young age of teenage sexters, they are not exempt from this law, and a number of adolescents have been arrested and tried under these child pornography laws.

Sexual apps.   Another method of engaging in sexual interactions via smartphones is the use of applications, commonly known as apps, with sexual content. Apps are computer software designed to help the user perform specific tasks. They can be obtained via downloads from the phone's manufacturer for a small fee, though many are available at no charge. Apps are available for a wide variety of purposes, from monitoring public transit to personal accounting to locating nearby businesses. Not surprisingly, many of the apps on the market contain sexual content, such as sexually themed games or suggestive imagery. This makes it possible for individuals to access sexual content on their phones at any time and in any location. However, in response to complaints from users, some companies have begun to place restrictions on the type of apps available. For example, Apple, the manufacturer of the iPhone and iPad, bans from its App Store the sale of apps featuring sexually suggestive content. Apple also offers parental controls to protect children from sexual content. Although many users have complained about this policy, Apple has remained firm. Apple's competitors have not followed suit, however, instead continuing to make sexually themed apps available to those who want them.

Websites

Of all media, websites provide the largest range of communication to be used in sexual interactions. Websites may be devoted solely to obtaining and purchasing sexually based content, such as pornographic images, and online sex shows. Some websites allow for interactive experiences, such as participating in sexual activities, including sexual perpetration through virtual world fantasy games (see the **Video Games [Rape Fantasy Games]** entry by Myers, Lamade, and Okada for more details), as well as those that allow paying consumers to request sexual acts to be enacted via webcamera. Additionally, sexual theme-based websites include newsgroups, message boards, and sites that support and provide information about various sexual activities, ranging from educational, to promoting paraphilic sexual actives (e.g., The North American Man/Boy Love Association). The entry on **Websites for Perpetrators** by Lamade and Okada also discusses these opportunities. There are a plethora of websites dedicated to assisting victims of sexual abuse and assault, which the **Websites for Victims** entry by Lamade discusses. Websites may also be used for the specific intent to meet, groom, and perpetrate a hands-on offense against an individual.

Cyber Activities

The combination of accessibility, affordability, and anonymity, dubbed the "Triple-A Engine" by Cooper (1998), make the Internet an attractive and efficient venue for gratifying all manner of sexual interests. Like any tool, the Internet can be used in a positive way to explore one's sexuality and experiment in cyber-sexual activities with a consenting adult. For individuals with social anxiety and limited communication and social skills, it can be extremely difficult if not impossible to initiate conversations with strangers. The shield of anonymity allows such individuals to experiment socially and still feel protected. For both shy and outgoing people, it provides the freedom to explore social situations, to be open without fear of being judged or labeled, and to explore different aspects of an existing persona or to create an entirely new persona. This type of anonymity may be especially attractive and helpful to those in sexually disenfranchised and isolated communities (e.g., transgendered). However, there are clearly dangerous manifestations, such as sexual exploitation of others, and acting on deviant sexual interests (e.g., child pornography/pedophilia), thereby abetting growth of deviant sex industries. Another potential negative outcome may originate from the general feeling among users that the Internet allows them to project whatever image they choose seemingly without consequence; i.e., no one truly knows who they are online, so they cannot be held accountable.

A range of websites are available that allow users to access sexual materials. Perhaps the most common are cyber pornography sites. Cyber pornography is sexually explicit imagery that is distributed via the Internet. Hundreds of thousands of such sites currently exist. Pornographic content can be found in various forms, including still images, videos, and live web shows. Such imagery can be retrieved using any device that can access the Internet, including computers, smartphones, and tablets such as the iPad. Imagery is available to suit a wide range of interests and tastes, from children to adults, mainstream to deviant and violent. For more detailed information, see the entry on **Pornography, Internet** by Gabriel and Lamade.

Politicians, legal experts, and academics have difficulty agreeing on a standard for defining pornography, in good measure because what constitutes pornography tends to be based in large part on personal opinion. The common definition of pornography is that it is any type of media (photos, video, etc.) depicting erotic content with the goal of causing sexual arousal. Though many forms of pornography are protected as free speech by the First Amendment and therefore considered to be legal, this is not true for pornography depicting children. The production, distribution, and possession of child pornography is a criminal offense. Child pornography is commonly defined as any type of media depicting nudity and any sexual activities involving individuals below the age of 17. The federal definition is simply any visual depiction, the production of which involved the use of a minor (below age 18) engaged in sexually explicit conduct (18 U.S.C. §§ 2252, 2256(2), 2256(8)).

Those who seek cyber pornography encounter few obstacles to doing so. Currently, hundreds of thousands of websites exist that feature some type of pornographic content. In the United States, visits to websites offering sexual content doubled in 2000, with some sites reporting more than 50 million hits annually (Worden, 2001). Such images are easily available and their distribution constitutes a sizable industry. Images are available for free as well as commercially, though recent years have seen a shift from commercial pay-per-view sites toward free, user-generated content in formats similar to that of YouTube. Images are available in a wide range of formats, the most popular being photos, videos, and live interactive shows via webcam. Pornography "users" (those who frequent pornography websites) typically use P2P (Peer to Peer) software, such as Limewire, Gnutella, or BeasrShare, that permit file sharing (exchanging pornographic images and videos). Once downloaded, files are stored using a wide range of electronic or magnetic mediums, from hard drives, flash drives, CD-ROMs, and digital video disks to PDAs (Personal Digital Assistants), MMCs (Multi Media Cards), smart cards, optical disks, or electronic notebooks. Many of these storage devices, such as hard drives, tapes, laser disks, and Bernoulli disks, can hold vast quantities of information.

From a criminal standpoint, the availability and accessibility of this imagery can be problematic. Seto et al., (2001) suggested that "individuals who are already predisposed to sexually offend are the most likely to show an effect of pornography exposure" (Seto, Maric, & Barbaree, 2001, p. 46). As the Internet makes it possible for individuals to spend more time viewing pornography, there is concern that there will be a corresponding increase in the incidence of sexual violence.

An additional concern is that individuals may be exposed to pornographic imagery unsolicited. Unsolicited pornography can be encountered in several ways. A simple Internet search of nonsexual content may inadvertently lead to sexual content. Through a process called "spamdexing" (a combination of "spam" and "indexing"), it is possible for website operators to deliberately manipulate their rank so that they appear higher in the list of responses to an Internet search. This may trick individuals into unintentionally clicking on a pornographic link. Pornography may also be accidentally encountered when using video-sharing sites such as YouTube. Website operators may post links to pornographic sites in the comments sections or give a pornographic video a name that suggests it is nonsexual in nature. Perhaps the most common form of encountering unsolicited pornography is through spam e-mails that contain links to sites featuring sexual content. Although such e-mails have become sufficiently commonplace that many people can recognize and avoid them, they can often be misleading. As with other undesirable outcomes of technological advances, unsolicited cyber pornography may have a significant impact on youth exposed to sexual materials.

Also relevant to the topic of cyber pornography is the use of sexual images to embarrass, harass, and humiliate. A form of cyberbullying, such behavior typically takes one of two forms: (1) the offender repeatedly exposes the target, via e-mail or social networking sites, to unwanted pornography imagery, or (2) the offender releases to a wide audience sexual photos of the target, which may be either real or falsified. A tragic example of the latter is the case of Tyler Clementi, a student at Rutgers University who committed suicide after two classmates made public a video of Clementi's sexual encounter with a man; the classmate deemed primarily responsible was subsequently charged with 15 counts of criminal violations. It is under circumstances such as these that the production and distribution of adult cyber pornography begins to cross the line into sexual offending.

Harmful Cyber Behavior
Increased Opportunities for Perpetrating Sexual Violence
As mentioned, the features referred to as the "Triple-A Engine" (Cooper, 1998) make the Internet an attractive and efficient venue for gratifying all manner of sexual interests, including sexual urges and fantasies involving children, therefore fostering a growth in child pornography. Instead of having to leave the home and search for victims, perpetrators can search for victims in the comfort of their own home. Furthermore, various forms of cyber-sex are available without the

usual prerequisites of attractiveness or social skills. The anonymity that the Internet offers allows people to be free to explore, be open, and adopt different personas. Instead of being limited to the confines of a geographic area, one can find like-minded individuals on the Internet who share and support similar interests, including deviant sexual interests. This can foster a wide range of distorted cognitions and beliefs about sexual behavior, normalizing and supporting deviant sexual behavior.

Catching individuals who are responsible for illegal pornographic materials is challenging, because of the technology used to steal and block IP (Internet Protocol) addresses, as well as the ease with which one can misrepresent their physical location. Technology can be used to conceal one's identity or avoid detection by law enforcement officials. Technologically savvy individuals can conceal their identity online by using proxy or anonymous proxy servers to mask their IP address (Luders, 2007). For those who maintain websites with illegal sexual content, strategies such as the use of hexadecimal codes to encode the URL (uniform resource locator) can confuse people trying to track the source of the web page content (Luders, 2007). Another tactic is to use a redirection service in which the user thinks that the server is located in a particular county or region, when in fact the user is really redirected to another location or country (Luders, 2007). Once detected, analysis of confiscated storage devices is further complicated by the lengths to which users go to hide, compress, password protect, and encrypt incriminating files. Individuals who pay to download non-criminal pornography sometimes may get more than they bargained for when child pornographic images are included in the download file without the individual's knowledge or consent. This has led to arrest and prosecution of unsuspecting individuals.

Also, savvy pornography production teams will pick website names that appear to be something else. Consider the old pornographic website *whitehouse.com*, which many people keyed in to attempt to access information about the U.S. White House (instead of *whitehouse.gov*). The owner, Daniel Parisi, sold the website name in 2004 to a nonpornographic company.

Cyber Sexual Offenses

Cyber sexual offenses can be described generally as unsolicited, unwelcome, sexual communications taking place on the Internet. Some are clearly prohibited by law, such as cyber child pornography, while the legality of others is the source of some debate, such as cyber rape.

Child cyber pornography.   Federal law defines child pornography as any visual depiction of an individual below the age of 18 engaging in sexually explicit conduct. "Sexually explicit conduct" is a fairly broad term, and has been understood to include nude photos, sexual intercourse, and graphic abuse. In addition to manufacturing, child pornography laws also prohibit distributing, receiving, or possessing sexual images of children. Child pornography trafficking via the Internet has come to be understood as a separate offense. A cyber offense involves the use of the Internet for the production, distribution, or receipt of child pornography. In some states, this also includes disseminating sexual materials to minors in the form of distributing unsolicited pornography or engaging in a sexually explicit chat with the intent of soliciting a real-life sexual encounter. IRCs (Internet relay chats) are real time chat rooms providing perpetrators the opportunity to engage children. Currently, more than 100,000 websites have child pornography, generating $3 billion annually (Pennsylvania Attorney General, 2010), and 116,000 searches daily for "child pornography" on the internet (Ropelato, 2008).

Cyber rape. Cyber rape typically refers to the use of text or a game avatar to engage another individual in unwanted and assaultive sexual communications. It can take several forms: (1) sexual harassment or stalking in which perpetrators send their victims sexual messages that are perceived as inappropriate and predatory; (2) rape enactment in a role-playing game in which text or video graphics can be manipulated to depict a violent and nonconsensual sexual act; and (3) watching video clips showing either actual rape or actors portraying a rape. Such incidents have been the subject of considerable debate: although targets often feel victimized and violated, perpetrators argue that no real harm has taken place and that cyber rape is a safe means of expressing violent fantasies. For more information, see the entry on **Rape, Cyber**.

Vulnerable Populations for Increased Risk of Internet Sexual Victimization
Cyber sexual activity tends to be fairly common among teenagers and young adults who have grown up with this technology and for whom technology is a primary means of communication. Young people offer many explanations for engaging in cyber sexual activity. For many, it is a means of flirting with and eliciting attention and interest from potential partners, or increasing feelings of attractiveness and desirability when one receives a positive response to his or her sexual photo or message. Many teenagers report that they engaged in cyber sexual activity as a response to peer pressure or because their partner created a feeling of obligation (e.g., if you care about me, you will do this for me). Perhaps the simplest scenario is that the recipient of a sexual image or text is encouraged to reciprocate or feels obligated to reciprocate.

Whatever the motivation, engaging in cyber sexual activity presents many potential dangers to youth. Their activities may be discovered by parents or other authority figures, resulting in embarrassment, shame, social ostracism, punishment, and in some cases, arrest. The end of a friendship or romantic relationship could result in one angry party releasing sexual images of the other party, an act that can have negative consequences for all involved. In summary, the emotional consequences of engaging in such activities can lead to severe emotional distress and self-harm.

Legal Implications

The legal system is not keeping pace with the rapid changes in Internet technology. As a result, the legal system has relatively few laws in place that regulate activity on the Internet. Many behaviors that may be potentially dangerous or harmful, such as cyberbullying or virtual rape, remain legal. Often, these dangerous behaviors cannot be regulated, because they are so new that the potential consequences have not been adequately examined empirically. Clearly, this is an area where research is urgently needed. Effectively decreasing distribution of Internet child pornographic has been undermined, because of the technological advances enabling distributors to conceal their operations. Many federal and state sting operations were set up using undercover police officers posing as minors to trap individuals seeking minors for sexual liaisons. However, some courts have ruled that these defendants could not be charged with attempted sexual assault of a minor when they were instead talking to a police officer posing as a minor in a sting operation (Rogers, 2009).

Communications Decency Act

The Communications Decency Act (CDA) of 1996 marked the first attempt by Congress to regulate pornographic material on the Internet. This legislation aimed to affect the Internet in two ways: (1) by targeting materials deemed to be obscene and indecent and (2) by determining that website operators should not be held liable for the words of people who utilize their services. The first goal immediately became embroiled in controversy. Opponents argued that the meaning of "indecent" was unclear and misleading. Supporters of the CDA argued that the law would protect children from viewing materials that would be "indecent" or inappropriate given their age by imposing criminal sanctions on anyone using a computer to share sexually explicit materials with minors. Opponents of the CDA saw things differently. They argued that this definition of "indecent" would inadvertently criminalize information protected by the First Amendment. For example, under the CDA many arguably inoffensive and harmless resources, such as printed novels and medical information, would become illegal if posted online. After years of legal battles, the CDA was amended in 2003 to remove the indecency provision; it now regulates only obscenity (which includes pornography) and website operator liability.

Child Online Protection Act

The Child Online Protection Act (COPA) of 1998 was introduced as a direct response to the CDA being struck down by the courts. Like the CDA, its goal was to restrict access by minors to material on the Internet deemed harmful. It attempted to improve on the CDA by narrowing the range of content covered by the law, focusing on commercial speech. COPA required commercial distributors of potentially harmful materials to restrict minors' access to their websites. COPA was met with the same arguments faced by the CDA. It was struck down by the courts in 1999 after they determined that COPA's overly broad definition of harmful materials was in violation of the First Amendment.

Children's Internet Protection Act

Passed by Congress in 2000 and upheld by the Supreme Court in 2003, the Children's Internet Protection Act (CIPA) limits minors' exposure to online pornographic content by requiring libraries and schools receiving federal funds to purchase and implement "technology protection measures" for every computer connected to the Internet. The protections act as a filter and must be used during any Internet search conducted by a minor; the filters can be disabled for use by an adult or when an adult is supervising a minor. Though CIPA has been challenged by opponents, it has been upheld by the courts and remains in effect.

Deleting Online Predators Act

Similar to CIPA, the Deleting Online Predators Act (DOPA), introduced in 2006, requires schools receiving federal funding to protect minors when using the Internet onsite. DOPA is more specifically aimed at protecting children from online predators when using social networking sites and requires schools to either prohibit access to this type of site or create restrictions for use. Similar to CIPA, these restrictions can be removed for use by adults or minors being supervised by adults for educational purposes. DOPA met with opposition on the basis that in addition to blocking sites such as MySpace and Facebook, the label of "social networking" also applies to many sites believed to be harmless or educational, such as Yahoo or Amazon. As a result, though DOPA was passed by the House of Representatives in 2006, it remains under consideration in the Senate.

Adam Walsh Protection ACT and SORNA

On July 27, 2006, President Bush signed the Adam Walsh Protection Act (AWA) (H.R. 4472, United States Federal Law) intended to streamline the tracking of sex offenders and provide national standards for registration. Title 1 of AWA, the Sex Offender Registration and Notification Act (SORNA), established a comprehensive national system for the registration of all sex offenders, providing minimum standards for state compliance based on a three-tiered system. Sexually provocative pictures of juveniles transmitted over the Internet, irrespective of whether they are exchanged between peers in a consensual context, are considered child pornography by the law, and may result in very serious sanctions under SORNA. Designation of tier level is based upon the governing offense. Juveniles may be "subject to tier III classification, with the proviso that they may be removed after 25 years if there have been no new felony offenses," and the offender has complied with supervised release and treatment orders. (Prentky et al., 2010, p. 24). SORNA potentially leaves offenders vulnerable to harassment, victimization, and stress, substantially undermining their ability to reintegrate back into society. The overall impact on juveniles is profoundly negative, severely limiting opportunities for anything remotely approaching normal development.

Public Health and Larger Social Implications

The accessibility and availability of sexual content on the Internet is unprecedented. We do not know the impact of this smorgasbord of sexual material, particularly on (1) vulnerable adults, including adults prone to, or at risk for, sexually inappropriate or sexually offensive behavior, (2) normal children and adolescents who are at crucial stages in their psychosocial and sexual development, and (3) at-risk children and adolescents who have been and are continuing to be abused. This new era, which has opened up the information floodgates, particularly with regard to sexuality, has potential ramifications on multiple levels.

The wide variety and virtually unlimited access to sexual material that the Internet provides may be detrimental for individuals with addictive or antisocial personality characteristics, as well as those who lack adequate impulse control or self-regulation. The Internet may be the perfect vehicle to "act out" sexual issues online. Likewise, for individuals with compulsive sexual interests, the Internet may be an inexhaustible supply of sexual material, thereby temporarily satisfying, but over the long term exacerbating a preexisting mental disorder. For some individuals, particularly for those who are predisposed and for those with traits of antisocial personality disorder, the Internet's Triple A engine may provide the perfect combination of factors to increase the risk of committing a sexual offense. The Internet may also promote unhealthy and unrealistic ideas about sexuality and intimacy, especially in children and adolescents who are exploring their own sexuality. Deviant sexual behaviors are often normalized and supported. Although there is a debate about the potential adverse impact of sexually explicit content on children, little is known about the long-term consequences of sexually explicit materials, particularly violent and deviant content on developing youth. Safe sexual practices are rarely displayed or promoted, fostering a dangerously unhealthy view of sexual practices that potentially puts experimenting youth at risk for contracting sexually transmitted diseases.

Technology related to the Internet and information storage and transfer is racing ahead, leaving woefully behind (1) enactment of informed laws that govern and regulate such technology, (2) social policy regarding such technology, and perhaps most of all (3) the empirical research that is required to inform new legislation and social policy.

Raina V. Lamade and Adeena M. Gabriel

Further Reading

Cooper, A. (1998). Sexuality and the Internet: Surfing its way into the new millennium. *CyberPsychology and Behavior, 1*, 181–187.

Family Research Council (2009, May 30). *1 in 5 teens and 1 in 3 young adults are sexting*. Retrieved from http://www.opposingviews.com/articles/research-1-in-5-teens-and-1-in-3-young-adults-are-sexting

Luders, W. (2007). Child pornography web sites. Techniques used to evade law enforcement. *FBI Law Enforcement Bulletin*, July, 17–21.

National Campaign to Prevent Teen and Unplanned Pregnancy (2008). *Sex and tech: Results from a survey of teens and young adults*. Retrieved from http://www.thenationalcampaign.org/sextech/pdf/sextech_summary.pdf

National Center for Education Statistics (2006). *Computer and Internet use by students in 2003: Statistical analysis report*. Retrieved from http://nces.ed.gov/pubs2006/2006065.pdf

Pennsylvania Attorney General (2010). Cyber safety: Protecting your kids and teens online. Retrieved from http://www.attorneygeneral.gov/uploadedfiles/crime/cybersafety.pdf

Prentky, R. A., Li, N.-C., Righthand, S., Schuler, A., Cavanaugh, D., & Lee, A. F. (2010). Assessing risk of sexually abusive behavior among youth in child welfare sample. *Behavioral Sciences and the Law, 28*, 24–45.

Rogers, A. (2009). Protecting children on the Internet: Mission impossible? *Baylor Law Review, 61*, 323–354.

Ropelato, J. (2008). Internet pornography statistics. *Top Ten Reviews*. Retrieved from http://internet-filterreview.toptenreviews.com/internet-pornography-statistics.html

Seto, M. C., Maric, A., & Barbaree, H. E. (2001). The role of pornography in the etiology of sexual aggression. *Aggression and violent behavior, 6*, 35–53.

Worden, S. (2001, March 1). E-trafficking. *Foreign Policy*, 92–97.

Selected Websites

U.S. Census Bureau (2012). *The 2012 Statistical Abstract*. Information and communications: Internet publishing and broadcasting and Internet usage [Data file]. Retrieved from http://www.census.gov/compendia/statab/cats/information_communications/internet_publishing_and_broadcasting_and_internet_usage.html

Teen Dating Abuse

Teen dating abuse is a problem that has gained attention in recent years. About one in five teens reports physical abuse in a relationship, one in three reports being pressured into a sexual act, and even more report some level of emotional abuse (Teenage Research Unlimited, 2006). There are several types of abuse, including emotional, physical, and sexual, but one aspect unique to dating relationships is the use of technology in controlling one's partner. Technological abuse can overlap with sexual abuse, and while awareness is growing in this area, sexual abuse among teenagers is often overlooked. Some other important aspects of teen dating abuse include understanding the progression of abuse and understanding the differences between men and women and even racial groups in perpetration and victimization.

Teen dating abuse can include physical, emotional, or sexual abuse, and sexual abuse is defined as forcing a partner to engage in a sex act when he or she cannot or does not consent. This may be sexual intercourse, but can include any level of sexual act from kissing and touching to some form of penetration. For those in dating relationships, sexual abuse by a partner is part of a wider pattern of controlling behavior from one partner to another.

While sexual abuse in dating abusive relationships is sometimes overlooked, there is a connection between this and other forms of abuse. Emotional abuse, also called psychological abuse, is a strong predictor of physical violence; being a victim of physical abuse is a strong predictor of being victimized sexually. Abuse progresses from warning signs to emotional abuse, and then sometimes to physical abuse and sexual abuse. Not every victim will experience physical or sexual abuse, but if they do, it typically occurs after experiencing less aggressive forms of abuse. Teasing and name-calling are sometimes considered part of a normal relationship, but when considered in the broader context of an abusive relationship, these can be the warning signs. It can progress to yelling, screaming, and throwing objects, which may in turn become physical by hitting, slapping, or pushing. These behaviors are a violation of an individual's emotional and physical boundaries, and a lack of respect for these boundaries may mean the partner could be capable of crossing sexual boundaries. Sexual abuse may occur when a partner tries to pressure the other person to perform some kind of sexual act by asking repeatedly, making the person feel guilty, or blackmailing the partner with threats of revealing secrets. Sexual assault exists as a form of abuse within teen dating relationships. It can occur at any level of sexual interaction, and be the result of pressure from a partner. It often progresses from other, less aggressive forms of violence. Certain groups are more likely to be victims, including women, blacks, and Hispanics.

Technological abuse has gained particular attention due to its prevalence among dating abusive relationships. Technological abuse can include behaviors such as checking social networking websites and looking through a person's phone to view text messages or the call log. Constantly texting or calling a person to see where he or she is can turn into harassment or even be considered stalking in some states. When texts become sexual in nature, also known as sexting, this can be considered sexual abuse as well. This may be written texts or pictures. When sexting occurs in relationships where either party is under 18, there are serious legal implications. Around the United States, teenagers have been charged with possession and distribution of child pornography when found with pictures of an underage partner. While in some cases this may have been consensual, in an abusive relationship there may have been pressure to send such texts or pictures by one partner to another, the pictures may have been sent to others without consent, or they may have been used as blackmail.

Circumstances around dating violence have some tendencies by gender. About 10 to 15 percent of females and 5 percent of males report sexual violence victimization (Bergman, 1992; Foshee, 1996). Almost one-third of girls report having been pressured into a sexual act they did not want to perform (Teenage Research Unlimited, 2006). Males are more likely to perpetrate sexual violence and women are more likely to be victims. Women are more likely to sustain injuries from their partners. Additionally, black and Hispanic teenagers report higher rates of being forced to have sexual intercourse than white teens.

Corinne D. Warrener

See also Date Rape; Intimate Partner Violence; Prevention, Dating Violence; Sexting; Stalking

Further Reading

Bergman, L. (1992). Dating violence among high school students. *Social Work, 37*(1), 21.

Centers for Disease Control and Prevention. (2009). Youth Risk Behavioral Surveillance. *Surveillance Summaries, 59*, No. SS-5.

Foshee, V. A. (1996). Gender differences in adolescent dating abuse prevalence, types and injuries. *Health Education Research, 11*(3), 275–286.

Teenage Research Unlimited (2006). *Liz Claiborne Inc. Topline findings: Teen relationship abuse survey*. Northbrook, IL: Author.

Selected Websites

Love Is Not Abuse. Retrieved from http://www.loveisnotabuse.com/ (includes warning signs and how teens can talk to adults about dating violence; has smartphone app)

Love Is Respect: National Teen Dating Abuse Helping. Retrieved from http://www.loveisrespect.org (offers resources on identifying abuse and getting help)

Teen dating violence. Centers for Disease Control and Prevention. Retrieved from http://www.cdc.gov/violenceprevention/intimatepartnerviolence/teen_dating_violence.html (provides definitions, data, risk and protective factors, and prevention strategies)

A Thin Line. Retrieved from http://www.athinline.org/ (MTV's website focuses on technological aspects of dating abuse such as stalking and sexting)

Theories (Overview)

Sexual violence is widely recognized as a major social problem worldwide, including the United States. We know that sexual violence comes in many shapes and forms, and that it impacts all types of individuals regardless of gender, age, ethnicity, religion, or income. We also know that the consequences of sexual violence are often devastating and insidious, impacting the lives of millions of survivors in multiple ways. Although most people would agree that sexual violence is a serious problem, we still do not have a clear understanding of why sexual violence occurs. Throughout the last century, a variety of theories have been proposed to provide a causal explanation for the occurrence of sexual violence. These theories are derived from a number of disciplines, including psychology, biology, public health, social work, women's and gender studies, criminal justice, and more. Each theory offers a different conceptualization of sexual violence and its causes, based on different perspectives and philosophies about issues such as gender, violence, and sex more generally.

Theoretical frameworks are important because they help us to define the problem of sexual violence and provide a context for understanding some of its causes or factors. The theoretical perspective adopted by individuals influences the way they view the problem of sexual violence and the way in which they will respond. While none of the proposed sexual violence theories have been able to completely explain the cause of sexual violence, each has shaped the course of research on the issues, prevention and intervention efforts, policies, and societal responses. Many of these theories offer competing explanations for understanding sexual violence, and all of the theories have support as well as critiques in the literature.

In her review of theoretical explanations for violence against women, Jana Jasinski (2001) provides a helpful categorization of theories as belonging to one of three groups, including *micro-oriented*, *macro-oriented*, and *multidimensional* theories. This framework can also be applied to understanding different types of theories proposed to explain sexual violence. Therefore the entries on sexual violence theories in this topic area are grouped according to these categories. Below, each of these is further discussed.

Micro-Oriented Theories

Micro-oriented theories are based on the view that there are characteristics of individuals that make them more likely to perpetrate sexual violence. This group of theories includes criminal, sociobiological and biological, and psychological theories, which purport that a person's character plays a role in increasing the propensity of an individual to commit an act of sexual violence. The common thread among these theories is their emphasis on the role of the individual in causing sexual violence, although some of these theories have begun to integrate other factors such as the individual's interaction with his or her environment.

In their review of the **Theory, General Theory of Crime**, Gibbs and Schwartz explain that this perspective views low self-control as the root cause of all criminal behavior, including sexual offending. Based on this framework, perpetrators of sexual violence are regarded as making a rational decision to commit a crime of sexual violence, based on the desire for immediate sexual gratification, without considering the long-term consequences. Thus this theory focuses on individual actions and decisions as leading to sexual violence. Gibbs and Schwartz provide a full critique of the theory, emphasizing that other factors need to be considered when understanding crimes such as sexual violence, which are so heavily gender based. They suggest that a feminist analysis may help in understanding issues such as the connection between men's sexual aggression and patriarchal attitudes.

Sociobiological and biological theories represent another framework for understanding the causes of sexual violence. In his discussion of these theories in his entry, **Theories, Sociobiological**, Michael Bemes explains that there exist a range of sociobiological and biological perspectives that are built on the assumption that sexual violence is a function of genetic factors that have adapted over time. These theories range in the emphasis they place on the role of genetics in the perpetration of sexual violence. For example, evolutionary theories have posited that sexual violence occurs as a result of men's desire to pass along their genes. Bemes points out that the evolutionary theories have been regarded as controversial. Other theories, such as biosocial theories, move away from an exclusive focus on the individual's biology and purport a mixture of social and genetic factors that contribute to sexual violence perpetration. Finally, Bemes also presents physiological/neurophysiological theories as another perspective that emphasizes the role of brain injury, trauma, and substance use.

Gannon and Ó Ciardha review psychological theories (see **Theories, Psychological**), a large and well-developed group of perspectives that explain the occurrence of sexual violence based on a number of developmental, cognitive, social, behavioral, or affective mechanisms. Psychological theories represent a wide variety of ideas about sexual violence, and Gannon and Ó Ciardha utilize Ward and Hudson's (1998) categories of single factor, multifactor, and microfactor to help organize the various theories used to explain the role of psychology in sexual offending. *Single-factor* psychological theories focus on some maladaptive aspect of the individual as leading to sexual violence perpetration, such as poor impulsivity control. *Multifactor* theories move beyond just a focus on individual characteristics and take into account the interaction with other factors such as biological or social. *Microfactor* theories focus on understanding an individual's account of what led to an incidence of sexual offending, and typically includes a look at the sequence of events and factors that occurred for a particular offender. As Gannon and Ó Ciardha explain, microfactor theories are less prevalent than single-factor or multifactor theories and focus more on how the offending occurred than on why.

Macro-Oriented Theories

As opposed to micro-level theories that focus on characteristics of individuals as the primary cause of sexual violence, *macro-oriented theories* focus on the role of societal structures and conditions that contribute to the occurrence of sexual violence. These theories generally argue that there are certain aspects of our culture, such as sexism, that support violence, especially against women and girls. Included in this group of theories are feminist theories, sociocultural theories, and continuum of violence theories, which all point to conditions in our society that provide a foundation for the perpetration and acceptance of sexual violence.

Feminist theories contend that to understand sexual violence, we must move beyond a focus on the isolated individual to also examine the influence of social groups, culture, and institutions. As explained by Sheila McMahon in her entry **Theory, Feminist**, feminist theories also reconceptualize rape as an issue of power, control, and violence rather than sex or perversion. Refuting the idea that race and class are central characteristics among rapists, feminist theories concentrate on the role of gender, patriarchy, and sexism.

Sociocultural theories have emerged largely in response to the micro, individual-focused theories and attempt to redefine rape etiology. As opposed to microlevel theories, sociocultural theories of violence explain that sexual violence is not just a function of individual rapists, but occurs because it is supported by societal-level actions, beliefs, and standards. These can include family values, group beliefs and behavior, media messages, organizational structures and policies, and larger social norms. As Sarah McMahon explains in her entry, **Theory, Sociocultural**, sociocultural theories of violence maintain that there are certain aspects of our culture that tolerate, support, and thereby contribute to the occurrence of sexual violence. These theories are rooted largely in a feminist framework that contends that our society is structured in ways such that rigid gender roles are supported and violence is glorified, which creates an atmosphere ripe for sexual violence to occur.

A related perspective on sexual violence based on feminist and sociocultural theories is the Continuum of Violence theory. As explained by Sarah McMahon in her entry (**Theory, Continuum of Violence**), this framework is used to understand multiple forms of sexual violence and their relationship to one another. This is based on a feminist perspective that conceptualizes various forms of sexual violence against women not as separate, discrete acts but rather as connected and all based in patriarchal (male) power and control. The concept of a continuum of violence explains that there exists a range of behaviors that escalate in severity and violence and that are linked to one another. Overt, violent acts exist at one end of the continuum (such as rape) and more covert, subtle acts are placed at the other end (such as sexist language). While behaviors on the less overt end of the continuum are not regarded as imposing immediate harm to victims, these acts are significant because they contribute to a culture of violence that supports and tolerates the more severe forms of violence against women. Theorists from this standpoint contend that we are living in a "rape-supportive culture" that sustains gender stereotypes and sexism, and thus normalizes certain behaviors acts of violence against women.

Multidimensional Theories

There has been a trend toward viewing microlevel and macrolevel theories as incomplete in explaining sexual violence, and therefore multidimensional models are offered as a way to combine various aspects of these theories. *Multidimensional theories* integrate individual- and societal-level aspects of violence and conceptualize sexual violence as a multilevel problem influenced by a variety of factors. Multidimensional theories discussed below include hegemonic masculinity theory, male peer support theory, coercive control theory, and socio-ecological frameworks.

As an outgrowth of feminist theory, theories of masculinity offer a potential contribution to the discussion about the causes of sexual violence. In her entry **Theory, Hegemonic Masculinity**, Sarah McMahon explains how, in particular, hegemonic masculinity theory may be helpful for understanding how some men define masculinity to include domination over others, with violence against women, girls, and other men as an outcome. She explains that there are certain characteristics of the dominant or "hegemonic" form of masculinity in our culture that promote the use of violence. The underlying concepts of this theory provide a foundation for understanding the relationship between sexual assault and gender construction. This theory is multidimensional because it takes into account the individual's actions, the influence of the particular context on the construction and demonstration of gender, and the larger societal definitions of masculinity. The role of context is especially salient in understanding the role of hegemonic masculinity, as gender is constructed differently in various situations, and may illuminate the situational aspect involved with the occurrence of sexual violence.

A related perspective is Male Peer Support (MPS) theory, a gender-based theory that includes micro, individual factors and macro, cultural factors. As described by Schwartz and DeKeseredy in their entry (**Theory, Male Peer Support**), MPS argues that sexual violence occurs in part because of the behaviors of men who receive social support from their peers for sexual and physical violence. In addition, the theory takes into account other contributions such as patriarchal beliefs, excessive alcohol consumption, membership in organizations that support abuse, and the absence of deterrence. In this sense, the theory is multidimensional because it highlights the interaction of individual-, group-, and cultural-level factors.

Yet another perspective that interweaves individual- and societal-level factors is Stark's Coercive Control theory (see **Theory, Coercive Control**). In his entry, Stark draws on human rights literature and explains how structural gender inequality and discrimination at the societal level are tied to women's personal experiences of violence and abuse. He describes the Coercive Control model as a series of controlling or coercive tactics used in addition to sexual and physical abuse by a perpetrator to entrap a woman in an abusive situation. Sexual assault and humiliation are utilized as tactics to dominate women. Stark emphasizes that the perpetrator's use of these tactics are in part successful because of the larger, societal-level supports of gender discrimination that limit a woman's ability to change her situation.

Another multidimensional theory described in this topic area is the socio-ecological perspective. Increasingly, researchers and practitioners in the field of sexual violence are proposing an ecological model that is multilevel and incorporates aspects of various theories to explain the occurrence of sexual violence. In her entry on socio-ecological theories (see **Theory, Ecological Approach**), Casey explains that these theories suggest that human behavior is mutually shaped by influences at several widening layers of individuals' environments, including family, peer, community, and societal levels. Further, ecological theories posit that influences across these levels interact to increase or diminish the likelihood of developmental or behavioral problems. Ecological theories are fluid, dynamic theories that focus on the interaction of a number of factors and consider the person in his or her environment.

In conclusion, a variety of theories have been proposed to explicate sexual violence toward women, yet none have been proven to fully explain its occurrence. Micro-oriented theories focus on individual characteristics, such as psychological, sociobiological, and crime theories. These theories may be useful in helping to pinpoint aspects of individuals that make them more likely to perpetrate sexual violence. From another perspective, macro-oriented theories emphasize the role of societal structures and standards that may contribute to the occurrence of sexual violence. Feminist, socio-structural, and continuum of violence are examples of these theories. While these perspectives may shed light on the larger societal issues that foster sexual violence, they are also incomplete, as not all individuals exposed to the same societal-level factors commit sexual violence. As a result of these gaps, multidimensional theories offer a perspective that allows for both individual- (micro) and societal- (macro) level factors to interact and contribute to a greater propensity for committing sexual violence. Examples of multidimensional theories discussed in this topic area include hegemonic masculinity theory, male peer support theory, coercive control theory, and socio-ecological frameworks.

Sarah McMahon

Theories, Psychological

Numerous psychological theories of sexual violence and abuse have been developed over the past few decades. Psychological theories focus on explaining human thought and behavior via numerous developmental, cognitive, social, behavioral, or affective mechanisms. The vast majority of psychological theories of sexual violence and abuse focus on adult male-perpetrated rape and child molestation, although a small number focus on subcategories of offences (e.g., sexual sadism or female-perpetrated abuse). There are no psychological theories available to exclusively explain child-perpetrated sexual violence or abuse, although many refer to adolescent sexual offending. Psychological theories provide a conceptual model of the psychological problems facilitating sexual violence and abuse. This makes such theories helpful for structuring assessments or tailoring treatment interventions in order to achieve optimal rehabilitation success.

Psychological theories of sexual violence and abuse vary according to how much they generally recognize or incorporate other theoretical stances (e.g., biological or societal factors). Ward and Hudson (1998) have usefully divided theories of sexual offending into three categories: single-factor, multifactor, and microlevel. *Single-factor* psychological theories examine only a single component empirically associated with sexual violence/abuse (e.g., intimacy deficits). *Multifactor* psychological theories combine numerous single-factor explanations into a comprehensive account of the factors and causal relationships associated with sexual violence/abuse. Although such accounts are psychologically focused, they will generally incorporate some nonpsychological explanations as well (e.g., biological). *Microlevel* psychological theories focus on the sequence of unfolding cognitive, affective, behavioral, and contextual events that result in a single episode of sexual violence/abuse. They are generally descriptive accounts developed from offenders' own descriptions of their offending. Because microlevel theories focus on *how* rather than *why* offending occurs, such theories are generally much less prevalent than single- or multifactor theories. However, they are psychologically focused and may be useful for identifying the offense styles of offenders, or for developing initial theory where little or no single- or multifactor theories exist.

Single- and multifactor psychological explanations of male-perpetrated rape and child molestation are well established. Research indicates that single factors such as intimacy problems, inappropriate sexual interests, emotional control, and offense-supportive thinking are all psychological components associated with the perpetration of sexual assault against adult or children (Ward, Polaschek, & Beech, 2006). Numerous multifactor psychological theories describe the relations of these factors—alongside nonpsychological mechanisms—to varying degrees of complexity in the facilitation of sexual offending.

The most recent multifactor psychological theory constructed specifically to explain child molestation is Ward and Siegert's pathways model (2002). This theory combined the stronger parts of previous theories into a theory designed to explain five specific routes or pathways to offending via complex interactions between learning, biological, and cultural factors. In other words, five subtypes of child molester are described and each is predicted to hold a unique configuration and prominence of single psychological factors or vulnerabilities. The five subtypes are typically labeled according to the psychological factor predicted to be most dysfunctional for that subtype (i.e., *emotional regulation*, *sexual scripts*, *intimacy*, *antisocial thinking*, and *multiple dysfunction*). So, for example, the intimacy subtype refers to individuals whose most prominent psychological vulnerability motivating their sexual offending against children is a lack of intimacy with adults and associated loneliness. Multiple-dysfunction perpetrators, on the other hand, refer to child molesters who hold problems on all four psychological factors.

A particularly prominent multifactor theory has been constructed specifically to explain rape by Malamuth (1996). Within this theory, which has been subject to numerous appraisals and refinements, both sociocultural feminist and evolutionary perspectives are amalgamated with key psychological factors in order to explain male propensity toward sexual aggression via ultimate and proximate causes (i.e., *why* vs. *how* mechanisms develop). The reason *why* men hold a propensity to rape is predicted to be because they are evolutionarily programmed to prefer impersonal sex, which is likely to be optimized by coercive sex. In relation to *how* factors culminate to cause rape, it is predicted that a confluence of risk factors motivate, disinhibit, and provide the general context for sexual offending (e.g., hostile masculinity, antisocial personality).

Numerous other theories of sexual violence and abuse are available, but they are not developed specifically to explain rape and instead focus on both rape and child sexual assault. One such theory, developed by Marshall and Barbaree (1990), pays particular attention to offending that develops during adolescence. During adolescence, it is predicted that as hormonal activity increases so too do aggressive impulses. While the majority of males are predicted to successfully control and suppress such impulses, psychological vulnerabilities created via numerous avenues (e.g., biological, developmental) are predicted to interact with contextual factors (e.g., intoxication, sexual arousal) and impair normal inhibition processes, heightening the likelihood of sexual aggression. A more recent theory—the integrated theory of sexual offending (Ward & Beech, 2006)—integrates biological factors, ecological factors, and neuropsychological factors in its broad explanation of sexual violence and abuse.

While male-perpetrated rape and child molestation are associated with numerous multifactor psychological theories, very little theory is available to explain particular facets of sexual violence or abuse. For example, behaviors such as frotteurism, exhibitionism, voyeurism, and online offending are almost exclusively associated with a very small number of single-psychological-factor theories. In such cases, it is generally presumed that multifactor psychological theories of sexual offending hold application. However, in other areas such as female sexual offending, it is presumed that existing multifactor theories are not sufficient to account for the gender differences of female perpetrators.

Psychological theories provide a neat conceptualization of the range of cognitive, social, developmental, and behavioral factors associated with sexual violence and abuse at the individual level. As such they enable professionals working with perpetrators of sexual violence/abuse to (1) pinpoint the range of psychological factors that facilitate sexual offenses and (2) highlight those psychological factors that require treatment interventions. One limitation of such theories, however, is that psychological factors tend to be emphasized over and above societal or biological mechanisms. Nevertheless, even the most complex multifactor psychological theories at least acknowledge these factors to some extent.

Theresa A. Gannon and Caoilte Ó Ciardha

See also Child Sexual Abuse; Perpetrators (Overview); Sexual Molestation; Voyeurism

Further Reading

Gannon, T. A., Ward, T., Collie, R. M., & Thakker, J. (2008). Rape: Psychopathology, theory and treatment. *Clinical Psychology Review, 28*(6), 982–1008. doi:10.1016/j.cpr.2008.02.005

Laws, D. R., & O'Donohue, W. T. (2008). *Sexual deviance: Theory, assessment and treatment* (2nd ed.). London, England: Guilford Press.

Malamuth, N. M. (1996). The confluence model of sexual aggression: Feminist and evolutionary perspectives. In D. B. Buss & N. M. Malamuth (Eds.), *Sex, power, conflict: Evolutionary and feminist perspectives* (pp. 269–295). New York, NY: Oxford University Press.

Marshall, W. L., & Barbaree, H. E. (1990). An integrated theory of sexual offending. In W. L. Marshall, D. R. Laws, & H. E. Barbaree (Eds.), *Handbook of sexual assault: Issues, theories and treatment of the offender* (pp. 363–385). New York, NY: Plenum Press.

Ward, T., & Beech, A. R. (2006). The integrated theory of sexual offending. *Aggression and Violent Behavior, 11*, 44–63. doi:10.1016/j.avb.2005.05.002

Ward, T., & Hudson, S. M. (1998). The construction and development of theory in the sexual offending area: A meta-theoretical framework. *Sexual Abuse: A Journal of Research and Treatment, 10*, 47–63. doi:10.1023/A:1022106731724

Ward, T., Polaschek, D. L. L., & Beech, A. R. (2006). *Theories of sexual offending.* Chichester, England: Wiley.

Ward, T., & Siegert, R. (2002). Toward a comprehensive theory of child sexual abuse: A theory knitting perspective. *Psychology, Crime, and Law, 8*, 319–351. doi:10.1080/10683160903535917

Selected Websites

Association for the Treatment of Sexual Abusers. Retrieved from http://www.atsa.com (various useful resources relating to the assessment, theory, and treatment of abusers)

Theories, Sociobiological

Sexual violence is a widespread global problem that affects all genders, ages, and cultures. Sexually related violence is not new and is much greater than most believe. Globally, there is a lack of research emphasis necessary to bring about significant social changes, and the research base is still smaller regarding childhood sexual violence in developing countries. Sexual violence comes in many forms and multiple settings, which increases the difficulties to define it. Its pervasiveness causes physical and mental health problems, a vast array of sexual and reproductive health complications, increases in suicides, HIV transmission, and murder, and the toll it takes on families and communities is undefinable (Centers for Disease Control and Prevention [CDC], 2011). Understanding the common causes or theoretical principles, sometimes called tenets, of sexual violence is very important in developing solutions to these problems within global communities. This comprehension can bring clarity to individual cases and the appropriate roles of both victims and perpetrators in such situations (Shoemaker, Tankard, & Lasorsa, 2004).

Theories are the building blocks of assimilating knowledge that provides a logical use to research through understanding, predictions, and control. They allow practitioners, educators, researchers, and policy makers the framework to apply data, continue to accumulate developmental knowledge, and make social change through this process.

Sexual violence has a history of theories that provide explanations to why and how these events occur. The sociobiological and biological theories are descriptions of social behaviors that have evolved as genetically essential and have adapted over time. The basis for these theories is essentially grounded in the context that behavioral characteristics are inherited (genetics) and that these traits have been developed through the process of natural selection as an adaptive process to the environment. The following sociobiological and biological theories represent a more common list of such theories that have varying application regarding acts of sexual violence.

Evolutionary Theory

One of the more debated models is evolutionary theory, which has grown from Darwin's theory of natural selection and more specifically the idea of adaptation.

The foundation of this theory suggests that sexual violence has developed through stages to adapt to the changing environment and is a by-product of the male's desire to pass on his genes as well as sexual selection to ensure mating success. This theory suggests that this is what advances the underlying psychology of sexually violent perpetrators. Evolutionary theories are very controversial and especially criticized and rejected by religious, feminist, political, and academic groups. These groups have varying concerns and denunciations, but most feel that evolutionary theory lacks academic integrity, it is considered a soft science, its framework justifies the perpetuation of sexual violence, and it supports competing radical political viewpoints ancillary to the status quo while ignoring social justice issues.

A recent adaptation to this theory is the feminist evolutionary theory, which asserts that sexual violence does possess an element of sex and considers social, environmental, and developmental factors as concurrent causes of this violence. It purports that sexual violence is not solely based upon power and control. This line of thought supports aspects of Darwinian theory with the perspective being more of an evolutionary science model.

An evaluation of the theory's major principles suggests the lack of academic rigor necessary to be a scientific, testable, and replicative model. More importantly, it justifies sexual violence as normal human activity and does not account for environmental and cultural factors that influence sexually aggressive behaviors.

Biosocial Theory

Typically considered a combination of theories, biosocial theory focuses on combining biological and social tenets. These tenets include that sexual violence is truly sexual in nature and learned, that natural selection dictates that male sex drives are stronger than female, that male hormones create intense sexual urges that must be satisfied in any manner possible, and that sexual violence is not exclusive to males. This theory is based in genetics for its root causes.

An analysis of the biosocial model embraces a broad application possessing elements of adaptation, cultural and social influences, as well as genetic and biological explanations for sexual violence. Biosocial theory attempts to widen the explanation of motivations toward sexual violence focusing on the goal of sexual acts rather than on tactics such as domination and aggression.

Physiology/Neurophysiology Theories

These theories generally suggest that hormones and chemical imbalances, as well as brain trauma or abnormalities, are the reasons for sexual violence. These physiological problems create impulsivity, lack of control, and aggression. Most of this research has been developed with animals so the causality of these findings is not well recognized at this time. Although illuminating the hormonal, chemical, and brain or head abnormality influences upon sexual violence, it does not consider cultural, learned, genetic, adaptive, or environmental impacts on sexually violent behaviors.

One example of a physiology theory is the belief that alcohol or substance abuse distorts rational thought, creates negative social interactions, and alters brain chemistry. Some researchers believe there is a genetic relationship, while others suggest that alcohol combined with mental problems creates the violence. While alcohol and drug abuse has been directly related to violent crimes, it does not clearly explain the many sexually criminal acts committed without the influence of alcohol or other substances.

Michael S. Bermes

See also Alcohol and Drug Abuse, Perpetration; Perpetrators (Overview)

Further Reading

Centers for Disease Control and Prevention (2011, January 26). In Division of Violence Prevention (Ed.), *Sexual violence*. Retrieved from http://www.cdc.gov/Violence Prevention/sexual violence/

Ellis, L. (1991). A synthesized (biosocial) theory of rape. *Journal of Consulting and Clinical Psychology, 1*(59), 631–642.

Shoemaker, P., Tankard, J., & Lasorsa, D. (2004). *How to build social science theories.* Thousand Oaks, CA: Sage.

Vandermassen, G. (2011). Evolution and rape: A feminist Darwinian perspective. *Sex Roles, 64*(1), 732–747.

Theories, Sociocultural

Sociocultural theories of violence maintain that there are certain aspects of our culture that tolerate, support, and thereby contribute to the occurrence of sexual violence. By definition, sociocultural refers to a combination of social and cultural factors that shape a certain phenomenon. These theories are rooted largely in a feminist framework that contends that our society is structured in ways that rigid gender roles are supported and violence is glorified, which creates an atmosphere ripe for sexual violence to occur. Sociocultural theories are used by some researchers to explain the cause of sexual violence, as well as understanding the ways in which our society responds to sexual violence.

Sociocultural theories of violence explain that sexual violence is not just a function of individual rapists, but occurs because it is supported by societal-level actions, beliefs, and standards. These societal aspects occur at many levels in our culture and include but are not limited to: family values and socialization (such as teaching boys to be "tough" and girls to be "nice"); group beliefs and behavior (for example, rituals at a fraternity that may include the use of sexist language or getting girls drunk to have sex); media messages (such as depicting women or girls as sexual objects in advertisements); organizational structures (for example, religious or community organizations that view women and girls as subservient); and larger social norms (for example, societal beliefs that violence occurring in a relationship is a private matter or that a rape victim is partly at fault for her assault).

Many times sociocultural supports of violence are subtle and normalized in our culture, such as the use of sexist language, which is widely accepted in our society and often not regarded as a serious problem. However, sociocultural theorists would argue that the use of sexist language creates a culture where the denigration of girls and women is viewed as harmless and even comical, and therefore sets a foundation for the perpetration of more serious violence. Additionally, sexist norms may influence the attitudes of those professionals who are supposed to provide support to victims of sexual violence. There is research indicating that helping professionals (such as health workers, police officers, judges, and counselors) who hold sexist beliefs are more likely to blame victims of sexual violence and therefore fail to provide much needed support to survivors (Campbell, 1998).

Sociocultural theories are largely related to the idea of gender role socialization, where males and females learn from the dominant culture to fulfill certain roles based on gender. Through the socialization process, girls and women are often taught among other characteristics to be demure, to be nice, to value their worth based on their appearance, and to be submissive to men. Similarly, boys and men learn to be dominant, tough, and aggressive, including sexually. In our society, the normative, heterosexual, masculine sexual "script" includes expectations that boys try to have sex with girls and that this demonstrates manhood. As boys enter adolescence, they are under pressure to demonstrate their heterosexual masculinity to their peers, including engaging in heterosexual sex. Hence, to be "one of the boys" and to be accepted, boys must behave in certain ways that dramatize their masculinity and solidify their masculine identities; often that behavior is linked to sexual activity.

Feminist theorists in particular argue that these socialization messages are deeply embedded in our culture and are transmitted through conduits such as the media, peers, family, and other social institutions. While recent years have witnessed some altering of gender role expectations to include greater flexibility for boys and girls to explore other gender roles, there is evidence that they are still deeply embedded and are taught from an early age. As a result of this socialization based in unequal gender relations, feminist scholars contend that we are living in a culture that sustains gender stereotypes and normalizes certain behaviors, such as violence against women and girls. A number of studies have demonstrated that those communities in which there are higher levels of sexist beliefs and norms, there are also higher rates of violence against women (see Casey & Lindhorst, 2009, for a review).

In her important sociological work on rape cultures, Sanday (1981) coined the term "rape-prone" cultures. She argues that rape is a culturally shaped event, and that throughout history, there have been certain cultures that are "rape-prone" and others that are "rape-free." These phrases are also used to describe various cultures in our contemporary society. *Rape-prone cultures* are those where there is a higher incidence of rape, accompanied by rigid gender roles characterized by inequality, with men in dominant roles. *Rape-free cultures* are those where rape is infrequent or nonexistent, typically characterized by a social structure that includes gender equality in decision making. Rape-free cultures demonstrate beliefs, rituals, and actions that do not tolerate sexism or violence, and where individuals in the community express their social disapproval of these behaviors.

In addition to identifying our general culture as rape supportive, some researchers have identified certain "subcultures" or groups where specific cultural norms legitimize violence against women. For example, feminist scholars have conducted extensive research on fraternities and found some of them to be "rape-prone cultures" where group activities, language, rituals, and practices contribute to the creation of an atmosphere that tolerates or even promotes violence against women (see Martin & Hummer, 1989; Sanday, 2007). A similar identification of athletic and military culture as "rape-prone" has been suggested.

Critics of sociocultural theories argue that there is a lack of evidence of a causal relationship between the exposure to violent or sexist aspects of society and the actual perpetration of sexual violence. Most individuals who use sexist language, view pornography, or believe women are subservient do not perpetrate sexual violence. On the other side, sociocultural theorists argue that while societal-level factors may not present a complete picture of why some people commit sexual violence, it does provide an atmosphere where sexual violence is more likely to be committed or tolerated. These theorists have concluded that effective sexual violence prevention efforts must therefore address the underlying assumptions about gender and sexual violence, and that changing rape-supportive ideologies and social norms will ultimately decrease sexual violence perpetration.

Sarah McMahon

See also Fraternities and Sororities; Rape Myths; Sports Teams; Theory, Continuum of Violence; Theory, Social Norms; Victims, Blaming

Further Reading

Berkowitz, A. D. (2001). Critical elements of sexual assault prevention and risk reduction programs for men and women. In C. Kilmartin (Ed.), *Sexual assault in context: Teaching college men about gender* (pp. 75–99). Holmes Beach, FL: Learning Publications.

Campbell, R. (1998). The community response to rape: Victims' experiences with the legal, medical, and mental health system. *American Journal of Community Psychology, 36*(3), 355–379.

Casey, E. A., & Lindhorst, T. P. (2009). Toward a multi-level, ecological approach to the primary prevention of sexual assault. *Trauma, Violence, & Abuse, 10*(2), 91–114.

Fabiano, P., Perkins, H. W., Berkowitz, A. D., Linkenbach, J., & Stark, C. (2004). Engaging men as social justice allies in ending violence against women: Evidence for a social norms approach. *Journal of American College Health, 52*(3), 105–112.

Martin, P. Y., & Hummer, R. A. (1989). Fraternities and rape on campus. *Gender and Society, 3*, 457–473.

Sanday, P. R. (1981). The socio-cultural context of rape: A cross-cultural study. *Journal of Social Issues, 37*(4), 5–27.

Sanday, P. R. (2007). *Fraternity gang rape* (2nd ed.). New York, NY: New York University Press.

Theory, Coercive Control

Coercive control is a theory of abuse that attempts to encompass the range of strategies employed to dominate individual women in personal life and link them to persistent sexual inequalities in the larger society. Coercive control provides a unique framework for understanding sexual violence because sexual assault and humiliation are key components of coercive control and because sex/gender identity is the central focus of coercion and control. Alternately referred to as coerced persuasion; conjugal, patriarchal, or intimate terrorism; emotional or psychological abuse; indirect abuse; or emotional torture, coercive control theory describes an ongoing pattern of sexual mastery by which male abusive partners primarily interweave repeated physical and sexual violence with intimidation, sexual degradation, isolation, and control and highlights a range of harms to dignity, liberty, autonomy, and personhood in addition to physical injury and psychological trauma. The theory is grounded in the empirical claim that the majority of women who seek outside assistance for abuse are victims of coercive control as opposed to simple domestic violence.

The coercive control theory defines abuse as a malevolent course of conduct rather than as a discrete incident of violence, and it emphasizes the frequency and "routine" nature of violence and other abusive tactics rather than their severity. Additionally, the theory assesses a victim's risk as the cumulative result of multiple tactics employed over time rather than as a reaction to a specific incident. Thus the probability that a victim will be seriously injured or killed is understood as a by-product of her socially constructed inability to escape or effectively resist abuse. This is measured by the extent to which she is isolated, deprived of basic resources, and micromanaged ("control") and by the subjective level of fear elicited by violence, threats, and sexual degradation.

The coercive control theory draws on the human rights literature to subdivide the tactics deployed in abusive relationships into violence, intimidation, isolation, and control. For example, intimidation encompasses the tactics used to induce fear and humiliation and extends from literal threats, stalking, and other forms of surveillance through varied forms of sexual abuse (such as inspections) to subtle threats understood only by victims and based on the unique knowledge a partner has because of his privileged access to his victim. Literal rapes by abusive partners are commonplace in coercive control and are often repeated, with 24 percent of abused women in shelters reporting they were raped "often" or "all the time" and 27 percent reporting they were forced to engage in anal sex. Importantly, many abuse victims report that their compliance with sexual demands they find degrading is coerced by more subtle means that make sex "feel like rape" even though there is no direct use of threats or violence. Control includes the deprivation of basic resources (such as money, food, or transportation); limitations on speech and movement; and the regulation of a victim's everyday life. Isolation refers to a subset of control tactics that constrain victims' access to friends, family, coworkers, helping professionals, and other forms of support. Within a broad justice framework, it is useful to link violence to the right to security, intimidation to the right to dignity and to live without fear, isolation to the right to autonomy, and control to liberty rights. Security, dignity, autonomy, and liberty are rights that are universally recognized as worthy of state protection.

The emphasis on the violation of rights and liberties shifts the terms by which abuse is discussed from a psychological language of victimization and dependence to a political language of domination, agency, resistance, and subordination. Against this background, what men do to women is less important than what they prevent women from doing for themselves. Women's right to use whatever means are available to liberate themselves from coercive control derives from the right afforded to all persons to free themselves from tyranny. The theory does not minimize sexual, physical, or psychological trauma, but insists that the deprivation of liberty merits an aggressive societal response irrespective of whether a victim has required medical care or police protection from violence. The theory holds that we have failed to recognize the harms to liberty and autonomy created by coercive control; hence, we need to accord women the same liberty rights we would accord men in a similar situation.

This new model is rooted in the same tenets that gave birth to the battered-women's movement—that the abuse of women in personal life is inextricably bound up with their standing in the larger society and therefore that women's entrapment in their personal lives can be significantly reduced only if sexual discrimination is addressed simultaneously. The theory draws a distinction between coercive control as a specific form of abuse that builds on and exacerbates sexual inequality and other forms of interpersonal violence that do so only to a limited extent, such as assaults, "fights," same-sex violence, or women's violence against male partners. However often women may hurt or abuse male or female partners, they rarely are able to deprive them of basic resources, rape them or degrade them sexually, regulate their enactment of gender roles, or systemically isolate them from the supports needed for autonomy. The theory holds that men's capacity to deploy coercive control in personal life reflects the advantages they derive from persistent sexual inequalities rather than from their greater physical strength or a greater propensity for violence than women. Because it builds on and exacerbates inequality, coercive control merits a level of societal response that goes beyond the response to the illegitimate use of violence by partners in other contexts. Outside prison or a similar institutional setting, there is no counterpart in men's lives to women's entrapment by men in personal life due to coercive control.

Coercive control shares general elements with other capture or course-of-conduct crimes such as kidnapping, stalking, and harassment, including the facts that it is ongoing and its perpetrators use various means to hurt, humiliate, intimidate, exploit, isolate, and dominate their victims. But unlike other capture crimes, coercive control is personalized, extends through social space as well as over time, and is gendered in that it relies for its impact on women's vulnerability as women due to sexual inequality. This is obvious not only from the gender specific distribution of coercive control but also from the fact that the major form of control deployed involves the microregulation of behaviors associated with stereotypic female roles, such as how women dress, cook, clean, socialize, care for their children, or perform sexually.

The claim that coercive control is largely a gender crime has yet to be empirically validated. Critics have also questioned whether shifting the focus to domination might alienate supporters of the antiviolence movement or distract attention from the emphasis on sexual violence. Framing criminal laws that target the harms inflicted by coercive control also remains a challenge.

Evan Stark

See also Intimate Partner Violence; Sexual Coercion; Sexual Freedom; Sexual Harassment; Stalking; Theory, Continuum of Violence

Further Reading

Bancroft, Lundy (2002). *Why does he do that?: Inside the minds of angry and controlling men*. New York, NY: Berkeley Books.

Dutton, M. A., & Goodman, L. A. (2005). Coercive control in intimate partner violence: Towards a new conceptualization. *Sex Roles: A Journal of Research, 52,* 743–756.

Ferraro, Kathleen (2006). *Neither angels nor demons: Women, crime and victimization*. Boston, MA: Northeastern University Press.

Johnson, Michael P. (2009). *Typology of domestic violence: Intimate terrorism, violent resistance, and situational couple violence*. Chicago, IL: Northwestern University Press.

Stark, Evan (2007). *Coercive control: How men entrap women in personal life*. New York, NY: Oxford University Press

Theory, Continuum of Violence

The continuum of violence is a framework used to understand multiple forms of sexual violence and their relationship to one another. This is based on a feminist perspective that conceptualizes various forms of sexual violence against women not as separate, discrete acts but rather as connected and all based in patriarchal (male) power and control. The concept of a continuum of violence explains that there exists a range of behaviors that escalate in severity and violence and that are linked to one another. At one end of the continuum are those behaviors that are generally considered sexually violent in our society including rape, sexual assault, and criminal sexual contact. These acts are more overt, often pose immediate harm to potential victims, are recognized as crimes in our culture with legal ramifications and punishment, and are judged more harshly. However, even for these severe acts of violence that are often regarded as crimes in our society, there is variation in how serious individuals and society perceive these behaviors to be. For example, there is ample evidence that a sexual assault committed by a stranger is often viewed as more serious than one committed by someone known to the victim.

Toward the middle of the continuum exist sexual actions that imply a threat of violence toward women and girls but are typically not regarded as posing the same serious level of harm as crimes such as rape. In this category, girls and women may experience stalking, verbal or physical threats of violence, obscene phone calls or text messages, lewdness, coercion, and harassment. Sheffield (1987) explains that these nonviolent behaviors contribute to a sense of "sexual terrorism," whereby girls and women are limited in their actions because they must constantly function in fear of the actual sexual violence that may occur. For example, girls and women may refrain from walking in certain places or at certain times because of the threat of sexual violence. In this sense, the threat of sexual violence alone restricts girls and women and supports male dominance.

At the other end of the continuum are behaviors that contribute to the existence of sexual violence that are more commonly accepted in our society, including the use of sexually degrading language, sexually violent pornography, and the sexual objectification of girls and women in media images. The behaviors at this end of the continuum are less overt and often do not pose immediate harm to victims and are often normalized as a part of our culture. Hence, their connection to sexual violence is covert and not widely recognized nor judged as harmful.

While these behaviors on the less overt end of the continuum are not regarded as imposing immediate harm to victims, there is a growing body of sociocultural theoretical literature that emphasizes the significance of these acts because they contribute to a culture of violence that supports and tolerates the more severe forms of violence against women. Theorists from this standpoint contend that we are living in a "rape-supportive culture" that sustains gender stereotypes and sexism, and thus normalizes certain behaviors acts of violence against women. A number of studies have demonstrated that in those communities in which there are higher levels of sexist beliefs and norms, there are also higher rates of violence against women (see Casey & Lindhorst, 2009, for a review).

As with analyses of other sociocultural, macrolevel theories, critics argue that sexual violence cannot be explained solely by addressing the role of societal influences. Some point to the fact that not everyone engaging in behaviors on the less overt side of the continuum of violence will then commit more serious acts of violence, so there must be other factors at play in understanding perpetration.

Others argue that although these behaviors are not as serious, their influence on the larger culture needs to be discussed. Because behaviors at the less overt end of the continuum are often normalized in our culture, it may be difficult for individuals to recognize them as problematic. Research suggests that the concept of a continuum of violence may be too abstract for individuals to grasp without explicit discussion, concrete examples, and evidence. Therefore some argue that we must teach individuals to recognize the potential harm of these situations as well as how to intervene.

Sarah McMahon

See also Pornography; Sexual Assault; Sexual Coercion; Sexual Harassment

Further Reading

Brownmiller, S. (1975). *Against our will: Men, women, and rape*. New York, NY: Simon & Schuster.

Buchwald, E., Fletcher, P., & Roth, M. (1993). Introduction. In E. Buchwald, P. Fletcher, & M. Roth (Eds.), *Transforming a rape culture* (pp. 1–3). Minneapolis, MN: Milkweed Editions.

Casey, E. A., & Lindhorst, T. P. (2009). Toward a multi-level, ecological approach to the primary prevention of sexual assault. *Trauma, Violence, & Abuse, 10*(2), 91–114.

Kelly, L. (1987). The continuum of sexual violence. In J. Hanmer & M. Maynard (Eds.), *Women, violence and social control* (pp. 46–60. Atlantic Highlands, NJ: Humanities Press International.

Leidig, M. J. (1992). The continuum of violence against women: Psychological and physical consequences. *Journal of American College Health, 40*(4), 149–155.

Sheffield, C. (1987). Sexual terrorism. In B. B. Hess & M. M. Ferree (Eds.), Analyzing gender: A handbook of social science research (pp. 171–189). London, England: Sage.

Stout, K. D., & McPhail, B. (1998). *Confronting sexism and violence against women: A challenge for social work.* New York, NY: Longman.

Theory, Diffusion of Innovations

Diffusion of innovations theory is a theory that explains how new ideas spread; this theory has been studied and tested in many fields, ranging from agriculture and international development to education and public health. While sources citing diffusion as a theoretical concept date back to French sociologist Gabriel Tarde's *The Laws of Imitation* (1902), Bryce Ryan and Neil Gross's 1943 study on how two U.S. farming communities developed the use of hybrid corn seeds to make crops resistant to drought provided an important framework for theorizing on how to encourage communities to adapt and change. Their researched helped make the study of *diffusion* central to sociologists and other social scientists. Understanding how diffusion works helps to explain how new ideas and technologies become popular.

Rural sociologist Everett Rogers, perhaps the most well-known thinker on the diffusion of innovations, describes innovation as an idea, behavior, or object that is perceived as new. Innovations are often context-specific, and can be useful for one person or population but harmful to another. For example, the introduction of the GPS locator on cell phones can be helpful to locate someone who is lost; however, this same innovation can increase the danger for individuals who are caught in controlling relationships with significant others who use this function to keep track of a person's every move.

Innovations create uncertainty because they are perceived as new by a person, group, or organization. As a result of this uncertainty, people seek more information through social networks with other individuals, resulting in the spread and adoption of the innovation. It can take a long time for innovations, or new ideas, to be accepted and adopted. This is particularly important to consider when the innovation is in conflict with the prevailing norms of the culture in which the innovation is introduced. For example, when women activists in the 1970s began speaking publicly about the problem of sexual violence as a societal problem rather than a family secret, they challenged the shared cultural norms that valued silence around these issues. Over time, these activists were able to change public opinion, and, eventually, even change state and federal legislation (e.g., the Violence Against Women Act [VAWA]) that attempts to significantly reduce incidents of violence against women through law enforcement, education, and increased support services.

So, how do individuals decide whether to adopt an innovation? According to Rogers, the *innovation-decision process* involves five steps: (1) knowledge, which occurs when a person is exposed to an innovation and gains some basic under-standing of it; (2) persuasion, which includes when a person or group forms a positive or negative opinion toward the innovation; (3) decision, which is when individuals take steps that result in adoption or rejection of the innovation; (4) implementation, which occurs when they use the innovation; and (5) confirma-tion, which happens when individuals look for support for an innovation decision. At this point, a person may reverse his or her decision about the innovation in the face of conflicting messages or opinions. For example, a woman may learn about Twitter from friends and establish a Twitter account, allowing friends to keep track of her every activity. However, if she finds that a jealous former boyfriend is following her on Twitter and showing up unexpectedly as a result, she may reverse the decision to adopt this innovation for her own safety.

How do communities adopt an innovation? Decisions to adopt or reject a new idea or innovation can be made by individuals, group consensus, or a few author-ities. Those who are earliest to adopt an innovation are called "innovators" and often do so because of the novelty associated with an innovation. Innovators share the new idea or object with "early adopters," a subset of opinion leaders. If early adopters give an innovation a positive appraisal, other opinion leaders will also adopt the change and an imitative effect then occurs, in which the majority mimic the opinion leaders, and subsequently adopt an innovation. Opinion leaders exist at the center of interpersonal communication networks, and rely on informal lead-ership and are often able to influence others in their social system. Because they tend to conform to the norms of a given structure, opinion leaders also embody the system's structure. Opinion leaders are people who have a high level of infor-mal authority in a community and others rely on them when making decisions.

For example, the activists mentioned above identified change agents from the National Organization for Women Education and Legal Defense Fund who then identified political leaders who could champion the cause of fighting violence against women. When then Senator Joe Biden proposed VAWA in 1994, he did so with the help of many change agents and then influenced other opinion leaders in Congress to support this landmark legislation.

Diffusion of innovations (DOI) theory has not been explicitly tested in the field of sexual violence prevention but has been tested in the HIV/AIDS prevention field. Much like sexual violence, HIV is a source of enormous stigma and shame, thus requiring multiple intervention strategies. Empirical studies of HIV prevention efforts using DOI theory highlight the importance of opinion leaders, saturation, and influence of peer behavior on individuals. For example, in 1981, at the outset of the AIDS crisis, gay men in San Francisco used DOI theory in the establishment of the STOP AIDS group, which recruited local gay male opinion leaders and provided them with education about the causes and spread of HIV and AIDS. Activists worked with opinion leaders to reach out to members of the community who respected opinion leaders' points of view. They then met in small groups to learn and provide peer support for safer sex practices, which helped reduce the spread of HIV in the local community. As a result of this education, the numbers of new HIV infections in San Francisco were cut in half. This is a powerful example of how diffusion of innovations works to allow social and individual behavior changes to occur in large communities.

Sheila McMahon

See also The Green Dot (Program); Impact, Community; SCREAM Theater (Program); Theory, Social Norms

Further Reading

Cox, P. J., Lang, K. S., Townsend, S. M., & Campbell, R. (2010). The rape prevention and education (RPE) theory model of community change: Connecting individual and social change. *Journal of Family Social Work, 13*(4), 297–312.

Dearing, J. W. (2009). Applying diffusion of innovation theory to intervention development. *Research on Social Work Practice, 19*(5), 503–518.

Rogers, E. M. (1995). *Diffusion of innovations* (4th ed.). New York, NY: The Free Press.

Rogers, E. M. (2004). A prospective and retrospective look at the diffusion model. *Journal of Health Communication, 9*, 13–19.

Theory, Ecological Approach

Sexual violence is a complex problem with multiple and interrelated contributing factors. Accordingly, sexual violence and its consequences have increasingly been conceptualized using ecological theories. Ecological theories suggest that human behavior is mutually shaped by influences at several widening layers of individuals' environments, including family, peer, community, and societal levels. Further, ecological theories posit that influences across these levels interact to increase or diminish the likelihood of developmental or behavioral problems. Ecological frameworks provide a comprehensive way of organizing multidimensional knowledge about risk factors for violence and for analyzing how factors at different levels may act together to create risk for sexual assault or abuse.

Ecological Frameworks

Although numerous ecological theories have emerged from disciplines within the social sciences, the models share a focus on reciprocal influences between individual, family, community, and societal contexts. One of the most common ecological frameworks applied to understanding violence is adapted from the work of developmental psychologist Urie Bronfenbrenner (1979). Bronfenbrenner identifies four nested layers of environmental influences on human behavior, typically signified by concentric circles surrounding the biological, psychological, and social characteristics of an *individual*. These include the *microsystem*, or characteristics of and interactions between family members and peers in a person's immediate environment; the *mesosystem*, which is generated by interactions between microsystem members and institutions in the environment; the *exosystem*, or the larger organizations and systems in an individual's community (such as schools, workplaces, social service agencies, or legal system), and the *macrosystem*, which consists of overarching social and cultural norms and political structures within a society. Many ecological conceptualizations of violence and other social problems merge the mesosystem and ecosystem levels of analysis. Bronfenbrenner later added the *chronosystem* to this model, suggesting that individuals are shaped by their cumulative experiences over time within the various layers of their environments. Applying an ecological model involves both identifying characteristics that may contribute to a problem within each of these layers and examining how the layers interact to exacerbate or ameliorate that problem.

Applying an Ecological Framework to Understanding Sexual Violence

In the context of sexual violence, ecological theories have perhaps most often been used to understand who may be at greatest risk for perpetrating abuse. To illustrate the use of an ecological framework, some of the risk factors for perpetration at each layer of Bronfenbrenner's model will be briefly summarized below, followed by a discussion of how risks may interact across layers.

Individual factors. Individual risk factors for perpetrating sexual violence include being male, experiencing or witnessing sexual or other kinds of violence as a child, developing "deviant" sexual arousal patterns to coercive or abusive situations and having an impersonal, non-intimacy-based approach to sexual relationships. Research has also shown that men who report hostile attitudes toward women, who believe that sexual coercion is sometimes justified (i.e., who endorse rape myths), and who distrust women are at greater risk for perpetrating sexual violence.

Microsystem factors. Men who are embedded in families characterized by a strong belief in patriarchal power arrangements may be more at risk of perpetrating sexual violence. Association with peers who engage in delinquency or who express support for sexually coercive behavior is also a strong predictor of sexually aggressive conduct.

Meso- and exosystem factors. Community-based risk factors for sexual violence perpetration include poverty, living in an environment with few avenues for meaningful employment or self-actualization, and a lack of community or criminal justice sanctions for the mistreatment of girls and women.

Macrosystem factors. Broad social norms that devalue or objectify women, that associate notions of masculinity with dominance and aggression, or that reinforce patriarchal power structures are associated with higher rates of sexual violence. Additionally, societies with higher crime rates, with greater general acceptance of violence, or who are experiencing armed conflict may experience a "spillover" into higher levels of violence against women. Finally, sexual violence may be reinforced in societies with absent or ineffective structures for holding perpetrators accountable.

The chronosystem and interaction between levels of the ecological framework. A key aspect of employing an ecological framework to understand sexual violence is examining the interplay between influences from different levels over time. For example, a young man who is exposed to abuse as a child and who goes on to associate with delinquent peers who reinforce negative, exploitive attitudes toward women may be at greater risk of perpetrating sexual assault than a young man who is exposed to childhood abuse, but who is subsequently exposed to supportive family, school, peer, or community contexts that explicitly prohibit the mistreatment of women.

Other Applications of the Ecological Framework to Sexual Violence

Increasingly, ecological theories have been applied to understanding multiple aspects of sexual violence, including vulnerability to victimization, postassault coping and service utilization among victims, and prevention. For example, Campbell, Dworkin, and Cabral (2009) apply the ecological model to understanding mental health outcomes for survivors of sexual assault. They find that individual coping style, level of postassault support from family and friends, the nature of legal system response, and levels of societal rape myth acceptance (among other factors) are all related to the likelihood of developing depression, post-traumatic stress disorder, and suicidality among victims.

Strengths and Limitations of Ecological Theories

Ecological frameworks offer the advantage of capturing complex, multidimensional, and interrelated influences on sexual violence. In doing so, ecological frameworks can help us to identify diverse and multiple possible "pathways" for the development of perpetrating behavior over time. Further, these models move beyond focusing on individual behavior and highlight factors at peer, community, and societal levels that must be addressed to reduce violence against women. A limitation of ecological frameworks is that they do not specify the particular psychological or sociological mechanisms that link risk factors within or across individual, family, and community levels. Rather, ecological models simply provide an organizing framework for representing a wide range of influences on the problem of sexual violence. Understanding the specific ways in which risk factors interact, or how to intervene to alter these risk factors, requires the application of additional theoretical and conceptual models.

Erin A. Casey

See also Prevention, Ecological Model of; Theory, Coercive Control

Further Reading

Bronfenbrenner, U. (1979). *The ecology of human development: Experiments by nature and design.* Cambridge, MA: Harvard University Press.

Campbell, R., Dworkin, E., & Cabral, G. (2009). An ecological model of the impact of sexual assault on women's mental health. *Trauma, Violence, & Abuse, 10,* 225–246.

Casey, E. A., & Lindhorst, T. (2009). Toward a multi-level, ecological approach to the primary prevention of sexual assault: Prevention in peer and community contexts. *Trauma, Violence, & Abuse, 10,* 91–114.

Heise, L. L. (1998). Violence against women: an integrated, ecological framework. *Violence Against Women, 4,* 262–290.

World Health Organization (2002). Sexual violence. In *World report on violence and health* (pp. 147–181). Geneva, Switzerland: Author.

Selected Website

Sexual violence. Centers for Disease Control and Prevention. Retrieved from http://www.cdc.gov/ViolencePrevention/sexualviolence/index.html (provides links to several resources related to sexual violence, including information about applications of ecological models to sexual assault)

Theory, Feminist

Because violence against women is a complex problem, there are many theories that have been used to explain it. One such theory, feminist theory, examines the relationship between gender and power, as well as societal structures and socialization methods that reinforce gender roles and encourage male dominance. Such sociocultural or macro explanations of violence against women include a focus on cultural and structural issues to explain sexual violence. Hence, violence against women, as viewed by feminists, is a form of social control, maintaining male dominance over women. Feminists commonly identify rape as a crime that is not about sex, but rather a way of exerting control through physical domination and humiliation of another person. Accordingly, violence against women is not an inevitable outcome of inherent biological differences between men and women, but rather the result of a social phenomenon whereby men control women through degrading actions such as physical or sexual abuse. While feminism as a movement for social change has existed in the United States for centuries, it was during the second wave of the movement, beginning in the 1960s, that feminist activists brought issues of violence against women to the political forefront. This resulted in improvements to laws to protect women who were victims of sexual and physical violence and provided the impetus for federal funding of women's rape crisis centers and domestic violence shelters. Out of this productive time in the women's movement, feminist theory also developed and expanded across many academic disciplines.

Feminist scholars articulated questions about the nature of violence against women, including an analysis of power differences between women and men. Gender, in this context, is a cultural identity that maintains imbalanced social relations between men and women. Hence, from a young age, boys are encouraged to use violence to get their way, a pattern that ensures the reproduction of unequal exchanges between men and women. Moreover, because of the division of society into categories of male versus female, sexuality becomes a central difference that serves as a means for maintaining an unjust gendered social order.

Accordingly, feminist theories of sexual violence often focus on social forces and structural concerns that fuel violence against women, particularly sexual violence. Patriarchy, which can be defined as a sexual system of power in which the male possesses superior power and economic privilege, is often central to feminists' explanations of sexual violence. Power imbalances in gender relations, within the patriarchal system, are part of this broad approach to understanding violence against women (as opposed to a narrow, legalistic approach). In this system, men's power, exercised through sexual, physical, psychological, and economic abuse, is a way of maintaining control over women. In some sense, this prevalence of this system explains the pervasive levels of sexual violence against women. While these crimes may not receive widespread attention, they are all too common. Feminist theory accounts for this reality by exploring the culture, systems, and structures that make violence against women possible. For example, while viewing pornography does not cause rape, viewing repeated degrading sexual images of women can desensitize individuals to the continuum of behaviors from cat calls and groping to sexual assault and rape that constitute violence against women.

Feminist theories take seriously women's experience as a starting point for investigation and understanding the phenomenon of sexual violence and violence against women. As feminist theories have grown and developed beyond the vision of radical feminists, feminist theories now also look for explanations of sexual violence through examination of multiple levels of influence, resulting in multidimensional theories of sexual violence and violence against women more broadly.

Critics of feminist approaches to explaining violence against women, particularly sexual violence, argue that feminists' emphasis on patriarchal structures as the cause of violence unnecessarily assumes that the macrostructure of patriarchy could explain or predict individual actions. For example, some advocates of the family violence perspective would argue that many men who batter their wives are suffering from personality disorders, psychological conditions that predispose them to violence, not as a result of exposure to any larger societal influence that condones this type of abuse. Additionally, the family violence perspective critiques feminists' emphasis on violence against women because the feminist perspective does not account for violence done by women against their partners or spouses. Advocates of the family violence perspective argue that feminists' unilateral view of men's abuse of their female spouses does not account for individual differences, such as men who are not violent, men who are only slightly violent, and men who are very violent.

Sheila M. McMahon

See also Feminism, Influence of; Pornography; Theory, Coercive Control; Theory, Continuum of Violence

Further Reading

DeKeseredy, Walter S., & Schwartz, Martin D. (2011). Theoretical and definitional issues in violence against women. In C. M. Renzetti, J. L. Edeleson, & R. K. Bergen (Eds.), *Sourcebook on violence against women* (2nd ed., pp. 3–21). Thousand Oaks, CA: Sage.

Jasinski, J. L. (2001). Theoretical explanations for violence against women. In C. M. Renzetti, J. L. Edleson, & R. K. Bergen. (2001). *Sourcebook on violence against women* (pp. 5–21). Thousand Oaks, CA: Sage.

Theory, General Theory of Crime

In 1990, Michael Gottfredson and Travis Hirschi proposed "a general theory of crime." Reducing any complex theory to a simple proposition is risky, but their essential, unique claim is that low self-control can be seen as the root cause of all crime and comparable behavior—including sexual assault. This theory has become one of the most popular in general criminology. More specifically, while researchers have found low self-control an important part of the explanation for some crimes, it does not do as well for sexual violence, which is much more complex than simple low self-control. A feminist analysis would seem to make this theory more useful.

Crime was defined by Gottfredson and Hirschi as "acts of force or fraud undertaken in pursuit of self-interest" (1990, p. 15), although they claimed that their theory could explain other behaviors that were not necessarily against the law, such as extensive sex outside relationships, masturbation, or reading pornography. Crimes, they claim, are characterized by several elements. They (1) provide immediate gratification; (2) are easy and simple; (3) are exciting, risky, or thrilling; (4) have few or meager long-term benefits; (5) require little skill or planning; and (6) often result in pain or discomfort for the victim.

Overall, criminals are "impulsive, insensitive, physical (as opposed to mental), risk-taking, short-sighted, and non-verbal" (Gottfredson & Hirschi, 1990, p. 90). Gottfredson and Hirschi concluded that these characteristics constitute a stable construct of low self-control, which is useful in explaining crime. However, hailing back to his earlier social bond theory, Hirschi later argued that bonding with others does prevent people from committing crimes, but that those with short-term views do not take the time to consider the consequences of losing or breaking social bonds. Thus what seemed in 1990 to be unthinking rapists with a particular psychological trait later became (at least for Hirschi) a rational thinking actor who makes a choice to commit rape, albeit without sufficient consideration of the long-term effects of this choice (Lilly, Cullen, & Ball, 2011).

The theory has been very widely tested, and there has been some support for it, although not as much as for other causes of crime. However, few attempts have been made to apply this theory to sexual assault, perhaps because of Gottfredson and Hirschi's early difficulties in conceptualizing sexual assault as a crime. Unlike most criminologists, they claim that acquaintance, intimate, and marital rapes are "relatively rare" events. With no evidence cited, they assert that the amount of non-stranger rape is overstated, because typically what is claimed as an acquaintance is someone the woman barely knows. Such acquaintance rapes are often not reported, they claim, which does raise the question of how they are overstated. Further, they believe that sexual assault is caused by a lack of self-control in which offenders look for shortcuts to immediately satisfy their sexual needs, which they called "sex without courtship." It is difficult to determine whether they truly meant to reduce violent sexual assault to a form of masturbation, or simply used an unfortunate metaphor.

However, feminist scholars such as Miller and Burack (1993) contend that Gottfredson and Hirschi ignore gender as a power relationship and mischaracterize male violence against women. Sexual assault involves gendered power differences and inequalities, and disregarding these social relations and power disparities creates a false sense of gender neutrality. Asserting that sexual violence is only a need one fulfills by immediate gratification ignores the complexities of this crime and overlooks the reality that sexual violence is an act of power, control, and domination.

Turning to research evidence, low self-control has definitely been found to be associated with true "sex without courtship" such as masturbation, having numerous sexual partners outside relationships, or reading pornography. With more serious offenders, one set of researchers found that serious sexual offenders tend to lack personal constraint for both general and sexual offenses, based on a survey of 209 Canadian inmates convicted of sexual assault, most of whom were recidivists (Lussier, Proulx, & LeBlanc, 2005). Perhaps the most direct study of the relationship between low self-control and sexual violence was conducted by Shawna Cleary (2004), who interviewed 295 inmates in two prisons in Oklahoma. The confounding problem that imprisonment or treatment might be based on low self-control (as opposed to rape itself) is illustrated by her study, where the offenders housed in the Sexual Residential Offender Treatment Program tested lower in self-control than prisoner sex offenders who were not in treatment or non-sex-offender prisoners. There was no attempt in these studies to test whether low-self-control inmates were more likely to receive prison time, or treatment, or to have committed their crime in the context of other crimes, such as burglary, which would make imprisonment more likely.

In short, Cleary (2004) found that some sex offenders had low self-control while others did not. Thus various research has found that low self-control does seem to be related to extensive masturbation or consensual casual sex, or reading pornography. It also may be a causative factor in some cases of serious recidivist stranger rape, but even there it is certainly not the only or perhaps even the primary driving force. So far there has not been good evidence showing that the typical rape offender has low self-control, and particularly those who are not incarcerated. Altogether, this research lends some support to Gottfredson and Hirschi's theory, but not much. Rather, it is part of a consistent finding that other factors also play a role.

In summary, as with many other theories, lack of self-control as the main cause of crime has many valid points but does not work for crimes with gender issues. A feminist version of this theory would add motivation, for example, and explain why so many men see women as legitimate objects for their crimes (see, e.g., Schwartz & Pitts, 1995). Another fertile avenue is Tittle, Ward, and Grasmick's (2004) suggestion that our motivation to exercise self-restraint can be as important as the more psychological capacity for self-control that Gottfredson and Hirschi discuss. A feminist analysis might center on the extent to which men's desire to control their own sexual aggression can be reduced if they adopt patriarchal attitudes that support using women as objects.

Jennifer C. Gibbs and Martin D. Schwartz

See also Pornography; Stranger Rape; Theory, Feminist

Further Reading

Cleary, S. (2004). *Sex offenders and self-control: Explaining sexual violence*. New York, NY: LFB Scholarly Publishing.

Goode, E. (Ed.). (2008). *Out of control: Assessing the general theory of crime*. Stanford, CA: Stanford University Press.

Gottfredson, M. R., & Hirschi, T. (1990). *A general theory of crime*. Stanford, CA: Stanford University Press.

Hirschi, T. (2004). Self-control and crime. In R. E. Baumeister & K. D. Dobbs (Eds.), *Handbook of self-regulation: Research, theory and applications* (pp. 537–552). New York, NY: Guilford Press.

Lilly, J. R., Cullen, F. T., & Ball, R. A. (2011). *Criminological theory: Context and consequences* (5th ed.). Thousand Oaks, CA: Sage.

Love, S. R. (2006). Illicit sexual behavior: A test of self-control theory. *Deviant Behavior, 27*, 505–536.

Lussier, P., Proulx, J., & LeBlanc, M. (2005). Criminal propensity, deviant sexual interests and criminal activity of sexual aggressors against women: A comparison of alternative explanatory models. *Criminology, 43*, 249–282.

Miller, S. L., & Burack, C. (1993). A critique of Gottfredson and Hirschi's general theory of crime: Selective (in)attention to gender and power positions. *Women and Criminal Justice*, 4, 115–134.

Schwartz, M. D., & Pitts, V. L. (1995). Toward a feminist routine activities theory on campus sexual assault. *Justice Quarterly, 12*, 9–31.

Tittle, C. R., Ward, D. A., & Grasmick, H. G. (2004). Capacity for self-control and individuals' interest in exercising self-control. *Journal of Quantitative Criminology, 20*, 143–172.

Theory, Hegemonic Masculinity

Hegemonic masculinity theory states that there are certain characteristics of the dominant form of masculinity in our culture that promote the use of violence against girls, women, and other men, including sexual violence. Its underlying concepts provide a foundation for understanding the relationship between sexual violence, gender, and power. In particular, the notion of hegemonic masculinity may be helpful for understanding how some men define masculinity in certain situations to include domination over others, with violence against women, girls, and other men as an outcome.

Understanding hegemonic masculinity is related to understanding larger, postmodern gender theories. Common understandings and depictions of gender in our society typically define gender as either "male" or "female." Recently, however, this assumption has been challenged by scholars who propose a new conceptualization of gender, which regards it as socially constructed, multidimensional, and able to change based on the situation and context. They propose that there exists not just one, objective quality called "masculinity" or "femininity" but rather that there are different types of masculinities and femininities that occur in different situations, time periods, and by culture, class, religion, and their interplay. The role of context is especially salient in theories of masculinity, and may illuminate the situational aspect involved with the occurrence of sexual assault and violence against women. For example, a man may show his masculinity differently in a locker room than he would in his workplace; how he acts may also be influenced by who else is in the room, as well as individual aspects such as his culture, class, religion, and many other variables.

One of the types of proposed masculinity is hegemonic masculinity. Borrowing from Antonio Gramsci's Marxist analysis of class relations, R. W. Connell (1995) applies the term to address the role of power, which is absent in many other previous gender theories, and to explain masculinity as multiple and hierarchical. Hegemonic masculinity is the dominant, ascendant form of masculinity that is defined in relation to the subordination of others, including women and other men. This is the type of masculinity that is regarded as the "ideal" masculinity at any given point in time.

According to Connell, the characteristics of hegemonic masculinity change throughout history but consistently reinforce global male domination over women. This domination results in what Connell terms "patriarchal dividend," which provides men with benefits including honor, prestige, the right to command, and a material dividend such as higher incomes (Connell, 1995). In our contemporary Western culture, hegemonic masculinity is defined through its relationship of dominance over other males, such as gay men, and also over women and girls (Connell, 1995). Men subscribing to hegemonic masculinity feel compelled to demonstrate that they are men through showing their power over others that they regard as insubordinate. As Connell notes, this results in some men utilizing violence as a method for asserting dominance over women and other men as a claim to hegemonic masculinity.

The hegemonic masculinity in our contemporary culture is characterized by heterosexuality, strength, and sexual prowess. To be a man in our culture often means to be tough, responsible, and able to "get" women (Katz, 2006). Evidence suggests that men are required to "do gender"—or act in ways that demonstrate the hegemonic notion of masculinity—in certain group contexts (West & Zimmerman, 1987). In these contexts, boys and men may feel pressure by others to demonstrate their dominance and strength, to act tough. Acting "feminine" in these situations is regarded as weak and gay. Homophobia and the fear of being perceived as gay is largely connected to hegemonic masculinity, as boys and men are compelled to demonstrate that they are indeed not gay. This is often accomplished through sexual conquests with girls and women, which may be discussed with other men or may even occur in front of other men. Certain group rapes of girls or women may occur in part because boys or men who are witnessing the assault feel compelled to demonstrate to others that they are "one of the boys."

Certain contexts have been identified by researchers as being especially supportive of hegemonic masculinity, including some college fraternities, male athletic teams, gangs, and military groups. In these group settings, researchers have shown that sometimes there is language, rituals, and beliefs that support hegemonic masculinity including strength, dominance, and power. Sometimes these group situations include acts and beliefs that denigrate women through means such as displaying pornography, using sexist language, ranking the appearances of girls and women, and encouraging peers to have sex with women.

However, it is important to recognize that researchers have also found that not all men in these situations subscribe to demonstrating hegemonic masculinity. Critics of masculinity theories argue that not all men adhere to behavior that supports dominance, even if they belong to a group where the value of masculine strength is emphasized. For example, not all men in a particular fraternity or on an all-male athletic team will agree that men need to be strong, or they may have different definitions of masculinity and what it means to be a man. Many men who appear stereotypically masculine are actually outspoken against the perpetration of violence against women and girls. In addition to pinpointing those situations and contexts where boys and men are encouraged to engage in violence as a way to demonstrate hegemonic masculinity, there has also been a recent and clear call from the theoretical literature on masculinity and violence to better understand the ways in which hegemonic masculinity is resisted or challenged by some boys and men.

Sarah McMahon

See also Fraternities and Sororities; Homophobic Acts; Sports Teams; Theory, Male Peer Support; Theory, Social Norms

Further Reading

Connell, R. W. (1995). *Masculinities*. Berkeley, CA: University of California Press.

Katz, J. (2006). *The macho paradox*. Naperville, IL: Sourcebooks.

West, C., & Zimmerman, D. H. (1987). Doing gender. *Gender and Society, 1*, 125–151.

Theory, Male Peer Support

Why do some men see some women as potential targets for sexual assault? Male peer support (MPS) theory claims that men who have friends who proclaim patriarchal attitudes and approve of physical and sexual abuse of women (at least some women, under some circumstances) are more likely to themselves engage in sexual assault. Unlike victimization theories on sexual assault, this theory suggests that the focus of our inquiry should not be on women's actions, but on men's beliefs, attitudes, and behavior. It has received extensive empirical support, with both a national representative sample and community populations, although it has been mostly tested with white college-age men in the United States and Canada.

Of course, a complex and multidimensional phenomenon such as sexual assault cannot be reduced to a single cause that explains all antisocial behavior. However, although different names are used, some discussion of MPS is common in the literature. Popular early theories include Kanin's (1957) reference group theory, Bowker's (1983) standards of gratification perspective, and Sanday's (1990) psychoanalytic theory.

The term "male peer support" (MPS) was introduced by DeKeseredy, who in 1990 explained that it has two parts. The first, *attachments* to other abusive men, is congruent with a broad array of literature that discusses the importance, particularly to young men, of maintaining their public face before other men. The second is *resources* that these others provide, which includes verbal or emotional support or demands. The theory is based on a psychological social support model that argues that people who receive social support from others are more psychologically healthy, but argues that such models are too focused on individual models, leaving out sociological insights.

The basic model began with the argument that men who received social support for the physical or sexual abuse of women were more likely to engage in this behavior. Such men are provided with a vocabulary of motive that defines some women as legitimate objects of abuse and sexual assault. This always present rationalization is available to be called upon in a variety of specific situations, whether the peers are present or not. What is most important here is that relatively few men who commit sexual aggression are abusing total strangers. Rather, for the most part they abuse friends, lovers, and acquaintances. This vocabulary of motive enables and convinces them that they are not rapists, but ordinary men. Rapists attack strangers in dark places, but if women actually enjoy sexual violence, or women deserve it, or women act wrongly in denying sex, then these men see no reason to believe that they are rapists.

Thus later additions to the model included such factors as patriarchal beliefs (such as "men who pay for dinner deserve sex as a reward"); excessive alcohol consumption; membership in formal organizations that support abuse (such as some fraternities or sports teams); and the one most often forgotten: the absence of deterrence. This lack of consequence is essential: simply put, if men believe that they can get away with rape, it is because most often they can and do. Universities with dozens (if not hundreds) of rapes a year of acquaintances rarely see a single conviction, even under campus judiciaries. Similarly, in studies of urban public housing, male residents were not part of formal organizations but were similarly acting to maintain or gain status among peers, or just to fulfill perceived masculinity challenges. Still, low reporting and the failure of many police officers to believe that acquaintances can be raped means that in a wide variety of North American contexts there is little deterrence. These factors come together to support a narrow conception of masculinity (a real man is athletic, can hold his drink, has money to spend, and is in charge), the sexual objectification of women (which makes it possible to rape wives, girlfriends, dates, and others the man actually likes), and group secrecy (by both men and women, which supports the lack of deterrence). Thus no matter how many women are victims of sexual assault (and many studies have claimed up to 25% of college women are assaulted), few men in North America see themselves as rapists.

There have been many empirical tests of elements of this theory, and some broader tests of the model. Almost invariably, male peer support can be found to be a predictor of sexual violence against women. Although most of the studies have been of college-age men, similar results have been found in work with juvenile offenders, men in public housing, and men in rural communities. In a variety of studies of local and national samples, DeKeseredy and Schwartz have found (together and independently) that male peer support significantly predicts which men admit (anonymously) to committing sexual assault. For example, in a national survey they found that men who drank often and had male friends who verbally supported the emotional, physical, and sexual abuse of women, were almost 10 times as likely to report being sexual aggressors than those who did not drink as often and did not have such male peer support (Schwartz, DeKeseredy, Tait, & Alvi, 2001).

This theory has broad implications for public policy and practice. Extraordinary amounts of money have been spent in the past 20 years on sex offender treatment in prison, and batterer intervention programs in the community. Although there are few signs of these programs working, they have become the preferred model of how to deal with the small percentage of offenders who are officially sanctioned. The problem is that these models all deal with the individual problems of the single offender. Either they never leave, or after treatment are then returned to their patriarchal families, their patriarchal places of work, and their patriarchal places of leisure. "It is hard to imagine that there will ever be any change in their attitudes, and eventually in their behavior. And, of course, this is exactly what we have been finding" (Schwartz & DeKeseredy, 2008, p. 181).

Martin D. Schwartz and Walter S. DeKeseredy

See also Fraternities and Sororities; Pornography; Prevention, Involving Men; Sports Teams; Theory, Masculinity; Theory, Social Norms

Further Reading

Bowker, L. (1983). *Beating wife-beating*. Lexington, MA: Lexington Books.

DeKeseredy, W. S. (1990). Male peer support and woman abuse: The current state of knowledge. *Sociological Focus, 23*, 129–139.

DeKeseredy, W. S., & Schwartz, M. D. (2009). *Dangerous exits: Escaping abusive relationships in rural America*. New Brunswick, NJ: Rutgers University Press.

DeKeseredy, W. S., & Schwartz, M. D. (2013). *Male peer support and violence against women: History and verification of a theory*. Boston: Northeastern University Press.

Kanin, E. J. (1957). Male aggression in dating-courtship relations. *American Journal of Sociology, 63*, 197–204.

Sanday, P. R. (1990). *Fraternity gang rape*. New York, NY: New York University Press.

Schwartz, M. D., & DeKeseredy, W. S. (1997). *Sexual assault on the college campus: The role of male peer support*. Thousand Oaks, CA: Sage.

Schwartz, M. D., & DeKeseredy, W. S. (2008). Interpersonal violence against women: The role of men. *Journal of Contemporary Criminal Justice, 24*, 178–185.

Schwartz, M. D., DeKeseredy, W. S., Tait, D., & Alvi, S. (2001). Male peer support and a feminist routine activities theory. *Justice Quarterly, 18*, 623–650.

Sinclair, R. L. (2002). *Male peer support and male-to-female dating abuse committed by socially displaced male youth*. Doctoral dissertation, Carleton University, Ottawa, Ontario, Canada.

Therapeutic Interviewing Strategies

A therapeutic interview is one in which the element of empathy has been introduced that, in turn, results in the interviewee feeling safe enough to recall the information and feelings that will allow healing to begin and, potentially, a legal case to be processed. When dealing with survivors of sexual violence, there are many cultural, social, and environmental considerations that must be addressed before a successful interview can even take place.

Due to the intensely intimate nature of a sexual assault, the cultural and religious mores involving sex, and the high percentage of cases where the survivor knew the perpetrator (estimates are between 82% and 90%), the crime of sexual violence is unique in that the *victim* is often made to feel shame and guilt, despite not having done anything to provoke the attack. Particularly among the most vulnerable populations—which include minors, individuals with disabilities, immigrants (documented and undocumented) who have limited English proficiency, senior citizens, lesbian, gay, bisexual, and transgender individuals, and Native Americans—fears surrounding additional humiliation, judgment, and social or financial repercussions may affect the survivor's recall of events. This, coupled with the effects of rape trauma syndrome, as evidenced by post-traumatic stress disorder (PTSD), dictates that therapeutic interviewing strategies be divided into two categories: prior to the interview, and interview procedures.

Prior to the interview, it is important to address the following. First, make sure the interview takes place in a safe, discreet location respectful of the survivor's privacy. Second, be aware of trauma's impact. Each time survivors recount what happened, it can be painful and retraumatizing. They may have frozen in shock during the event and have difficulty recalling the details, or they may actually relive the trauma as they are recounting the assault. The degree of trauma experienced will vary for each person and can greatly impact their recall. This is the mind's way of protecting the survivor. Finally, be mindful of your own cultural, religious, and sociological views of sexual violence and leave them at the door. Understand that no matter what the age or culture of the survivor, he or she will be worried about being judged by family, friends, colleagues, and significant others. One of the primary intents of a therapeutic interview is to validate the survivor's experience, reactions, and believability.

Procedures to use during the therapeutic interviewing include the following. First, give survivors enough physical space to feel comfortable. This also means refraining from touching the survivor unless he or she gives permission and being aware of your own body language. Second, empower the survivor by offering choices, such as where to sit, whether water is wanted, if the physical space between you is all right. Sexual violence strips personal power away; you have the opportunity to begin to restore that in a therapeutic setting. Third, choose your words carefully, avoiding blame and advice giving. Discussing sexual violence is difficult in all cultures, and most survivors have misguided feelings of self-blame, shame, and self-disgust. Fourth, be prepared for any type of emotional reaction, which can range from compulsive talking, crying, and angry outbursts to partial or complete withdrawal. Avoid interpreting a survivor's calm as an indication that the sexual assault did not occur. The survivor could still be in shock. Fifth, model confidence and respect, being careful not to patronize or overprotect the survivor, but rather reassure him or her that he or she is strong and is capable of positive coping skills. Next, do not "clean up" or correct the survivor's language. The successful therapeutic interviewer will be comfortable talking about sexual violence as well as body parts and the broad range of acts. A survivor who is continually corrected will begin to feel judged. Finally, remember that a sexual assault is a shock to the victim. When humans go into shock, the part of the brain responsible for executive decision making and minute details is drained of blood that is allocated elsewhere so the "fight or flight" response can take over. For that reason, open-ended questions regarding feelings surrounding the incident will be available for recall much more readily than a specific timeline.

This is especially true when minors have been assaulted. An interview protocol developed by the Eunice Kennedy Shriver National Institute of Child Health and Human Development (NICHD) focuses on having the child talk about the target incident in a narrative stream, as opposed to answering direct questions. Nearly a decade of research confirms that when interviewers encourage narratives, survivors young or old can give more and better-quality information while feeling empowered to begin healing.

Denise Lang-Grant

See also Individuals with Disabilities; Native Americans; Rape, Older Adult; Recovery; Remembrance and Mourning

Further Reading

Deblinger, Esther, & Heflin, Anne Hope (1996). *Treating sexually abused children and their non-offending parents*. Los Angeles, CA: Sage.

Harris, Sara (2010). Toward a better way to interview child victims of sexual abuse. Retrieved October 10, 2011, from http://www.nij.gov/journals/267/child-victim-interview.htm

Reiter, Michael D. (2008). *Therapeutic interviewing: Essential skills and contexts of counseling*. Old Tappan, NJ: Merrill/Pearson Education.

Selected Websites

Office for Victims of Crime. Department of Justice. Retrieved from http://www.ojp.usdoj.gov/ovc/

Southern Poverty Law Center. Retrieved from http://www.splcenter.org

Therapeutic Communication Skills. Retrieved from http://www.slideshare.net/consgp/therapeutic-communications-skills

Trafficking in Persons

This entry provides an overview of trafficking in persons (also known as human trafficking). Although labor trafficking is mentioned to provide clarification about this topic, this entry is focused on trafficking of persons as it relates to sexual violence and abuse.

Over the past decade trafficking in persons, or modern-day slavery, has become a major criminal, social justice, and human rights issue around the world. In 2010, the U.S. Department of State estimated that 12.3 million adults and children were victims of forced and bonded labor and forced prostitution worldwide. Girls and women make up 56 percent of all trafficking victims, the vast majority of victims whom are sexually exploited, assaulted, and abused. According to the United

Nations Children's Fund (UNICEF) 150 million girls and 73 million children are sexually assaulted every year (http://www.unicef.org). The National Human Trafficking Hotline estimates that 200,000 American minors are at risk for human trafficking (http://www.polarisproject.org), the vast majority of whom are commercially sexually exploited and abused by adults.

People are trafficked for two primary reasons—for the purposes of sex exploitation and or forced labor. Areas of particular concern include bonded labor, involuntary domestic servitude, forced child labor, child sex trafficking, and child soldiers. Subjugated victims in the sex industry are often forced into activities such as prostitution, peep shows, and or other forms of pornography. Labor trafficking may involve exploitation through domestic servitude or forced labor in industries such as tourism, fine jewelry, agriculture, manufacturing, service industry (restaurants, hotels, etc.), and construction. Because female victims (adult and children) and male perpetrators are the foundation of the sex-trafficking trade, gender-focused strategies to combat sex trafficking are necessary.

The difference between smuggling and trafficking in people requires clarification. The major difference between smuggling and trafficking is subjugation; by definition trafficking involves force, fraud, or coercion. Smuggling involves illegally crossing a border, and the person who is smuggled is considered to have committed a crime. Smuggling may also involve deceit on the part of the smuggler, and people smuggled across borders may be vulnerable to many types of victimization. Individuals who are willingly smuggled into the United States may later become trafficking victims through forced labor or commercial sexual exploitation, but unlike people who are smuggled, certified victims of human trafficking are considered victims of federal and state crimes and entitled to protections as crime victims.

In this entry, survivors of human trafficking may be referred to simply as "victims" for narrative efficiency and in recognition of the criminality of this social ill. However, this label is not meant to be demeaning or judgmental. The authors recognize that victims are individuals who have survived a significant combination of physical, emotional, and sexual abuse and trauma. We honor their stories and them as survivors.

According to the U.S. Department of State's Trafficking in Persons (TIP) report in 2011, 33,113 victims of trafficking were identified worldwide in 2010 (29% were identified in African countries, 27% were identified in Europe, and 20% were identified in the Western Hemisphere [the Americas]). Despite the renewed attention to this global issue, the literature on human trafficking is relatively scarce. What is available largely focuses on the definition the problem, calls for increased attention to the issue, or ranking countries where trafficking in persons are of major concern. While these issues are important, additional research is needed to understand victimization including risk factors and vulnerability, the impact of trauma and assault, and needed resources for restoration and prevention strategies. Research is very difficult because victims are hidden and highly controlled emotionally, physically, and sexually by their traffickers. Consequently, victims are very difficult to identify and rescue or extract from their traffickers.

Sex trafficking involves the commercial sexual exploitation of children and adults and includes both U.S. citizens and foreign-born victims. Under the Trafficking Victims Protection Act (TVPA), a child who is being sexually exploited is considered a victim of human trafficking without having to meet the standard of force, fraud, or coercion. In other words, laws prohibit children and youth from being able to consent to sexual contact, intercourse, or activities. Any adult sexual contact with a child or youth is considered illegal. The forced prostitution of children is sometimes referred to as domestic minor sex trafficking (DMST) or commercial sexual exploitation of children (CSEC). Child sex trafficking includes any child involved in commercial sexual exploitation. Although not always, sex trafficking of minors generally involves small pimp-run operations that exploit chronic runaways or other vulnerable youth and children. Adult victims of sex trafficking may be prostituted by a pimp operating individually or may be forced to work in a more extensive "service" establishment with other victims such as a brothel, strip club or bar, adult entertainment establishment, or other venues.

Customers of prostituted victims, often referred to as "johns," contribute to the overall demand for the availability of sex for hire, including sex with children and youth. The use of online social media through a variety of websites and outlets has shifted the way some forced prostitutions operate. Many pimps now advertise the victim online, then "deliver" her to the john at a hotel or other location. Also, events that draw large crowds to cities (such as sporting and entertainment events, conventions, and business meetings) increase the likelihood of sex trafficking, and specifically the exploitation of minor victims of sex trafficking. Victims often report being transported by their trafficker(s) to "work" a particular event.

Trafficking does not have to involve moving victims from one location to another nor does it have to involve crossing an international border. The United States' landmark Trafficking Victims Protection Act (TVPA) signed by President Clinton in 2000 (reauthorized in 2003, 2005, and 2008) set domestic and international standards for antitrafficking efforts, including prevention, prosecution of traffickers, and protection of victims. The TVPA defines human trafficking as: "the recruitment, harboring, transporting, provision, or obtaining of a person for labor or services, through the use of force, fraud, or coercion for the purpose of subjection to involuntary servitude, peonage, debt bondage, slavery, or forced commercial sex acts" (TVPA, section 103[8]). The TVPA entitles trafficked persons to benefits and services, and for foreign-born victims protection from deportation. Although foreign-born and American citizen victims are protected under the TVPA, funding for specialized services for foreign-born victims is more widely available. As an international antitrafficking response, the Palermo Protocol to Prevent, Suppress, and Punish Trafficking in Persons, Especially Women and Children, Supplementing the United Nations Convention against Transnational Organized Crime has been adopted by 128 countries worldwide.

Since 2000, the U.S. Department of State has published the *Trafficking in Persons Report* (TIP) to assess and rank governments' efforts to address the crime of human trafficking. In 2011, 184 countries were included in the identified as Tier 1, Tier 2, Tier 2 Watch List, and Tier 3. Tier 1 countries are considered to be in full compliance with standards to eradicate human trafficking. Countries ranked as Tier 2 are not considered to be in full compliance, yet they are making significant efforts to comply, and Tier 2 Watch List countries are similarly working on compliance but there are significant numbers of victims or a growing number of victims, evidence for increased efforts is lacking, and the ranking is based on the country's commitment to continue to work toward full compliance with the minimum of the TVPA. Tier 3 includes countries not in compliance and not making significant efforts to comply, and these countries may be subject to monetary sanctions. For the last two years, since the State Department included the United States in its ranking, the United States has ranked as Tier 1. Although the response has been relatively swift over the last decade, gaps about effective prevention, investigative strategies, and responsive social services for victims remain.

Less is known about traffickers than the victims that they exploit, but what is known is that traffickers see their victims as lucrative commodities. Although there are no universal agreed-upon cost estimates, most experts agree that the economic gains for those that profit from human trafficking are exceptionally large— in the billions of dollars every year; it is considered one of the most profitable organized crimes in the world. One of the challenges involved in studying human traffickers, similar to human trafficking victims, is that traffickers are also a relatively hidden population primarily because criminal justice systems have difficulty holding them accountable for their crimes. Anti-human trafficking law enforcement agents report that sex traffickers tend to be males and older than their female victims. Law enforcement also reports that human trafficking is often linked to other criminal networks such as illegal drugs and prostitution. Traffickers who exploit U.S. citizens tend to be associated with small criminal groups, gangs, and criminal entrepreneurs while traffickers who move victims from across borders may be linked with national or transnational organized crime syndications.

Traffickers use a variety of methods to lure victims including the development of a direct relationship with the victim (particularly in the case of a single pimp of a sexually exploited victim) or through a "facilitator" (someone that connects potential victims with the trafficker). Women, who comprise the majority of victims, are sometimes coerced into recruiting positions or "promoted within the trafficking organization" to recruit new victims and avoid further sexual assault victimization themselves. For many American citizen victims, particularly minor victims, the trafficker often coerces the victim by befriending her, taking care of her, and buying her gifts. The trafficker often becomes the victim's "boyfriend"; it is not until this attention and often loving relationship is formed that the trafficker begins to exploit and demand the victim be prostituted and that she give all the earning from her sexual assault to him. For foreign-born victims there are often promises of legitimate employment and wage-earning opportunities. Victims are often rendered completely helpless for a variety of reasons, but traffickers maintain control over victims by using physical and sexual violence, isolation and entrapment, drug addiction, psychological and emotional abuse, and threats to other family members' well-being. The psychological coercion cannot be understated. Victims have been rescued after years of enslavement without chains because of the fear and threats of retaliation from their traffickers, against them or their family members, if they escape.

Victims of human trafficking need short- and long-term services to rebuild their lives. Acute or immediate needs include safety, housing, medical care, food, and clothing. Crisis intervention and trauma-informed mental health services may also need to be accessed immediately after a victim has been freed from her or his traffickers. Victims have cited the need for long-term employment assistance, legal services, independent and permanent housing, ongoing mental health care, and, for foreign-born victims, English-language acquisition and family reunification.

The Office for Victims of Crime (OVC) provides funding for critical services to newly identified victims of human trafficking and the Office of Refugee Resettlement (ORR) provides funding for long-term services. Specific funding for American citizen victims is less centralized and more elusive than this available funding for foreign-born victims.

The National Human Trafficking Resource Center is a hotline (1-888-3737-888) that accepts tips about potential trafficking situations; provides urgent and nonurgent referrals for victim services; offers technical assistance to law enforcement and social service professionals; and provides comprehensive general information and anti-trafficking resources.

A criminal justice system response to this crime has been the thrust of many efforts over the past decade. Federal legislation and prosecution of traffickers have also led heightened awareness among Americans that modern-day slavery exists. The TIP (2011) reports 6,017 prosecutions (of which 90% were for sex-trafficking crimes) and 3,619 convictions (of which 94% were for sex-trafficking crimes) worldwide. In the United States two visa categories are provided for foreign-born trafficking victims—T and U Visas. The T Visa is given to an adult victim who has been certified by a law enforcement agent as a severe victim of severe trafficking. The victim must cooperate with law enforcement in the criminal case although victims under the age of 18 years old are not required to cooperate with law enforcement. Employment authorization document is given with the T Visa, and holders are eligible for assistance through the refugee programs administered by the U.S. Department of Health and Human Services (HHS) and the Office of Refugee Resettlement (ORR). The U Visa is given to victims of violent crimes who endured substantial physical or psychological abuse during the crime that can be documented and verified by a governmental entity. It gives victims temporary legal status and work eligibility in the United States.

Noël Busch-Armendariz, Maura B. Nsonwu, Laurie Cook Heffron, and
Neely Mahapatra

See also Violence Against Women Act (VAWA)

Further Reading

Batstone, D. (2010). *Not for Sale*. New York, NY: HarperCollins.

Lloyd, R. (2010). *Girls like us: Fighting for a world where girls are not for sale, an activist finds her calling and heals herself*. New York, NY: HarperCollins.

Kara, S. (2009). *Sex trafficking: Inside the business of modern slavery*. New York, NY: Columbia University Press.

Trafficking Victims Protection Act of 2000, H.R. 3244, 107th Cong., 1st Sess (2000). Retrieved from http://www.polarisproject.org/images/docs/Trafficking%20Victim's% 20Protection%20Act,%20Public%20Law%20106-386%20(Oct.%2028,%202000).pdf

Trafficking Victims Protection Reauthorization Act of 2003, H.R. 2620, 108th Cong., 1st Sess. (2003). Retrieved from http://www.polarisproject.org/images/docs/TVPA% 20Reauthorization%20Act%20of%202003,%20Public%20Law%20108-193%20(Dec.% 2019,%202003).pdf

Trafficking Victims Protection Reauthorization Act of 2005, H.R. 972, 109th Cong., 1st Sess. (2005). Retrieved from http://www.polarisproject.org/images/docs/TVPA% 20Reauthorization%20Act%20of%202005,%20Public%20Law%20109-164%20(Jan.% 2010,%202005).pdf

Trafficking Victims Protection Reauthorization Act of 2008, S. 3061, 110th Cong., 2nd Sess. (2008). Retrieved from http://frwebgate.access.gpo.gov/cgi-bin/getdoc.cgi ?dbname=110_cong_public_laws&docid=f:publ457.110.pdf

U.S. Department of State. (n.d.). *Trafficking in Persons Report* (*TIP*). Retrieved from http://www.state.gov/g/tip/rls/tiprpt/2009/

Selected Websites

Campaign to rescue and restore victims of human trafficking. U.S. Department of Health and Human Services. Administration for Children and Families. Retrieved from http://www.acf.hhs.gov/trafficking/index.html

Characteristics of suspected human trafficking incidents, 2007–8. The U.S. Department of Justice, Office of Justice Programs, Bureau of Justice Statistics. Retrieved from http://bjs.ojp.usdoj.gov/index.cfm?ty=pbdetail&iid=550

Coalition against Trafficking in Women. Retrieved from http://www.catwinternational.org

Free the Slaves. Retrieved from http://www.freetheslaves.net

Girls Educational and Mentoring Services. Retrieved from http://www.gems-girls.org/

Human trafficking North Carolina. University of North Carolina at Chapel Hill. http://humantrafficking.unc.edu/

Polaris Project: For a World without Slavery. Retrieved from http://www.polarisproject.org

Shared Hope International: Leading a Worldwide Effort to Eradicate Sexual Slavery. Retrieved from http://www.sharedhope.org

Slavery Footprint. Retrieved from http://www.slaveryfootprint.org

Trafficking in Persons Report 2011. U.S. Department of State. Retrieved from http://www.state.gov/g/tip/rls/tiprpt/2011

UNICEF. Retrieved from http://www.unicef.org

United Nations Office on Drugs and Crime on human trafficking and migrant smuggling. Retrieved from http://www.unodc.org/unodc/en/human-trafficking/index.html

Trauma, Secondary

Secondary traumatic stress is the broadest among several frameworks that describe the effects on human service professionals and other helpers of working with people who have experienced traumatic life events. Related concepts include *compassion fatigue*, *vicarious traumatization*, *burnout*, and *countertransference*. Although preventable and treatable, secondary traumatic stress is a serious occupational hazard of direct work with specific populations, such as victims of child abuse, rape, interpersonal violence, war, violent crime, terrorism, as well as naturally occurring disasters. Helpers who are affected most commonly report symptoms that are markedly similar to those of post-traumatic stress disorder (PTSD), in particular feeling numb or disconnected and experiencing flashbacks, intrusive images, or dreams about the traumatic event. Secondary traumatic stress is prevalent among helpers, such as child welfare workers, psychologists, social workers, nurses, relief workers, as well as volunteers. Those who are at higher risk for developing secondary traumatic stress are helpers with a personal history of trauma, helpers who are less experienced, and helpers who have heavier exposure to traumatized clients, often through larger caseloads. If secondary traumatic stress goes untreated, helpers may be diagnosed with PTSD, may have difficulty establishing meaningful relationships, and may run the risk of leaving the trauma field prematurely. Strategies for addressing secondary traumatic stress include practicing self-care, having a balance between work and home, and participating in supportive supervision.

As an umbrella term, secondary traumatic stress includes the following categories of indirect exposure: compassion fatigue, vicarious traumatization, burnout, and countertransference. Compassion fatigue is often understood as synonymous with secondary traumatic stress in which a helper becomes "fatigued" through empathically connecting with others. Vicarious traumatization describes changes in a helper's inner life and worldview in response to working with traumatized people, often those victimized by rape, interpersonal violence, or child sexual abuse. Burnout describes the effect of concrete workplace stressors that are often associated with contact with traumatized populations, including low pay, long hours, and poor working conditions. Burnout can also develop when helpers are confronted with particularly challenging, difficult, or resistant clients where they feel they are unable to make a difference. Finally, countertransference describes a helping professional's reaction and response to a particular client based on the professional's personal history and personality. Countertransference is not necessarily specific to clients with trauma histories.

When not used as an umbrella term to frame different consequences of indirect exposure, secondary traumatic stress is a syndrome of symptoms that are nearly identical to PTSD, although the traumatic event is the hearing about, not actually experiencing, a specific traumatic event. Figley (1995) defines secondary traumatic stress as "the natural consequent behaviors and emotions resulting from knowledge about a traumatizing event experienced by a significant other. It is the stress resulting from helping or wanting to help a traumatized or suffering person" (p. 10). Although most often the term is associated with those whose work exposes them to trauma, family members and friends are also at risk for developing symptoms.

Helpers engaged in direct practice with trauma victims are likely to experience PTSD with the development of symptoms following exposure to an extreme traumatic event involving direct personal experience of an event that involves actual or threatened death or serious injury. The rate of PTSD in social workers is twice that of the general population (Bride, 2007). Secondary traumatic stress includes symptoms nearly identical to PTSD, including thinking about clients outside of sessions, reliving or reexperiencing the client's story through dreams, hyperarousal, numbing, and attempts to distance oneself from the trauma. Helpers most commonly report intrusion symptoms, such as unwelcome recollections of the events, distressing dreams, nightmares, or flashbacks. Avoidance symptoms include feeling numb, avoiding people or places that may trigger memories of the event, and/or consciously avoiding thinking about the event, resulting in a loss of connection with others. Impairment in daily functioning and an overall sense of doom are also common among helpers, as well as feelings of denial, disbelief, disconnection, and withdrawal from intimate relationships.

Secondary traumatic stress is so prevalent among mental health professionals that a diagnosis of secondary post-traumatic stress disorder (SPTSD) has been proposed for inclusion in the *Diagnostic and Statistical Manual of Mental Disorders* (*DSM*). However, it has not yet been accepted for inclusion.

A growing awareness of secondary traumatic stress among those in the helping professions has led the way to a range of response strategies. For example, the Secondary Traumatic Stress Scale has 17 questions that measure intrusion, avoidance, and arousal symptoms in helpers. This self-administered test allows helpers to assess their level of secondary traumatic stress. Using this scale, helpers respond to statements such as: "I had trouble sleeping; I felt discouraged about the future; I felt jumpy; reminders of my clients upset me; I was easily annoyed" (Bride, Robinson, Yedidis, & Figley, 2004).

Helpers in the trauma field need to pay careful attention to secondary traumatic stress. Untreated, secondary traumatic stress may lead to PTSD, resulting in helpers leaving the trauma field prematurely, or, if they remain, experiencing an inability to empathize with and effectively help those in need. Secondary traumatic stress is preventable through specific self-care strategies, including establishing a balance between work and home, getting support through supervision, peer groups, or other avenues, and paying attention to aspects of work satisfaction.

Shantih E. Clemans

See also Burnout in Human Services; Countertransference (Therapists); Vicarious Traumatization

Further Reading

Bride, B. E., Robinson, M. M., Yegidis, B., & Figley, C. R. (2004). Development and validation of the Secondary Traumatic Stress Scale. *Research on Social Work Practice, 14*, 27–35.

Figley, C. R. (1995). Compassion fatigue as secondary traumatic stress disorder: An overview. In C. R. Figley (Ed.), *Compassion fatigue* (pp. 1–20). New York, NY: Brunner-Mazel.

McCann, I., & Pearlman, L. (1990). Vicarious traumatization: A framework for understanding the psychological effects of working with victims. *Journal of Traumatic Stress, 3*, 131–149.

Pearlman, L. A., & Saakvitne, K. W. (1995). *Trauma and the therapist: Countertransference and vicarious traumatization in psychotherapy with incest survivors*. New York, NY: Norton.

Selected Web Sites

Charles Figley Institute. Retrieved from http://www.figleyinstitute.com/

Compassion Fatigue Awareness Project. Retrieved from http://www.compassionfatigue.org/pages/reading.html

U.S. Department of Veterans Affairs, National Center for PTSD. Retrieved from http://www.healthquality.va.gov/Post_Traumatic_Stress_Disorder_PTSD.asp

Trauma Therapy

Trauma therapy is the process of healing the specific symptoms trauma can leave behind. The objective is to eliminate or decrease the unpleasant effects left after a distressing experience. Through minimizing and eliminating trauma-related symptoms, an individual may reclaim his or her sense of security and emotional balance, and generally live a healthy, calm life.

Trauma occurs after a critically stressful event in one's life, such as severe accidents, death of a loved one, war-related activities, domestic violence, sexual assault, and being the victim of a crime. Trauma can also occur when witnessing these types of events happening to others. Trauma symptoms can last for days, weeks, months, or even years after the trauma is over. The intensity and duration of the trauma impacts the length of time these symptoms last.

Trauma therapy has specific goals that are intended to help the victim overcome the effects of the trauma. Effects that are addressed in therapy often include depressive symptoms, anger, anxiety, changes in sleeping and eating habits, heightened startle response and flashbacks. Initially, therapy creates a healing relationship between the client and the therapist. This, in and of itself, may be a corrective experience in which a healthy relationship is demonstrated. Such a therapeutic foundation will help clients begin to address the trauma narrative. The trauma narrative describes the thoughts and internal dialogue that a survivor often experiences subsequent to the trauma. The main thoughts and feelings include hopelessness, helplessness, and fear. The narrative plays in the survivor's mind in phrases, such as, "I will always feel this way." After these thoughts occur, the emotions follow, and can grow to the point of interfering and negatively impacting the survivor's life. Through therapy, one works on identifying negative or distorted narratives, and works to reverse them in an effort to change any damaging effects. The desired result is a more positive narrative that has a healthy perspective on past events.

Trauma is stored differently in our minds and bodies than regular memory. Trauma can have lasting effects on the brain, specifically regarding memory and emotion. This impact may include heightened stress response, difficulty retrieving memory, and dissociation. This has long-term implications for children growing up witnessing or being subjected to violence. Therapy and appropriate therapeutic interventions can reverse these effects. Through support, validation, and healthy modeling, children and adults alike can recover from trauma.

In children and adolescents, therapy has similar goals, but often different methodologies. Similar emotions are exhibited differently in youths, and therapy will be sensitive to such differences. For example, a depressed child may show more anger or out-of-control behaviors than sadness. These behaviors include physical aggression toward others and vocal outbursts. For children and adolescents, talk therapy is frequently supplemented with activity, reading, and nonverbal expression. This nonverbal expression is an essential piece of trauma therapy. It may include drawing, coloring, music, or physical activity. For younger children, playing is a common and appropriate medium for healing to take place. This may mean therapeutic card games or with dolls, action figures, or toy models of common household items. All transactions occur in a secure and protected place where healthy and appropriate boundaries are established and respected.

Addressing and challenging victim mythology is also an integral process of trauma therapy. Survivors are encouraged to explore topics such as what it means to be a victim, how this experience will change them, and what defines the person they are, as well as the roles they play in the lives of others.

There are varied settings for trauma therapy. Individual therapy is the most common, and allows survivors to heal privately in a supportive and healthy atmosphere. For children and adolescents, family therapy may be a necessary component to healing. Family therapy increases tolerance, understanding, and respect for a victim. This is done through enhancing interaction between family members through insight and empathy. Group therapy is also beneficial to survivors of trauma, although mainly for adults. Hearing another group member share his or her story is helpful in reducing isolation, which can reduce confusion and shame. It is essential that trauma therapy, be it with individuals, families, or groups, provide a safe place for survivors to share these stories. Additionally, trauma therapy should be directed toward healing people's wounds and helping survivors identify healthy and positive coping skills to deal with trauma related symptoms. Finally, trauma therapy recognizes that the reactions to trauma, such as depression and anxiety, are normal reactions to an abnormal situation. Frequently, these symptoms will diminish with time.

Larissa Boianelli

See also Group Therapy; Impact, Brain Functioning; Play Therapy

Further Reading

Hall, G. C. N., & Hirschman, R. (1991). Toward a theory of sexual aggression: A quadripartite model. *Journal of Consulting and Clinical Psychology, 59*, 662–669.

Kihlstrom, J. F. (2010). Self-reference effect. In D. Matsumoto (Ed.), *The Cambridge dictionary of psychology* (pp. 480–481). New York, NY: Cambridge University Press.

McEwen, B. S., Conrad, C. D., Kuroda, Y., Frankfurt, M., Magarinos, A. M., & McKittrick, C. (1997). Prevention of stress-induced morphological and cognitive consequences. *European Neuropsychopharmacology, 3*, 322–328.

Miranda, R. M., & Kihlstrom, J. F. (2005). Mood congruence in childhood and recent autobiographical memory. *Cognition & Emotion, 19*, 981–998.

Putnam F. W., & Trickett P. K. (1993). Child sexual abuse: A model of chronic trauma. *Psychiatry, 56*, 82–95.

Traumatic Bonding

In the field of sexual violence and abuse, traumatic bonding has been observed between child abuse victims and their abusive caregivers (Nader, 2001), and between battered women and their abusive partners (Dutton & Painter, 1981). Traumatic bonding involves the development of an ultrastrong emotional tie that defies logic to the outside observer. Traumatic bonding requires repeated or prolonged exposure to trauma and occurs after an abuse victim has been taken into captivity using some form of coercive control that involves a combination of force, intimidation, or entice- ment (Herman, 1992). A similar bonding process, labeled Stockholm Syndrome, was also noted to occur between hostages and bank robbers in Sweden after the hostages were freed and paradoxically showered their Stockholm captors with compassion, loyalty, and love despite being held gunpoint and threatened with death.

Since the conditions of captivity necessary for traumatic bonding to occur are emulated during childhood, abused infants and children can be considered hos- tages held captive by their dependence and lack of alternatives. The context for traumatic bonding involves an imbalance of power where the more powerful abuser uses coercive control involving a continuous pattern of intermittent abusive acts (i.e., degradation, manipulation of perceptions, physical and sexual assault, deprivation of rights and freedoms) and intimidation to control and dominate his or her less powerful victim. The abuser randomly alternates between abuse behav- iors and nurturing behaviors such as access to water, personal hygiene, food, and freedoms that were previously restricted, or a reprieve from violence and sometimes an apology. The acts of nurturing and kindness give the victim hope and further strengthen the traumatic bond.

Susceptibility to becoming traumatically bonded to the abuser is not tied to personality deficits and instead is accounted for by the features in the relationship context itself. The victim's feelings of terror and perceived isolation as well as the level of resistance she or he mounts will depend upon the coercive control pattern and other factors including the victim's age, social connections, coping response patterns, victimization history, and access to resources. Since the victim's normal emotional bonds and social connections with others threaten the durability of the traumatic bond, the abuser acts to isolate the victim from potential sources of support or intervention in order to reduce outside influences that may overcome the victim's negative self-perceptions and feelings of hopeless- ness, worthlessness, and self-blame.

One of the most recently discovered childhood sexual assault cases where a paradoxical attachment was evident involved the kidnapping case of Jaycee Lee Dugard. Ms. Dugard formed a traumatic bond to David Garrido after he kidnapped Jaycee at age 11, raped her on numerous occasions, and forced her to bear two children during 18 years of captivity in the Garrido backyard. Initially, Garrido intimidated and threatened Jaycee to stop her from escaping. Garrido also manipulated her to feel sorry for him by telling her that she was helping him with his sexual appetite while saving others from the same fate by staying with him. When she became pregnant, the Garridos allowed her to start sleeping inside the house so that she saw the children as blessings. During her captivity, Jaycee assisted Garrido with his business files, greeted his customers at the door, and had opportunities to go out in public although she never tried to escape.

Over time, the victim internalizes the abuser's worldview and perceptions while perceiving his or her own agency and options for escape as severely constrained or nonexistent. Consequently, when the victim stays connected to the abuser despite the appearance of a clear path for exit, the "choice" to stay or love the abuser is considered survival oriented as an act of self-preservation in an effort to avoid the threatened consequences delivered in the past and present, or promised in the future.

The more the victim becomes hyperfocused on her abuser's behavior in order to ward off danger and increase her chance of survival, the less able she is to focus on and distinguish her own needs from his, the more interested she is in placating his every mood, and the more vulnerable she becomes to his control. As her resistance is met with the futility of escape, her identity is subsumed to his and she cannot bear to be separated from him. Her behaviors may include taking up his causes, protecting him, absolving him of responsibility and following his lead and his will in all she does including compromising her value system. She may commit crimes of larceny, theft, selling or using drugs, as well as engaging in abuse and neglect of her children, which contributes to the corruption of the self and leads to extreme anger and self-loathing.

One of the most notorious examples of traumatic bonding involved Hedda Nussbaum and the paradoxical attachment to her abuser and live-in lover, Joel Steinberg. The case was brought to light in 1987 by police when Lisa, Joel Steinberg's illegally adopted six-year-old daughter, was found battered and close to death on the bathroom floor. Hedda was also severely battered by Joel, her face almost unrecognizable when compared to her photo prior to entering the relationship. Hedda's internalization of Joel's beliefs and perceptions as well as her blind obedience to Joel's demands demonstrated an extreme loss of self-agency and autonomy to act on her own behalf to extract herself from the traumatic bond she had with Joel. Hedda's traumatic bond contributed directly to her inability to act on behalf of her adopted daughter to obtain medical help. Lisa died a few days after she was initially discovered by authorities. During Joel's trial for Lisa's murder, Hedda testified that she loved Joel more than ever, and 15 years later Hedda reported that she still had some positive feelings for him.

Cynthia Wilcox Lischick

See also Coping Mechanisms; Theory, Coercive Control; Victims, Guilt and Shame

Further Reading

Bancroft, L., & Silverman, J. (2002). *The batterer as parent*. Thousand Oaks, CA: Sage.

Dutton, D. G., & Painter, S. (1981). Traumatic bonding: The development of emotional attachments in battered women and other relationships of intermittent abuse. *Journal of Victimology, 6*, 139–155.

Fitzpatrick, Laura (2009, August 31). Stockholm syndrome. *Time*. Retrieved from http://www.time.com/time/magazine/article/0,9171,1920301,00.html

Herman, J. (1992). *Trauma and recovery*. New York, NY: Basic Books.

Jones, A. (1994). *Next time, she'll be dead: Battering and how to stop it*. Boston, MA: Beacon Press.

Nader, K. (2001). Treatment methods for childhood trauma. In J. Wilson, M. Friedman, & J. Lindy (Eds.), *Treating psychological trauma and PTSD* (pp. 278–334). New York, NY: Guildford Press.

Roberts, Laura (2011, July 8). Jaycee Lee Dugard talks of painful birth in pedophile's backyard. *Mail Online*. Retrieved from http://www.dailymail.co.uk/news/article-2011896/Jaycee-Lee-Dugard-talks-painful-birth-paedophile-David-Garridos-yard.html

Russo, Francine (1997). *The New York Times Magazine* (March 30). The faces of Hedda Nussbaum. Retrieved from http://www.nytimes.com/1997/03/30/magazine/the-faces-of-hedda-nussbaum.html?pagewanted=all&src=pm

Stark, E. D. (2007). *Coercive control*. New York, NY: Oxford University Press.

Treatment Programs for Sexual Offenders

Although public policy has generally moved toward more punitive approaches to sex offender management, therapeutic treatment of sexual offenders is also common, either within prison or in community settings. Among court-order models of intervention, group counseling approaches are far more common than individual treatment, likely due to cost and staffing considerations. In addition, group models can allow offenders the opportunity to hold one another accountable, provide support to, and engage in positive confrontation with others who may be perceived to be like themselves. Although there are a wide variety of treatment models available, a few of the most common will be addressed here.

Relapse Prevention

Traditional rehabilitation approaches often use a cognitive behavioral model, focusing on building empathy for the victims and relapse prevention. Models such as these have been adapted from traditional substance abuse models. These models are built on the assumption that building empathy for actual and potential victims can assist in relapse prevention by developing a more accurate understanding of the meaning and impacts of their behaviors. In addition, this empathy may provide an avenue for disrupting cognitive distortions that neutralize social and emotional barriers to sexual offending. These distortions include the belief that an offender cannot control his or her sexuality, the sense that he or she is entitled to have the sexual relationships he or she desires, and that children are sexual beings. These distortions may also be related to his or her own victimization history, in which prior victimization is reconceptualized as loving interaction or the impact minimized as a coping technique.

These cognitive approaches are typically implemented using a strong confrontational approach. Accountability for maladaptive thoughts and behaviors, without minimizations or externalized blame, are central requirements in moving forward through the intervention. Offenders then begin to identify emotional and behavioral cues or situations that put them at risk for future perpetration. This may include such things as negative emotional states or use of fantasy or pornography. The goal is to replace maladaptive behaviors with more appropriate thoughts and actions and to develop strategies to avoid and manage risk factors.

These interventions are found to be generally successful; however, motivation among mandated participants is noted as an important barrier. This is believed to be particularly true of approaches that use more confrontative strategies to achieve accountability. More recent adaptations of the relapse prevention model incorporate more supporting and holistic methods of engaging the offender in the intervention prior to the onset of the cognitive behavioral techniques. This is intended to overcome resistance to intervention and improve motivation for change.

Criticisms of the approach primarily focus on the "one-size-fits-all" approach in which offenders with a variety of histories and offense patterns are treated simultaneously using the same manualized intervention strategy. This approach may not attend to underlying issues such as trauma exposure and the differences between types of offenders, such as low- and high-risk offenders or violent and nonviolent offenders. In addition, some have criticized the model for taking an approach to rehabilitation that is too punitive.

Behavioral Approaches

A modification of classic relapse prevention approaches adjusts the focus of the intervention away addressing the cognitive elements of relapse prevention, to provide more behavioral strategies designed to increase prosocial behavior. Some elements of the cognitive approach are maintained to address the distortions and minimizations that allow sexual offending. However, this model devotes greater attention to the development of social skills and relationship building. This can involve addressing issues such as loneliness, low self-esteem, and social deficits that may contribute to offending behavior through the use of role plays and other activities designed to develop prosocial skills.

The good lives model (Ward & Stewart, 2003) is a more recent treatment approach that attempts to utilize these behavioral interventions to assist offenders in developing a balanced, fulfilled life. In this model, the therapist works with each individual to develop a list of personalized goals, based on his or her own interests and strengths. This approach is intended to be more holistic and personal to the offender, working to develop coping skills as part of a more adaptive personal identity. This is done through the exploration of life history, self-worth, acceptance of responsibility, exploration of dynamic risk factors, development of coping strategies, and relationship building (both sexual and nonsexual). Although the intervention may develop limited self-management plans to avoid risk of relapse, the focus of the plans is instead on the development of the personalized goals.

A strength of this approach is increased motivation for treatment and lower attrition as compared to relapse prevention models. However, the approach has also been criticized for placing the emotional needs of the offender above the risk management concerns of the community. Specifically, the model may not do enough to equip offenders with the skills necessary to deal with the inevitable setbacks or potentially risky situations that could lead to future offending.

Treatment with Juvenile or Adult Offenders

Although similar models of intervention are used with both adult and juvenile sexual offenders, some differences do exist. Research indicates that due to social and biological development, the capacity for moral reasoning and ability to regulate risk-taking impulses may not be fully developed until early adulthood. For this reason, the juvenile justice program is built on a model that is generally more rehabilitative and less punitive than the adult system.

This is reflected in the prevalence of trauma-informed care models in the treatment of juvenile sex offenders. These models are developed to be sensitive to the traumatic histories of offenders and address the post-traumatic stress symptoms. The intervention then attempts to identify the ways in which the trauma has contributed to maladaptive coping strategies, in these cases involving the abuse of others. More positive coping strategies are developed while attending to the feelings of pain, betrayal, and fear caused by the traumatic childhood experiences.

Rates of recidivism have been found to be lower for juvenile sex offenders who complete treatment than adults. It is not clear if the lower recidivism rates are due to the developmental process of the adolescent or the use of trauma-informed care. It is possible that the development of the regions of the brain associated with decision making and moral reasoning may make juveniles more responsive to treatment. However, the success of trauma-informed therapy with this population is resulting in the expansion of these models to adult offenders and exploration of the efficacy.

Through the course of the intervention, depression and suicidality are also common as offenders face the realities of their behavior and the social stigma associated with being labeled a sexual offender. Although it is not a common component of many cognitive behavioral or psychoeducational approaches, addressing these experiences will provide a greater foundation for the development of a more positive self-concept and coping strategies.

Coexisting Issues

In general, sex offender treatment approaches are designed to address only the maladaptive sexual behaviors. However, other issues that may be relevant to treatment often coexist with sexual offending. This includes such things as trauma, substance abuse, mental illness, and developmental or cognitive disability. Each of these may present a barrier to the completion of the treatment program as well as provide additional challenges in emotional and behavioral change. However, little research is available to address how these issues can be addressed within the intervention. Instead, it is often proposed that simultaneous intervention should be provided to address the coexisting issues.

Although little research has explored the efficacy of such approaches, an increasing number of approaches have been explored that integrate trauma resolution with sex offender treatment. Offenders with histories of victimization in their own childhood may be further traumatized by exposure to and interaction with violent sexual offenders in group treatment. In addition, these offenders may be resistant to interventions that require complete accountability while denying the potential impact of their own victimization history. In most cases, intervention such as eye movement desensitization and reprocessing are used as a supplement to other forms of sex offender treatment. It is hypothesized that decreasing the trauma symptoms, such as compulsivity and maladaptive survival strategies, can increase the receptivity of the offender to cognitive or behavioral treatment strategies.

Voluntary Participation in Treatment

Although it is believed that the majority of participants in sex offender treatment are mandated to participate through Child Protective Services or criminal court, it is difficult to assess the number of individuals who may be voluntarily participating in interventions. Individual and family counseling is one avenue in which an offender may voluntarily seek help. Mandatory reporting laws require most helping professionals to report sex offenders to the child protection agencies, which may prevent many offenders from seeking help to change their behavior.

However, other sources of support may be available through anonymous sources such as Sex Addicts Anonymous and Sex and Love Addicts Anonymous. These community organizations, based on the 12-step model similar to Alcoholics

Anonymous, provide an avenue for seeking support without the threat of legal interventions. The Internet has also provided an avenue for offenders to confidentially receive support and connect with others in a safe environment. The Internet provides an important opportunity for those who may feel shame or fear about seeking help in a setting that is not anonymous. However, due to the anonymous nature of 12-step program and Internet-based self-help groups, measurement of the prevalence of the utilization of these services is not available. Additionally, research has not sufficiently examined the impacts of participation.

A variety of criticisms of these approaches exist, many similar to those of other 12-step models. Because they are not commonly led by a trained mental health professional, concern exists that they may not be able to adequately address the history of trauma, mental health issues, or the severe underlying distortions of some participants. Without this ability to adequately address these underlying issues, true change may not be possible. In addition, voluntary programs may not provide the accountability to maintain the intervention when it becomes painful or difficult for the individual. Concern also exists that bringing together individuals with these abusive histories may result in collusion and support for the continuation of harmful cognitions and behaviors when there is not the oversight of a professional therapist.

Effectiveness

For sex offender treatment, effectiveness is typically defined in a decrease in recidivism rates among sexual offenders. However, these rates can be measured in a variety of ways. These differences can result in highly varied reports of recidivism. The first consideration involves whether to include all criminal recidivism or just sexual crimes. The majority of rearrests and convictions for sexual offenders are for nonsexual crimes, accounting for up to 75 percent of all recidivism, particularly when technical violations of parole or registration are included. This can inflate the perception of the ability to treat or change sexually abusive behavior. However, these criminal acts may actually be more reflective of the difficulties of reentering following incarceration.

Recidivism can also be measured as either the rate of arrest, conviction rates, or subsequent incarceration. Each holds advantages and disadvantages in representing the actual rates of behavior. As arrest, conviction, and incarceration rates are low for all sexual crimes, with an increasingly low percentage moving through each stage of the legal process, it is likely that these will underrepresent the actual levels of violence perpetrated. However, arrest rates may also include some proportion of individuals who are arrested but are not actually found to have committed the crime.

All of these are likely to have largely underestimated the recidivism rates due to low reporting rates. It is estimated that fewer than one-quarter of sexual assaults are ever reported to the police. A few other forms of data on recidivism have been attempted. These include self-report surveys with the use of polygraph, which have been found to reveal recidivism rates that are more than twice as high. Alternatively, effectiveness can be measured by examining offense-related behaviors, such as use of pornography or loitering near schools. These may indicate at the very least that there is a threat of reoffenses, indicating that the treatment may not have been fully effective.

In order to accurately assess the impact of treatment, several elements are considered essential in the design of a rigorous research study. First, the results of the group receiving treatment are more meaningful if compared against a similar group that does not receive the intervention. However, ethical issues arise as this requires withholding treatment from potentially dangerous individuals. Second, a lengthy follow-up is needed as it may be several years or longer before an individual will reoffend. In addition, criminal records may not provide a complete measure of recidivism as offenses may be committed for which the individual is never reported or convicted. However, self-reports may also be biased. Last, it is necessary to examine recidivism rates for different types of offenders separately. Recidivism patterns may vary for juvenile versus adult offenders, or between child molesters, rapists, and other offenders, such as exhibitionists.

An examination of the results of more than 20 evaluation studies shows a great deal of inconsistency in the effectiveness of intervention. In a review of prison-based research, it was found that offenders who participated in cognitive behavioral treatment while in prison had significantly lower recidivism rates for sexual offenses. However, when all forms of recidivism, including nonsexual and nonviolent offenses, are included, research indicates that there is no significant difference in recidivism rates for those who complete treatment and those who do not. Some research indicates that barriers to reintegration, such as stigma and alienation associated with community notification and restrictive residency policies, may lead to unemployment, social isolation, and housing instability. These may increase the likelihood of recidivism for nonsexual crimes. Community-based offender treatment programs were found to be effective in decreasing recidivism for both sexual and nonsexual crimes. This may be due to the ongoing support with successful reintegration following prison.

A Cure for Sexual Offenses?

Discussion exists on whether it is truly possible to "cure" a sexual offender. This discussion is complex in that there is not one homogeneous population of sexual offenders. The offenders that draw the greatest amount of media attention are pedophiles. This diagnostic criterion relates to those over the age of 16 who have a primary or exclusive sexual attraction to prepubescent children. Similarly, hebephilia refers to those with primary attraction to youth in the early stages of puberty, generally 10 to 14. A third category, ephebophilia, refers to the attraction of adults to older adolescents, generally ages 15 to 20. This is far more acceptable in American society, and may actually be encouraged through media representations of the sexuality of young adults and teen girls. Yet laws and social norms vary on the age of consent for sexual behavior in statutory rape laws, ranging from 15 to 18 years of age. In addition, although some attraction to teens may be seen as normal and acceptable, a primary attraction to this age group may be seen as problematic. However, this is rarely diagnosed.

In considering pedohebephilic disorders, it is thought that the sexual attractions can be described much like sexual orientation, in that it is not a choice, but a stable personality trait. Some evidence indicates that there are neurobiological connections that may cause or contribute to the orientation. Although individuals with this diagnosis may be able to develop adaptive coping strategies to reduce the risk of abusive or predatory behavior, it is thought that it is not possible to remove these desires and attractions completely.

However, some research indicates that only a very small percentage, fewer than 10 percent of sexual offenders are diagnosable with pedohebephilic disorders. The remaining offenders are far more amenable to treatment and may, in fact, be able to live prosocial, nonviolent lives without attraction to or risk of predatory or violent behaviors. Underlying issues of trauma, cognitive distortions or self-concept may be addressed in treatment in order to change cognitions, attitudes, and ultimately behaviors. A wide range of factors is considered in determining the risk of recidivism, even among those who do not possess the characteristics of pedohebephilic disorders, including victim and perpetrator characteristics and the nature of the offense. Most sex offenders do not differ dramatically from the general criminal population in terms of their treatment needs and risk of recidivism. Some literature suggests that, with the exception of perpetrators of incest, the more effective strategy may be the implementation of prisoner reentry supports and interventions made available to the general prison population.

Conclusions

"Sex offender" refers to a wide and varied range of behaviors and characteristics. Risk assessment that includes the characteristics of the offender as well as the type of offense is necessary in determining the most appropriate intervention. Perpetrators of incest, public exhibitionists, and statutory rapists, for example, may have very difference offense patterns and therapeutic needs. However, it is common, in both prison and community-based offender treatment groups, to include all types of offenders in one group. This may not be the most effective or appropriate means of treating offenders. Some may require extensive therapy and possibly pharmacological intervention. Others may be better served through a more psychotherapeutic, trauma-informed approach. The needs in terms of the duration of the intervention also vary widely, with some benefiting from short-term intervention and others necessitating lifelong care.

Many characteristics are typically associated with recidivism risk and treatment needs, including characteristics of the victim, such as age, gender, and relationship to the perpetrator, and characteristics of the offender, such as impulsive or antisocial behavior, number of prior offenses, and the level of violence. These characteristics should guide the intervention approach. In addition, treatment should consider factors such as the cultural and social environment of the offender, including cultural norms and expectations, and social support. Coexisting conditions such as substance abuse and mental illness must also be considered in individual treatment planning.

Poco Donna Kernsmith

See also Alcohol and Drug Abuse, Perpetration; Criminal Justice and Perpetrators; Reporting, Mandated and Abuse Registries

Further Reading

Furby, L., Weinrott, M. R., & Blackshaw, L. (1989). Sex offender recidivism: A review. *Psychological Bulletin, 105*(1), 3–30.

Marshall, W. L., Marshall, L. E., Serran, G. A., & O'Brien, M. D. (2008). Sexual offender treatment: A positive approach. *Psychiatric Clinics of North America, 31*, 681–696.

Polizzi, D. M., MacKenzie, D. L., & Hickman, L. J. (1999). What works in adult sex offender treatment? A review of prison- and non-prison-based treatment programs. *International Journal of Offender Therapy and Comparative Criminology, 43*(3), 357–374.

Ward, T., & Stewart, C. A. (2003). The treatment of sex offenders: Risk management and good lives. *Professional Psychology: Research and Practice, 34*(4), 353–360.

U

Underreporting

Research on sexual violence against women, men, and children is integral to understanding the nature and extent of the problem as well as the most effective prevention and intervention approaches. However, sexual violence is one of the most difficult types of victimization experience to measure due to underreporting in the three main data sources: service agency data, police statistics, and population-based prevalence studies.

Many victims of sexual violence do not tell anyone about their experiences for a number of reasons: not recognizing the event as violence or fearing that others will not see it as a crime, fear of being blamed or judged, being scared or intimidated, or not wanting anyone to know what happened. When they do tell someone, most tend to first turn to friends and family rather than the police or helping agencies such as rape crisis centers, shelters, and counselors. Data collected by these service agencies counts only those individuals who come to them for help; hence, this type of data does not represent all victims who experience sexual violence. Particularly, women and children who are marginalized by social factors like race, ethnicity, sexual orientation, level of ability, age, refugee or immigration status, and colonization face barriers in accessing services due to discrimination, language, poverty, social isolation, or lack of information about what services are available. Men may be particularly unlikely to come forward with experiences of sexual victimization, especially victimizations that happened in childhood, due to the stigma attached to male victims. Data collected at health service agencies, such as hospitals or doctors' offices, tend to represent individuals who present to medical services with an injury or who explicitly disclose that they have been sexually assaulted.

Police statistics do not accurately measure sexual violence because these crimes are very unlikely to be reported to police. The International Violence Against Women Survey found that less than one-third of women who experienced violence reported to police (Johnson, Ollus, & Nevala, 2008). The U.S. National Crime Victimization Survey found that about 39 percent of female victims of rape or sexual assault report to police. Police are contacted in about 30 percent of cases of sexual violence against children (Finklehor, Hammer, & Sedlak, 2008). Rates of sexual violence reported to the police are significantly higher for women than men, and constitute up to 90 percent of victims who report to police. Most women who do not report to the police believe that the police will not be able to do anything to help; they may not want the perpetrator arrested or prosecuted because he is known to them, or they fear or distrust the police. Children may not report sexual violence due to feelings of guilt and blame, particularly if they were engaging in behaviors of which their caregivers would disapprove when the assault happened (e.g., drinking alcohol). In addition to underreporting, police exercise considerable discretion about what cases to investigate. Compared to other crimes, a relatively high proportion of sexual violence incidents that are reported to police are dismissed as "unfounded." Unfounding occurs when police decide there is not enough evidence to suggest that an offence took place. Different countries also use different definitions of sexual violence in their laws and practices. Some do not consider rape by husbands to be a crime or do not differentiate between offenses against adults and offenses against children in their statistics.

Prevalence studies interview representative samples of women, men, and children in the general population to produce more reliable estimates of the true nature and extent of sexual violence. For example, according to the U.S. National Violence Against Women Survey, 18 percent of American women and 3 percent of American men have experienced sexual violence at some point in their life. These type of studies likely also underrepresent the actual number of victims because many victims feel embarrassed talking about sexual victimization, especially those from different social and cultural groups. Victimization surveys may not measure violence committed against very young children, who are a particularly vulnerable group. There are ethical and safety considerations that prevent researchers from talking to children about sexual violence. Permission to interview children must be obtained from their parents, and children's responses are likely to be affected by the presence of their parents during the interview. It is more common to obtain estimates of child abuse by interviewing adults about abuse that happened in their childhood, but memories of past events are not always accurate. To improve the disclosure of sexual violence researchers should use knowledgeable, well-trained, and empathetic interviewers in a face-to-face interview; conduct the interview at a time and place that is safe, private, and comfortable for the participant; and use a well-established measurement tool, such as the Sexual Experiences Survey. While it is unlikely that researchers will ever be able to uncover the true extent of sexual violence against women, men, and children, using a combination of data sources with an awareness of why many victims underreport these crimes adds to an understanding of this social problem.

Jennifer Fraser

See also Discretion, Law Enforcement; Help Seeking, Barriers to; Reporting Rates; Victims, Disclosure

Further Reading

Ellsberg, M., & Heise, L. (2005). *Researching violence against women: A practical guide for researchers and activists.* Geneva, Switzerland: World Health Organization.

Finklehor, D., Hammer, H., & Sedlak, A. J. (2008). *Sexually assaulted children: National estimates and characteristics.* NISMART. Washington, DC: U.S. Department of Justice, Office of Justice Programs.

Johnson, H., Ollus, N., & Nevala, S. (2008). *Violence against women: An international perspective.* New York, NY: Springer.

Kelly, L., Lovett, J., & Regan, L. (2005). *A gap or a chasm? Attrition in reported rape cases.* London, England: Home Office Research, Development and Statistics Directorate.

Laws, S., & Mann, G. (2004). *So you want to involve children in research? A toolkit supporting children's meaningful and ethical participation in research relating to violence against children.* Stockholm, Sweden: Save the Children.

Lievore, D. (2005). *No longer silent: A study of women's help-seeking decisions and service responses to sexual assault.* Canberra, Australia: Australian Institute of Criminology.

Tjaden, P., & Thoennes, N. (2000). *Full report of the prevalence, incidence, and consequences of violence against women: Findings from the National Violence Against Women Survey.* Washington, DC: U.S. Department of Justice, Office of Justice Programs.

Selected Websites

Reporting rates. RAINN (Rape, Abuse & Incest National Network). Retrieved from http://www.rainn.org/get-information/statistics/reporting-rates

U.S. Department of Justice, Criminal Victimization in the United States. Retrieved from http://bjs.ojp.usdoj.gov/index.cfm?ty=pbse&sid=58

Undetected Rapists

There are two ways to define the term "undetected rapist." One definition could describe a rapist whose crime has not been reported to law enforcement, and whose crime, therefore, is undetected by law enforcement. Yet another type of undetected rapist is a person who committed his crime without the victim even being aware that an assault has taken place. This entry will touch briefly on both definitions of the term and then explore the implications of undetected rapists.

Rape is a notoriously underreported crime. It is generally agreed among mental health practitioners and researchers that the numbers of rapes reported to law enforcement are not representative of the total number of rapes that occur. A government report from the Department of Justice's Bureau of Justice Statistics stated that 55 percent of sexual assault victims report their victimizations to law enforcement (Rand & Truman, 2010). There are other studies that detail reporting rates as low as 19 percent for female sexual assault victims and 13 percent for male sexual assault victims (Tjaden & Thoennes, 2006). These percentages indicate that estimates of the yearly incidence of rape, if based on reports to law enforcement, are almost always gross underestimates.

Child sexual abuse can be just as difficult to detect. Most sexual abuse of children is committed by a person known to the child, which can make disclosures difficult for children. With 22 percent of female and 48 percent of male victims of abuse reporting being sexually victimized before the age of 12, the scope of the problem of undetected child sexual abusers is substantial (Tjaden & Thoennes, 2006).

To obtain an accurate estimate of the number of rapes that are committed each year, scholars prefer to survey the general population where victims can identify themselves. The most recent statistics where a sample of the general population was used estimated that approximately 126,000 of rapes or sexual assaults occurred in 2009 (Rand & Truman, 2010).

While sobering, the numbers reflected above represent only those crimes where a victim is able to determine that an assault occurred. As indicated, some undetected rapists commit their crime without even the knowledge of the victim, such as through drug-facilitated sexual assaults. Alcohol is the most common substance used by offenders to commit a drug-facilitated sexual assault. Yet "date rape" drugs, such as Rohypnol ("Roofies") and GHB, are other substances used to commit undetected sexual assaults (see entry on **Rape Drugs**). These drugs are generally tasteless, colorless, and odorless so that the victim is unaware of its presence. One review estimated that GHB is used in 3 to 4 percent of rapes (Németh, Kun, & Demetrovics, 2010). Date rape drugs leave the system rapidly and this quick excretion increases chances that a rape will be undetected. Still other rapists engage in the sexual abuse of elderly adults in nursing homes or rape cognitively impaired individuals who are unable to understand the nature of what has occurred.

Considering either definition, the issues surrounding undetected rape have implications for treatment for offenders, policy, and services to victims. Of course, when rapists are undetected they skirt legal responsibility for their actions and any punishment that may have been handed down by the judicial system. Undetected rapists tend to be repeat offenders with one study reporting an average of more than five rapes for offenders who never were prosecuted by the criminal justice system (Lisak & Miller, 2002). While it goes without saying that these offenders could benefit from treatment, current research illustrates that those who participate in sex offender treatment are overwhelmingly involved with the criminal justice system. Very few mental health practitioners or scholars would argue that substantial numbers of undetected rapists attempt to mitigate their risk by seeking treatment on their own.

By skirting legal repercussions for their actions, undetected rapists also "fly under the radar" of policies aimed at reducing the frequency of repeat sexual offending. For example, sex offender registries, which were made public through Megan's Law and then enhanced through the Adam Walsh Act, apply only to sex offenders who have been convicted of a sexual crime. Since undetected rapists do not register their addresses with law enforcement, their offense history is not available in the public domain. Therefore when rapes are not reported to police, the utility of such laws is undercut.

Finally, if a rapist goes undetected, it can actually influence the funding for services provided to the sexual assault victim. The Victims of Crime Act provides states with funding that is obtained from criminal fines and forfeited appearance bonds to help the states compensate their victims of crimes. Sexual assault victims, along with victims of other crimes, can ask for compensation for matters such as lost wages, mental health treatment, and the treatment of medical injuries they sustained as a result of their victimization. State victim compensation boards generally maintain that crime victims must report the crime committed against them to law enforcement and cooperate with the investigation to receive reimbursement. The majority of sexual assault crisis centers that provide counseling will not require the victim to seek funding from this board to pay for treatment; however, it does help cover expenses when the funding is received.

Sarah W. Craun

See also Alcohol-Facilitated Sexual Assault; Drug-Facilitated Rape; Individuals with Disabilities; Rape, Older Adult; Rape Drugs; Underreporting

Further Reading

Date rape drugs: Frequently asked questions (2008). Office of Women's Health. U.S. Department of Health and Human Services. Retrieved from http://www.womenshealth.gov/faq/date-rape-drugs.pdf

Lisak, D., & Miller, P. M. (2002). Repeat rape and multiple offending among undetected rapists. *Violence and Victims, 17*(1), 73–84.

Németh, Z., Kun, B., & Demetrovics, Z. (2010). The involvement of gamma-hydroxybutyrate in reported sexual assaults: a systematic review. *Journal of Psychopharmacology, 24*(9), 1281–1287.

Rand, M., & Truman, J. (2010). Criminal victimization, 2009 (NCJ 231327). U.S. Department of Justice. Retrieved on January 26, 2011, from http://bjs.ojp.usdoj.gov/index.cfm?ty=pbdetail&iid=2217

Tjaden, P., & Thoennes, N. (2006). Extent, nature, and consequences of rape victimization: findings from the national violence against women survey (NCJ 210346). U.S. Department of Justice. Retrieved on January 26, 2011, from http://www.ncjrs.gov/pdffiles1/nij/210346.pdf

Selected Websites

Bureau of Justice Statistics. Retrieved from http://www.bjs.gov

National Association of Crime Victim Boards. Retrieved from http://www.nacvcb.org

Office of Violence Against Women. U.S. Department of Justice. Retrieved from http://www.ovw.usdoj.gov

Unintended Rape

The term "unintended rape" is sometimes used to describe a sexual assault in which the perpetrator did not know the victim did not consent to sexual activity. This is also sometimes referred to as *unintentional rape*. This term is somewhat misleading in that it could be interpreted to mean that engaging in the sexual activity was unintentional. Rather, this term refers more to the context in which the sexual activity occurred. More specifically, it denotes a situation in which miscommunication about sexual activity occurred—namely, the perpetrator perceived the victim to have given consent when she had not. Thus while is it not possible for rape to occur unintentionally, it is possible for miscommunication about consent to occur.

Regarding communication of consent, studies have found that nonverbal behaviors are more frequently used than verbal behaviors to initiate sex and indicate consent to another's advances. For example, Humphreys (2000) found that the most common behaviors men report using to seek their partner's consent to sexual intercourse are kissing, moving closer, and touching sexually. Two other studies indicated that the way in which women most commonly communicate consent to sexual intercourse is by not responding, that is, by not saying "no" or resisting a partner's initiation of sexual activity (Beres, Herold, & Maitland, 2004; Hickman & Muehlenhard, 1999). Interestingly, men and women agree that verbal communication (as opposed to nonverbal) provides clear expression of consent (Lim & Roloff, 1999). However, the vast majority of men and women find verbally asking for consent awkward (Humphreys, 2000). Thus sex tends to be both initiated and consented to in rather indirect ways, creating a potential for miscommunication.

As sexual consent cannot be legally established by a lack of resistance, there exists a disconnect between the way in which people actually behave in sexual situations and the way in which the law defines sexual consent behavior. Therefore although miscommunication *is not a cause of rape*, the discrepancy between the legal requirements for consent and people's actual behavior may lead some to presume that rape can "unintentionally" occur.

Christopher T. Allen

See also Consent; Laws, Rape; Rape Myths

Further Reading

Beres, M. A., Herold, E., & Maitland, S. B. (2004). Sexual consent behaviors in same-sex relationships. *Archives of Sexual Behavior, 44*, 475–486.

Hickman, S. E., & Muehlenhard, C. L. (1999). "By the semi-mystical appearance of a condom": How young women and men communicate sexual consent in heterosexual situations. *Journal of Sex Research, 36*, 258–272.

Humphreys, T. P. (2000). *Sexual consent in heterosexual dating relationships: Attitudes and behaviors of university students.* Doctoral dissertation, University of Guelph, Guelph, Ontario, Canada.

Lim, G. Y., & Roloff, M. E. (1999). Attributing sexual consent. *Journal of Applied Communication Research, 27*, 1–23.

V

The Vagina Monologues

The Vagina Monologues (TVM) is an episodic play written by playwright, political activist, and actress Eve Ensler in 1994. Ensler, a survivor of sexual assault, was keenly aware of the social and cultural stigma associated with sexual violence and wanted to produce a piece that would speak to all women and bring awareness about violence against women. In a 1995 interview with Random House, Ensler stated that her fascination with vaginas began because of she understood that rape, incest, and battery against women are connected to sexuality and subsequently vaginas.

Ensler conducted over 200 interviews with women from all different racial, ethnic, age, religious, and employment backgrounds; *TVM* vignettes are based on all those interviews. She asked questions regarding their experiences with sex and relationships, and their thoughts about sexual violence and domestic abuse, and compiled the information to write the piece to "celebrate the vagina." The vignettes include an elderly woman, an angry woman, a six-year old girl, a female Bosnian rape victim, a woman's experience watching a childbirth, and a female sex worker just to name a few.

On Valentine's Day 1998, Ensler established V-Day. *The Vagina Monologues* was the cornerstone of the V-Day movement, whose participants stage benefit performances of *TVM* and/or host other related events in their communities. V-Day was established to allow the public to put on individual performances of *TVM* to broaden the reach that increases awareness to the general public, as well as raise money for existing antiviolence organizations. Ensler realized the power of the production, and the purpose of the piece changed from a celebration of vaginas and femininity to a movement to stop violence against women.

V-Day's mission is an organized response against violence toward women. Every year, during the months of January through April, groups around the world are allowed to produce a benefit performance of the TVM, as well as other works created by Ensler (*A Memory, a Monologue, a Rant and a Prayer"* or *Any One of Us: Words from Prison*), and the proceeds are donated to local individual projects and programs that work to end violence against women and girls; often battered women's shelters and rape crisis centers are chosen.

TVM ran off-Broadway for five years in New York and has continued to tour throughout the United States. After a few years of performances, Ensler found scores of women who would line up to speak with her about their own violence.

The Vagina Monologues became the catalyst that gave women words for their experience as well as a voice. Ensler knew that this was the beginning of her vision to use *The Vagina Monologues* to move people to speak about the violence and subsequently work to end the violence. The production has been staged internationally, and a television version featuring Ensler was produced by cable TV channel HBO.

Beginning in 2003, V-Day launched a new campaign called "Spotlight Campaign" in which Ensler wrote a new monologue about the plight of women in Afghanistan under Taliban rule; the monologue is titled "Under the Burqa." Due to its tremendous success, each year a new monologue has been written to include: "Native American and First Nations Women" (2003), "Missing and Murdered Women in Juarez, Mexico" (2004), "Women of Iraq, Under Siege" (2005), "Justice to 'Comfort Women'" (2006), "Women In Conflict Zones" (2007), "The Women of New Orleans" (2008), "The Women and Girls of the Democratic Republic of Congo" (2009 and 2010), and "The Women of Haiti" (2011).

Today, the productions range in scope from a performance in a small-group setting among students to one in a stadium in New Orleans at the Louisiana Super Dome. Through V-Day campaigns, local volunteers and college students produce annual benefit performances of *The Vagina Monologues* to raise awareness and funds for antiviolence groups within their own communities, and *The Vagina Monologues* has been translated into over 48 languages and performed in over 140 countries. Over 5,400 V-Day benefit events are taking place, produced by volunteer activists in the United States and around the world, educating millions of people about the reality of violence against women and girls and raising over $80 million for antiviolence programs around the globe.

Eve Ensler was awarded the Obie Award in 1996 for Best New Play and in 1999 was awarded a Guggenheim Fellowship Award in Playwriting. She has also received the Berrilla-Kerr Award for Playwriting, the Elliot Norton Award for Outstanding Solo Performance, and the Jury Award for Theater at the U.S. Comedy Arts Festival.

To learn more about putting on a benefit production of *The Vagina Monologues*, visit http://www.vday.org.

Jill Kracov-Zinckgraf

Vicarious Traumatization

Vicarious traumatization is a phenomenon that characterizes the emotional, psychological, social, and spiritual changes on helpers of working with clients who have experienced traumatic life events, in particular child sexual abuse, rape, incest, and interpersonal violence. Most commonly, helpers who are affected are those who work in a professional capacity, such as psychologists, social workers, and child welfare workers. Based on constructivist self-development theory that maintains a person's unique history shapes his or her reactions to traumatic events, vicarious traumatization is "the cumulative transformation in the inner experience of a therapist [or other helper] that comes about as a result of empathic engagement with client's traumatic material" (Pearlman & Saakvitne, 1995, p. 31). Vicarious traumatization is an emotionally damaging process that, over time, interferes with a helper's ability to genuinely empathize and assist clients. Although preventable and treatable with supportive supervision, helpers' own therapy, and other specific self-care strategies, vicarious traumatization is a serious occupational hazard of working directly with clients affected by traumatic life events.

There are three specific ways of conceptualizing vicarious traumatization: (1) it is an individual phenomenon that affects each helper differently, based on factors such as gender, past abuse, personality, and length of time in a trauma-specific job; (2) it is a process that develops over time and through exposure to numerous clients with trauma histories; and (3) it is a pervasive process that affects all areas of helpers' lives, including their feelings of safety, their experiences in personal relationships, and how they view the world.

Vicarious traumatization is sometimes experienced when helpers have symptoms that are similar to those of their clients, such as difficulty sleeping, nightmares, flashbacks, feeling numb, and other symptoms of post-traumatic stress disorder (PTSD). This process is also referred to as secondary traumatic stress. Characterized by inner emotional and existential changes in helpers that extend beyond PTSD symptoms, vicarious traumatization occurs when helpers deeply care, connect, and empathize with their clients. This empathic connection, necessary to assist clients in their healing, puts helpers at risk for vicarious traumatization on three levels: (1) their feelings about themselves, (2) their feelings about others, and (3) their feelings about the world. Hearing the details about another person's assault or abuse may cause helpers to fear their own victimization. Other documented symptoms include increased feelings of vulnerability, inability to trust others, changes in one's view of the world, and intrusive images of violence. These symptoms may make it difficult for a helper to separate from work, as seen in the following example:

Ellie works in a sexual assault treatment program where she provides therapy to sexually abused adults. After a long day seeing clients, Ellie wants to be able to rest when she gets home. However, she finds that as soon as she closes her eyes, images of her client's abuse emerge, making her feel vulnerable, afraid, and unable to get relief.

Helpers' relationships with their children, spouses, friends, and colleagues are also changed through the process of vicarious traumatization. Helpers may feel overprotective of children and overly concerned and fearful that they will be harmed in some way. Some helpers report changes in their sexual or intimate lives, such as avoiding sexual contact as a way of self-protection or fearing that all sexual relationships are abusive. In addition to emotional and relationship changes, helpers also experience painful transformations in their view of the world. Through ongoing exposure to accounts of abuse and violence, specifically accounts of human cruelty, helpers are at risk of becoming cynical and angry at the injustices of the world. As a result, they may feel unable to make a difference in client's lives, as illustrated in the following example:

> Ruth always prided herself on being a caring, compassionate, and sensitive person. Since working with sexually abused children, she has begun to feel overwhelmed with anger at the injustices of child abuse. Ruth feels as though her compassionate, optimistic view of the world has been replaced by rage, hatred, and anger. She no longer sees the world as a good and safe place.

A growing awareness of the dangers of and responses to vicarious traumatization is present among organizations that serve traumatized populations. Helpers in the trauma field need to pay careful attention to vicarious traumatization. Effective response strategies include peer groups, supportive supervision, establishing a healthy work-home balance, and other self-care techniques such as eating well, spending time with supportive people, and getting adequate rest.

Shantih E. Clemans

See also Burnout in Human Services; Countertransference (Therapists); Trauma, Secondary

Further Reading

Clemans, S. E. (2004). Recognizing vicarious traumatization: A single session group model for trauma workers. *Social Work with Groups, 27*(2/3), 55–74.

McCann, I., & Pearlman, L. (1990). Vicarious traumatization: A framework for understanding the psychological effects of working with victims. *Journal of Traumatic Stress, 3*, 131–149.

Pearlman, L. A., & Saakvitne, K. W. (1995). *Trauma and the therapist: Countertransference and vicarious traumatization in psychotherapy with incest survivors.* New York, NY: Norton.

Saakvitne, L. A., & Pearlman, K. W. (1996). *Transforming the pain: A workbook on vicarious traumatization.* New York, NY: Norton.

Selected Website

A video series on vicarious traumatization. Cavalcade Productions. The website offers a two-part training video for professionals working with clients who have experienced trauma. The content includes: "Vicarious Trauma I: The Cost of Empathy," where definitions, causes, and contributing factors are explained by trauma therapists; and "Vicarious Trauma II: Transforming the Pain," which discusses specific ways of responding to vicarious trauma, such as supervision and the creation of a healthy work-life balance. Retrieved from http://www.cavalcadeproductions.com/vicarious-traumatization.html

Victimization, Prevalence of

Estimating the prevalence of sexual victimization is challenging because most acts of sexual violence and abuse go unreported to authorities (e.g., health care providers, law enforcement personnel) and victims do not always seek help or services for the violence. However, information about sexual victimization prevalence is tremendously helpful to sexual assault advocates, policy makers, and others attempting to prevent sexual violence or to provide services to sexual assault victims. Prevalence information helps advocates and policy makers to understand the extent and nature of the problem and know which groups of persons in our society are most at risk of sexual victimization. In turn, such information is helpful in developing effective sexual victimization prevention and intervention services. Therefore many researchers have studied the prevalence of sexual victimization to help document the extent and nature of the problem.

National survey studies have found widely varying estimates of prevalence, ranging from about 18 to 44 percent of U.S. women reporting some form of sexual victimization in their lifetime (Russell & Bolen, 2000; Tjaden & Thoennes, 2000). The National Violence Against Women (NVAW) Survey, a general victimization survey, suggests that approximately 17.7 million American women have been victims of an attempted or completed rape, the majority perpetrated by a male intimate partner (Tjaden & Thoennes, 2000). Conversely, about 2.8 million men in the United States reported being sexual assault victims. This translates into 1 in 6 U.S. women (17.6%) and 1 in 33 U.S. men (3.0%) as victims of an attempted or completed rape as either a child or an adult.

Most acts of sexual violence occur during childhood. In the NVAW Survey, more than half (54%) of the 14.8 percent of women who reported a completed rape first experienced rape before the age of 18, with the majority of first rapes occurring before the age of 12 (21.6%). For male victims who reported completed rapes, 71 percent experienced rape before the age of 18 (48% before the age of 12; Tjaden & Thoennes, 2000). Despite these alarming estimates, child welfare data collected by the National Child Abuse and Neglect Data System found that in 1999, 92,000 children experienced sexual abuse, a 39 percent decrease in sexual assault cases over a seven-year period (Jones, Finkelhor, & Kopiec, 2001). According to the study, the decline may be due to several factors including: changes in screening or investigation procedures; caseworkers being more cautious about what they investigate or substantiate; less vigilance by reporters; improvement in caseworkers' ability to successfully intervene; and successful prevention efforts.

Hence, sexual violence is a widespread problem affecting many people in the United States. However, there are certain groups of persons who are at increased risk of victimization. For example, researchers report a range of 30 to 45 percent of military-related sexually violent assaults among female veterans (Zinzow, Grubaugh, Monnier, Suffoletta-Maierle, & Frueh, 2007). Sexual violence is also a major concern on college campuses. The National College Women's Sexual Victimization Study estimated that about 1 in 36 college women (2.8%) experienced a completed or attempted rape during the academic year. Further, over the course of their college years, it is expected that the percentage of completed or attempted rape among women in college will climb to about 1 in 5 college women (Fisher, Cullen, & Turner, 2000).

Women with disabilities are also a vulnerable population when considering sexual violence. A study using the NVAW Survey found that women with severe disability impairments (i.e., women who suffered from a chronic disease or health condition, serious injury, or chronic mental health disease or condition that significantly interfered with their normal activities during the past week) were four times more likely to be sexually assaulted than women with no reported disabilities (2.1% vs. 0.5%; Casteel, Martin, Smith, Gurka, & Kupper, 2008). Among women with a serious mental illness, 21 to 76 percent report an experience of adult sexual victimization (Goodman, Rosenberg, Mueser, & Drake, 1997).

In terms of race and ethnicity, there is some limited evidence that American Indian women are more likely to report rape relative to other racial and ethnic groups (Tjaden & Thoennes, 2000; Wahab & Olson, 2004). However, this evidence may not be accurate given the small number of American Indian women who participate in sexual victimization studies. Specifically, the NVAW Survey found that 34 percent of American Indian women reported a completed or attempted rape at some point in their lives compared to 6.8 percent of Asian American women, 18.8 percent of African American woman, and 17.7 percent of white women (Tjaden & Thoennes, 2000). This finding is similar to estimates from the National Crime Victimization Survey, which determined American Indians were more likely to experience rape when compared to people of other races and ethnicities (Rennison, 2001).

Given the majority of nationally based studies that examined prevalence of sexual victimization were conducted in mid- to late 1990s, there is a need for more current research that investigates sexual victimization prevalence. More current research can aid in determining whether sexual victimization rates have increased or decreased, and whether there is a need for better sexual victimization interventions. Although the evidence suggests a decline in child sexual assault cases, the reason for this decline is uncertain. Further, this decline is specific to the child welfare population and may not extend to the children in the general population. Therefore it is important that, in the future, researchers investigate sexual victimization rates among children who are not involved with child welfare. In addition, identifying why sexual victimization rates have decreased in the child welfare population can help to determine effective child sexual abuse prevention efforts. Further investigations in these areas will provide helpful information for dealing with sexual victimization.

Ijeoma Nwabuzor

See also Colleges and Universities; Native Americans; Individuals with Disabilities; Military Sexual Trauma; Reporting Rates; Underreporting

Further Reading

Casteel, C. Martin, S. L., Smith, J. B., Gurka, K. K., & Kupper, L. L. (2008). National study of physical and sexual assault among women with disabilities. *Injury Prevention, 14*, 87–90.

Fisher, B. S., Cullen, F. T., & Turner, M. G. (2000). *The sexual victimization of college women* (NCJ182369). Washington, DC: U.S. Department of Justice, National Institute of Justice.

Goodman, L. A., Rosenberg, S. D., Mueser, K. T., & Drake, R. E. (1997). Physical and sexual assault history in women with serious mental illness: Prevalence, correlates, treatment, and future research directions. *Schizophrenia Bulletin, 23*(4), 685–696.

Jones, L. M., Finkelhor, D., & Kopiec, K. (2001). Why is sexual abuse declining? A survey of state child protection administrators. *Child Abuse and Neglect, 25*, 1139–1158.

Rennison, C. (2001). *Violence victimization and race, 1993–98* (NCJ 176354). Washington DC: U.S. Department of Justice, Office of Justice Programs.

Russell, D. E. H., & Bolen, R. M. (2000). *The epidemic of rape and child sexual abuse in the United States*. Thousand Oaks, CA: Sage.

Tjaden, P., & Thoennes, N. (2000). *Full report from the prevalence, incidence, and consequences of violence against women: Findings from the National Violence Against Women Search* (NCJ 183781). Washington, DC: U.S. Department of Justice, National Institute of Justice.

Wahab, S., & Olson, L. (2004). Intimate partner violence and sexual assault in Native American communities. *Trauma, Violence, & Abuse, 5*, 353–366.

Zinzow, H. M., Grubaugh, A. L., Monnier, J., Suffoletta-Maierle, S., & Frueh, B. C. (2007). Trauma among female veterans: A critical review. *Trauma, Violence, & Abuse, 8*, 384–400.

Selected Websites

Rape and sexual assault. Bureau of Justice Statistics. Retrieved from http://bjs.ojp
.usdoj.gov/index.cfm?ty=tp&tid=317

Who are the victims? RAINN (Rape, Abuse & Incest National Network). Retrieved
from http://www.rainn.org/get-information/statistics/sexual-assault-victims

Victims (Overview)

Sexual abuse and sexual violence are complex, multifaceted, and serious issues.
To comprehend the phenomenon of sexual abuse and sexual violence fully, it is
essential to know about the victims of these types of violence. As Gilbert
describes in her entry on **"Real Rape" and "Real Victims"—Correcting Misinformation**, there is considerable misinformation, which is known as "rape myths,"
in our society about sexual abuse and sexual violence. These rape myths have led
to serious misunderstandings of sexual abuse and sexual violence victimization. In
this entry, we seek to help to clarify and correct these misunderstandings by presenting the best available and most current information on sexual abuse and sexual
violence victims.

Unfortunately, many people experience sexual victimization. In her entry concerned with victimization prevalence, Nwabuzor discusses how one national study
showed that nearly 18 percent of women and 3 percent of men in the United States
are victimized by attempted or completed rape over the course of their lives
(Tjaden & Thoennes, 2000). These numbers show that sexual victimization is a
widespread problem. However, Ermentrout and Nwabuzor state in their entries
on **Victims, Male** and **Victimization, Prevalence of** respectively that such
research statistics may actually be lower than in reality because sexual abuse and
sexual violence often go unreported to authorities (e.g., health care providers,
law enforcement) and to researchers. Thus the most current and rigorous research
on sexual abuse and sexual violence might not provide an accurate and complete
picture of the prevalence of these problems. Nevertheless, the research shows that
sexual abuse and sexual violence are significant problems that affect many people.

One reason why our knowledge about sexual victimization is incomplete is that
only in the past 20 to 30 years have sexual abuse and sexual violence become considered pressing problems worthy of societal concern. In addition, some victim
advocates have argued that less attention has been given to funding, preventing,
researching, and providing services for sexual abuse and sexual violence relative
to other health and social issues (Macy, Giattina, Parish, & Crosby, 2010). Advocates describe the challenges of raising public awareness for and increasing policy
attention to these issues because human sexuality and violence are difficult to discuss, especially when they intersect as sexual abuse and sexual violence.

Fortunately, public awareness of and policy attention to the issues of sexual abuse and sexual violence are growing. In addition, increasing research attention to these issues is helping to answer important questions about sexual victimization. Researchers have been actively trying to answer questions such as: (1) who can be a victim (2) why are some groups of people at heightened victimization risk relative to other groups; (3) what happens to victims after an assault; and (4) what helps victims? To begin to address these questions, this overview summarizes and highlights some of the critical information about sexual victimization. For detailed information on these topics, see the specific entries cited throughout this overview.

Who can be a victim? Anyone can be a victim of sexual abuse and sexual violence, regardless of age, (dis)ability, ethnicity and race, gender, geography, and socioeconomic status. However, some groups of people are at greater victimization risk in comparison to other groups. Greater or increased risk means that some people are more likely to experience sexual victimization because of their group memberships, personal characteristics, or situational circumstances. Nwabuzor discusses in her entry the specific groups of people who are at heightened risk of sexual victimization, including children, adolescents and young adults; people with disabilities; and American Indians. In addition, people involved in certain institutions are at a heightened risk of sexual violence. Female university students and female military personnel tend to report greater sexual victimization relative to other groups of women. In addition, Ermentrout's entry describes how males in institutionalized settings (e.g., prison), as well as males who live on the streets, in military conflict zones, and in refugee camps tend to be more vulnerable to (i.e., at greater risk of) sexual victimization in comparison to males who do not live is such settings.

Not only are certain groups of people at heightened risk, prior experiences of violent victimization can also lead to increases in sexual victimization risk. Rizo's **Victims, Repeat** entry explains that people who have been sexually victimized once are at increased sexual violence risk relative to people who have never experienced sexual abuse or sexual violence. In other words, people who have experienced sexual abuse or sexual violence once in their lives might be likely to experience victimization again sometime in the future.

The knowledge and information about who is most at risk of sexual victimization are considerable. However, more research is needed before there will be a full understanding of what characteristics, circumstances, factors, and situations place people at heightened sexual victimization risk. As discussed earlier, many incidents of sexual victimization go unreported. Gilbert's entry explains how societal rape myths and misinformation about sexual abuse and sexual violence might mean that some individuals do not consider themselves to be victims, even when the violence they experienced meets legal definitions of rape. Ermentrout's entry explains how underreporting among males might especially be a problem.

Bryant's entry on **Victims, Disclosure** discusses how and why many victims never even tell their most trusted family and friends about their abuse and assault experiences. Likewise, Johnson's entry about **Victims, Guilt and Shame** explains how victims tend to blame themselves. Along with feelings of embarrassment about victimization and fear of the perpetrator, self-blame might prevent victims' disclosure to authorities, family, and friends. Given that many victims never discuss their abuse and assault experiences with trusted others, it is not surprising that victims might also not report such violence to authorities or researchers. In their entries, both Bryant and Johnson offer recommendations on how close others can help to support victims. For example, family and friends should help victims by offering positive, nonjudgmental emotional support. The widespread adoption of such efforts is needed to help facilitate victims' disclosure and reporting if and when victims choose to do so.

Why are some groups of people at heightened victimization risk? Current research and conceptualizations of sexual victimization put forward that personal characteristics, situational factors, cultural factors, and social factors all combine to place some groups of people at heightened victimization risk. Detailed information about why some groups are at higher victimization risk relative to others is presented in the **Theories (Overview)** entry in this encyclopedia.

Rizo's entry explains that the ecological perspective is valuable for understanding revictimization because this framework highlights the multiple, dynamic factors that play a role in a person's repeated victimizations over the life course. Consider a woman who is homeless as an example of how many complex and dynamic factors interact to increase an individual person's risk of victimization and revictimization. A young homeless woman who is living on the streets may have run away from home because of family violence and sexual abuse in her family. Thus she is at risk of sexual revictimization because she has already been victimized earlier in her life. Now that this young woman is homeless, she lives in a dangerous environment where she may be frequently exposed to potential perpetrators on a regular basis. If she is sexually assaulted while living homeless, she might not report this assault to law enforcement or seek help for the assault because she believes that people will not take her experiences seriously or that people will blame her because she is living on the streets.

Similar to other aspects of victimization, the research about why some groups of people are at higher victimization risk has been limited so far. Accordingly, three entries—**Victims, Male Victims**; **Victimization, Prevalence of**; and **Victims, Repeat**—argue that more research is needed to provide a full explanation about why victimization occurs to some groups of people more often than others. This lack of research evidence means that there is limited information about the following issues: (1) the various risk pathways that might lead to sexual victimization; (2) how sexual victimization risk changes over the course of people's live; (3) what characteristics, factors, situation and/or contexts might protect people against sexual victimization; and (4) what factors or processes might help promote victims' resilience and well-being in the aftermath of an assault. In the meantime, readers should keep in mind that victimization occurs because of the interaction of various factors at different levels of the social environment (e.g., individual, family, community) in a dynamic way. Thus there is no one reason why sexual victimization occurs.

What happens to victims? Sexual abuse and sexual violence victims can experience serious emotional problems (e.g., anxiety, depression, trauma), physical problems (e.g., injuries, gastrointestinal problems, headaches, reproductive health problems, sleep disturbances), social problems (e.g., withdraw from family and friends), and economic consequences (e.g., not completing education because of an assault at college/university, loss of income because the victim cannot work after the assault; Martin, Macy, & Young, 2010). Additional information about the health, social, and economic consequences of sexual violence is also presented in the **Impact and Consequences (Overview)** entry of this encyclopedia.

Johnson's entry on **Victims, Blaming** describes how victims might struggle with profound feelings of guilt and shame that are often related to feelings of self-blame about sexual victimization. Pollock's entry concerned with **Sexually Acting Out** describes a consequence of sexual abuse that is often associated with child victims. As Pollack explains, *sexually acting out* includes sexualized activities that are developmentally inappropriate or that are markedly outside generally accepted sexual behaviors. Thus, even sexual victims of one abuse incident or assault might experience significant problems because of this violence.

In addition, as Rizo discusses in her entry (**Victims, Repeat**), people who have experienced sexual abuse and/or sexual violence repeatedly are more likely to struggle with negative consequences relative to victims of onetime abuse and/or violence. Sexual abuse and sexual violence victims also often experience other forms of abuse and violence, such as emotional and physical. These additional experiences of violence might worsen the problems with which sexual abuse and sexual violence victims struggle. For example, a child who is sexually victimized by a primary caregiver might also experience emotional abuse from this caregiver (e.g., the caregiver calls the child names, puts the child down with words). As another example, a woman who is physically victimized by her intimate partner (e.g., she is hit, kicked, pushed, strangled by her partner) might also be sexually victimized by him (e.g., forced to have sexual intercourse when she does not want to do so). The topic area **Intersections with Other Forms of Abuse (Overview)** will be useful for readers interested in the various types of violence that people who have been sexually victimized might also experience.

What helps victims? As discussed above, sexual abuse and sexual violence victims might struggle with serious emotional, health, social, and economic problems that are related directly to their experiences of violent victimization. Importantly however, readers should be mindful that not all victims struggle with the problems described above. Some sexual abuse and sexual violence victims return to their usual ways of behaving, feeling, and functioning despite the terrible trauma(s) that they experienced. For example, child sexual abuse victims often show such resilience when they have primary caregivers who: (1) believe their children's reports of abuse; (2) act quickly to protect their children from perpetrators and future abuse; and (3) provide positive emotional support to their children.

Services for children who have been sexually abused are also offered at Child Advocacy Centers. These community-based, nonprofit organizations work with professionals from various disciplines (e.g., child protection, criminal justice, health care, mental health care) to help facilitate investigations and prosecutions of child abuse perpetrators, while also providing treatment services to child victims and their nonoffending family members. The National Children's Alliance is a resource for finding information about local community child advocacy centers. (See the National Children's Alliance website listed at the end of this overview.)

Research also shows that adult victims of sexual violence benefit from advocacy services that are offered by community-based, nonprofit rape crisis and sexual assault programs (Campbell, 2006). The goal of advocacy services is to support victims after sexual violence by offering them two interventions types. First, sexual assault advocates offer victims information and emotional support, which are provided in one-on-one discussions and meetings on the telephone and in person. Sexual assault advocates also offer victims help through referral to and coordination with other community organizations that provide valuable services and supports to promote victims' recovery and well-being in the aftermath of an assault (e.g., counseling, health care, and legal services).

In addition to advocacy, there are behavioral health interventions (e.g., cognitive behavioral therapies) and physical health treatments (e.g., sexual assault nurse examiners) that can help ensure victims' health and well-being. The entry on **Victims and Interventions** in this encyclopedia is useful for readers interested in helpful services, strategies, and supports to promote resilience among victims following abuse and assaults. Bryant's entry, **Victims, Disclosure**, also describes the import of disclosure for victims' emotional well-being. As mentioned earlier, it is unfortunate that limited knowledge exists concerning what factors or processes might help promote victims' resilience in the aftermath of an assault. Other, yet undetermined interventions, services and treatments might also help promote resilience among sexual abuse and sexual violence victims. Thus, additional research is needed to determine what most helps promote victims' resilience and well-being in the aftermath of an assault.

To conclude, there is no one reason why sexual victimization occurs. Rather, people become sexual abuse and sexual violence victims because of the interaction of various factors at different social levels in a dynamic way (e.g., individual, family, community). Some groups of people and some people in particular circumstances or situations are at higher risk of sexual abuse and sexual violence relative other groups. Nonetheless, anyone can be sexually victimized.

Victims of sexual abuse and sexual violence might struggle with emotional, physical, social, and economic problems. However, there are community services and supports for victims to help them with such problems. Good places for victims to begin to seek help—no matter the type of sexual abuse or sexual violence they experienced—are at local communities' rape crisis and sexual assault programs (for adult victims), as well as at local communities' Child Advocacy Centers (for child victims and their nonoffending caregivers and parents). Such programs can help ensure that victims have access to information, emotional support, and referrals to other helpful community services. The Rape, Abuse & Incest National Network (RAINN) is a resource for finding information about local community's rape crisis and sexual assault programs. (See the RAINN website listed at the end of this overview.)

Many victims might experience feelings of guilt, shame, and self-blame. Because of such feelings, victims are often reluctant to disclose about their victimization to authorities, researchers, as well as families and friends. Gilbert's discussion of rape myths explains how misinformation about sexual abuse, sexual violence, and victimization contributes to victims' feelings of self-blame. Individuals, organizations, and communities can help to diminish victims' feelings of self-blame by working to correct such misinformation and dispel rape myths in their everyday activities. In addition, not all victims struggle with difficult feelings or problems because of sexual abuse and sexual violence. Sexual victims can also show resilience in the aftermath of these horrible experiences. Family and friends, as well as communities and organizations, can help to promote victims' resilience and well-being by placing the blame for such violence on perpetrators (and not victims), by holding perpetrators accountable, and by offering victims understanding and support.

Rebecca J. Macy

Further Reading

Campbell, R. (2006). Rape survivors' experiences with the legal and medical systems: Do rape victim advocates make a difference? *Violence Against Women, 12*, 30–45.

Macy, R. J., Giattina, M., Parish, S., & Crosby, C. (2010). Domestic violence and sexual assault services: Historical concerns and contemporary challenges. *Journal of Interpersonal Violence, 25*(1), 3–32.

Martin, S. L., Macy, R. J., & Young, S. (2010). The impact of sexual violence against women: Health and economic consequences. In J. White & M. Koss (Eds.) *Violence against women and children: Consensus, critical analyses, and emergent priorities: Vol. 1. Mapping the terrain* (pp. 173–195). Washington DC: American Psychological Association.

Tjaden, P., & Thoennes, N. (2000). *Full report from the prevalence, incidence, and consequences of violence against women: Findings from the National Violence Against Women Survey* (NCJ 183781). Washington, DC: U.S. Department of Justice, National Institute of Justice.

Selected Websites

National Children's Alliance: Empowering local communities to serve victims of child abuse. Retrieved from http://www.nationalchildrensalliance.org/

RAINN (Rape, Abuse & Incest National Network). Retrieved from http://www.rainn.org/

Rape and sexual violence. National Institute of Justice: Office of Justice Programs. Retrieved from http://www.nij.gov/topics/crime/rape-sexual-violence/welcome.htm

Sexual violence. Centers for Disease Control and Prevention, Injury Prevention and Control, Violence Prevention. Retrieved from http://www.cdc.gov/Violenceprevention/sexualviolence/index.html

Victims, Blaming

Victim blame is reflected in attitudes, beliefs, and statements that place responsibility for sexual violence on the person who experienced the abuse and assault. Victim blaming is a devaluing act that occurs when the victim(s) of a crime or an accident is held responsible, in whole or in part, for the crimes that have been committed against them. Victim blaming can occur in many forms, including negative responses from friends, family, law enforcement, courts, medical and mental health professionals, and the media.

Victim blame diminishes the perpetrator's responsibility for sexual violence and thus is often use by perpetrators to justify their actions. Examples of victim-blaming statements that might come from perpetrators include "She led me on to expect that we were going to have sex and then changed her mind at the last moment" or "How could I help it? She wore a really low-cut shirt."

Societal norms, as well as typical but inaccurate perceptions of sexual abuse and rape victims, also perpetuate victim blaming. There are various examples of such societal norms, including the belief that victims provoke rape through their clothing and actions. Other examples include the belief that victims should have done more to prevent and stop sexual assault. Victims who disclosed their experiences of abuse and violence to family and friends may be faced with victim-blaming responses such as: "How drunk were you when this happened?"; Why did you go off with that guy by yourself?"; or "Why didn't you fight back?"

Sexual violence, including child sexual abuse, sexual assault, and rape, are crimes that are often misunderstood. Consequently, myths about sexual violence exist in our culture and society. Examples of such sexual violence myths include the belief that when a man pays for all the expenses on a date with a woman that he should expect sex. Likewise, a myth about child sexual abuse is that young girls can be sexually provocative and thus invite sexual advances from adults. Unfortunately, such sexual violence myths perpetuate the victim blaming. Therefore victims become the target of blame because of their clothing, reputation, or the circumstances such as location and time of the assault, whereas the perpetrators are seen to be sexually frustrated or misled by the victim.

Blaming the victim is more often seen in cases when the victim and perpetrator know each other and less in cases of stranger rape. However, stranger rape cannot be excluded from victim blame. In some instances, victims are blamed for leaving the door unlocked or walking alone at night. All of these negative attitudes and comments toward the victim can be perceived by the victim, as well as by others, as releasing perpetrators from any responsibility for their violent behaviors.

Victims might also look for a reason as to why they were abused, assaulted, or raped. In seeking such reasons, victims might experience a sense of powerlessness and shame that can also manifest into self-blame. In addition, victims are exposed daily to sexual violence myths from the media, friends, and family. Consequently, victims might internalize such myths as their own beliefs and feelings, which in turn will also lead to self-blame for the sexual violence that they experienced.

The impact of victim blaming affects not only the victim but society as a whole. With the pervasiveness of sexual violence myths and victim blame in our culture, victims might feel vulnerable and unwilling to disclose about the violence. To be able to tell someone else about the violence, victims must address realistic fears, including (1) disbelief from others, (2) the possibility of being held responsible for the violence, and (3) the reality of being stigmatized as a sexual violence victim. By not informing legal authorities about the assault because of such fears, victims might not be able to avail themselves of legal actions or remedies to address the assault. Without information about sexually violent assaults and abuse, legal authorities cannot hold perpetrators accountable for their crimes. In addition, family and friends might choose not to believe victims if they decide not to report the assault to police. Further, when victims do not disclose about their experiences of abuse, assault, or violence, they might not be able to access needed physical and mental health services. Without appropriate services to support their recovery, victims might struggle in their everyday lives, as well as in their roles as family members, friends, students, and employees.

Even when the intent of victim blaming is not malicious but rather uninformed, the outcome is the same. Victim blaming can prevent the victim from fully recovering, and it prevents our society from holding perpetrators accountable for their actions and crimes. Victim blaming indicates the victim deserved to be sexually violated. However, no one deserves to be raped, sexually abused, or sexually assaulted. More so, victim blame allows perpetrators and those who blame the victim to be excused from any responsibility for their crimes and actions. Placing blame on the victim also increases the opportunity for the perpetrator to continue victimizing. Not every rapist goes to prison, but accountability is necessary to stop the violence.

Monika Johnson Hostler

See also Bias, Police and Prosecution; "Justifiable Rape"; Rape Myths; Revictimization, Individuals; Revictimization, Organizations

Further Reading
Andrew, B., Brewin, C. R., & Rose, S. (2003). Gender, social support, and PTSD in victims of violent crime. *Journal of Traumatic Stress, 4*(16), 421–427.

Joyce, E. (2003/2004). Teen dating violence: Facing the epidemic. Networks. National Center for Victims of Crime. Retrieved from http://www.ncvc.org/ncvc/AGP.Net/Components/documentViewer/Download.aspxnz?DocumentID=38039

Madigan, L., & Gamble, N. (1991). *The second rape: Society's continued betrayal of the victim.* New York, NY: Lexington Books

McCaul, K. D., Veltum, L. G., Boyechko, V., & Crawford, J. J. (1990). Understanding attributions of victim blame for rape: Sex, violence, and foreseeability. *Journal of Applied Social Psychology, 20,* 1–26.

Victim blaming (2009). Canadian Resource Center for Victims of Crime. Retrieved from http://crcvc.ca/docs/victim_blaming.pdf

Selected Website
Santa Clara University: Ethics Home Page. Retrieved from http://www.scu.edu/ethics/publications/iie/v3n2/justworld.html

Victims, Credibility

Sexual assault is one of the few crimes in which victim credibility is subject to close scrutiny, both within the legal system and by the general public. A victim's actions before, during, and after a sexual assault are called into question, particularly when these actions do not conform to societal notions of who is a victim, who is an offender, and how a victim should behave.

Sexual assault cases are difficult to investigate and prosecute because victim credibility is such a polarizing issue. Conviction rates for sexual assault are among the lowest for any serious felony (Bryden & Lengnick, 1997). These low rates persist despite legal reforms (i.e., rape shield laws) designed to counter stereotypes about sexual assault victims as well as research showing few incidences of false reporting (Lisak, Gardinier, Nicksa, & Cote, 2010; Lonsway, Archambault, & Lisak, 2009).

Questions about credibility are fueled by rape myths, specifically stereotypes or false beliefs about victims and perpetrators of sexual assault. These myths surface in defense arguments and in popular media. According to rape myths, a "true" victim immediately contacts law enforcement, always resists the sexual assault, and becomes anxious when asked to recount the crime. Myths also suggest that strangers account for most sexual assaults when in fact data from the Bureau of Justice Statistics at the National Institute of Justice, among others, show that the vast majority of offenders are known to the victim. Defendants exploit all of these myths to plant doubt by insisting that a victim whose behavior departs from these expected responses must have something to hide, is telling a lie, or seeks revenge against someone.

Some of the challenges to victim credibility rely on general misconceptions about responses to traumatic events. People respond to trauma in a variety of ways depending on several interrelated factors including the nature of the trauma, the persons involved, history of trauma, cultural considerations, and much more. Exposure to trauma can also significantly impact memory. Victim credibility, however, remains attached to the very specific reactions to trauma perpetuated through rape myths. In reality, each victim's response is distinct.

The specific facts of a case can dictate the extent to which a victim's credibility will be examined. For example, the victim's ability to accurately recount events will be debated during investigation and prosecution if alcohol or drug use is involved (voluntarily or not). Sometimes victims black out or have a hazy recollection of events, which may lead them to doubt their own ability to judge whether a sexual assault occurred. They anticipate that others may characterize the encounter as "drunk sex." This uncertainty exists even when there are signs of injury or witness accounts suggesting nonconsensual activity. Dismissive responses from friends or family members further fuel a victim's self-blame and embarrassment, which in turn deters reporting.

Overall, a dangerous attitude prevails that these victims "got what was coming to them" because they deliberately placed themselves in vulnerable or socially unacceptable situations. This perspective is particularly apparent when the victim is sexually assaulted while engaged in an illegal activity such as drug use or prostitution. Some people dismiss the report as the victim's way of deflecting attention from his or her own crimes. Others harbor the inhumane notion that a prostitute cannot be sexually assaulted, no matter the circumstances.

Victim credibility is challenged most vigorously when the offender is well known. Star athletes, celebrities, politicians, community leaders, and other high-profile figures enjoy particularly strong benefit of the doubt. The general public is more likely to assign ulterior motives to the reporting victim than to believe that a famous or respected person is capable of sexual assault. Often victims who do come forward in these situations are subject to extreme personal attacks. Other victims who see these attacks play out in public, particularly in the media, are reticent to report their own sexual assaults for fear of enduring the same treatment, even if their assailant is not a well-known person.

Victim credibility often boils down to the oft-used term "he said/she said" (or insert whatever pronoun applies to the gender identitie of the parties). This is a dismissive characterization of a sexual assault because it implies that a misunderstanding—and not a crime—occurred. The societal and systemic response must treat these matters as the crimes they are. This requires the stance of assuming, rather than questioning, a victim's credibility.

Caroline Palmer

See also Disclosure, Seeking Help; Help Seeking, Barriers to; Rape Myths; "Real Rape" and "Real Victims"—Correcting Misinformation; Revictimization, Organizations; Victims, Guilt and Shame

Further Reading

Bryden, D., & Lengnick, S. (1997). Criminal law: Rape in the criminal justice system. *Criminal Law & Criminology, 87*, 1194–1384.

Campbell, R., Dworkin, E., & Cabral, G. (2009). An ecological model of the impact of sexual assault on women's mental health. *Trauma Violence Abuse, 10*, 225–246.

Kilpatrick, D. G., Edmunds, C. N., & Seymour, A. (1992). *Rape in America: A report to the nation*. Arlington, VA: National Center for Victims of Crime.

Lisak, D., Gardinier, L., Nicksa, S. C., & Cote, A. M. (2010). False allegations of sexual assault: An analysis of ten years of reported cases. *Violence Against Women, 16*(12), 1318–1334.

Long, J. G. (2007). Introducing expert testimony to explain victim behavior in sexual and domestic violence prosecutions. Retrieved from http://www.ndaa.org/pdf/pub_introducing_expert_testimony.pdf (last visited June 14, 2011).

Lonsway, K., Archambault, J., & Lisak, D. (2009). False reports: Moving beyond the issues to successfully prosecute non-stranger sexual assault. *The Voice, 3*(1).

Selected Websites

End Violence Against Women International. Retrieved from http://www.evawintl.org/

National Judicial Education Program: A right to justice for victims. Legal Momentum. Retrieved from http://www.legalmomentum.org/our-work/vaw/njep.html

National Sexual Violence Resource Center. Retrieved from http://www.nsvrc.org

Victims, Disclosure

The silence that shrouds crimes of rape and sexual abuse has been a long-standing problem throughout our history. This entry provides an overview of the reasons why victims of sexual violence choose not to remain silent, who they disclose to, and the ways in which they disclose. This entry also addresses the reasons why victims may remain silent.

Sexual violence, sexual abuse, and victimization are not typically discussed openly because of societal norms. In particular, a widely accepted but inaccurate norm is that victims are personally responsible for the abuse and violence they suffered. Consequently, victims report that feelings of guilt and shame prevented their disclosures. Another long-standing but inaccurate norm in our culture has been that children and women, who constitute the majority of victims of sexual abuse and violence, frequently make false reports. The normalization of false reporting has been codified into our laws and policies. For example, in the most recent 30 years in the United States "... a woman could not testify that she was raped unless there was corroboration in three forms: an eye-witness, evidence of injury, and clear medical evidence linking the accused to the rape" (O'Malley, 1997, p.78). Thus victims also report that the fear of not being believed or taken seriously prevented their disclosures.

Over the past 40 years, however, personal stories of rape, sexual assault, and sexually violent victimization have become less taboo and are more openly and widely discussed in the United States. This cultural shift can be credited to a 1971 "speakout" against rape organized by a group called the New York Radical Feminists. This speakout provided a venue for a crowd of over 300 to hear women break their silence for the first time and tell their personal stories of rape, assault, and abuse. The 1971 speakout helped to create an environment in which women of various ages and cultures could openly discuss their experiences of sexual victimization, their postassault struggles with identity, and their journey to survivorship.

Although today, victims of sexual violence face a more positive environment in which to disclose, in addition to the societal norms previously discussed there are still several reasons why victims remain silent. The decision to disclose is influenced by a victim's sexual orientation, race, ethnicity, religion, and a variety of other identifying factors. The more marginalized a victim's identity the less likely she or he is empowered to disclose sexual violations and therefore is more at risk for a lifetime of further marginalization. For example, the use of "corrective rape" has been used as a means to target gay-identified persons in an attempt to "turn them straight." Furthermore, because male rape is highlighted in the traditional cultural definition of rape, males who are assaulted outside of prison are not often believed. Finally, in war-torn nations women and children have consistently been victimized as a means of humiliation, to increase the perpetrator's sense of power and control and to taint bloodlines; for these victims, disclosure could mean rejection by their families and communities. In some instances victims of war are often raped in front of their husbands and fathers, eliminating the opportunity to disclose to a loved one and causing further humiliation.

The various ways in which victims both self-identify and are stereotyped in society influence whether they choose to disclose to if they disclose at all. While victims may disclose to a trusted family member or friend, they may also choose not to disclose nor seek support from legal authorities and health care providers. Disclosure for victims is an acknowledgment that a crime has been committed against them and that they are a victim. Because of this, disclosure does not always occur immediately following victimization. Disclosure can take months or years, while some victims never disclose at all. The immediacy with which a victim discloses sexual abuse is dependent upon many factors, the most significant of which is safety. The issue of safety is further exacerbated by the victim's age. Children and teen victims are often coerced and threatened and thus fearful that their parents and friends will find out about the abuse. Adults can also be coerced and threatened by their abuser thus experiencing deep feelings of shame and guilt leading them to question their behavior and actions leading up to the assault.

Disclosure provides victims a way to acknowledge that a crime has been committed against them and to begin the process of healing. Victims typically disclose in three main ways: directly, indirectly, or through third-party communication. Direct disclosure can be verbal or written communication and is often intentional and deliberate. Victims who directly disclose are generally seeking help and support and possibly even validation of their victimization. Victims who use indirect disclosure or disguised disclosure hint that they may have experienced victimization without directly stating it. For example, a child might ask, "What would happen if someone was being touched in a way they don't like?" or may consistently indicate discomfort with being alone with a particular individual. Lastly, third-party disclosure involves someone other than the victim, a third party, disclosing suspected or proven victimization on behalf of the victim. This method of disclosure is more commonly used when a third party is trying to provide help and support for the victim.

Disclosure also occurs when a victim is reporting to law enforcement; however, one of the most startling aspects of sex crimes is how many go unreported. The most common reasons given by victims for not reporting these crimes to legal authorities is the belief that sexual violence is a private matter and that they fear reprisal from the assailant. "Of sexually abused children in grades five through twelve, 48 percent of the boys and 29 percent of the girls had told no one about the abuse, not even a friend or sibling" (Schoen et al., 1997).

Ultimately, the act of disclosure to any individual, not just law enforcement, allows victims the potential to recover the power and control that is lost post sexual victimization. Disclosure enables victims to acknowledge the devastation and impact of sexual violence, sexual abuse, and victimization and to receive help as they recover. Whether victims disclose or not they may experience a lifelong battle with denial, self-blame, and a debilitating sense of self-worth; disclosure is just one tool that can make this battle easier. The barriers that prevent victims from disclosing continue to reinforce cultural norms that support violence against women and children and silence their victimization. Disclosure is a powerful tool through which victims can begin the journey to survivor-hood and ultimately heal from the trauma of sexual violence.

Shamecca Bryant

See also Feminism, Influence of; Help Seeking, Barriers to; Rape Myths; Recovery; Underreporting; Victims, Guilt and Shame

Further Reading

O'Malley, Suzanne (1997, August). The new reason rapists are going free. *Redbook Magazine*, 76–79, 107–108.

Rainn.org (2011). *Crime and Punishment in America: 1999*. National Center for Policy Analysis http://rainn.org/get-information/statistics/reporting-rates.

Schoen, Cathy, Davis, Karen, Scott, Karen, et al. (1997). Commonwealth Fund Survey of the Health of Adolescent Girls. New York, NY: Commonwealth Fund.

U.S. Department of Justice, Bureau of Justice Statistics (2005). National Crime Victimization Survey, 2005. ICPSR22746-v2. Ann Arbor, MI: Inter-university Consortium for Political and Social Research.

Selected Websites

Survivor rights. Orange County Rape Crisis Center. Retrieved from http://ocrcc.org/resources/survivors/survivor-rights/

Talking about sexual assault: Society's response to sexual assault survivors. National Sexual Violence Resource Center [Podcast]. Retrieved from http://www.nsvrc.org/podcasts/sarah-ullman

Victims, Guilt and Shame

Sexual violence victims experience significant emotional trauma. As a result, victims experience a wide range of feelings. Primary among these feelings are guilt and shame. Guilt and shame are rarely experienced separately, and guilt is experienced almost universally after experiencing a traumatic event such as sexual assault. To help victims experiencing guilt and shame, it is helpful to understand how guilt and shame are defined and how they affect sexual violence victims.

Though guilt and shame are often discussed as distinctly different emotions, differences between shame and guilt may be less distinguished in some cultures. For example, in non-Western, collectivistic cultures in which the self is viewed as less separate from relationships with others and context, guilt and shame are less differentiated. Even among sexual violence victims who experience guilt and shame as different emotions, there may be variation in how they are experienced.

Researchers who conceptualize guilt and shame as different explain *guilt* as negative judgments and feelings about *actions, behaviors, or omissions* in a certain situation (Kurtz, 2007; Lewis & Haviland-Jones, 2000; Middleton-Moz, 1990). Therefore, a sexual violence victim may judge what they did or did not do while the abuse was happening and may feel guilty for their actions or behaviors during the abuse. For example, sexual violence victims may feel they should have tried to stop the abuse or might believe that they said or did something that invited the abuse.

Shame is described as more intensely negative than guilt, having the ability to impair one's thoughts, behaviors and capacity to communicate. Authors who distinguish between guilt and shame explain *shame* as negative feelings and judgments about one's *character, being, or self* as it relates to living up to external standards (Kurtz, 2007; Lewis & Haviland-Jones, 2000; Middleton-Moz, 1990). Shame also involves feelings of not living up to or falling short of an expectation that significant others may have of us or that we have of ourselves. Therefore when sexual violence victims experience shame, they feel bad about *who they are*, or *their value and status*, as opposed to feeling bad about *what they did* in a certain situation as with guilt. As a result, they may conclude that they are worthless, inferior, unlovable, and/or defective as a person.

Guilt is primarily a personal and internal process that is not easily seen by others. Shame is experienced as being exposed, vulnerable, and open to examination by others and often has a visible posture associated with it such as slumped posture, looking away or down, and shrinking. Noticing postures can be helpful in differentiating between a victim's experience of guilt or shame.

It is almost impossible to discuss guilt without discussing self-blame as they are often closely related. Questioning one's fault in the abuse is a normal reaction for all trauma survivors. Blaming oneself for abuse can serve as a way to cope with the atrocity of the abuse and help the victim gain a sense of control. If a victim believes that the abuse happened as a result of something she or he did, she or he then can change that behavior. This belief, though erroneous, might give victims a sense of power or protection that they can prevent the abuse from happening again. Likewise, child victims of sexual abuse often blame themselves in an attempt to make sense of the abuse they experienced. Herman (1997) explains that creating a justifiable reason for the abuse can help a victim of abuse make sense of why or how the happened to them, and what they can change about themselves that will keep the abuse from happening to them in the future; thus allowing them to "preserve a sense of meaning, hope, and power" (p. 103).

Initially, guilt and self-blame can serve a positive role in helping sexual violence victims give meaning to the experience and reclaim a sense of power over their lives. However, guilt and self-blame can also take an emotional toll on victims over time. Feelings of shame often increase at the time that a victim discloses the abuse. Negative responses to disclosure of abuse can also increase a victim's feelings of guilt and shame. For example, when someone responds with shock, disbelief, and/or blames the victim, these responses reinforce the feelings of guilt and shame a victim is already feeling.

Feelings of guilt and shame that remain unresolved can have negative effects on sexual violence victims. Prolonged experiences of guilt and shame affect one's self-esteem, self-confidence, and feelings of self-worth and can eventually become debilitating. Therefore it is important that persons who wish to help victims who are experiencing guilt and shame understand what victims need to heal and recover from the violent trauma.

Talking about the abuse can be one of the most powerful and effective ways for a sexual violence victim to overcome these emotions because silence, secrecy, and continued self-blame perpetuate feelings of shame and guilt. The most significant need a victim has in addressing issues of guilt is support from someone who "is willing to recognize that a traumatic event occurred, will suspend their preconceived judgments, and simply bear witness to her tale" (Herman, 1997 p. 68). Overcoming guilt and shame associated with sexual violence can be a long process and may need different forms of treatment to help the survivors through this process. Nonetheless, having a safe, supportive, and nonjudgmental environment in which a victim can talk about the abuse is an important first step in healing and overcoming feelings of guilt and shame.

Kathryn Johnson

See also Help Seeking, from Family and Friends; Recovery; Victims, Disclosure

Further Reading

Fierling, C., & Taska, L. (2005). The persistence of shame following sexual abuse: A Longitudinal look at risk and recovery. *Child Maltreatment, 11*(4), 337–349.

Hensley, Laura G. (2002). Treatment for survivors of rape: Issues and interventions. *Journal of Mental Health Counseling, 24*(4), 330–347.

Herman, J. (1997). *Trauma and recovery: The aftermath of violence-from domestic abuse to political terror.* New York, NY: Basic Books.

Kurtz, E. (2007). *Shame and guilt* (2nd ed.). New York, NY: iUniverse.

Lewis, M., & Haviland-Jones, J. M. (Eds.). (2000). *Handbook of emotions* (2nd ed.). New York: Guilford Press.

Middleton-Moz, J. (1990). *Shame and guilt: Masters of disguise.* Deerfield Beach, FL: Health Communications.

Wong, Y., & Tsai, J. L. (2007). Cultural models of shame and guilt. In J. Tracy, R. Robins, & J. Tangney (Eds.), *The self-conscious emotions: Theory and research* (pp. 209–223). New York, NY: Guilford Press.

Selected Websites

Guilt and shame. Healthy Place. Retrieved from http://www.healthyplace.com/abuse/escaping-hades/guilt-and-shame-after-sexual-assault/menu-id-810/

MICAVA (Minnesota Center against Violence and Abuse). Retrieved from http://www.mincava.umn.edu/categories/911

RAINN (Rape, Abuse & Incest National Network). Retrieved from http://www.rainn.org/search/node/Guilt+and+Shame

Victims, Identifying

Women and children are at greatest risk for sexual deviance victimization. Sexual deviance encompasses child sexual abuse, sexual assault, rape, and other sexual offenses. Unfortunately, its victims are impacted in a variety of ways including incest, molestation, child pornography, exhibitionism and voyeurism (flashing and peeping), sex trafficking, prostitution, and violence. These underreported crimes create immediate and long-term consequences on victims and society. For example, sexual deviance victimization can alter victims' perceptions of themselves and others, which negatively affects relationships and psychological functioning. A victim's suffering and resiliency depends on multiple factors such as a victim's age, severity of events, and response of caretakers and authorities. In other words, individuals vary in how they might look, feel, and act prior to, during, and after sexual victimization. However, the aftermath of victimization frequently leads to anxiety, post-traumatic stress disorder (PTSD), depression, self-injurious behaviors, eating disorders, sleep problems, substance abuse, borderline personality disorder, and sexualized behaviors. Identifying victims of sexual deviance and preventing itsdevastating effects is an important responsibility.

Society plays an important role in identifying victims; therefore it is critical to understand potential warning signs that someone may have been victimized. Childhood victims reveal a range of warning signs as a result of sexual deviance. Again, these circumstances vary based on a child's personality and trauma. Children can exhibit physical symptoms such as stomachaches, bruises, markings, or regional pain on or around their genitals. For example, children with urinary tract infections, genital bleeding, or sexually transmitted diseases raise considerable suspicions. Alternatively, children might display psychological changes such as increased sexual knowledge, aggressiveness, fear of people or places, nightmares, or unexplained distress. Some children make verbal comments about sexual matters. Statements of this kind should not be disregarded, but gently discussed. In addition, general risk factors including females ages four and up, physical or mental disabilities, low socioeconomic status, and poor family supervision increases victim risk (Putnam, 2003; Salter, 2003). Hence, a range of physical and mental warning signs signify the possibility of child victimization, particularly in the context of common risk factors.

Adult victims warrant close attention as well. After all, any adult can be sexually victimized. National statistics show however that women aged 16 to 30 are at highest risk (Sadock & Sadock, 2007). This is perhaps due to an adult's increased social activities and exposure to offending males. Indeed, certain males have rape-oriented attitudes and use deviant strategies to attain sex (i.e., alcohol, peers, or coercion). If bystanders happen to identify these circumstances, intervention is required. When adult victimization takes place, victims often display intense symptoms. For instance, a victim's immediate reactions to rape may involve shock, anger, confusion, and extreme humiliation. To make matters worse, some victims feel revictimized upon disclosure, given multiple interviews, medical exams, and negative interactions with authorities. Consequently, a high percentage of adult victims choose not to report their abuse or seek treatment. Indeed many adult victims seek treatment years later or related to abuse that took place during childhood. Either way friends and family members close to the victim might be called upon for support and recovery.

In conclusion, many children and adults experience sexual victimization during their lifetime. Society needs to be aware of possible warning signs and risk factors. Identifying victims early in the process helps prevent these crimes and their unfortunate consequences.

Julian Cano

See also Bystander Intervention; Depression and Anxiety; Eating Disorders; PTSD and Stress

Further Reading

Holmes, S. T., & Holmes, R. T. (2002). *Sex crimes: Patterns and behavior* (2nd ed.). Thousand Oaks, CA: Sage.

La Fond, J. Q. (2005). *Preventing sexual violence: How society should cope with sex offenders*. Washington, DC: American Psychological Association.

Perry, B. D., & Szalavitz, M. (2006). *The boy who was raised by a dog: And other stories from a child psychiatrist's notebook*. New York, NY: Basic Books.

Putnam, F. W. (2003). Ten-year research update review: Child sexual abuse. *Journal of the American Academy of Child and Adolescent Psychiatry, 42*(3), 269–278.

Sadock, B. J., & Sadock, V. A. (2007). *Synopsis of psychiatry: Behavioral sciences/ clinical psychiatry* (10th ed.). Philadelphia, PA: Lippincott, Williams & Wilkins.

Salter, A. C. (2003). *Predators: Pedophiles, rapists, and other sex offenders: Who they are, how they operate, and how we can protect ourselves and our children*. New York, NY: Perseus Books.

Victims, Male

Sexual victimization of men and boys is a significant public health concern affecting more than two million males in the United States during their lifetimes (Basile, Chen, Black, & Saltzman, 2007). However, the topic receives less attention in research, public health surveillance statistics, and community advocacy efforts relative to female sexual victimization. Given that women and girls endure a highly disproportionate share of sexual violence, sexual victimization is largely associated with the violence against women movement and viewed as a security issue for women. Consequently, men's roles as perpetrators tend to overshadow their roles as victims. Increasingly however, such societal misperceptions about male sexual victimization are being challenged.

Sexual activity directed against men and boys without their consent is a significantly underreported phenomenon. Even so, several U.S. national surveys have investigated the prevalence of male sexual violence victims. A criminal victimization study using a large, nationally representative sample of U.S. households reports that nine percent of victims of sexual violence are male (Weiss, 2010). A recent review of studies describing rates of lifetime rape perpetrated against a male victim demonstrates estimates ranging from 3.8 percent to 22.2 percent (Tewksbury, 2007). When considering male sexual victimization across the life span, incidents of sexual violence are predominantly associated with younger males. Seventy percent of male victims experienced an incident of sexual assault prior to the age of 18 (Basile, Chen, Black, & Saltzman, 2007). Even though sizable estimates do exist, expert consensus supports the view that the true scope of male sexual victimization is unknown, and current numbers likely greatly underestimate the actual extent of the problem.

One of the most significant impediments to accurate and thorough data collection on male victimization rates is the scarcity of victim reports to police officers, therapists, and researchers. In one national study, only 14.9 percent of male victims described making an official report to police or other institutional officials (Weiss, 2010). Men queried about their reasons not to report cited embarrassment, fear of not being believed, concerns about harassment, and fear of retaliation by the perpetrator as reasons to remain silent. In addition to holding perpetrators accountable for their actions, reports by male victims offer evidence that sexual violence is a salient concern for men and that communities must attend to the unique needs of male victims. As a consequence of the lack of reporting, community resources, victim outreach, therapeutic treatment options, and even legal remedies remain largely geared toward female victims.

The lack of reporting by male survivors of sexual assault underscores the stigma faced by victims of sexual violence generally, and male victims in particular.

Frequent misperceptions, prejudices, as well as societal norms about the male gender challenge public opinion of male victims of sexual violence. Notably, acceptance of myths about male rape is widespread in U.S. society. Men and women surveyed on the topic of male victims acknowledged beliefs that (1) men should be able to protect themselves from unwanted sexual advances, based on their size and strength; (2) male rape is extremely rare, with the exception of sexual violence in prisons; (3) female perpetrators are "harmless"; and (4) homosexuality is a defining feature of male-male victimization and perpetration.

As a result of limited data, widespread misinformation, and myths about male sexual victimization, little is known about male survivors and the contexts and circumstances of their abuse. In a national study, male survey respondents described the perpetrator of their first ever assault as acquaintances (32.3%), family members (17.7%), friends (17.6%), and intimate partners (15.9%; Basile, Chen, Black, & Saltzman, 2007). The most commonly reported perpetrator by gender was male, although 46 percent of male victims reported being victimized by women. Female perpetrators were most often friends, acquaintances, or coworkers of the victim, and least often a parent or stepparent. Similar to female victims of sexual assault, male victims reported being victimized at home, but other contexts for sexual violence diverged from sites typical for violence against women. Sexually victimized men described being more vulnerable to sexual assault in institutionalized settings (e.g., prison, police custody, military installations, fraternities, mental health facilities, schools, and the workplace), the streets (i.e., sites frequented by the homeless or runaways), military conflict zones, and refugee camps. Perpetrators from these settings use rape as a weapon of war, an activity for amusement or sexual gratification, a punishment, a method for asserting dominance, a tool of discipline, and a means for establishing the local hierarchy.

Physical and mental health consequences for male victims of sexual violence are pervasive and lifelong. Survivors of sexual assault may suffer from traumatic physical injuries (e.g., rectal tears) or chronic health concerns (e.g., migraines, gastrointestinal disorders, sexual dysfunction/discomfort, activity limitations, and sexually transmitted infections, including HIV). Findings from a recent national violence survey show that 16.1 percent of adult male victims reported that they had sustained a physical injury as a result of rape (Tjaden & Thoennes, 2006). Possible negative psychological outcomes are numerous and include immediate effects (e.g., shock, shame, anger, fear, withdrawal, and grief) and long-term conditions (e.g., depression, PTSD, sexual/gender identity confusion, poor self-concept, suicidal ideation, distrust). The aftermath of sexual victimization may also interrupt normal social functioning, disrupting relationships with family, friends, and intimate partners. Victims may seek and receive less emotional support, avoid contact with usual associates, or absent themselves from obligations. It is also likely that harmful health behaviors may follow. Male victims may uncharacteristically engage in high-risk sexual behavior, self-injury, substance use, or violence.

Given the limited utility of available data on male sexual victimization, prevention strategies and therapeutic services targeting male victims of sexual violence require systematic efforts of data surveillance. The research agenda for sexual violence must also be expanded to explore critical topics related to male victims such as the impact of male sexual victimization across populations, revictimization, access to services, perpetrator profiles, and risk of future perpetration (victim to offender). Investments in these areas will result in valuable information for addressing male sexual victimization.

Dania M. Ermentrout

See also Child Sexual Abuse; Child Sexual Abuse, Adult Survivors of; Male-on-Male Sexual Violence; Rape Myths; Underreporting; Victims, Guilt and Shame

Further Reading

Basile, K. C., Chen, J., Black, M. C., & Saltzman, L. E. (2007). Prevalence and characteristics of sexual violence victimization among U.S. adults, 2001–2003. *Violence and Victims, 22*(4), 437–448.

Choudhary, E., Coben, J., & Bossarte, R. M. (2010). Adverse health outcomes, perpetrator characteristics, and sexual violence victimization among U.S. adult males. *Journal of Interpersonal Violence, 25*, 1523–1541. doi:10.1177/0886260509346063

Putnam, F. W. (2003). Ten-year research update review: Child sexual abuse. *Journal of the American Academy of Child and Adolescent Psychiatry, 42*(3), 269–278.

Tewksbury, R. (2007). Effects of sexual assaults on men: Physical, mental, and sexual consequences. *International Journal of Men's Health, 6*(1), 22–35. Retrieved from http://www.mensstudies.com/content/120391/

Tjaden, P., & Thoennes, N. (2006). *Extent, nature, and consequences of rape victimization: Findings from the National Violence Against Women Survey* (NIJ Publication No. NCJ210346). Retrieved from http://www.ncjrs.gov/pdffiles1/nij/210346.pdf

Weiss, K. G. (2010). Male sexual victimization: Examining men's experiences of rape and sexual assault. *Men and Masculinities, 12*, 275–298. doi:10.1177/1097184X08 322632

World Report on Violence and Health (2002). World Health Organization. Retrieved from http://whqlibdoc.who.int/publications/2002/9241545615_eng.pdf

Selected Websites

For men only: For male survivors of sexual assault. University of Texas at Austin Counseling and Mental Health Center. Retrieved from http://cmhc.utexas.edu/booklets/maleassault/menassault.html

Male sexual assault [search page]. National Sexual Violence Resource Center. Retrieved from http://www.nsvrc.org/publications?tid=277&tid_1=All

MaleSurvivor: Overcoming Sexual Victimization of Men and Boys. Retrieved from http://www.malesurvivor.org/

No escape: Male rape in U.S. prisons. Human Rights Watch. Retrieved from http://www.hrw.org/legacy/reports/2001/prison/

Resources. STOP IT NOW! (Together We Can Stop the Sexual Abuse of Children). Retrieved from http://www.stopitnow.org/resources

Resources for male survivors. Men Can Stop Rape: Creating Cultures Free from Violence. Retrieved from http://www.mencanstoprape.org/Resources/resources-for-male-survivors.html

Where we stand: Male victims. National Alliance to End Sexual Violence. Retrieved from http://endsexualviolence.org/where-we-stand/male-victims

Victims, Repeat

The problem of sexual revictimization is a real and serious concern for all victims. Individuals who have been sexually victimized are at a heightened risk of future sexual victimization relative to persons who have never been victimized. Sexual assault revictimization has been defined in many ways. Whereas some researchers characterize revictimization as the subsequent sexual assault of child sexual abuse (CSA) survivors, others have defined revictimization as the successive sexual assault of adult sexual assault survivors. This entry takes a broad conceptualization of revictimization to include any subsequent sexual victimization of individuals who have experienced sexual abuse at some previous point in their lives, regardless of the life developmental period in which the first incident occurred.

Research shows that revictimization is a considerable problem for both male and female sexual abuse victims (Coxell & King, 2010). Overall, revictimization ranges from 10 to 69 percent and approximately two of three individuals who are sexually victimized will be revictimized (Classen, Palesh, & Aggarwal, 2005). A nationally representative study examining the revictimization experiences of men and women found that women with a CSA history were nearly twice as likely to have experienced sexual revictimization in adulthood compared to those with no such history, whereas men with a CSA history were nearly six times as likely to have experienced sexual revictimization in adulthood (Desai, Arias, Thompson, & Basile, 2002). A recent longitudinal study examining revictimization among adolescents and adults found that women who had experienced CSA were almost twice as likely to have experienced revictimization compared to women without this history (Barnes, Noll, Putnam, & Trickett, 2009). In addition, preliminary research suggests that different minority groups (e.g., African Americans, Latinos/Hispanics) may be at an increased risk for revictimization

(Classen, Palesh, & Aggarwal, 2005). However, the research examining the revictimization experiences of persons from diverse ethnic and racial groups is limited and additional focus on this topic is needed.

Repeated experiences of sexual violence undermine victims' recovery from the first experience of violent trauma. In addition, revictimization is associated with serious problems for victims' health and well-being. Revictimized persons exhibit greater trauma and higher levels of psychological distress compared to persons who experience only either CSA or adult sexual abuse (Arata, 2002). For instance, revictimized persons display higher levels of trauma symptoms and are more likely to have a lifetime diagnosis of post-traumatic stress disorder (PTSD). Revictimization is also associated with increased emotional difficulties and mental illness (e.g., depression, anxiety) and greater comorbidity of mental disorders. Revictimized persons also report more sexual problems, somatic complaints, interpersonal problems (e.g., interpersonal sensitivity, hostility), self- and societal blame, and suicide attempts compared to single-incident sexual abuse victims.

Various theories have been applied to the problem of revictimization to understand the phenomenon and explain causal pathways. Until recently, most of the theories applied to revictimization focus on individual factors without attending to social and environmental contexts. In addition, most theoretical explanations of revictimization lack empirical support and do not explain revictimization from multiple partners. Fortunately, recent theories are beginning to consider social and environmental risk factors outside of the individual (e.g., homelessness, social norms that support violence, poverty). Grauerholz's (2000) theory of revictimization uses the ecological perspective and proposes four levels for understanding revictimization: (1) ontogenic development, (2) the microsystem, (3) the exosystem, and (4) the macrosystem. Ontogenic development consists of an individual's personal history and considers factors such as early family experiences and the initial victimization experience. The microsystem refers to the context in which revictimization occurs (e.g., factors increasing the victim's interactions with potential perpetrators and perception of the victim as an easy target). The exosystem consists of the formal and informal social structures surrounding the victim (e.g., lack of family support), and the macrosystem represents societal and cultural factors (e.g., cultural tendency to blame the victim). Overall, the ecological perspective is a useful framework for understanding revictimization because it diminishes the tendency to focus on characteristics and actions of the victim. Further, the perspective reflects the complex and multifaceted nature of revictimization.

Although the ecological perspective is gaining favor among researchers, most of the research on revictimization risk and protective factors to date has focused on the victim's history, characteristics, and behaviors. Vulnerability-enhancing past events and situational variables are the risk factors that have garnered the most empirical evidence. Among these risk factors are characteristics of prior sexual victimization. For instance, risk for revictimization is increased when prior experiences of sexual victimization are (1) more intrusive, (2) perpetrated by someone close to the victim, (3) frequent, (4) of long duration, (5) violent, and (6) recent. Other vulnerability-enhancing past events associated with revictimization include childhood physical abuse and multiple traumas. Some evidence suggests that the combination of CSA and childhood physical abuse increases the risk for revictimization more so than CSA alone. In general, as the number of traumatic experiences increases, so does one's risk of revictimization.

A number of family-of-origin characteristics have been associated with sexual revictimization. For instance, intrafamilial conflict (e.g., parental conflict), drug and alcohol problems, mental health problems, and poor family functioning (e.g., less cohesive, less expressive, more controlling) increase the likelihood of revictimization. Substance abuse (either alcohol or drugs) and certain sexual activities also increase one's risk of sexual revictimization. For instance, having first consensual intercourse at an early age and having multiple consensual sexual partners are known risk factors for revictimization. Another factor that increases the likelihood for revictimization is problems in assessing the dangerousness of situations, persons, and relationships, which is known as impairments in threat detection.

Although limited research has focused on social-contextual factors, preliminary evidence suggests lack of resources (e.g., low income, limited educations, limited support) and being mobile are risk factors for revictimization. Equally underresearched are factors that reduce a person's risk of revictimization. However, evidence highlights the importance of self-efficacy, sense of mastery, and situation assertiveness factors that might protect against revictimization.

Cynthia F. Rizo

See also Cumulative Abuse; Revictimization, Individuals; Revictimization, Organizations; Risk for Future Violence

Further Reading

Arata, C. M. (2002). Child sexual abuse and sexual revictimization. *Clinical Psychology: Science and Practice, 9*(2), 135–164. doi:10.1093/clipsy/9.2.135

Barnes, J. E., Noll, J. G., Putnam, F. W., & Trickett, P. K. (2009). Sexual and physical revictimization among victims of severe childhood sexual abuse. *Child Abuse & Neglect, 33*(7), 412–420. doi:10.1016/j.chiabu.2008.09.013

Classen, C. C., Palesh, O., & Aggarwal, R. (2005). Sexual revictimization: A review of the empirical literature. *Trauma, Violence, & Abuse, 6*(2), 103–129. doi:10.1177/1524838005275087

Coxell, A. W., & King, M. B. (2010). Adult male rape and sexual assault: prevalence, re-victimisation and the tonic immobility response. *Sexual & Relationship Therapy, 25*(4), 372–379. doi:10.1080/14681991003747430

Desai, S., Arias, I., Thompson, M. P., & Basile, K. C. (2002). Childhood victimization and subsequent adult revictimization assessed in a nationally representative sample of women and men. *Violence and Victims, 17*(6), 639–653. doi:10.1891/vivi.17.6.639.33725

Grauerholz, L. (2000). An ecological approach to understanding sexual revictimization: Linking personal, interpersonal, and sociocultural factors and processes. *Child Maltreatment, 5*(1), 5–17. doi:10.1177/1077559500005001002

Selected Websites

Male sexual abuse. Alive and Well News Online. Retrieved from http://www.aliveandwellnews.com/web%20reports/mental%20health/male_sexual_abuse.shtml

Multiple victimization of rape victims. Rape Crisis Information Research Pathfinder. Retrieved from http://www.ibiblio.org/rcip/mvrv.html

Recovery from Abuse. Retrieved from http://www.recoveryfromabuse.com/wordpress/?page_id=23

Revictimization. Pandora's Project. Retrieved from http://www.pandys.org/articles/revictimization.html

Victims and Interventions (Overview)

The impact of sexual violence on an individual is often immediate, pervasive, and long term. People experience sexual violence differently and their needs may be compounded depending on their individual history, what actually occurred during the violence, and the response they received afterward. These needs can be addressed in a short- or long-term therapeutic setting. This overview outlines a variety of different types of intervention for survivors of sexual violence.

There are many different types of services available for survivors of sexual violence including short- and long-term counseling, crisis intervention, and hotline counseling. Short-term counseling may be defined as counseling that focuses on the causes of the feelings or issues a person is having rather than the symptoms of the problem. It may also be defined by the length of time the service is provided. For instance, counseling through a hotline will be immediate and focused and is not intended to be used for ongoing support. Some of the interventions will depend on the demographics of the survivor. Age and relation to the perpetrator may impact what services the survivor accesses. Additionally, survivors may choose interventions based on their socioeconomic status or their personal beliefs about counseling or therapy. For instance, in most states, crisis counseling for victims of sexual violence is free of cost. Many long-term therapeutic interventions are provided at cost by trained practitioners; some survivors will not have the ability to access such services.

Regardless of the type of intervention, there are some basic theories that are associated with victim intervention. These theoretical approaches guide many service providers in their work with survivors and how they approach assisting victims in recovering from sexual violence. This overview begins with a summary of the entries outlining different theoretical approaches to intervention and then presents how victims are identified by practitioners. Next, an overview of the entries on immediate or short-term interventions is discussed. This overview concludes with a review of the longer-term or therapeutic interventions.

Theoretical Approaches

There are a number of theoretical approaches that can impact victim intervention. These approaches can be looked at as the overarching framework that service providers utilize in addressing survivors of sexual violence within the healing process. It is important to first understand that there is a process for healing from sexual violence. Regardless of whether the survivor is a child or an adult, the idea of sexual violence recovery exists.

Individuals recover from sexual violence in different ways and in different time frames. This is true for all survivors regardless of gender, age, race, and socioeconomic status. Theories that exist around sexual violence recovery address recovery in phases or stages. In her entry on **Recovery**, Koenick highlights two different phase or stage approaches most commonly referred to by practitioners—Burgess and Holmstrom's "rape trauma syndrome" and Judith Herman's three-stage recovery. While these theories are different, there are commonalities among the ideas. For example, both approaches focus on a period of time in which the survivor would focus on sadness or mourning the loss of her or his life prior to the act of violence. Additionally, both theories address the time a survivor spends on addressing safety and security issues. Recovery is also impacted by physical and psychological reactions to the trauma, how others react to disclosure of the trauma, and other co-occurring issues present in the life of the survivor. The main understanding of any theory around sexual assault recovery is that it is possible to move forward and feel healed from an act of sexual violence.

While helping survivors recover from a sexual violence experience, three main theoretical approaches are frequently used by practitioners including empowerment, feminist theory, and the strengths perspective. These three theoretical approaches overlap in the core tenets. For example, the strengths perspective is the belief that all people have within themselves the capacity and skill to make the decisions and take actions that are best suited for them. In her entry, **Strengths Perspective**, Lang-Grant highlights the 10 significant principles that define the strengths perspective in the therapeutic setting. In both short- and long-term intervention with a survivor, following the core principles of the strengths perspective will allow the survivor to focus on her or his own needs and make decisions that work best.

Empowerment is often seen as part of the strengths perspective. As highlighted by Chiarelli-Helminiak, **Empowerment** can be seen in a number of ways. The basic approach within sexual violence work is that the perpetrator has taken away the power and control of the victim. The goal of the advocate or counselor is to provide information and support so that the survivor can regain control by making decisions that are best for that person. Survivors, upon making decisions and choices for themselves, may begin to regain a sense of worth and confidence, which are often damaged by sexual violence.

Using an empowerment or strengths perspective approach is important with all survivors of sexual violence and abuse, regardless of age. However, when working with children or minors who are victims of sexual violence, these theories may not work as well since children and minors may not be able to make certain decisions for themselves. In a counseling or supportive setting, it is important to provide a space for survivors to explore their feelings and acknowledge their abilities. Even though children cannot make some decisions, older children can still be helped to feel good about their strengths.

The use of empowerment within a counseling setting also allows for a balanced or egalitarian relationship between the survivor and the service provider. Such balance is also an important aspect of **Feminist Practice Theory** as outlined by Salerno Wallace. Similarly, both empowerment and feminist theory purport that sexual violence and abuse is rooted in our patriarchal history and the social norms of our society. Salerno Wallace discusses both the theoretical understanding of the feminist perspective about sexual violence as an issue as well as the use of feminist theory in the therapeutic setting. Feminist theory within the therapeutic setting focuses on being supportive, nonjudgmental, and valuing the experience and perspective of the survivor.

Identifying Victims

With national statistics indicating that approximately 18 percent of all women and 3 percent of all men will be sexually victimized in their lifetime (Tjaden & Thoennes, 2000), it is reasonable to assume that many people are suffering from the aftereffects of such victimization. Victims are identified in a number of ways based on several different factors. Some victims of sexual violence or abuse will self-identify. This means they will understand that they have been victimized or harmed by the behavior in some way and seek services. Victims who self-identify may engage in the various organizations that are involved in sexual violence as a health or criminal justice issue. For instance, an adult victim may reach out to a rape crisis center for information or support or to other organizations (see **Organizational Response [Overview]**).

Victims may also be identified by other individuals or agencies. This might include treatment providers for a medical or mental health issue, a teacher, a nonoffending family member, or Child Protective Services within state government. For example, an adult victim may present at her or his primary care physician with a medical complaint, such as an inability to sleep. If that provider does a complete screening of the patient, he or she may find that the change in the sleeping pattern comes from nightmares that are the result of a previous sexual assault. In the entry **Victims, Identifying**, Cano highlights the importance of all members of society identifying victims in an effort to address sexual violence and support survivors. Cano suggests that everyone should understand potential warning signs for both adult and child victims of sexual violence. Another responsibility of members of society is to notify authorities of child victims of abuse. Luciano outlines this responsibility, as well as the responsibility of state Child Protective Services to document and provide services to child victims in the entry **Reporting, Mandated**. In the case of child victimization, an individual or agency may identify that child as a victim and engage the child in the state child protective systems that exist to address child sexual abuse. While any individual community member may report a suspected incident of child abuse, there are specific individuals or entities that are required to do so. Teachers, social workers, child care providers, and health care professionals are some of the designated mandated reporters in most states.

Along with identifying victims, practitioners may also conduct a risk assessment to identify the potential for revictimization. In **Risk Assessments**, Marandino outlines the often controversial practice of completing risk assessments. Risk assessments are a tool that is used mainly in cases of child abuse in which the determination of whether the offender should have access to the child is being made. Risk assessments are completed by trained clinicians. They are often conducted by completing interviews with involved parties as well as relying on statistics and dynamic factors. Additionally, standardized tools and scales are often used by the clinician. While the completion of a risk assessment cannot completely determine future risk, they can be a helpful tool in determining if dynamic factors, such as a violation of a court order, have changed or if the level of risk has increased for an individual.

Immediate or Short-Term Interventions

Once a victim has self-identified or has been identified by a helping professional, there are a variety of interventions that can be utilized by victims, depending on their need, comfort level, access, and response to each service or therapy. Short-term interventions are typically immediate and focused interventions for victims. Many victims' first encounter with an intervention in the aftermath of an act of sexual violence is considered crisis response. There are four topics within this section that focus on crisis response: Hotlines, Crisis Intervention, Crisis Counseling, and Advocacy.

In **Crisis Intervention**, Roebuck defines it as the prompt, time-limited, and focused response to a victim of sexual violence. Crisis intervention can occur in person or through the use of a hotline service. There are several purposes for crisis intervention including reducing the often intense feelings and behavioral reactions, helping the victim identify coping strategies, addressing the psychological, medical, and legal concerns, and connecting individuals with referrals to further assist them through both the logistical and emotional recovery process. Service providers who offer crisis intervention also focus on the immediate safety of the victim and help the victim identify a plan for ongoing safety.

Similar to crisis intervention, crisis counseling is also immediate and time limited. The goal of crisis counseling is similar to that of crisis intervention—to provide a supportive and nonjudgmental environment for a survivor. In **Crisis Counseling**, Roebuck outlines the importance of crisis counseling as individuals are often more responsive to intervention during or immediately following a crisis, such as an act of sexual violence. Crisis intervention focuses on addressing a survivor in three ways: helping the survivor to reduce the often overwhelming emotional and psychological impact of the trauma; providing education about sexual violence and the variety of issues that result from victimization; and providing support for that person. This immediate, positive intervention often provides the survivor with a sense of ongoing support and encouragement in making decisions for further interventions, such as longer-term therapeutic interventions.

Within crisis intervention or crisis counseling, one may use therapeutic interviewing strategies to assist the survivor in providing a detailed narrative of what has happened. **Therapeutic Interviewing Strategies**, written by Lang-Grant, is a technique used to allow for a safe space for a survivor to share the experiences with a supportive, empathetic person. As Lang-Grant highlights, the first part of this strategy is ensuring that there is a safe location that will allow for privacy. The second part is allowing the survivor physical and emotional space so that they can to share as little or as much about what has happened. It is important for the advocate to provide a nonjudgmental response, options, and validation. This will allow both child and adult survivors to feel empowered and supported as they move through a medical or criminal justice process.

Oftentimes, crisis intervention and crisis counseling also takes the form of or leads to advocacy services for a survivor. In the field of sexual violence, advocacy refers to a person or group taking action on behalf of or for the benefit of survivors. Advocacy encompasses two forms including individual advocacy and systems advocacy. As Roebuck highlights in **Advocacy**, the actions a group or individual may take to facilitate support or change has many forms.

Individual advocacy focuses on providing support to a survivor who is engaged in the system in the immediate aftermath of an assault. Advocacy on this level is provided by trained individuals typically from the community-based sexual assault programs or rape crisis centers for adults and teen survivors and Child Advocacy Centers for children. These individuals are typically referred to as advocates within the system (see entry on **Advocates**). Individual advocacy often includes: providing information about medical, legal, and civil options for survivors; accompanying the survivor to medical or forensic exams and/or criminal or civil proceedings; and providing resources and referrals. Advocates often respond as one part of the sexual assault response team (SART), which may also include a sexual assault nurse examiner (SANE) and a member of law enforcement. (See the entries on **SARTs [Sexual Assault Response Team] and SANE [Sexual Assault Nurse Examiner]**.) Each individual within this team represents a particular need for a victim in the immediate aftermath of an act of sexual violence. The advocate plays an important role for survivors within and outside of the SART process. Research indicates that the presence of the advocate is positive for the survivor. Survivors that worked with an advocate report receiving more services and less retraumatization from medical and legal systems. They also report less distress after their contact with the legal system when they had an advocate present (Campbell, 2006).

While individual advocacy focuses on one survivor and their individual needs, systems advocacy focuses on the overarching issues surrounding sexual violence and victims of sexual violence. Systems advocacy addresses the broader scope of sexual violence and encourages community awareness, influencing law and public policy and improving the systematic response to sexual violence in both intervention and prevention efforts. There are many strategies for engaging in system advocacy that includes working individually or as a group.

Advocacy or crisis intervention and counseling are often completed through the use of hotlines. **Hotlines**, as described by Wilson Lischick, are a service that any victim with access to a phone can utilize. The services provided from the hotlines are free, confidential, and can be anonymous. Typically, hotlines are provided by a social service agency, such as a sexual violence program, and are available 24 hours a day, 7 days a week, 365 days a year. They are used by a variety of people for a variety of reasons. For example, an individual may call a hotline to seek validation that what happened to her or him was an act of sexual violence. A family member or loved one may call a hotline seeking ways to be helpful to a survivor. Finally, a recent victim may call a hotline to assess her or his options. Hotline workers receive training on crisis response and have access to a variety of resources and referrals to provide to callers. Hotlines are a benefit to survivors because they can utilize the service at any time of day and can do so anonymously. Hotlines can be seen as a gateway to other services as referrals are often given during the call. Many communities have local hotlines, and there are also state hotlines and some national hotline services. In response to our cyber-focused society, some providers have created online hotlines that allow for interaction between hotline advocates and survivors via a "chat" feature through a website. Regardless of how the hotline service is delivered, the goal is to provide immediate information and support to anyone regarding sexual violence.

In addition to providing support and information about options, an immediate need to address with any victim of sexual violence is her or his current and future safety. One strategy to assist victims in addressing short- and long-term safety needs is providing an opportunity to develop a safety plan. As outlined in **Safety Plans**, Smith identifies a safety plan as an individualized plan that focuses on reducing further risk from violence. Most individuals use safety planning in their daily lives without much thought. Many of the strategies that are used by individuals are done so because we have been sent the message that doing these things may keep us safe. Safety planning as an intervention is often associated with domestic violence. There is much research that highlights the risk victims of domestic violence encounter both within the relationship and upon leaving an abusive partner. It is important to focus on safety planning with victims of sexual violence for a number of reasons. First, sexual violence may occur as part of domestic violence. Second, it is important for victims to do things that help them feel safe and secure. Part of gaining the feeling of safety and security is making decisions that allow the person to feel in control and physically safe. Safety planning is a fluid process that once developed can be reassessed should changes occur; and often once focused on, it becomes ingrained or automatic for a time or indefinitely. It is also important to remember that while safety planning may reduce risk, it does not prevent sexual violence from occurring. Additionally, if a victim does or does not employ safety planning strategies, she or he is never at fault for the violence committed against her or him.

Therapeutic Interventions

There are a variety of therapeutic interventions that are offered by clinicians to address the long-term, psychological impact that the trauma of sexual violence has on an individual. While the modalities mentioned in this overview are not an exhaustive list of every type of therapy available, it does provide a well-rounded sample of the types of therapy most frequently utilized by therapists working with adult and child survivors of sexual violence. Most of the treatments mentioned are a form of psychotherapy. Psychotherapy can be defined simply as a process that an individual with a mental health issue or an issue that is impacting his or her emotional, behavioral, or physical health address while working with a trained professional through the use of psychological techniques based on specific theories.

Many therapeutic inventions use post-traumatic stress disorder (PTSD) as the basis for treatment. Whether a person is diagnosed with this mental health issue or not, many child and adult survivors of violence experience a number of the symptoms related to PTSD. These symptoms include emotional, psychological, and behavioral challenges for a survivor, including experiencing intrusive thoughts or images, strong feelings of detachment from others, or difficulty feeling safe and secure. (See entry on **PTSD and Stress**.)

There are both similarities and differences in these therapies including the theory behind each modality, the suggested length of sessions, and which individuals benefit most from the particular type of intervention. Many therapies can be provided in an individual or group setting. The most important factors for a survivor when determining what treatment is best suited for him or her is that the survivor is comfortable with the treatment and the clinician. Being as comfortable as possible will provide the survivor with a strong foundation for processing the trauma of sexual violence with the therapist in a safe and supportive environment.

The most closely aligned therapy to the many immediate interventions, such as crisis counseling, is trauma therapy. Trauma therapy is the process of healing the specific symptoms that occur when an individual experiences a trauma. As is discussed in Koenick's entry, **Recovery**, trauma can impact an individual in many different ways and in differing lengths of time. **Trauma Therapy**, as outlined by Boianelli, allows for use in a variety of settings, such as individual, group, or family therapy, and for both children and adults. The goal of trauma therapy is to assist a survivor in minimizing or eliminating the trauma-related symptoms. Trauma therapy also focuses on these symptoms as a natural or common reaction to an abnormal experience. It is similar to narrative therapy, as the telling of the trauma narrative is an important aspect for the survivor.

As Scala discusses in the entry, **Narrative Therapy**, the purpose of this type of therapy is to tell or retell stories. An important aspect of the retelling or recalling traumatic memories is highlighted in the entry, **Remembrance and Mourning**. In this section Bender Zuckerman addresses Herman's third phase of recovery (Herman, 1992). The phase also focuses on the importance of recalling the traumatic memories and then working to deal with the feelings associated with that trauma. While often difficult due to the way in which traumatic memories store in the brain, it is important for a survivor not to avoid these memories. The loss associated with sexual violence, such as loss of trust in others, loss of a sense of power or control over self, or loss of relationships, can be seen in the phase of mourning. It is important for clinicians to allow space for the survivor to address the feelings of loss and to acknowledge and name that loss.

Narrative therapy is an approach to psychotherapy and is intended to recognize that the client is the expert in his or her own life and that the therapist should provide a respectful, non-blaming environment for the survivor. This therapy allows for clients to tell their stories and focus on the "externalization" or identify the difference between the person and the problem. For survivors of sexual violence, the act of violence and the reaction by self and others could be identified as the problem. It is after the problem is identified that the therapist can assist survivors in understanding how their story impacts who they are and how they see the world. It is then that the survivor and therapist can work together to address the inner strengths of the survivor in constructing future narratives.

Regardless of the type of therapeutic intervention that is being used by a survivor, it is important to consider the factors in addition to the act of sexual violence or abuse that influence the survivor. These factors include culture, family of origin, and spirituality. Spirituality can have a significant impact, both positive and negative, on a survivor's healing process. If spirituality has a role in a victim's life, it is important to allow space for that to be addressed in a therapeutic setting for a number of reasons. As outlined by Evan and Luciano in **Spirituality**, survivors may use aspects of their faith as a healthy coping mechanism. As developing healthy coping skills is an important aspect of trauma work, this would be beneficial for survivors. Additionally, survivors may have a positive sense of belonging and support within their spiritual or religious community. These feelings may help counter negative feelings of isolation, or self-blame. Spiritual beliefs may also cause conflicts internally or externally for a survivor. Clinicians should be aware of this and help the survivor process such conflict within the clinical setting.

Two evidence-based therapeutic interventions are **Cognitive Behavioral Therapy** (CBT) and **EMDR (Eye Movement Desensitization and Reprocessing)**. These two therapies are explored in the topics of the same name. EMDR and CBT are used with both child and adult survivors. Evidence based means that there has been scientific research with individuals engaged in the therapy that proves that the therapy is effectively treating the client. Marandino writes that there are a number of variations of CBT that are used with survivors of sexual violence, including trauma-focused CBT, exposure therapy, and prolonged exposure (PE). CBT is a short-term form of psychotherapy based on the concept that the way we think about things affects how we feel emotionally and therefore how we behave. The components of CBT, exposure therapy, and PE include: educating the survivor; reducing stress by using healthy coping strategies; eliminating the PTSD symptoms; and exposing the survivor to the traumatic memories in an effort to relive the traumatic experience in a controlled environment. This allows for the processing of the memory and of the feelings associated with that memory. Depending on the survivor and her or his ability to tolerate the traumatic memories, PE is often done slowly and over a long period of time. Additionally, **Exposure Therapy**, addressed by Oreski, offers three types of exposure, each designed to allow for the survivor to retell and reexperience in a supportive environment with the goal to access those memories and process the negative thoughts and feelings associated with that experience.

Eye movement desensitization and reprocessing or EMDR also helps to relieve and reprocess thoughts, feelings, and images associated with traumatic experiences. As Heinman writes, EMDR is a relatively new therapy that uses "bilateral stimulation," meaning engaging both sides of the brain. This is done through eye stimulation, ear stimulation, or touch. It encourages a survivor to notice thoughts, images, or feelings that come up and then discuss them. This is a therapy that is relatively short term and does not require, as other treatments do, the survivor to complete work outside of the clinical setting.

The use of neurobiology in CBT, EMDR, and other therapies is important. As Sarid highlights in the **Neurobiology, Interventions Using** entry, the impact of trauma on the brain is significant. Traumatic experiences do not immediately store in the brain as a memory. Oftentimes, survivors indicate the presence of nightmares, flashbacks, and other intrusive thoughts about the traumatic experience. Such experiences are distressing for survivors but help the brain process the experience and store it as a memory. Using neurobiology within the therapeutic setting allows for the traumatic experiences to begin changing into memories in a controlled way. By using a variety of techniques including flooding or exposure or guided imagery, the therapist can assist the survivor in moving the thoughts into a memory in a way that will be the most helpful for the survivor.

Two additional shorter-term therapeutic interventions are **Stress Inoculation Training** and **Solution-Focused Brief Therapy** (highlighted by Lang-Grant and Tasiopoulos respectively). Stress inoculation training or SIT focuses on relieving the symptoms that result from the anxiety and stress caused by an act of sexual violence through the use of healthy coping skills and relaxation techniques. This type of therapy is flexible and tailored to each individual. SIT is typically complete in 10 or less sessions and is often used in conjunction with other therapeutic modalities.

Solution-focused brief therapy or SFBT is typically conducted within 4 to 12 sessions and focuses on goal-oriented solutions for a client, rather than the problems. This type of therapy may be helpful for survivors of violence in focusing on solutions that they have control over, such as who they disclose the abuse to or how they manage their symptoms of post-traumatic stress disorder. This allows survivors to identify their own abilities and strengths, which may empower them. The therapist offers validation and feedback throughout the process, which may give the survivor a renewed sense of control in her or his life.

There are two types of interventions that may occur in the group setting: **Group Therapy** and **Support Groups** (highlighted in entries of the same name written by Labbad and Seay respectively). Support groups or group therapy bring together a group of survivors to share their experiences and provide support and encouragement for each other. Support groups, whether they occur in person or online, should be led by a professional. Group therapy can use many different treatment therapies, depending on the clinician and members of the group. While not appropriate for all survivors, support groups can be offered independently or in conjunction with other therapies. Groups can be offered for a specific group of survivors (for instance, a "survivors of childhood sexual abuse" group may be offered), or group survivors of many forms of violence together. A main benefit of a support group for survivors of sexual violence is the ability to allow for survivors to recognize the universality of their experience, which assists in decreasing feelings of "why me?" and isolation. Breaking down the isolation or the belief that they are alone in this experience is challenging in an individual therapy setting.

A type of therapy that is specific and helpful for child survivors is **Play Therapy**. This type of therapy is especially useful for children ages 3–12 and those who are nonverbal and typically occurs within about 20 sessions. As indicated by Briggs and Gil, therapists who utilize play therapy believe that children will eventually act out or bring issues up through toys and play. There are many different theories that guide how play therapy can be used, and the therapist's role is often nondirective during the play, allowing the child to guide the play.

In addition to many types of psychotherapies that are utilized in the treatment of survivors of sexual violence, many alternative therapies are also used. Alternative therapies are often nontraditional techniques that are used by therapists or survivors to aid in the healing process. There are many different types of alternative therapies such as art therapy, relaxation, massage, meditation, and acupuncture. One promising alternative therapy is the use of yoga. As discussed in **Yoga Therapy** by Lang-Grant, yoga's emphasis is focusing on being present with the self and focusing on individual strength; hence, it is of benefit to survivors who may struggle with such focus. Yoga programs exist for both children and adults and are now being linked to reducing symptoms of PTSD. Alternative therapies are not appropriate for everyone, but survivors can explore what might be helpful for them as an individual to enhance their healing process.

In conclusion, there are many immediate and therapeutic interventions that exist for survivors of sexual violence and abuse. Immediate interventions focus on the immediate needs and feelings of the survivor. Therapeutic interventions vary in length and often address ways to manage post-trauma symptoms and address thoughts and feelings related to the memories of the sexual violence. While each intervention has benefits, survivors should explore what intervention would work best for them. Regardless of the type of intervention, it is important for survivors to work with professionals who are supportive and nonjudgmental in their approach.

Laura Luciano

Further Reading

Burgess, A., & Holmstrom, L. (1979). *Rape crisis and recovery*. Bowie, MD: Robert J. Brady Co.

Campbell, R. (2006). Rape survivors' experiences with the legal and medical systems: Do rape victim advocates make a difference? *Violence Against Women, 12*, 31–45.

Corey, G. (2001). *Theory and practice of counseling and psychotherapy*. Belmont, CA: Wadsworth/Thomson Learning.

Herman, J. (1992). *Trauma and recovery*. New York, NY: Basic Books.

Holmstrom, L., & Burgess, A. (1985). Rape trauma syndrome and post traumatic stress disorder. In A. Burgess (Ed.), *Rape and sexual assault: A research handbook* (pp. 46–60). New York, NY: Garland.

Tjaden, P., & Thoennes, N. (2000). Full report from the prevalence, incidence and consequences of violence against women: Findings from the National Violence Against Women Survey (NCJ 183781). Washington, DC: U.S. Department of Justice, National Institute of Justice.

Warshaw, R. (1988). *I never called it rape.* New York, NY: Harper/Perennial.

Selected Websites

MaleSurvivor: Overcoming Sexual Victimization of Men and Boys. Retrieved from http://www.malesurvivor.org/

National Sexual Violence Resource Center. Retrieved from http://www.nsvrc.org/

RAINN. (Rape Abuse and Incest National Network.) Retrieved from http://rainn.org/

Sidran Institute: Traumatic Stress Education and Advocacy. Retrieved from http://sidran.org/

Video Games (Rape Fantasy Games)

Video and rape fantasy games include virtual games that permit players to engage in sexually explicit demeaning and/or violent acts, including perpetration (i.e., rape) that may or may not involve other real players.

Illusion Software is a Japanese video company that specializes in Hentai, a Japanese word that refers to sexually explicit animation of Japanese origin. Illusion Software has produced a variety of sexual fantasy games, all enabling the player to engage in a wide range of sexual behaviors with apparently willing but clearly objectified females. At least one of these games goes well beyond objectification.

The most controversial game produced by Illusion Software is *RapeLay*, where players take on the role of a sexual predator who stalks a family of three young women with the intent of raping them. Aspects of this game also include suicide, murder, and abortion. *RapeLay* was intended for sale exclusively in Japan but became accessible in other countries through Amazon. After receiving complaints, Amazon banned the sale of *RapeLay*. In 2010, women's advocacy and human rights groups called for a complete ban of these video games.

Other examples, however, can be found in *Grand Theft Auto: San Andreas*, whereby a normally inaccessible mini-game entitled *Hot Coffee* was available, allowing the player to control the main character's actions during sex. These games target males as the main players, providing them with the opportunity to sexually exploit female characters. Content analysis has found that video games, particularly ones that are sexually explicit, convey exaggerated negative gender stereotypical roles: hypermasculine, dominant, aggressive, sexually violent males and sexually provocative, passive females with unrealistically overdeveloped breasts and buttocks, dressed in tight and revealing clothing (Robinson, Callister, Clark, & Phillips, 2008; Yao, Mahood, & Linz, 2010).

MMORPGs (massively multiplayer online role-playing games) evolved from early virtual world text games called multiuser dungeons (MUDs) that were modeled after the role-playing game *Dungeons and Dragons*. MUDs evolved into graphic games and finally into MMORPGs. Currently, there are hundreds of MMORPGs that allow players the opportunity to control their character and interact with other people in a virtual world (e.g., *World of Warcraft*). *Second Life* is a newer game, whereby players are not restricted by game parameters and can essentially do almost anything they wish, creating a virtually unlimited number of possibilities, including engaging in sexual activities, such as prostitution and rape, as well as drug use, and murder. Avatars (a player's representation of him or herself as a graphic image in Internet games or other forums, usually with a fictitious name) can engage in "Dolcett play," whereby they are killed and canni-balized. Avatars can also rape other avatars. In this case, the rape is twice removed, once from a real-life offense to a virtual "offense" (as in the game *RapeLay*), and then again to a virtual representation of oneself (avatar). Age play is a phenomenon whereby players take on different ages (e.g., one is a child and one is an adult) and engage in pedophilic sexual activity. A teenage version of *SecondLife*, called *Teen SecondLife*, is available for those who do not meet the minimum age requirements for *SecondLife*. Anyone can falsify their age, however, and gain access to *SecondLife* and the virtual sex it offers. For example, a 13-year-old can state that he is 21 and gain access to *SecondLife*. Players can engage in a variety of sexual activities that unfold graphically on their computer screen. Other sites (e.g., RedLightCenter.com) allow players to engage in virtual sex for pay. Although virtual rape perpetrated in a cyberspace fantasy game may not presently qualify as a criminal offense, it certainly offends the moral sensibilities of many people. Although this new domain of fantasy crime is largely unaddressed by current statutes governing criminal pornography, there is evidence to suggest adverse psychological consequences for victims of virtual offenses like cyber rape (Brenner, 2008; Whitaker & Bushman, 2009). There is also research documenting the negative consequences of fantasy games, such as compulsive gaming, damage to real-world relationships, and poorer school performance (Hussain & Griffiths, 2009). The extent to which these negative effects translate into real-world aggres-sion toward others, however, is inconclusive, with some studies failing to find a relationship between violent video game play and an increase in real-world aggression (i.e., Williams & Skoric, 2005). Little is known, however, about the long-term consequences of such games, particularly on developing youth dealing with issues of sexual identity, intimacy, and social relationships.

Jarell Myers, Raina V. Lamade, and Kei Okada

See also Pornography, Internet; Rape, Cyber; Websites for Perpetrators

Further Reading

Brenner, S. W. (2008). Fantasy crime: The role of criminal law in virtual worlds. *Vanderbilt Journal of Entertainment and Technology Law, 11*, 1–76.

Hussain, Z., & Griffins, M. D. (2009). The attitudes, feelings, and experiences of online gamers: A qualitative analysis. *CyberPsychology & Behavior, 12*(6), 747–753.

Malamuth, N., & Huppin, M. (2007). Drawing the line on virtual child pornography: Bringing the law in line with the research evidence. *New York University Review of Law & Social Change, 31*(4), 773–827.

Robinson, T., Callister, M., Clark, B., & Phillips, J. (2008). Violence, sexuality, and gender stereotyping: A content analysis of official video game web sites. *Web Journal of Mass Communication Research, 13*, 1–17.

Whitaker, J. L., & Bushman, B. J. (2009). Protecting virtual playgrounds: Children, law, and play online: Online dangers: Keeping children and adolescents safe. *Washington & Lee Law Review, 66*, 1053–1063.

Williams, D., & Skoric, M. (2005). Internet fantasy violence: A test of aggression in an online game. *Communications Monographs, 72*(2), 217–233.

Wilson, R. F. (2009). Protecting virtual playgrounds: Children, law and play online: Sex play in virtual worlds. *Washington & Lee Law Review, 66*, 1127–1169.

Yao, M. Z., Mahood, C., & Linz, D. (2010). Sexual priming, gender stereotyping, and likelihood to sexually harass: Examining the cognitive effects of playing a sexually-explicit video game. *Sex Roles, 62*, 77–88.

Violence Against Women Act (VAWA)

The Violence Against Women Act (VAWA) is a piece of comprehensive legislation that introduced a variety of laws to improve criminal justice and community response to crimes commonly committed against women. Particularly, VAWA focuses on crimes pertaining to sexual violence, domestic violence, dating violence, and stalking. Though the act's name specifies "women," both men and women are eligible to receive services under the act. VAWA was originally passed in 1994, with two revisions that later followed in 2000 and 2005, respectively. VAWA is being considered for reauthorization in 2012.

The first version of VAWA, passed in 1994, focused on joining the efforts of the criminal justice system, social services, and nonprofit domestic and sexual violence organizations. Federal prosecution of interstate domestic violence and sexual assault crimes, interstate enforcement of protection orders, and immigration protections for domestic violence victims were included. The 1994 version of VAWA also provided a federal civil remedy for victims of gender-based crime but was later struck down on constitutional grounds by the U.S. Supreme Court. Also established was the Office on Violence Against Women (OVW), an office contained within the U.S. Department of Justice, with the purpose of providing grant support to organizations that serve victims of sexual and domestic violence.

In 2000, VAWA was reauthorized with some important changes from the original 1994 act. Legal programs for victims, expanded protections for immigrant and trafficked victims, and dating violence and stalking as types of violence were added.

In VAWA 2005, new focus areas for victims with disabilities, culturally specific communities and prevention of violent crime were created. This included an authorization to collect DNA samples from individuals arrested or otherwise detained by federal authorities, funding programs addressing sexual assault against Native American women, and an initiative to increase workplace safety and support for employees who have suffered abuse. This reauthorization of VAWA also created the first federal funding source for rape crisis centers and legislation to remedy remaining victim immigration issues.

VAWA addresses many types of issues that may arise from gender-based crimes. Below is a more detailed explanation of those provisions.

Immigration

VAWA has a large number of provisions relating to issues of violence against immigrant women. Due to the unique circumstances of several groups of immigrant women, specific provisions are in place to better regulate their immigrant status. Some special circumstances include: undocumented women who are threatened with deportation by lawfully residing abusers; trafficked women; and recipients of fiancée visas.

VAWA specifically addresses the problem of abusers threatening their victims with deportation. For example, an abuser may threaten his spouse that if she reports his violent behavior to law enforcement, he will report her undocumented status to the proper authorities. In an attempt to restructure the abuser-victim balance of power, VAWA allows the battered spouse of a resident abuser to apply for U.S. legal status without the aid of the abuser through a process called self-petitioning.

For victims of human trafficking, VAWA also provides several protections and exemptions to ease the process of obtaining legal residency in the United States. For example, a trafficking victim receives exceptions to the penalties of being in the United States unlawfully as long as the trafficking was a central reason for his or her presence. Trafficking victims are also allowed to obtain T Visas for their family members living abroad and can obtain VAWA visas for their children.

There is also no requirement to cooperate with law enforcement if the victim's physical or psychological trauma impedes his or her ability to do so.

Many fiancée visas are obtained by those using international marriage brokers (IMBs). IMBs are agencies hired by men with lawful permanent residency for the purpose of matching them with foreign women. VAWA 2000 placed new regulations on IMBs in order to reduce the amount of violence on this group of immigrant women. VAWA 2005 furthered these regulations by including in its language the International Marriage Broker Regulation Act (IMBRA). IMBRA requires that IMBs must now run background checks on clients, including a check with the national sex offender registry, before giving them the addresses of women they would like to contact. IMBs are also required to have clients fill out personal-history questionnaires. The questionnaire and the background check results must be given to the woman and translated into her native language, if necessary. IMBs are not allowed to give clients any information regarding minors. IMBRA also placed a lifetime limit of two fiancée visas.

VAWA also addresses issues that arise for immigrant victims when cases are within the purview of the Department of Homeland Security (DHS). VAWA prohibits disclosure to third parties of any information relating to an immigrant victim's application for relief. Also, information from an abuser cannot be the sole reason to arrest or deport an immigrant victim. DHS must be in full compliance with these provisions. Finally, VAWA provides opportunities for child abuse victims to obtain visas up until the age of 25 as long as the abuse was one of the reasons for the filing delay.

Housing

A high rate of homelessness among abused women led to a variety of housing provisions in VAWA. Many abused women become homeless due to evictions following acts of violence in the home. To combat this, there are several VAWA provisions to address discrimination in public housing. For instance, public housing authorities (PHAs) are not able to deny housing access to victims of domestic violence, dating violence, or stalking. If an abuser commits a criminal activity, the victim may not be evicted as long as the abuser's crime was connected to the abuse. PHAs may split a lease to maintain the victim's tenancy while evicting the abuser. PHAs must give notice to tenants of these VAWA requirements.

Along with discrimination issues, other housing protections have increased with each version of VAWA. Currently, eligible victims may receive transitional housing assistance grants that pay for rent, relocation expenses, and supportive services for up to 24 months. VAWA also gives grants to organizations for services to women. These include grants for providing transitional housing and self-sufficiency training to victims of domestic violence as well as training PHAs to not discriminate against victims and appropriately respond to reports of sexual assault and domestic violence.

Tribal Programs

In order to address sexual assault committed against Native American women, VAWA created two programs that would offer funding and services for women living on reservations. VAWA 2005 created the Tribal Domestic Violence and Sexual Assault Coalitions Grant Program (Tribal Coalitions Program) to increase the number of survivors, advocates, and Indian women's organizations or coalitions. This program gives grants to applicants creating programs with the intent to end violence against American Indian and Alaskan Native women.

The Grants to Indian Tribal Governments Program works to better the response to crimes against Indian women. This program also increases, and develops new forms of, education and prevention for Indian women who are victims of domestic and/or sexual violence. Examples include providing transitional housing and giving legal advice and/or representation to victims of violence.

Criticisms of VAWA

The different reauthorizations of VAWA have faced criticisms related to its constitutionality and fairness. The American Civil Liberties Union (ACLU) has argued that the provision making DNA tests mandatory for accused abusers in federal custody is unconstitutional. Specifically, their argument is that a required DNA exam for those in custody is a violation of the Fourth Amendment to the U.S. Constitution, which protects against unreasonable search and seizure. The ACLU is supportive of many other VAWA provisions.

The organization R.A.D.A.R. (Respecting Accuracy in Domestic Abuse Reporting) has argued that VAWA does not adequately address female-on-male domestic violence and that its provisions block gender neutrality in domestic violence reporting.

In 2000, a portion of VAWA was determined to be unconstitutional by the U.S. Supreme Court in the case *U.S. v. Morrison*. In *Morrison*, the Supreme Court decided that Congress had exceeded its power under the U.S. Commerce Clause by providing a federal civil remedy for victims of gender-based crime. No other portions of VAWA were affected by this ruling.

Ebony Tucker

See also Individuals with Disabilities; Intimate Partner Violence; Native Americans; Refugee Women in the United States; Stalking; Trafficking in Persons

Further Reading

Immigrant victims of domestic abuse (n.d.). National Coalition against Domestic Violence. Retrieved from http://www.hope-eci.org/_documents/immigrantvictims.pdf

Meyer-Emerick, N. (2001). *The Violence Against Women Act of 1994: An analysis of intent and perception*. Santa Barbara, CA: Praeger.

Meloy, M. L. (2010). *The victimization of women: Law, policies, and politics*. New York: Oxford University Press.

The Safeguards in the Violence Against Women Act (VAWA) (2011). National Task Force to End Sexual and Domestic Violence Against Women. Retrieved from http://www.ncdsv.org/images/NatlTFEndSDVAW_Safeguards%20in%20VAWA_2011.pdf

Shriver, S. (2006). *A look at VAWA housing provisions*. National Center on Poverty Law, 9(12). Retrieved from http://www.ncdsv.org/images/ALookgatVAWAHousing Provisions.pdf

Violence Against Women Act: 10 years of progress and moving forward (2006). National Task Force to End Sexual and Domestic Violence Against Women. Retrieved from http://www.ncdsv.org/images/VAWA10YearsProgress.pdf

Selected Websites

National Center on Domestic and Sexual Violence. Retrieved from http://www.ncdsv.org/

Office on Violence Against Women. U.S. Department of Justice. Retrieved from http://www.ovw.usdoj.gov/

Violence Against Women Act: Issues and more. Legal Momentum. Retrieved from http://www.legalmomentum.org/our-work/vaw/violence-against-women-act-issues.html

Voyeurism

Sexual voyeurism is the repeated act of watching others who do not know they are being watched and who are naked, undressing, or engaging in sexual intercourse. Such viewing is for the purpose of sexual arousal. An individual who practices sexual voyeurism is referred to as a voyeur, and can also be referred to as a peeping tom. Voyeurism has also been named spying and "the male gaze." It is believed that almost all voyeurs are men gazing at women.

The American Psychiatric Association (APA) defines "voyeurism" as observing an unsuspecting individual (usually a stranger) who is naked, or in the process of dressing, undressing, or engaging in sexual activity, for the purpose of sexual arousal. The APA notes that sometimes voyeurs fantasize that they are with the person they are watching, that these behaviors usually begin before the age of 15, and that voyeurism is a chronic disorder. Voyeurism is classified as a sexual and gender identity disorder.

The stereotypical sexual voyeur is a man who hides in the bushes and watches women inside of a neighboring house. However, with technological advances, voyeurism is accomplished through secret photography, hidden cameras, peep holes, and two-way mirrors. In the United States, voyeurism is illegal as per state and federal regulations. Acts of sexual voyeurism are prosecuted under the category of invasion of privacy, and in some states may require the voyeur (perpetrator) to register on the sex offender registry.

Sexual voyeurism is a form of paraphilia, which is a preference for or obsession with unusual sexual practices. Paraphilia is classified as intense, recurring sexual fantasies, urges, or behaviors that involve nonhuman objects, children or nonconsenting adults, suffering, or humiliation (to self or to others).

Sexual voyeurism is believed to be on the obsessive-compulsive spectrum because of the nature of the behaviors, which are often referred to as immoral, sadistic, and a sign of mental imbalance or deviance. Treatment of voyeurs is often difficult because as in any paraphilia, there is a resistance from the individual.

Using the Freudian theory, voyeurism appears to be rooted in Oedipal development, in particular the castration crisis. The Freudian Oedipus complex is the repressed, unconscious thoughts of young boys to be with their mother and desires to kill their father. Freud explained that each individual works through such a complex as part of healthy development and that when this does not occur paraphilia may develop. In the case of sexual voyeurism, compulsively looking at the sex organs and activities of others takes the place of personal sexual experiences, and becomes a means of deflecting awareness of the emptiness in the self.

Although Freud was the first to address parophilias like voyeurism in the early 1900s, voyeurism can be traced to the erotic literature of the Enlightenment period, which lasted from the late 1600s until the early 1800s. Voyeurism was regarded in literature not as a perversion or deviation, but as a way to expose the inexperienced to sexuality and eroticism. Directly following this time period were the Modern and Romantic eras in which two aspects of voyeurism, curiosity and imagination, were freed from religious limitations and were often expressed in literature and visual art. During this time period women were often objectified, and in many cases gazed at by men in works of art.

Sexual voyeurism should not be confused with scopophilia, which is the basic pleasure of watching others, i.e., people watching. Although many popular television shows and films do showcase sexual voyeurism (e.g. *American Pie*, *Rear Window*, *Disturbia*), for male viewing pleasure, it is much more common for shows to showcase scopophilia through reality TV (e.g., *Survivor*, *The Real World*, *Big Brother*). One can determine if a movie or TV show is voyeuristic or scopophilistic by determining if the gaze is sadistic or assaultive, or if it is loving, passionate, or simply curious.

In conclusion, sexual voyeurism a form of paraphilia and is the act of watching unsuspecting others as a source of sexual gratification. It is currently illegal, but is commonly expressed in current and historical visual arts, language, and film.

Jennifer A. Martinez

See also Megan's Law; Sex Offender Registries

Further Reading

American Psychiatric Association. (2000). *Diagnostic and statistical manual of mental disorders* (4th ed., text rev.). Washington, DC: American Psychiatric Publishing.

Kilman, P. R., Sabalis, R. F., Gearing, M. I., Bukstel, L. H., & Scovern, A. W. (1982). The treatment of sexual paraphilias: A review of the outcome research. *The Journal of Sex Research, 18*(3), 193–252.

Metzi, J. M. (2004). From scopophilia to survivor, a brief history of voyeurism. *Textual Practice, 18*(3), 415–434.

Steigerwald, J. (2008). Curious imagination or the rise of voyeurism: Mirabeau's Le Rideau levé. *MLN, 123*(4), 924–946.

Tudor, R. J. (2010). Romantic voyeurism and the modern idea of the savage. *Texas Review, 31*(1/2), 94–113.

W

War, Tactic of

There is no one single definition of violence accepted and used worldwide, as norms, values, customs, and laws that shape perceptions about violence vary from culture to culture. The concept of violence has been defined in different ways depending on the purpose of the definition. For the criminal justice system, the definition would have a different focus from that of social services and human rights perspectives. For the public health system, violence is defined in a way that captures criminals' actions as well as the subjective experiences of the victims. According to the World Health Organization (WHO, 2002), violence is:

> The intentional use of physical force or power, threatened or actual, against oneself, another person, or against a group or community, that either results in or has a high likelihood of resulting in injury, death, psychological harm, maldevelopment or deprivation.

Drawing from this definition, sexual violence involves diverse acts that use sex to cause harm, place victims in a position to be harmed by sex, or negatively affect a person's sexual integrity. In addition to rape, examples of such acts range from sexual harassment, child sexual abuse, sexual trafficking, child marriage, and female genital mutilation, to coercion of young men into sex by older women. The physical and/or mental scars of sexual violence may linger for years, and mortality may be the result of HIV infection, suicide, or murder.

Throughout centuries, sex has been used to subdue those who are deemed inferior, less powerful, oppressed, or vulnerable. For example, conquistadores and colonizers used sexual violence against native women; landlords against female peasants; slave owners against female slaves; prison guards or powerful prisoners against weak prisoners; men against women, adolescents, and children; priests against children; bosses against employees; teachers against students; pimps against sexual workers; warriors against victims; and so forth. Sexual violence may occur both as an act of interpersonal violence (at the individual level) as well as collective violence in conflict situations. It may be inflicted within the domestic realm by relatives or acquaintances, as much as by strangers who may act alone or in groups. Sexual violence may be a random or a systematic act. Despite all the forms and contexts in which this kind of violence manifests itself, it has traditionally been characterized by the silence of its victims and impunity of the crime.

There are several theories that explain violent sexual behavior. Some theories argue that aggressive behavior is learned in society and through one's upbringing. Other theories focus on childhood or other trauma that cause someone to inflict violence through sex. Cultural expectations of how men and women should behave are the reasons stated by some theorists about men's use of sexual violence against women. Deviant behavior or psychiatric explanations have also been used to understand sexual violence, as well as theories of group cohesion among men. Sexual violence is more prevalent in societies that have rigid gender roles, beliefs of male's sexual entitlement, high impunity of sexual crimes, and a generalized culture of violence (WHO, 2002). However, no one theory seems to explain the use of sexual violence as a weapon of war.

The concept of sexual violence as a weapon of war has been accepted by different entities, organizations, and individuals interested in the analysis of war conflict and all its implications. From the United Nations and the World Health Organization, to activists, nongovernmental organizations, academics, and the media, sexual violence as a weapon of war is understood as the use of forced sex, in all its manifestations, during wartime, including internal conflict situations. This means that war may occur within a country, as much as between countries. Some of the manifestations of sexual violence during war include sexual slavery, forced prostitution, forced pornography, and systematic rape. The reason why sexual violence is effective as a weapon during wartime is due to the cultural perception that women's sexuality is subject to public ownership. Therefore an attack against one woman becomes an attack against an entire community or ethnic group. Furthermore, the difficulty of proving rape in many cases facilitates the use of this crime to terrorize during war time.

Sexual violence is considered a war crime under international law, and when used systematically, it is a crime against humanity, second to genocide. Although the perpetrators and victims could be women, children, and men, sexual violence as a weapon of war is committed mainly by men against adult women and the girl child. Thus the acknowledgment that this crime occurs during violent conflict is also a demonstration of the many forms in which power, usually male power, may be exercised over other humans, as both individual and political forms of aggression. However, sexual violence against men during conflict situations is not uncommon, just silent. This was the case of men of different ethnic backgrounds throughout the Balkan war who were "beaten across the genitals, forced to be naked, raped, and castrated" (Petchesky, 2005, p. 311). The media reported very little about this. On the contrary, when the perpetrator was a woman soldier and the victims were male prisoners at Abu Ghraib prison in Iraq, much media attention was given to the role the woman soldier played (Petchesky, 2005).

Systematic sexual violence, particularly systematic rape of women, has been documented in international conflicts such as in Korea during World War II and during Bangladesh's independence war. However, systematic rape has become more prevalent in internal violent conflicts such as those in India (Kashmir), Rwanda, Uganda, Liberia, Algeria, Indonesia, the former Yugoslavia, and Bosnia and Herzegovina, where between 10,000 and 60,000 women were raped by soldiers (WHO, 2002). Widespread rape of women has also been established in Myanmar and Somalia (Shanks & Schull, 2000). More recently, systematic sexual violence has been documented in Colombia, where a 50-year internal conflict between the military, paramilitary, and guerrilla fighters has displaced more than four million people. Most of the internally displaced are women and children who flee their rural territories and seek refuge mainly in urban centers of Colombia. Two out of 10 women displaced abandon their home due to sexual violence (Oxfam International, 2009).

Systematic sexual violence is used for several purposes: to humiliate, to take revenge, to punish, to intimidate, to terrorize, to control, to impart a "lesson," among other reasons. The perpetrators purposefully inflict harm on women, not just to victimize them, but to show dominance and control upon the men related to the women. Thus women are used as a means to a greater end: the moral defeat of enemy men to facilitate the achievement of a military objective. An example of a military objective used in Rwanda was "ethnic cleansing" through systematic rape. From the enemy's point of view, this ensured a new "clean" generation of Rwandans. In reality, it created unwanted children labeled as "children of bad memories;" other children were abandoned, and others murdered by their mothers as newborns, which is called infanticide (Shanks & Schull, 2000).

In the Colombian conflict, impunity, fear of retaliation, lack of protective measures, and lack of services to women and girls who are victims have acted as deterrents to report sexual crimes. This underreporting makes it impossible to have an accurate count of the magnitude of this problem or establish the degree of responsibility of each one of the armed actors. In the meantime, many internally displaced women and girls who are victims of systematic sexual violence endure unwanted pregnancies that may result in maternal morbidity and even maternal mortality. Other women interrupt their pregnancies, and many other acquire sexually transmitted infections (Oxfam International, 2009).

According to Doctors without Borders (DWB), there are some strategies to reduce barriers to reporting sexual crimes in conflict situations. They include: (1) ensure a sufficient number of female health care workers, ideally 50 percent; (2) allow sufficient time to establish rapport; (3) train health care workers in treatment protocols; and (4) provide a safe and confidential environment for disclosure. DWB also offers protocols to manage victims of sexual violence in complex emergencies (see DWB website).

Thanks to many women's organizations around the world, progressive legislation within countries, and the role of international entities such as the International Criminal Court, public awareness will continue to be raised about the use of sexual violence as a weapon of war. This in turn will increase the demand for accountability, justice, and appropriate services for victims.

Mónica M. Alzate

See also Comfort Women; Military Sexual Trauma; Prostitution; Theories, Sociocultural

Further Reading

Alakija, P. (2000). Ravages of war. *Canadian Medical Association Journal, 163*(9), 1148–1149.

Kirby, P. (In press). How is rape a weapon of war?: Feminist international relations, modes of critical explanations, and the study of wartime sexual violence. *European Journal of International Relations.*

Oxfam International. (2009). Sexual violence in Colombia: Instrument of war. *Oxfam Briefing Paper.*

Pankhurst, D. (2010). Sexual violence in war. In Laura J. Shepherd (Ed). *Gender matters in global politics: A feminist introduction to international relations* (pp. 148–160). New York, NY: Routledge.

Petchesky, R. (2008). Editorial. Conflict and crisis settings: Promoting sexual and reproductive rights. *Reproductive Health Matters, 16*, 31, 4–9.

Petchesky, R. (2005). *Rights of the body and perversions of war: Sexual rights and wrongs ten years past Beijing.* Unpublished manuscript. UNESCO.

Shanks, L., & Schull, M. J. (2000). Rape in war: The humanitarian response. *Canadian Medical Association Journal, 163*(9), 1152–1156.

World Health Organization. (2002). *World report on violence and health.* Geneva, Switzerland: Author.

Selected Websites

Amnesty International. Retrieved from http://www.amnesty.org

Comisión Colombiana de Juristas. Retrieved from http://www.coljuristas.org

Doctors without Borders. Retrieved from http://www.doctorswithoutborders.org

Human Rights Watch. Retrieved from http://www.hrw.org

International Criminal Court. Retrieved from http://www.icc-cpi.int/Menus/ICC/About+the+Court/

Oxfam International. Retrieved from http://www.oxfam.org

UN Women. Retrieved from http://www.unwomen.org/

Women's Refugee Commission. Retrieved from http://womensrefugeecommission.org/

World Health Organization. Retrieved from http://www.who.org

Websites for Perpetrators

The Internet is used in various ways to perpetrate actual criminal sexual offenses, as well as engage in virtual sexual offenses (see **Rape, Cyber**). Perpetrators of sexual violence typically take advantage of victim vulnerability or isolation to exploit or harm a victim by committing a battery (hands-on) offense. It is also possible, however, for harm to occur when vulnerable individuals, typically children and adult victims of sexual abuse, are exposed to websites containing sexually violent content. Such websites include those that (1) support or promote sexual victimization, abuse, or trafficking and/or (2) are used to commit virtual sexual offenses or aid in connecting perpetrators to potential victims.

The Internet provides a variety of ways for users with criminal intent to connect with likeminded individuals to exchange "how to" tips about best sources (i.e., websites, chat rooms) for finding and grooming victims, eluding apprehension, garnering support and validation, and meeting others with similar interests. Websites that specifically support sexual victimization include pro-rape message boards and pages, such as the now defunct *pro-rape* Facebook page, created by college students at an Australian university, and the *North American Man/Boy Love Association* (*NAMBL*), which promotes sexual activity with boys.

Sexual offenses may be enacted online (e.g., see **Pornography, Internet**), allowing users to engage in the perpetration of virtual sex offenses. Cases where deviant sexual fantasies are discussed and/or enacted online and subsequently enacted in the real world with partners from the Internet have occasionally resulted in criminal outcomes. Dating and social networking sites (e.g., MySpace, Facebook) have the potential to lead to cybercrimes (e.g., cyberstalking) and real crimes (sexual assault). Under the terms of agreement, most social networking sites release themselves from responsibility for content, leaving parents and users to monitor usage. Stalkers and predators use social networking websites to gather information about potential victims, and search for victims who live nearby. Sites specializing in "mail-order brides" or "Internet brides" post profiles of women from around the world, many of whom are part of a sex-trafficking industry that lures vulnerable women from impoverished environments. These sites purport to provide young brides, some in the 15- to 17-year-old range. These sites may charge an extra fee for a virgin.

Do-it-yourself sex videos and amateur websites such as YouPorn.com and RedTube.com provide a fertile environment for anyone to display sexual content, providing another avenue for potential perpetration. Actual or doctored sexual images of individuals, for example, can be posted without consent or used to harass or extort victims. Prank films displayed for fun, originally called "happy slapping," now include rape and sexual assault videos. Pornographic websites broker interactive live sex shows, wherein a user requests that sexual acts be performed in real time over webcams. Although these requests are often demeaning, many who rely on this service for income are unlikely to deny requests for fear of losing clients.

Of great concern is the use of the Internet to connect perpetrators to potential child victims for online and hands-on offenses. Predators seek children and adolescents who appear emotionally needy, isolated, and lonely, in a word—vulnerable. The disbanded *Wonderland Club* consisted of hundreds of members worldwide that used websites to exchange, discuss, and transmit images of such children, including child pornography and live child-sex shows. Web forums for pedophiles support and justify pedophilia, providing an "advocacy" service, promoting pedophilia, and providing advice about engaging and carrying out pedophilic activities without being detected by the authorities. For individuals with antisocial tendencies, or those lacking adequate impulse control or self-regulation, these websites may increase the risk of committing a sexual offense.

Additionally, two public health concerns exist. First, although there is some research to suggest that youth who are sexually harassed or receive unwanted sexual solicitations suffer negative health consequences, little is known about the long-term consequences of sexually explicit content, particularly violent content, on developing youth (Wilson, 2009). Second, websites promoting sexual activity seldom, if ever, promote or display safe sex practices. This potentially puts experimenting youth at risk for contracting sexually transmitted diseases. Perhaps the most critical concern, however, is the extent to which these websites increase the likelihood that rape-prone users will commit a battery sexual offense on a real victim.

Raina V. Lamade and Kei Okada

See also Pornography, Internet; Rape, Cyber; Video Games (Rape Fantasy Games)

Further Reading

Fisher, W. A., & Barak, A. (2000). Online sex shops: Phenomenological, psychological, and ideological perspectives on internet sexuality. *CyberPsychology & Behavior, 3*(4), 575–589.

Jackson, S. H. (2002). To honor and obey: Trafficking in "mail-order brides". *The George Washington Law Review, 70,* 475–565.

Holt, T. J., Blevins, K. R., & Burkert, N. (2010). Considering the pedophile subculture online. *Sexual abuse: A journal of research and treatment, 22*(1), 3–24.

McGrath, M. G., & Casey, E. (2002). Forensic psychiatry and the Internet: Practical perspectives on sexual predators and obsessional harassers in cyberspace. *Journal of the American Academy of Psychiatric Law, 30*(1), 81–94.

Wilson, R. F. (2009). Protecting virtual playgrounds: Children, law and play online: Sex play in virtual worlds. *Washington & Lee Law Review, 66,* 1127–1169.

Websites for Victims

Websites for victims include those that provide resources, information, support, and referrals to health care and human service providers for victims of virtual and hands-on sexual offenses. Also related are websites aimed at preventing sexual violence—particularly Internet sexual violence. The number of websites for victims is overwhelming.

Sites Promoting Healthy Sexual Behavior

Websites dedicated to facilitating the development of healthy sexual behavior and preventing sexual violence target adolescents and young adults. They often contain educational information and resources about sexuality, safe sex practices, protection from sexually transmitted diseases, as well as information about the development of healthy sexuality and relationships, including the prevention of sexual perpetration. Examples of such websites include: Sexuality Information and Education Council of the U.S. (http://www.siecus.org/), the Coalition for Positive Sexuality (http://www.positive.org/Home/index.html), Gay Teen Resources (http://www.gayteenresources.org), and Advocates for Youth (http://www.advocatesforyouth.org).

Sites for Protection of Children and Young People

The Federal Bureau of Investigation, Crimes against Children (http://www.fbi.gov/about-us/investigate/vc_majorthefts/cac) has a web page dedicated to providing parents, guardians, and teachers with information and resources to prevent, protect from, and eliminate child Internet sexual victimization. Additionally, documents such as "A Parent's Guide to Internet Safety" (http://www.fbi.gov/stats-services/publications/parent-guide/parentsguide.pdf) and "Social Networking sites: Online Friendships Can Mean Offline Peril" (http://www.fbi.gov/news/stories/2006/april/social_networking040306) can be downloaded through the FBI website. Also included are links to the sex offender registry websites for each state and U.S. territory (http://www.fbi.gov/scams-safety/registry), and to the National Center for Missing and Exploited Children (http://www.missingkids.com), which contains a plethora of research and resources. On the commercial end of prevention, websites that sell filter products, such as Net Nanny (http://www.netnanny.com/), iProtectYou (http://www.softforyou.com/ip-index.html), and InternetSafety.com, formerly known as Safe Eyes (http://www.internetsafety.com/index.php), are designed to block websites containing pornographic and potentially victimizing materials, and contain educational information about perpetrators of sexual violence. Watch groups run by volunteers, such as Perverted Justice (http://www.perverted-justice.com/), are dedicated to exposing adult predators searching for children in chat rooms.

General Sites for Information on Sexual Violence and Victimization

General websites also exist on the national level that have dedicated sections for sexual and cyber-victimization to provide educational and legal information as well as links to resources to assist victims and help reduce sexual victimization. These include the U.S. government's National Criminal Justice Reference Service/Justice Information Center (http://www.ncjrs.gov), the National Organization for Victim Assistance (http://www.try-nova.org/), the National Center for Victims of Crime (http://www.ncvc.org), and the U.S. government Office for Victims of Crime (http://www.ojp.usdoj.gov/ovc/). The National Criminal Justice Reference Service/Justice Information Center, for example, contains Internet safety sections entitled "Internet Safety for children" and "Cyberbullying and Cyberstalking" where individuals can download publications (e.g., Bureau of Justice statistics, congressional testimonies) as well as find links to similar resources and organizations. Websites specifically dedicated to assisting victims of sexual offenses (e.g., providing counseling center locations, education) include the National Sexual Violence Resource Center (http://www.nsvrc.org/), the National Center on Domestic and Sexual Violence (http://www.ncdsv.org/), and the sexual violence prevention web page on the Centers for Disease Control and Prevention website (http://www.cdc.gov/ViolencePrevention/sexualviolence/index.html). RAINN, an acronym for Rape, Abuse & Incest National Network (http://www.rainn.org/), provides a list of rape crisis centers in all U.S. states and many foreign countries with their corresponding information (e.g., address, phone, website). An online hotline allows victims of sexual violence to securely, anonymously, and instantly communicate with trained professionals. In addition to providing educational resources (e.g., legal, supportive), information for those who would like to volunteer for projects preventing sexual violence is also available.

Government and State-Related Sites

Many states have websites for sexual victimization, as well as federal government websites that provide state-level information. Examples of federal websites include the U.S. Department of Justice's Office on Violence Against Women website (http://www.ovw.usdoj.gov/) and its page on state programs (http://www.ovw.usdoj.gov/statedomestic.htm). Examples of state websites include the New Jersey Coalition against Sexual Assault (http://www.njcasa.org/), the New York State Coalition against Sexual Assault (http://nyscasa.org/), the Sexual Violence Center in Minnesota (http://www.sexualviolencecenter.org/), and the California Coalition against Sexual Assault (CALCASA; http://calcasa.org/).

College and University Sites

Besides national and state level agencies, virtually all college and university campuses have information on their websites about sexual victimization and acquaintance (date) rape, including policies and resources for victims (e.g., the University of Chicago's page on sexual violence at http://sexualviolence .uchicago.edu/assault.shtml). Information may include where to obtain help (e.g., on and off campus, such as the local police and emergency room), education about sexual assault (e.g., unwanted physical contact of a sexual nature) and rape (unwanted sexual penetration), downloadable policy and resource documents, legal options, and related topics such as stalking. Additionally the U.S. Department of Justice has posted a bulletin about campus sexual assault titled "Sexual Assault on Campus: What Colleges and Universities Are Doing about It" (http://www.ncjrs.gov/pdffiles1/nij/205521.pdf).

Recovery Sites

Websites to assist victims in recovering from sexual victimization include newsgroups (i.e., alt.abuse.recovery, hosted by Google groups), support groups, such as Survivors of Incest Anonymous (http://www.siawso.org/), After Silence (http://www.aftersilence.org/), and MaleSurvivor (http://www.malesurvivor.org/ default.html). Adult Survivors of Child Abuse (http://www.ascasupport.org/) is an international support group. Websites specifically dedicated to various forms of cyber-victimization (sexual violence, cyberstalking, etc.) include Wiredsafety (http://www.wiredsaftey.org), which provides links to assistance.

Victims should be warned, however, that they run the risk of being exposed to predators who frequent websites designed for victims, especially those that have message boards or some means where members can communicate with each other. Sexual perpetrators pose as victims and search for potential future victims. Once potential victims are identified, predators begin the grooming process. Since this risk is well understood, victims should receive some preliminary preventive education before spending any significant amount of time on these websites.

Raina V. Lamade

See also Child Abuse Hotlines; Disclosure, Seeking Help; Help Seeking, Formal and Informal; Victims, Male

Y

Yoga Therapy

There are several traditional, cognitive behavioral types of anxiety management therapies in use; however, more practitioners and survivors are discovering that the ancient practice of yoga has the ability to induce a calming of the neurophysiology of stress and empower survivors to get back in touch with their bodies in a positive way. Yoga has become such a viable alternative therapy that it has been endorsed not only by the Veterans Administration for PTSD but also by the United Nations, which, in January 2011, released a letter supporting the innovative Project Air and yoga as a means of trauma relief and trauma prevention, as it is being used to heal the thousands of women and children who suffered rape and sexual violence during the genocide in Rwanda. This official support recognized that when one suffers a sexual assault or prolonged sexual abuse, the survivor's body and mind are subjected to a neurophysiological response that overwhelms the person's normal coping skills. The human body is hardwired to respond to danger and attack by fighting or fleeing, but during a sexual assault, that natural survival response is often suppressed because to flee or fight could mean injury or death. As a result many survivors talk about "freezing" or "checking out"—both normal survival reactions to extreme danger. Problems arise, however, after the sexual violence is over because the survivor's body and mind remain in a hyper state of alertness (fight) or numbing (flight). Flashback can be triggered by reminders of the abuse that thrust the survivor right back in his or her memory and body to the sights, sounds, and sensations present at the time of the abuse. Indeed, some scholars describe sexual trauma as "hijacking the body."

Further, while a normal reaction is to move away from the trigger of anxiety, because a sexual assault is so personal the survivor's *own body* can serve as a trigger. As a result, most sexual violence survivors report disliking their bodies intensely. Hence, one of the long-term realities of assault and abuse is disassociation—where the survivor experiences a "splitting off" or "checking out" from her or his body and from the present. The experience of practicing yoga, with its gentle unity of the participant's mind, breathing, and body, slowly brings the fragments of the survivor's psyche back together and assists it in withstanding the destructive forces of flashbacks. Since yoga's emphasis is on letting the past and future remain in their respective places and focuses only on the present moment, survivors learn to be grounded and rediscover the innate strengths and coping skills that contributed to their survival. Learning yoga's calming techniques such as mindfulness, breathing, meditation, and physical poses, which require focus, allows the body to send impulses to the brain that no one is in danger anymore.

Yoga programs targeting child and adolescent survivors of sexual abuse, such as the Healing Childhood Sexual Abuse with Yoga Program (HCSAY), founded by Mark Lilly in Portland, Oregon, in conjunction with the Child Services Family Sexual Abuse Treatment team, focus on building safety, strength, and assertiveness in young survivors. Since, as they move through the curriculum, the survivors grow in developing healthy boundaries and integrating the focus and coping skills found in yoga's best practices, the program—and those like it—also serve as a prevention tool, reducing the survivor's chances of being revictimized.

Empirical studies are just emerging but have affirmed yoga's value in reducing the symptoms of PTSD in trauma survivors, and specifically sexual trauma survivors. In one study, researchers found that a group of female patients who completed eight hatha yoga classes showed significant improvement in symptoms—including lessening the frequency of intrusive thoughts and the severity of anxiety—than a similar group that had undergone eight sessions of regular talk therapy. The study also reported that yoga can improve heart-rate variability, which is a strong indicator of a person's ability to calm oneself (Yehuda, 2006).

Denise Lang-Grant

See also Depression and Anxiety; PTSD and Stress; Recovery; Trauma Therapy

Further Reading

Abadula, Lensay (2010). Yoga helps Rwandan victims of sexual trauma. Spirit Voyage. Retrieved July 2, 2011, from http://www.spiritvoyage.com/blog/index.php/yoga-helps-rwandan-victims-of-sexual-trauma.

Emerson, David, & Hopper, Elizabeth (2011). *Overcoming trauma through yoga: Reclaiming your body.* Berkeley, CA: North Atlantic Books.

Forbes, Bo (2011). *Yoga for emotional balance: Simple practices to help relieve anxiety and depression.* Boston, MA: Shambhala.

Haines, Staci (2007). *Healing sex: A mind-body approach to healing sexual trauma.* Berkeley, CA: Cleis Press.

Miller, Richard (2007). *Integrative restoration: The ancient practice of yoga nidra for easing stress, healing trauma and awakening to your timeless presence* (Audio Book on CD). Sebastopal, CA: Anahata Press.

Wills, D. K. Healing life's traumas. *The Yoga Journal.* Retrieved from http://yogajournal.com/health/2532?print=1

Yehuda, Rachel (2006). *Psychobiology of post-traumatic stress disorder: A decade of progress.* New York, NY: New York Academy of Sciences.

Selected Websites

Project Air. Retrieved from http://www.project-air.org

Street Yoga. Retrieved from http://www.streetyoga.org

The Trauma Center at Justice Resource Institute (click on Training and Education). Retrieved from http://traumacenter.org.

Jim Hopper, PhD, Harvard Medical School psychologist and therapist, lists several articles on his opening page regarding trauma and mindfulness. Retrieved from http://www.jimhopper.com

Recommended Resources

Books

Bevacqua, M. (2000). *Rape on the public agenda: Feminism and the politics of sexual assault*. Boston, MA: Northeastern University Press.

Brownmiller, S. (19795). *Against our will: Men, women and rape*. New York, NY: Bantam Books.

Buchwald, E., Fletcher, P., & Roth, M. (1993). *Transforming a rape culture*. Minneapolis, MN: Milkweed Editions.

Burgess, A. W. (1985). *Rape and sexual assault: A research handbook*. New York, NY: Garland.

Courtois, C. A. (1988). *Healing the incest wound: Adult survivors in therapy*. New York, NY: Norton.

Draucker, C. B. (2000). *Counseling survivors of childhood sexual abuse*. Thousand Oaks, CA: Sage.

Estrich, S. (1987). *Real rape*. Cambridge, MA: Harvard University Press.

Finkelhor, D. (1986). *Sourcebook on child sexual abuse*. Thousand Oaks, CA: Sage.

Herman, J. (1997). *Trauma and recovery*. New York, NY: Basic Books.

Myers, J. E. B., Berliner, L., Briere, J., Hendrix, C. T., Jenny, C., & Reid, T. A. (2002). *The APSAC handbook on child mistreatment* (2nd ed.). Thousand Oaks, CA: Sage.

O'Toole, L. L., & Schiffman, J. R. (1997). *Gender violence: Interdisciplinary perspectives*. New York, NY: New York University Press.

Parrot, A., & Bechhofer, L. (1991). *Acquaintance rape: The hidden crime*. New York, NY: Wiley.

Renzetti, C. M., Edleson, J. L., & Bergen, R. K. (2001). *Sourcebook on violence against women*. Thousand Oaks, CA: Sage.

Russell, D. E. H., & Bolen, R. M. (2000). *The epidemic of rape and child sexual abuse in the United States*. Thousand Oaks, CA: Sage.

Sanday, P. R. (2007). *Fraternity gang rape* (2nd ed.). New York, NY: New York University Press.

Ullman, S. E. (2010). *Talking about sexual assault: Society's response to survivors*. Washington, DC: American Psychological Association.

Warshaw, R. (1988). *I never called it rape.* New York, NY: HarperCollins.

Weisz, A. N., & Black, B. M. (2009). *Programs to reduce teen dating violence and sexual assault: Perspectives on what works.* New York, NY: Columbia University Press.

Articles

Sexual Assault

Ahrens, C. E. (2006). Being silenced: The impact of negative social reactions on the disclosure of rape. *American Journal of Community Psychology, 38,* 263–274.

Amar, A. F. (2004). Prevalence estimates of violence in the dating experiences of college women. *Journal of National Black Nurses Association, 15*(2), 23–31.

Banyard, V. L., Moynihan, M. M., Walsh, W. A., Cohn, E. S., & Ward, S. (2010). Friends of survivors: The community impact of unwanted sexual experiences. *Journal of Interpersonal Violence, 25,* 242–256.

Banyard, V. L., Eckstein, R. P., & Moynihan, M. M. (2010). Sexual violence prevention: The role of stages of change. *Journal of Interpersonal Violence, 25*(1), 111–135.

Burt, M. (1980). Cultural myths and supports for rape. *Journal of Personality and Social Psychology, 38*(2), 217–230.

Campbell, R. (2008). The psychological impact of rape victims' experiences with the legal, medical, and mental health systems. *American Psychologist, 63*(8), 702–717.

Campbell, R., Dworkin, E., & Cabral, G. (2009). An ecological model of the impact of sexual assault on women's mental health. *Trauma, Violence, & Abuse, 10*(3), 225–246.

Campbell, R., Sefl, T., & Ahrens, C. E. (2004). The impact of rape on women's sexual health risk behaviors. *Health Psychology, 23*(1), 67–74.

Campbell, R., Sefl, T., Barnes, H. E., Ahrens, C., Wasco, S. M., & Zaragoza-Diesfeld, Y. (1999). Community services for rape survivors: Enhancing psychological well-being or increasing trauma? *Journal of Consulting and Clinical Psychology, 67*(6), 847–858.

Casey, E. A., & Lindhorst, T. P. (2009). Toward a multi-level, ecological approach to the primary prevention of sexual assault: Prevention on peer and community contexts. *Trauma, Violence, & Abuse, 10*(2), 91–114.

Clay-Warner, J., & Burt, C. H. (2005). Rape reporting after reforms: Have times really changed? *Violence Against Women, 11*(2), 150–176.

Dobie, K. (2011, February). Tiny little laws: A plague of sexual violence in Indian country. *Harpers Magazine,* 55–64.

Donat, P., & D'Emilio, J. (1992). A feminist redefinition of rape and sexual assault: Historical foundations and change. *Journal of Social Issues, 48*(1), 9–22.

Du Mont, J., Miller, K.-L., & Myhr, T. L. (2003). The role of "real rape" and "real victim" stereotypes in the police reporting practices of sexually assaulted women. *Violence Against Women, 9*(4), 466–486.

Girschick, Lori. (2002). No sugar, no spice: Reflections on research on woman-to-woman sexual violence. *Violence Against Women, 8*(12), 1474–1499.

Haydon, A. A., McRee, A. L., & Halpern, C. T. (2011). Unwanted sex among young adults in the United States: The role of physical disability and cognitive performance. *Journal of Interpersonal Violence, 26*(17), 3476–3493.

Jackson, S. M., Cram, F., & Seymour, F. W. (2000). Violence and sexual coercion in high school students' dating relationships. *Journal of Family Violence, 15*(1), 23–36.

Katz, J., & Tirone, V. (2010). Going along with it: Sexually coercive partner behavior predicts dating women's compliance with unwanted sex. *Violence Against Women, 16*, 730–742.

Kaukinen, C., & DeMaris, A. (2009). Sexual assault and current mental health: The role of help-seeking and police response. *Violence Against Women, 15*(11), 1331–1357.

Lee, M. J., Hust, S., Zhang, L., & Zhang, Y. (2011). Effects of violence against women in popular crime dramas on viewers' attitudes related to sexual violence. *Mass Communication & Society, 14*, 25–44.

Lee, M. Y., & Law, P. F. M. (2001). Perception of sexual violence against women in Asian American Communities. *Journal of Ethic & Cultural Diversity in Social Work, 10* (2), 3–25.

Lewis, S. (2003). Sexual assault in rural communities. Harrisburg, PA: VAWnet, a project of the National Resource Center on Domestic Violence/Pennsylvania Coalition against Domestic Violence. Retrieved from http://www.vawnet.org

Logan, T. K., & Cole, J. (2011). Exploring the intersection of partner stalking and sexual abuse. *Violence Against Women, 17*(7), 904–924.

Low, G., & Organista, K. C. (2000). Latinas and sexual assault: Towards culturally sensitive assessment and intervention. *Journal of Multicultural Social Work, 8*(1/2), 131–157.

Martin, E. K., Taft, C. T., & Resick, P. A. (2007). A review of marital rape. *Aggression and Violent Behavior, 12*, 329–347.

McMahon, S. (2010). Rape myth beliefs and bystander attitudes among incoming college students. *Journal of American College Health, 59*(1), 3–11.

Neville, H. A., & Pugh, A. O. (1997). General and culture-specific factors influencing African American women's reporting patterns and perceived social support following sexual assault. *Violence Against Women, 3*(4), 361–381.

Patterson, D., Greeson, M., & Campbell, R. (2009). Understanding rape survivors' decisions not to seek help from formal social systems. *Health & Social Work, 34*(2), 127–136.

Riger, S., & Gordon, M. T. (1981). The fear of rape: A study in social control. *Journal of Social Issues, 37*(4), 71–92.

Ruback, R. Barry, & Kim S. Menard. 2001. Rural-urban differences in sexual victimization and reporting: Analyses using UCR and Crisis Center data. *Criminal Justice and Behavior, 28*(2), 131–155.

Sanday, P. R. (1981). The socio-cultural context of rape: A cross-cultural study. *Journal of Social Issues, 37*(4), 5–27.

Tillman, S., Bryant-Davis T., Smith, K., & Marks, A. (2010). Shattering silence: Exploring barriers to disclosure for African American sexual assault survivors. *Trauma, Violence, & Abuse, 11*, 59–70.

Tjaden, P., & Thoennes, N. (2006). *Extent, nature, and consequences of rape victimization: Findings from the National Violence Against Women Survey*. Washington, DC: National Institute of Justice.

Todahl, J. F., Linville, D., Bustin, A., Wheeler, J., & Gau, J. (2009). Sexual assault support services and community systems: Understanding critical issues and needs in the LGBTQ community. *Violence Against Women, 15*(8), 952–976.

Washington, P. A. (2001). Disclosure patterns of black female sexual assault survivors. *Violence Against Women, 7*(11), 1254–1283.

Weiss, K. G. (2010). Male sexual victimization: Examining men's experiences of rape and sexual assault. *Men and Masculinities, 12*(3), 275–298.

Wyatt, G. E. (1992). The sociocultural context of African American and white American women's rape. *Journal of Social Issues, 48*(1), 77–91.

Child Sexual Abuse

Alaggia, R. (2005). Disclosing the trauma of child sexual abuse: A gender analysis. *Journal of Loss and Trauma, 10*, 453–470.

Banyard, V. L., Williams, L. M., Siegel, J. A., & West, C. M. (2002). Childhood sexual abuse in the lives of black women: Risk and resilience in a longitudinal study. *Women & Therapy, 25*(3–4), 45–58.

Barnitz, L. (2001). Effectively responding to the commercial sexual exploitation of children: A comprehensive approach to prevention, protection, and reintegration services. *Child Welfare, 80*(5), 597–610.

Daro, D. (2002). Public perception of child sexual abuse: Who is to blame? *Child Abuse & Neglect, 26*(11), 1131–1133.

Day, A., Thurlow, K., & Woolliscroft, J. (2003). Working with childhood sexual abuse: survey of mental health professionals. *Child Abuse & Neglect, 27*(2), 191–198.

Durham, A. (2003). Young men living through and with child sexual abuse: A practitioner research study. *The British Journal of Social Work, 33*(3), 309–323.

Finkelhor, D. (2009). The prevention of childhood sexual abuse. *The Future of Children, 19*(2), 169–194.

Fontes, L. A., Cruz, M., & Tabachnick, J. (2001). Views of child sexual abuse in two cultural communities: An exploratory study among African Americans and Latinos. *Child Maltreatment, 6*(2), 103–117.

Fong, R., & Cardoso, J. B. (2010). Child human trafficking victims: Challenges for the child welfare system. *Evaluation and Program Planning, 33*, 311–316.

Freeman, K. A., & Morris, T. L. (2001). A review of conceptual models explaining the effects of child sexual abuse. *Aggression and Violent Behavior, 6*, 357–373.

Goodman-Brown, T. B., Edelstein, R. S., Goodman, G. S., Jones, D. P. H., & Gordon, D. S. (2003). Why children tell: A model of children's disclosure of sexual abuse. *Child Abuse & Neglect, 27*(5), 525–540.

Hyman, B., & Williams, L. (2001). Resilience among women survivors of child sexual abuse. *Affilia, 16*(2), 198–219.

Kellogg, N. D. (2002). Child sexual abuse: A marker or magnifying glass for family dysfunction? *The Social Science Journal, 39*(4), 569–582.

Kendall-Tackett, K. A., Meyer Williams, L., & Finkelhor, D. (1992). Impact of sexual abuse on children: A review and synthesis of recent empirical studies. *Psychological Bulletin, 113*, 164–180.

Ligiero, D. P., Fassinger, R., McCauley, M., Moore, J., & Lyytinen, N. (2009). Childhood sexual abuse, culture and coping: A qualitative study of Latinas. *Psychology of Women Quarterly, 33*, 67–80.

Lowe, W., Pavkov, T. W., Casnova, G. M., & Wetcheler, J. L. (2005). Do American ethnic cultures differ in their definitions of child sexual abuse? *The American Journal of Family Therapy, 33*, 147–166.

McCloskey, L. A., & Bailey, J. A. (2000). The intergenerational transmission of risk for child sexual abuse. *Journal of Interpersonal Violence, 15*(10), 1019–1035.

McGee, H., O'Higgins, M., Garavan, R., & Conroy, R. (2011). Rape and child sexual abuse: What beliefs persist about motives, perpetrators and survivors? *Journal of Interpersonal Violence, 26*(17), 3580–3593.

Nelson-Gardell, D. (2001). The voices of victims: Surviving child sexual abuse. *Child & Adolescent Social Work Journal, 18*(6), 401–416.

Plummer, C. A. (2001). Prevention of child sexual abuse: A survey of 87 programs. *Violence and Victims, 16*(5), 575–588.

Renk, K., Liljequist, L., Steinberg, A., Bosco, G., & Phares, V. (2002). Prevention of child sexual abuse: Are we doing enough? *Trauma, Violence, & Abuse, 3*, 68–84.

Robboy, J., & Anderson, K. G. (2011). Intergenerational child abuse and coping. *Journal of Interpersonal Violence, 26*(17), 3526–3541.

Ross, G., & O'Carroll, P. (2004). Cognitive behavioural psychotherapy intervention in childhood sexual abuse: Identifying new directions from the literature. *Child Abuse Review, 13*, 51–64.

Swenson, C. C., & Chaffin, M. (2006). Beyond psychotherapy: Treating abused children by changing their social ecology. *Aggression and Violent Behavior, 11*, 120–137.

Tutty, L. M. (2000). What children learn from sexual abuse prevention programs: Difficult concepts and developmental issues. *Research on Social Work Practice, 10*(3), 275–300.

Ulibarri, M. D., Ulloa, E. C., & Camacho, L. (2009). Prevalence of sexually abusive experiences in childhood and adolescence among a community sample of Latinas: A descriptive study. *Journal of Child Sexual Abuse, 18*(4), 405–421.

Winder, J. H. (1996). Counseling adult male survivors of childhood sexual abuse: A review of treatment techniques. *Journal of Mental Health Counseling, 18*, 123–133.

Wurtele, S. K. (2009). Preventing sexual abuse of children in the twenty-first century: Preparing for challenges and opportunities. *Journal of Child Sexual Abuse, 18*(1), 1–18.

Offenders

Craissati, J. (2005). Sexual violence against women: A psychological approach to the assessment and management of rapists in the community. *Probation Journal, 52*(4), 401–422.

Freeman, N. J., & Sandler, J. C. (2008). Female and male sex offenders: A comparison of recidivism patterns and risk factors. *Journal of Interpersonal Violence, 23*(10), 1394–1413.

Garrett, T., Oliver, C., Wilcox, D. T., & Middleton, D. (2003). Who cares? The views of sexual offenders about the group treatment they receive. *Sexual Abuse: A Journal of Research and Treatment, 15*(4), 323–338

Marshall, W. L., Ward, T., Mann, R. E., Moulden, H., Fernandez, Y. M., Serran, G., & Marshall, L. E. (2005). Working positively with sexual offenders maximizing the effectiveness of treatment. *Journal of Interpersonal Violence, 20*(9), 1096–1114.

Newbauer, J. F., & Blanks, J. W. (2001). Group work with adolescent sexual offenders. *Journal of Individual Psychology, 57*(1), 37–50.

Polizzi, D. M., MacKenzie, D. L., & Hickman, L. J. (1999). What works in adult sex offender treatment? A review of prison- and non-prison-based treatment programs. *International Journal of Offender Therapy and Comparative Criminology, 43*(3), 357–374.

Thompson, M. P., Koss, M. P., Kingree, J. B., Goree, J., & Rice, J. (2011). A prospective meditational model of sexual aggression among college men. *Journal of Interpersonal Violence, 26*(13), 2716–2734.

Ward, T., & Stewart, C. A. (2003). The treatment of sex offenders: Risk management and good lives. *Professional Psychology: Research and Practice, 34*(4), 353–360.

Williams, J. R., Ghandour, R. M., & Kub, J. E. (2008). Female perpetration of violence in heterosexual intimate relationships: Adolescence through adulthood. *Trauma, Violence, & Abuse, 9*(4), 227–249.

Videos

Dreamworlds 3: Desire, sex, and power in music video. (2007). Sut Jhally, writer, narrator, and editor. 60 mins. Media Education Foundation. Available at http://www.mediaed.org

The greatest silence: Rape in the Congo. (2007). Lisa Jackson, producer. 76 mins. A Women Make Movies Release. Available at http://www.wmm.com

Price of pleasure. (2008). Chyng Sun, producer, director, and writer. 55 mins. Media Education Foundation. Available at http://www.mediaed.org

Rape is … (2003). Margaret Lazarus and Renner Wunderlich, producers and directors. 30 mins. Cambridge Documentary Films. Available at http://www.cambridgedocumentary films.org/

A survivor's story. (2004). A Betsy Cox Production, O.R.T. Solutions, Alexandria, VA.

Tough guise: Violence, media, and the crisis in masculinity. (1999). Sut Jhally, executive producer and director; Jackson Katz and Jeremy Earp, writers. Media Education Foundation. Available at http://www.mediaed.org

Websites

Aequitas: The Prosecutors' Resource on Violence Against Women. Retrieved from http://www.aequitasresource.org

Center for Sex Offender Management (CSOM). Retrieved from http://www.csom.org/

Centers for Disease Control and Prevention (CDC): Sexual Violence. Retrieved from http://www.cdc.gov/ViolencePrevention/sexualviolence/index.html

Child Welfare Information Gateway. U.S. Department of Health and Human Services. Retrieved from http://www.childwelfare.gov

Coalition to Abolish Slavery and Trafficking (CAST). Retrieved from http://www.castla.org/

Love Is Respect. Retrieved from http://blog.loveisrespect.org/

MaleSurvivor: Overcoming Sexual Victimization of Men and Boys. Retrieved from http://www.malesurvivor.org/default.html

Men Can Stop Rape: Creating Cultures Free from Violence. Retrieved from http://www.mencanstoprape.org/

Minnesota Center against Violence and Abuse (MINCAVA) electronic clearinghouse. Retrieved from http://www.mincava.umn.edu

National Alliance to End Sexual Violence. Retrieved from http://endsexualviolence.org/

National Center on Elder Abuse. Administration on Aging. Retrieved from http://www.ncea.aoa.gov/ncearoot/Main_Site/index.aspx

National Center for Victims of Crime. Retrieved from http://www.ncvc.org/ncvc/Main.aspx

National Network to End Violence Against Immigrant Women. Retrieved from http://www.immigrantwomennetwork.org/

National Online Resource Center on Violence Against Women. Retrieved from http://www.vawnet.org

National Sexual Violence Resource Center. Retrieved from http://www.nsvrc.org

Pandora's Project Support and Resources for Survivors of Rape and Sexual Abuse. Retrieved from http://www.pandorasaquarium.org

PreventConnect: A National Online Project Dedicated to the Primary Prevention of Sexual Assault and Domestic Violence. Retrieved from http://preventconnect.org/

RAINN (Rape, Abuse & Incest Network). Retrieved from http://www.rainn.org

Stalking Resource Center: A Program of the National Center for Victims of Crime. Retrieved from http://www.ncvc.org/src/main.aspx

Stop It Now! Together We Can Prevent the Sexual Abuse of Children. Retrieved from http://www.stopitnow.org/

Workplaces Respond to Domestic and Sexual Violence: A National Resource Center. Retrieved from http://www.workplacesrespond.org/

Index

Page numbers for main entries in the encyclopedia are indicated in **boldface**.

Families, sexual violence and, 752
  attachment disorder and, 248–49
  forced marriage and, 194–95
  help seeking from, 217–18, 219,
    225, 228–30
  impacts of SVA on, 250, 261–63
  incest, 130, 249, 272–73,
    278–79, 476
  Japanese, 296
  Latino, 309–10
  reactions of, 219, 250, 261, 473–75
  sibling abuse, 130, 203, 283, 581–86
  South Asian, 232, 594
  See also Child sexual abuse; Parents,
    CSA and
Family therapy, 692
Farmer v. Brennan (1994), 434
FBI (Federal Bureau of Investigation),
    323, 357–58, 607, 769
  Uniform Crime Report (UCR),
    504–5, 510, 606
Feder, Elyssa, 311–13, 319–20
Federal Communications
    Commission, 395
Female-on-female sexual violence,
    183–86
  in prisons, 432–34
Female prisoners, 111
Female sex offenders, 109, **187–89**,
    382, 384, 654
Feminism, 396, 495, 496,
    500, 554
  Buddhism and, 45, 46, 494
  rape prevention and, 402–3, 729
  rape terminology and, 128, 327
  second-wave, 190, 234, 671
Feminism, influence of, **189–91**, 234
Feminist practice theory, **192–93**,
    737–38
Feminist theory of sexual violence,
    649, 670–72

evolutionary theory, 656
  gender roles and, 658, 670, 673
Figley, C. R., 689
Filipas, H. H., 225, 226
Finkelhor, David, 70, 124
Fishbein, Martin, 405, 486, 487
Fisher, Bonnie S., 27, 408, 413–14,
    546–47
  on research, xxx, 508–15
Forced marriage, 173–74, **193–96**
  See also Marital rape
Forensic medical exams, 197, 198, 369,
    375, 462, 530
  child abuse and, 60, 372–73
  rape kits and, 323, 468–70, 568
Forensic nursing, **197–98**, 375,
    548–49
  See also SANE (sexual assault nurse
    examiner)
Forensic psychology, **199–200**, 322
Forrester, Trina, 123–24
Foster and group homes, **201–3**
Foubert, John D., 205, 345, 407
Fraser, Jennifer, 703–4
Fraternities and sororities,
    96, **204–6**, 413, 659, 677
Freudian psychology, 234,
    506, 760
Friedan, Betty, 190
Friends, help seeking from, 217–18,
    219, 225, 228–30
  reactions of, 473–75
Frierson, Damien T., xxvii, 331–33
Frohwirth, L., 401
Fuentes, Milton A., 57–58, 320, 408–9,
    410–12
Fuldeore, Rupali, 131–33, 246–47
Futures without Violence
    (FWV), 407, 428
Future violence, risk of. *See* Risk, for
    future violence

Gabriel, Adeena M., xxxi, 454–55,
633–44
on Internet pornography,
397–99, 637
Galupo, M., 201–2
Gang rape, 128–29, **207–8**, 234, 354,
600, 677
Gannon, Theresa A., 648, 652–54
Garrido, David, 693–94
Gay and bisexual men, 331, 571, 667
homophobic acts and, xxvii, 237–40,
332, 676
Gender, rape law and, 316
Gender hierarchy, 42–43
See also Patriarchy
Gender roles, 471, 662, 670
socialization and, 658, 675–76
See also Masculinity
General Crimes Act (1817), 357
General Social Survey
(1996–2000), 239
General theory of crime, 648, 672–74
Geneva Convention, 208
Genovese, Kitty, 50
GHB (gamma-hydroxy butyrate), 126,
145–46, 464–65, 706
Gibbs, Jennifer C., 648, 672–74
Gidyez, Christine, 424
Gil, Eliana, 392–94, 745
Gilmore, Anne, 600
Golding, J. M., 273
Good lives model (treatment), 697
Gossett, J. L., 555
Gottfredson, Michael, 672, 673, 674
Gover, Angela R., 137–39, 217, 219,
476–78
GPS monitoring, 603, 665
of offenders, 108, 391
Gramsci, Antonio, 676
Grauerholz, L., 751
Gravdal, Kathryn, 327

Greek letter organizations, 96, 204–6
See also Fraternities and sororities
The Green Dot (program), **209**, 407, 427
Greene, Michele G., 245, 400–401
Grooming the victim, **210–12**, 385
Gross, Neil, 665
Grossman, Stephanie L., 153–55, 247
Group homes, 201–3
Group rape. *See* Gang rape
Group therapy, **212–14**, 628–30,
692, 745
Grove, Jennifer, 404, 429–31
Gruskin, S., 563
Guilt and shame, of victims, 720, 723,
729, 731–33
Guthrie, D., 273

Hagemeister, Annelies K., 321, 607–9
Hahn, Sur Ah, 97–99
Hale, Matthew, 335
Haller, Kimberly, 565–66
Harassment. *See* Sexual harassment
Hartman, Jennifer L., 54–56, 220–21
Hathaway, S. R., 200
Hausbeck, K., 562
Health belief model, **215–16**, 405, 406
Hebrew Bible, 41–42, 298–99, 495
See also Biblical legacy
Hegemonic masculinity theory, 650,
675–77
Heiman, Marsha, 154–56, 744
Help seeking (overview), xxviii, **216–21**
Help seeking, 216–30
cultural group and, 169–70
disclosure and, 137–39, 217, 222,
225, 226
shame and, 228–29
stigma of rape and, 218, 235
See also Hotlines
Help seeking, barriers to, 218,
221–24, 540

About the Editor and Contributors

The Editor

Judy L. Postmus is an associate professor at the School of Social Work, Rutgers University in New Brunswick, New Jersey. She is also the director of the Center on Violence Against Women and Children. She is published widely in national and international journals and has presented her research at local, national, and international conferences on the impact of policies and interventions on survivors of violence. She holds a PhD from the State University of New York–Albany and an MSW from Barry University in Miami, Florida.

The Contributors

Diana Ali is a postdoctoral fellow in psychology at Princeton House Behavioral Health Women's Program, Brunswick, New Jersey, where she specializes in providing psychotherapy for survivors of sexual trauma.

Christopher T. Allen is a postdoctoral associate at the Center on Violence Against Women and Children at Rutgers University. He earned his PhD in clinical-community psychology at the University of South Carolina where he specialized in the study of intimate partner violence and sexual assault in college populations.

Mónica M. Alzate was a tenured associate professor at the University of Oklahoma School of Social Work and Women's and Gender Studies Program when she contributed for this publication. She has presented her research on women's reproductive health and rights and policies that affect women and girls in the US, Mexico, Barbados, Colombia, and Germany. She holds PhD, MSW and MA degrees from the US and a BA from Colombia and is currently an independent consultant.

Victoria L. Banyard, PhD, is a professor in the University of New Hampshire Department of Psychology and research and evaluation consultant for Prevention Innovations: Research and Practices for Ending Violence Against Women. Her research focuses on consequences of interpersonal violence, understanding resilience of survivors, and evaluating community prevention efforts.

Kareen Bar-Akiva is the training coordinator at the New Jersey Coalition against Sexual Assault. She earned her JD from New England School of Law and was the 2008–9 clinical teaching fellow at Northeastern University School of Law's Domestic Violence Institute. She is responsible for the development of sexual violence training curricula for criminal justice professionals.

Joanne Belknap is a professor of sociology at the University of Colorado–Boulder. Her interests are the issues of violence against women and girls and incarcerated women and children. She is the author of *The Invisible Woman: Gender, Crime, and Justice* (2006).

Tricia B. Bent-Goodley, Ph.D., is a professor of social work at Howard University, and has practiced in the area of violence against women and girls as a clinician, administrator, and a researcher. She is the author of *The Ultimate Betrayal: A Renewed Look at Intimate Partner Violence* (2011). She holds a PhD from Columbia University and MSW from the University of Pennsylvania.

Katharine M. Bergacs is a licensed clinical social worker with extensive experience in working with children and families in nonprofit organizations and schools providing both prevention education and clinical work.

Alan D. Berkowitz, PhD, has received five national awards for scholarship and innovative programs on substance abuse and sexual assault prevention, bystander intervention, and social justice. He is a cofounder of the social norms approach, has authored a book on bystander intervention theory and skills, and currently works advising institutions of higher education and the U.S. military on sexual assault prevention strategies.

Michael S. Bermes is the Coordinator, for the Military Social Work program and a doctoral candidate at the University of Central Florida, Orlando. He earned his master's at UCF and is an internationally licensed addiction professional. His research focus and specialty is early life trauma and neglect, PTSD, and military, veterans, and families.

Larissa Boianelli is a licensed psychotherapist working in private practice, specializing in sexual trauma. She is currently a member of the NASW, National

Association of Social Workers, and ATSA, the Association for Treatment of Sexual Offenders.

Jackson Tay Bosley works to reduce interpersonal violence by developing specialized treatment programs for adolescent and adult sexual offenders in prisons, hospitals, and the community. Dr. Bosley currently works for the University of Medicine and Dentistry of New Jersey administering a statewide, community-based treatment program for adult sexual offenders under lifetime supervision by the State Parole Board.

Sharon Elizabeth Bowland, PhD, LCSW, is an assistant professor of social work, Kent School of Social Work in Louisville, Kentucky. She conducts research on the intersection between trauma, spirituality/religion, and mental health. An intervention she conducted with older survivors won the Dissertation of the Year award from the Society for Social Work and Research in 2009, and appears in *Social Work*, January 2012.

Emily Brandt was the founder and director of Take Back the News, a nonprofit organization that worked to counter media misrepresentation of sexual violence. She is a Brooklyn-based writer, educator, and activist.

Maria F. Brandt, former Take Back the News board member, earned her PhD in English from Boston College. She currently teaches creative writing; women in literature; and violence, art, and activism at Monroe Community College in Rochester, New York, and is an active member of the Greater Rochester Consortium of Women and Gender Studies.

Vicki Breitbart is the director of the health advocacy program at Sarah Lawrence College in Bronxville, New York. She earned her doctorate in organization development and leadership from Columbia University and has published extensively on women's reproductive health issues.

Kristin Briggs, EdD, a psychologist employed at Child Abuse Research and Education Services (CARES) Institute at UMDNJ, is also an executive committee member on the New Jersey Governor's Advisory Council against Sexual Violence. Her most recent publication is "The Use of Play in Trauma-Focused Cognitive-Behavioral Therapy" (2010), in *Play in Clinical Practice: Evidence-Based Approaches*, ed. S. W. Russ and L. N. Niec (New York: Guilford Press, 2010).

Kenly Brown is a doctoral student in sociology at the University of California–Santa Barbara. She has received numerous awards, including the University of Colorado Jacob Van Ek Award for academics and service.

Shamecca Bryant, MA, is the executive director of the Orange County Rape Crisis Center in Chapel Hill, North Carolina. She has worked at the Center for five years helping to provide rape prevention education to and provide survivors of sexual violence with counseling and healing techniques.

Noël Busch-Armendariz is an associate professor at The University of Texas at Austin School of Social Work and the director of the Institute on Domestic Violence and Sexual Assault. She has been working in the anti-interpersonal violence field for more than 19 years. She has managed six research projects on human trafficking.

Rebecca Campbell, PhD, is a professor of psychology and program evaluation at Michigan State University. Her research examines how the legal, medical, and mental health systems and rape crisis centers respond to the needs of adult, adolescent, and pediatric victims of sexual assault. Her current work, funded by the National Institute of Justice, focuses on sexual assault nurse examiner (SANE) programs and the criminal justice system.

Julian Cano is a mental health clinician and social science researcher specializing in sexual deviance. He is a doctoral candidate at The University of Texas at Austin and an active-duty clinical social worker for the United States Air Force.

Erin A. Casey, PhD, is an Associate Professor of social work at the University of Washington–Tacoma. She has over 10 years of practice experience in the fields of domestic and sexual violence. Her research centers on examining ecological approaches to violence prevention and on efforts to engage men in the primary prevention of violence.

Griselda Chapa is an epidemiologist in private industry where she is the director of outcomes research. She is also a full-time doctoral student at Tulane University's School of Public Health and Tropical Medicine. The focus of her research is health disparities. Her last peer-reviewed publication examined predictors of hospital readmission among a Medicaid disabled population (*Journal for Healthcare Quality*, 2010).

Sanjukta Chaudhuri is Project Manager at Moving to End Sexual Assault, Boulder, Colorado. She is accredited with a master's degree in Women, Gender, and Development from ISS, Hague, Netherlands. Her expertise is community-level organizing and advocacy. She has worked internationally, as a scholar, researcher, and a non-profit program consultant to end gender-based violence.

Christina M. Chiarelli-Helminiak is a doctoral student at the University of Connecticut School of Social Work, where she also teaches in the MSW program. Ms. Chiarelli-Helminiak led the development of a rural children's advocacy center, providing community-based services to abused children, influencing her dissertation topic on compassion fatigue among forensic interviewers.

Janice Chisholm is an adjunct instructor and DPH candidate at City University of New York. She is ABD and holds a master's in Applied Educational Psychology from New York University, and a master's in Public Health from Columbia University. Ms. Chisholm serves as the Assistant Commissioner/Director of Contracts at New York City's Department of Health and Mental Hygiene.

Shantih E. Clemans, LCSW, DSW, is an assistant professor/mentor in community and human services at Empire State College, State University of New York, Brooklyn Unit, where she mentors students and teaches in the areas of trauma, group work, and clinical practice. A former director of a rape crisis program, Dr. Clemans's research focuses on group work models to address vicarious traumatization, democratic teaching strategies, feminist practice, and mentoring adult students.

Erin B. Comartin, LMSW, Ph.D., earned her PhD in social work at Wayne State University in Detroit, Michigan. She is an assistant professor at Oakland University in Rochester, Michigan. Her research includes public attitudes of sanctions for sex offenders, with a specific interest in juvenile or young adult sex offenders. She has also explored the impacts that public registration has on family members of young adult sex offenders.

Sarah W. Craun is a behavioral analyst for the National Sex Offender Targeting Center in the United States Marshals Service. She obtained her PhD in social welfare from the University of California–Los Angeles. She has published several articles on sex offender registration.

Leah E. Daigle is an associate professor of criminal justice and criminology at Georgia State University. She has published extensively in the areas of sexual victimization and life-course criminology. She is author of *Victimology: A Text/Reader* and coauthor of *Unsafe in the Ivory Tower: The Sexual Victimization of College Women*, which was named the 2010 Outstanding Book of the Year by the Academy of Criminal Justice Sciences.

Dr. Shir Daphna Tekoah, PhD, is a researcher and a lecturer at the School of Social Work, Ashkelon Academic College, and a researcher at the Program for

Children at Risk, Kaplan Medical Center. Her most recent publication is "The Role of Perinatal Dissociation as Predictor of PTSD Symptoms Following Childbirth," *Journal of Loss and Trauma* (2010). She is specializing in trauma, post-traumatic growth, violence, sexual abuse, and health and gender.

Shamita Das Dasgupta is a cofounder of Manavi, an organization focusing on violence against South Asian immigrant women. She teaches at NYU Law School. Shamita is the author of four books, *The Demon Slayers and Other Stories* (1995), *A Patchwork Shawl* (1998), *Body Evidence* (2007), and *Mothers for Sale* (2009).

Anindita Dasgupta, MPH, is a doctoral student in the Joint Doctoral Program in Public Health at the University of San Diego, California and San Diego State University. Prior to entering this program, Anindita worked as research coordinator on NIH intervention projects in the United States and India on HIV and on gender-based violence.

Rebecca Davis, PhD, LCSW, is a lecturer at and the director of the Center for International Social Work, School of Social Work, Rutgers, The State University of New Jersey. She managed several U.S. government child welfare reform initiatives in Romania, Bosnia and Herzegovina and currently directs a study abroad program at Babes-Boylai University in Romania.

Jacqueline M. Deitch-Stackhouse is a licensed clinical social worker with dual master's degrees in social service and in law and social policy from Bryn Mawr College. Previously at The College of New Jersey, she now directs campus-wide prevention initiatives and advocates for power-based personal violence victims and survivors at Princeton University.

Walter S. DeKeseredy, PhD, is a professor of criminology at the University of Ontario Institute of Technology. He has published 15 books and over 70 refereed journal articles. He has also received awards for his work from two divisions of the American Society of Criminology and one from the Institute on Violence, Abuse and Trauma.

Renae Diegel is a forensic nurse examiner, and the program administrator for Turning Point's Forensic Nurse Examiner Program in Macomb County, Michigan. She has lectured both nationally and internationally on the topic of forensic nursing and has cared for patients of sexual assault, domestic violence, child abuse, elder abuse, and other trauma.

Louis Donnelly is a doctoral student at Rutgers University School of Social Work and a graduate research assistant at the Institute for Families.

Lynn B. D'Orio is an attorney and on the Professional Advisory Board, which advises the Michigan Coalition for a Useful Registry on ways to improve the Michigan's Sex Offender Registry laws. Her most recent publication on the subject is "Invisible Stripes: Juveniles and the Sex Offender Registry," *Res Ipsa Loquitur*, January 2010.

Sapna Doshi, PhD, is a clinical psychologist in private practice at Potomac Behavioral Solutions in Arlington, Virginia. She completed her pre-doctoral internship training at Duke University Medical Center and earned her doctoral degree from Drexel University. She specializes in the treatment of eating disorders and obesity.

Dania M. Ermentrout is a clinical instructor in the School of Social Work at the University of North Carolina at Chapel Hill.

Deidre Evans is working toward her master's degree in clinical social work and certificate on violence against women and children at Rutgers.

Elyssa Feder is a recent graduate of London School of Economics, where she earned an MSc in Comparative Politics. She also holds a BA from The George Washington University in international affairs and women's studies.

Bonnie S. Fisher is a professor of criminal justice at the University of Cincinnati. She has written extensively about the victimization of students and the measurement of sexual victimization. Her 2011 coauthored book, *Unsafe in the Ivory Tower: The Sexual Victimization of College Women*, won the Outstanding Book Award from the Academy of Criminal Justice Sciences.

Trina Forrester has earned an MA from the University of Ottawa in Criminology and currently works for Correctional Service Canada.

John D. Foubert, PhD is the Anderson, Farris and Halligan Professor of College Student Development at Oklahoma State University. He has published eight books and over 33 refereed journal articles about ending men's violence against women, the harms of pornography, and college student development theory.

Jennifer Fraser is a PhD candidate in Criminology at the University of Ottawa and an assistant professor in Criminal Justice and Criminology at Ryerson

University. Her research interests include feminist activism and socio-political responses to violence against women.

Damien T. Frierson, MA, MSW is a PhD candidate at the Howard University School of Social Work and adjunct instructor in the African American studies department at Temple University. His research interests include the intersections of race, gender, and sexual orientation among LGBT people of color and same-sex intimate partner violence.

Milton A. Fuentes, PsyD, is an associate professor of psychology at Montclair State University and a licensed psychologist in New Jersey and New York. Dr. Fuentes's interests are in the areas of Latino and multicultural psychology, child psychology, and family psychology.

Rupali Fuldeore is a clinical outcomes analyst at WellPoint Inc. She is a physician from India and has a master's in epidemiology from Medical College of Wisconsin. Her most work is in disease management programs.

Adeena M. Gabriel, PhD, is a clinical psychologist in New York City. She has conducted research under the mentorship of Dr. Prentky in the areas of sexual violence and childhood Internet victimization.

Theresa A. Gannon is an HPC registered forensic psychologist and Professor of forensic psychology at the University of Kent, UK. She has published extensively on the topic of male and female perpetrated abuse, including general theory development and theory evaluations, as well as the application of cognitive theory and methods to the study of sexual violence.

Jennifer C. Gibbs is an assistant professor at West Chester University. She received her PhD in criminology and criminal justice from the University of Maryland, College Park. Her research interests include violence against women, policing, terrorism, and the scholarship of teaching and learning.

Eliana Gil, PhD, is in private practice in Fairfax, Virginia, at the Gil Center for Healing and Play. She has specialized in working with traumatized children for 38 years and she integrates expressive therapies (including sand, play, and art therapies) with cognitive behavioral approaches and other evidence-based practices. Dr. Gil is also the director of Starbright Training Institute.

Wendy Perkins Gilbert is an assistant professor at Urbana University and is the director of Criminal Justice Graduate Studies. Her research interests are sexual victimization, police decision making, and criminal justice theory.

Angela R. Gover is Professor in the School of Public Affairs at the University of Colorado–Denver. Her research interests include violence against women, gender and crime, and the criminal justice system response to violence against women. Her recent work has appeared in *Violence Against Women*, *Journal of Interpersonal Violence*, and *Violence and Victims*.

Michele G. Greene, DrPH, is professor in the Department of Health and Nutrition Sciences at Brooklyn College, professor at the CUNY School of Public Health, and adjunct professor of public health in medicine at the Weill Medical College of Cornell University. Her research focuses on communication between physician and patients. She has a long-standing interest in humanism in medicine and women and the health care system.

Stephanie L. Grossman is a recent graduate from Amherst College. She is currently working as a research coordinator for Drexel University's Program on Eating Disorders and Obesity Research and plans to pursue a degree in clinical psychology.

Jennifer Grove is the prevention outreach coordinator for the National Sexual Violence Resource Center. Working in the anti-sexual violence movement for over 13 years, she currently develops resources and provides training at the national level on effective primary prevention approaches.

Annelies K. Hagemeister is an associate professor of social work at Minnesota State University–Mankato. Previously, she was project coordinator for the Minnesota Center against Violence and Abuse and a child therapist at the Domestic Abuse Project in Minneapolis. She has published and presented research in domestic violence, poverty, and grief.

Sur Ah Hahn has earned an MA in women's studies in South Korea and is currently a PhD student in social work at the University of Kansas. She has published several articles on violence against women and women's health issues.

Kimberly Haller, BA, is a clinical psychology PhD candidate at Fairleigh Dickinson University working under the mentorship of Dr. Prentky and is interested in juvenile delinquency.

Jennifer L. Hartman is an associate professor in the Department of Criminology and Criminal Justice at the University of North Carolina at Charlotte. She received her PhD in criminal justice from the University of Cincinnati. Her research involves studying victimization research as it relates to domestic violence, stalking, and sexual assault.

Laurie Cook Heffron is a social worker and the director of research with the Institute on Domestic Violence and Sexual Assault at The University of Texas at Austin School of Social Work. She is also working toward a doctoral degree and has managed research projects on human trafficking for IDVSA.

Marsha Heiman, PhD, is a licensed clinical psychologist in private practice in Metuchen, New Jersey. Dr. Heiman specializes in the area of sexual abuse and trauma providing treatment, training, and supervision, as well as lecturing and publishing. She has been using EMDR since 1995 and is an EMDRIA Approved Consultant.

Karen Herman, PhD, is the author of *Art, Violence, & Social Change: Challenging Violence Against Women and Girls through Entertainment Education*. She is the director of sexual assault services for the New Mexico Coalition of Sexual Assault Programs, developing policy and providing technical assistance and resources for rape crisis centers and community mental health centers in New Mexico.

Melanie Lowe Hoffman is a program coordinator at the Center on Violence Against Women and Children at Rutgers University School of Social Work. Melanie has a master's in public administration from the Robert F. Wagner School of Public Service at NYU.

Gretchen L. Hoge is a doctoral student in social work at Rutgers, The State University of New Jersey. She serves as a graduate research assistant at the Center on Violence Against Women and Children, where her work focuses on domestic violence prevention and intervention.

Beth Lynn Greene Hollander is a postdoctoral psychology fellow at North Shore–Long Island Jewish Hospital, where she treats patients with mood, anxiety, and personality disorders. Dr. Hollander has a history of treating patients with PTSD, particularly those who have been victims of crimes and military and law enforcement personnel.

Jonathan Horowitz is a sociology PhD student at the University of North Carolina–Chapel Hill and conducts research on fraternity systems, prevention and grassroots activism.

Monika Johnson Hostler, MPA is the executive director of the North Carolina Coalition against Sexual Assault. She has been an anti-sexual violence advocate for 15 years. Prior to working at NCCASA, she worked at rape crisis centers as a victim advocate and school educator.

Mihai Bogdan Iovu earned his PhD at Babeş-Bolyai University, Cluj-Napoca, Romania. During 2010–11 he was a Junior Fulbright Scholar at Rutgers University. He is currently a postdoctoral fellow focusing on child abuse and neglect in Romania.

Hazel Jamieson is a licensed primary therapist at the University Medical Center of Princeton at Plainsboro, Princeton Healthcare System, Princeton House Behavioral Health Women's Programs in Hamilton, New Jersey.

Véronique Jaquier earned her PhD in criminology at the University of Lausanne, Switzerland, where she teaches a class on women and crime and is currently pursuing research on sexual violence, mental health problems, and risk behaviors through a Swiss National Science Foundation fellowship at Yale University, Division of Prevention and Community Research.

Robert Jensen is a professor in the School of Journalism at the University of Texas at Austin. He is the author of *Getting Off: Pornography and the End of Masculinity* (South End Press, 2007) and co-writer/producer of an educational slide show in PowerPoint about pornography, "Who wants to be a porn star? Sex and violence in today's pornography industry." Information about the show is available at http://stoppornculture.org/. Jensen was a consultant to the filmmakers of the 2008 documentary "The Price of Pleasure: Pornography, Sexuality, and Relationships."

Kathryn Johnson is a licensed marriage and family therapist and has worked in the field of domestic and sexual violence since 1991. She is the associate executive director of InterAct (The Family Violence Prevention Center, Inc.) in Raleigh, North Carolina, providing clinical program development and oversight and professional training.

Alexis Jemal, JD, MSW, is a PhD student in social work at Rutgers University. Her general area of interest for clinical work and research is trauma, justice, and punishment with a specific focus on victim offenders, children in the court system, and human trafficking.

Jackson Katz, PhD, is cofounder of Mentors in Violence Prevention (MVP), the most widely utilized sexual and domestic violence prevention initiative in college and professional athletics. He is the creator of the film *Tough Guise* and author of *The Macho Paradox*. He lectures widely in the United States and around the world on violence, media, and masculinities.

Catherine Kaukinen is an Associate Professor in the School of Public Affairs at the University of Colorado, Colorado Springs. Dr. Kaukinen received her PhD in Sociology in 2001 from the University of Toronto. Her research interests include intimate partner violence, adolescent and college dating violence and campus intervention and prevention, and risk and protective factors for violent victimization. She is currently funded by the Office on Violence Against Women to implement a multi-campus violence prevention program.

Kathleen Kelley is a doctoral graduate student at the University of Delaware. She received her master's degree from Michigan State University where she worked on research evaluating the effectiveness of sexual assault nurse examiners. Her current research interests include violence against women, masculinity, intersectionality, and qualitative methods.

Poco Donna Kernsmith, PhD, is an associate professor in the School of Social Work at Wayne State University. Her research includes intervention and policy approaches for the prevention and treatment of violence in families and intimate partner relationships, with an emphasis on gender differences in perpetration of violence.

Roger Kernsmith is a professor in the Department of Sociology, Anthropology, and Criminology at Eastern Michigan University. He specializes in criminology, juvenile delinquency, and deviance. His Ph.D. is from Vanderbilt University.

Ruth Anne Koenick is the director of the Rutgers University Office for Violence Prevention and Victim Assistance. She has worked in the antiviolence field for over 40 years and teaches in the Rutgers School of Social Work, Department of Women and Gender Studies, and the Graduate School of Education.

Jill Kracov-Zinckgraf earned her master's in public administration at Rutgers, The State University of New Jersey where she specialized in violence against women and children. She has worked and volunteered in the field of violence against women and children for over 25 years.

Raina V. Lamade, MA, received her Master's Degree in Psychology from Teachers College, Columbia University. She is a clinical psychology doctoral candidate at Fairleigh Dickinson University in Teaneck, New Jersey, working under the mentorship of Dr. Prentky on various projects involving sexual violence, juvenile justice, and childhood Internet victimization.

Denise Lang-Grant is a licensed professional therapist specializing in sexual trauma and author of nine nonfiction books on health, family relationships, and true crime. Director of the Morris County Sexual Assault Center for Atlantic

Health, she is a certified dispute mediator and also serves as an adjunct instructor for Seton Hall University's master's in counseling program.

Robert D. Laurino, Esq., is an attorney who has served as a career prosecutor. He has written and lectured extensively in the area of sexual violence, forensic evidence, and the abuse of individuals with disabilities.

Melissa F. Lavin earned her PhD at University of Connecticut–Storrs, and she is currently an adjunct professor in the Connecticut State University system. She has researched extensively in the area of sex work and drug use. Her areas of expertise within sociology include crime and deviance, gender and sexualities, qualitative methods, and sociological psychology.

Jodie M. Lawston is associate professor of women's studies at California State University–San Marcos. She has published extensively on women's incarceration. She is the author of *Sisters Outside: Radical Activists Working for Women Prisoners* (2009) and coeditor of *Razor Wire Women: Prisoners, Activists, Scholars, and Artists* (2011), both SUNY Press.

Irene Lebbad is a licensed clinical social worker and the director of Somerset County, New Jersey's sexual assault support services program. She chairs the county's Violence Prevention Advisory Council and serves on the county's Sexual Assault Response Team Board. Ms. Lebbad has also been a special guest on WOR and BBC radio.

Shawna J. Lee is an assistant professor of social work at The University of Michigan, Ann Arbor. Her research examining the role of fathers in the etiology of physical child abuse and neglect was funded by the Centers for Disease Control and Prevention. She is currently funded by the United States Air Force to develop parent education for fathers.

Judith Leitch is a PhD student in social work and specializes in the study of intimate partner violence. She has direct service experience in the fields of violence in relationships, mental health, GLBTQ counseling, curriculum development, and public health.

Cynthia Wilcox Lischick earned an MA/PhD in psychology from Rutgers University and an MA in psychological counseling from Monmouth University, New Jersey. She is a licensed professional counselor. She provides expert testimony on domestic violence matters part-time, and works full-time as the director of psychological health for the New Jersey National Guard.

Shelley Johnson Listwan is an Associate Professor in the Department of Criminal Justice and Criminology at the University of North Carolina Charlotte. Her research focuses on the relationship between criminology and correctional rehabilitation, with an emphasis on individual level differences. Her work has appeared in JQ, *Criminology and Public Policy, Criminal Justice and Behavior*, *Crime and Delinquency*, and *Journal of Offender Rehabilitation*

Laura Luciano is the assistant director for the Office for Violence Prevention and Victim Assistance at Rutgers, The State University of New Jersey. She has been working in the anti-violence against women field for 14 years.

Rebecca J. Macy, PhD, ACSW, LCSW, is an associate professor at the University of North Carolina at Chapel Hill School of Social Work. Her research is concerned with child maltreatment, partner and sexual violence, and human trafficking. She particularly focuses on the development of community-based interventions to promote violence survivors' resilience and well-being.

Neely Mahapatra is an assistant professor at the University of Wyoming College of Health Sciences Division of Social Work. Her areas of expertise include violence against women with a specific focus on Asian women. She was previously a postdoctoral fellow with IDVSA and worked on research related to human trafficking.

Sophia Marandino has a master's degree in counseling psychology and is program coordinator for the Center for Family Services, Services Empowering Rights of Victims (SERV) program. She is currently pursuing her PsyD in clinical psychology at the Philadelphia College of Osteopathic Medicine.

Jennifer A. Martinez earned her master's degree in social work at Rutgers, The State University of New Jersey in 2011.

Karen M. Matta Oshima is a doctoral candidate at the George Warren Brown School of Social Work at Washington University in St. Louis. Her research focuses on risk and protective factors of adolescent sexual violence and violent delinquency and early adult outcomes for these youth.

Thelma Pepper McCoy is a PhD candidate at The University of Texas at Austin School of Social Work. Her research and teaching interests are in children exposed to intimate partner violence and related psychopathology to trauma, adolescent mental health, homeless dually diagnosed women, and family policy.

Sarah McMahon, MSW, PhD, is an assistant professor at the Rutgers University School of Social Work, where she also serves as the associate director of the Center on Violence Against Women and Children. She has published widely and provided numerous presentations locally and nationally on sexual violence prevention.

Sheila M. McMahon, MDiv, is a PhD student at the Rutgers School of Social Work, where she is also a graduate research assistant at the Center on Violence Against Women and Children (VAWC). Her research focuses on bystander intervention as a primary prevention strategy to address sexual assault on college campuses.

Myrna McNitt lectures at Dominican University's Graduate School of Social Work, River Forest, with extensive work in child protection, serving as a trustee for the International Foster Care Organization with the publications "Foster Parent Development and Support: Finding and Keeping Resource Families" (in press) and "Child Welfare Challenges for Developing Nations" in *Child Welfare: Connecting Research, Policy, and Practice* (2011).

Sara Meger is a PhD researcher at the University of Melbourne, where she conducts research on the use of sexual violence in contemporary conflicts. She has published several articles on sexual violence in the Democratic Republic of Congo and currently teaches at The University of Queensland in international relations.

Terri L. Messman-Moore, PhD, is an associate professor at Miami University. Her research focuses on women's experiences with sexual revictimization, rape, and child sexual abuse.

Silke Meyer is a postdoctoral research fellow at the Institute for Social Science Research (The University of Queensland, Australia). Her research interests center on violence against women, including intimate partner violence, sexual exploitation, and human rights violation.

Leticia Miranda is a writer and former media research associate at the Media Literacy Project.

Diane Moyer, Esq., is the legal director for the Pennsylvania Coalition against Rape. She has spent 15 years advocating for the rights and needs of victims of sexual violence through policy work at the state and federal level.

Sadie J. Mummert is currently pursuing her PhD in criminal justice and criminology at Georgia State University. Her main research interests are in sexual victimization and sexual revictimization. Her work has been published in the

Journal of Criminal Justice Education and the *International Criminal Justice Review.*

Jarell Myers, BA, is a clinical psychology PhD candidate at Fairleigh Dickinson University working under the mentorship of Dr. Prentky on a project looking at the antecedents of aggressive behavior in adolescent females.

Yukiko Nakajima, RN, WHNP-BC, is a PhD student, School of Social Work, University of Minnesota. She is a SANE (sexual assault nurse examiner) and has been working in the field of sexual violence in Asia and the United States extensively.

Holly Nelson-Becker, PhD, LCSW, Hartford faculty scholar in geriatric social work, is professor at Loyola University Chicago with an ongoing focus in gerontology. Her scholarship and research center on spirituality and aging as well as end-of-life care. She holds a PhD from the University of Chicago and an MSW from Arizona State University.

Jennifer Nix is the director of government and policy affairs at the New Jersey Coalition against Sexual Assault, where she develops and advocates for sexual assault survivor-friendly policy. She has a law degree from Northeastern University School of Law and a master's of public health from Tufts University.

Ashley Nolan earned her MA in community social psychology and a certificate in domestic violence prevention from the University of Massachusetts at Lowell. She continues to be an individual advocate, as well as a member of community organizations that provide public awareness and support for victims of rape and sexual assault.

Maura B. Nsonwu is an assistant professor at North Carolina Agricultural & Technical State University in the Department of Sociology and Social Work and a research fellow with the Center for New North Carolinians. Her research has focused on working with refugee and immigrant communities and issues of human trafficking.

Ijeoma Nwabuzor is a doctoral candidate at the University of North Carolina at Chapel Hill School of Social Work. Her research interests include: the co-occurrence of domestic violence and child abuse/neglect; child welfare; domestic violence; and African American children and families.

Caoilte Ó Ciardha is a research associate in forensic psychology at the University of Kent, UK. He has published on theoretical and empirical aspects of sexual offender cognition.

Brian O'Connor is the director of public education campaigns and programs at Futures Without Violence. A former marketer of global brands like Gatorade and Lucky Charms, and reporter for the *Village Voice*, in New York City, he engages men to teach boys positive masculinity and that violence against women and girls is wrong.

Kei Okada, BA, MA, received her Master's Degree in Forensic Psychology at Fairleigh Dickinson University working under the mentorship of Dr. Prentky.

Jessica S. Oppenheim, Esq., is the director of the Criminal Justice Advocacy Program of The Arc of New Jersey and as an assistant prosecutor and deputy attorney general in the Division of Criminal Justice, Department of Law and Public Safety, drafted and implemented the attorney general's Megan's Law Guidelines and prosecuted Megan's Law and domestic violence cases.

Stephen Oreski, LCSW, is a psychotherapist in private practice with more than fifteen years experience working with survivors of sexual violence.

Melanie D. Otis has a PhD in sociology and is the Richard K. Brautigam Professor of Criminal, Juvenile, and Social Justice in the College of Social Work at the University of Kentucky. She has published extensively on the psychosocial and sociocultural impact of victimization and discrimination.

Caroline Palmer is the staff attorney at the Minnesota Coalition Against Sexual Assault and an adjunct professor at the Hamline University School of Law.

Jane E. Palmer, MSW, is a doctoral candidate in justice, law, and society at American University. She is also a research associate at the National Institute of Justice where she works on a Congressionally-mandated violence against Native women research project. Her dissertation is on the role of bystanders in preventing and responding to violence against women.

Debra Patterson is an assistant professor of social work at Wayne State University. Her research examines the social, medical, and legal systems' response to sexual assault victims/survivors, as well as the impact of sexual assault nurse examiner (SANE) programs on legal outcomes and survivor' emotional well-being.

Stacey Plichta, ScD, CPH, is a Professor of Public Health at the CUNY School of Public Health at Hunter College in New York City. She has written extensively about survivors of intimate partner violence and rape and their interactions with the health care system. She is currently working on a study of how domestic violence and rape crisis services are organized at the state level.

Sara-Beth Plummer, PhD, MSW, is a project coordinator and instructor at the Center on Violence Against Women and Children at the School of Social Work, Rutgers University. Her experience includes being an assistant director at an agency that provided services to individuals with disabilities who were survivors of abuse.

McLean D. Pollock is a licensed clinical social worker who has worked in the field of violence against women for over seven years. She is currently a PhD candidate at the Gillings School of Global Public Health at the University of North Carolina at Chapel Hill.

Ráchael Powers, PhD is an assistant professor in the Department of Criminology at the University of South Florida. Her research interests include violent victimization, gender, and quantitative methodology.

Robert A. Prentky, PhD, is a professor of psychology and the Director of the MA program in Forensic Psychology at Fairleigh Dickinson University in Teaneck, New Jersey. He has been doing research in the area of sexual violence for over 30 years.

Andrea Quijada is the executive director of the Media Literacy Project in Albuquerque, New Mexico. She presents nationally on media literacy topics including media policy, media ownership, and gender, race, and class representation. She is a 2010 alum of Women's Media Center Progressive Women's Voices.

Anita Raj, PhD, is a professor in the Division of Global Public Health, University of California at San Diego (UCSD), and Senior Fellow at the Center on Global Justice at UCSD. Dr. Raj has over 15 years of experience conducting research in the areas of sexual and reproductive health and gender-based violence in vulnerable populations, including immigrants and refugees, in the United States and internationally.

Alexandra Redcay is a consultant trainer and guest lecturer at Rutgers University in New Brunswick, NJ. She has over 17 years of direct practice, management, research and training experience working in child welfare, juvenile justice, and education systems. She is particularly interested in measurement design and LGBTQ youth issues.

Colleen J. Reed, PhD, MSW, consults with healthcare and human service organizations focused on capacity building and leadership development with Compass Group in Denver, Colorado. Dr. Reed is an educator, practitioner, and researcher in the areas of mental health and aging as well as mind-body-spirit practices.

Cynthia F. Rizo is a doctoral student in the School of Social Work at the University of North Carolina–Chapel Hill. Her research focuses on Latina survivors of violence against women.

Selena T. Rodgers, PhD, LCSW-R, is an assistant professor of social work at York College of The City University of New York. Her research and scholarly writing focuses on issues of posttraumatic growth, including child sexual abuse, historical trauma, secondary trauma, intimate partner violence, and United States immigration.

Julie Roebuck is a licensed clinical social worker with an extensive background in supervision in a variety of settings such as mental health clinics, hospitals, and trauma centers. She is currently self-employed as a therapist with private offices in both Morris and Bergen counties in New Jersey.

Brady Root is pursuing a graduate degree at the Rutgers University School of Social Work. She has studied and worked in the field of violence prevention for five years and is currently the Prevention Education Assistant for the Office for Violence Prevention and Victim Assistance at Rutgers University.

Maria Roth, PhD, a professor at Babeş-Bolyai University, Cluj-Napoca, Romania, was one of the founders and later the chair of the social work department. She has published several books, articles, and research reports on children's rights and child welfare services.

Ratonia C. Runnels, PhD, is a licensed master social worker and postdoctoral teaching faculty at Baylor University School of Social Work. Her research focuses on the intersection of spirituality and culture and its impact on social work research, education, and practice.

Orly Sarid, PhD, a senior lecturer at Ben Gurion University of the Negev, Israel has studied the association between psychological risk factors and immunological factors during short-term stress and investigated triggers that initiate depressive states and incur disease in women experiencing traumatic birth. Recently, she wrote on similarities and differences of art therapy and cognitive behavioral interventions in dissipating negative image/memories.

Jeanne Scala is a psychotherapist in private practice in Morristown, New Jersey. She has extensive training and experience in treating perpetrators and victims of sexual abuse and violence.

Martin D. Schwartz is a Visiting Professor at George Washington University and professor emeritus at Ohio University. The 2008 Academy of Criminal Justice Sciences Fellow, he has several distinguished scholar awards and won the Ohio title of Presidential Research Scholar. Often with DeKeseredy, he has written/edited 21 editions of 14 books, 70 journal articles, and 65 chapters and reports.

Rachel Schwartz is a program coordinator at the Center on Violence Against Women and Children at Rutgers University, School of Social Work. She has a master's in social work from Rutgers, The State University of New Jersey.

Kristen D. Seay is a social work doctoral student at Washington University in St. Louis. Her research interests include child abuse and neglect, Child Protective Services investigations, and parental substance abuse. She is the recipient of the Doris Duke Fellowship for the Prevention of Child Abuse and Neglect and a National Institute on Drug Abuse STAR Predoctoral Fellow.

Denise R. Shaw is an associate professor of English and women's studies at the University of South Carolina–Union. Her areas of specialty include southern literature and the twentieth-century American novel. Her first book, *The Rape Narrative and the American South* (2007), explores the proliferation of sexual violence in modern southern literature.

Narae Shin is a doctoral candidate in the School of Social Work at the University of Minnesota–Twin Cities. She has practiced and published on violence against women and children.

Rupesh Shirore MBSS, MPH is a Senior Scientific Writer/Evidence Analyst – Health Economics and Outcomes Research (HEOR), at Novartis Healthcare Pvt. Ltd. He is a physician by training from India has a Masters in PH from East Tennessee State University, USA.

Elithet Silva-Martínez earned her PhD at the University of Iowa. She has worked with survivors of interpersonal violence in Puerto Rico, Mexico, and the United States. Her most recent publication is "Ethics and Cultural Competence in Research with Battered Immigrant Latina Women," *Journal of Ethic and Cultural Diversity in Social Work* (2011): 223–39.

Cassandra Simmel, MSW, PhD, is an assistant professor at the School of Social Work at Rutgers University. Her research and scholarly interests include child welfare policies, programs, and services as well as the long-term developmental and mental health outcomes of child maltreatment.

Lisa J. Smith is the coordinator of domestic violence services in the Office for Violence Prevention and Victim Assistance at Rutgers, The State University of New Jersey. She has worked in the field of interpersonal violence for 20 years and is certified as a domestic violence specialist in New Jersey.

Joanne P. Smith-Darden, PhD, MSW, is an assistant professor of research at Wayne State University. Her work is driven by over 25 years of experience working with vulnerable youth and focuses on the interface between relational trauma, attachment, and cognitive processing—or how individuals who have experienced relational trauma process the world around them.

Elisabeth Snell is a former sexual assault advocate and sexual assault response team (SART) director. She currently works for New York City's Department of Health and Mental Hygiene while pursuing her master's in public health.

Andrea Spencer-Linzie, MDiv, MPhil is the executive director of the New Jersey Coalition against Sexual Assault. Spencer-Linzie is a trustee of the National Alliance to End Sexual Violence, cochair of the New Jersey Governor's Advisory Council against Sexual Violence, and has been an adjunct professor in women's studies, philosophy, ethics, and the humanities.

Marcia Spira, PhD, LCSW, is a professor of social work at Loyola University–Chicago. She directs the Institute on Aging, Intergenerational Study and Practice. Her scholarship includes several articles on the impact of aging and cognitive decline on family relationships. Her current research focuses on the needs of grandmothers raising grandchildren. She holds a Ph.D. from the University of Chicago.

Vidya Sri is the founder of Gangashakti.org, a community advocacy organization working to cause social and policy change in the United States on the issue of forced marriage. Vidya Sri uses her own experience of being in a forced marriage to give talks and workshops to raise awareness.

Noelle M. St. Vil, PhD, is a post doctoral fellow at John Hopkins University. Her dissertation was on the impact of social networks on African American marital satisfaction. Her research interests lie in the areas of violence against women, women's issues and healthy relationships.

Evan Stark is a founder of an early shelter for battered women in the United States, an award-winning researcher, and a forensic social worker who has served as an expert in more than 100 criminal and civil cases. He is a professor at the School of Public Affairs and Administration at Rutgers–Newark.

Sabrina Starkman is a master's of social work candidate and resident hall director at Rutgers, The State University of New Jersey. Her academic and clinical interests include college student mental health, the development and treatment of psychopathology, and women's issues.

Jessica Steier, MPH, is a doctoral candidate in public health at the Graduate Center of the City University of New York where she specializes in health policy. She also serves as the research coordinator of Hofstra University's physician assistant program, and an assistant professor of epidemiology and research design and analysis.

Megan Stewart earned her PhD in criminal justice from the University of Cincinnati, and is an assistant professor of criminal justice at Georgia Gwinnett College. Her primary area of interest is violence against women.

Jessica Strong, MSW, is a PhD student in social work at Rutgers University, studying issues related to military veterans and their families, particularly female veterans and those returning from the conflicts in Iraq and Afghanistan. She is also a military family member whose husband is currently serving in the army.

Amanda Mathisen Stylianou, MSW, LCSW, is a doctoral research assistant at the Center for Violence Against Women and Children at Rutgers University, School of Social Work. Ms. Stylianou focuses her research on the intersection of trauma and mental health and runs a private practice in Pennington, New Jersey.

Aimee Sutherlin is the associate director at TESSA, in Colorado Springs, Colorado. She has worked in the social services for almost 20 years, concentrating in the field of family violence. She holds a master's in social work from the University of Hawaii, at Manoa.

Deborah V. Svoboda is an assistant professor in social work at Eastern Washington University. Her research interests include the workings of feminist organizations and the policy development related to gender-based violence.

Chrisula Tasiopoulos, MSW, LCSW, is the senior director of the rape crisis center at the YWCA Bergen County in New Jersey. She has over 10 years' experience in the field of sexual and domestic violence, from direct services to nonprofit management.

Louise A. Taylor earned her PhD in psychology at Rutgers University. She was an assistant professor of social, cultural, and gender psychology at Ramapo College of New Jersey and served as full-time teaching faculty at Rutgers, The State University of New Jersey. She is editorial consultant at Forensic Associates in New

Jersey. She is working on a book about Dinnerstein's theory of misogynistic culture.

Elizabeth A. Tomsich is a doctoral candidate in the School of Public Affairs at the University of Colorado–Denver. Elizabeth earned her BA in psychology from the University of Minnesota and her MS in social psychology from Purdue University. She has broad research interests including, but not limited to, violence against women, family violence, and reproductive health policy.

Michelle Marie Truffin earned her MA in educational psychology and post-BA certificate in child advocacy and policy at Montclair State University, where she is currently an adjunct professor. Her research interests include child sexual abuse prevention and intervention efforts, children's rights, and forensic psychology. She plans to pursue a doctorate degree in psychology.

Ebony Tucker received her JD from the Florida State University College of Law. She was previously a civil rights attorney for the state of Florida and is now the Assistant Executive Director for the Florida Council Against Sexual Violence.

Rebecca Morrison Van Voorhis retired in 2009 from university teaching after 35 years of teaching, primarily at Indiana University School of Social Work. Her presentations and publications reflect her particular interests in oppression, women, gay and lesbian people, and social justice. Her professional consultation and service focus on developing social services and evaluating programs for several domestic and international organizations.

Armanda Venezia earned an MS in criminal justice at the University of Cincinnati. She works for the Charlotte-Mecklenburg Police Department in North Carolina.

Jyoti Venketraman is the prevention director at the New Jersey Coalition against Sexual Assault.

Stéphanie Wahab is an associate professor in social work at Portland State University. She has published extensively on female commercial sex work and intimate partner violence. Her body of work revolves around the intersections of race, class, gender, and sexuality situated within social justice issues and movements.

Nicolette Salerno Wallace, Ed, is an adjunct professor of psychology and a board certified life coach, specializing in life transitions, parenting and women's issues. Her current area of specialization is the impact of chronic illness on relationships.

Corinne D. Warrener, MSW, LSW, is currently a doctoral candidate at Rutgers University. She is working on her dissertation, focusing on sense of entitlement and abusive behaviors among college dating relationships. Her research and practical backgrounds involve dating and domestic violence, prevention, and community and professional education.

Sharon M. Wasco, PhD, is a community psychologist with over 17 years of experience in the fields of sexual assault and violence prevention research. Dr. Wasco works as an independent evaluator and consultant helping organizations use evidence to make decisions, improve sexual violence prevention and intervention programs, and solve community problems.

Arlene N. Weisz is a professor and director of the doctoral program at the School of Social Work, Wayne State University. Her research focuses on domestic violence, teen dating violence, and sexual assault prevention, including a coauthored book disseminating practice wisdom and research from teen dating violence and sexual assault prevention programs.

Elizabeth Whalley is a doctoral student in sociology at the University of Colorado–Boulder. Her interests are sexual abuse and women in prison.

Rachael White is a licensed social worker with a certificate in violence against women and children from the Rutgers School of Social Work. She works at a nonprofit crisis center where she provides counseling to individuals and families who have been affected by domestic violence and sexual assault.

Natalie Williams (MTS, Vanderbilt University) is a PhD student in religion and society at Drew University in Madison, New Jersey. Her areas of research include Christian social ethics and feminist ethics, focusing on the topics of violence against women, marriage reform movements, and heterosexism.

Elizabeth A. Winter, PhD, LSW is a faculty member in the Child Welfare Education and Research Programs in the School of Social Work at the University of Pittsburgh. Her interests include child maltreatment, addiction, traumatic stress, child welfare-involved sexual minority youth, and child welfare workforce development. She has provided clinical services since 1998.

Peter B. Wood (MA, PhD, Vanderbilt) is a professor of sociology at Eastern Michigan University and the editor-in-chief of *Sociological Inquiry*. He is currently chair of the Academy of Criminal Justice Sciences Public Policy

Committee and a member of the ASC/ACJS Criminology and Criminal Justice Policy Coalition. Wood also serves on the editorial board of *Justice Quarterly*.

Kathryn S. Woods is the assistant director of the Women and Gender Advocacy Center at Colorado State University. She is responsible for coordinating victim services on campus for survivors of sexual assault, relationship violence and stalking. She also teaches in the women's studies and social work programs at Colorado State University.

Theresa R. Wyatt is a forensic clinical specialist and an adjunct professor at University of Detroit Mercy and St. Clair County Community College. She earned her master of science in forensic nursing at Fitchburg State College and is currently a doctoral student at the Medical University of South Carolina.

Sun Young Yoon is a research associate at the University of Southern Maine Muskie School of Public Service. She is currently working on the VAWA Measuring Effectiveness Initiative project. She earned her PhD in child and family studies from the University of Wisconsin at Madison.

Liz Zadnik is currently the education and resource coordinator at the Pennsylvania Coalition against Rape (PCAR), and has worked in the violence prevention and reproductive justice movements. Liz recently received her master's in community psychology and social change from The Pennsylvania State University, concentrating on community diversity and gender issues.

William J. Zaorski is the director of legal and police studies with Career Development Institute, Kendall Park, New Jersey. He retired as a deputy attorney general with the New Jersey Division of Criminal Justice where he developed and conducted workshops for law enforcement officers and prosecutors on domestic violence and search and seizure issues.

Sharon Zucker is the prevention education coordinator at the Rutgers University Office for Violence Prevention and Victim Assistance. She holds a master's in public administration with a certificate in domestic violence studies, and helped develop the *SCREAMing to Prevent Violence* curriculum for SCREAM Theater.

Monna Bender Zuckerman is a licensed clinical social worker who has worked in the field of family violence for over 20 years as a therapist, educator, and consultant. Zuckerman, who received her PhD in social work from the State University of New York at Albany, conducts research on intimate partner violence.